The
NATURAL
FOOD
COOKBOOK

The
NATURAL
FOOD
COOKBOOK

George Seddon & Jackie Burrow

EXETER BOOKS ★ NEW YORK

Executive Editor	Glorya Hale
Editors	Gail Howell-Jones
	Sally Walters
Art Editor	Sue Casebourne
Assistant Editor	Nicola Hemingway
Assistant Art Editor	Javed Badar
Designers	Suzanne Stevenson
	Jackie Whelan
Picture Research Editor	Susan Pinkus
Picture Researcher	Bridget Alexander
Editorial Assistant	Charlotte Kennedy
Production	Barry Baker
Publisher	Bruce Marshall
Art Director	John Bigg
Production Director	Michael Powell
Consultant	John Rivers

ISBN 0-671-07228-5

Filmset by Servis Filmsetting Limited,
Manchester
Reproduction by Sackville Press,
Billericay Limited
Printed and bound in Spain by
Printer Industria Grafica S.a., Barcelona
D.L.B. 28533-1984

Eating is one of the great pleasures of life. It is not just a source of pleasure, however, because life itself depends on it. The food we eat greatly affects how we feel, so a healthy diet is important, but too much concern about eating the right foods can be fatal to enjoyment. This book, therefore, is about eating good food, enjoying it and avoiding the worry.

Anyone who is desperately hungry will eat the most unpalatable food, and will stop as soon as the pangs of hunger have been appeased. Appealing food, however, tempts us to go on eating after our needs are satisfied. We all eat too much sometimes, with no harm done, but if we consume even a little more than we need day after day we are in grave danger of becoming unhealthily fat. So the first target is to control our greed.

The next step is to realize that our affluent Western diet is not as healthy as it should be. Food processing, for example, has decreased the amount of roughage in our diet and our overdependence on animal products means we eat too much rich, fatty food that may also be high in cholesterol. The answer is not only to cut down on fat consumption, but to have a more varied diet.

The authors of this book firmly believe that the basis of a good meal—one that tastes good as well as being nutritious—is wholesome, natural food that is prepared at home. But they have no desire to turn anyone into a kitchen slave. You will find that only a little extra effort will be needed to end dependence on the supermarket deep-freeze and on the can opener—and it will be amply rewarded by the extra pleasure you will have. In fact, cooking wholesome food can soon become part of the enjoyment of eating it.

The plan of the book is as straightforward as its aim. It begins with an outline of the foods we require and goes on to explain where, and why, our diet has gone wrong. It explodes all the popular myths about various foods, and tells you how bad eating habits can be easily corrected.

The heart of the book, however, is a survey of the cornucopia of good ingredients that are available and shows you how you can use them to make delectable dishes.

The recipes are comparatively low in cholesterol, fats and sugar and they use natural foods, unadulterated by processing techniques. The cooking methods used in the recipes ensure that as much flavor and as many vitamins and minerals as possible are retained for maximum benefit and the greatest enjoyment.

Finally, the fact-finding charts provide an easy-to-follow guide to some of the essential information you will need to eat well and stay healthy.

NUTRITIONAL MEASUREMENTS

Throughout this book the nutritional value of each of the foods has been given as the number of grams (g) of each nutrient in one hundred grams of food (shown as a cube divided into one hundred squares). One hundred grams (which is equivalent to about three and a half ounces) is the standard amount of food used in food tables because it is the simplest way of calculating the percentage of protein, fat, carbohydrate and water in a particular food.

Although the amount of major nutrients can be expressed in grams per hundred grams of food, minerals and vitamins must be given in milligrams (mg), which are thousandths of a gram, or, for even more minute quantities, in micrograms (mcg), which are millionths of a gram.

There are complications, however, with vitamin A. This has often been expressed in international units (i.u.), but it is now given in retinol equivalents. Retinol is the form of vitamin A found in animal products. Carotene, which is contained in fruit and vegetables, can be converted into vitamin A in the body, but less efficiently; so while one milligram of retinol provides one milligram of retinol equivalent, it takes six milligrams of carotene to provide one milligram of retinol equivalent.

It is simple to convert international units into retinol equivalents. One milligram of retinol equivalent is equal to 3,330 international units of retinol, or 10,000 international units of carotene.

For large weights, such as the amount of sugar a person consumes in a week or how much a person should weigh, the metric measurements must be in units of thousands of grams, or kilograms (kg). One thousand grams is equal to one kilogram, which is about 2.2 pounds.

Calories as an expression of the energy values of foods are already being abandoned by scientists in favor of the Système International unit (SI) the joule, but calories are too well established in popular use to disappear immediately.

One thousand calories make up the Calorie in general use. The Calorie, also called a kilocalorie (kcal), represents the amount of heat required to raise the temperature of a kilogram of water one degree centigrade. The joule, abbreviated to J, is such a minute unit that the kilojoule (kJ), which is one thousand joules, is more widely used. One Calorie equals 4.186 kilojoules. For larger amounts than a kilojoule, the megajoule (MJ), one thousand kilojoules, or one million joules, is used.

RECIPE MEASUREMENTS

All the ingredients in the recipes in this book are given in both United States standard measurements and metric quantities. Use either the standard or the metric quantities; do not mix them. The metric quantities are not exact conversions of the standard quantities, but are in correct proportion to the other metric quantities in the same recipe.

Standard measuring spoons have been used to measure small quantities of liquid and dry ingredients. All spoon measurements are level. Standard measuring spoons of one-quarter teaspoon, one-half teaspoon, one teaspoon and one tablespoon and standard metric spoons of two and a half, five, ten and fifteen milliliters (ml) capacity have been used.

The recipes have been tested in standard-sized baking dishes. Although the equivalent metric measurements have been given, dishes in these sizes may not be easy to obtain and the nearest sized dish available may be substituted.

Fish is one of the most wholesome of foods and the more recently caught it is the more delicious it will taste.

TASTE IS A PRECIOUS SENSE that we shamefully neglect. Indeed today's average Western diet corrupts it. Natural honest flavors are replaced by blandness or by artificial flavorings, whose impact has all the subtlety of a sledge hammer. Many of the foods we eat have lost not only their agreeable flavor but some of their nutritional value as well. A return to wholesome food would give us more enjoyment, as well as a sense of well-being—the most desirable sixth sense we can hope for. Eating, unlike some human activities, can be good for us and can also be extremely pleasurable.

The basis of good, pleasurable eating is honesty—natural ingredients, their natural flavors and nutrients retained as much as possible. Nothing you like need be excluded from your diet. Some foods, of course, are more nutritious than others and some should be eaten in moderation, but there is nothing that a healthy person need avoid completely. Even sugar is maligned for the wrong reasons. Its virtue is that it can help to make some other foods palatable; but that virtue can be turned into a vice if sugar is eaten to excess. The same can be said of fats and oils; they are not harmful until excess makes them so. It is our eating habits rather than the foods we eat that are bad for us.

Although in theory we may accept that all food is good, only a person who is starving will put the belief into practice. For most of us there are a vast number of foods we reject with feelings that range from slight distaste to revulsion. Because they are largely irrational, our prejudices are all the more firmly held and harder to overcome. Local customs, submerged taboos, fads, aversions acquired in childhood and a fear of experimenting impose quite unnecessary restrictions on our diet. It is unrealistic to expect that overnight we can sweep away all these self-imposed barriers, but we might occasionally demolish a few and explore new areas of taste.

The first step is to realize how sloppy and uncritical most people have become over the last two decades about the food they buy and eat. The growth of vast chains of supermarkets epitomizes the decline. But supermarkets are obviously here to stay and are the places to shop if you want predictable, prepackaged and processed food. They have made shopping faster but impersonal. They have made food safer, so that our stomachs and our palates are unlikely to be upset. They can almost guarantee unchanging quality by the control they exercise over the growing, processing and transporting of the food they sell. They have cut time spent in the kitchen by as much as three-quarters since Grandma's day. But in the process much of the individuality of our diet has been lost and the great variety of flavors which were enjoyed only a generation ago has been reduced to a comparative few. Creativity in the kitchen has been sacrificed for convenience.

In France housewives shop every day to ensure that the fruit and vegetables they buy will be as fresh as possible.

It is still possible, however, to break out of the straitjacket of taste imposed by technology. If you are lucky enough to have a garden you can grow vegetables and eat them when they are at their best. If not, there are still stores that sell vegetables that are not sweating heavily under their plastic wraps. There are still butchers who sell excellent meat, although fresh fish becomes harder to find. In larger towns you can still find exciting, though expensive, specialty food stores that sell wholesome food. For some delicious "unfashionable" foods you may have to search in "health-food" stores. Although their prices are often inflated, their booming business may be a sign that a growing number of people think it worth the extra trouble and expense to shop for honest-to-goodness food and worth the extra time to cook it, too.

A wholesome diet is not just a question of taste. Even Brillat-Savarin, the eighteenth-century lawyer and gourmet, who argued that of all the senses taste gives most delight, added that along with the pleasure of eating there is the satisfaction of knowing that the wear and tear on the body is being made good and life is being prolonged.

A wholesome diet is not a cranky health-food regime, conjuring up the image of devotees endlessly chewing raw vegetables. While some foods can be enjoyed raw, many are more digestible and palatable when they are cooked. A chart of the nutritive value of food shows that raw asparagus, for example, has a reasonably high vitamin C content and that half of it is lost when the stalks are cooked. But unless asparagus is cooked it is not fit to eat and when it is cooked it is fit for the gods. Similarly, sound though it might be nutritionally, it would be difficult to savor raw artichokes, beets, kale, lentils, turnip tops, squash or potatoes.

Wholesome cooking, like the ingredients it uses, is honest. It does not dress nut cutlets up as lamb. It makes no pretense of imitating *haute cuisine*, but that does not mean that it is crude fare. Appreciation of the natural flavors of food, and doing justice to them, demand considerable skill on the part of the cook. Like French provincial cooking its appeal will be to those who have, or who develop, fairly sophisticated palates and to those for whom eating is something more than filling a ravenous hole in the stomach. A healthy gourmet does not demand elaborate meals, but can appreciate, for example, the simple flavors of home-baked bread, a bowl of crisp crudités or tart homemade preserves.

As Elizabeth David, the great English cook and writer, wrote in her book *French Provincial Cooking*: "The feeling of our time is for simpler food, simply presented; not that this is necessarily easier to achieve than *haute cuisine*; it demands less time and expense, but, if anything a more genuine feeling for cookery and a truer taste."

Traditional butcher stores, such as this famous one in London, hang meat properly so that it is tender and flavorsome.

THE ENERGY GIVERS

According to many experts our diet should include many more polyunsaturated fatty acids than saturated ones. Generally, this means using vegetable or fish oils instead of animal fats.

More than 50 percent of the fatty acids in sunflower seed oil are polyunsaturated. Only safflower seed oil has a marginally higher percentage.

Most vegetable oils are high in polyunsaturated fatty acids, but coconut oil and olive oil are the exceptions. Coconut oil contains only 2 percent, and olive oil contains from 4 to 14 percent, depending on the particular crop. All vegetable oils are, however, superior to animal fats from a health point of view, because they do not contain cholesterol, which is thought to contribute to heart disease.

WE EAT FOOD, but our bodies absorb nutrients. Therefore to help us to decide what to eat we must know what nutrients our food contains. Although it is easy to get bogged down in the details of nutritional research the basic outline is fairly simple.

Our diet contains carbohydrates, fats, proteins, minerals and vitamins, plus water, alcohol and fiber, or roughage. Each has a role, separately or in cooperation with another. Carbohydrates and fats are the body's main sources of energy. The role of proteins, minerals and vitamins is in body building and maintenance. Proteins can also provide energy. Fiber is needed for the efficient functioning of the digestive system, while water is necessary for all of the body's functions.

As a rough guide it can be reckoned that carbohydrates and proteins provide a similar amount of energy (110 Calories per ounce or 4 Calories from every gram), while fat provides more than double that amount (250 Calories per ounce or 9 Calories from every gram). In practice, even in the fat-rich diets of the Western world, the greater part of most people's energy is derived from carbohydrates.

Carbohydrates are chemical substances made up of carbon, hydrogen and oxygen. They are manufactured in the green leaves of plants from carbon dioxide and water through the action of sunlight. This process is known as photosynthesis. Carbohydrates that plants do not need for energy accumulate in fruits and seeds and in roots and tubers. Animals cannot carry out the remarkable process of photosynthesis, and obtain most of their carbohydrates by eating plants.

Sugars, starch and cellulose are the main forms of carbohydrates produced by plants. The two simplest sugars in the diet are glucose, which occurs in such plants as corn and onions and is

formed in the body during the digestion of other carbohydrates, and fructose, a sweeter sugar found in honey and fruit. Other sugars are sucrose, obtained from sugar cane and sugar beet; lactose, found in the milk of cows and humans; and maltose, the sugar in malt, which is produced from the starch of grain when it germinates.

Starches, chemically more complex than sugars, are the main source of carbohydrate throughout the world—although in industrialized countries sugars run a close second. In Europe and the United States, for example, some 40 percent of the carbohydrates eaten are sugars, and 60 percent are starches, mainly from cereals and potatoes.

A large proportion of the fibrous parts of plants consists of cellulose, which humans cannot digest. The virtue of cellulose in the human diet is that it provides bulk or roughage to help in the working of the bowel. But ruminants such as cattle have rumen bacteria in one of their stomachs which can digest cellulose, and when we eat beef we are eating the cellulose that they have converted into protein and fat.

All carbohydrates, except cellulose, are broken down in the body during digestion into simple

People on diets should beware of the avocado, which is a nutritional rogue. It contains 17 percent fat, while most other vegetable fruits contain less than 1 percent

COOKING MEANS CALORIES

Although raw potatoes provide 87 Calories per hundred grams, the calorific value of a potato rises when it is cooked. The explanation is simple—the potato loses some of its water content. Frying in oil or butter increases the calorific value even more. One hundred grams of raw potato produces 85 grams of baked potato (providing 87 Calories). The same amount of raw potato makes 50 grams of French fries (which provide 120 Calories) or 44 grams of potato chips (which provide 245 Calories)

sugars, mainly glucose. In a complicated series of chemical reactions the glucose is broken down and combined with oxygen to form carbon dioxide, water and energy.

Fats are a more concentrated source of energy than carbohydrates. In a Western diet they may provide 40 percent or more of the energy requirement, while in the rest of the world, either because of poverty or choice, they contribute 10 percent or less. Fats and oils are provided by both animals and plants, and although the basic constituents of all of them are carbon, hydrogen and oxygen, the way in which these are chemically linked and the number of hydrogen atoms in the molecule alters the character of the fat, even when it does not affect the energy value. An understanding of these differences will clarify current concern about the types of fat that should and should not be eaten.

Almost all the fats we eat are triglycerides, which are made up of one glycerol molecule and three fatty acid molecules. Of the forty or more fatty acids found in nature, those with a full quota of hydrogen atoms are called "saturated." These form a large proportion of animal fats and are held responsible for the high blood cholesterol levels that increase the risk of coronary disease. Cholesterol itself is essential for the functioning of the body. It is important in the manufacture of sex hormones and vitamin D. But because the body makes all the cholesterol it requires we do not need it in our diet. Common saturated fatty acids, which make up a high proportion of animal fats, include palmitic acid, found in all fats and oils, but especially in mutton fat; stearic acid, found in beef fat, mutton fat and lard; and butyric acid, found in butter. Most saturated fats are solid at room temperature.

Fatty acids with fewer hydrogen atoms and with carbon atoms joined together by double instead of single bonds are called "unsaturated." These form a high proportion of the fatty acids in most vegetable oils. Those fatty acids with two or more double bonds (polyunsaturated acids) tend to lower the cholesterol level of the blood. Those fatty acids that have only one double bond (monounsaturated fatty acids) do not have this effect. Most unsaturated fatty acids are liquid at room temperature. Unsaturated fatty acids include the monounsaturated fatty acid oleic acid, found in all oils, the polyunsaturated fatty acid linoleic acid, which is in all vegetable oils, particularly soybean, safflower, sunflower and cottonseed oil, the polyunsaturated fatty acid linolenic acid, which is in some vegetable oils, but especially linseed oil, and the polyunsaturated arachidonic acid, found in polyunsaturated fats of animal origin, especially eggs, liver and the "invisible" fat of meat. Linoleic acid cannot be synthesized in the body; it has to be provided by the food we eat, and is described as an essential fatty acid.

Besides providing energy, fats add to the flavor of food, giving a feeling of fullness after a meal and, since they are digested more slowly, stave off hunger for a longer period of time than carbohydrates. Like carbohydrates and proteins, fats that are not needed for immediate conversion into energy are used to build up body fat. Some body fat is invaluable because it forms an insulating layer under the skin, a protective covering for such organs as the kidneys and a reserve of energy.

Animal and vegetable fats and oils are the most obvious sources of fat. Visible fat—such as that on meat, and in butter and cream—accounts for up to half of the average fat consumption in the Western diet. The rest—"invisible" fat—comes from such foods as lean meat, fish and eggs.

THE VALUE OF PROTEINS

DO YOU GET ENOUGH OF THE RIGHT KIND OF PROTEIN?

Most protein in the average Western diet comes from animal products.

Vegetables contribute about 10 percent of the daily protein requirement.

Cereals are surprisingly rich in protein and because most people eat so much of them they may supply almost one-third of the protein in the diet.

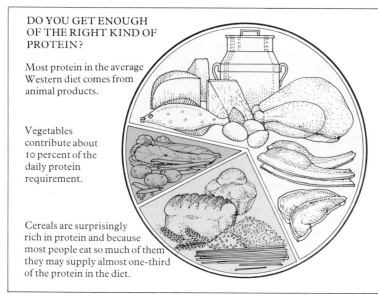

Most vegetable proteins lack one or more of the essential amino acids and are considered second-class proteins. But a pairing of certain foods, each of which makes up for the other's deficit, produces a first-class protein with the full complement of amino acids.

Bread is low in lysine, but is fairly rich in methionine. Baked beans are the reverse and on toast are a good protein meal.

Cornflakes and milk are an excellent protein combination. Milk contributes tryptophan and corn methionine.

PROTEINS ARE PRIMARILY BODY BUILDERS, and we need them not only when we are growing up but all our lives. The tissues of the body are always being renewed, although diminishingly so as we get older. Between 1 and 2 percent of the tissue protein is replaced each day, but the rate varies for different parts of the body. The renewal of heart, liver and kidney tissue, for example, is rapid; that of muscle and bone much slower.

The word protein was first used in 1837 by a Dutch chemist, G. J. Mulder, who made the error of thinking of it in terms of an unvarying nitrogen-rich substance. The great German chemist Justus von Liebig perpetuated the error, which became accepted doctrine. Later research showed that proteins vary greatly according to the different combinations and amounts of the basic building blocks, or amino acids, of which they are composed.

The building blocks, like those of carbohydrates and fats, are constructed of carbon, hydrogen and oxygen, but in addition they include nitrogen. In some proteins there may be other elements present, such as sulfur. Of the hundreds of amino acids present in proteins only about twenty commonly occur and are of particular importance to us. Some of these are described as "essential" because they cannot be manufactured in the body and must therefore be included in the diet. Eight such amino acids are essential for adults. These are isoleucine, leucine, lysine, methionine, phenylalanine, threonine, tryptophan and valine. Very young children need an additional two—arginine and histidine. The "nonessential" proteins are just as important, but these are made in the body.

The value of protein foods depends on the relative amounts of essential amino acids they contain, and the value may be limited simply by a shortage of one amino acid. Bread protein, for example, is deficient in lysine, corn and legumes are deficient in tryptophan and leafy vegetables in methionine. The protein we eat is broken down in digestion into its constituent amino acids in order to be recreated as body protein. Body protein can only be formed if all the necessary amino acids are available at the same time. There is no store to call upon, for excess amino acids are used up as energy or converted into fat. By eating a mixture of protein-rich foods in the same meal, however, you can help to ensure that you get enough of the essential amino acids needed to form body protein.

Estimates of the daily requirements of protein vary widely, but both estimates and consumption in the West are way above the minimum. This, for most adults, ranges between one to one and a half ounces (about 25 to 45 g); for mothers who are breastfeeding it rises to almost two ounces (55 g). Usually the recommended daily intakes are based on the calculation that 10 percent of an individual's energy requirements should be provided by protein. By this rather arbitrary calculation the recommended intakes for adults range between two to three ounces (55 to 85 g). A varied diet will include more than enough protein, with adequate amounts of the essential amino acids.

To talk of a food as being rich in protein may be true but it is, nonetheless, misleading; it all depends on how much of that food we eat. Lobster, for example, is undoubtedly rich in protein, but the contribution it makes to most people's protein needs is minimal. Potatoes, however, which we think of as a starchy food, give most people about 5 percent of their daily protein. More surprisingly, 20 percent of the protein in the average American diet comes from bread and other flour products, which are always regarded

It's difficult to persuade people to try new foods, particularly the new protein foods, which frequently masquerade as meat.

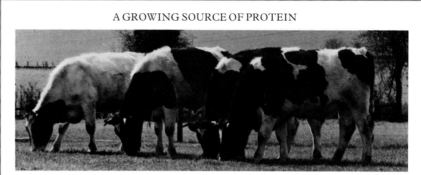

In the future the new vegetable protein foods, such as soybean products, are likely to become more important in our diet because they are so much cheaper to produce than animal protein. An acre of soybeans can produce almost thirty times the amount of protein as an acre on which beef cattle are reared.

as carbohydrate foods. The percentage of protein from vegetables is about 10 percent for both the United States and Britain. The rest of our protein comes from animal products—meat, fish, milk, cheese and eggs. Today Americans eat about 7 percent more animal protein than the British do.

Researchers are now urgently looking for new sources of protein that will add to or substitute for such protein-rich foods as meat, fish, eggs and milk, which are both scarce and expensive. So far the alternative protein foods intended for human consumption have been manufactured from existing food sources, notably soybeans. In one process soy flour is made into a dough, heated and extruded through a nozzle under pressure, dried and then cut into pieces that have a texture similar to meat. Another method produces fine threads of soy protein, which can be spun to give different textures. Flavor, color and fat can be added at will and the end product can be dried, canned or frozen. Soy protein is also used to make nondairy coffee whiteners.

Beans and other seeds now generally used for animal feeds will in the future undoubtedly also be used to provide human food with a high crude protein content of at least 50 percent.

Even more novel protein foods may be in the offing. Since green leaves are so efficient in synthesizing food it is a pity that humans cannot digest the inedible fiber of such plants as grass. The protein-rich juice, however, can be extracted and processed, but the result is as yet unattractive.

All our food ultimately comes from plant life and researchers have even learned how to obtain food from plant life that died millions and millions of years ago and now exists as oil. Yeasts, bacteria and fungi can all manufacture protein by being cultivated on waste petroleum products.

Some of these proteins are already being used experimentally in Britain and abroad as animal feeds. A group of Dutch researchers have for some years been feeding yeast/petroleum protein to pigs and poultry. As a sign of the courage of their convictions they and their families have been eating the meat and eggs of their experimental animals, and no harm has befallen them.

The ever increasing demand for protein can never be solved through meat—the world's resources are too limited to squander on the uneconomical conversion of plant to animal to human protein. Increasingly, people all over the world will have to rely on vegetable protein.

Various forecasts are that by 1980 between 5 and 10 percent of meat will have been replaced by textured vegetable proteins, largely because they are cheaper. This estimate is probably optimistic because people are not willing to accept a product that pretends to be something it isn't. The novel proteins so far introduced are being projected in the image of meat, even though they do not taste or even chew like meat. That is the prerogative of meat alone. Until the new protein foods stop being produced as "meat" and their own worth is established in a palatable form, people will not regularly or willingly make use of them as a source of protein.

THE OTHER ESSENTIALS

Vitamin A is needed to make the pigment that enables the retina of the eye to adjust from a bright to a dim light. It is found in such animal products as eggs and such vegetables as spinach and carrots. Two average-sized carrots, for example, supply our daily needs.

Vitamin D is the vitamin that nearly isn't, because provided that we get sunlight we do not need it. We produce compounds in our skin that are changed by even dull sunlight into vitamin D. Without sun, we depend on such foods as fatty fish and dairy products, with our daily requirement coming, for example, from one egg.

There are seven B vitamins that are important in our diet —thiamine, niacin, riboflavin, folic acid, pantothenic acid, B_6 and B_{12}. Two ounces of peanuts and two ounces of liver for example, give us all the B vitamins that we need in one day.

Vitamin C, or ascorbic acid, is provided by fruit and vegetables. Recommended daily amounts vary from 30 to 60 milligrams—the upper limit can be obtained from a glass of orange juice.
Many people, however, take from ten to fifty times as much in the hope that excess vitamin C will prevent or at least ameliorate the common cold. The theory arose originally out of the observation that in scurvy—vitamin C deficiency—infections were more common. It was regarded as untrue by most nutritionists until in 1970 Nobel Prizewinner Professor Linus Pauling published a book backing what he called megavitamin therapy—the idea that very large doses of vitamin C specifically protect you against the common cold. Despite the boost given by Pauling's reputation the theory still remains "unproven."

MAN CANNOT LIVE by carbohydrates, fats and, proteins alone; but scientists were a long time discovering why. It is only since the beginning of the twentieth century that the other essential elements in food have been tracked down; some of them little more than twenty years ago. These other elements are minerals and vitamins, and although the amounts we need of them are small, their importance to our health is immense. Lack of vitamins is responsible, for example, for such deficiency diseases as anemia, scurvy, rickets, pellagra, beriberi and blindness.

The minerals needed in the largest amounts are known as the major elements. They include calcium and phosphorus, the chief elements in the bones of the body. Of the total weight of our bones, more than two pounds is calcium and about one and a half pounds is phosphorus. For the body to absorb calcium, vitamin D has to be present. Absorption is reduced by the presence of phytic acid, which is found particularly in whole-wheat. Calcium is unavoidably removed in the milling of white flour and in many countries it is put back to ensure that there is no lack of calcium in the diet. Milk and cheese are excellent sources of calcium, and water in hard-water areas also makes a fair contribution. There is little risk of a shortage of phosphorus because it is present as phosphate in many of the foods we eat.

Other elements that are needed are iron, magnesium, sodium, chlorine, potassium and sulfur. Liver and eggs are the best sources of iron. Bread, however, provides much of most people's daily requirement not because it is rich in iron but because they eat so much of it. Magnesium is found in almost all foods and par-

ticularly in cereals, legumes, fish, green vegetables and potatoes. Sodium and chlorine, largely provided by common salt (sodium chloride), are also found in most foods. Meat, milk and green vegetables are rich sources of potassium. Sulfur is supplied by meat, fish, poultry, eggs and the cabbage family (hence the smell). Minerals needed in the diet in only minute quantities, and found in many foods, are called trace elements; these are iodine, fluorine, zinc, copper, manganese, chromium, cobalt and molybdenum.

It is hard to believe that before 1911 there was no such word as vitamin. More than half a century and the discovery of thirteen major vitamins later there are still great gaps in the knowledge of vitamins; even the precise function of the first to be named, vitamin A, is not known. Recommenda-

tions of the amounts we should eat are largely guesswork and are generous, to be on the safe side. But the knowledge we do have has meant that scurvy can be cured with vitamin C, beriberi with thiamine, pellagra with niacin and rickets with vitamin D. These are the more dramatic aspects of the role vitamins play, but just as important is their everyday role in the body's functions.

Unlike minerals, which are inorganic, vitamins are organic substances. Although essential they are not magical, at least no more than anything else in our diet. The amounts we eat range from minute to merely small, and it is a fallacy to believe that because small amounts of vitamins are good for us more would be better. A well-balanced diet provides a generous amount of vitamins, and it is a waste of money to stuff our bodies with vitamin pills. Indeed an excess of vitamin A and vitamin D may be harmful.

Vitamin A is needed for vision, healthy skin and the linings of the throat and bronchial tubes. The most important sources of vitamin A include liver, butter and fortified margarine. While most vegetables contain no vitamin A, they provide carotene, from which the body can make vitamin A.

There are, so far, seven B vitamins known to be necessary in our diet. One of the main roles of B vitamins is the part they play in the release of energy from carbohydrates, fats and proteins. They are also involved in the making of red cells in the blood and the working of the nervous system. B vitamins include thiamine (B_1) found in flour, cereals, meat and vegetables, especially potatoes. There can be heavy losses of thiamine during cooking. The richest sources of riboflavin (B_2) are liver and kidney, but we get our largest supplies from other meats and from milk. While niacin is found in meat, fish and whole grains, in practice the main sources are meat, vegetables and enriched flour. Beer drinkers consume a fair amount. Vitamin B_6 is found in many foods; rich sources include nuts, meat, fish and whole-wheat flour. Pantothenic acid is found in almost all foods, folic acid in green vegetables and liver and B_{12} is found most notably in liver, kidney, fish and eggs.

Vitamin C helps to make the tissue that binds the cells of the body together. For some reason it is given star rating by many people, who swallow vitamin C pills in the mistaken belief that they will cure all ills. Good sources of vitamin C are berries and citrus fruits, peppers, vegetables of the cabbage family, potatoes and fresh beans. Regrettably, this vitamin dissolves in water and much is lost in cooking. Further losses occur by exposure of cut fruit and vegetables to the air.

The role of vitamin D is to assist the body to build bones and teeth, and it controls the absorption of calcium from the digestive system and excretion of calcium from the kidneys. The body can make vitamin D through the action of the sun's ultraviolet rays on the skin. Food sources are such fatty fishes as fresh herring, kippers and sardines and fortified margarine and dairy products.

The effect of vitamin E on the fertility of mice, rabbits and turkeys and unsupported claims for its value in treating heart disease are scarcely reasons for it to become one of the pet vitamins of food faddists. Little of certainty is known about the vitamin, but the body does seem to need it, although in what quantity no one can say. It is present in most food, notably vegetables, fats and the germ of cereal grains.

Vitamin K is required for the clotting of blood. It is found particularly in green leafy vegetables and is manufactured by bacteria in the intestine.

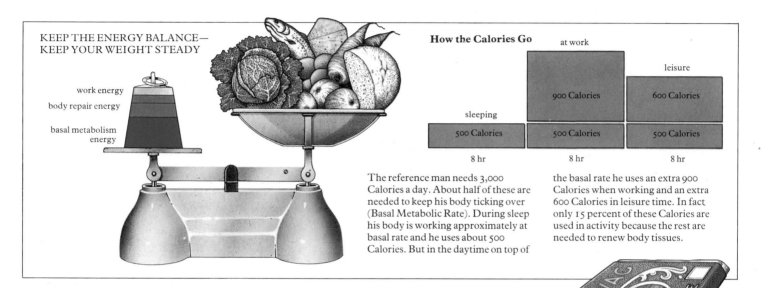

KEEP THE ENERGY BALANCE—
KEEP YOUR WEIGHT STEADY

work energy
body repair energy
basal metabolism energy

How the Calories Go

at work

leisure

sleeping

900 Calories

600 Calories

500 Calories

500 Calories

500 Calories

8 hr   8 hr   8 hr

The reference man needs 3,000 Calories a day. About half of these are needed to keep his body ticking over (Basal Metabolic Rate). During sleep his body is working approximately at basal rate and he uses about 500 Calories. But in the daytime on top of the basal rate he uses an extra 900 Calories when working and an extra 600 Calories in leisure time. In fact only 15 percent of these Calories are used in activity because the rest are needed to renew body tissues.

There has to be a balance between the amount of food energy (calories) we eat and the amount we expend. Even if we take in only a few more calories than we use up—protein calories, fat calories or carbohydrate calories—we become fat.

HAVING DIGESTED the basic facts of nutrition and diet, the next step is to turn this knowledge into meals that you enjoy and from which you will benefit. If only nutrition were an exact science it might be possible to establish a theoretically "perfect diet," but even that would not work in practice because it would ignore individual likes and dislikes. There are, however, certain guidelines to be followed to achieve a balanced diet.

Food and health are indissolubly related. Too often, however, our approach to a healthy diet is negative. We are always lectured about the foods that are "bad" for us and, according to which nutritional theory is currently in favor, we give up potatoes, bread, fat, sugar, eggs or meat, hoping thereby that we will put off illness for as long as possible. But health is more than the state of not being ill.

The World Health Organization has ambitiously defined health as "a state of complete physical, mental and social well being and not merely the absence of disease or infirmity." Not even a "perfect diet" would achieve that, whatever food faddists claim, but there is no doubt that a reasonably balanced diet makes a major contribution to overall health.

The first balance that has to be achieved in a diet is between the energy your food provides and the energy your body uses up. The reason why people become fat is that carbohydrates, fats and proteins—in excess of the body's needs—are turned into fat.

Appetite, controlled by two small areas in the lower part of the brain, is one way of regulating how much you eat, but it is easily led astray. A scale is far more reliable, for if you overeat you will gain weight. The eighteenth-century scholar Dr. Samuel Johnson, speaking with the authority of one who was grossly overweight, was perfectly right when he said to his chronicler Boswell, "Nay sir, whatever may be the quantity that a man eats

Obesity does not necessarily come from gluttony or sloth. A half ounce piece of chocolate in excess per day, for example, is equal to a gain of 28,000 Calories per year or eight pounds of body fat.

it is plain that if he is too fat he has eaten more than he should have done."

But how fat is "too fat"? The chart on page 225 indicates the considered optimum weights for people of various ages, heights and builds. If you are reasonably close to the suggested figures, regular weighing will act as a check on your energy balance. If you are already overweight you should aim to gradually slim down by losing no more than two pounds a week. It should be possible to achieve this with a daily intake of 1,000 fewer Calories than you expend.

Although the energy output of each individual differs, averages have been calculated for people of the same age and weight living in comparable conditions and engaged in a whole range of activities. One such set of calculations has been made by the World Health Organization, taking as the basis a hypothetical reference man. He lives in a temperate zone with a mean annual temperature of 50°F (10°C), is twenty-five years of age and weighs an unchanging 143 pounds (65 kg). He works eight hours a day, not too strenuously, and for the rest of the day he spends four hours sitting around, one and a half hours walking, another one and a half hours in active leisure and then he sleeps. The reference woman is also

People cannot live by bread alone, or indeed on any other single food apart from breast milk. No one food combines all of the vitamins, minerals, amino acids and essential fatty acids in the amounts that we need. Thus it is fortunate that we eat meals rather than food, because it is often the mixture of foods that we choose to eat which provides the balance we need. Even relatively cheap combinations can be well balanced—fish and French fries, spaghetti bolognese or moussaka, for example. Alone the versatile American hamburger is not a balanced meal; but in a bun (which adds extra B vitamins and the carbohydrate that is not found in meat) and eaten with a layer of cheese (which has the calcium and vitamins A and D that meat lacks) and a garnish of red and green peppers (for added vitamin C) it is a perfectly balanced meal.

A balanced diet in pill form would require at least six hundred pills a day.

twenty-five, weighs 120 pounds (55 kg) and is busy doing housework or is employed in a moderately active job.

The reference man is reckoned to have an energy output of 3,000 Calories a day, and the woman one of 2,200 Calories. These estimates are high by American standards (2,800 Calories for men and 2,000 for women). Even 100 Calories a day more than you need can add ten pounds a year to your weight.

Energy is needed simply to keep your heart, lungs and other organs and tissues working, and this, calculated under precisely defined conditions, is known as the Basal Metabolic Rate. Energy output rises as soon as you indulge in any activity, from thinking (a negligible increase), to running upstairs (a large upsurge). Researchers have estimated that playing Beethoven's *Appassionata Sonata* on the piano takes almost twice as much energy as playing one of Mendelssohn's *Songs Without Words* for the same length of time.

Fats, proteins and carbohydrates are our sources of energy. But fats and proteins have nutritional roles that carbohydrates cannot fulfill. So a diet must have a balance between the three nutrients. Proteins are essential for body maintenance, but to consume more than is needed is pointless, for excess protein is converted into fat; one gram of protein provides the same number of Calories (four) as one gram of carbohydrate.

The amount of protein required each day varies considerably according to age. It reaches a peak among teenagers, drops marginally in adulthood and decreases in old age. By the time you are seventy your needs are the same as those of a seven-year-old. The estimated figure for an adult man's daily intake of protein is just over two ounces (60 g) in the United States. A simple rule of thumb for ensuring an adequate (indeed generous) supply of protein is to reckon it as about one-tenth of total energy intake. Thus, if you need 3,000 Calories a day, proteins should provide 300 Calories—that is nearly three ounces (85 g) at 110 Calories an ounce.

But some proteins, depending on the relative amounts of essential amino acids they contain, are more valuable than others. A balance of amino acids is needed in a balanced diet. Wheat, for example, is low in the amino acid lysine, but this can be made good by combining it with such lysine-rich foods as cheese or beans. A diet should be varied to ensure an adequate intake of amino acids. Vegetarians, especially those who do not include milk, cheese and eggs in their diet, must be particularly careful to eat a wide range of vegetables and cereals.

In the West we eat too much fat. Nutritionists generally agree that fats should contribute between 30 to 40 percent of our energy intake. In the United States the proportion has reached over 40 percent of the daily Calorie intake—that means about five ounces (150 g) of fat a day. Fortunately, we are beginning to eat more vegetable fats than animal fats. This means that the diet is less likely to be short of one of the essential fatty acids, linoleic acid, which is low in most visible animal fats, but high in vegetable fats. The invisible fats of animal products do, however, contain some of the other essential fatty acids.

No diet is balanced unless it has an adequate supply of minerals and vitamins. In the main, if we balance our diet by eating a wide range of carbohydrates and proteins plus a discriminating choice of fats we need not worry about consuming enough minerals or vitamins. What we have to guard against is that we do not, by the careless preparation and cooking of food, destroy too many of those precious vitamins.

One other balance has to be achieved—the balance between eating what we like and what is best for us. The solution is to try to make them the same thing.

TABOOS AND ADDICTIONS

Our diets are limited by our refusal to regard all that is edible as food. Most Europeans, for example, refuse to eat horseflesh, not knowing that the origin of the taboo was a directive from the Pope in the eighth century A.D.

Economics and fashion interact. In the nineteenth century oysters, then plentiful, were eaten by London's poor.

Fish Fridays, illustrated in this nineteenth-century painting by Walter Sadler, began as a day of abstaining from meat. Originated by the Roman Catholic Church during the Middle Ages, it now survives as a habit few people question.

SEVERAL MILLION YEARS OF HISTORY have shaped our diet. To go back about seventy-five thousand years Neanderthal man hunted and fished and gathered plants and was not averse to eating his fellow men, although possibly only in times of dire need. The Neanderthals lasted some forty thousand years, and by the end of that time the foundations had been laid for the Neolithic revolution in which man basically changed from hunter-gatherer to farmer.

Experts have rival theories to explain why and how domestication of plants and animals began and developed. But there is no doubt that domestication shifted the emphasis in man's diet from animal to vegetable. Even in the modern, affluent, meat-loving West that has not changed. Indeed it cannot be otherwise if there is to be any hope of feeding soaring populations.

Some of our food habits are entirely irrational, since they merely perpetuate ancient taboos and myths, which have now lost any relevance. They are frequently of religious origin. Throughout recorded history, and probably before, the gods have taken a hand in deciding what we may eat. According to the book of Leviticus in the Old Testament the Lord gave to Moses and Aaron an enormously complex list of forbidden foods. The meat of pig, camel, hare and rock badger was unclean. So was the flesh of any swimming creature without fins and scales. Forbidden birds ranged from eagles to ostriches, with bats included. Winged creatures that "creep, going upon all four" were an abomination unless they also had legs; this let out the locust—a wise provision since more than 50 percent of dried locust is protein and about 20 percent is fat.

The Jewish and Muslim prohibition of pork is based on its being "unclean" meat, but in India the taboo against beef arose because the cow was

Unfortunately, a childhood aversion to certain foods may last through a lifetime.

considered sacred. In ancient Egypt religious taboos limited the meat eaten by royalty to veal and goose.

While most of the taboos and myths apply to animal products there are also aversions to eating certain vegetables. The Jains, an ancient religious sect in India, will not eat vegetables that grow underground, and there are similar taboos in parts of Africa.

The choice of food may also be circumscribed for reasons that have lost any validity. Most Britons, for example, have an aversion to eating horsemeat. By contrast, the early Britons were avid eaters of horse, and it was Pope Gregory III who put a stop to that. In the eighth century, in support of St. Boniface's great missionary campaigns in Germany and England, he ordered that Christians should abstain from eating horseflesh so that they would stand apart from the unconverted pagans. (The British, however, readily send horses to be slaughtered and eaten abroad.)

The English and Americans now eat far less

WEALTH VERSUS HEALTH

During the last century, increasing economic wealth has not only encouraged us to eat more but also to eat the wrong kinds of foods. We now tend to eat an excessive amount of fat, which because of its high calorific value can easily lead to obesity. Even worse, there has been a trend toward eating less vegetable oil and more animal fat, thus unfortunately shifting the balance toward the high cholesterol, saturated kind. Furthermore, we now obtain more calories from sugar than from starchy foods, which do at least contain other nutrients.

On average we eat about five ounces (140 g) of fat a day—two and a half tons in a lifetime.

We eat about four and a half ounces (130 g) of sugar a day—more in two weeks than in a year a century ago.

Ice cream sums up what is wrong with modern eating. A super nonfood made from sugar and saturated fat, it has no other nutrients and provides energy in its least nutritious form.

fish than they do meat. In the Middle Ages in Britain it was the other way around, because the Roman Catholic Church dictated that all Fridays, certain Wednesdays and Saturdays, other occasional days and the forty days of Lent were days on which meat was forbidden but fish was allowed. With the Reformation official fish days disappeared. This change had such disastrous effects on the fishing industry that eventually two fish days were restored, but by the end of the sixteenth century the attempt to enforce them was abandoned. Friday remains the popular unofficial fish day even though today it has little religious significance even for Catholics.

Our choice of staple foods—wheat, rice, potatoes, corn and other grains—is largely decided by where we live and what will grow in that climate. Our food habits are also under strong pressures from national and regional eating habits. Just as important are the likes and dislikes acquired in childhood or as we grew up. Of all the irrational factors that decide what we eat, our fads and fancies can be the most treacherous.

In the affluent West the most obvious dietary vice we have is that we eat so much of what we like that we grow fat. Gluttony and obesity are not, of course, the prerogative of twentieth-century man. The ancient Egyptians overate, but believed that by setting aside three days during each month for vomiting they would remain healthy. (The modern equivalent is to flee periodically to a health farm.) Medieval man was an enormous eater, but he compensated by leading an energetic life. Similarly, although the gluttony of well-to-do Victorians almost matched that of ancient Romans, the Victorians may have been reprieved by the nonexistence of the car.

Modern Western man not only overeats, he is also sedentary and a worrier. His current dietary obsessions center mainly on his obesity and on his fear of early death from heart troubles. The Western woman is also worried about growing fat, as much concerned with her fashionably slim figure as with her health.

While animals in their natural state tend not to overeat, the human appetite may need to be consciously regulated, for there are siren foods that will lead it astray. The most seductive of these are fat and sugar; even monkeys in captivity will quickly develop an excessively sweet tooth.

The Western diet is high in both fat and sugar. Sugar, once an expensive luxury, is now a cheap and large part of our diet. Since the beginning of the twentieth century world consumption of sugar has tripled. The British and Americans are notorious addicts; on average each man, woman and child eats about two pounds of sugar every week. Sugar may be a good source of energy, but it contains no vitamins or minerals. Taken in such large quantities it spoils the appetite for more balanced foods and plays havoc with teeth.

More fat is now being eaten, but the rise in its consumption has been less spectacular than that of sugar. Even in the wealthy United States consumption of fat has risen only 12 percent since the beginning of the twentieth century, while sugar consumption has shot up by 120 percent. It is, however, the combined increase in the amounts of sugar and fat eaten that is important; for example, there are large amounts of both sugar and fat in cakes, puddings, sticky pastries and ice cream. It is unfortunate that sugar and fat are so attractive to the palate and so satisfying to the appetite and that the penalty for over-indulgence is obesity and ill health.

IN THE GRIP OF TECHNOLOGY

The free-range chicken is rapidly becoming a food of the past. "Factory farming" (inset right) is economically so successful that it produces 98 percent of the chicken sold in the United States. The argument for factory farming is simple—that chicken is no longer a luxury food but one that is relatively cheap and available. The argument against is just as clear—for cheaper chicken we have sacrificed flavor.

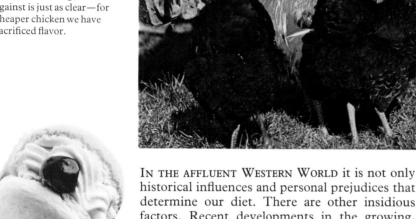

Perhaps it is fortunate that food labels are often imprecise: food technologists may be able to spray-dry blood plasma and mix it with locust bean kernel, thus producing an acceptable alternative to egg white. But would you enjoy eating meringues labeled "containing blood protein"?

IN THE AFFLUENT WESTERN WORLD it is not only historical influences and personal prejudices that determine our diet. There are other insidious factors. Recent developments in the growing, processing and retailing of food are of the greatest significance to our eating habits and health, even though we may be only dimly aware of them.

Immediately disturbing is the quality and taste of the food produced by "factory farming." This cliché describes the new intensive system of raising animals. Pigs, for example, are raised along factory lines, and with machinery for feeding and manure removal one person can look after as many as three thousand pigs. Veal calves are raised intensively and fed solely on milk substitutes until they are killed at three months old. Beef calves may never be allowed out to graze, but are fed lavishly indoors and sold soon after they are a year old.

Intensive production of meat has a considerable, but generally unrealized, effect on our diet. Cattle that graze at large have a high proportion of muscle—that is, lean meat—and very little fat. Intensively fed beef may be one-third fat, even when it looks lean, because of the fat embedded in the muscle—the marbling, which gives much of the succulence to meat. Thus, while we worry about our own obesity we are eating obese meat.

Heavy use of artificial fertilizers, particularly if no organic fertilizers are used as well, can, by affecting the amount of nutrients absorbed by the plants from the soil, reduce the amount of trace elements in our diet. While nitrogen, used by plants to make protein, will increase yield, excessive nitrogen will lower the percentage of protein in a crop, decrease the vitamin content and affect the taste.

Plant breeders have never been so preoccupied with developing varieties that crop heavily, resist disease, mature rapidly, can be harvested by machines and travel well. This may seem praiseworthy, but not when texture and flavor are ruined, as has happened, for example, with potatoes, strawberries and tomatoes.

It was less than two centuries ago that people started eating canned food and barely half a century since their pets did. People had to get along without instant coffee until 1900, frozen vegetables until the 1920s and instant potatoes until 1939. Frozen fish sticks and frozen French fries did not exist twenty years ago. And we have had to wait until the last few years before being able to "enjoy" substitute meat spun out of soybeans. How did the human race ever survive?

Some methods of preserving food have an incredibly long history. Early man observed that food that was dried either by sun or wind did not putrefy or rot. This is because bacteria, yeast and molds that cause food to go bad need moisture to develop. Meat, fish, green vegetables and fruit are now dried in a mechanically produced current of hot air. In the more expensive freeze-drying the food is first frozen, then dried in a near-vacuum, causing the ice to be driven off as vapor without first turning into water. The best instant coffee is made in this way.

Freezing is both the oldest and almost the newest method of preserving food. But until ways of making ice artificially were discovered reliable refrigeration was out of the question. One of the most radical changes in the eating habits of the Western World came about because an American named Clarence Birdseye went on a fur-trading expedition to Labrador in 1912, and realized the commercial possibilities of frozen food. After years of experimenting, in 1924 he put his packaged frozen foods on the market and went on

Technological improvements in food processing are efficient but unromantic. Butter advertisements may feature rural landscapes (below) and farmhouse settings to imply their butter is "naturally" produced. Today commercial butter is never made in such pastoral settings. A modern dairy (right) resembles an operating theater more than a rural landscape by Constable. Technology makes food production more efficient, and hence reduces cost. It also minimizes the chance of bacterial contamination of food. But the price we pay for cheaper, more hygienic food is the loss of much of its original taste and texture.

The proliferation of convenience foods can all too easily seduce you away from good natural food.

to make millions. If you seek a monument to the father of frozen food, look around you in any supermarket.

The convenience-food explosion of the last two decades has changed the Western diet as much as frozen foods have. A convenience food is something that is almost literally handed to you on a plate. All you have to do to the cooked, dried, frozen or canned product is to warm it, add water or milk to it and eat or drink it (the most strenuous part of the operation). The appeal starts early; on the average every baby in the United States eats more than one can or package of baby food a day.

Many people are becoming rightly suspicious about what goes into convenience food. There has, of course, hardly ever been a time when someone has not been tampering with food. It was usually done to cheat, and it was called adulteration. It reached a scandalous peak in the first half of the nineteenth century. There was alum and ground bones in bread, chalk in milk, sulfuric acid in beer and in sugar, floor sweepings in pepper, verdigris and black lead in tea, brick dust in cocoa powder, copper in pickles and red lead in Gloucester cheese.

Today there is less reason to fear such adulteration, but now we have what is called enrichment, which means adding to food substances that have

been lost in processing. White bread, for example, is supplemented with iron, thiamine and niacin, as well as vitamin D and calcium; just some of the nutrients lost in the production of flour. Never have so many permitted substances been added to food. Many countries throughout the world add vitamins and calcium to their basic cereals on nutritional grounds. But additives may also be used to make food acid or alkaline, ensure that it stays moist, or firm and crisp, or glazed to give an appealing shine, while some merely prevent the food from sticking to surfaces while it is being processed. Additives can enhance the flavor of food, or change it completely, and give it irresistible color. The result is that the end product has little resemblance to the original.

To the raw meat basis of "luncheon meat" may be added potato starch (to give texture), sodium caseinate (a stabilizer), salt, emulsifying fats, spices, monosodium glutamate (a flavor enhancer), sodium nitrite (a preservative) and coloring. At least luncheon meat has some meat in it, but artificial cream has none of the ingredients of real cream; instead it is refined sugar, methyl ethyl cellulose, polyoxethylene, sorbitan stearate, salt, sodium alginate, coloring and, of course, synthetic mouth-watering flavoring.

The greater the amount of food that is processed the more additives we are going to consume. While there is no doubt that many additives have a corrupting influence on our appreciation of the true taste of food it is impossible to say with certainty that they are either harmful or harmless; the danger is that we are woefully ignorant about many of the additives we use. A quarter of a century ago about fifteen hundred processed foods were being sold; now the number has increased more than sixfold. Give us this day our daily additives.

TECHNOLOGICAL FISH

The modern fisherman hunts with all the paraphernalia of modern technology. Huge trawlers track down their quarry with electronic devices, hauling in ton after ton of fish to be quick-frozen by the accompanying factory ship. Back in port, skinned fillets are molded and frozen into solid blocks of fish, then sawn into steaks to boil in the bag or cut into strips. The strips progress through a curtain of batter, a shower of brightly colored crumbs, a half-minute dip in a tank of hot fat and finally another quick freeze down to −40°F (−40°C) in a blast of cold air. Ten fish sticks weigh about two hundred and twenty grams, of which about one hundred and fifty grams are water, thirty-five protein and twenty fat. Each fish stick, therefore, provides almost 40 Calories as well as an unidentifiable texture. To label them fish is an affront to one of nature's most wholesome foods.

21

Food Fads

A vegetarian diet is perfectly acceptable if it is not taken to extremes. In Dr. J. H. Kellogg's Battle Creek Sanitarium in Michigan patients were allowed no meat and ended their strictly regimented day with the Grand March (right). Dr. Kellogg (inset right) was, however, careful to ensure that his patients had a varied, and therefore healthy, diet. To add variety he invented many cereal and peanut products which now allow us to enjoy such foods as peanut butter and cornflakes.

THE GROWING REVOLT against the way commercialism desecrates our food is a healthy sign. Unfortunately, the forms the reaction takes are often irrational. One of Brillat-Savarin's aphorisms was: "Animals feed: man eats: only the man of intellect knows how to eat." How wrong he was. People who are otherwise intelligent readily take leave of their senses over their diet, and turn eating first into a fad, then into a cult, then possibly into a way of life and even into a religion. There are no cranks so impervious to reason as food cranks.

History is littered with them. In the second century A.D. the Greek Athenaeus reports in his food guide and cookbook *The Sophists at Dinner* that two of the Sophists lived entirely on figs. Even the fact that they were ostracized at the public baths because they smelled so rank did not persuade them to change their diet.

At the end of the fifteenth century the Venetian Luigi Cornaro decided, after forty years of excessive eating and drinking, to give abstemiousness a chance. For years afterward his diet consisted of exactly twelve ounces of food and fourteen ounces of wine a day. As he grew older he was able to subsist, he claimed, on one egg a day. He lived to be a hundred.

Although vegetarianism attracts innumerable food faddists, the vegetarian diet is a perfectly valid and acceptable one. You may be a vegetarian because, like the Greek philosopher Pythagoras, you believe in the transmigration of souls and respect the sanctity of animals: "Beware, I implore you in the name of the Gods, of expelling their souls, which are cognate to you, from their housings, in order that blood might not be nourished by blood." Many of the world's religions have the deepest respect for animal life, but in the West it is rare. Western vegetarians are more likely to have other motives; they may have an ethical objection to slaughtering animals, a revulsion to the idea of eating their flesh or the belief that, in a world short of food, it would be more economical if grain was fed directly to people. These reasons are to be respected; the argument, however, that it is healthier to eat only vegetables is not proven. Nor is there any evidence that vegetarians are less aggressive and more sweet-tempered than meat-eaters. They are in fact often rather violent in expressing their views.

Dr. Sylvester Graham, the nineteenth-century American "natural" food faddist, whose name lives on in Graham flour, declared: "The enormous wickedness and atrocious violence and outrages of mankind immediately preceding the Flood, strongly indicate, if they do not prove, an excessive indulgence in animal food." His perfect diet went even farther back, to that of the Garden of Eden. "Fruits, nuts, farinaceous seeds and roots, with perhaps some milk and it may be honey, in all rational probability, constituted the food of the first family and the first generations of mankind." He pointed out that the only processing needed in that diet was to crack the nuts.

In the nineteenth century in both Britain and the United States there were strongly religious and puritanical elements in vegetarianism. Dr. Graham, described by the nineteenth-century writer Ralph Waldo Emerson as "the poet of bran bread and pumpkins," advocated not only natural foods but temperance, chastity, hard mattresses, cold showers and cheerfulness at meals.

Vegetarianism is closely connected with the Seventh Day Adventists. Dr. J. H. Kellogg, when he was the director of the Battle Creek Sanitarium in Michigan, toward the end of the nineteenth century, invented eighty or more

Grapefruit has no magic properties, although some people believe that eating a grapefruit before a meal will burn up all the calories they'll consume afterward.

Zen Macrobiotics are based on the traditional diet of the vegetarian Zen Buddhist monks in Japan (right). Unfortunately the diet has too often been taken to extremes, notably by Western youth in the 1960s, until the devotee has finished up on an unnourishing diet exclusively of brown rice. Such a diet inevitably leads to malnutrition. Zen Macrobiotics in fact recognizes the importance of vegetables in the diet and even considers small amounts of fish and poultry to be acceptable secondary foods.

grain and peanut products to give variety to the patients' vegetarian diet. These included peanut butter and cornflakes, the basis of the vast food industry developed by his brother, W. K. Kellogg.

One of the pioneers of the vegetarian movement in Britain was the nineteenth-century Scot Dr. George Cheyne, who was disgustingly obese. When he reached four hundred and forty-eight pounds he decided that something must be done, and for several months he adopted a light diet of vegetables and milk. Of course he lost weight, but this was because he was eating less, not because he had given up meat. In fact many of the claims for all kinds of diets are more likely to be arguments against overeating.

Some food cults concentrate on the eating of raw vegetarian foods. The twentieth-century Swiss physician Dr. Bircher-Benner did so because he held that all heating of food was bad.

Many modern fads are connected with the obsession to be thin. Various foods—peanuts, honey, bananas and milk—have their bigoted disciples. The myth attached to grapefruit is the most odd; to it is attributed the magical quality of burning up fat inside the body. Even seemingly reasonable people believe this.

Americans are particularly susceptible to fad diets and their commercial exploitation is one of the country's great growth industries. The Germans are not far behind, and some of their cults are based on American fads. In the 1950s the American "Separating Diet" fad was introduced into Germany. Various foods could not be mixed, and had to be taken separately in three meals a day: one of milk, vegetables and fruit; one of starchy foods; and one of such protein foods as meat and eggs. The concept is ridiculous if only because many natural foods contain all three

types of nutrient. The "Point Diet" was introduced in the late 1960s and had some resemblance to the "Drinking Man's Diet" in the United States. It was high in fat and alcohol and low in vegetables and fruits, so cutting down the intake of vitamins and minerals.

The United States Food and Drug Administration blames the addiction of Americans to food cults on four "myths," which are said to have misled the American public. These are that faulty diet is the cause of all disease; that foods are overprocessed; that chemical fertilizers are bad for health; and that depletion of the soil leads to malnutrition.

Yet in each of those "myths" there is some truth. A faulty diet is likely to cause ill health. Food is overprocessed to the point of boredom, if nothing more. Chemical fertilizers and depletion of the soil do affect the composition of foods. It is the irrational conclusions drawn from such facts that make people fall prey to health quacks and commercial operators, who make fortunes out of the fears of the gullible.

"It would be a good deal better for these people," said the British nutrition expert Sir Jack Drummond, who became well known during the Second World War, "if they would adopt a simple and more rational diet in their everyday life." But a "simple diet" must not involve restricting the variety of foods eaten, as Dr. William Stark demonstrated. In 1769 he set out to discover whether "a pleasant and varied diet is equally conducive to health with a more strict and simple one." The simple diets he chose included bread and water for two weeks, bread, water and sugar for a month, bread and olive oil, and finally honey puddings and Cheshire cheese. The honey pudding and Cheshire cheese diet was his last because after suffering from scurvy and digestive troubles for six months he died at the age of thirty. One obituary notice read that "he fell a victim to his enthusiasm."

There could be no clearer evidence of the need for eating as wide a range of foods as possible. In such a diet the only restraint to be exercised is in the amount you eat.

THE GOOD INGREDIENTS

"NOTHING TO EAT BUT FOOD" runs one line of a nineteenth-century poem called *The Pessimist*, and what a fantastic choice that still gives us. But the staple food of most of the world is derived from just a handful of grasses. Grains, therefore, which are plentiful and nutritious, have pride of place among the good ingredients.

The climate of the part of the world in which we live usually decides what grains we eat. In temperate climates they will be mainly wheat and rye, with some oats and barley. In the tropics and subtropics they will be rice, corn and millet. Only from wheat and rye can a good bread flour be obtained; the other crops are eaten as grain or are ground to make gruels and porridges or flat breads.

Whatever the grain, and however it is eaten, it is the cheapest and most important source of our energy. And because we eat grain products in large amounts they also contribute a fair proportion of the proteins we require.

The major sources of protein in Western countries are animal products. These foods are high in good-quality protein, but whereas there is comparatively little fat in most fish and poultry, there is a substantial amount in meat and only a small proportion of it is polyunsaturated. So while meat can be considered to be among the good ingredients, except by vegetarians, most people who can afford it probably eat too much of it. Conventional American meals make excessive meat-eating almost inevitable. And the "meat and two vegetable" syndrome quite unnecessarily denigrates the role vegetables should have. The French have a better way with vegetables, which are served on their own and not as part of the meat course.

The importance given to meat in Western diets is curious considering that the choice of meat is limited almost to the point of monotony; beef, lamb, pork and chicken—only a minority of people venture beyond these. By comparison plants can give an infinite variety of natural flavors to a diet, without the need of elaborate artifice by the cook.

Some vegetables that are dug out of the ground rate as staple foods in many parts of the world. These include potatoes, yams, cassava, taro and sweet potatoes, all of which are rich in carbohydrates. Other roots and tubers—carrots, turnips, rutabaga, parsnips, beets, Jerusalem artichokes—provide sweetness and different flavors. They are invaluable, too, because they can be stored for use in the winter. They are not particularly rich in vitamins, but these can be found in greater profusion in leaf vegetables and brassicas. Cabbage, kale, turnip tops, broccoli and spinach are, above all, good sources of vitamin C.

The onion family is in a class of its own among

vegetables, and has been for thousands of years. Quite why is not clear. A boiled onion contains very little protein, even less fat, few calories and only a token amount of vitamins. Even its showing on minerals is only fair and it is beaten hands down by celery. In spite of that it is hard to envisage a diet that lacks the flavor of onions. Substituting ethyl thiocyanate for real onions and diallyl disulphide for garlic is a bad second best.

Delicious and satisfying, the seeds and pods of leguminous plants—peas, beans and lentils—are rich in protein and can help us to escape from our overdependence on meat. They are also delicious and satisfying, either fresh in summer or dried in winter.

Stalks and shoots—asparagus, artichokes, kale and, of course, celery—give us some of the most delicate and desirable flavors. The fruits of vegetable plants—tomatoes, squashes, eggplant, peppers, cucumbers and avocados—contribute pleasure as well as nutrients to the diet. For the overfed, tomatoes have the negative virtue of being low in carbohydrate, while avocados and olives are unique among fruits in having up to 17 percent fat, instead of the usual trace amount.

There are many vegetables that can be eaten raw, thus avoiding the loss of nutrients in cooking. They add variety to the established salad plants— the inevitable lettuce and cress, chicory and endive, or to the less frequently encountered dandelion, corn salad and celtuce.

Without doubt vegetables rank high among the good ingredients. There is one great drawback. They are never as good, either in food value or in flavor, when you buy them as when they are harvested. The answer is to grow your vegetables yourself.

If you can grow some fruit as well, so much the better, but unfortunately, few people can or do. In fact the average American eats little more than one and a half pounds of fruit a week. Americans would be healthier and thinner if only they could be persuaded to abandon starchy, sugar-saturated desserts in favor of fruit, preferably uncooked.

Completing the cornucopia of good ingredients are herbs, spices and flavorings. Tactfully used they will enhance or complement the flavors of other foods. Although chemists can identify and imitate their flavors, the imitations are but crude approximations of the originals.

It would be pointless taking all the care in the world to eat wholesome food if we swilled it down with poison. With the proliferation of synthetic soft drinks there is every opportunity to do so.

Furthermore, as Socrates used to remind his pupils, we should eat only when we are hungry and stop long before we feel bloated. The Christian grace before meals could well be changed to make us truly thankful for what we are about to receive—in moderation.

WHEAT/The Most Versatile Grain

a head of durum wheat

a head of bread wheat

a head of English wheat

THE WORLD WE KNOW TODAY could not have come into existence without grain; no other food could have supported such vast populations. The six main crops—wheat, rice, rye, oats, corn and barley—would provide enough grain, if shared out equally, for each person in the world to have nearly six hundred pounds (270 kg) a year. Western city dwellers may take their bread and pasta for granted, but to the peasant the grain harvest is as worthy of veneration as it was to the ancients.

Of all the grains wheat is the most venerable and valuable. Although barley has as long a history it is not so widely used, and rice is more recent. Only rye approaches wheat as a bread grain.

From the wild species of wheat that evolved at the end of the last Ice Age came the first cultivated wheat, einkhorn, and the first bread wheat, emmer. Selective breeding of emmer has produced today's two great wheats—*Triticum aestivum*, which, in its thousands of varieties, is the wheat used in bread making, and *Triticum durum*, the basis of pasta.

A field of ripe wheat is staggeringly beautiful, but totally inedible. Before humans can digest it the grain has to be threshed to separate it from the stalks and chaff, and then milled and cooked.

In milling the first of a succession of rollers breaks open the whole grain and the outer coat is sifted out. What is left is then passed through more rollers, each grinding being followed by a sifting. The fineness of the sieve decides the so-called extraction rate, which is simply the percentage of the original wheat that remains in the flour. If nothing, not even the coarse bran, is sieved out, the extraction rate is 100 percent and the flour is used for whole-wheat bread. Other brown bread is baked from flour with extraction rates of between 80 and 90 percent. The whitest bread has an extraction rate of about 72 percent. Usually all bread, except whole-wheat, is enriched with calcium, iron, niacin and thiamine.

Most people prefer white bread. Yet brown bread is certainly more nutritious because it contains more protein, fat, iron, thiamine, riboflavin and niacin. Protagonists of white bread point out that whole-wheat bread has more indigestible fiber and that the phytic acid in the fiber combines with the calcium in the flour to prevent the absorption of calcium in the intestine. The brown-bread supporters retort that roughage is good for you, that it is far cheaper eaten in bread than in breakfast cereals and that in any event the amount of bread we eat does not raise phytic acid to dangerous levels. Actually the choice between brown and white bread is usually made as a matter of taste, and there is no reason why we should not enjoy the flavors and textures of both.

To taste bread as it should be, however, you should make your own. Most of the bread sold in stores is made by a process in which a pre-fermented brew is mixed into the flour by blades working at very high speeds. The operation takes about sixty seconds and produces a continuous stream of oven-ready dough. Such technologically processed bread can be relied on not to vary greatly from day to day.

Home-baked bread has no such uniformity. Two people making bread according to the same recipe are liable to produce loaves of widely different taste and texture, each having an individual character that is totally lacking in mass-produced, sliced and wrapped bread.

The magic ingredient, shared by wheat and rye

flour, is gluten, a complex of two proteins, which becomes viscous when water is added and so produces a dough. The dough is made to rise by the use of carbon dioxide, traditionally produced by the slow fermentation of yeast; the trapped bubbles of gas are responsible for the mass of small holes in the bread. Kneading stretches the gluten fibers and this, combined with the action of carbon dioxide gas, gives the dough elasticity and a fine, smooth texture.

Soft water gives a better dough than hard water, which slows down the fermentation of the yeast. Salt may make a dough sticky, but, on the other hand, it gives flavor and helps to form a crisp crust.

STRUCTURE OF WHOLE-WHEAT

The germ, or seed, of a wheat grain is nourished by a starchy endosperm and protected by a coat of indigestible fiber, or bran. In the milling of whole-wheat flour the bran and germ are retained; whole-wheat bread, therefore, provides roughage, B vitamins and iron as well as starch. White flour is often fortified with nutrients.

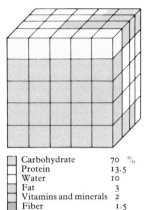

bran

endosperm

germ

The Nutrients in Wheat
Wheat contains more protein than any other cereal and is high in calories. Three and a half ounces (100 g) provide about 330 Calories.

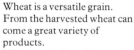

Carbohydrate	70 %
Protein	13.5
Water	10
Fat	3
Vitamins and minerals	2
Fiber	1.5

Wheat is a versatile grain. From the harvested wheat can come a great variety of products.
Wheat can be bought not only in its processed forms but also as a whole grain. The grain must be cooked in water or other liquid before it can be eaten.
Pasta in its simplest form is made from semolina and water. Semolina is the endosperm removed from coarsely ground durum wheat. Pasta comes in innumerable shapes, from tubular macaroni to flat lasagne.
Ready-to-eat cereals are made from wheat grains that have been cooked as they are processed. To make good the nutrient losses in processing some cereals are enriched with vitamins, iron or protein. The high-gluten content of wheat makes it the best cereal grain for bread making. The type of bread made depends upon the variety of wheat used and the amount of bran and germ removed in the manufacture of the flour.

THERE IS SOMETHING immensely gratifying about producing a loaf of bread, from kneading the dough and seeing it rise to removing the baked loaf from the oven, brown, crusty and fragrant.

The basic ingredients for bread baking are flour, yeast, salt and water or milk.

FLOUR
Use all-purpose flour, which has a high gluten content, for the lightest bread; and whole-wheat, granary or rye flour for the tastiest. Bread made only with whole-wheat or rye flour is rather close and heavy textured, while a mixture of whole-wheat or rye and all-purpose flour produces a lighter loaf with a rich color and flavor. Cake flour or self-rising flour is unsuitable for bread baking because it is made from soft wheat and lacks the gluten necessary.

YEAST
Yeast is a living organism that grows when it is provided with warmth and moisture. As it grows it produces carbon dioxide, which causes the bread dough to rise.

Fresh yeast is available from some bakers and from health-food stores. It looks like pale cream-colored putty and should be smooth and moist. It can be stored in a sealed plastic bag in the refrigerator for up to two weeks, or in the freezer for up to one year.

Generally, fresh yeast is sold in the form of a small "cake" that weighs two-thirds of an ounce (19 g). Throughout this book when a cake of compressed yeast is specified, it refers to a two-third-ounce cake of fresh yeast.

Dried yeast, which is more widely available, must be reconstituted before it can be used in bread baking. Dissolve one teaspoon of sugar in a little lukewarm water, then add the yeast. Leave it in a warm, draft-free place for ten to twenty minutes, or until the mixture becomes frothy.

Dried yeast will keep for up to six months if it is stored in an airtight container in a cool place.

When substituting dried yeast for fresh yeast, two teaspoons of dried yeast equals two-thirds of an ounce of fresh yeast.

Although yeast is the most commonly used rising agent, or leavening, baking powder, sour milk or baking soda are also used.

SALT
A little salt, about two teaspoons to every pound (four cups) of flour, is added to improve the flavor of the bread. Too much salt will, however, slow down the growth of the yeast.

LIQUID
The liquid used to bind the dough is usually water, but milk or a mixture of milk and water may be used. Always use tepid liquid—if it is too hot it will kill the yeast—and add it all at one time. Extra flour may be added if the dough is too sticky.

A batter may be made from the yeast, the liquid and one-third of the flour specified in the recipe. Let the mixture stand for twenty minutes, or until it is puffed up and frothy, then add the rest of the flour with the other ingredients. This method of incorporating the yeast is best suited to rich doughs.

ENRICHED DOUGH
Fat, molasses or honey, malt and eggs may also be added to bread dough. Butter or oil improves the flavor of bread and helps it to stay fresh longer, but polyunsaturated margarine, which has the same effect, can always be substituted. Molasses, honey or malt also add flavor and give the bread a good, dark color. Eggs may be added to bread dough to give it a yellow color and a rich flavor.

MIXING THE DOUGH
Put the flour and salt into a mixing bowl. Make a well in the flour and pour in the yeast, then stir thoroughly with a wooden spoon. Continue to bind the dough with your hands until it comes away cleanly from the sides of the bowl.

KNEADING
Thorough kneading of the dough is very important to develop the elasticity of the gluten. Turn the dough out onto a lightly floured surface and knead by lifting and folding one end of the dough toward you into the center, then pushing it down and away from you with the heel of your hand. Give the dough a quarter turn after each fold and continue kneading for ten minutes, or until the dough is firm and elastic and no longer sticks to your hands.

RISING
Shape the dough into a ball and put it into a lightly greased bowl. To keep the dough from drying out while it is rising, cover it lightly with greased plastic wrap, or oil the inside of a large plastic bag and put the dough inside it.

Put the dough in a warm place to rise until it has doubled in bulk and springs back into shape if you press it lightly with a floured finger.

In a warm place the dough will rise in forty-five to sixty minutes. At room temperature it will take about two hours, in a cool place it will take twelve hours and in a refrigerator it will take about twenty-four hours.

Dough that has risen in the cold should be brought back to room temperature before it is knocked back.

KNOCKING BACK
When the dough has risen, knead it again for two to three minutes to knock out the air bubbles and to reduce the dough to its original size.

SHAPING
Roll the dough up, or shape it into a rectangle by folding each side under, to fit into a loaf pan. The dough should come no higher than halfway up the sides of the pan.

Alternatively, the dough may be formed into a variety of shapes such as a cottage loaf, a round loaf, a French loaf or individual rolls and put onto a greased baking sheet.

MAKING BREAD DOUGH

Make a well in the flour and pour in the yeast liquid.

Knead the dough; push away with the heel of the hand.

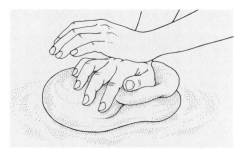

Lift and fold the end of the dough toward you. Repeat.

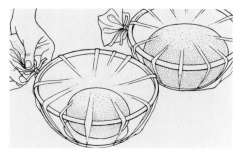

Put the dough in a warm place to double in bulk.

PROVING

After shaping the dough, cover it lightly with greased plastic wrap and put it in a warm place to rise for twenty to thirty minutes, or until it has doubled in bulk or has reached the top of the loaf pan.

GLAZES AND FINISHES

The top of the loaf may be left plain, dusted with flour for a soft crust or glazed with beaten egg mixed with a little milk for a shiny crust. A saltwater glaze gives a crisp, hard crust. The loaf may also be sprinkled with cracked wheat, sesame seeds or poppy seeds.

BAKING

Bread must be baked in a very hot, preheated oven. A shallow baking pan filled with water and placed in the bottom of the oven hardens the crust and improves the texture of the bread.

Bread is done when it shrinks slightly from the sides of the pan and sounds hollow when it is removed from the pan and tapped sharply with the knuckles underneath. Cool the loaf on a wire rack.

STORAGE

Risen dough may be wrapped in a greased plastic bag and stored in the refrigerator for a couple of days before it is shaped and baked.

Baked loaves must be thoroughly cooled before being stored in a covered, but ventilated, container.

FREEZING

Risen or unrisen dough may be frozen, but it is advisable to use 50 percent more yeast than is stated in the recipe.

Put the dough in a greased plastic bag, insert a straw into the opening and suck out the air before sealing the bag.

Unrisen plain dough may be frozen for two months and enriched dough for one month. Risen dough may be frozen for up to one month.

Baked plain bread may be frozen for one month and enriched bread for two months. The bread must be left to cool completely before being wrapped in foil or sealed in a plastic bag.

Basic Bread

Whole-wheat flour, white flour or a mixture of flours may be used for this easy-to-make, traditional bread.

In a large bowl mix 6 cups of whole-wheat flour and 1 tablespoon of salt. Add 1 tablespoon of margarine or butter and rub it into the flour.

Blend 1 cake of compressed yeast with 2 scant cups of tepid water. Mix until the yeast has dissolved. Make a well in the flour and pour in the yeast liquid. Mix the ingredients together until they form a firm dough. After the initial stirring with a wooden spoon it is best to bind the dough with your hands.

Turn the dough out onto a lightly floured surface. Knead the dough well for 10 minutes, or until it becomes firm and elastic and no longer sticks to your fingers.

Lightly grease a large bowl. Shape the dough into a ball and put it into the bowl. Cover the bowl lightly with greased plastic wrap and put it in a warm place to rise for 45 to 60 minutes, or until the dough has doubled in bulk.

When the dough has risen, turn it out onto a floured surface and knead it again for 2 to 3 minutes. Shape the dough into a loaf and place it in a well-greased, large loaf pan or in two 5- by 9-inch (13- by 23-cm) pans.

Preheat the oven to 450°F (230°C).

Cover the pan with greased plastic wrap. Put the dough in a warm place to rise for 20 to 30 minutes, or until it rises to the top of the pan.

Remove the plastic wrap and place the loaf in the center of the oven. If the loaf is browning too quickly, after 15 minutes reduce the oven temperature to 400°F (200°C) and continue baking for 15 to 25 minutes more.

Remove the loaf from the oven and turn it out of the pan. Tap the base of the loaf. If it sounds hollow it is ready. Cool the loaf on a wire rack.

INGREDIENTS TO MAKE ONE LARGE LOAF:
6 cups (750 g) whole-wheat flour
1 tablespoon (15 ml) salt
1 tablespoon (15 g) margarine or butter
1 cake compressed yeast
2 scant cups (450 ml) tepid water

Granary Loaf

This wholesome whole-wheat bread contains cracked wheat, wheat germ and malt, which give the loaf its grainy texture and rich flavor.

In a large bowl mix 2½ cups of whole-wheat flour with 2½ cups of all-purpose flour and 1 tablespoon of salt.

Add 1 tablespoon of margarine or butter to the flour and rub it in. Add ¾ cup of cracked wheat and ⅔ cup of wheat germ to the flour and mix in well.

In a bowl blend 1 cake of compressed yeast with 1 scant cup of tepid water and 1 scant cup of tepid milk. Mix until the yeast is dissolved. Make a well in the flour and pour in the yeast liquid. Add 2 tablespoons of malt. Mix all the ingredients to form a soft dough.

Turn the dough out onto a floured surface and knead it well for 10 minutes, or until it becomes firm and elastic and is no longer sticky.

Lightly grease a large bowl. Place the dough in the bowl and lightly cover it with greased plastic wrap. Put the dough in a warm place to rise for 45 to 60 minutes, or until it has doubled in bulk.

When the dough has risen, knead it again for 2 to 3 minutes. Divide the dough in half and shape each half into a round loaf. Place the loaves on a greased baking sheet. Sprinkle 2 tablespoons of cracked wheat over the loaves.

Preheat the oven to 425°F (220°C).

Cover the baking sheet with greased plastic wrap and put the dough in a warm place to rise for 20 to 30 minutes, or until the dough has doubled in bulk.

Remove the plastic wrap and place the loaves in the oven. After 15 minutes lower the oven temperature to 375°F (190°C) and continue baking for 20 to 25 minutes more.

Remove the loaves from the oven. Tap the base of each loaf. If it sounds hollow the bread is ready. Cool the loaves on a wire rack.

INGREDIENTS TO MAKE TWO SMALL LOAVES:
2½ cups (350 g) whole-wheat flour
2½ cups (350 g) all-purpose flour
1 tablespoon (15 ml) salt
1 tablespoon (15 g) margarine or butter
¾ cup plus 2 tablespoons (125 g) cracked wheat
⅔ cup (50 g) wheat germ
1 cake compressed yeast
1 scant cup (225 ml) tepid water
1 scant cup (225 ml) tepid milk
2 tablespoons (30 ml) malt

English Muffins

The muffin man was once a familiar sight in English streets, selling fresh muffins hot from the oven. Today authentic English muffins are less easy to buy, but fortunately these unsweetened, soft, round buns are simple to make at home.

Put 4 cups of all-purpose flour into a mixing bowl with 1 teaspoon of salt. Blend 1 cake of compressed yeast with $1\frac{1}{4}$ cups of warm milk. Mix until the yeast is dissolved. Make a well in the center of the flour and pour in the yeast liquid. Mix the ingredients together to form a soft dough.

Turn the dough out onto a floured surface and knead it well for 10 minutes, or until it becomes firm and elastic and is no longer sticky.

Lightly grease a large bowl. Put the dough in the bowl and cover it with greased plastic wrap. Put the dough in a warm place to rise for 45 to 60 minutes, or until it has doubled in bulk.

When the dough has risen, knead it again for 2 to 3 minutes. Roll the dough out until it is about $\frac{1}{2}$ inch (1 cm) thick. Cut 3-inch (8-cm) rounds out of the dough and put them on a floured baking sheet. Dust the rounds with flour and put them in a warm place to rise for 20 to 30 minutes.

Cook the muffins gently on a griddle or in a large, greased frying pan for about 5 minutes on each side until they are golden brown. Alternatively, preheat the oven to 400°F (200°C) and bake them for 15 to 20 minutes.

Serve the muffins hot and spread with butter, or split them in half and toast them.

INGREDIENTS TO MAKE TWELVE MUFFINS:
4 cups (500 g) all-purpose flour
1 teaspoon (5 ml) salt
1 cake compressed yeast
$1\frac{1}{4}$ cups (300 ml) warm milk

Garlic and Herb French Bread

Eat French bread on the day it is baked. Older loaves are delicious if warmed in the oven, 400°F (200°C), for 20 minutes.

Put 6 cups of all-purpose flour into a large mixing bowl with 1 tablespoon of salt.

Blend 1 cake of compressed yeast with 2 scant cups of tepid water. Mix until the yeast is dissolved. Make a well in the flour and pour in the yeast liquid. Mix the ingredients together until they form a firm dough.

Turn the dough out onto a floured surface and knead it well for 10 minutes, or until the dough becomes firm and elastic and is no longer sticky.

Lightly grease a large bowl. Put the dough in the bowl and cover it lightly with greased plastic wrap. Put the dough in a warm place

to rise for 45 to 60 minutes, or until it has doubled in bulk.

Meanwhile soften $\frac{1}{2}$ cup of margarine or butter in a bowl. Add 3 or 4 finely chopped garlic cloves (depending on taste), 1 tablespoon of dried mixed herbs and 1 tablespoon of chopped parsley and mix well.

When the dough has risen, turn it out onto a floured surface and knead it again for 2 or 3 minutes. Divide the dough in two and roll each half out to form an oval as long as a baking sheet, about 10 by 14 inches (25 by 35 cm).

Spread half of the prepared butter mixture on each piece of dough, leaving a 1-inch (2-cm) margin all around the edges. Roll each oval up tightly lengthwise and seal the edges.

Preheat the oven to 425°F (220°C).

Put the loaves with the seams underneath on a well-greased baking sheet. Make diagonal slits into the top of the loaves at 2-inch (5-cm) intervals. Cover the baking sheet with greased plastic wrap and put the dough in a warm place to rise for 20 to 30 minutes.

Remove the plastic wrap from the loaves. For a crisp crust, brush the loaves with 1 teaspoon of salt dissolved in 4 tablespoons of water.

Bake the loaves for 15 minutes, or until they are crisp and golden brown. Remove the loaves from the oven. Tap the base of each loaf. If it sounds hollow the bread is ready. Cool the loaves on a wire rack.

INGREDIENTS TO MAKE TWO LOAVES:
6 cups (750 g) all-purpose flour
1 tablespoon (15 ml) salt
1 cake compressed yeast
2 scant cups (450 ml) tepid water
$\frac{1}{2}$ cup (100 g) margarine or butter
3 or 4 garlic cloves
1 tablespoon (15 ml) dried mixed herbs
1 tablespoon (15 ml) chopped parsley

ADDING FLAVOR TO FRENCH LOAVES

Spread the filling over the dough and roll it up.

Franciscan Pizza

Put 2 cups of all-purpose flour and 1 teaspoon of salt into a mixing bowl. Blend $\frac{1}{2}$ cake of compressed yeast with $\frac{2}{3}$ cup of tepid water until the yeast is dissolved. Make a well in the flour and pour in the yeast liquid. Mix the ingredients together until they form a firm dough.

Turn the dough out onto a floured surface and knead it well for 10 minutes, or until the dough becomes firm and elastic and is no longer sticky.

Lightly grease a large bowl. Put the dough into the bowl and cover it with greased plastic wrap. Put the dough in a warm place to rise for 45 to 60 minutes, or until it has doubled in bulk.

Meanwhile, heat 1 tablespoon of corn oil in a frying pan. Add 2 cups of sliced onions to the pan and fry them gently for 5 minutes, or until they are soft. Remove the onions from the pan, add a little more oil if necessary and fry $\frac{1}{2}$ cup of sliced mushrooms for 2 minutes.

Thinly slice 3 ounces of salami, 2 blanched and peeled tomatoes and 2 ounces of Bel Paese or Mozzarella cheese.

When the dough has risen, turn it out onto a lightly floured surface and knead it for 2 to 3 minutes. Roll out the dough to form a 9-inch (23-cm) round and put it on a greased baking sheet.

Preheat the oven to 425°F (220°C).

Spread the cooked onions over the dough and arrange the slices of salami around the edge. Put the cooked mushrooms over the onions, cover them with the tomato slices and top the tomatoes with the cheese. Sprinkle with 1 teaspoon of dried oregano and freshly ground black pepper. Put the pizza in a warm place to rise for 15 minutes.

Bake the pizza for 20 to 25 minutes, or until it has risen and is lightly browned around the edges.

INGREDIENTS TO MAKE ONE 9-INCH (23-CM) PIZZA:
2 cups (250 g) all-purpose flour
1 teaspoon (5 ml) salt
$\frac{1}{2}$ cake compressed yeast
$\frac{2}{3}$ cup (150 ml) tepid water
1 tablespoon (15 ml) corn oil
2 cups (250 g) sliced onions
$\frac{1}{2}$ cup (75 g) sliced mushrooms
3 oz (75 g) salami
2 tomatoes
2 oz (50 g) Bel Paese or Mozzarella cheese
1 teaspoon (5 ml) dried oregano
freshly ground black pepper

Orange Savarin

Here is a simple recipe for an impressive dessert that can be made several days in advance.

In a large bowl mix together 4 tablespoons of all-purpose flour, 1 cake of compressed yeast and ⅔ cup of warm milk. Put the bowl in a warm place for about 20 minutes, or until the mixture has become puffed up and frothy.

Add 1 cup of all-purpose flour, ¼ teaspoon of salt, 1 tablespoon of sugar, 1 beaten egg and 2 tablespoons of softened margarine or butter to the yeast mixture. Beat all the ingredients together thoroughly for 3 minutes.

Preheat the oven to 400°F (200°C).

Grease a 4-cup (7-inch) ring mold and spoon the mixture into it. Cover the mold with greased plastic wrap and put the mixture in a warm place to rise for 20 to 30 minutes, or until it almost reaches the top of the pan. Remove the plastic wrap. Bake the savarin for 20 to 25 minutes, or until it is firm and golden brown.

Allow the savarin to cool for 5 minutes before turning it out onto a serving dish. Prick it all over with a fork. Add 2 tablespoons of rum to 2 cups of orange juice and pour this mixture over the warm savarin. Let the savarin cool.

Warm 3 tablespoons of honey and brush it over the surface of the savarin. Peel and remove the pith from 3 oranges and cut the membrane away from the segments of fruit. Mix the orange segments with ½ pound of seedless grapes and pile them into the center.

Prick the savarin then brush with honey.

INGREDIENTS TO SERVE SIX:
1¼ cups (125 g) all-purpose flour
1 cake compressed yeast
⅔ cup (150 ml) warm milk
¼ teaspoon (1 ml) salt
1 tablespoon (15 ml) sugar
1 egg
2 tablespoons (25 g) margarine or butter
2 tablespoons (30 ml) rum
2 cups (450 ml) orange juice
3 tablespoons (45 ml) honey
3 oranges
½ lb (250 g) seedless grapes

Savory Country Loaf

Broil 8 slices of bacon. Chop it finely.

In a large bowl mix together 3 cups of all-purpose flour, 3 cups of whole-wheat flour, 1 tablespoon of salt and a large pinch of pepper. Grate ¼ pound of sharp Cheddar cheese and mix three-quarters of it into the flour together with the bacon and 1 tablespoon of chopped sage leaves.

Blend 1 cake of compressed yeast with 2 scant cups of tepid water. Mix until the yeast is dissolved. Make a well in the dry ingredients and pour in the yeast liquid. Mix the ingredients together until they form a firm dough.

Turn the dough out onto a lightly floured surface and knead it well for 10 minutes, or until it is firm and elastic and is no longer sticky.

Place the dough in a lightly greased bowl and cover it with greased plastic wrap. Put the dough in a warm place to rise for 45 to 60 minutes, or until it has doubled in bulk.

When the dough has risen, turn it out onto a lightly floured surface and knead it for 2 to 3 minutes.

Cut off a quarter of the dough. Shape the larger piece of dough into a ball and place it on a greased baking sheet. Shape the smaller piece of dough into a ball and place it on top of the larger ball. Flour the handle of a wooden spoon and push it through the center of both balls, then pull it out again quickly.

Preheat the oven to 425°F (220°C).

Cover the baking sheet with greased plastic wrap and put the dough in a warm place to rise for 20 to 30 minutes, or until it has doubled in bulk.

Sprinkle the loaf with the remaining grated cheese. Bake the loaf for 30 minutes, or until it is well risen, browned and sounds hollow when tapped underneath. Cool the loaf on a wire rack.

INGREDIENTS TO MAKE ONE LARGE LOAF:
8 slices bacon
3 cups (350 g) all-purpose flour
3 cups (350 g) whole-wheat flour
1 tablespoon (15 ml) salt
pepper
¼ lb (100 g) sharp Cheddar cheese
1 tablespoon (15 ml) chopped sage
1 cake compressed yeast
2 scant cups (450 ml) tepid water

Pitta Bread

Pitta is a traditional Middle Eastern bread with a soft white crust and a chewy inside that is ideal for absorbing sauces. The pitta must be baked in a hot oven, where it will puff up with a pocket of air inside. It is often slit in half and the pocket inside filled with hot kebabs, onions, tomatoes and coriander leaves.

Put 4 cups of all-purpose flour into a mixing bowl with 1 teaspoon of salt. Dissolve 1 cake of compressed yeast in 1¼ cups of tepid water. Make a well in the flour and pour in the yeast liquid. Mix the ingredients together until they form a firm dough.

Turn the dough out onto a floured surface and knead it well for 10 minutes, or until the dough becomes firm and elastic and is no longer sticky.

Lightly grease a large bowl. Shape the dough into a ball and put it into the bowl. Brush the dough with oil to keep it from becoming crusty. Cover the bowl lightly with plastic wrap and put the dough in a warm place to rise for 45 to 60 minutes, or until it has doubled in bulk.

Put 2 greased baking sheets in the oven and preheat the oven to 450°F (230°C).

Turn the risen dough out onto a lightly floured surface and knead it for 2 to 3 minutes. Divide the dough into 6 pieces. Dust each piece with flour and roll it out to form an oval approximately 8 by 5 inches (20 by 13 cm) and ¼ inch (6 mm) thick. Put the pieces of dough on a floured board and dust them with flour.

Cover the dough with greased plastic wrap and put it in a warm place to rise for 20 to 30 minutes.

Remove the plastic wrap and transfer the pitta very quickly to the hot baking sheets in the oven. Bake for about 10 minutes, or until they are just beginning to turn light brown. If the oven and baking sheets are not very hot, the pitta will not puff up as they should.

INGREDIENTS TO MAKE SIX PITTA LOAVES:
4 cups (500 g) all-purpose flour
1 teaspoon (5 ml) salt
1 cake compressed yeast
1¼ cups (300 ml) tepid water

Chelsea Buns

Traditionally these buns are placed so that they stick together when baked and have to be pulled apart for serving.

In a large bowl beat together ½ cup of all-purpose flour, 1 cake of compressed yeast and ½ cup of warm milk. Put the bowl in a warm place for 20 to 30 minutes, or until the mixture becomes puffed up and frothy.

Meanwhile in another bowl mix 1½ cups of all-purpose flour with ½ teaspoon of salt and ½ teaspoon of sugar. Add 2 tablespoons of margarine or butter and rub it into the flour.

When the yeast batter is frothy, stir in 1 beaten egg and the flour mixture. Mix the ingredients well until they form a dough.

Turn the dough out onto a lightly floured surface and knead well for 10 minutes, or until the dough becomes firm and elastic and is no longer sticky.

Put the dough in a lightly greased bowl and cover it with greased plastic wrap. Put the dough in a warm place to rise for 45 to 60 minutes, or until it has doubled in bulk.

When the dough has risen, turn it out onto a floured surface and knead it again for 2 to 3 minutes. Roll the dough out to form an oblong about 9 by 12 inches (23 by 30 cm). Melt 2 tablespoons of margarine or butter and brush it over the dough.

In a small bowl combine ¼ pound of chopped mixed dried fruit, ⅓ cup of brown sugar and 1 teaspoon of ground mixed spice. Sprinkle this mixture evenly over the dough.

Roll the dough up lengthwise to form a neat long sausage. Cut the sausage into 9 equal pieces and put them flat and close together on a greased baking sheet or in a greased cake pan.

Preheat the oven to 400°F (200°C).

Cover the baking sheet with greased plastic wrap and put the dough in a warm place to rise for 20 to 30 minutes, or until it has doubled in bulk.

Remove the plastic wrap. Bake the buns for 20 to 30 minutes, or until they have risen and are golden brown. Put the buns on a wire rack to cool.

INGREDIENTS TO MAKE NINE BUNS:
2 cups (250 g) all-purpose flour
1 cake compressed yeast
½ cup (125 ml) warm milk
½ teaspoon (2.5 ml) salt
½ teaspoon (2.5 ml) sugar
4 tablespoons (50 g) margarine or butter
1 egg
¼ lb (100 g) mixed dried fruit
⅓ cup (50 g) brown sugar
1 teaspoon (5 ml) ground mixed spice

Apple Cinnamon Braid

This attractive braid, filled with apples, raisins and hazelnuts, can be served warm or cold.

In a large bowl beat together ½ cup of all-purpose flour, 1 cake of compressed yeast and ½ cup of warm milk. Put the bowl in a warm place for 20 to 30 minutes, or until the mixture has become puffed up and frothy.

In another bowl combine 1½ cups of all-purpose flour with 2 teaspoons of ground cinnamon, ½ teaspoon of salt and 2 tablespoons of sugar. Add 2 tablespoons of margarine or butter and rub it into the flour mixture.

Stir 1 beaten egg and the flour mixture into the frothy yeast batter to form a dough.

Turn the dough out onto a lightly floured board and knead it well for 10 minutes, or until it becomes firm and elastic and is no longer sticky. The dough will be pale brown because of the cinnamon.

Lightly grease a bowl. Put the dough into the bowl and cover it with greased plastic wrap. Put the dough in a warm place to rise for 45 to 60 minutes, or until it has doubled in bulk.

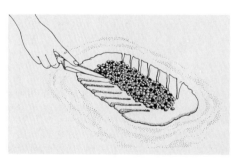

Make diagonal cuts along the sides of the dough.

Lift the short sides of the dough over the filling.

Braid the cut strips of dough over the filling.

Meanwhile, peel, core and slice 1 pound of tart apples. Put the apple slices into a small pan. Add the grated rind and juice of ½ lemon, ⅔ cup of seedless raisins, ⅓ cup of brown sugar and ⅓ cup of coarsely chopped hazelnuts to the pan. Cover the pan and cook gently for 5 minutes, or until the apples are just tender. Remove the pan from the heat and allow the mixture to cool.

When the dough has risen, turn it out onto a floured board and knead it again for 2 to 3 minutes. Roll the dough out to form an oblong about 12 by 9 inches (30 by 23 cm).

Spread the prepared apple mixture down the center of the dough not quite to the short ends, leaving a 3-inch (8-cm) margin of dough on each long side. With a sharp knife, make 2-inch (5-cm) diagonal cuts, 1 inch (2 cm) apart, into the longer margins. Lift the shorter sides and fold them over the filling. To make the braid start at one end, take a strip of dough from each side alternately and cross it over the filling. Continue along the sides until the whole bread is braided and the filling is just visible between the strips.

Preheat the oven to 400°F (200°C).

Put the braid on a greased baking sheet and cover it with greased plastic wrap. Put the braid in a warm place to rise for 20 to 30 minutes, or until it has doubled in bulk.

Remove the plastic wrap. Bake the braid for 30 minutes, or until it is golden brown. Remove the braid from the oven and tap the bottom. If it sounds hollow it is ready. Put the braid on a wire rack to cool.

INGREDIENTS TO MAKE ONE LARGE BRAID:
2 cups (250 g) all-purpose flour
1 cake compressed yeast
½ cup (125 ml) warm milk
2 teaspoons (10 ml) ground cinnamon
½ teaspoon (2.5 ml) salt
2 tablespoons (30 ml) sugar
2 tablespoons (25 g) margarine or butter
1 egg
1 lb (500 g) tart apples
½ lemon
⅔ cup (100 g) seedless raisins
⅓ cup (50 g) brown sugar
⅓ cup (50 g) coarsely chopped hazelnuts

Kugelhopf

A Viennese speciality, kugelhopf is traditionally baked in a fluted ring mold so that the cake looks very dramatic when it is turned out, but it may be baked in any equivalent-sized cake pan.

Combine 2 cups of all-purpose flour, ½ teaspoon of salt and 1 tablespoon of sugar in a mixing bowl.

Blend 1 cake of compressed yeast with ⅔ cup of warm milk. Mix until the yeast is dissolved. Make a well in the flour and pour in the yeast liquid with 2 tablespoons of melted margarine or butter and 2 egg yolks. Mix the ingredients well until they form a stiff batter.

Stir the grated rind and juice of 1 orange, ⅔ cup of seedless raisins and ⅓ cup of blanched split almonds into the batter. In a small bowl beat the egg whites until they are just stiff and fold them into the mixture.

Brush a 4- to 5-cup (7- to 9-inch) fluted ring mold with oil and spoon the prepared mixture into it until the mold is three-quarters full.

Preheat the oven to 375°F (190°C).

Cover the mold with greased plastic wrap and put the mixture in a warm place to rise for 20 to 30 minutes, or until it has risen almost to the top of the mold.

Bake the kugelhopf for about 45 minutes, or until the top is browned. Cool the cake for a few minutes before turning it out onto a wire rack.

When the kugelhopf is cool, dust it with sifted confectioner's sugar.

INGREDIENTS TO SERVE EIGHT :
**2 cups (250 g) all-purpose flour
½ teaspoon (2.5 ml) salt
1 tablespoon (15 ml) sugar
1 cake compressed yeast
⅔ cup (150 ml) warm milk
2 tablespoons (25 g) melted margarine
   or butter
2 eggs
1 orange
⅔ cup (100 g) seedless raisins
⅓ cup (50 g) blanched, split almonds
confectioner's sugar**

Soda Bread

Baking soda is used as the rising agent in this bread.

Preheat the oven to 400°F (200°C).

In a large bowl mix 4 cups of all-purpose flour with 1 teaspoon of salt, 1 teaspoon of baking soda and 1 teaspoon of cream of tartar. Add 2 tablespoons of margarine or butter and rub it into the flour. Make a well in the center of the flour and pour in 1¼ cups of buttermilk or milk. Stir the ingredients together to form a soft, spongy dough.

Turn the dough out onto a floured surface and shape it into a large round loaf or 2 smaller loaves about 2 inches (5 cm) thick. Put the loaf on a greased baking sheet and score the top into quarters with a sharp knife.

Bake the loaf for 30 to 35 minutes, or until it is golden brown and sounds hollow when tapped underneath. Put the loaf on a wire rack to cool.

INGREDIENTS TO MAKE ONE LARGE OR TWO SMALL LOAVES :
**4 cups (500 g) all-purpose flour
1 teaspoon (5 ml) salt
1 teaspoon (5 ml) baking soda
1 teaspoon (5 ml) cream of tartar
2 tablespoons (25 g) margarine or butter
1¼ cups (300 ml) buttermilk or milk**

Whole-wheat Apricot Braid

In a large bowl mix 2 cups of whole-wheat flour, 2 cups of all-purpose flour, 1 teaspoon of salt, ⅔ cup of chopped dried apricots and the grated rind of 1 lemon.

In another bowl blend 1 cake of compressed yeast with 1¼ cups of warm milk until the yeast is dissolved. Make a well in the flour and pour in the yeast mixture, 2 tablespoons of honey and 4 tablespoons of melted margarine or butter. Mix the ingredients together to form a firm dough.

Turn the dough out onto a floured surface and knead it well for 10 minutes, or until it becomes firm and elastic and is no longer sticky.

Lightly grease a large bowl. Put the dough into the bowl and cover it with greased plastic wrap. Put the dough in a warm place to rise for 45 to 60 minutes, or until it has doubled in bulk.

When the dough has risen, turn it out onto a lightly floured surface and knead it again for 2 to 3 minutes. Shape the dough into a sausage about 12 inches (30 cm) long. Cut it into 3 equal strands, leaving the dough joined at one end. Braid the strands of dough and pinch the ends together. Turn the ends under the braid. Place the braid on a greased baking sheet.

Preheat the oven to 425°F (220°C).

Cover the baking sheet with greased plastic wrap and put the braid in a warm place to rise for 20 to 30 minutes, or until it has doubled in bulk.

Brush the braid with milk and sprinkle it with 2 tablespoons of cracked wheat. Bake the braid for about 30 minutes, or until it is golden brown and sounds hollow when it is tapped underneath. Cool on a wire rack.

INGREDIENTS TO MAKE ONE LARGE BRAID :
**2 cups (250 g) whole-wheat flour
2 cups (250 g) all-purpose flour
1 teaspoon (5 ml) salt
⅔ cup (100 g) chopped dried apricots
1 lemon
1 cake compressed yeast
1¼ cups (300 ml) warm milk
2 tablespoons (30 ml) honey
4 tablespoons (50 g) melted margarine
   or butter
2 tablespoons (30 ml) cracked wheat**

MAKING A BRAID

Cut the dough into three strands joined at one end.

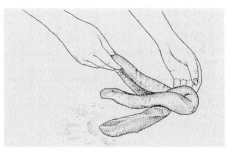

Cross the strands one over another alternately.

To make good pastry you need a light hand, a cool kitchen and cool ingredients (except for such pastry as choux and hot-water crust) and the correct proportion of flour to fat to liquid.

Use all-purpose flour. If the flour is fine there is no need to sift it. Or try whole-wheat flour or a mixture of whole-wheat and all-purpose flour; the result will be heavier but tastier.

Use margarine or butter. Pastry made with soft fats, however, requires a different technique—see the recipe for pastry made with polyunsaturated margarine. Butter or margarine taken from the refrigerator will be too cold and hard to use, so leave it at room temperature for a few minutes until it is soft but still firm.

Ice-cold water is the liquid most commonly used to bind the dough, although milk or a mixture of milk and water, or egg and water is sometimes used. Once the dough is formed handle it as little as possible.

Other ingredients may be added to a basic pastry for flavor. Grated cheese, chopped herbs, ground spices or ground nuts may be mixed with the dry ingredients.

Cover the dough and chill it in the refrigerator for at least thirty minutes before rolling it out. This makes the pastry lighter and helps to keep it from shrinking during baking.

Pastry dough may be refrigerated for up to two days; allow it to return to room temperature before using it. The dough may also be kept in the freezer for up to three months.

Roll the dough out on a smooth, clean, cool, lightly floured surface. Make light, short movements. And, finally, always preheat the oven to the required temperature.

Pastry dough is measured by the amount of flour used. For example, 1½ cups of pastry refers to pastry made with 1½ cups of flour and not to the total volume of the pastry.

To line an 8- to 9-inch (20- to 23-cm) flan ring or pie pan, 1½ cups (160 g) of pastry dough is sufficient.

A precooked pie shell is often required when the filling is uncooked or to keep the pastry from becoming sodden.

Shortcrust Pastry

The most popular pastry, and the easiest to make, is shortcrust. Traditionally the fat should consist of half butter and half lard, but it has a particularly good flavor if made with butter, or margarine can be used instead.

Put 1½ cups of all-purpose flour and ¼ teaspoon of salt into a mixing bowl. Add 6 tablespoons of margarine or butter and cut it into small pieces with a table knife. Rub the pieces of fat into the flour with your fingertips until the mixture resembles fine bread crumbs.

Sprinkle 2 tablespoons of cold water over the flour and mix quickly with a knife to a stiff dough. Turn the dough out onto a lightly floured board and knead it gently, with your fingertips, until it is smooth.

Cover and chill the dough until it is needed.

INGREDIENTS TO MAKE ONE AND A HALF CUPS (150 g) OF PASTRY:
1½ cups (150 g) all-purpose flour
¼ teaspoon (1 ml) salt
6 tablespoons (75 g) margarine or butter

MAKING SHORTCRUST PASTRY

Rub the fat and flour lightly with your fingertips.

Sprinkle with cold water and mix quickly.

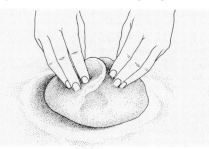

Knead gently to a smooth dough with your fingertips.

Lining a Flan Ring

A French quiche, or flan, is served in an open, free-standing pastry shell. The shell is formed in a metal flan ring, which is set on a baking sheet. When it is baked, the ring is removed and the quiche is slid onto a serving plate. A springform cake pan, 1 to 1½ inches (2 to 3 cm) deep, can be used instead of a flan ring.

Put a 7- to 8-inch (18- to 20-cm) flan ring

on a baking sheet. Grease the inside of the ring and the baking sheet.

Roll out 1½ cups of pastry dough on a lightly floured surface until it is about ⅛ inch (5 mm) thick and about 2 inches (5 cm) larger in diameter than the ring. Fold the dough in half and in half again to form a triangle. Lift the folded dough, lay it in the ring and unfold it. Alternatively, lift the dough up on the rolling pin and lay it over the ring.

Gently ease the dough into the ring. Use your knuckles to mold the dough, making sure no air is trapped between the dough and the ring. Trim off the excess dough around

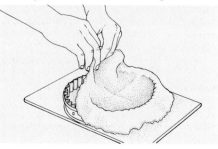

Lay the folded dough in the flan ring and unfold it.

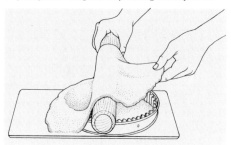

Or roll the dough around the rolling pin to lift it.

Press the dough into the flan ring with your knuckles.

Trim the dough by rolling the pin over the flan ring.

the edge of the ring with scissors or a sharp knife. If a fluted flan ring is being used, roll the rolling pin over the top of the ring to trim off the excess dough.

Baking Blind

Preheat the oven to 400°F (200°C).

When the flan ring or pie pan is lined, prick the dough all over with a fork. Line the dough with waxed paper or aluminum foil, then weight it down with dried beans, bread crumbs or rice (this is to keep the pastry from rising during baking). Beans or rice used in this way become very dry and hard, so keep some especially for this purpose.

Bake the pastry for 10 minutes, then remove the waxed paper or foil and the beans, bread crumbs or rice. Return the pastry to the oven for a further 5 minutes to dry out and color slightly.

Cool the pastry shell before filling it.

Baked pastry shells can be frozen for up to 6 weeks.

Weight the dough with beans to prevent it rising.

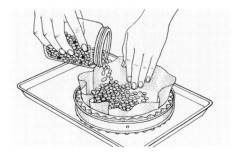

Polyunsaturated Shortcrust Pastry

Polyunsaturated and other soft margarines are too soft, even when refrigerated, to rub into flour easily. The following creamed method is best suited to soft margarines.

Put 6 tablespoons of chilled soft margarine into a mixing bowl with ½ cup of all-purpose flour and 2 tablespoons of cold water. Cream together with a fork until they are well mixed. Add 1 cup of all-purpose flour and ¼ teaspoon of salt and mix to form a firm dough.

Turn the dough out onto a lightly floured surface and knead gently until smooth.

Cover and chill the dough until it is needed.

INGREDIENTS TO MAKE ONE AND A HALF CUPS (150 g) OF PASTRY:
6 tablespoons (75 g) polyunsaturated margarine
1½ cups (150 g) all-purpose flour
¼ teaspoon (1 ml) salt

Sweet Pie Pastry

Although not as rich as *pâte sucrée*, the traditional French *tarte* pastry, this rich shortcrust pastry is excellent for sweet pies. Because this dough is slightly more sticky than ordinary shortcrust it must be chilled thoroughly before it is rolled out. For a spicier pastry add 1 tablespoon of ground mixed spice or cinnamon, or the grated rind of ½ lemon or orange to the flour.

Put 1½ cups of all-purpose flour into a mixing bowl. Add 6 tablespoons of margarine or butter and cut it into small pieces with a table knife. Rub the fat into the flour with your fingertips until the mixture resembles fine bread crumbs. Stir in 2 tablespoons of sugar.

In a small bowl beat 1 egg yolk with 1 tablespoon of cold water. Make a well in the flour mixture and pour in the egg and water. Mix the ingredients until they form a firm dough.

Turn the dough out onto a lightly floured surface and knead it gently until it is smooth. Cover and chill it until it is needed.

Sweet pie pastry is baked in the same way as shortcrust pastry.

INGREDIENTS TO MAKE ONE AND A HALF CUPS (150 g) OF PASTRY:
1½ cups (150 g) all-purpose flour
6 tablespoons (75 g) margarine or butter
2 tablespoons (25 g) sugar
1 egg yolk

Choux Pastry

If polyunsaturated margarine is used in this recipe, it will produce a very light, crisp pastry.

Over low heat melt ¼ cup of margarine or butter in ⅔ cup of water. Bring to the boil. Remove the pan from the heat immediately and pour in ½ cup plus 2 tablespoons of all-purpose flour all at once. Stir vigorously with a wooden spoon until the mixture is smooth and comes away from the sides of the pan.

Allow the mixture to cool slightly. Beat in 2 eggs, one at a time, with a wooden spoon, until they are completely absorbed and the mixture is smooth and shiny.

It is best to use the dough at once. Preheat the oven to 425°F (220°C). Thoroughly grease a large baking sheet.

Use either a pastry tube or a tablespoon to shape the dough onto the baking sheet.

Bake for 20 minutes. Remove from the oven and make a horizontal slit along the center of each piece of pastry to allow the steam to escape.

Lower the oven temperature to 375°F (190°C) and continue baking for 10 minutes more, or until the pastry is firm to the touch. Remove the pastry from the oven and cool on a wire rack before filling.

INGREDIENTS TO MAKE TEN TABLESPOONS (75 g) OF PASTRY:
¼ cup (50 g) margarine or butter
½ cup plus 2 tablespoons (75 g) all-purpose flour
2 eggs

Almond Pastry

The addition of ground almonds to a sweet pie pastry gives it a rich cookielike texture. Other ground nuts, such as walnuts or hazelnuts, may be substituted.

Put 1 cup of all-purpose flour into a mixing bowl. Add 6 tablespoons of margarine or butter and cut it into small pieces with a table knife. Rub the fat into the flour with your fingertips until the mixture resembles bread crumbs. Stir in ½ cup of ground almonds and ¼ cup of sugar.

In a small bowl beat 1 egg yolk with 2 teaspoons of cold water and 3 to 4 drops of almond extract. Make a well in the flour mixture and pour in the egg and water. Mix the ingredients until they form a soft dough.

Turn the dough out onto a lightly floured surface and knead it gently until it is smooth. Cover and chill the dough for at least 1 hour before using.

Almond pastry can be used instead of sweet pie pastry.

INGREDIENTS TO MAKE ONE CUP (100 g) OF PASTRY:
1 cup (100 g) all-purpose flour
6 tablespoons (75 g) margarine or butter
½ cup (75 g) ground almonds
¼ cup (50 g) sugar
1 egg yolk
3 to 4 drops almond extract

Gingerbread

Keep this gingerbread for 2 to 3 days before serving, for its spicy flavor and moist texture will improve. Gingerbread will stay fresh for 2 weeks in an airtight container.

Preheat the oven to 300°F (150°C). Grease a 7-inch (18-cm) square cake pan and line it with waxed paper. Grease the paper.

Put ½ cup of margarine or butter, ⅓ cup of brown sugar, ¼ cup of molasses and ¾ cup of light corn syrup into a saucepan. Stir over low heat until the butter has melted and the sugar has dissolved. Remove the pan from the heat and allow the mixture to cool slightly. Beat 2 eggs in a small bowl and add them to the pan with ⅔ cup of yogurt. Stir the ingredients well.

Combine 2 cups of all-purpose flour, 1 tablespoon of ground ginger, 1 teaspoon of ground allspice and ½ teaspoon of baking soda in a mixing bowl. Make a well in the flour and pour in the cooled butter and sugar mixture. Add 5 tablespoons of chopped preserved ginger and mix in well.

Pour the batter into the prepared pan. Bake for 1½ hours, or until the cake has risen and is firm to the touch.

Allow the gingerbread to cool slightly in the pan before turning it out onto a wire rack to cool completely.

INGREDIENTS TO MAKE ONE SEVEN-INCH (18-cm) CAKE:
½ cup (100 g) margarine or butter
⅓ cup (50 g) brown sugar
¼ cup (50 g) molasses
¾ cup (150 g) light corn syrup
2 eggs
⅔ cup (150 ml) yogurt
2 cups (250 g) all-purpose flour
1 tablespoon (15 ml) ground ginger
1 teaspoon (5 ml) ground allspice
½ teaspoon (2.5 ml) baking soda
5 tablespoons (75 g) chopped preserved ginger

Coffee Cheese Cake

Preheat the oven to 350°F (180°C). Grease two 8-inch (20-cm) cake pans. Measure 1½ cups of whole-wheat flour into a bowl.

In a large bowl cream ¾ cup of margarine and ¾ cup of sugar. Beat in 3 eggs alternately with 3 tablespoons of the flour. Mix 1½ teaspoons of baking powder with the remaining flour and fold into the mixture. Add 1 tablespoon of freeze-dried coffee dissolved in 1 tablespoon of warm water. Stir until the ingredients are well blended.

Divide the batter between the prepared pans and level the surfaces. Bake the layers for 20 to 25 minutes, or until they have risen and are brown and firm to the touch. Remove the layers from the pans and cool them on wire racks.

Meanwhile, beat together ¾ pound of pot cheese and ⅔ cup of yogurt until smooth. Reserving a little for decoration, divide the mixture in half. Sandwich the layers together with half of it. Stir 1 tablespoon of coffee extract into the other half of the cheese mixture and spread it over the top and sides of the cake.

Press ⅔ cup of coarsely chopped walnut halves around the sides of the cake. Using a pastry tube, pipe whirls of the reserved cheese mixture on top of the cake and decorate with some walnut halves.

INGREDIENTS TO MAKE ONE EIGHT-INCH (20-CM) CAKE:
1½ cups (150 g) whole-wheat flour
¾ cup (150 g) margarine
¾ cup (150 g) sugar
3 eggs
1½ teaspoons (7.5 ml) baking powder
2 tablespoons (30 ml) freeze-dried coffee
¾ lb (350 g) pot cheese
⅔ cup (150 ml) yogurt
⅔ cup (100 g) chopped walnuts
walnut halves

Yogurt Whole-wheat Biscuits

Yogurt is used to raise as well as to flavor these wedge-shaped biscuits.

Preheat the oven to 400°F (200°C).

In a bowl combine 2 cups of whole-wheat flour with ½ teaspoon of salt and 2 teaspoons of baking powder. Add 2 tablespoons of margarine or butter and rub it into the flour. Add ⅔ cup of yogurt and stir until a soft dough is formed.

Turn the dough out onto a floured surface and knead it lightly. Roll the dough out to form a round about 1 inch (2 cm) thick. Cut the round into 8 wedges and place the wedges on a greased baking sheet. Bake the wedges for 10 to 15 minutes, or until they have risen and are golden brown.

Remove the wedges from the oven, split them and serve immediately with butter or cottage cheese.

INGREDIENTS TO MAKE EIGHT BISCUITS:
2 cups (250 g) whole-wheat flour
½ teaspoon (2.5 ml) salt
2 teaspoons (10 ml) baking powder
2 tablespoons (25 g) margarine or butter
⅔ cup (150 ml) yogurt

Sunshine Fruit Cake

Preheat the oven to 350°F (180°C). Grease a large loaf pan and line it with waxed paper.

Put 2 cups of self-rising flour into a bowl. In another large bowl cream ¾ cup of margarine and ¾ cup of sugar until the mixture is pale and fluffy. Beat in 3 eggs alternately with 3 tablespoons of the flour. Fold in the remaining flour and ½ teaspoon of ground nutmeg. Grate the rind and squeeze the juice of 1 lemon and 1 orange and stir the rind and juice into the mixture.

Spoon the mixture into the prepared pan and level the surface. Bake the cake for 40 to 45 minutes, or until it has risen and is golden brown and firm to the touch. Remove the cake from the pan and cool it on a wire rack.

Meanwhile, mash 2 large bananas in a bowl. Beat in ¼ pound of pot cheese. Cut the cake into two layers. Spread half of the banana mixture on the bottom layer.

Peel and cut away the pith of 1 large grapefruit and 1 orange. Cut away the membrane from the fruit segments. Arrange half the segments on top of the filling. Replace the top layer of the cake and cover it with the remaining banana mixture. Decorate with the remaining grapefruit and orange segments.

INGREDIENTS TO MAKE ONE LARGE CAKE:
2 cups (250 g) self-rising flour
¾ cup (150 g) margarine
¾ cup (150 g) sugar
3 eggs
½ teaspoon (2.5 ml) ground nutmeg
1 lemon
2 oranges
2 large bananas
¼ lb (100 g) pot cheese
1 grapefruit

Coconut Wheat Cookies

Whole-wheat flour and shredded coconut give these cookies a nutty flavor and crisp texture.

Preheat the oven to 350°F (180°C). Lightly grease 2 baking sheets.

Cream ½ cup of margarine or butter and ⅔ cup of brown sugar in a mixing bowl until light and fluffy. Beat in 1 egg.

Mix in 2 cups of whole-wheat flour, 1 teaspoon of baking powder and ½ cup of unsweetened shredded coconut to form a firm dough.

Turn the dough out onto a lightly floured surface and knead it gently until it is smooth. Roll the dough out to about ¼ inch (6 mm) thick. Cut out round cookies with a 2½-inch (6-cm) fluted cutter and put them on the prepared baking sheets. Sprinkle a pinch of coconut on each cookie.

Bake the cookies for 15 minutes, or until

they are lightly browned. Allow the cookies to cool slightly before putting them on a wire rack to cool completely.

INGREDIENTS TO MAKE TWENTY-FOUR COOKIES:

½ cup (100 g) margarine or butter
⅔ cup (100 g) brown sugar
1 egg
2 cups (250 g) whole-wheat flour
1 teaspoon (5 ml) baking powder
½ cup plus 1 tablespoon (65 g)
   unsweetened shredded coconut

Lemon Whole-wheat Shortbread

Use butter to give this rich, crisp, Scottish shortbread a particularly good flavor.

Preheat the oven to 300°F (150°C). Lightly grease a baking sheet.

Combine 1 cup of whole-wheat flour, ½ cup of rice flour, ⅓ cup of brown sugar and the grated rind of 1 lemon in a mixing bowl. Add ½ cup of butter, cut into small pieces. Rub the fat into the flour mixture to form a dough.

Roll the dough out on a lightly floured surface to form a 7-inch (18-cm) circle. Carefully lift the round onto the baking sheet. Mark the top of the dough with a sharp knife, dividing it into 8 wedges. Prick the dough all over with a fork and crimp the edges.

Bake the shortbread for 40 to 50 minutes, or until it is just colored.

INGREDIENTS TO MAKE EIGHT LARGE COOKIES:

1 cup (100 g) whole-wheat flour
½ cup (50 g) rice flour
⅓ cup (50 g) brown sugar
1 lemon
½ cup (100 g) butter

Fruity Gingersnaps

Preheat the oven to 350°F (180°C). Lightly grease 2 baking sheets.

Combine 1 cup of all-purpose flour, ½ teaspoon of baking soda, 1 teaspoon of ground ginger and ½ teaspoon of ground cinnamon in a bowl. Mix in ⅓ cup of seedless raisins.

Melt ¼ cup of margarine or butter with 3 tablespoons of light corn syrup in a small saucepan over low heat. Make a well in the flour mixture and pour in the syrup. Stir the ingredients well.

Take spoonfuls of the mixture and roll them into balls, the size of walnuts, between your hands. Put the balls well apart on the prepared baking sheets and flatten them slightly.

Bake the cookies for 10 to 15 minutes, or until they are a deep golden brown. Cool the cookies for 5 minutes on the baking sheets, then put them on a wire rack to cool completely.

INGREDIENTS TO MAKE TWENTY TO TWENTY-FOUR COOKIES:

1 cup (100 g) all-purpose flour
½ teaspoon (2.5 ml) baking soda
1 teaspoon (5 ml) ground ginger
½ teaspoon (2.5 ml) ground cinnamon
⅓ cup (50 g) seedless raisins
¼ cup (50 g) margarine or butter
3 tablespoons (45 ml) light corn syrup

Elizabethan Layer Cake

Homemade lemon curd adds zest to this simple layer cake.

Preheat the oven to 350°F (180°C). Grease an 8-inch (20-cm) round cake pan.

Measure 1 cup of whole-wheat flour into a bowl.

In a large mixing bowl cream ½ cup of margarine with ⅔ cup of brown sugar until the mixture is pale and creamy. Beat in 2 eggs alternately with 2 tablespoons of the flour, then fold in 1 teaspoon of baking powder and the remaining flour.

Pour into the prepared pan and level the surface. Bake for 20 to 25 minutes, or until the cake has risen and is brown and firm to the touch. Remove the cake from the pan and put it on a wire rack to cool.

Cut the cake into two layers. Spread ½ cup of lemon curd (see page 180) on one layer, then cover with the second layer.

INGREDIENTS TO MAKE ONE EIGHT-INCH (20-CM) CAKE:

1 cup (100 g) whole-wheat flour
½ cup (100 g) margarine
⅔ cup (100 g) brown sugar
2 eggs
1 teaspoon (5 ml) baking powder
½ cup (100 g) lemon curd (see page 180)

Halva Cake

Cut into slices and wrapped in foil, this moist cake will keep for up to 3 weeks.

Preheat the oven to 350°F (180°C). Grease a 7-inch (18-cm) square cake pan and line it with waxed paper so that the paper comes up above the sides of the pan. Grease the paper. Put 1 cup of all-purpose flour into a bowl.

In a large bowl cream ¾ cup of margarine and ¾ cup of sugar. Beat in 4 eggs alternately with 4 tablespoons of the flour. Fold the remaining flour, 2 teaspoons of ground cinnamon, 1 cup of semolina, ¼ cup of unsweetened shredded coconut and the grated rind of 1 lemon into the mixture.

Spoon the mixture into the prepared pan and level off the surface. Sprinkle 1 tablespoon of poppy seeds over the top and press them in lightly.

Bake the cake for 40 to 45 minutes, or until it has risen and is golden brown and firm to the touch.

Meanwhile, in a small saucepan heat 2 tablespoons of clear honey with 1 tablespoon of lemon juice. Pour the syrup over the cake immediately after it is taken from the oven. Cool the cake in the pan.

Lift out carefully by the raised wax paper, remove the paper and serve.

INGREDIENTS TO MAKE ONE SEVEN-INCH (18-CM) CAKE:

1 cup (100 g) all-purpose flour
¾ cup (150 g) margarine
¾ cup (150 g) sugar
4 eggs
2 teaspoons (10 ml) ground cinnamon
1 cup (100 g) semolina
¼ cup (25 g) unsweetened shredded coconut
1 lemon
1 tablespoon (15 ml) poppy seeds
2 tablespoons (30 ml) clear honey

TURNING OUT A MOIST CAKE

Gently lift the cake out by the paper.

Cottage Cheese Coffee Cake is moist and fruity and is made with an unusual combination of ingredients, including cottage cheese, dates and walnuts.

Cottage Cheese Coffee Cake

This is a light, moist coffee cake made with cottage cheese instead of butter.

Preheat the oven to 350 F (180 C). Grease a large loaf pan and line it with waxed paper. Grease the paper.

Sieve ½ pound of cottage cheese into a mixing bowl. Add 1 cup of brown sugar and beat until creamy. Add 3 eggs and beat them into the mixture.

Reserving a few for decoration, coarsely chop ½ cup of walnuts. Add the chopped walnuts to the creamed mixture with 1 cup of chopped, pitted dates. Fold 2 cups of self-rising flour into the mixture.

Spoon the mixture into the loaf pan and level the surface. Press the reserved walnuts into the top of the loaf in a line down the center. Bake the coffee cake for 45 to 50 minutes, or until it is firm and golden brown. Turn it out of the pan onto a wire rack to cool.

INGREDIENTS TO MAKE ONE LARGE COFFEE CAKE:
½ lb (250 g) cottage cheese
1 cup (150 g) brown sugar
3 eggs
½ cup (50 g) walnuts
1 cup (100 g) chopped, pitted dates
2 cups (250 g) self-rising flour

Farmhouse Fruit Cake

Whole-wheat flour and brown sugar give this moist, crumbly fruit cake a rich dark color. It will keep for at least a week in an airtight container.

Preheat the oven to 350 F (180 C). Grease an 8-inch (20-cm) round cake pan and line it with waxed paper.

Mix 1 cup of whole-wheat flour, 1 cup of all-purpose flour, 2 teaspoons of baking powder and 1 teaspoon of ground nutmeg in a large bowl. Add 6 tablespoons of margarine or butter. Cut it into small pieces with a table knife and rub it into the flour with your fingertips until the mixture resembles fine bread crumbs.

Stir in ½ cup of brown sugar, 1 cup of seedless raisins, ¼ cup of chopped candied lemon peel and orange peel, ¼ cup of chopped candied cherries and the grated rind and juice of ½ lemon. In a small bowl, beat 2 eggs with ⅔ cup of milk. Make a well in the fruit mixture and pour in the beaten egg and milk. Stir the ingredients until they are thoroughly mixed.

Spoon the mixture into the prepared cake pan and level the surface. Arrange ⅓ cup of split blanched almonds on the top.

Bake the cake for 1 to 1¼ hours, or until it is brown and firm to the touch. Allow the cake to cool slightly before turning it out of the pan onto a wire rack to cool completely.

INGREDIENTS TO MAKE ONE EIGHT-INCH (20-CM) CAKE:
1 cup (100 g) whole-wheat flour
1 cup (100 g) all-purpose flour
2 teaspoons (10 ml) baking powder
1 teaspoon (5 ml) ground nutmeg
6 tablespoons (75 g) margarine or butter
½ cup (75 g) brown sugar
1 cup (150 g) seedless raisins
¼ cup (50 g) chopped candied lemon peel and orange peel
¼ cup (50 g) chopped candied cherries
½ lemon
2 eggs
⅔ cup (150 ml) milk
⅓ cup (50 g) blanched and split almonds

Macaroons

Macaroons are traditionally baked on edible rice paper to keep them from sticking to the baking sheet. If rice paper is not available, use any nonstick baking paper.

Preheat the oven to 350 F (180 C). Line baking sheets with rice paper or nonstick baking paper.

In a mixing bowl beat 1 egg white until it forms stiff peaks. Add ½ cup of ground almonds, 6 tablespoons of sugar and ½ teaspoon of almond extract and fold in gently to form a smooth, stiff mixture.

Put spoonfuls of the mixture on the prepared baking sheets, leaving enough room for each spoonful to spread. Put a split almond in the center of each macaroon.

Bake the macaroons for 15 to 20 minutes, or until they are just beginning to color. Cool them on a wire rack.

INGREDIENTS TO MAKE TEN TO TWELVE MACAROONS:
1 egg white
½ cup (50 g) ground almonds
6 tablespoons (75 g) sugar
½ teaspoon (2.5 ml) almond extract
12 blanched and split almonds

Dutch Apple Cake

A layer of spiced apples tops this moist sponge cake. Baked in an oblong pan, it is cut into slices before serving.

Preheat the oven to 350 F (180 C). Lightly grease a 4- by 9-inch (10- by 23-cm) loaf pan.

Put ½ cup of margarine or butter into a mixing bowl with ½ cup of sugar. Beat until light and creamy. Add 2 eggs, one at a time, beating the mixture well after each addition. Fold in 1½ cups of self-rising flour. Add a little milk to give the mixture a soft dropping consistency. Spoon the mixture into the prepared baking pan.

Peel, core and thinly slice 1 pound of apples. Arrange the slices on top of the cake batter. In a bowl mix together the grated rind of ½ lemon, 2 teaspoons of ground ginger and 1 tablespoon of sugar. Sprinkle this mixture over the apple slices.

Bake for 30 minutes, or until the topping is golden brown and the apples are tender. Cool the cake on a wire rack.

INGREDIENTS TO MAKE ONE SMALL CAKE:
½ cup (100 g) margarine or butter
½ cup (100 g) plus 1 tablespoon (15 ml) sugar
2 eggs
1½ cups (150 g) self-rising flour
milk
1 lb (500 g) apples
½ lemon
2 teaspoons (10 ml) ground ginger

A selection of favorite cakes and cookies, clockwise: Gingerbread, Fruity Gingersnaps, Macaroons, Farmhouse Fruit Cake and Dutch Apple Cake and, for a special occasion, Coffee Cheesecake.

Crêpes

Crêpes can be kept for up to 2 days in the refrigerator. Let them cool, then wrap them in foil and store them. Crêpes may be frozen for up to 2 months. Interleave the cooled crêpes with lightly oiled waxed paper or plastic wrap so that single crêpes can be separated and defrosted. To defrost crêpes, leave them in their packaging at room temperature for 2 to 3 hours or in the refrigerator overnight. To reheat crêpes, preheat the oven to 375°F (190°C) and put a pile of crêpes, wrapped in aluminum foil, in the oven for 20 to 30 minutes.

Put 1 cup of all-purpose flour and ¼ teaspoon of salt into a mixing bowl. Make a well in the flour and pour in 1 egg and ⅔ cup of milk. Stir the ingredients well with a wooden spoon until the batter is smooth. Beat in another ⅔ cup of milk. This batter can be used immediately or left to stand for up to 2 hours.

Heat ½ teaspoon of safflower oil, just enough to coat the bottom of an 8-inch (20-cm) frying pan. Less oil will be needed if a nonstick frying pan is used. When the oil is very hot, quickly pour enough batter into the pan to thinly coat the bottom. Tilt the pan so that the batter spreads evenly.

Cook until the top of the batter is set and the underside is golden brown. Turn, or toss, the crêpe over and cook the other side. Slide the crêpe onto a warmed dish, cover with an upturned bowl or wrap in a clean dish towel to keep hot. Repeat, adding more oil to the pan if needed, until the batter is used up. About 8 crêpes can be made from 1¼ cups of batter.

INGREDIENTS TO MAKE ONE AND A QUARTER CUPS (300 ml) OF BATTER:
1 cup (100 g) all-purpose flour
¼ teaspoon (5 ml) salt
1 egg
1⅓ cups (300 ml) milk
safflower oil

Savory Crêpe Stack

These crêpes are sure to satisfy the heartiest of appetites.

Melt 6 tablespoons of margarine or butter in a saucepan. Add 1 chopped onion and 4 chopped stalks of celery and fry gently for 10 to 15 minutes, or until they are soft. Stir in ½ cup of flour. Gradually pour in 2 scant cups of milk and continue stirring until the mixture begins to boil. Add 1½ cups of chopped cooked ham and 2 teaspoons of prepared English mustard. Season to taste

Spread a layer of filling over the cooked crêpes.

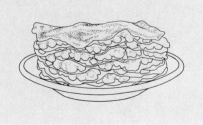

Stack the crêpes with filling between each one.

with salt and pepper. Reduce the heat and simmer for 2 minutes. Remove the pan from the heat and set aside.

Put 1 cup of whole-wheat flour and ¼ teaspoon of salt into a mixing bowl. Make a well in the flour and pour in 1 egg, 5 tablespoons of milk and 5 tablespoons of water. Stir well with a wooden spoon until the batter is smooth. Beat in another 5 tablespoons of milk and 5 tablespoons of water. Because whole-wheat flour tends to make a thicker batter, add 2 to 3 tablespoons more water if necessary.

Heat ½ teaspoon of safflower oil in an 8-inch (20-cm) frying pan. When the oil is very hot quickly pour enough batter into the pan to thinly coat the bottom. Tilt the pan so that the batter spreads evenly.

Cook until the top of the batter is set and the underside is golden brown. Turn, or toss, the crêpe over and cook the other side.

Put the crêpe onto a hot flameproof dish and spread with a layer of the prepared filling. Continue making the crêpes, stacking one above the other and spreading the filling between each layer, until the batter and the filling are used up. (This recipe should make

7 or 8 crêpes.) Sprinkle the pile with 4 tablespoons of grated Cheddar cheese. Put the dish under a hot broiler until the cheese has melted. Alternatively, bake in a 400°F (200°C) oven for 5 to 10 minutes.

Serve cut into wedges like a cake.

INGREDIENTS TO SERVE FOUR:
6 tablespoons (75 g) margarine or butter
1 onion
4 celery stalks
½ cup (50 g) flour
2½ cups (400 ml) milk
1½ cups (250 g) chopped cooked ham
2 teaspoons (10 ml) English mustard
salt
pepper
1 cup (100 g) whole-wheat flour
1 egg
safflower oil
4 tablespoons (60 ml) grated Cheddar cheese

Mediterranean Crêpes

These crêpes are ideal to serve as a first course for a dinner party or as a main dish for lunch or supper.

Make 1¼ cups of batter and cook 8 crêpes. Put the crêpes onto a hot plate as they are cooked and cover with an upturned bowl or wrap them in a dish towel or foil.

Preheat the oven to 375°F (190°C).

Prepare 4 cups of peeled and sliced onions. Heat 2 tablespoons of margarine or butter and 1 tablespoon of corn oil in a saucepan. Add the onions to the pan and fry gently for 5 minutes. Stir in 4 blanched, peeled and chopped ripe tomatoes, the drained and chopped anchovies from a small can, 3 tablespoons of tomato paste and 8 sliced stuffed olives. Season to taste with salt and pepper. Cover the pan and simmer gently for 20 minutes, stirring occasionally.

Spread each crêpe with the mixture, roll them up and put them into an ovenproof dish. Cover and bake for 15 minutes.

Alternatively, allow the crêpes and filling to cool until they are needed. Fill the crêpes and bake for 25 minutes.

Garnish with stuffed olives and tomato slices and serve immediately.

INGREDIENTS TO SERVE EIGHT AS A FIRST COURSE:
1¼ cups (300 ml) crêpe batter
4 cups (500 g) sliced onions
2 tablespoons (25 g) margarine or butter
1 tablespoon (15 ml) corn oil
6 ripe tomatoes
1 small can anchovies
3 tablespoons (45 ml) tomato paste
16 small stuffed olives
salt
pepper

Apple and Cottage Cheese Crêpes

Yogurt makes an excellent accompaniment to these cheese-filled crêpes.

Make 1¼ cups of crêpe batter and cook 8 crêpes on one side only.

Peel, core and slice ¾ pound of tart apples. Put the apples into a saucepan with the grated rind and juice of ½ lemon, 1 tablespoon of water, 1 tablespoon of sugar, 3 tablespoons of seedless raisins and ½ teaspoon of ground mixed spice. Cover and, stirring occasionally, cook gently for 5 minutes, or until the apple slices are cooked but are still slightly crisp. Remove the pan from the heat and add ¼ pound of cottage cheese. Mix the ingredients thoroughly.

Spread the apple and cheese mixture over the cooked side of each crêpe. Roll the crêpes up, folding in the edges.

Heat 2 tablespoons of margarine or butter with 1 tablespoon of corn oil in a frying pan. Add the rolled crêpes and fry them until they are golden brown. Serve immediately.

INGREDIENTS TO SERVE FOUR:
1¼ cups (300 ml) crêpe batter
¾ lb (350 g) tart apples
½ lemon
1 tablespoon (15 ml) sugar
3 tablespoons (25 g) seedless raisins
½ teaspoon (2.5 ml) ground mixed spice
¼ lb (100 g) cottage cheese
2 tablespoons (25 g) margarine or butter
1 tablespoon (15 ml) corn oil

FILLING ROLLED CRÊPES

Roll the crêpes enclosing the filling.

Spicy Scotch Pancakes

These pancakes, also called drop scones, are served with butter or with clear honey poured over them.

Combine 1 cup of self-rising flour, 2 tablespoons of sugar and 2 teaspoons of ground mixed spice in a mixing bowl. Beat 1 egg in a small bowl. Make a well in the flour mixture and pour in the beaten egg and ⅔ cup of milk. Stir the ingredients well; the batter should have the consistency of thick cream.

Lightly grease a griddle or a heavy frying pan and heat it over low heat. Drop 1 tablespoonful of batter onto the hot griddle. Cook for 2 to 3 minutes, or until bubbles appear on the surface. Turn the pancake over using a spatula and cook the other side until it is golden brown.

Remove the pancake from the pan and put it between the folds of a clean dish towel to keep warm and moist. Continue to cook the pancakes until the batter is used up. Serve immediately.

INGREDIENTS TO MAKE TWELVE TO SIXTEEN PANCAKES:
1 cup (100 g) self-rising flour
2 tablespoons (25 g) sugar
2 teaspoons (10 ml) ground mixed spice
1 egg
⅔ cup (150 ml) milk

Toad in the Hole

Meatballs cooked in a batter pudding look just like toads in holes when the batter puffs up around them.

Preheat the oven to 425°F (220°C).

In a large bowl combine ¾ pound of ground beef with 1 cup of fresh bread crumbs, ½ teaspoon of dried mixed herbs and 1 grated onion. Season to taste with salt and pepper. Mix the ingredients thoroughly.

In a small bowl beat 1 egg and add just enough to the meat mixture to bind it. Divide the meat mixture into 8 pieces and shape each one into a ball.

Put 2 tablespoons of corn oil into a small roasting pan or a shallow baking dish. Heat in the oven for 5 minutes. Add the meatballs to the hot oil and return the pan to the oven for 10 minutes.

Meanwhile, make up 1¼ cups of crêpe batter. Pour it over the meatballs. Return the pan to the oven and cook for another 30 to 40 minutes, or until the batter is well risen, crisp and brown.

INGREDIENTS TO SERVE FOUR:
¾ lb (350 g) ground beef
1 cup (50 g) fresh bread crumbs
½ teaspoon (2.5 ml) dried mixed herbs
1 onion
salt
pepper
1 egg
2 tablespoons (30 ml) corn oil
1¼ cups (300 ml) crêpe batter

Grapefruit Crêpes

Put 1 cup of all-purpose flour and ¼ teaspoon of salt into a mixing bowl. Make a well in the flour and pour in 1 egg and ⅔ cup of milk. Stir well until the batter is smooth. Beat in ⅔ cup of water.

Make 8 crêpes.

Squeeze the juice of 4 large oranges into a frying pan, add 2 tablespoons of honey and heat gently until the honey is dissolved. Simmer for 30 seconds. Remove the pan from the heat and stir in 2 tablespoons of Cointreau or Grand Marnier.

Peel and remove the pith from 1 grapefruit. Cut the membrane from the segments of fruit. Fold each crêpe in half, then in half again to form a triangle. Fill the pockets of the triangles with grapefruit segments. Put the crêpes into the frying pan and return to the heat. Simmer the crêpes gently for a few minutes, spooning the sauce over them several times, until they are heated through. Arrange the crêpes in a serving dish.

Alternatively, put the crêpes into a baking dish, pour the sauce over them and bake at 375°F (190°C) for 15 minutes, or until heated through.

In a small saucepan heat 2 tablespoons of brandy and pour it over the crêpes. Ignite the brandy and serve the crêpes flaming.

INGREDIENTS TO SERVE FOUR:
1 cup (100 g) all-purpose flour
¼ teaspoon (1 ml) salt
1 egg
⅔ cup (150 ml) milk
4 large oranges
2 tablespoons (30 ml) honey
2 tablespoons (30 ml) Cointreau or Grand Marnier
1 grapefruit
2 tablespoons (30 ml) brandy

FILLING FOLDED CRÊPES

Fill the pockets of the crêpes with fruit.

PASTA DOUGH IS MADE with flour and water and sometimes eggs. It is, of course, the base for a large number of simple but superb dishes.

Although homemade pasta is traditionally made with all-purpose flour, whole-wheat flour or a mixture of whole-wheat and all-purpose flours may be used.

The dough may be stored, well wrapped in plastic wrap, in the refrigerator for up to two days or in the freezer for as long as two months.

When making pasta dough it is useful to have a large working surface, preferably of marble. A long rolling pin is necessary and well worth the expense of buying.

MAKING PASTA DOUGH

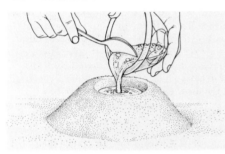

Make a well in the flour and pour in the liquid.

Draw the flour into the liquid to form a dough.

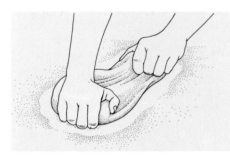

Knead well in the same way as bread dough.

Homemade Pasta

Put 4 cups of sifted flour mixed with 1 teaspoon of salt onto a large working surface. In a small bowl beat 4 eggs with 2 tablespoons of water. Make a well in the flour and pour in the beaten eggs and water. Using your hands, gradually draw the flour into the egg mixture, adding up to 2 tablespoons more water if necessary, until a stiff dough is formed.

Knead the dough in the same way as for bread for 10 minutes, or until it is smooth and elastic.

INGREDIENTS TO MAKE FOUR CUPS (500 g) OF PASTA:
4 cups (500 g) flour
1 teaspoon (5 ml) salt
4 eggs

Spinach Pasta Dough

Spinach gives this pasta its attractive green color and fine flavor.

Thoroughly wash 6 ounces of spinach in cold water. Drain well and put into a large saucepan. Add 1 teaspoon of salt, cover and cook for 10 minutes, or until the spinach is tender. Drain well and chop coarsely. Put the spinach into a small bowl. Add 2 eggs and beat well.

Put 4 cups of sifted flour mixed with 2 teaspoons of salt onto a large working surface. Make a well in the flour and pour in the spinach and egg mixture. Using your hands, gradually draw the flour into the spinach and egg mixture until a stiff dough is formed.

Proceed as for homemade pasta.

INGREDIENTS TO MAKE FOUR CUPS (500 g) OF PASTA:
6 oz (150 g) spinach
3 teaspoons (15 ml) salt
2 eggs
4 cups (500 g) flour

Tagliatelle

After this pasta is cooked you may add such ingredients as sautéed mushrooms, crisply broiled chopped bacon, garlic, herbs or bolognese sauce.

Divide 4 cups of pasta dough into a number of pieces. Roll each piece out very thinly on a lightly floured surface. Dust the dough and the working surface frequently with flour. Lift the rolled-out dough—it should be quite pliable and easy to handle without tearing—and spread it on a clean cloth over the back of a chair or on a table. Let the dough rest for 15 minutes.

Roll up each piece of dough loosely, jelly-roll style, and cut it crosswise at ¼-inch

(6-mm) intervals. Unroll the noodles and let them dry for 10 minutes or longer—up to 24 hours.

Bring a large pan of salted water to the boil. Add the tagliatelle gradually so that the water does not stop boiling. Boil for 5 minutes, or until the tagliatelle is tender but still slightly firm—this is aptly described by the Italians as *al dente*, to the tooth, or chewy.

Drain the tagliatelle. Put it into a serving bowl with ½ cup of butter or margarine and toss it quickly. Serve immediately with a bowl of grated Parmesan cheese.

INGREDIENTS TO SERVE FOUR:
4 cups (500 g) pasta dough
½ cup (100 g) butter or margarine
grated Parmesan cheese

CUTTING PASTA

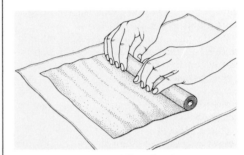

Roll the dough up gently, jelly-roll style.

Slice the rolled pasta into noodles.

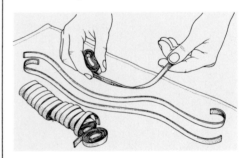

Unroll the noodles and leave to dry.

Baked Noodles with Cheese

Nourishing and tasty, this version of an old favorite calls for whole-wheat pasta.

First, prepare, roll out and cut 2 cups of whole-wheat pasta dough (see tagliatelle).

Heat $\frac{1}{4}$ cup of oil or butter in a saucepan. Add 1 cup of sliced small mushrooms and fry for 2 minutes. Stir in 2 tablespoons of flour. Gradually add $2\frac{1}{2}$ cups of milk, stirring constantly, and bring to the boil. Continue boiling and stirring until the mixture thickens. Stir in $\frac{1}{2}$ cup of chopped cooked ham, $\frac{1}{2}$ cup of peanuts and $\frac{3}{4}$ cup of grated sharp Cheddar cheese. Season to taste with salt and pepper. Remove the pan from the heat.

Bring $2\frac{1}{2}$ quarts of salted water to the boil. Add the pasta and cook it for 5 minutes, or until it is just tender. Drain the pasta and fold it into the hot sauce. Put it in a greased flameproof dish and sprinkle $\frac{1}{4}$ cup of grated sharp Cheddar cheese over the top.

Put the dish under a hot broiler until the sauce is bubbling and golden brown on top or bake at 400 F (200 C) for 20 to 30 minutes.

Serve immediately.

INGREDIENTS TO SERVE FOUR:
2 cups (250 g) whole-wheat pasta
(see tagliatelle)
$\frac{1}{4}$ cup (50 g) oil or butter
1 cup (100 g) small mushrooms
2 tablespoons (30 ml) flour
$2\frac{1}{2}$ cups (600 ml) milk
$\frac{1}{2}$ cup (100 g) chopped cooked ham
$\frac{1}{2}$ cup (75 g) peanuts
1 cup (100 g) grated sharp Cheddar
cheese
salt
pepper

Lasagne Verdi al Forno

This rich and satisfying dish requires no accompaniment other than a crisp green salad.

Divide 2 cups of spinach pasta dough into two pieces. Roll each piece out very thinly (see tagliatelle) and let the dough rest.

Meanwhile, finely chop 4 slices of bacon, 1 medium-sized onion, 1 celery stalk and 1 carrot. Heat 1 tablespoon of corn oil in a saucepan. Add the chopped bacon and the vegetables and fry for 5 minutes.

Add $\frac{3}{4}$ pound of ground beef and continue frying for 3 minutes. Stir in 4 tablespoons of flour. Add $1\frac{1}{4}$ cups of beef stock, 2 tablespoons of tomato paste and $\frac{1}{2}$ teaspoon of dried oregano. Season to taste with salt and pepper and bring to the boil, stirring frequently. Reduce the heat, cover the pan and simmer for 30 minutes.

Preheat the oven to 400 F (200 C).

Meanwhile, make a béchamel sauce. Halve 1 small onion and put it into a saucepan with 2 scant cups of milk, 2 parsley sprigs and 1 bay leaf and bring to the boil. Remove the pan from the heat and let the milk absorb the flavor for 10 minutes.

Melt 2 tablespoons of margarine or butter in another saucepan. Stir in 4 tablespoons of flour. Strain the milk and add it to the pan gradually, stirring constantly. Bring to the boil and continue to cook for 1 minute, stirring. Season to taste with salt and pepper and $\frac{1}{4}$ teaspoon of ground nutmeg. Remove the pan from the heat and set aside.

Cut the pieces of pasta dough into 2-inch (5-cm) wide strips and let the dough dry for 10 minutes.

Bring a large pan of salted water to the boil. Add the lasagne strips gradually and boil for 5 minutes, or until they are just tender. Drain the lasagne and immediately immerse in cold water. Drain again and spread the lasagne on a clean dish towel to dry.

Grease an ovenproof dish or a lasagne pan and spoon a thin layer of meat sauce on the bottom. Cover completely with a layer of béchamel sauce, then put a layer of lasagne on top. Repeat these layers until the dish is full, finishing with a layer of béchamel sauce. Sprinkle 1 tablespoon of grated Parmesan cheese over the top.

Bake the lasagne for 20 to 30 minutes, or until it is bubbling and golden brown on top.

INGREDIENTS TO SERVE FOUR:
2 cups (250 g) spinach pasta dough
(see tagliatelle)
4 slices (50 g) bacon
1 medium-sized onion
1 small onion
1 celery stalk
1 carrot
1 tablespoon (15 ml) corn oil
$\frac{3}{4}$ lb (350 g) ground beef
8 tablespoons (50 g) flour
$1\frac{1}{4}$ cups (300 ml) beef stock
2 tablespoons (30 ml) tomato paste
$\frac{1}{2}$ teaspoon (2.5 ml) dried oregano
salt
pepper
2 scant cups (450 ml) milk
2 parsley sprigs
1 bay leaf
2 tablespoons (25 g) margarine or butter
$\frac{1}{4}$ teaspoon (1 ml) ground nutmeg
1 tablespoon (15 ml) grated Parmesan
cheese

Chicken Canneloni

Divide 2 cups of pasta dough into 2 pieces. Roll each piece out very thinly (see tagliatelle) and let the dough rest.

Preheat the oven to 400 F (200 C).

Heat 1 tablespoon of corn oil in a small saucepan. Add 1 chopped onion and fry for 3 minutes. Take the pan off the heat and mix in 2 cups of ground, or finely minced, cooked chicken, 1 cup of fresh bread crumbs, 2 tablespoons of chopped parsley and the grated rind of $\frac{1}{2}$ lemon. Season to taste with salt and pepper. Stir until well mixed. Beat 1 egg in a small bowl and add enough to bind the chicken mixture.

Cut the pieces of pasta dough into 8 rectangles about 3 by 4 inches (8 by 10 cm) and let dry for 10 minutes.

Bring a large pan of salted water to the boil. Gradually add the canneloni and boil for 5 minutes, or until they are just tender. Drain the canneloni and immerse in cold water. Drain again and separate the canneloni on a clean cloth.

Divide the stuffing mixture into 8 sausage-shaped pieces. Put one on each piece of canneloni and roll tightly to form tubes.

Put the tubes into a greased ovenproof dish. Pour $1\frac{1}{4}$ cups of tomato sauce (see page 108) over the tubes. Bake the canneloni for 20 to 30 minutes, or until the sauce is bubbling.

Serve immediately with a bowl of grated Parmesan cheese.

INGREDIENTS TO SERVE FOUR:
2 cups (250 g) pasta dough (see
tagliatelle)
1 tablespoon (15 ml) corn oil
1 onion
2 cups (250 g) ground or finely minced
cooked chicken
1 cup (50 g) fresh bread crumbs
2 tablespoons (30 ml) chopped parsley
$\frac{1}{2}$ lemon
salt
pepper
1 egg
$1\frac{1}{4}$ cups (300 ml) tomato sauce
(see page 108)
grated Parmesan cheese

Ravioli with Ricotta

Freshly made, these delicate little "cushions" of pasta are superb. Pot cheese or sieved cottage cheese may be substituted for ricotta.

Put 2 cups of pasta dough on a lightly floured surface and divide it into two. Roll each half out very thinly to form a rectangle about 12 by 14 inches (30 by 35 cm). Let the dough rest for 15 minutes.

Meanwhile, put ½ pound of ricotta cheese into a large bowl with 4 tablespoons of grated Parmesan cheese, ¼ teaspoon of dried marjoram, ¼ teaspoon of nutmeg, 1 beaten egg and a pinch of salt and pepper. Mix thoroughly.

Brush one half of the pasta with water and at 2-inch (5-cm) intervals put teaspoonfuls of the ricotta mixture. Cover with the other half of the pasta and seal by pressing along the edges and between the mounds of ricotta filling. Using a 2-inch (5-cm) fluted pastry wheel, cut around each mound to make squares (about 28). Let the ravioli dry for 10 minutes before cooking it.

Add the ravioli to a large pan of boiling salted water and cook for 5 minutes, or until it is just tender. Drain the ravioli and put it

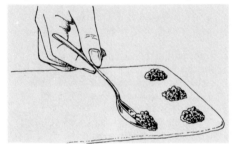

Put spoonfuls of filling at intervals on the pasta.

Cover with pasta and seal around the filling.

Cut around the mounds of filling.

into a warm serving bowl. Sprinkle with 4 tablespoons of grated Parmesan cheese and 1 tablespoon of chopped parsley. Serve immediately.

INGREDIENTS TO SERVE FOUR:
2 cups (250 g) pasta dough
½ lb (250 g) ricotta cheese
½ cup (50 g) grated Parmesan cheese
¼ teaspoon (1 ml) dried marjoram
¼ teaspoon (1 ml) nutmeg
1 egg
salt
pepper
1 tablespoon (15 ml) chopped parsley

Eggplant and Pasta Casserole

In this dish the vegetables are layered with the pasta and then topped with yogurt, which sets on the top like cheese. Macaroni, spaghetti or noodles may be used.

Cook ½ pound of pasta in a large pan of salted boiling water until it is just tender. Drain well.

Preheat the oven to 375°F (190°C).

Cut 1 large eggplant into thin slices. Spread the slices on a plate and sprinkle them liberally with salt. Leave for at least 30 minutes. Wash the slices and drain them well.

Slice 2 medium-sized tomatoes. Finely chop 1 small onion and mix it with 1 crushed garlic clove.

In a casserole arrange layers of eggplant, tomato and cooked pasta, sprinkling each layer with a little of the onion and garlic and salt and pepper. Finish with a layer of eggplant, arranged with the slices overlapping.

Spread ⅔ cup of yogurt over the top. Sprinkle with 2 tablespoons of grated Parmesan cheese.

Bake for 40 to 45 minutes, or until the eggplant is cooked and the top is golden brown.

INGREDIENTS TO SERVE FOUR:
½ lb (250 g) pasta
1 large eggplant
2 medium-sized tomatoes
1 small onion
1 garlic clove
salt
pepper
⅔ cup (150 ml) yogurt
2 tablespoons (30 ml) grated Parmesan cheese

Pasta al Pesto

This dish may be made with any pasta, although the thin, stringlike varieties are best. If you are making your own pasta follow the instructions for rolling and cutting given in the recipe for tagliatelle. The pesto sauce is mixed in at the table.

Remove the stems from a large bunch of basil and put the leaves into a mortar or small mixing bowl with 1 crushed garlic clove, ⅓ cup of chopped walnuts, ½ cup of grated Parmesan cheese and a little salt. Pound the ingredients with a pestle until they form a thick purée.

Beat in 3 tablespoons of olive oil, a little at a time, until the sauce is well blended and thick like creamed butter. Alternatively, put all the ingredients, except the oil, into a blender and mix to a purée. Slowly add the oil and blend at high speed until the sauce is smooth.

Add 2 cups of freshly made pasta to a large pan of boiling salted water and cook for 5 minutes, or until just tender. Drain the pasta and pile it into a warmed serving bowl.

At the table spoon the sauce over the pasta and top with a piece of butter or margarine.

Serve immediately with a bowl of grated Parmesan cheese.

INGREDIENTS TO SERVE FOUR:
1 large bunch basil
1 garlic clove
⅓ cup (25 g) chopped walnuts
1¼ cups (150 g) grated Parmesan cheese
salt
3 tablespoons (45 ml) olive oil
2 cups (250 g) freshly made tagliatelle or spaghetti
butter or margarine

Tomato Gnocchi

Pour 2½ cups of milk into a saucepan with 1 small onion, cut in half, 1 bay leaf and 1 pinch each of ground nutmeg, salt and pepper. Bring to the boil. Remove the pan from the heat and discard the bay leaf and the onion.

Sprinkle 1 cup of semolina into the milk. Cook over very low heat, stirring constantly, until the mixture is very thick. Remove the pan from the heat and beat in 2 eggs, ½ teaspoon of Dijon mustard and ½ cup of grated Parmesan cheese.

Turn the mixture into a greased shallow bowl and spread to a thickness of ½ inch (1 cm). Set the bowl aside until the mixture is cool, preferably overnight.

Preheat the oven to 400°F (200°C). Grease a shallow baking dish.

Slice 4 tomatoes thinly. Put the tomato slices into the prepared dish. Cut the semolina dough into 1½-inch (3-cm) squares. Arrange the squares on the tomatoes, letting them overlap slightly. Sprinkle the top with ¼ cup of grated Parmesan cheese.

Bake for 15 minutes, or until the top is crisp and brown.

INGREDIENTS TO SERVE FOUR:
2½ cups (600 ml) milk
1 small onion
1 bay leaf
ground nutmeg
salt
pepper
1 cup (100 g) semolina
2 eggs
½ teaspoon (2.5 ml) Dijon mustard
¾ cup (75 g) grated Parmesan cheese
4 tomatoes

PREPARING TOMATO GNOCCHI

Cut the set gnocchi into squares.

Arrange the squares on the tomato slices.

Singapore Noodles

Cook ½ pound of noodles or spaghetti in a large saucepan of boiling, salted water until tender. Drain well.

Meanwhile, finely chop or crush 1 large garlic clove, prepare 1 cup of sliced mushrooms, 1 cup of finely shredded cooked pork and ½ cup of cooked shelled shrimp. Peel and finely chop ¼-inch (6-mm) slice of ginger root. Heat 1 tablespoon of peanut oil in a large saucepan. Add the garlic, mushrooms and ginger and fry for 2 minutes. Add the pork and the shrimp and stir-fry for 1 minute.

Stir in ⅔ cup of chicken stock and 2 tablespoons of dry sherry or 1 tablespoon of soy sauce. Add 1½ cups of shredded cabbage

and 2 chopped scallions and bring to the boil.

Add the drained noodles and stir-fry for 3 to 5 minutes, or until the noodles are heated through and are lightly browned. Transfer to a serving bowl, garnish with chopped coriander or parsley and serve immediately.

INGREDIENTS TO SERVE FOUR TO SIX:
½ lb (250 g) of noodles or spaghetti
1 large garlic clove
1 cup (100 g) sliced mushrooms
1 cup (100 g) finely shredded cooked pork
½ cup (100 g) cooked shelled shrimp
ginger root
1 tablespoon (15 ml) peanut oil
⅔ cup (150 ml) chicken stock
2 tablespoons (30 ml) dry sherry or 1 tablespoon (15 ml) soy sauce
1½ cups (100 g) shredded cabbage
2 scallions
chopped coriander or parsley

Spaghetti with Tuna Sauce

Cook ½ pound of spaghetti in a large pan of boiling, salted water until tender.

Meanwhile, prepare the sauce. Heat 1 tablespoon of corn oil in a saucepan. Add 1 chopped large onion and 1 crushed garlic clove and fry for 3 minutes, or until the onions are tender but not brown.

Add 1¼ cups of chicken or fish stock and 3 tablespoons of dry white wine or vermouth to the pan. Bring to the boil and cook for 2 minutes, or until the stock has reduced slightly.

Drain and flake 7 ounces of canned tuna fish into the pan and simmer for 2 to 3 minutes. Season to taste with salt and pepper.

Drain the pasta well and put it in a serving dish. Pour the hot sauce over the pasta and sprinkle with 2 tablespoons of chopped parsley.

INGREDIENTS TO SERVE FOUR:
½ lb (250 g) spaghetti
salt
1 tablespoon (15 ml) corn oil
1 large onion
1 garlic clove
1¼ cups (300 ml) chicken or fish stock
3 tablespoons (45 ml) dry white wine or vermouth
7 oz (198 g) canned tuna fish
pepper
2 tablespoons (30 ml) chopped parsley

Noodle Soup

Put 5 cups of well-seasoned chicken stock into a large saucepan and bring to the boil.

Finely slice 1 stalk of celery and add to the stock. Reduce the heat and simmer for 5 minutes.

Slice 4 scallions and add to the stock with ¼ pound of vermicelli and ¼ pound of bean sprouts. Add 1 cup of shredded cooked chicken.

Simmer the soup for 5 minutes, or until the noodles are tender but the vegetables are still crisp. Serve immediately.

INGREDIENTS TO SERVE FOUR TO SIX:
5 cups (1 liter) well-seasoned chicken stock
1 celery stalk
4 scallions
¼ lb (100 g) vermicelli
¼ lb (100 g) bean sprouts
1 cup (100 g) shredded cooked chicken

Orange Macaroni Pudding

A sharp, sweet sauce complements the bland pasta in this unusual macaroni pudding.

Melt 2 tablespoons of margarine or butter in a saucepan. Stir in 4 tablespoons of flour. Add 1¼ cups of milk and bring to the boil, stirring constantly. Continue boiling and stirring the mixture until the sauce thickens.

Reduce the heat to the simmering point and add the grated rind and juice of 2 oranges, 2 tablespoons of sugar, ⅔ cup of seedless raisins and ½ teaspoon of ground cinnamon. Mix well and continue to simmer for 2 minutes.

Add 1½ cups of macaroni shells to a large pan of boiling salted water and cook for 5 minutes, or until the shells are just tender. Drain the macaroni shells and fold them into the hot sauce.

Serve the pudding immediately.

INGREDIENTS TO SERVE FOUR:
2 tablespoons (25 g) margarine or butter
4 tablespoons (25 g) flour
1¼ cups (300 ml) milk
2 oranges
2 tablespoons (30 ml) sugar
⅔ cup (100 g) seedless raisins
½ teaspoon (2.5 ml) ground cinnamon
1½ cups (150 g) macaroni shells

RICE, LIKE WHEAT, has its gods and even more disciples. In the East it is the staple diet of millions of people and is a symbol of happiness and fertility. The grain, which like oats and barley is surrounded by a tough outer husk, has a lower protein content than wheat, but is otherwise nutritionally similar.

Brown rice is the grain with only the husk removed. More than 2 percent of the protein and almost all the fat and minerals in brown rice are lost in the manufacture of white rice. But the most serious loss is of the vitamin thiamine, because it is lack of this vitamin that leads to the deficiency disease beriberi.

The connection between rice and beriberi is a classic example of the way science can stumble on a major discovery without realizing its full significance. Beriberi was rampant in the Dutch East Indies in the late nineteenth century and a young army doctor, Christian Eijkman, was sent to investigate the cause of the disease. For economy's sake, Eijkman fed hens on which he was carrying out research with polished rice left over from meals in the military hospital in Java. The fowls developed a paralysis remarkably similar to that of the patients suffering from beriberi. When a new director at the hospital put a stop to the doctor's supply of scraps the hens were fed on rice still in the husk, and, as if by a miracle, they recovered. It took almost half a century of investigation, however, before the full significance of thiamine in preventing beriberi became known.

The loss of thiamine in milled rice is minimized by a process known as parboiling, and it is estimated that in India more than half the rice is treated in this way. The method is to steep the unmilled rice in warm water for several days, then to steam-heat it and finally to dry it. Thiamine and other valuable vitamins and minerals in the husk and bran dissolve in the warm water and are carried into the endosperm, which makes up three-quarters of the grain, so that they are not lost in milling. The grain, which is milled after this treatment, is not so strikingly white, but it contains more than twice as much thiamine as untreated milled grain.

Most of the world's rice is produced in the tropics, where, since it is an aquatic plant, it is usually grown in standing water—the vast paddies with laborers bent double over the plants provide the universal image of rice growing. But the rice grown in warm temperate zones is more likely to be grown on dry land.

India was probably the birthplace of rice, but the first clear evidence of its cultivation comes from China in about 3000 B.C. For more than the four thousand years of Imperial China the

The Nutrients in Rice
Rice is more than three-quarters starch and is a good energy source. Three and a half ounces (100 g) provide about 360 Calories.

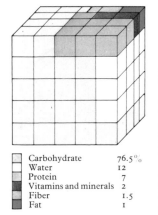

Carbohydrate	76.5%
Water	12
Protein	7
Vitamins and minerals	2
Fiber	1.5
Fat	1

Brown rice, which is the whole grain with just the husk removed, is more nutritious than white rice because it retains the protein, fat, minerals and B vitamins of the bran and germ. Short-grain and long-grain white rice have a much higher starch content because the bran and germ are removed in the process of pearling and polishing.

a panicle of rice

Most rice is grown in the monsoon belt where heavy rains and irrigation methods, like these terraces in Sri Lanka, provide the conditions required by many varieties of the grain.

Emperor and other members of the hierarchy took part in an annual symbolic ceremony of plowing a rice field. The Arabs introduced the cultivation of rice to Spain, and it spread to Italy in the fifteenth century. Rice reached America in 1700, and South Carolina, where it was first cultivated, was for a long time the most important rice-growing region.

There are several thousand varieties of rice, but the basic distinction in cooking is between three main types—long, medium and short grains. The long grains of Patna and Basmati rice are fluffy and separate when cooked and are therefore best used for savory rice dishes and for plain boiled rice. Medium and short grains, such as Java, Italian and Carolina rice, are stickier and more moist grains, and are used to make molds, stuffings and rice pudding.

Rice has an important role in sophisticated cuisines both of the East and the West. Many national rice dishes, or corruptions of them, have become almost universal. Pilav, basically a mixture of rice, meat and vegetables, is a national peasant dish in Turkey, but it turns up as plov in the USSR, pilaw in Poland and pilaf in most of western Europe. For this dish, under whatever name, long-grained rice is essential.

Risotto, of Italian origin, is creamy and thick, and is best made with short-grained rice, preferably the Piedmontese variety, which does not become soggy with slow cooking. Like missionaries, Italian restaurateurs have spread the dish throughout the West. Spanish paella, yet another rice dish, was most probably the progenitor of jambalaya, the popular Southern dish.

In all these dishes other ingredients, such as poultry, fish and vegetables, are integral parts, but rice provides the foundation. For real appreciation of rice, however, one has to turn to Chinese and Japanese cooking. There rice is a vital part of a meal, rather than part of a dish. In Japan the three main meals are called morning rice, afternoon rice and evening rice, and the test of a good cook is in the immaculate quality of the rice. To the Chinese gourmet there is nothing to surpass the sweet natural flavor (*hsien*) of perfectly cooked rice.

Rice has its other uses, too. Cooked under pressure at very high temperatures it is converted into a breakfast cereal. The Swedes, Norwegians, Danes and Belgians make rice porridge, and all their recipes have in common a sprinkling of cinnamon. Norwegians serve it with a drink of raspberry cordial and Danes eat it with melted butter and nonalcoholic beer.

Inevitably, like other grains, rice is made into an alcoholic drink. The Japanese brew is sake and the Chinese samshu. Little wonder that the most respectful Japanese name for rice is *gohan*, meaning "honorable food."

In a gesture to please the rice gods the Balinese display charms, like the figure made of coins above, at harvest festivals. Such symbols are common in some countries of Asia, where millions of people's lives depend on the success of the rice crop.

Boiled White Rice

Of the many methods of cooking rice this is the most nutritious because any nutrient that is lost into the cooking water is reabsorbed into the rice.

Cold cooked rice may be stored, covered, in the refrigerator for up to 1 week.

Put the rice and the water into a saucepan in the proportions of 1 to 2. This may be 1 bowl of rice to 2 bowls of water, or 1¼ cups of rice to 2½ cups of water. Add ½ teaspoon of salt and bring to the boil.

Cover the pan, reduce the heat and simmer gently for 15 to 20 minutes, or until the rice is tender, there is no hard core in the center of the grains and all the water has been absorbed.

INGREDIENTS TO SERVE FOUR:
1¼ cups (250 g) white rice
2½ cups (600 ml) water
½ teaspoon (2.5 ml) salt

Boiled Brown Rice

Brown rice is the whole unpolished grains of rice with only the inedible hull removed. It is more nutritious than white rice because it contains more fiber and more vitamin B. It takes about twice as long to cook as white rice and has a chewy texture and nutty flavor.

Put 1¼ cups of brown rice into a large saucepan with 2½ cups of water. Add ½ teaspoon of salt and bring to the boil.

Cover the pan, reduce the heat and simmer for 30 to 40 minutes, or until the rice is chewy but tender and all the liquid has been absorbed.

INGREDIENTS TO SERVE FOUR:
1¼ cups (250 g) brown rice
2½ cups (600 ml) water
½ teaspoon (2.5 ml) salt

Oven-cooked Rice

This method of cooking rice can also be used to reheat cold cooked rice. Put the cooked rice into an ovenproof dish, cover and bake for 10 to 15 minutes.

Preheat the oven to a moderate 350°F (180°C).

Put 1¼ cups of rice into an ovenproof dish. Add 2½ cups of boiling water (twice as much water as rice) and ½ teaspoon of salt.

Cover the dish and put it into the oven. Bake brown rice for 60 to 80 minutes and white rice for 30 to 40 minutes, or until the rice is tender and all the water has been absorbed.

INGREDIENTS TO SERVE FOUR:
1¼ cups (250 g) rice
2½ cups (600 ml) boiling water
½ teaspoon (2.5 ml) salt

Rice Minestrone

Heat 1 tablespoon of safflower oil in a large saucepan. Add 1 chopped onion, 1 diced carrot, 1 chopped stalk of celery and 1 crushed garlic clove. Fry for 3 minutes, stirring frequently. Stir in 5 cups of well-seasoned chicken or vegetable stock and bring to the boil. Lower the heat and simmer for 20 minutes.

Add ½ cup of rice with 2 blanched, peeled, chopped, medium-sized tomatoes, ¼ of a small cabbage, shredded, ⅓ cup of sliced green beans and ⅓ cup of shelled peas. Simmer for 15 minutes, or until the rice is tender.

Sprinkle with grated Parmesan cheese and serve immediately.

INGREDIENTS TO SERVE FOUR:
1 tablespoon (15 ml) safflower oil
1 onion
1 carrot
1 celery stalk
1 garlic clove
5 cups (1 liter) chicken or vegetable stock
½ cup (75 g) rice
2 medium-sized tomatoes
¼ small cabbage
⅓ cup (50 g) green beans
⅓ cup (50 g) shelled peas
grated Parmesan cheese

Paella

Cut 1 small chicken into 8 pieces. Slice 1 onion. Chop 4 slices of bacon. Remove the seeds and pith from 1 small green pepper. Chop the pepper.

Heat 3 tablespoons of corn oil in a large, heavy frying pan. Add the onion and bacon and fry for 3 minutes. Add the chicken pieces and cook until they are lightly browned. Add

1 crushed garlic clove, the chopped green pepper and 1¼ cups of long-grain white rice. Continue to cook the mixture for 1 minute, stirring constantly.

Blend 2 pinches of powdered saffron with 4 scant cups of well-seasoned chicken stock and stir into the rice mixture. Bring to the boil, stirring occasionally.

Shell and devein ½ pound of uncooked shrimp. Beard and scrub ½ pint (300 ml) of mussels. Add the mussels and shrimp to the rice mixture. Cover the pan, reduce the heat and simmer gently for 15 minutes.

Add ⅔ cup of shelled peas to the pan and continue to simmer for 5 minutes more, or until the rice and chicken are tender, the stock has been absorbed and the mussels have opened.

Discard any mussels which remain closed. Serve immediately.

INGREDIENTS TO SERVE FOUR:
1 small chicken
1 onion
4 slices (50 g) bacon
1 small green pepper
3 tablespoons (45 ml) corn oil
1 garlic clove
1¼ cups (250 g) long-grain white rice
powdered saffron
4 scant cups (850 ml) chicken stock
½ lb (250 g) raw shrimp
½ pint (300 ml) mussels
⅔ cup (100 g) shelled peas

PREPARING SHELLFISH

Scrape any beard off mussels with a sharp knife.

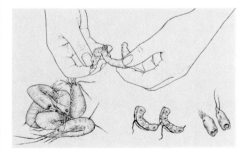

Remove the head and shell and devein prawns.

Savory Brown Rice

Put 1¼ cups of brown rice into a saucepan with 2½ cups of water or vegetable stock. Bring to the boil, cover, lower the heat and simmer for 30 minutes.

Add ½ cup of corn kernels with 4 chopped scallions and ¾ cup of peanuts to the rice. Simmer for 5 to 10 minutes more, or until the rice and corn are tender, adding more water if necessary. Season to taste with salt and pepper. Serve immediately.

INGREDIENTS TO SERVE FOUR:
1¼ cups (250 g) brown rice
2½ cups (600 ml) water or vegetable stock
½ cup (100 g) corn kernels
4 scallions
¾ cup (100 g) peanuts
salt
pepper

Persian Rice with Herbs

A delicious accompaniment to fish, this rice dish is traditionally served at New Year in Iran because its greenness is believed to ensure happiness in the year ahead. Any fresh herbs may be added, although if dried herbs are substituted only half the quantity given should be used because they have a much stronger flavor.

Put 1¼ cups of Basmati or long-grain rice into a saucepan. Cover with 2½ cups of water and bring to the boil. Lower the heat and simmer for 5 minutes.

Add 1 tablespoon of chopped chives, 1 tablespoon of chopped parsley and 2 tablespoons of chopped mixed herbs such as tarragon, thyme, marjoram and basil to the rice. Stir in the grated rind of ½ lemon and season with salt and pepper. Mix well, cover the pan and simmer gently for 10 minutes, or until the rice is tender and the water has been absorbed.

INGREDIENTS TO SERVE FOUR:
1¼ cups (250 g) Basmati or long-grain rice
1 tablespoon (15 ml) chopped chives
1 tablespoon (15 ml) chopped parsley
2 tablespoons (30 ml) chopped mixed herbs
½ lemon
salt
pepper

Fried Rice

This rice dish is a good accompaniment to many foods, but cooked meat, fish and vegetables may be added.

In a small bowl beat together 2 eggs and season with salt and pepper. Heat 1 tablespoon of peanut oil in a *wok* or a large, heavy frying pan. Pour the eggs into the pan and cook as an omelet until they are almost set. Slide the omelet onto a plate and chop it coarsely.

Add another tablespoon of peanut oil to the pan with ⅓ cup of chopped bacon and 1 chopped onion. Stirring frequently, fry for 3 to 5 minutes, or until the bacon is cooked and the onion is tender. Add 4 cups of cold cooked rice with ¼ cup of cooked peas, 4 coarsely chopped scallions and the chopped omelet. Stirring continuously, fry for 2 to 3 minutes, or until the ingredients are heated through. Stir in 1 tablespoon of soy sauce and serve immediately.

INGREDIENTS TO SERVE FOUR:
2 eggs
salt
pepper
2 tablespoons (30 ml) peanut oil
⅓ cup (50 g) chopped bacon
1 onion
4 cups (250 g) cold cooked rice
¼ cup (50 g) cooked peas
4 scallions
1 tablespoon (15 ml) soy sauce

STIR-FRYING

Heat the rice mixture in a wok *and stir continuously.*

Nasi Goreng

Chopped chilies may be added to this spicy Indonesian dish, but be careful because they are very hot.

Heat 2 tablespoons of corn oil in a large frying pan. Add 1 chopped onion and 1 crushed garlic clove and fry for 3 minutes, stirring constantly. Add ½ teaspoon of chilli powder, ¼ teaspoon of ground coriander and ¼ teaspoon of ground cumin and fry for 1 minute, stirring constantly.

Add 4 cups of cold cooked rice with ½ cup of chopped cooked ham, ¼ cup of cooked shelled shrimp, ¼ cup of peanuts and a 1-inch piece of cucumber, diced. Fry for 5 minutes, stirring constantly, or until the ingredients are heated through. Serve immediately.

INGREDIENTS TO SERVE FOUR:
2 tablespoons (30 ml) corn oil
1 onion
1 garlic clove
½ teaspoon (2.5 ml) chilli powder
¼ teaspoon (1 ml) ground coriander
¼ teaspoon (1 ml) ground cumin
4 cups (250 g) cold cooked rice
½ cup (75 g) chopped cooked ham
¼ cup (50 g) cooked shelled shrimp
¼ cup (50 g) peanuts
1-inch (2.5-cm) piece of cucumber

Pilau

This Middle Eastern rice dish is often served with kebabs.

Heat 2 tablespoons of corn oil in a saucepan. Add 1 chopped onion and fry, stirring frequently, for 5 minutes, or until the onion is lightly browned.

Add 1¼ cups of Basmati or long-grain rice, ⅓ cup of seedless raisins, ⅓ cup of chopped dried apricots and ⅓ cup of chopped walnuts.

Pour 2½ cups of chicken or vegetable stock over the rice mixture. Stir in ½ teaspoon of ground cinnamon and season to taste with salt and pepper. Bring to the boil, stirring occasionally. Lower the heat, cover and simmer for 15 minutes, or until the rice is tender and the stock has been absorbed.

INGREDIENTS TO SERVE FOUR:
2 tablespoons (30 ml) corn oil
1 onion
1¼ cups (250 g) Basmati or long-grain rice
⅓ cup (50 g) seedless raisins
⅓ cup (50 g) chopped dried apricots
⅓ cup (50 g) chopped walnuts
2½ cups (600 ml) chicken or vegetable stock
½ teaspoon (2.5 ml) ground cinnamon
salt
pepper

Kedgeree

Put ¾ pound of smoked haddock (finnan haddie) into a saucepan with 2½ cups of water, 2 peppercorns, 1 bay leaf, 2 parsley sprigs and the grated rind and juice of ½ lemon. Bring to the boil. Cover, lower the heat and simmer gently for 10 minutes, or until the haddock is tender. Drain the fish. Strain and reserve the liquid.

Add water if necessary to make the fish liquid up to 2½ cups. Put the liquid and 1¼ cups of long-grain white rice into a saucepan. Bring to the boil. Cover, lower the heat and simmer for 15 to 20 minutes, or until the rice is tender and all the liquid has been absorbed.

Coarsely chop 2 hard-boiled eggs. Flake the fish and add it with the chopped eggs to the rice. Stirring constantly, heat gently for 3 to 5 minutes, or until the ingredients are heated through.

Garnish with 1 sliced hard-boiled egg and 1 tablespoon of chopped parsley. Serve immediately.

INGREDIENTS TO SERVE FOUR:
¾ lb (350 g) smoked haddock (finnan haddie)
2 peppercorns
1 bay leaf
2 parsley sprigs
½ lemon
continued

POACHING AND SKINNING FISH

Simmer fillets of fish in water and lemon juice.

Scrape toward the head to skin poached fish.

1¼ cups (250 g) long-grain white rice
3 hard-boiled eggs
1 tablespoon (15 ml) chopped parsley

Apricot Lamb Polo

Preheat the oven to 350°F (180°C).

Heat 1 tablespoon of corn oil in a large saucepan. Add 1 chopped large onion and fry for 5 minutes, stirring frequently, until the onion is lightly browned. Cut 1 pound of lean boneless neck or leg of lamb into 1-inch (2-cm) cubes. Add the cubes to the pan and continue frying until the meat is brown.

Add ½ teaspoon of ground cinnamon, salt and pepper to taste, 2½ cups of water and 1 tablespoon of lemon juice to the pan. Mix well.

Bring to the boil, stirring constantly. Stir in 1 cup of dried apricots. Cover, reduce the heat and simmer for 1 to 1½ hours, or until the meat and the apricots are tender. If there is still quite a lot of liquid in the stew, boil it rapidly, uncovered, until the liquid has reduced but the stew is still moist.

Meanwhile, put 2½ cups of water into a large saucepan. Add 1¼ cups of long-grain white rice and 1 teaspoon of salt. Bring to the boil. Cover, reduce the heat and simmer for 10 minutes. Drain the rice.

Put a layer of the parboiled rice into an ovenproof dish, then put in a layer of the meat mixture. Continue making layers, finishing with a layer of rice.

Cover the dish and bake for 20 minutes. Serve immediately.

INGREDIENTS TO SERVE FOUR:
1 tablespoon (15 ml) corn oil
1 large onion
1 lb (500 g) lean boneless neck or leg of lamb
½ teaspoon (2.5 ml) ground cinnamon
salt
pepper
1 tablespoon (15 ml) lemon juice
1 cup (150 g) dried apricots
1¼ cups (250 g) long-grain white rice

Spinach and Chestnut Rice

Preheat the oven to 350°F (180°C).

Put 1¼ cups of rice and 2½ cups of water into a large saucepan. Add ½ teaspoon of salt and bring to the boil. Cover the pan, reduce the heat and simmer for 15 to 20 minutes, or until the rice is tender and all the water has been absorbed.

Meanwhile, thoroughly wash 1 pound of spinach in cold water and put it into a large saucepan. Add 1 teaspoon of salt, cover the pan and cook for 10 minutes, or until the spinach is tender. Drain the spinach well and chop it coarsely.

Make two cuts through the shells of ½ pound of chestnuts (about 20). Put them into a saucepan with water to cover. Bring to the boil and cook until the shells split. Drain the chestnuts and peel off the shells and inner skins while they are still warm.

Combine the rice, spinach and chestnuts in a mixing bowl and season to taste with salt and pepper. Transfer the mixture to an ovenproof dish. Sprinkle with 2 cups of fresh bread crumbs and dot with 1¼ cups of margarine or butter.

Bake for 35 minutes, or until the top is crisp and golden.

INGREDIENTS TO SERVE FOUR:
1¼ cups (250 g) rice
salt
1 lb (500 g) spinach
½ lb (250 g) chestnuts
pepper
2 cups (100 g) fresh bread crumbs
¼ cup (50 g) margarine or butter

Spanish Rice Casserole

This colorful rice dish makes an excellent accompaniment to chicken.

Heat 1 tablespoon of corn oil in a saucepan. Add 4 slices of chopped bacon and 1 chopped onion and fry, stirring frequently, for 5 minutes. Cut 1 green pepper into strips and add to the pan with 1¼ cups of long-grain white rice. Fry, stirring constantly, for 1 minute.

Stir 1¾ cups of chicken stock and 4 blanched, peeled and chopped, ripe, medium-sized tomatoes into the rice mixture. Add ¼ teaspoon of dried mixed herbs, salt and pepper. Bring to the boil and cover. Lower the heat and simmer gently for 15 minutes, or until the rice is tender and the liquid has been absorbed.

Alternatively, put into an ovenproof casserole, cover and bake at 375°F (190°C) for 20 to 30 minutes.

INGREDIENTS TO SERVE FOUR:
1 tablespoon (15 ml) corn oil
4 slices bacon
1 onion
1 green pepper
1¼ cups (250 g) long-grain white rice
1¾ cups (300 ml) chicken stock
4 ripe medium-sized tomatoes
¼ teaspoon (1 ml) dried mixed herbs
salt
pepper

Risotto Milanese

Heat 2 tablespoons of margarine or butter with 1 tablespoon of corn oil in a large saucepan. Add 1 chopped medium-sized onion and ½ cup of chopped bacon and fry for 5 minutes, stirring frequently, until the onion is beginning to brown.

Add 1 cup of sliced mushrooms and 1¼ cups of rice to the pan and fry for 1 minute, stirring constantly.

Add 2½ cups of chicken or vegetable stock to the rice and season to taste with salt and pepper. Continue stirring and bring to the boil. Cover, reduce the heat and simmer gently, adding more stock if necessary, for 15 to 20 minutes, or until the rice is cooked and the stock has been absorbed.

Add ½ cup of grated Cheddar cheese to the rice mixture. Stir the rice until the cheese has melted.

Turn the mixture into a warmed serving dish. Sprinkle with ½ cup of grated Cheddar cheese and serve.

INGREDIENTS TO SERVE FOUR:
2 tablespoons (25 g) margarine or butter
1 tablespoon (15 ml) corn oil
1 medium-sized onion
½ cup (15 g) chopped bacon
1 cup (100 g) sliced mushrooms
1¼ cups (250 g) rice
2½ cups (600 ml) chicken or vegetable stock
salt
pepper
1 cup (100 g) grated Cheddar cheese

Braised Onions and Rice
Preheat the oven to 350°F (180°C).

Peel and thinly slice 6 medium-sized onions. Separate the slices into rings and put half of them into a casserole or an ovenproof dish.

Sprinkle the onion rings with ⅔ cup of long-grain white rice, 4 sage leaves, 1 bay leaf, salt and pepper. Cover with the remaining onion rings, then pour in 1¼ cups of water.

Cover and bake for 1 hour, or until the rice and onions are tender and the water has been absorbed. Stir once or twice during cooking to mix the rice with the onions.

Serve hot.

INGREDIENTS TO SERVE FOUR:
6 medium-sized onions
⅔ cup (100 g) long-grain white rice
4 sage leaves
1 bay leaf
salt
pepper

Rice and Nut Ring
An elegant way to serve rice for a dinner party, this rice ring can be prepared in advance and kept chilled for up to 2 days before reheating.

Preheat the oven to 350°F (180°C). Lightly grease a 7- to 8-inch (18- to 20-cm) ring mold.

Heat 2 tablespoons of margarine or butter with 1 tablespoon of corn oil in a saucepan. Add ⅓ cup of coarsely chopped blanched

almonds, 2 tablespoons of chopped walnuts and 2 tablespoons of shelled and split pistachio nuts. Fry, stirring constantly, for 30 seconds until the nuts are golden brown.

Spoon the nuts into the prepared mold. Press 4 cups of cold cooked rice into the mold on top of the nuts.

Bake the mold for 15 minutes. Turn the mold out onto a plate and serve immediately.

MAKING A RICE AND NUT RING

Spoon nuts into the lightly greased mold.

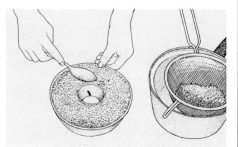
Cover with cooked rice and press into the mold.

Turn the mold out onto a plate and serve.

INGREDIENTS TO SERVE FOUR:
2 tablespoons (25 g) margarine or butter
1 tablespoon (15 ml) corn oil
⅓ cup (50 g) coarsely chopped blanched almonds
2 tablespoons (25 g) chopped walnuts
2 tablespoons (15 g) shelled split pistachio nuts
4 cups (250 g) cold cooked rice

Orange Rice Salad
This cold rice salad will keep well in the refrigerator for up to 2 days, but add more dressing before serving.

Prepare the dressing. Pour 3 tablespoons of wine vinegar into a small bowl and add 5 tablespoons of safflower oil, 1 tablespoon at a time, beating the mixture vigorously with a fork after each addition. Add the juice of 1 orange and 1 tablespoon of chopped mixed herbs and beat again.

Put 4 cups of warm cooked rice into a large mixing bowl. Add ⅓ cup of the dressing to the rice and mix thoroughly. The warm rice will absorb the dressing.

Peel and remove the pith from 2 oranges. Cut away the membrane from the segments of fruit. Add the segments to the rice with 1 chopped stalk of celery, ⅓ cup of seedless raisins and ⅓ cup of chopped walnuts. Mix well. Chill before serving.

INGREDIENTS TO SERVE FOUR TO SIX:
3 tablespoons (45 ml) wine vinegar
5 tablespoons (75 ml) safflower oil
3 oranges
1 tablespoon (15 ml) chopped mixed herbs
4 cups (250 g) warm cooked rice
2 oranges
1 celery stalk
⅓ cup (50 g) seedless raisins
⅓ cup (50 g) chopped walnuts

Cherry Rice Pudding
Preheat the oven to 350°F (180°C).

Put ½ cup of short-grain white rice and 2½ cups of milk into a saucepan. Add 2 tablespoons of sugar, the grated rind of ½ lemon, ½ teaspoon of grated nutmeg and ⅓ cup of seedless raisins. Mix well. Bring to the boil. Reduce the heat and simmer, stirring occasionally, for 15 minutes, or until the rice has swollen and the mixture is creamy.

Stir 2 egg yolks into the rice. Beat 2 egg whites until stiff and fold into the rice. Pit ½ pound of cherries and put them into an ovenproof dish. Pour the rice mixture over the cherries.

Bake the pudding for 20 to 30 minutes, or until the top is puffed up and brown.

INGREDIENTS TO SERVE FOUR:
½ cup (75 g) short-grain white rice
2½ cups (600 ml) milk
2 tablespoons (30 ml) sugar
½ lemon
½ teaspoon (2.5 ml) grated nutmeg
⅓ cup (50 g) seedless raisins
2 eggs
½ lb (250 g) cherries

TWO GRAINS—RYE AND OATS—which probably made their first appearance as weeds in wheat fields are now among the world's noteworthy cereals. They also have in common great hardiness in cold climates, an ability to thrive in poor soil and a more pronounced flavor than wheat, rice or corn. They differ from each other in that rye can be made into bread and is eaten by humans, while most of the world's oat crop is fed to animals. Human beings thus deprive themselves of one of the cereals which is rich in protein and fat and which is also well endowed with the B vitamins.

The original home of rye is believed to have been Asia Minor. By the Iron Age it was grown farther north and by the Middle Ages it was established as a major crop in central and northern Europe. From there it was taken to America, where it was used to make an alcoholic drink as well as to provide food.

The production and popularity of rye is greatest in a broad belt running south from the Arctic Circle through Scandinavia and the Soviet Union and into northeastern Europe, Germany and parts of France. In Finland, for example, the harvest is celebrated with a rye porridge, which is sometimes served with stewed pork and is an acquired taste.

Rye has never been a popular grain in England, where people have always hankered for as white a loaf of bread as they could get. Nevertheless, until the eighteenth century all but the wealthy English had to be content with bread made from maslin, a flour milled from a mixture of wheat and rye, or even from barley and rye or from oats and rye.

Perhaps it was because the English mixed rye with other grains that they escaped the disastrous outbreaks of poisoning, caused by eating rye bread, that periodically swept through Europe. The first serious outbreak was in A.D. 857, when thousands of people died in the Rhine Valley. The last was in 1951 in the Rhône Valley, where hundreds of people appeared to go mad overnight.

These disasters are now known to have been caused by a virulent fungus called ergot which can infect the ripe heads of rye. The fungus contains several poisonous alkaloids, one of which is closely allied to LSD. Any further outbreaks of ergotism seem unlikely because strict precautions are now taken to ensure that infected rye is not milled.

The protein value of rye bread is considerably lower than that of wheaten bread. There is also

MUESLI—A WELL-BALANCED MEAL

There are few more nutritious dishes than muesli, whose basic ingredients —rolled oats, raw apple, lemon juice, hazelnuts and milk—make a perfectly balanced meal. Muesli was devised early in the twentieth century by the

Swiss physician Dr. Bircher-Benner, at his famous clinic. Different ingredients may be added, but all muesli recipes are based on the traditional raw goodness that the doctor revered.

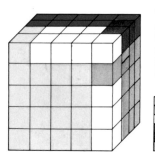

The Nutrients in Oats
As a cereal oats are very high in fat and also rich in protein and three and a half ounces (100 g) provide almost 400 Calories.

Carbohydrate	66	%
Protein	11.5	
Water	10	
Fat	9	
Vitamins and minerals	2	
Fiber	1.5	

a panicle of oats

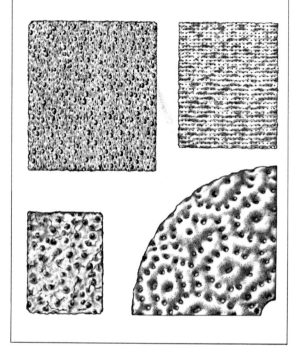

no comparison in the flavor or texture. The
readiness with which rye ferments gives the bread
its distinctive sour flavor—and this flavor you
may either like or dislike. The Poles, Scandinavians, Germans, French and also many Americans are among those who enjoy it.

In England rye bread has never managed to
shake off its association with poverty. Rye crisp
bread, however, has a following among British as
well as American dieters, who seem to believe
that it is endowed with magical properties. Manufacturers, however, are not permitted to make
extravagant claims for it and may only recommend it as an aid to weight loss.

There is as great a variety of rye breads as of
those made from wheat. Depending on the rate
of extraction the flour will vary from pale to rich
and dark. But because of the grain's low gluten
content, all rye breads have a dense texture. The
heaviest and blackest rye bread is the German
pumpernickel, which is made from coarsely
ground rye. Although it was a favorite of Napo-
leon's horse, few people appreciate its flavor.
Mixing wheat flour, which is richer in gluten,
with rye flour gives a more open texture to the
otherwise solid loaf.

Among the milled grains there is no flavor to
compare with the nutty sweetness of oats. In
spite of this oats are one of the least popular of
cereals, except in Ireland and in Scotland where
the addiction to oats has long been a source of
jibes by English writers. In the eighteenth century, Dr. Johnson, in his *Dictionary of the English
Language*, defined the oat as "a grain, which in
England is generally given to horses, but in
Scotland supports the people."

The fearsome names of some of the oat-based
Scottish and Irish dishes could have come
straight out of Tolkien's *Lord of the Rings*. There
is brose, a Scottish porridgy soup, and brotchán,
an Irish version; crowdie, a Scottish dish made
with oatmeal and buttermilk, and the Irish–
Scottish sowans, a fermented gruel that is
probably made more palatable when eaten, as at
Christmas, with whiskey. Haggis, which is basically a mixture of oatmeal and the heart, liver and
blood of a sheep, was known to the Romans, but
it is now as Scottish as the tartan. The Irish make
an oatmeal-based sausage called white pudding,
while the Scottish version is mealie pudding, or,
more enticingly, skirlie. A hodgils is a Scottish
oatmeal dumpling, and so is the mysteriously
named fitless cock.

Generally, the consumption of oatmeal was,
until recently, largely in the form of real porridge,
but this has now lost much of its breakfast-time
supremacy to convenience cereals made mainly
from corn, wheat and rice. These are ready-to-
serve, while the coarse oatmeal, that makes the
best porridge, needs long, slow cooking and
constant stirring. And, according to a tradition
that goes back to the Druids, porridge must
always be stirred to the right.

Oatmeal is lacking in gluten and cannot be
made into bread, but it does make delicious oatcakes. Here again the Scots excel with their
bannocks and broonies. Parkin, a sticky cake of
oatmeal and treacle, has its devotees. In the north
of England it is traditionally eaten around the
bonfires on Guy Fawkes's night. And in the
United States oatmeal is made into delicious
raisin-studded cookies.

a head of rye

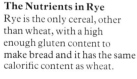

The Nutrients in Rye
Rye is the only cereal, other
than wheat, with a high
enough gluten content to
make bread and it has the same
calorific content as wheat.

Carbohydrate	72 %
Water	15
Protein	7.5
Vitamins and minerals	2
Fat	2
Fiber	1.5

Pumpernickel

Of German origin, this recipe makes a firm black bread. Because rye has little gluten it will not rise as much as bread made from wheat flour.

In a large bowl mix 6 cups of rye flour with 1 tablespoon of salt. Add 4 tablespoons of margarine. Cut the fat into small pieces with a table knife and rub it into the flour.

Put 2 tablespoons of molasses into a small saucepan with 1¼ cups of milk. Cook over very low heat until the molasses has dissolved and the milk is lukewarm.

Blend 1 cake of compressed yeast with ⅔ cup of tepid water. Mix until the yeast dissolves. Make a well in the flour mixture and pour in the yeast liquid and the warm milk and molasses. Mix until a sticky dough has formed.

Turn the dough out onto a floured surface and knead it well for 10 minutes, or until the dough is firm and no longer sticky. Add more flour if necessary.

Put the dough into a lightly greased bowl and cover with greased plastic wrap, or put it into a large greased plastic bag. Put the dough in a warm place to rise for 45 to 60 minutes, or until it has doubled in bulk.

Preheat the oven to 400°F (200°C).

When the dough has risen turn it out onto a lightly floured surface and knead it again for 2 to 3 minutes. Divide the dough in half, shape it into 2 ovals and put them on a lightly greased baking sheet. Alternatively, put the dough into two 5- by 9-inch (13- by 23-cm) loaf pans. Sprinkle 1 tablespoon of caraway seeds over the loaves and press the seeds lightly into the dough. Cover the dough and put in a warm place to rise until it has doubled in bulk, or risen to the top of the pans.

Bake for 45 minutes, or until the loaves are dark brown and sound hollow when tapped underneath. Cool on a wire rack.

INGREDIENTS TO MAKE TWO SMALL LOAVES:
6 cups (750 g) rye flour
1 tablespoon (15 ml) salt
4 tablespoons (50 g) margarine
2 tablespoons (30 ml) molasses
1¼ cups (300 ml) milk
1 cake compressed yeast
⅔ cup (150 ml) tepid water
1 tablespoon (15 ml) caraway seeds

Sourdough Rye Bread

Heat 2 scant cups of milk until it is lukewarm. Put 1 cake of compressed yeast into a large mixing bowl, pour in a little of the milk and stir until the yeast has dissolved. Stir in the remaining milk and 2 cups of rye flour. Cover and leave in a warm place for at least 12 hours, until the mixture smells sour.

Stir 1 cup more of rye flour, 2 cups of all-purpose flour and 1 tablespoon of salt into the mixture to make a firm dough. Turn the dough onto a floured surface. Knead it for 10 minutes, adding more flour if necessary, until the dough has become firm and elastic. Put the dough into a lightly greased bowl. Cover it with greased plastic wrap and leave it in a warm place for about 1 hour, or until the dough has risen and doubled in bulk.

When the dough has risen, turn it out onto a lightly floured surface and knead again for 2 to 3 minutes. Divide the dough in half and shape into 2 loaves. Put the loaves on a greased baking sheet or into two 5- by 9-inch (13- by 23-cm) loaf pans. Cover with greased plastic wrap and let rise in a warm place for 20 to 30 minutes, until the dough has doubled in bulk, or reached the top of the pans.

Preheat the oven to 425°F (220°C).

Bake the loaves for 15 minutes, then reduce the oven temperature to 375°F (190°C) and bake for 20 to 25 minutes more, or until the loaves are brown and sound hollow when tapped underneath. Cool on a wire rack.

INGREDIENTS TO MAKE TWO SMALL LOAVES:
2 scant cups (450 ml) milk
1 cake compressed yeast
3 cups (350 g) rye flour
2 cups (250 g) all-purpose flour
1 tablespoon (15 ml) salt

Peasant Bread

In a large mixing bowl combine 4 cups of whole-wheat flour, 1 cup of rye flour, ¾ cup of cornmeal and 1 tablespoon of salt. Mix well.

Into a small saucepan pour 1¼ cups of milk, ⅔ cup of water and 2 tablespoons of molasses. Cook over low heat until the molasses has dissolved and the mixture is warm enough to hold your finger in without discomfort.

Put 1 cake of compressed yeast into a bowl. Stirring, gradually add the warm milk mixture. Mix until well blended.

Pour the yeast liquid onto the dry ingredients. Mix until a sticky dough is formed. Turn the dough out onto a floured surface and knead it, adding more flour if necessary, for 10 minutes, or until the dough is firm and no longer sticky.

Put the dough into a lightly greased bowl, cover with greased plastic wrap and leave in a warm place for about 1 hour, or until the dough has risen and doubled in bulk. When

the dough has risen turn it out of the bowl and knead it again for a few minutes.

Divide the dough in half and shape it into 2 oval loaves. Put the loaves on a greased baking sheet, or into two 5- by 9-inch (13- by 23-cm) loaf pans. Make 3 diagonal cuts in the top of each loaf. Cover with greased plastic wrap and let rise until the dough has doubled in bulk or reached the top of the pans.

Preheat the oven to 400°F (200°C).

Bake for 35 minutes, or until the loaves are dark brown, firm to the touch and sound hollow when tapped underneath. Cool on a wire rack.

INGREDIENTS TO MAKE TWO SMALL LOAVES:
4 cups (500 g) whole-wheat flour
1 cup (100 g) rye flour
¾ cup (100 g) cornmeal
1 tablespoon (15 ml) salt
1¼ cups (300 ml) milk
2 tablespoons (30 ml) molasses
1 cake compressed yeast

SHAPING BREAD

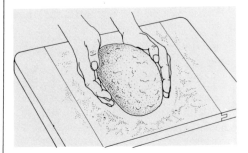

Mold the dough into loaves with your hands.

Old-fashioned Parkin

This Scottish oatcake may be stored for 2 to 3 weeks in an airtight container. It improves with age.

Preheat the oven to 325°F (170°C). Grease a 10- by 8- by 2-inch (25- by 20- by 5-cm) cake pan and line it with waxed paper.

Put ½ cup of margarine or butter into a saucepan with ⅓ cup of brown sugar, ½ cup of molasses and ½ cup of light corn syrup. Heat gently until the fat has melted and the sugar has dissolved. Set aside until cool.

Beat 2 eggs with ⅔ cup of milk and stir into the cooled melted ingredients.

In a large bowl mix together 2 cups of whole-wheat flour, 1 cup of medium oatmeal, ½ teaspoon of baking soda and 2 teaspoons of ground ginger.

Make a well in the flour mixture and pour in the melted ingredients. Stir until well mixed. Spread the mixture in the prepared pan. Bake for 1 to 1¼ hours, or until the cake is firm to the touch. Cool on a wire rack.

Wrap the cake in foil and keep it for at least 1 day before serving.

INGREDIENTS TO MAKE ONE LARGE CAKE:
½ cup (100 g) margarine or butter
⅓ cup (50 g) brown sugar
½ cup (120 ml) molasses
½ cup (120 ml) light corn syrup
2 eggs
⅔ cup (150 ml) milk
2 cups (250 g) whole-wheat flour
1 cup (150 g) medium oatmeal
½ teaspoon (2.5 ml) baking soda
2 teaspoons (10 ml) ground ginger

Harvest Oatcake

This golden country cake is made with oats, whole-wheat flour and wheat germ, and is flavored with oranges and honey. It is very easy to make; everything is mixed together in one bowl.

Preheat the oven to 350°F (180°C). Grease a 7-inch (18-cm) square cake pan.

In a large mixing bowl blend together 1 egg, 4 tablespoons of corn oil, 6 tablespoons of honey and 1 teaspoon of vanilla extract. Grate the rind of 1 orange into the bowl. Squeeze the juice from 3 oranges and stir it into the mixture.

Blend in 2 teaspoons of baking powder, 1 cup of whole-wheat flour, 2½ cups of rolled oats and 1⅓ cups of wheat germ. Mix well.

Turn the batter into the prepared cake pan. Level the surface and bake for 40 to 45 minutes, or until the cake has risen and the top is golden. Cool slightly before removing from the pan.

INGREDIENTS TO MAKE ONE SMALL CAKE:
1 egg
4 tablespoons (60 ml) corn oil
6 tablespoons (90 ml) honey
1 teaspoon (5 ml) vanilla extract
3 oranges
2 teaspoons (10 ml) baking powder
1 cup (100 g) whole-wheat flour
2½ cups (250 g) rolled oats
1⅓ cups (100 g) wheat germ

Oatwheels

Preheat the oven to 350°F (180°C).

In a large mixing bowl cream together ½ cup of margarine or butter with ⅔ cup of brown sugar until the mixture is pale and fluffy. Mix 1 teaspoon of baking powder with 1 cup of whole-wheat flour and stir it into the creamed mixture with 1¼ cups of rolled oats and the grated rind and juice of ½ lemon.

Press the mixture together with your hands. Carefully roll the mixture out on a floured surface to ¼-inch (6-mm) thick. Using a 3½-inch (9-cm) fluted cutter cut out 12 to 15 cookies, rerolling the dough as necessary. Using a spatula, carefully lift the cookies onto a lightly greased baking sheet.

Bake for 10 to 15 minutes, or until the oatwheels are just beginning to color at the edges. Allow them to cool slightly before transferring them to a wire rack.

INGREDIENTS TO MAKE TWELVE TO FIFTEEN COOKIES:
½ cup (100 g) margarine or butter
⅔ cup (100 g) brown sugar
1 teaspoon (5 ml) baking powder
1 cup (100 g) whole-wheat flour
1¼ cups (100 g) rolled oats
½ lemon

Scottish Oatcakes

Traditionally called farls in Scotland, these oatcakes may be served warm or cold with butter or jam.

Preheat the oven to 400°F (200°C).

Put ⅔ cup of medium oatmeal into a mixing bowl. Stir in a pinch of salt, ¼ teaspoon of baking soda and ¼ teaspoon of ground cinnamon.

Put 2 tablespoons of margarine into a small saucepan with 1 tablespoon of water and heat slowly until the margarine has melted. Bring to the boil, then pour into the oatmeal mixture. Stir to a soft dough.

Bind the dough together with your hands, then turn it onto a floured surface and knead lightly. Roll the dough out thinly to form a circle 8 inches (20 cm) in diameter. Cut the round into 8 wedges.

Using a spatula, carefully lift the wedges onto a greased baking sheet. Bake for 15 to 20 minutes, or until the oatcakes are crisp, lightly browned and the edges are beginning to curl up.

INGREDIENTS TO MAKE EIGHT OATCAKES:
⅔ cup (100 g) medium oatmeal
salt
¼ teaspoon (1 ml) baking soda
¼ teaspoon (1 ml) ground cinnamon
2 tablespoons (25 g) margarine

Herb Rye Crisp Bread

This wafer-thin crisp bread can be eaten as a cracker or as a substitute for bread.

Preheat the oven to 400°F (200°C).

Put 2 cups of rye flour into a mixing bowl and rub in ¼ cup of margarine. Mix in 1 teaspoon of dried mixed herbs and ½ teaspoon of salt. Stir in 4 tablespoons of milk or water and mix until the ingredients are thoroughly blended and the dough is firm.

Divide the dough in half. Knead each piece lightly on a floured surface. Roll each piece of dough out thinly to about 9 inches (23 cm) square. Cut into 3-inch (8-cm) squares. Put the squares onto lightly greased baking sheets. Prick each square well with a fork to keep it from rising and bubbling.

Bake the crisp bread for 10 to 15 minutes, or until the edges just begin to color, but do not let them brown. Cool slightly on the baking sheets, then transfer them to wire racks.

INGREDIENTS TO MAKE EIGHTEEN CRISP BREADS:
2 cups (250 g) rye flour
¼ cup (50 g) margarine
1 teaspoon (5 ml) dried mixed herbs
½ teaspoon (2.5 ml) salt
4 tablespoons (60 ml) milk or water

MAKING CRISP BREAD

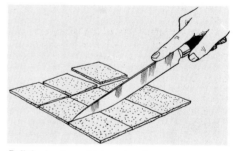

Roll the dough out thinly and cut into squares.

Prick the squares well to keep them from rising.

Oat Bars

These crunchy, sticky bars will keep well for up to 2 weeks if they are stored in an airtight container.

Preheat the oven to 375°F (190°C). Grease a 7- to 8-inch (18- to 20-cm) square cake pan.

Put 6 tablespoons of margarine or butter into a saucepan with ⅓ cup of brown sugar and 2 tablespoons of light corn syrup. Heat gently until the sugar has dissolved. Remove the pan from the heat and stir in 2 cups of rolled oats. Mix well.

Press the mixture into the greased pan and level the surface. Bake for 20 minutes, or until golden brown and firm to the touch.

Cut into 12 bars while still in the pan. Cool in the pan until the bars are hard, then put on a wire rack.

INGREDIENTS TO MAKE TWELVE BARS:
6 tablespoons (75 g) margarine or butter
⅓ cup (50 g) brown sugar
2 tablespoons (30 ml) light corn syrup
2 cups (150 g) rolled oats

MAKING OAT BARS

Press the mixture into the pan with a knife.

Cut into bars and cool in the pan.

Muesli

This nutritious cereal is not only a delicious breakfast dish but served with fresh fruit makes an excellent dessert. It can be stored in an airtight container for up to 1 month. To serve muesli, spoon it into serving bowls, add milk, yogurt or fresh orange juice and mix to a creamy consistency.

Combine 2½ cups of rolled oats with ⅔ cup of wheat germ and 4 tablespoons of brown sugar. Add 1 cup of mixed dried fruit, such as currants, raisins, apricots, apples, figs, dates or prunes, and ⅔ cup of chopped almonds, walnuts or hazelnuts. Mix well.

INGREDIENTS TO MAKE ONE AND A HALF POUNDS (700 g) OF MUESLI:
2½ cups (250 g) rolled oats
⅔ cup (50 g) wheat germ
4 tablespoons (60 ml) brown sugar
1 cup (250 g) mixed dried fruit
⅔ cup (100 g) nuts

Almond Crunch Granola

This crunchy breakfast cereal, made from toasted oats, nuts and honey, is more delicious than any you can buy. Serve it with milk and fresh or dried fruit.

Preheat the oven to 350°F (180°C).

Mix 5 cups of rolled oats with ⅔ cup of coarsely chopped blanched almonds or a mixture of nuts. Stir in 8 tablespoons of clear honey, 2 tablespoons of safflower oil and 1 teaspoon of vanilla extract. Mix well. Spread the mixture thinly on 2 lightly greased baking sheets.

Bake for 20 to 25 minutes, turning occasionally so that the oats are evenly and lightly browned.

Cool. Store in sealed jars or containers for up to 1 month.

INGREDIENTS TO MAKE ONE AND A HALF POUNDS (750 g) OF CEREAL:
5 cups (500 g) rolled oats
⅔ cups (250 g) blanched almonds
8 tablespoons (120 ml) clear honey
2 tablespoons (30 ml) safflower oil
1 teaspoon (5 ml) vanilla extract

Porridge

This traditional Scottish breakfast dish can be made from coarse, medium or fine oatmeal or from rolled oats. For a good flavor and creamy texture soak the oats in milk overnight.

Put 5 cups of milk or water into a saucepan and bring to the boil. Remove the pan from the heat and stir in ¾ cup of oatmeal or 1¼ cups rolled oats. Leave to soak, overnight if possible.

Return the pan to the heat and bring to the boil. Reduce the heat and simmer, stirring continuously, until the oats are swollen and tender. Simmer fine oatmeal or rolled oats for 5 minutes, medium oatmeal for 15 minutes and coarse oatmeal for longer.

Add salt to taste and water if a thinner consistency is preferred. Serve immediately.

INGREDIENTS TO SERVE FOUR TO SIX:
5 cups (1 liter) milk or water
¾ cup (100 g) oatmeal or 1¼ cups rolled oats
salt

Oat and Rye Raisin Bread

Preheat the oven to 400°F (200°C). Grease a large loaf pan.

Combine 2 cups of whole-wheat flour with 1 cup of rye flour and ¾ cup of oatmeal or 1¼ cups of rolled oats in a large mixing bowl. Add 1 teaspoon of baking soda, 1 teaspoon of baking powder, 1 teaspoon of salt and 2 tablespoons of brown sugar. Add ⅔ cup of seedless raisins and mix well.

Stir 1¼ cups of yogurt into the flour mixture and mix to a soft dough.

Turn the dough out onto a lightly floured board and knead it until it becomes smooth. Shape the dough into a loaf and put it into the prepared pan or on a greased baking sheet.

Bake for 40 to 45 minutes, or until the loaf has risen, is brown on top and sounds hollow when tapped underneath.

INGREDIENTS TO MAKE 1 LARGE LOAF:
2 cups (250 g) whole-wheat flour
1 cup (100 g) rye flour
¾ cup (100 g) oatmeal or 1¼ cups rolled oats
1 teaspoon (5 ml) baking soda
1 teaspoon (5 ml) baking powder
1 teaspoon (5 ml) salt
2 tablespoons (30 ml) brown sugar
⅔ cup (100 g) seedless raisins
1¼ cups (300 ml) yogurt

Delicious Date Bars

Preheat the oven to 375°F (190°C).

In a large bowl mix 2 cups of rolled oats with 1 cup of whole-wheat flour. Rub in ½ cup of margarine or butter until it is well mixed. Mold the mixture together with your hands until it forms a firm dough. Press half of the dough into a greased 7-inch (18-cm) square cake pan.

Coarsely chop ½ pound of pitted dates. Add 1 tablespoon of honey and 2 tablespoons of lemon juice to the dates and mix well. Spread the date mixture over the layer of dough. Spread the remaining dough over the date mixture, pressing down well so that some of the dates show through.

Bake for 30 to 40 minutes, or until the top is golden brown. Cut into bars while still warm and let cool in the pan.

INGREDIENTS TO MAKE TWELVE BARS:
2 cups (150 g) rolled oats
1 cup (100 g) whole-wheat flour
½ cup (100 g) margarine or butter
½ lb (250 g) pitted dates
1 tablespoon (15 ml) honey
2 tablespoons (30 ml) lemon juice

MAKING DATE BARS

Cover the dough in the pan with the date mixture.

Press the remaining dough on top with your fingers.

Brown Oatmeal Bread

In a large bowl mix together 4 cups of whole-wheat flour, 1⅔ cups of medium oatmeal or 3 cups of rolled oats, 1 tablespoon of salt and 1 tablespoon of brown sugar. Add 1 tablespoon of margarine and rub it into the flour.

Blend 1 cake of compressed fresh yeast with 2 scant cups of tepid water until the yeast has dissolved. Make a well in the flour and pour in the yeast liquid. Mix to a soft dough adding a little more oats or flour if the dough is too sticky.

Turn the dough out onto a lightly floured surface and knead well for 10 minutes, or until the dough is firm and elastic and no longer sticky.

Shape the dough into a ball and put it into a lightly greased bowl. Cover the bowl with greased plastic wrap. Put the dough in a warm place to rise for about 1 hour, or until it has doubled in bulk.

Preheat the oven to 425°F (210°C).

When the dough has risen, knead it again for 2 to 3 minutes. Divide the dough in half and shape each half into an oval loaf. Put the loaves on a greased baking sheet and make 3 diagonal cuts across the top of each loaf. Cover with greased plastic wrap and put in a warm place to rise for 30 minutes, or until the loaves have doubled in bulk.

Bake for 30 to 40 minutes, or until the loaves are lightly browned and sound hollow when tapped underneath.

INGREDIENTS TO MAKE 2 SMALL LOAVES:
4 cups (400 g) whole-wheat flour
1⅔ cups (300 g) medium oatmeal or
**   3 cups (300 g) rolled oats**
1 tablespoon (15 ml) salt
1 tablespoon (15 ml) brown sugar
1 tablespoon (15 g) margarine
1 cake (15 g) compressed fresh yeast
2 scant cups (450 ml) tepid water

Oatmeal Stuffing

This is a piquant version of a Scottish recipe that is traditionally used to stuff herring. It can be used to stuff any fat fish.

Combine 1¼ cups of rolled oats with 1 tablespoon of grated onion, 1 tablespoon of chopped thyme, 2 tablespoons of chopped parsley, the grated rind of 1 lemon, salt and pepper. Add 1 beaten egg with 2 tablespoons of milk and 1 teaspoon of lemon juice. Mix well.

INGREDIENTS TO STUFF FOUR MEDIUM-SIZED HERRING:
1¼ cups (100 g) rolled oats
1 tablespoon (15 ml) grated onion
1 tablespoon (15 ml) chopped thyme
2 tablespoons (30 ml) chopped parsley
1 lemon
salt
pepper
1 egg
2 tablespoons (30 ml) milk

Apple Oat Crumble

Preheat the oven to 375°F (190°C).

Peel and core 1 pound of tart apples. Cut the apples into thin slices. Put the apple slices into a 1-quart (850-ml) pie pan or baking dish and sprinkle with ⅓ cup of brown sugar. Scatter 6 cloves over the apples.

Melt 3 tablespoons of margarine or butter in a large saucepan. Add ⅓ cup of brown sugar and cook over low heat, stirring constantly, until the sugar has dissolved. Remove the pan from the heat and stir in 1¼ cups of rolled oats. Mix well.

Spoon the oat mixture over the apples and level the surface. Bake for 30 to 40 minutes, or until the crumble is golden brown.

INGREDIENTS TO SERVE FOUR:
1 lb (500 g) tart apples
⅔ cup (100 g) brown sugar
6 cloves
3 tablespoons (35 g) margarine or butter
1¼ cups (100 g) rolled oats

Danish Holecake

These crisp breads were eaten all through the winter by Danish peasants, who threaded them together by the holes cut in them and hung them from the rafters of their cottages.

Preheat the oven to 450°F (230°C). Grease 2 large baking sheets.

Put 4 cups of rye flour and 1 teaspoon of salt into a mixing bowl. Make a well in the flour and pour in 1¼ cups of tepid water. Mix to a dough.

Put the dough onto a lightly floured board and roll it out very thinly. Cut 4 large circles out of the dough using a dinner plate as a guide. Using a cookie cutter, cut a hole near the edge of each circle.

Transfer the circles to the baking sheets and bake for 10 minutes.

INGREDIENTS TO MAKE 4 CRISP BREADS:
4 cups (500 g) rye flour
1 teaspoon (5 ml) salt
1¼ cups tepid water

MORE CORN IS PRODUCED than any other cereal except wheat, but most of it is eaten by animals. It is the one cereal of American origin and the inhabitants of the middle Americas were growing corn three thousand years before Christopher Columbus brought it back to Spain from the Caribbean in 1496. It is now also grown in the warmer parts of Europe, and in Africa, Asia and Australia.

Corn is nutritionally inferior to wheat, largely because it contains less protein, and the protein it does have is of lower biological value since it has inadequate amounts of the amino acids tryptophan and lysine. Tryptophan is needed for conversion within the body to the vitamin niacin, a shortage of which may cause pellagra, a disease which may be prevalent in places where corn is the staple food. During the past three

In Africa where corn is the staple diet the people often suffer from pellagra, a disease caused by a deficiency of the B vitamin niacin. Corn contains niacin, but in a form the human body cannot make use of. There is no pellagra in Mexico, however, even though tortillas are the basis of most meals. These spicy pancakes are made of corn mixed with lime water which produces an alkaline condition that frees the niacin.

decades, however, plant breeders have produced mutants with more protein and a better balance of amino acids.

The other drawback to corn is that it does not contain sufficient gluten to produce a dough that will rise. Corn bread, therefore, bears no resemblance to a wheaten loaf. "Breads" made from cornmeal are popular in the United States, in Latin America and in parts of southwest France. Coarsely ground cornmeal is made into a porridge in the South where it is called hominy grits and in Italy where it is known as polenta.

But corn turns up in many other forms. It can be pulverized to make cornstarch, which is used to thicken sauces and soups (especially in Chinese cooking) and, mixed with wheat flour, to lighten cakes. Corn can also be exploded to make popcorn, hydrolyzed to make corn syrup and crushed to extract the excellent polyunsaturated corn oil.

For many people all over the world the introduction to corn was effected in childhood through the American Kellogg brothers and their cornflakes. In the modern large-scale manufacture of cornflakes the broken grains, or grits, are steamed, flavored with salt, malt and sugar, fortified with thiamine, riboflavin and niacin,

a panicle of sorghum

an ear of dent type corn used for flour

an ear of common millet

a head of barley

a stem of buckwheat

dried, rested for a day or two, flattened into flakes between rollers, toasted in rotary ovens, cooled and, finally, packed.

Grains that in one part of the world are a staple food may elsewhere provide only beer or birdseed. The most notable and most ancient are barley and the millet group of grains.

Barley may well be the oldest cultivated grain. In Neolithic times it was eaten as a paste, and it was still popular with the ancient Greeks. In Tibet a concoction of toasted barley flour, black tea and yak butter has survived into the twentieth century. In India, Japan and the Baltic States it is still an important food and in the Near East it is a staple. Barley meal is used in parts of Europe for porridge and malt breads. But in the United States and western Europe the grain is eaten mainly as pot barley or pearl barley. Pot barley is the whole grain minus the outer husk. It tastes nuttier than pearl barley, which lacks most of the bran and germ, as well as the husk. These barleys give a delicious flavor and smoothness to soups, notably to Scotch broth.

More than half of the world's barley crop is used as animal fodder and most of the rest is turned into beer and whiskey. Barley has been used for making beer since time immemorial. Barley wine was being brewed in Babylon in 2800 B.C.

The other grains are sorghum, millet and buckwheat. Although sorghum is mainly used for animal feed, it is nutritionally comparable to corn and is a basic food in many parts of Africa and Asia. Millet, which has a higher protein content than corn, barley or sorghum, is a staple in parts of Africa and India, where it is made into such foods as porridge, and unleavened bread, or chapatis. Buckwheat is a staple in the USSR and Poland where it is often served and cooked like rice. In the United States buckwheat flour is used to make pancakes.

MALT EXTRACT

Usually made from malted barley, malt extract has been given to children for more than a hundred years. The advertisement (right) shows a Victorian child eagerly stretching for it. The malt was often mixed with cod liver oil (high in vitamins A and D) the taste of which children loathed. This advertisement also recommended malt extract to nursing mothers and consumptives, implying that bouncing health was but a spoonful away. What it didn't say is that malt extract is only a good energy source because it is 50 per cent sugars.

The Nutrients in Barley

Barley is a good source of B vitamins, especially niacin, and three and a half ounces (100 g) provide about 350 Calories.

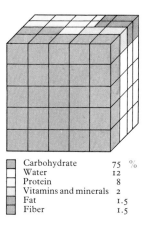

Carbohydrate	75	%
Water	12	
Protein	8	
Vitamins and minerals	2	
Fat	1.5	
Fiber	1.5	

The Nutrients in Millet and Corn

Millet is high in protein and, like corn, has a high fat content. Both calorie counts are similar to barley.

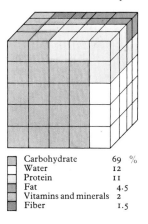

Carbohydrate	69	%
Water	12	
Protein	11	
Fat	4.5	
Vitamins and minerals	2	
Fiber	1.5	

Corn Muffins

Preheat the oven to a hot 425°F (200°C).

Put 1 scant cup of yellow cornmeal into a mixing bowl with ¾ cup of all-purpose flour, 1 tablespoon of baking powder and 1 tablespoon of sugar. Mix well.

Lightly beat 1 egg in a small mixing bowl. Beat in 1 cup of milk and 2 tablespoons of corn oil. Pour the liquid onto the dry ingredients and mix well.

Spoon the batter into 15 greased deep muffin pans, filling each three-quarters full. Sprinkle each one with ¼ teaspoon of grated Parmesan cheese.

Bake for 15 to 20 minutes, or until the muffins have risen and are golden brown. Remove the muffins from the pans and cool them on a wire rack.

INGREDIENTS TO MAKE FIFTEEN MUFFINS:
1 scant cup (125 g) yellow cornmeal
¾ cup (75 g) all-purpose flour
1 tablespoon (15 ml) baking powder
1 tablespoon (15 ml) sugar
1 egg
1 cup (250 ml) milk
2 tablespoons (30 ml) corn oil
1 tablespoon (15 ml) grated Parmesan cheese

MAKING MUFFINS

Spoon or pour the batter into muffin pans.

Mixed Grain Bread

In a large bowl mix 2 cups of all-purpose flour with 2 cups of barley or rye flour, ¾ cup of yellow cornmeal, 1¼ cups of rolled oats and 1 tablespoon of salt.

Blend 1 cake of compressed fresh yeast with 2 scant cups of tepid water. Mix until the yeast is dissolved. Make a well in the flour mixture and pour in the yeast liquid. Mix to a firm dough.

Turn the dough out onto a lightly floured surface and knead well for 10 minutes, or until the dough is firm and elastic and is no longer sticky.

Put the dough into a greased bowl and cover it lightly with greased plastic wrap, or put the bowl into a large greased plastic bag. Put the dough in a warm place to rise for 45 to 60 minutes, or until it has risen and

doubled in bulk. When the dough has risen turn it out onto a lightly floured surface and knead again for 2 to 3 minutes.

Preheat the oven to 425°F (280°C).

Divide the dough in half. Shape each half into an oval and place it on a greased baking sheet. The dough may, alternatively, be put into two greased 5- by 9-inch (13- by 23-cm) loaf pans. Make diagonal cuts across the top of the dough. Cover and put in a warm place until the dough has risen almost to the top of the pans and has doubled in bulk.

Bake in the center of the oven for 30 to 40 minutes, or until the loaves are golden brown and sound hollow when tapped underneath. Cool on a wire rack.

INGREDIENTS TO MAKE TWO SMALL LOAVES:
2 cups (250 g) all-purpose flour
2 cups (250 g) barley or rye flour
¾ cup (100 g) yellow cornmeal
1¼ cups (100 g) rolled oats
1 tablespoon (15 ml) salt
1 cake (15 g) compressed fresh yeast
2 scant cups (450 ml) tepid water

Spoonbread

Preheat the oven to 400°F (200°C).

Pour 2½ cups of milk into a saucepan and bring to the boil. Stir in ½ cup plus 2 tablespoons of cornmeal and 1 teaspoon of salt. Reduce the heat and simmer gently, stirring continuously, for about 5 minutes, or until the mixture thickens. Remove the pan from the heat and let the mixture cool until it is lukewarm.

Add 4 egg yolks to the mixture, stirring until well blended.

Beat 4 egg whites until stiff and then fold them into the mixture. Pour into a 2-quart (1½-liter) soufflé dish.

Bake for 40 to 45 minutes, or until the spoonbread is well risen and golden brown. Serve immediately.

INGREDIENTS TO SERVE FOUR:
2½ cups (600 ml) milk
½ cup plus 2 tablespoons (75 g) cornmeal
1 teaspoon (5 ml) salt
4 eggs

Whole-wheat Cornbread

Preheat the oven to 400°F (200°C).

Mix together ¾ cup of cornmeal with 1 cup of whole-wheat flour, 1 tablespoon of baking powder, 1 teaspoon of salt and 1 tablespoon of sugar.

In a mixing bowl lightly beat 1 egg. Stir in 1¼ cups of buttermilk or milk. Pour the liquid into the dry ingredients. Stir well until blended.

Pour the batter into a greased 7-inch (18-cm) square cake pan. Bake for 30 to 35 minutes, or until the cornbread has risen and is lightly browned and firm to the touch.

Allow to cool for a few minutes in the pan before turning out onto a wire rack.

INGREDIENTS TO MAKE ONE SMALL LOAF:
¾ cup (100 g) cornmeal
1 cup (100 g) whole-wheat flour
1 tablespoon (15 ml) baking powder
1 teaspoon (5 ml) salt
1 tablespoon (15 ml) sugar
1 egg
1¼ cups (300 ml) buttermilk or milk

Banana Malt Loaf

Malt gives this easy-to-make English tea bread a particularly rich flavor.

Combine 3 tablespoons of malt extract in a small saucepan with ⅓ cup of brown sugar, 2 tablespoons of margarine and ⅔ cup of milk. Cook over very low heat until the sugar has dissolved.

In a large bowl mix together 2 cups of whole-wheat flour, 2 teaspoons of baking powder and ¼ teaspoon of salt. Add the malt mixture and stir well to blend.

Stir in 2 finely chopped or mashed bananas and ½ cup of seedless raisins and mix well.

Preheat the oven to 325°F (170°C).

Spoon the batter into a greased 5- by 9-inch (13- by 23-cm) loaf pan and level the surface. Bake for 1 to 1¼ hours, or until the loaf is golden brown and firm to the touch. Remove it from the pan and cool on a wire rack.

INGREDIENTS TO MAKE ONE LARGE LOAF:
3 tablespoons (45 ml) malt extract
⅓ cup (50 g) brown sugar
2 tablespoons (25 g) margarine
⅔ cup (150 ml) milk
2 cups (250 g) whole-wheat flour
2 teaspoons (10 ml) baking powder
¼ teaspoon (1 ml) salt
2 bananas
½ cup (75 g) seedless raisins

Polenta Baked with Mushrooms

Preheat the oven to 400°F (200°C).

Put 5 cups of water into a large saucepan with 1 teaspoon of salt and bring to the boil.

Stir in 1½ cups of cornmeal. Simmer gently for 20 minutes, stirring occasionally, until the polenta is thick, smooth and soft. Stir in ½ cup of grated Parmesan cheese, ¼ teaspoon of grated nutmeg and salt and pepper to taste.

Poach 1½ cups of sliced mushrooms in boiling water for 5 minutes and then drain them.

Spread a third of the polenta in an ovenproof dish. Cover the polenta with half of the poached mushrooms. Spread another third of the polenta over the mushrooms in the dish. Sprinkle the remaining mushrooms on top and cover with the remaining polenta. Sprinkle ¼ cup of grated Parmesan cheese over the polenta.

Bake for 30 minutes, or until the polenta is browned on top.

INGREDIENTS TO SERVE FOUR TO SIX:
salt
1½ cups (250 g) cornmeal
¾ cup (75 g) grated Parmesan cheese
¼ teaspoon (1 ml) grated nutmeg
pepper
1½ cups (150 g) sliced mushrooms

Tortillas

Serve these Mexican corn pancakes in a napkin to keep them warm and moist. Tortillas may be reheated in an ungreased frying pan.

Mix 2 cups masa harina (flour made from corn) with 1 teaspoon of salt in a mixing bowl.

Make a well in the flour and pour in 1¼ cups of water. Mix to a soft dough. Turn the dough out onto a lightly floured surface and knead it, adding a little more flour if necessary, until the dough no longer sticks to your fingers.

Divide the dough into 12 pieces, roll each piece into a ball and flatten it slightly. Put the pieces of dough between 2 sheets of waxed paper, one at a time, and roll them out very thinly to 5-inch (13-cm) circles. Add more flour if the dough sticks to the paper.

Cook the tortillas in an ungreased frying pan for 1 minute on each side, or until they are lightly browned. Wrap the tortillas in aluminum foil and put them in a warm oven while the remainder are being cooked.

INGREDIENTS TO MAKE TWELVE TORTILLAS:
2 cups (250 g) masa harina
1 teaspoon (5 ml) salt

Chicken Enchiladas

Make 2½ cups of tomato sauce (see page 108). Add ⅓ cup of diced chilies or 1 teaspoon of chilli powder and 1 tablespoon of chopped oregano or basil and mix well.

Preheat the oven to 350°F (180°C).

Beat ¼ pound of pot cheese with 4 tablespoons of milk until smooth and creamy. Finely slice 4 small black olives and 2 scallions and add them to the cheese mixture with 1 tablespoon of chopped parsley. Stir in 2 cups of diced, cooked chicken. Season to taste with salt and pepper.

Make 12 tortillas.

Heat the tomato sauce in a large saucepan. Dip the tortillas, one at a time, into the sauce until the tortilla is heated through. Remove the tortilla and put some filling in the center of the sauce-covered side. Roll the tortilla up to form a cylinder. Repeat until all the tortillas have been filled and rolled.

Place the enchiladas in a baking dish. Pour the remaining tomato sauce over them and sprinkle with 2 tablespoons of grated Parmesan cheese.

Bake for 20 minutes, or until the enchiladas are heated through and lightly browned on top.

INGREDIENTS TO SERVE SIX:
2½ cups (600 ml) tomato sauce (see page 108)
⅓ cup (50 g) diced chilies or 1 teaspoon (5 ml) chilli powder
1 tablespoon (15 ml) chopped oregano or basil
¼ lb (100 g) pot cheese
4 tablespoons (60 ml) milk
4 small black olives
2 scallions
1 tablespoon (15 ml) chopped parsley
salt
pepper
2 cups (250 g) diced cooked chicken
12 tortillas
2 tablespoons (30 ml) Parmesan cheese

Barley and Mushroom Pilaf

It is best to begin to prepare this dish the day before serving so that the barley can soak overnight in the stock.

Heat 2 tablespoons of corn oil in a frying pan. Add 1 chopped large onion and cook, stirring frequently, for 3 minutes. Add 1 cup of sliced mushrooms to the onion in the pan and fry for 1 minute, stirring constantly. Add ¾ cup of pearl barley and fry for 1 minute more, stirring occasionally.

Transfer the barley mixture to an ovenproof dish. Pour in 2 cups of well-seasoned chicken or vegetable stock. Season to taste with salt and freshly ground black pepper. Put 1 bay leaf on top, cover the dish and refrigerate for at least 2 hours, but preferably overnight.

Preheat the oven to 375°F (190°C). Bake the casserole, covered, for 1 hour, or until the stock is absorbed and the barley is tender and slightly chewy.

Serve immediately, sprinkled with ¼ cup of grated Cheddar cheese.

INGREDIENTS TO SERVE FOUR:
2 tablespoons (30 ml) corn oil
1 large onion
1 cup (100 g) sliced mushrooms
¾ cup (150 g) pearl barley
2 cups (½ liter) well-seasoned chicken or vegetable stock
salt
freshly ground black pepper
1 bay leaf
¼ cup (25 g) grated Cheddar cheese

Barley Yogurt Soup

Soak ½ scant cup of pearl barley in water to cover for at least 12 hours.

Heat 1 tablespoon of corn oil in a large saucepan. Add 1 chopped large onion and fry over low heat, stirring frequently, for 5 minutes, or until the onion is soft and translucent. Add 5 cups of well-seasoned chicken or vegetable stock and bring to the boil. Add 1 bay leaf and the drained barley. Season to taste with salt and pepper. Cover the pan, reduce the heat and simmer gently for 50 to 60 minutes, or until the barley is tender and swollen. Remove the pan from the heat and stir in 2 tablespoons of chopped parsley. Adjust the seasoning.

Just before serving, beat 1¼ cups of yogurt in a small mixing bowl until it is smooth. Stir a little of the hot soup into the yogurt, then pour the yogurt mixture into the pan, beating well. Reheat the soup, but do not allow it to boil or the yogurt will curdle.

Serve immediately, sprinkled with chopped mint.

INGREDIENTS TO SERVE FOUR:
½ scant cup (75 g) pearl barley
1 tablespoon (15 ml) corn oil
1 large onion
5 cups (1 liter) well-seasoned chicken or vegetable stock
1 bay leaf
salt
pepper
2 tablespoons (30 ml) chopped parsley
1¼ cups (300 ml) yogurt
mint

The Nutrients in White Fish

The Nutrients in White Fish
White fish have excellent protein and little fat. Three and a half ounces (100 g) provide about 80 Calories.

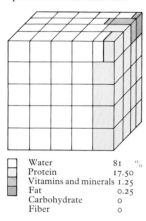

	Water	81	%
	Protein	17.50	
	Vitamins and minerals	1.25	
	Fat	0.25	
	Carbohydrate	0	
	Fiber	0	

FRESHLY CAUGHT FISH is one of the most wholesome, nutritious and delicious foods you could hope for.

Unfortunately, fish has one failing—it rapidly putrifies; so it is dried, salted, smoked and canned. But all these processes turn fresh fish into something different, however appetizing. The only way to retain some of the freshness of the fish caught in distant fishing grounds is to freeze it. The modern method of quick-freezing on board ship ensures that fish remains "fresh" for three to eight months. The nutritional value is not greatly diminished, but no one can pretend that the flavor and texture are the same. The vast quantities of fish caught nearer home, landed quickly and sold fresh are more likely to taste as fish should.

The edible part of fish can be from 15 to more than 20 percent protein. And the protein is of good quality because, like poultry and meat protein, it contains most of the essential amino acids. Its fat is polyunsaturated—a great plus mark over meat. Percentages of fat, however, vary widely according to the type of fish and the time of year it is caught. Such fat fish as herrings and mackerel, which grow fat on plankton near the surface of the sea, are about 20 percent fat in summer, when plankton is plentiful, but by the end of winter they are less than half that amount. Such fish as

turbot

lemon sole

halibut

cod, haddock and flatfish that live on the sea bed are low in fat. Plaice, for example, has only 2 percent, while halibut has 4 percent fat. Shellfish are also low in fat, but they contain almost twice as much cholesterol as fish, poultry and game.

The small flatfish include the firm-fleshed sole, found at its best in Britain, Norway and Denmark, and the softer-fleshed lemon soles, dabs, plaice and flounders. (The American sole is, in fact, a flounder, but it is superior to European flounders.) Of the large flatfish the giant is halibut, which flourishes off the Canadian Pacific coast, and in that stretch of the North Sea between Scotland and Norway. Others include the even more delicious and moist turbot of the English Channel, the French Atlantic coast and the Baltic and the smaller brill. Both turbot and brill are not to be found in American waters.

Other worthwhile nonfat fish are sea bass, porgy, the hideous-looking catfish, cod, haddock, John Dory, the fish reputedly caught by Saint Peter in the Sea of Galilee but at its best in the Mediterranean, monkfish, or angler fish, fearsome to look at but firm and sweet to eat, gray and red mullets, pompano, one compelling reason for visiting New Orleans, and whiting, if in childhood all the bones did not, sadly, put you off it for life.

Among fat fish there is nothing to approach the flavor of salmon, especially when it is eaten in its prime in early spring. Although the salmon spends most of its time at sea it is caught in fresh water. The most delicious fat fish of the sea is a really

crab

scallops

lobster

oysters

mussels

shrimp

Shellfish (above) are high in first-class protein, as well as in iron, calcium, riboflavin and niacin. They also contain up to 3 percent fat and, unlike fish, have a small amount of carbohydrate. Scallops, for example, are about 4 percent carbohydrate and oysters 5 percent. But shellfish are very high in cholesterol. Lobster has twice as much cholesterol as meat; oysters are even greater offenders with more than three times as much.

haddock

cod

whiting

rainbow trout

The Nutrients in Fat Fish
Fat fish contain more fat
than white fish but the
quantity varies. Three and a
half ounces (100 g) provide
about 200 Calories.

Water	68 %
Protein	17.50
Fat	13.25
Vitamins and minerals	1.25
Carbohydrate	0
Fiber	0

A meal planned around fish is far more healthful than one in which meat predominates. All fish contain as much high-quality protein as meat, but, unlike meat, white fish, above, have a negligible amount of fat and, therefore, they have half the number of calories.

fresh herring. If it is caught between July and October the creaminess of its flesh is a miracle of texture and taste. Other fat fish are mackerel, which is cheap and excellent if it is fresh, sprats, fresh sardines and pilchards.

To all the sea fish must be added some fresh-water fish—the estimable trout, grayling, perch, pike, carp and the fat-rich eel, which Izaak Walton described as a "dainty fish."

Shellfish are a particularly tasty but expensive source of protein. There are three types of shellfish that we eat. The crustaceans include the lobster of the Northern Hemisphere, the inferior crawfish of the Southern Hemisphere, crabs and shrimp (alias langoustines). Among the mollusks are the oysters, scallops, clams, cockles, mussels, whelks and winkles. Sea urchins are popular in France. The most expensive and the cheapest shellfish have one thing in common—they are fit to eat from the point of view of both taste and health only when they are fresh and have been taken from unpolluted waters.

Trout, carp and eels are among the few fish that have been cultivated so far. More than a hundred years ago the French scientist Coste forsaw the time when the seas and rivers would be thoroughly farmed, and there would be plentiful, cheap supplies not only of oysters but of salmon, trout and lobsters as well.

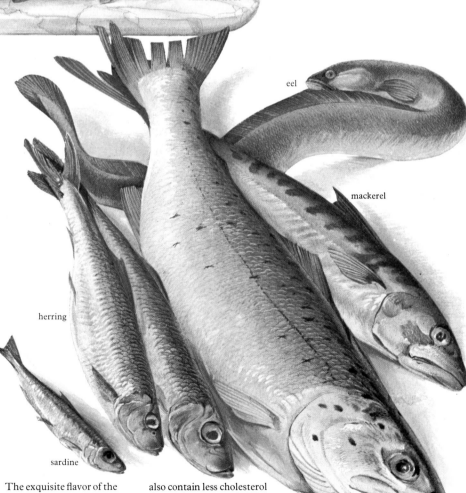

eel

mackerel

herring

sardine

salmon

The exquisite flavor of the fat fish (above) is matched by their excellent food value. Fortunately, the fat in these fish is polyunsaturated. They also contain less cholesterol than either meat or shellfish and provide niacin and vitamin D that are absent from white fish.

Poached Fish

Poaching is the simplest way to cook fish to retain its full flavor. It is suitable for fillets, steaks and whole fish.

First prepare a court bouillon. Pour 5 cups of water, or a mixture of dry white wine and water, into a saucepan. Slice 1 carrot, 1 onion and 1 stalk of celery and add them to the pan. Grate in the rind of ½ lemon and squeeze in the juice. Add a few parsley sprigs, 1 bay leaf, 2 peppercorns and salt. Bring to the boil, cover the pan, reduce the heat and simmer for 20 minutes. Strain the liquid and let it cool until it is lukewarm.

Put the fish into a pan. Pour in the court bouillon. (The fish may be tied loosely in cheesecloth for easy removal.) Cover the pan and cook over very low heat. The bouillon should barely bubble. Cooking time will vary according to the thickness of the fish, but allow 8 to 10 minutes per pound.

The fish may also be poached in an oven preheated to 350°F (180°C). A small whole fish or fish steaks will take 15 to 20 minutes to poach in the oven.

INGREDIENTS TO SERVE FOUR:
**5 cups (1 liter) water or a mixture of
   dry white wine and water
1 carrot
1 onion
1 celery stalk
½ lemon
parsley sprigs
1 bay leaf
2 peppercorns
salt
4 small whole fish, fillets or steaks,
   or 1 large whole fish**

POACHING FISH

Tie the fish loosely in cheesecloth for easy removal.

Fish Chowder

This fish soup makes a substantial meal. Any firm white fish, including cod, halibut, bass, turbot and hake, can be used.

Put ½ pound of fish fillets into a saucepan. Cover with 2½ cups of water and add the grated rind and juice of ½ lemon, salt, pepper and a bouquet garni, consisting of 1 bay leaf and sprigs of parsley and thyme tied together. Bring to simmering point and poach the fish gently for 10 to 15 minutes, or until it is tender.

Remove the fish from the pan with a slotted spoon. Discard the skin and flake the fish. Remove the bouquet garni from the cooking liquid.

Peel 2 medium-sized potatoes and cut into small dice. Add the potatoes to the cooking liquid with 1 medium-sized leek, thinly sliced, 3 tablespoons of rice and ¼ teaspoon of ground nutmeg. Cover the pan and simmer for 15 minutes, or until the potatoes and rice are tender.

Stir in the flaked fish and 1¼ cups of milk. Adjust the seasoning, reheat and serve.

INGREDIENTS TO SERVE FOUR TO SIX:
**½ lb (250 g) fillets of firm white fish
½ lemon
salt
pepper
1 bouquet garni, consisting of 1 bay leaf
   and parsley and thyme sprigs
2 medium-sized potatoes
1 medium-sized leek
3 tablespoons (25 g) rice
¼ teaspoon (1 ml) ground nutmeg
1¼ cups (300 ml) milk**

Baked Salmon Steaks

Preheat the oven to 350°F (180°C). Lightly grease an ovenproof dish.

Put 4 salmon steaks into the dish. Sprinkle them with salt, pepper and the juice of ½ lemon. Put 1 sprig of parsley or dill on each steak.

Cover the dish with foil and bake for about 20 minutes, or until the steaks are cooked.

Serve hot with yogurt hollandaise sauce (see page 93) or hot cucumber sauce (see page 109).

INGREDIENTS TO SERVE FOUR:
**4 salmon steaks
salt
pepper
½ lemon
parsley or dill sprigs
yogurt hollandaise sauce (see page 93)
cucumber sauce (see page 109)**

Mackerel Baked in Cider

Preheat the oven to 350°F (180°C).

Slice 1 large onion. Heat 1 tablespoon of corn oil in a frying pan. Fry the onion for 3 minutes, or until it is lightly browned. Peel and core 1 large tart apple and slice it into the pan. Fry gently for 2 minutes. Pour in 1 cup of hard cider, add ⅓ cup of seedless raisins and bring to the boil. Season to taste with salt and pepper.

Pour the cider mixture into a shallow ovenproof dish. Halve 4 medium-sized mackerel fillets. Roll up the 8 fillets so that the skin is outside. Secure the rolls with toothpicks.

Put the mackerel rolls into the dish. Bake for 25 to 30 minutes, basting occasionally with the sauce, until the mackerel is tender and the skin is browned on the top.

INGREDIENTS FOR FOUR:
**1 large onion
1 tablespoon (15 ml) corn oil
1 large (250 g) tart apple
1 cup (200 ml) hard cider
⅓ cup (50 g) seedless raisins
salt
pepper
4 medium-sized mackerel fillets**

Chinese Baked Snapper

Preheat the oven to 375°F (190°C).

Scrape the scales off 4 medium-sized red snapper. (Scrape with the back of a knife from the tail toward the head.) Cut off the fins. Gut the fish and wash well.

Shred 1 pound of cabbage and put it into a large ovenproof dish. Put ¼ pound of bean sprouts on top. Add salt and pepper to taste, 1 tablespoon of soy sauce and 1 tablespoon of lemon juice.

Put the snapper on top of the vegetables with 4 sprigs of coriander leaves.

Cover the dish with foil and bake for 15 to 20 minutes, or until fish and vegetables are tender.

INGREDIENTS TO SERVE FOUR:
**4 medium-sized red snapper
1 lb (500 g) cabbage
¼ lb (100 g) bean sprouts
salt
pepper
1 tablespoon (15 ml) soy sauce
1 tablespoon (15 ml) lemon juice
coriander sprigs**

Fish en Papillotte with Herbs

Enclosing whole fish in foil parcels is a delicious way to cook and serve them. The flavor is sealed in and the fish cook in their own juices. If red mullet is not available, mackerel, bluefish or snapper may be substituted.

Scrape the scales from 4 medium-sized red mullet, using the back of a knife and scraping from the tail toward the head. Cut off the fins but leave on the heads and tails. In each fish make a slit from underneath the head to halfway along toward the tail. Remove the guts.

Scrape fish from tail to head with the back of a knife.

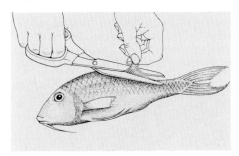

Cut the fins off with scissors leaving the tail.

Slit the fish for half its length and gut it.

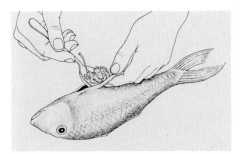

Spoon the stuffing into the cavity of the fish.

Preheat the oven to 375°F (190°C).

Wash the fish and stuff 1 slice of onion, 1 sprig of thyme, 1 sprig of parsley and 1 bay leaf into the cavity. Sprinkle each fish with salt and pepper and put a slice of lemon on top.

Put each stuffed fish onto a lightly greased square of foil or wax paper and fold it into a neat parcel. Put the parcels on a baking sheet and bake for 15 to 20 minutes, or until the fish is tender.

Serve the mullet in their parcels.

INGREDIENTS TO SERVE FOUR:
4 medium-sized red mullet
1 small onion
4 thyme sprigs
4 parsley sprigs
4 bay leaves
salt
pepper
4 lemon slices

Plaki

This is the Greek method of baking a whole fish with onions, tomatoes, olives and herbs.

Remove the fins and guts from 1 whole large fat fish, such as a mullet, and scrape away the scales if necessary. Wash well.

Preheat the oven to 350°F (180°C).

Slice 3 medium-sized onions. Spread half of them on the bottom of a shallow ovenproof dish large enough to hold the fish. Slice 2 medium-sized tomatoes and arrange half of them on top of the sliced onions. Sprinkle with 2 tablespoons of chopped parsley, salt and pepper.

Put the fish on top with the remaining onions and tomatoes. Put 8 pitted black olives around it. Slice 1 lemon and arrange the slices down the center of the fish. Top with 1 sprig of rosemary.

Pour ⅔ cup of dry white wine over the fish. Cover the dish with foil and bake for 40 to 45 minutes, or until the fish and vegetables are tender.

INGREDIENTS TO SERVE FOUR:
2½- to 3-lb (1¼- to 1½-kg) whole fat fish
3 medium-sized onions
2 medium-sized tomatoes
2 tablespoons (30 ml) chopped parsley
salt
pepper
8 pitted black olives
1 lemon
1 rosemary sprig
⅔ cup (150 ml) dry white wine

Fish Salad

This refreshing fish and shrimp salad can be served as a first course or as a luncheon dish. Halibut may be used instead of cod.

First make a court bouillon. Pour 5 cups of water into a saucepan. Add 1 bay leaf, 2 peppercorns, 2 parsley sprigs, 1 small onion stuck with 1 clove, 2 teaspoons of vinegar and ½ teaspoon of salt. Bring to the boil. Cover the pan, reduce the heat and simmer for 15 minutes. Strain the court bouillon.

Put 1 pound of cod fillets into a saucepan and add enough of the court bouillon to barely cover them. Cook over very low heat for 8 minutes, or until the cod is tender. Drain the fish and leave it to cool, then flake it coarsely into a mixing bowl.

Remove the seeds and pith from 1 small green pepper. Cut the pepper into thin strips. Thinly slice 1 small onion. Chop 2 stalks of celery. Add the pepper, onion and celery to the flaked fish with ½ cup of shelled cooked shrimp.

For the dressing, beat together 5 tablespoons of tomato juice, 1 tablespoon of lemon juice and 1 tablespoon of Worcestershire sauce. Add salt and pepper to taste. Spoon the dressing over the fish mixture. Refrigerate for at least 30 minutes before serving.

To serve, put 1 lettuce leaf in the bottoms of 4 individual bowls. Divide the fish mixture between the bowls and garnish with lemon slices.

INGREDIENTS TO SERVE FOUR:
1 bay leaf
2 peppercorns
2 parsley sprigs
2 small onions
1 clove
2 teaspoons (10 ml) vinegar
salt
1 lb (500 g) cod fillets
1 small green pepper
2 celery stalks
½ cup (100 g) shelled cooked shrimp
5 tablespoons (75 ml) tomato juice
1 tablespoon (15 ml) lemon juice
1 tablespoon (15 ml) Worcestershire sauce
pepper
4 lettuce leaves
4 lemon slices

Trout Baked with Grapefruit and Hazelnuts

Preheat the oven to 350°F (180°C).

Put ⅔ cup of hazelnuts under a hot broiler for 1 to 2 minutes, or until they brown. (Watch them carefully because they burn easily.) Remove the thin brown skins by rubbing the nuts together in a clean dish towel or a paper bag. Discard the skins.

Fill the cavities of 4 cleaned, medium-sized trout with the hazelnuts. Put the fish into a lightly greased, shallow ovenproof dish and sprinkle them with salt and pepper.

Cut the peel and white pith from 2 grapefruit. Cut the membrane away from the segments of fruit, working over the fish so that any juice pours over it. Put the grapefruit segments around the fish.

Bake uncovered for 20 to 30 minutes, or until the trout are tender.

INGREDIENTS TO SERVE FOUR:
⅔ cup (100 g) shelled hazelnuts
4 medium-sized trout
salt
pepper
2 grapefruit

Delicious and sophisticated, Trout Baked with Grapefruit and Hazelnuts makes an excellent main-course dish.

Stuffed Fish Rolls

This recipe brings out the delicate flavor of white fish. Lemon sole, Dover sole, flounder or haddock may be used. The cucumber sauce may be poured over the fish rolls or served separately in a gravy boat.

Preheat the oven to 350°F (180°C).

For the stuffing, finely chop or grate 1 small onion. Cut three-quarters of a large cucumber into small dice. (Reserve the rest of the cucumber.) Melt 1 tablespoon of margarine in a saucepan. Add the onion and the cucumber to the pan and fry over low heat for 5 minutes.

Remove the pan from the heat and stir in 1 cup of fresh bread crumbs, 3 tablespoons of chopped walnuts, the grated rind of 1 lemon and 2 tablespoons of chopped parsley. Lightly beat 1 egg and stir it into the stuffing mixture. Season to taste with salt and pepper.

Spread the stuffing on 4 large fillets of white fish. Roll the fillets up from the tail end. Secure each roll with a toothpick. Put the fish rolls into a shallow ovenproof dish.

Cover the dish and bake for 20 minutes, or until the fish is cooked.

For the sauce, cut the reserved cucumber into small dice. Stir the cucumber into ⅔ cup of warmed yogurt. Season to taste with salt and pepper.

Serve the fish hot, garnished with walnut halves.

INGREDIENTS TO SERVE FOUR:
1 small onion
1 large cucumber
1 tablespoon (15 g) margarine
1 cup (50 g) fresh bread crumbs
3 tablespoons (25 g) chopped walnuts
1 lemon
2 tablespoons (30 ml) chopped parsley
1 egg
salt
pepper
4 large fillets of white fish
⅔ cup (150 ml) yogurt
walnut halves

Mediterranean Fish Casserole

Chop 2 slices of bacon. Finely chop 1 large onion. Seed and remove the pith from 1 small green pepper and chop it finely. Blanch, peel and coarsely chop 5 ripe medium-sized tomatoes. Cut 1 pound of skinned fillets of firm white fish (cod, halibut, bass, Dover sole or lemon sole) into pieces.

In a large, heavy frying pan, over low heat, fry the chopped bacon until the fat runs. Add the chopped onion and green pepper to the pan with 1 crushed garlic clove and fry for 2 minutes, or until the onion is soft and translucent.

Stir in 1 tablespoon of flour. Stirring

constantly, gradually pour in $\frac{2}{3}$ cup of dry
white wine and $\frac{2}{3}$ cup of water. Add the
chopped tomatoes, $\frac{1}{2}$ teaspoon of dried basil,
salt and pepper.

Still stirring, boil the sauce until it thickens.
Add the fish. Cover the pan, reduce the heat
and simmer gently for 10 to 15 minutes, or
until the fish is cooked.

Serve hot, garnished with 2 tablespoons of
chopped parsley and 4 tablespoons of
chopped roasted peanuts.

INGREDIENTS TO SERVE FOUR:
2 slices bacon
1 large onion
1 small green pepper
5 ripe tomatoes
1 lb (500 g) fillets of firm white fish
5 ripe medium-sized tomatoes
1 lb (500 g) firm white fish fillets (cod,
  halibut, bass, Dover sole or lemon
  sole)
1 garlic clove
1 tablespoon (15 ml) flour
$\frac{2}{3}$ cup (150 ml) dry white wine
$\frac{1}{2}$ teaspoon (2.5 ml) dried basil
salt
pepper
2 tablespoons (30 ml) chopped parsley
4 tablespoons (25 g) chopped roasted
  peanuts

Fish Steaks with Fennel

Preheat the oven to 350°F (180°C).

Heat 1 tablespoon of corn oil in a saucepan.
Add 1 thinly sliced large fennel bulb to the
pan. Fry the fennel for 3 minutes, or until it is
lightly browned. Stir in 2 medium-sized
tomatoes, which have been blanched, peeled
and chopped, the grated rind and juice of
$\frac{1}{2}$ lemon, 1 tablespoon of chopped parsley,
$\frac{1}{2}$ teaspoon of ground coriander, salt and
pepper. Stirring frequently, bring to the boil.
Cover the pan, reduce the heat and simmer
for 10 minutes, stirring occasionally.

Transfer the sauce to a shallow ovenproof
dish. Arrange 4 haddock or halibut steaks on
top. Cover the dish and bake for 20 to
25 minutes, or until the fish is cooked.

INGREDIENTS TO SERVE FOUR:
1 tablespoon (15 ml) corn oil
1 large fennel bulb
2 medium-sized ripe tomatoes
$\frac{1}{2}$ lemon
1 tablespoon (15 ml) chopped parsley
$\frac{1}{2}$ teaspoon (2.5 ml) ground coriander
salt
pepper
4 haddock or halibut steaks

*Soused Herring is a favorite with Scandinavians,
who know all there is to know about cooking herring.
Serve with toast as a tasty first course.*

Soused Herring

This dish can be made in advance. Make
double the quantity and pack the fish into a
jar. Pour in the cooking liquid and seal the
jar. The herring will keep for up to 1 week.

Preheat the oven to 350°F (180°C).

Remove the heads, fins and guts from
4 herring. Clean the fish and remove the
backbones without removing the tails. Season
the herring with salt and pepper, then roll
each fish up toward the tail. Put the rolled
herring into a shallow ovenproof dish with
the tails pointing upward.

Thinly slice 1 medium-sized carrot and
1 medium-sized onion and scatter the slices
over and around the fish with 6 peppercorns
and 2 bay leaves. Pour in $\frac{2}{3}$ cup of water and
$\frac{2}{3}$ cup of wine vinegar.

Cover the dish and bake for 30 minutes.
Cool the fish in the cooking liquid. Serve
cold.

INGREDIENTS TO SERVE FOUR:
4 herring
salt
pepper
1 medium-sized carrot
1 medium-sized onion
6 peppercorns
2 bay leaves
$\frac{2}{3}$ cup (150 ml) wine vinegar

Orange Capered Halibut

Steaks of any firm white fish, such as cod,
may be substituted for the halibut.

Cut $1\frac{1}{2}$ to 2 pounds of halibut into 4 pieces
and wash well. Put into a large saucepan or
deep frying pan and barely cover with
water. Add 1 tablespoon of vinegar,
1 teaspoon of salt, 1 bay leaf and 1 sprig of
parsley. Bring to simmering point and poach
the halibut gently for 15 to 20 minutes, or
until it is tender. Carefully lift out the halibut
with a spatula. Remove the skin, put the fish
on a warm serving dish and keep it hot.

Heat 1 tablespoon of corn oil in a small
saucepan. Add 1 finely chopped small onion
and fry it for 3 minutes, or until it is lightly
browned. Stir in the juice of 2 oranges,
1 tablespoon of capers, salt and pepper.
Bring to the boil, stirring constantly. Reduce
the heat and simmer for 30 seconds. Pour the
sauce over the halibut and serve immediately,
garnished with parsley.

INGREDIENTS TO SERVE FOUR:
$1\frac{1}{2}$ to 2 lbs (750 g to 1 kg) halibut
1 tablespoon (15 ml) vinegar
salt
1 bay leaf
parsley sprigs
1 tablespoon (15 ml) corn oil
1 small onion
2 oranges
1 tablespoon (15 ml) capers
pepper

Baked Cod Steaks

Preheat the oven to 350°F (180°C).

Wash $\frac{1}{2}$ pound of small mushrooms and
put them into a shallow ovenproof dish.
(Leave small mushrooms whole and halve or
quarter larger mushrooms.) Sprinkle the
mushrooms with salt and pepper. Put 4 cod
steaks on top.

Beat $1\frac{1}{4}$ cups of yogurt until it is smooth,
then spread it over the cod steaks. Sprinkle
the top with 2 tablespoons of chopped
parsley.

Cover the dish with foil and bake for 20 to
30 minutes, or until the fish is tender.

Serve garnished with parsley sprigs.

INGREDIENTS TO SERVE FOUR:
$\frac{1}{2}$ lb (250 g) small mushrooms
salt
pepper
4 cod steaks
$1\frac{1}{4}$ cups (300 ml) yogurt
2 tablespoons (30 ml) chopped parsley
parsley sprigs

Watercress and Lemon Rolled Sole

Preheat the oven to 350°F (180°C). Skin 4 large fillets of Dover or lemon sole.

Make the stuffing. Put 1 cup of fresh bread crumbs into a mixing bowl. Remove the coarse stalks from a small bunch of watercress. Chop the leaves and tender stalks. Add to the bread crumbs. Grate in the rind of 1 lemon, then add 1 tablespoon of lemon juice. Lightly beat 1 small egg and stir it in. Season with salt and pepper.

Spread the stuffing on the skinned sides of the fish fillets. Roll the fillets up from the tail end and secure with toothpicks.

Put the fish rolls into a lightly greased, shallow ovenproof dish, cover and bake for 15 to 20 minutes, or until the fish is tender.

Serve hot, garnished with sprigs of watercress and twists of lemon.

INGREDIENTS TO SERVE FOUR:
4 large Dover or lemon sole fillets
1 cup (50 g) fresh bread crumbs
1 bunch watercress
1½ lemons
1 small egg
salt
pepper

PREPARING FISH ROLLS

Skinned side up, spread stuffing over the fillets.

Secure the rolled fillets with toothpicks.

Indonesian Broiled Spiced Fish

Clean 4 whole medium-sized fish, such as red mullet or snapper. Put the fish on a large plate. Cut a few diagonal gashes along the sides of the fish to allow the marinade to penetrate.

For the marinade, crush 1 garlic clove and grate 1 small onion into a small bowl. Add 2 tablespoons of lemon juice, 1 teaspoon of soy sauce, ½ teaspoon of chilli powder, ¼ teaspoon of ground coriander, salt and pepper. Mix well. Pour the marinade over the fish. Marinate the fish for about 45 minutes, turning and basting them occasionally.

Cook the fish under a moderately hot broiler, basting them occasionally and turning them once, for about 15 minutes, or until the fish is cooked and the skin is crisp and browned.

INGREDIENTS TO SERVE FOUR:
4 medium-sized red mullet or snapper
1 garlic clove
1 small onion
2 tablespoons (30 ml) lemon juice
1 teaspoon (5 ml) soy sauce
½ teaspoon (2.5 ml) chilli powder
¼ teaspoon (1 ml) ground coriander
salt
pepper

Steamed Mussels

This is the simplest and most delicious way to cook mussels—in a little white wine with garlic and parsley.

Wash 2 quarts of mussels under cold running water. Scrub each mussel well with a small stiff brush. Using a knife scrape off any weed that is clinging to the shells. Discard any mussels that remain open. Put the mussels into a colander and wash them again under cold running water.

Put the mussels into a large saucepan. Finely chop 1 small onion and add it to the pan with 1 crushed garlic clove, salt and pepper. Pour in ⅔ cup of dry white wine and ⅔ cup of water.

Cover the pan, bring to the boil and cook for 5 minutes. Remove the mussels, take off the top shells and arrange the mussels in individual serving bowls. Discard any mussels that have not opened.

Stir 1 tablespoon of chopped parsley into the cooking liquid, adjust the seasoning and pour it over the mussels. Serve at once.

INGREDIENTS TO SERVE FOUR:
2 quarts (1½ liters) mussels
1 small onion
1 garlic clove
salt
pepper
⅔ cup dry white wine
1 tablespoon (15 ml) chopped parsley

Shrimp Filled Avocados

First make the filling. Put ⅔ cup of yogurt into a mixing bowl. Add 1 teaspoon of chopped parsley, 1 teaspoon of chopped mint, 1 teaspoon of chopped chives and 1 teaspoon of chopped lemon verbena, if it is available. Stir in the juice of ½ small lemon. Season to taste with salt and pepper and mix well.

Stir in ½ cup of cooked shelled shrimp and leave to marinate for at least 30 minutes.

Just before serving, cut 2 avocados in half lengthwise. Remove the seeds and rub the cut surfaces with lemon juice to keep

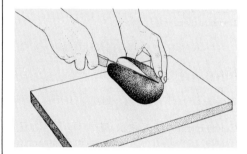

Use a sharp knife to cut avocados in half.

Lever out the seed with the point of a knife.

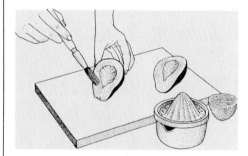

Brush with lemon juice to keep from browning.

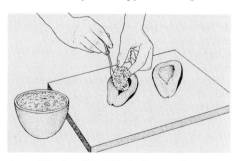

Spoon filling into the cavities in the avocados.

the avocados from turning brown.

Divide the filling between the avocado halves and serve.

INGREDIENTS TO SERVE FOUR:
⅔ cup (150 ml) yogurt
1 teaspoon (5 ml) chopped parsley
1 teaspoon (5 ml) chopped mint
1 teaspoon (5 ml) chopped chives
1 teaspoon (5 ml) chopped lemon verbena (optional)
½ small lemon
salt
pepper
½ cup (100 g) cooked shelled shrimp
2 avocados

Shrimp Provençal

Chop 1 small onion and 1 small green pepper. Blanch and peel 2 medium-sized tomatoes. Cut them into halves and remove the seeds. Coarsely chop the tomatoes.

Heat 1 tablespoon of corn oil in a saucepan. Add the onion and green pepper and fry over low heat for 5 minutes. Add the tomatoes to the pan with ⅔ cup of dry white wine, 1 tablespoon of chopped basil or oregano, salt and pepper. Cover the pan, reduce the heat and simmer gently for 15 minutes.

Add ¾ pound of shelled raw shrimp and cook for 5 minutes more.

Serve immediately, sprinkled with 1 tablespoon of chopped parsley.

INGREDIENTS TO SERVE FOUR:
1 small onion
1 small green pepper
2 medium-sized tomatoes
1 tablespoon (15 ml) corn oil
⅔ cup (150 ml) dry white wine
1 tablespoon (15 ml) chopped basil or oregano
salt
pepper
¾ lb (350 g) shelled raw shrimp
1 tablespoon (15 ml) chopped parsley

Taramasalata

This Greek fish pâté made from smoked cod's roe is delicious as a first course or as a dip for raw vegetables. Traditionally it is made with lots of olive oil, but this recipe substitutes yogurt, which gives a more refreshing flavor.

Pour boiling water over ½ pound of smoked cod's roe, then peel off the skin. Put the roe into a mixing bowl.

Trim the crusts from 2 slices of white bread and soak the bread in 2 tablespoons of milk or water for 2 to 3 minutes. Drain the liquid from the bread by squeezing it well. Add the bread to the roe. Beat in ⅔ cup of yogurt,

1 crushed garlic clove and the juice of 1 lemon. Beat well until the mixture is smooth or put all the ingredients into a blender and blend until smooth. Season to taste with salt and pepper.

Spoon the taramasalata into a serving bowl, cover and chill in the refrigerator for several hours before serving. (It will keep up to 5 days in the refrigerator.)

Sprinkle with 1 tablespoon of chopped parsley and serve with toast or a selection of raw vegetables.

INGREDIENTS TO SERVE FOUR:
½ lb (250 g) smoked cod's roe
2 slices of white bread
2 tablespoons (30 ml) milk or water
⅔ cup (150 ml) yogurt
1 garlic clove
1 lemon
salt
pepper
1 tablespoon (15 ml) chopped parsley

Smoked Haddock Mousse

Thinly slice 1 small onion and 1 carrot and put them into a saucepan with ⅔ cup of water, salt, pepper, 1 bay leaf, 3 parsley sprigs and the grated rind of ½ lemon. Bring to the boil, reduce the heat and simmer gently for 10 minutes.

Add 1 pound of smoked haddock fillets to the pan. Simmer for 10 minutes, or until the haddock is cooked. Remove the fish from the pan. Skin it and flake it into a mixing bowl.

Reduce the fish stock by boiling until 4 tablespoons remain in the pan. Remove the pan from the heat and sprinkle in 1½ tablespoons of powdered gelatin. Soak the gelatin for 2 minutes then cook over low heat, stirring, until the gelatin is dissolved.

Add 1¼ cups of yogurt to the flaked fish. Beat until smooth. Add the juice of ½ lemon and salt and pepper to taste. Pour in the dissolved gelatin and mix well.

Pour the mousse into 4 individual dishes or 1 large soufflé dish. Chill in the refrigerator for at least 4 hours before serving.

INGREDIENTS TO SERVE FOUR:
1 small onion
1 carrot
salt
pepper
1 bay leaf
3 parsley sprigs
1 lemon
1 lb (250 g) smoked haddock fillets
1½ tablespoons (15 g) powdered gelatin
1¼ cups (300 ml) yogurt

Kipper Pâté Lemons

This pâté can be stored in the refrigerator for up to 1 week or frozen for up to 1 month.

Cook ½ pound of kippers under a low broiler for 4 minutes on each side. Remove the skins and flake the kippers into a mixing bowl.

Cut 2 large lemons into halves. Using a grapefruit knife scoop out the fruit. Reserve the lemon rinds. Using a sharp knife cut the fruit away from the membrane. Work over a bowl to catch the juice. Coarsely chop the lemon and add it with the juice to the flaked kippers. Add ¼ pound of pot or cream cheese. Beat until the ingredients are well blended. Season to taste with salt and pepper.

Alternatively, purée the ingredients in a blender until smooth, adding 2 tablespoons of yogurt or milk if necessary.

Cut a small piece off the bottom of each lemon rind so it will stand. Spoon the pâté into the lemon rinds. Serve with toast.

INGREDIENTS TO SERVE FOUR:
½ lb (250 g) kippers
2 large lemons
¼ lb (100 g) pot cheese or cream cheese
salt
pepper

PREPARING LEMON CUPS

Cut the fruit from a lemon with a grapefruit knife.

Trim the bottoms to make the cups stand upright.

THE CHICKEN, which has traveled far since the domestication in prehistoric times of its ancestor, the Indian jungle fowl, is now the world's ubiquitous culinary bird. When it is alive it is a bird of many images, from the scrawny barnyard fowl, which has to scratch for its living, to the pampered castrato known as a capon. When it is cooked, the chicken appears in hundreds of guises. But however the flavor of the chicken and the way it is cooked varies the flesh remains high in protein, low in fat and is easily digested.

The youngest table chicken, eaten at three weeks old, is the tasteless *petit poussin*. When the bird is slightly older and weighs about one and a half pounds, it becomes a *poussin*, and, although tender, it is still fairly tasteless. The United States counterpart is the somewhat heavier broiler. The spring chicken, or *poulet*, is up to three months old, weighs about three pounds ($1\frac{1}{2}$ kg) and it has much more flavor if it is not overcooked. A roasting chicken is up to eight months old and weighs four to five pounds (2 to $2\frac{1}{4}$ kg). A neutered hen, or *poularde*, has firm white flesh and is five and a half pounds ($2\frac{1}{2}$ kg), while a castrated cockerel, or capon, can weigh almost twice as much.

The Roman consul Fannius must be thanked for unwittingly introducing the capon to the world. Worried that the gluttonous Romans were eating hens almost to extinction he forbade his subjects to eat them. But the Fannius Law forgot to mention cocks. The ingenious Romans, well aware of the physical changes that overcame eunuchs, began castrating the cock. The bird, its aggression lost, not only grew larger than the prohibited hen, but acquired the excellent culinary reputation that it still has today.

At the other extreme is the oven-ready bird, wretched in life and insipid in death. Nevertheless it is largely responsible for the great increase in the eating of chicken over the last two decades. Today, on average each American eats about thirty-three pounds (15 kg) of chicken a year, more than two and a half times as much as in the 1930s.

Turkeys and ducks have suffered less than chickens from intensive farming and industrial technology, and so far geese have escaped.

The huge turkeys that star in Dickens's novels are now out of favor and the British and Americans are turning to smaller birds, which are also the favorites of the Italians and Spanish. The

The Nutrients in Chicken and Turkey

These birds contain first-class protein and three and a half ounces (100 g) provide about 220 Calories.

□ Water	63%
□ Protein	20
▨ Fat	16
▨ Vitamins and minerals	1
Carbohydrate	0
Fiber	0

THE OVEN-READY CHICKEN

The oven-ready chicken is likely to have led a life that is nasty, hygienic and short. It will live in a shed along with five or ten thousand others, scratching around in a deep layer of wood shavings, often dosed to keep it healthy until it is fat enough to die at twelve to sixteen weeks. Carried along a conveyor track, it is stunned, killed, bled, scalded, plucked by a sequence of rubber fingers and flails, eviscerated, decapitated, plunged into ice water, trussed, packed into a plastic bag and quick-frozen. To enhance its minimal flavor it may be dusted, sprayed or injected with the inevitable monosodium glutamate. Despite all that its nutritional value, if not its flavor content, is still high.

large birds are now mainly for such ceremonial occasions as Christmas and Thanksgiving Day.

While chicken and turkey are high in protein and low in fat, the domestic duck and goose are rich in fat and flavor. They are birds of antiquity. In ancient Egypt both were sacrificed to the gods and the goose had a role in the myths of creation.

The best English table duck is the white Aylesbury; the best American breed is the Long Island, which is descended from nine Peking ducks imported in the late nineteenth century, and the best French ducks are the Rouen and Nantes ducks. Unlike most other breeds, French ducks are very lean and have a gamy flavor.

Goose is no longer popular in the United States or in Great Britain, but remains so in Germany, Sweden, Norway, Denmark, Holland and Hungary. The large white goose is the one generally preferred. A goose will live to a ripe old age, but if it is to be eaten it should not be allowed to live more than two years.

To this rather limited choice of poultry, or domesticated birds, can be added the neglected guinea fowl, or guinea hen. This is a West African bird, still found wild, but which is greatly superior as the domesticated version. Its flavor is reminiscent of the American Bronze turkey, with a slight hint of gamyness. But its size is that of the pheasant, to which it is related.

Pheasant, partridge and the minute quail are game birds that have succumbed to a certain amount of domestication. If pheasant is not eaten on the day it is killed it must be hung from four to ten days to give it taste and make it tender again. A young plump partridge is at its delicately flavored best when hung for only three to five days. Quail should be eaten at the latest the day after they have been killed.

The Nutrients in Duck and Goose
Both birds are high in fat as well as protein and three and a half ounces (100 g) provide about 340 Calories.

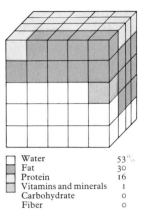

☐ Water	53%
☐ Fat	30
☐ Protein	16
☐ Vitamins and minerals	1
Carbohydrate	0
Fiber	0

Chicken, whether fresh or frozen, is an excellent source of protein, B vitamins and iron. Nevertheless free-range chickens undoubtedly have the better flavor. Turkey (top, far left) is equally as nutritious as chicken. Unfortunately, both contain some cholesterol. West African guinea fowl (top left) are related to the pheasant and have a slightly gamy flavor. Geese (bottom left) and ducks (center left) have almost twice as much saturated fat as chicken and turkey. They are also moderately high in cholesterol.

Boiled Chicken

Boiling, or more accurately poaching, is an excellent way to cook a chicken. The meat is succulent and the rich stock is useful. A boiling fowl or a roasting chicken may be cooked this way. A boiling fowl, however, should be barely covered with water and simmered for 2 to 3 hours.

Remove the giblets and any excess fat from inside a 2½-pound roasting chicken. Put the chicken, breast upward, into a large saucepan. Add the giblets. Pour in water to come halfway up the chicken breast.

Add the grated rind and juice of 1 lemon, salt, 6 peppercorns, 1 blade of mace and 1 bay leaf. Peel and quarter 1 onion, thickly slice 1 carrot and 1 stalk of celery and add to the pan with 1 sprig of thyme and 2 sprigs of parsley.

Cover the pan and bring to the boil. Reduce the heat and simmer gently for about 1 hour, or until the chicken is tender. Transfer the chicken to a serving dish, strain the stock into a bowl and leave to cool. Then skim off the fat.

The chicken may be served hot, with a sauce or gravy made from the stock, or cold. For a recipe needing cooked chicken meat, let the chicken cool, remove the skin and cut the meat off the bones. This should give 1 pound of cooked chicken meat.

INGREDIENTS TO SERVE FOUR:
2½-lb (1.2-kg) roasting chicken
1 lemon
salt
6 peppercorns
1 mace blade
1 bay leaf
1 onion
1 carrot
1 celery stalk
1 thyme sprig
2 parsley sprigs

Chicken and Noodles

Cut 1 small chicken, about 2 pounds, into quarters. Blanch, peel and coarsely chop 4 ripe medium-sized tomatoes. Coarsely chop 2 medium-sized onions. Put the chicken pieces into an ovenproof casserole with the chopped tomatoes and onions and 1½ cups of water, 1 crushed garlic clove, ½ teaspoon of dried oregano, salt and freshly ground black pepper. Cover the pan and simmer over very low heat for 45 minutes.

Take the chicken pieces from the pan. Remove the skin and cut the meat off the bones. Cut the chicken meat into pieces.

Add 2 cups of freshly made spinach noodles (see tagliatelle, page 42) to the liquid in the pan and cook for 5 minutes, or until the pasta is just tender. Add the chicken meat and cook for 5 minutes, or until the chicken is

heated through. Season to taste.

Sprinkle 3 tablespoons of grated Parmesan cheese over the chicken and noodles and serve immediately.

INGREDIENTS TO SERVE FOUR:
1 small chicken (about 2 lbs/1 kg)
4 ripe medium-sized tomatoes
2 medium-sized onions
1 garlic clove
½ teaspoon (2.5 ml) dried oregano
salt

continued

Preparing Chicken Quarters

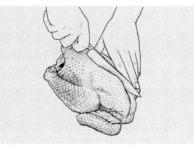

Lay the chicken on its back and cut it in half.

Lay each half flat and cut into two pieces.

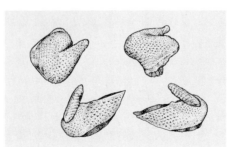

Each quarter will serve one person.

freshly ground black pepper
2 cups (250 g) freshly made spinach
  noodles (see tagliatelle, page 42)
3 tablespoons (45 ml) grated Parmesan
  cheese

Lemon and Herb Baked Chicken

Preheat the oven to 350°F (180°C).

Put 4 chicken breasts into an ovenproof casserole and bake, uncovered, for 30 minutes.

Meanwhile, finely chop 2 medium-sized

onions. Put the chopped onion into a mixing bowl with the grated rind and juice of 1 large lemon. Add 4 tablespoons of chopped parsley, 1 tablespoon of chopped thyme, 1 tablespoon of chopped sage and 1 tablespoon of chopped mint. Season to taste with salt and pepper.

Remove the chicken from the oven and pour off any fat that is in the pan. Pour ⅔ cup of well-seasoned chicken stock over the chicken. Press the herb mixture on top of the chicken breasts. Bake the chicken for 15 to 20 minutes more, or until the herb topping is crisp and lightly browned.

Serve hot or cold.

INGREDIENTS TO SERVE FOUR:
4 chicken breasts
2 medium-sized onions
1 large lemon
4 tablespoons (60 ml) chopped parsley
1 tablespoon (15 ml) chopped thyme
1 tablespoon (15 ml) chopped sage
1 tablespoon (15 ml) chopped mint
salt
pepper
⅔ cup (150 ml) chicken stock

Chicken Jerusalem

Heat 1 tablespoon of corn oil in a large saucepan. Add 4 chicken quarters and fry them until they are browned. Remove the chicken from the pan. Add 2 chopped medium-sized onions and fry gently for 3 minutes. Add 1¼ cups of chicken stock with the grated rind and juice of ½ lemon, 4 sprigs of thyme, salt and pepper.

Peel 1 pound of Jerusalem artichokes. Coarsely dice the artichokes and add them to the pan. Bring to the boil and add the chicken pieces. Cover, reduce the heat and simmer gently for 30 minutes.

Add 2 cups of sliced small mushrooms to the pan. Cover and cook for 10 minutes more, or until the chicken is tender.

Remove the chicken pieces to a warmed serving dish. Garnish with a few of the sliced mushrooms and diced artichokes. Put the remaining vegetables and the stock into a blender and blend to a smooth purée.

Pour the purée over the chicken, garnish with sprigs of watercress and serve.

INGREDIENTS TO SERVE FOUR:
1 tablespoon (15 ml) corn oil
4 chicken quarters
2 onions
1¼ cups (300 ml) chicken stock
½ lemon
4 thyme sprigs
salt
pepper
1 lb (500 g) Jerusalem artichokes
2 cups (150 g) sliced small mushrooms
watercress sprigs

Chicken à la Grècque

A marvelous dish for a buffet, this cold chicken dish should be made 1 day in advance.

Coarsely chop 1 large onion. Thinly slice 1 large carrot. Heat 2 teaspoons of olive oil in a saucepan. Add the onion and the carrot to the pan and fry over low heat until the onion is soft but not colored. Add 1 crushed garlic clove, $\frac{2}{3}$ cup of dry white wine and 1 bouquet garni, consisting of 1 bay leaf and sprigs of parsley and thyme. Season with salt and pepper.

Blanch and peel 2 medium-sized tomatoes. Cut the tomatoes into quarters and remove the seeds. Add the tomatoes to the pan with $2\frac{1}{2}$ cups of small mushrooms. Bring to the boil, reduce the heat and simmer gently, uncovered, for 15 minutes.

Remove the bouquet garni from the pan and add 4 cups of cooked chicken meat, coarsely chopped, and 1 thinly sliced red pepper. Stir well. Marinate in the refrigerator for 12 hours.

Sprinkle with 2 tablespoons of chopped parsley before serving.

INGREDIENTS TO SERVE FOUR:
1 large onion
1 large carrot
2 tablespoons (30 ml) olive oil
1 garlic clove
$\frac{2}{3}$ cup (150 ml) dry white wine
1 bouquet garni, consisting of 1 bay leaf and parsley and thyme sprigs
salt
pepper
2 medium-sized tomatoes
$2\frac{1}{2}$ cups (250 g) small mushrooms
4 cups (500 g) cooked chicken meat
1 red pepper
2 tablespoons (30 ml) chopped parsley

Deviled Chicken Legs

For the marinade, combine in a small mixing bowl 2 tablespoons of corn oil, 2 tablespoons of tarragon or wine vinegar, 2 tablespoons of water, 1 tablespoon of French mustard, 1 tablespoon of chopped sweet mango chutney, 1 grated onion, $\frac{1}{2}$ teaspoon of curry powder, $\frac{1}{2}$ teaspoon of ground ginger, salt and pepper. Mix well.

Score 4 chicken legs, or 8 drumsticks, with a sharp knife to allow the marinade to penetrate the meat. Put the chicken into a large bowl and pour in the marinade. Marinate for at least 12 hours in the refrigerator or 4 hours at room temperature, turning the chicken pieces occasionally.

Remove the chicken from the marinade and put on a broiler pan under a hot broiler. Broil the chicken for 15 minutes, or until the pieces are crisp and golden brown, turning once and basting frequently with the

marinade. Serve hot or cold, garnished with sprigs of watercress or parsley.

INGREDIENTS TO SERVE FOUR:
2 tablespoons (30 ml) corn oil
2 tablespoons (30 ml) tarragon or wine vinegar
1 tablespoon (15 ml) French mustard
1 tablespoon (15 ml) sweet mango chutney
1 onion
$\frac{1}{2}$ teaspoon (2.5 ml) curry powder
$\frac{1}{2}$ teaspoon (2.5 ml) ground ginger
salt
pepper
4 chicken legs or 8 drumsticks
watercress or parsley sprigs

Chicken Tandoori

This is a famous Indian dish. Its name comes from the *tandur*, the very hot charcoal oven in which it is traditionally cooked.

First make the marinade. Put $1\frac{1}{4}$ cups of yogurt into a mixing bowl. Add 1 grated small onion, 1 crushed garlic clove, the grated rind and juice of 1 small lemon and 1 tablespoon of tomato paste. Add 2 teaspoons of cayenne pepper, 2 teaspoons of paprika, $\frac{1}{2}$ teaspoon of ground ginger, salt and pepper. Mix well. Remove the skin from 4 chicken quarters. Put the chicken pieces into a bowl and pour the marinade over them. Cover, put in the refrigerator and leave to marinate for 24 hours. Baste the chicken occasionally.

To cook, remove the chicken pieces from the marinade and put them under a hot broiler. Cook for 15 to 20 minutes, turning frequently and basting with the marinade, until the chicken is cooked through. Alternatively, the chicken may be baked in a very hot oven for 20 to 30 minutes, basting frequently.

Serve immediately.

INGREDIENTS TO SERVE FOUR:
$1\frac{1}{4}$ cups (300 ml) yogurt
1 small onion
1 garlic clove
1 small lemon
1 tablespoon (15 ml) tomato paste
2 teaspoons (10 ml) cayenne pepper
2 teaspoons (10 ml) paprika
$\frac{1}{2}$ teaspoon (2.5 ml) ground ginger
salt
pepper
4 chicken quarters

Chicken Véronique with Yogurt

Chicken pieces cooked with green grapes and ginger and served with a creamy yogurt sauce make this a light and refreshing dish for a summer dinner.

Preheat the oven to 350°F (180°C).

Put 4 chicken quarters into an ovenproof casserole and sprinkle with $1\frac{1}{2}$ teaspoons of ground ginger, salt and pepper. Cut $\frac{1}{2}$ pound of green grapes into halves and remove the seeds. Scatter the grapes over the chicken. Add $1\frac{1}{4}$ cups of water, cover the casserole and bake for 1 hour, or until the chicken is tender.

Remove the chicken and the grapes to a warmed serving dish.

Pour $1\frac{1}{4}$ cups of yogurt into a mixing bowl and stir in 1 tablespoon of cornstarch. Slowly pour the liquid from the casserole into the yogurt, beating well. Return the yogurt mixture to the pan and cook over very low heat, stirring constantly, until the sauce is thickened. Season the sauce to taste and pour it over the chicken. Sprinkle $\frac{1}{3}$ cup of browned sliced almonds on top and serve immediately.

INGREDIENTS TO SERVE FOUR:
4 chicken quarters
$1\frac{1}{2}$ teaspoons (7.5 ml) ground ginger
salt
pepper
$\frac{1}{2}$ lb (250 g) green grapes
$1\frac{1}{4}$ cups (300 ml) yogurt
1 tablespoon (15 ml) cornstarch
$\frac{1}{3}$ cup (50 g) browned sliced almonds

French Chicken Casserole

Preheat the oven to 350°F (180°C).

Arrange 4 chicken quarters in an ovenproof casserole with $\frac{1}{2}$ pound of small onions, 2 stalks of celery, sliced, 4 sprigs of rosemary and 6 blanched, peeled and chopped ripe medium-sized tomatoes. Season to taste with salt and pepper. Pour in $\frac{2}{3}$ cup of water.

Cover and bake for 30 minutes. Stir in 12 stuffed olives and cook for 30 minutes more, or until the chicken is tender.

Serve hot.

INGREDIENTS TO SERVE FOUR:
4 chicken quarters
$\frac{1}{2}$ lb (250 g) small onions
2 celery stalks
4 rosemary sprigs
6 ripe medium-sized tomatoes
salt
pepper
12 stuffed olives

Cherry and Orange Duck

For this dish the duck is first roasted to brown the skin and to melt away some of the fat and is then braised with cherries in orange juice.

Preheat the oven to 400°F (200°C).

Put 1 halved onion into the cavity of a 4-pound duck. Put the duck on a rack in a roasting pan. Prick the skin all over with a fork to allow the fat to run out. Rub the skin with salt. Roast the duck for 1 hour.

Pit 1 pound of cherries. Put the pitted cherries into a bowl. Add the grated rind of 1 orange and the juice of 2 oranges to the cherries.

When the duck has cooked for 1 hour, drain off the fat that has collected in the roasting pan. Remove the rack and put the duck back in the pan. Pour the cherries and orange juice around the duck with ⅔ cup of chicken stock. Cover the pan with foil and roast for 30 minutes more.

Remove the duck to a warmed serving platter. Drain half of the cherries, put them around the duck and keep it warm.

For the sauce, put the remaining cherries into a blender with the cooking liquid and blend until smooth. Reheat the sauce, season to taste with salt and pepper and serve with the duck.

INGREDIENTS TO SERVE FOUR:
1 onion
4-lb (1.8-kg) duck
salt
1 lb (250 g) cherries
2 oranges
⅔ cup (150 ml) chicken stock
pepper

Chinese Chicken with Ginger and Bean Sprouts

Coarsely chop 2 slices of bacon. Peel and coarsely chop 1 medium-sized onion. Cut 2 thin slices of ginger root. Peel off the skin and cut the ginger into thin strips. Cut the meat from 4 chicken breasts, about 1½ pounds, and slice it into strips. Slice 1 cup of mushrooms.

Heat 1 tablespoon of peanut oil in a large, heavy frying pan. Add the bacon to the pan and fry over high heat, stirring constantly, for 1 minute. Add the chopped onion and 1 crushed garlic clove and fry, still stirring, until the onion is tender. Add the ginger and the chicken and fry for 3 minutes, stirring all the time. Add the mushrooms and ¼ pound of bean sprouts. Stir-fry for 1 minute.

Blend 1 teaspoon of cornstarch with ⅔ cup of chicken stock and 1 teaspoon of soy sauce and add it to the chicken mixture. Season to taste with salt and pepper. Continue to stir-fry for 2 more minutes, or until the chicken is cooked.

Garnish with sprigs of parsley or coriander and serve immediately.

INGREDIENTS TO SERVE FOUR:
2 slices bacon
1 medium-sized onion
ginger root
4 chicken breasts
1 cup (100 g) sliced mushrooms
1 tablespoon (15 ml) peanut oil
1 garlic clove
¼ lb (100 g) bean sprouts
1 teaspoon (5 ml) cornstarch
⅔ cup (150 ml) chicken stock
1 teaspoon (5 ml) soy sauce
salt
pepper
parsley or coriander sprigs

Orange Chicken Parcels

Preheat the oven to 400°F (200°C).
Cut 4 pieces of foil, each large enough to enclose a portion of chicken.

Rub 4 chicken quarters with ½ teaspoon of salt. Slice 1 medium-sized onion. Put the onion slices on the pieces of foil and put the chicken quarters on top.

Peel and remove the pith from 1 orange. Cut the membrane from the segments of fruit. Put the orange segments on top of the chicken pieces. Grate the rind from another orange and sprinkle it over the chicken. Squeeze the juice from the orange, mix it with 1 tablespoon of Worcestershire sauce and pour it over the chicken.

Lightly fold the foil over the chicken pieces. Put the parcels on a baking sheet. Bake for 45 minutes, or until the chicken is tender.

To serve, remove the chicken from the foil and garnish with sprigs of watercress.

INGREDIENTS TO SERVE FOUR:
4 chicken quarters
½ teaspoon (2.5 ml) salt
1 medium-sized onion
2 oranges
1 tablespoon (15 ml) Worcestershire sauce
watercress sprigs

pan with 1 bay leaf and the grated rind and juice of 1 lemon. Half-cover the pan, reduce the heat and simmer for 30 minutes.

Remove the pits from 8 black olives. Cut each olive into quarters and add to the pan. Adjust the seasoning, adding salt or pepper if necessary. Cook for 15 minutes more, or until the stock is absorbed and the rice is cooked.

Garnish with lemon slices and serve immediately.

INGREDIENTS TO SERVE FOUR:
1 small chicken (about 2 lbs/1 kg)
2 tablespoons (30 ml) corn oil
2 medium-sized onions
1¼ cups (250 g) brown rice
4 scant cups (850 ml) well-seasoned
  chicken stock
1 bay leaf
2 lemons
8 black olives
salt
pepper

Cocky-Leeky

This Scottish chicken and leek soup is traditionally made with prunes, which add a rich flavor.

Put 1 small chicken, about 2 pounds, or 2 large chicken quarters, into a large saucepan with 5 cups of water. Add ¼ pound of pitted prunes and a bouquet garni, consisting of 1 bay leaf and sprigs of parsley and thyme. Season to taste with salt and pepper. Bring to the boil. Cover the pan, reduce the heat and simmer gently for 1 hour.

Remove the chicken from the pan. Add 3 cups of sliced leeks to the soup and continue to simmer, covered, for 15 minutes. Meanwhile, skin the chicken and remove the meat from the bones. Coarsely chop the chicken meat. Add the chopped chicken to the soup with 2 tablespoons of chopped parsley and simmer for 5 minutes longer. Correct the seasoning. Serve immediately.

INGREDIENTS TO SERVE FOUR TO SIX:
1 small chicken (about 2 lbs/1 kg)
¼ lb (100 g) pitted prunes
1 bouquet garni, consisting of 1 bay leaf
  and parsley and thyme sprigs
salt
pepper
3 cups (500 g) sliced leeks
2 tablespoons (30 ml) chopped parsley

Poultry is extremely versatile and is the basis of many marvelous dishes, such as Cherry and Orange Duckling, left, and Chinese Chicken with Ginger and Bean Sprouts, right.

Chicken Liver with Snow Peas and Orange

This dish makes a delicious and unusual first course.

Cut ½ pound of chicken livers into ½-inch (1-cm) slices. Put 1 teaspoon of cornstarch into a mixing bowl and stir in 1 tablespoon of soy sauce and the grated rind and juice of 1 orange. Add the sliced chicken livers and marinate for at least 10 minutes.

Meanwhile, remove the tops and strings from ½ pound of snow peas. Blanch in boiling water for 2 minutes, or until tender but still crisp. Drain.

Heat 1 tablespoon of peanut oil in a heavy frying pan. Add 2 chopped scallions and fry over high heat, stirring constantly, for 30 seconds. Add the liver and marinade and fry, stirring, for 2 to 3 minutes, or until the liver is cooked and lightly browned. Add the blanched snow peas and cook, stirring constantly, for 2 minutes.

Serve immediately in warmed individual serving dishes, garnished with thin slices of orange.

INGREDIENTS TO SERVE FOUR AS A FIRST COURSE:
½ lb (250 g) chicken livers
1 teaspoon (5 ml) cornstarch
1 tablespoon (15 ml) soy sauce
1½ oranges
½ lb (250 g) snow peas
1 tablespoon (15 ml) peanut oil
2 scallions

Moroccan Chicken Rice

Cut the meat from 1 small chicken, about 2 pounds. Slice the meat into strips. (The skin and bones can be used to make chicken stock.)

Heat 2 tablespoons of corn oil in a large saucepan. Add 2 chopped medium-sized onions and fry over high heat, stirring frequently, for 5 minutes, or until the onions have browned. Stir in 1¼ cups of brown rice and then add 4 scant cups of well-seasoned chicken stock. Add the chicken strips to the

Congo Chicken

This African-style dish may be served hot or cold.

Preheat the oven to 350°F (180°C).

Put 4 chicken quarters into an ovenproof dish or a small roasting pan and bake uncovered for 30 minutes, or until the chicken is lightly browned.

Meanwhile, remove the seeds and pith from 1 green pepper. Cut the pepper into strips. Immerse the pepper strips in boiling water for 1 minute and then rinse in cold water.

Put 1½ cups of chopped, roasted salted peanuts into a mixing bowl. Stir in ⅔ cup of yogurt, 4 tablespoons of chopped parsley and salt and pepper to taste.

Remove the chicken from the oven and spread the pieces with the peanut mixture. Arrange the strips of pepper around the chicken and return it to the oven for 15 minutes, or until the topping is crisp and lightly browned.

INGREDIENTS TO SERVE FOUR:
4 chicken quarters
1 green pepper
1½ cups (250 g) chopped roasted salted
peanuts
⅔ cup (150 ml) yogurt
4 tablespoons (60 ml) chopped parsley
salt
pepper

Chicken and Thyme Pie

Boil a 2½- to 3-pound chicken (see boiled chicken, page 72). Allow the chicken to cool. Strain and reserve 1¼ cups of the stock and the uncooked chicken liver.

Make 3 cups of shortcrust pastry with whole-wheat flour (see page 34). Reserving one-third of the pastry for the lid, roll the rest out on a lightly floured surface and line an 11- by 4- by 2½-inch (28- by 10- by 6-cm) rectangular pan. Let the excess pastry overlap the edges of the pan.

Preheat the oven to 400°F (200°C).

Cut the chicken into pieces, remove and discard the skin and cut the meat from the bones. Coarsely chop the meat and put it into a mixing bowl.

Coarsely chop 8 slices of bacon and the chicken liver.

Add the bacon and liver to the chicken meat with the grated rind and juice of ½ lemon, 2 tablespoons of chopped parsley, 1 tablespoon of chopped thyme, salt and freshly ground black pepper. Mix well.

Spoon half of the chicken mixture into the pie shell. Arrange ½ pound of sliced cooked ham on top then spoon in the remainder of the chicken mixture. Fold the edges of the pastry shell over the filling.

Put the reserved pastry onto a lightly floured surface and roll it out large enough to cover the pie. Dampen the edges of the pie shell and the edges of the lid with water. Lift the lid carefully onto the pie shell. Trim the lid to fit the pie and seal the edges well by pressing them with a fork. Cut a hole in the center of the lid.

Reroll any pastry trimmings and make leaves and a tassel for decoration. Fit the tassel into the hole in the lid and arrange the leaves at each end of the pie. Beat 1 egg and brush it on the pie.

Bake the pie for 1 hour. If the top of the pie browns too quickly cover it with aluminum

Cover the pie with rolled-out pastry to form a lid.

Cut a hole in the lid and make a pastry tassel.

Decorate the pie with leaves cut from pastry.

Lift the tassel and pour jellied stock into the pie.

foil. Cool the pie in the pan.

Meanwhile, in a small saucepan, stir 1½ tablespoons of powdered gelatin into the reserved chicken stock. Heat gently until the gelatin has dissolved. When the stock is just beginning to set, remove the pastry tassel from the lid of the pie and pour in the jellied stock. Replace the tassel. Refrigerate the pie overnight to set.

INGREDIENTS TO SERVE EIGHT:
2½- to 3-lb (1.20- to 1.40-kg) boiled
chicken
1¼ cups (250 ml) chicken stock
1 chicken liver
3 cups (350 g) shortcrust pastry made
with whole-wheat flour (see page 34)
8 slices bacon
½ lemon
2 tablespoons (30 ml) chopped parsley
1 tablespoon (15 ml) chopped thyme
salt
freshly ground black pepper
½ lb (250 g) sliced cooked ham
1 egg
1½ tablespoons (15 g) powdered gelatin

Chicken with Celery and Cheese

This is an old English recipe. The chicken is braised with celery and the sauce is thickened with cheese.

Heat 2 tablespoons of corn oil in a large flameproof casserole. Add 4 chicken quarters and fry them until they are browned. Remove the chicken pieces from the casserole. Add 2 sliced medium-sized onions and fry them for 3 minutes.

Wash 1 head of celery and cut off the leaves. Cut the stalks into pieces about 2 inches (5 cm) long and add them to the casserole. Reserve the best celery leaves for garnish and add the rest to the casserole with ⅔ cup of chicken stock and the browned chicken pieces. Cover the casserole and simmer over low heat for 45 minutes.

Remove the chicken pieces to a warmed serving dish. Add 1 cup of grated Cheddar cheese to the celery sauce. Heat gently, stirring, until the cheese has melted and thickened the sauce. Pour the sauce over the chicken, garnish with the reserved celery leaves and serve.

INGREDIENTS TO SERVE FOUR:
2 tablespoons (30 ml) corn oil
4 chicken quarters
2 medium-sized onions
1 head celery
⅔ cup (150 ml) chicken stock
1 cup (100 g) grated Cheddar cheese

Turkey and Cranberry Casserole

Preheat the oven to 350°F (180°C).

Prepare 1½ cups of thickly sliced leeks. Scrape 3 medium-sized carrots and cut them into thick slices. Peel and quarter 2 medium-sized potatoes, 2 medium-sized turnips and 3 medium-sized onions.

Stick 3 cloves into one of the onion quarters. Put it inside the cavity of a 7- to 10-pound turkey with a thick slice of lemon and a few sprigs of parsley.

Put half the prepared vegetables into an ovenproof casserole or a roasting pan. Put the turkey on top of the vegetables. Mix the remaining vegetables with ¼ pound of cranberries and arrange them around the turkey. Wash the giblets and add them to the casserole with a bouquet garni, consisting of 1 bay leaf and sprigs of parsley and thyme. Pour in 5 cups of turkey or chicken stock.

Cover the casserole and bake for 2½ to 3 hours. Uncover and cook for 20 minutes more, or until the turkey is tender and brown.

Skim any fat from the top of the chilled stock.

Transfer the turkey to a serving dish and arrange the vegetables around it. Discard the bouquet garni and giblets. Serve some of the stock with the turkey.

Pour the remaining stock into a bowl and chill it until the next day. Skim any fat from the top and pour the stock into a saucepan. Chop leftover turkey and vegetables and add to the stock with ⅓ cup of white rice. Simmer for 15 minutes, or until the rice is cooked. Serve as a hot soup.

INGREDIENTS TO SERVE EIGHT TO TWELVE:
1½ cups (250 g) thickly sliced leeks
3 medium-sized carrots
2 medium-sized potatoes
2 medium-sized turnips
3 medium-sized onions
3 cloves
7- to 10-lb (3- to 4.5-kg) turkey
1 thick lemon slice
parsley sprigs
¼ lb (100 g) cranberries
1 bouquet garni, consisting of 1 bay leaf and sprigs of parsley and thyme
5 cups (1 liter) turkey or chicken stock
⅓ cup (50 g) white rice

Chicken and Pork Adobo

Cut 1 pound of boneless shoulder or neck of pork into 2-inch (5-cm) cubes. Put them into a large saucepan. Cut 1 small chicken into quarters and add them to the pan.

Slice 2 onions and add them to the pan with 1 crushed garlic clove, 1 bay leaf, salt and pepper. Add 1¼ cups of water, 5 tablespoons of cider vinegar or wine vinegar and 1 tablespoon of soy sauce. Bring to the boil. Cover the pan, reduce the heat and simmer for 1 hour, or until the meat is tender.

Mix in 1 cup of small mushrooms. Continue to cook, uncovered, for about 10 minutes, or until the mushrooms are cooked and the sauce has reduced and thickened.

Sprinkle with 1 tablespoon of chopped parsley and serve immediately.

INGREDIENTS TO SERVE FOUR:
1 lb (500 g) boneless shoulder or neck of pork
1 small chicken
2 onions
1 garlic clove
1 bay leaf
salt
pepper
5 tablespoons (75 ml) cider vinegar or wine vinegar
1 tablespoon (15 ml) soy sauce
1 cup (100 g) small mushrooms
1 tablespoon (15 ml) chopped parsley

Normandy Pheasant

The pheasant is first roasted to brown the skin and then braised in hard cider, with apples and raisins, to make a well-flavored and succulent dish.

Preheat the oven to 425°F (220°C).

Put 1 cock pheasant or 2 hen pheasants into a roasting pan and roast for 30 minutes, or until lightly browned.

Add to the pan 2 sliced medium-sized onions, 2 large cooking apples, sliced, and ⅓ cup of seedless raisins. Pour 1¼ cups of hard cider over the pheasant and sprinkle with salt and pepper.

Cover the pan with foil. Lower the oven temperature to 375°F (190°C) and cook the pheasant for 30 to 40 minutes more.

Remove the pheasant from the roasting pan and cut it into serving pieces. Put the pheasant pieces on a warmed serving dish with some of the apples, onions and raisins. Keep warm.

Pour the liquid and the remaining vegetables and fruit into a saucepan. Add 1 tablespoon of red currant jelly and bring to the boil, stirring. Reduce the heat and simmer gently for 5 minutes, or until the sauce has thickened slightly and the jelly has melted.

Pour the sauce over the pheasant, garnish with sprigs of watercress and serve.

INGREDIENTS TO SERVE FOUR:
1 cock or 2 hen pheasants
2 medium-sized onions
2 large cooking apples
⅓ cup (50 g) seedless raisins
1¼ cups (300 ml) hard cider
salt
pepper
1 tablespoon (15 ml) red currant jelly
watercress sprigs

Chicken with Prunes

Rabbit can be substituted for chicken in this tasty casserole.

Soak ½ pound of pitted prunes overnight.

Cut 4 slices of bacon into 1-inch (2-cm) pieces and fry over low heat in a large saucepan for 3 minutes, or until the fat runs. Add 2 cups of sliced onions, or whole small onions if available, and fry them until they are lightly browned.

Cut a large chicken into pieces and coat them in 1 tablespoon of seasoned flour. Add the chicken pieces to the pan and brown lightly. Then add 1¼ cups of chicken stock, 1 tablespoon of wine vinegar, salt and pepper. Drain the prunes and add them to the pan.

Cover the pan and simmer gently for 1 hour, or until the chicken is tender.

INGREDIENTS TO SERVE FOUR:
½ lb (250 g) pitted prunes
4 slices bacon
2 cups (250 g) sliced onions or whole small onions
1 large chicken
1 tablespoon (15 ml) seasoned flour
1¼ cups (300 ml) chicken stock
1 tablespoon (15 ml) wine vinegar
salt
pepper

The Nutrients in Meat
Meat is high in protein and in fat and three and a half ounces (100 g) of beef steak, for example, provide about 250 Calories.

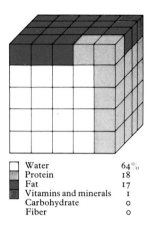

Water	64%
Protein	18
Fat	17
Vitamins and minerals	1
Carbohydrate	0
Fiber	0

To SOME PEOPLE the eating of flesh is abhorrent; to others a diet without meat is unthinkable. Both meat and meatless diets can be perfectly healthy. Vegetarians must make sure that their non-animal proteins are balanced to provide all the essential amino acids. Lovers of meat should be careful not to be seduced by its succulence into eating too much—a common failing in Western diets.

Much of the reputation of meat rests on its being such a good source of protein and well-balanced in amino acids. There are other things in its favor, too. It is rich in B vitamins—thiamine (especially in pork), niacin and B_{12}, and it is a good source of iron, phosphorus, potassium, sodium and magnesium. It is also digested slowly, thus delaying the return of hunger soon after a meal. And its smell when it is cooked is a remarkable stimulus to the digestive juices.

The aroma and flavor of meat are intimately connected, as you can discover by eating with your nose held tightly closed. So far science has been unable to explain exactly either smell or flavor. About one hundred and eighty substances have been tracked down in the odor of cooking beef, and separately some of them smell quite unpleasant. The cooked fat appears to account for the difference of flavor between such meats as beef, lamb and pork, but there are, in fact, many variables that decide the flavor of meat. These include the breed, the sex and the age of the animal, the food it ate and the way the meat was stored after slaughter. The difference that age makes is obvious in comparing veal with beef and lamb with mutton. The flavor of lamb also reveals where the lamb has grazed: lamb from the mountains is herby and sweet; from the marshes it has a tang of salt; and lamb from the chalk downs of England is spicy. These subtle and distinctive flavors can be lost if the lamb is fattened on roots or concentrates. Pork is liable to taste of fish if the pig was reared on large amounts of fish products. The beef from an intensively raised cow is more tender, more tasteless and fattier than that from a free-range cow.

Freshly killed meat is insipid, but the flavor improves during the next twenty-four hours. Thereafter, the meat should be aged for about ten days to allow the action of enzymes to make it more tender.

There is no meat that is the universal favorite. The English, Americans, French and Dutch like beef, which is forbidden to Hindus who consider the cow sacred. The English, however, have never been fond of veal, but it is popular in the United States and on the Continent. The best veal is reckoned to be that from a calf two and a half to three months old which has been fed only on milk. The Italians like it even younger, while veal in Spain is more likely to be one- to two-year-old

baby beef; it is at least better than Spanish beef, which may well be vanquished bull.

Pork is the most popular meat in Germany, and it is increasingly being eaten throughout the West. It is the basic meat of the Chinese, but it is rejected by both Muslims and Jews. They are happy, however, to eat the flesh of sheep; lamb and mutton have, indeed, escaped most meat taboos.

Strictly speaking, lamb is from a sheep under a year old and thereafter it becomes mutton. But the English often give the courtesy title of lamb to anything reasonably tender. A certain austerity produces the sweetest flavor as in the lamb reared in Iceland, Norway, the highlands of Britain and in Greece, and it limits the amount of fat.

The goat has a certain following, but only when a kid, for it becomes inedible if it is more than three months old, which may explain why the ancients so willingly sacrificed their goats to the gods.

Beef, lamb and pork contribute high-quality protein, B vitamins and iron to the diet. Unfortunately, these meats, and particularly pork, also contain a high proportion of saturated fat as well as a moderate amount of cholesterol. They should, therefore, be eaten in moderation. Deposits of fat, or "marbling," between the muscle fibers is even greater in the meat of intensively reared animals than that of free-grazing herds. Organ meats, such as liver and kidney, have the advantage of being lower in fat than muscle meat. They are equal in protein value and higher in iron and vitamins A, thiamine and riboflavin. But they have more than twice the amount of cholesterol.

Although there are more wild than domesticated animals their contribution to Western diets is relatively small. Furred game, to distinguish it from feathered game, includes rabbit, hare, deer, boar and bear—all of which have lean meat.

Meat, like fish, rapidly putrifies. The salting of meat is one of the oldest and most effective ways of preserving it for the winter. Today meat is salted, and also smoked, predominantly to make bacon and ham, because we enjoy the taste. There is little to choose between the energy and protein values of bacon and fresh pork, but some of the vitamins thiamine and niacin are lost in the salting.

By comparison with salting, canning is an infant in the history of preservation, dating only from the end of the eighteenth century. Some of the early canned meats were revolting—coarse meat and lumps of fat in a thin gravy. The British Navy had a macabre name for them—"Sweet Fanny Adams," after a woman whose body had been hacked to pieces by her murderer. Since then canned meat has become more spuriously palatable, but even further removed from the wholesome original.

Hamburgers and beefburgers are in the tradition of the cooked or easy-to-cook meats that have been around for several thousand years. The Greeks and Romans were as fond of sausages as are present-day Americans, who manage to consume an average of eighty hot dogs per head every year. There were cooked-meat shops in London as far back as the Middle Ages and William Cobbett, in the early nineteenth century, fulminated against the laziness of the rural laboring classes for patronizing them instead of cooking wholesome food at home. The taste for "convenience" meats was not confined to the working classes. One of England's most famous Prime Ministers, William Pitt the younger, is reputed to have said on his death bed: "I think I could eat one of Bellamy's veal pies."

Lancashire Hot Pot

Preheat the oven to 350°F (180°C).

Cut any excess fat from 8 rib lamb chops. Put the chops into an ovenproof casserole. Peel and remove the central core of 2 lamb kidneys. Slice the kidneys and add them to the casserole with 2 cups of sliced onions and 1 sliced large carrot. Sprinkle with 2 tablespoons of chopped mint and salt and pepper to taste.

Arrange 4 cups of peeled, thinly sliced potatoes, with the slices overlapping, on top of the lamb and vegetables. Pour in 1¼ cups of well-seasoned lamb or beef stock. Brush the potatoes lightly with corn oil.

Cover the casserole and bake for 1½ hours, or until the meat is tender. Uncover and bake for an additional 20 to 30 minutes, or until the potatoes are golden brown.

INGREDIENTS TO SERVE FOUR:
8 rib lamb chops
2 lamb kidneys
2 cups (250 g) sliced onions
1 large carrot
2 tablespoons (30 ml) chopped mint
salt
pepper
4 cups (500 g) sliced potatoes
1¼ cups (300 ml) lamb or beef stock
corn oil

PREPARING LANCASHIRE HOT POT

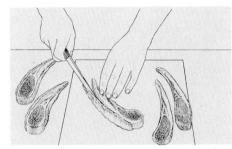

Trim any excess fat from lamb chops.

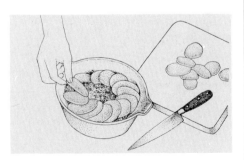

Cover the meat and vegetables with potato slices.

Lamb Curry

Heat 3 tablespoons of corn oil in a large saucepan. Add 2 finely chopped onions and fry, stirring, for 3 minutes. Peel and finely chop a 1-inch (2-cm) piece of ginger root and add it to the pan with 2 crushed garlic cloves and 1 finely chopped, seeded green chili and continue frying.

In a small bowl mix 1 teaspoon of turmeric, 2 teaspoons of ground coriander, 1 teaspoon of ground cumin, ½ teaspoon of cayenne and 1 teaspoon of paprika with enough cold water to make a paste. Add the paste to the pan and fry, stirring, for 5 minutes. Stir in 1 to 2 teaspoonfuls of water if the mixture gets too dry.

Cut 2 pounds of lean boneless shoulder or leg of lamb into 1-inch (2-cm) cubes. Add the cubes to the pan and fry, stirring, for 5 minutes.

Pour in 2½ cups of chicken stock. Stir to mix, season to taste with salt and pepper and bring to the boil. Cover the pan, reduce the heat to low and simmer for 40 minutes.

Add ½-inch (1-cm) slice of creamed coconut to the pan and stir until it is completely dissolved. Continue simmering for 20 minutes more, or until the lamb is tender.

INGREDIENTS TO SERVE FOUR TO SIX:
3 tablespoons (45 ml) corn oil
2 onions
1-inch (2-cm) piece ginger root
2 garlic cloves
1 green chili
1 teaspoon (5 ml) turmeric
2 teaspoons (10 ml) ground coriander
1 teaspoon (5 ml) ground cumin
½ teaspoon (2.5 ml) cayenne
1 teaspoon (5 ml) paprika
2 lb (1 kg) lean boneless shoulder or leg of lamb
2½ cups (600 ml) chicken stock
salt
pepper
½-inch (1-cm) slice creamed coconut

Moussaka

This adaptation of a popular Greek dish uses a yogurt sauce rather than the traditional béchamel.

Preheat the oven to 350°F (180°C).

Cut 3 medium-sized eggplant into ¼-inch (6-mm) slices. Put the slices into a colander set over a bowl. Sprinkle the eggplant generously with salt to draw out the juice, which can be bitter. Let drain for at least 30 minutes. Rinse and pat the slices dry with paper towels.

Brush the slices lightly with corn oil and put them on a lightly greased baking sheet or broiler pan. Put under a hot broiler for 5 minutes, or until they are golden brown, turning the slices over once.

Heat 1 tablespoon of corn oil in a large saucepan. Add 1 chopped large onion and fry for 3 minutes. Add 1 pound of ground lamb and fry, stirring constantly, for 5 minutes more, or until the meat is no longer red.

Stir in 1 tablespoon of tomato paste and ⅔ cup of lamb or beef stock. Season to taste with salt and freshly ground black pepper. Bring to the boil. Cover the pan, reduce the heat and simmer for 15 to 20 minutes, or until the meat is cooked.

Put a layer of eggplant slices into a deep baking dish. Pour over half of the meat mixture. Add another layer of the eggplant followed by the other half of the meat mixture. Arrange the last of the eggplant slices on top.

To make the sauce, beat 2 eggs in a bowl. Beat in 1¼ cups of yogurt, 4 tablespoons of flour, salt and pepper. Pour the sauce over the eggplant and meat. Sprinkle ½ cup of grated Cheddar cheese over the top.

Bake for 30 minutes, or until the sauce is set and brown on top.

INGREDIENTS TO SERVE FOUR:
3 medium-sized eggplant
salt
corn oil
1 large onion
1 lb (500 g) ground lamb
1 tablespoon (15 ml) tomato paste
⅔ cup (150 ml) lamb or beef stock
freshly ground black pepper
2 eggs
1¼ cups (300 ml) yogurt
4 tablespoons (25 g) flour
½ cup (50 g) grated Cheddar cheese

Navarin of Lamb

The meat and vegetables in this French lamb dish are cooked together in a casserole, making a complete and satisfying meal. Put ¼ cup of flageolets or navy beans and ¼ cup of pearl barley into a bowl. Cover with cold water and let soak overnight.

Cut any excess fat off 2 pounds of boneless shoulder of lamb, and then cut the meat into 8 pieces.

Heat 1 tablespoon of corn oil in a large saucepan. Add the meat and fry until it is brown on all sides. Remove the meat and put it on paper towels to drain off the fat. Put the meat into a large casserole.

Pour off all but 1 tablespoon of the oil from the pan. Add 1 chopped largo onion and fry for 3 minutes, or until the onion is golden. Stir in 1 tablespoon of flour. Stirring continuously, gradually add 2½ cups of lamb or beef stock. When all the stock has been added stir in 1 tablespoon of tomato paste. Season to taste with salt and pepper.

Bring to the boil. Reduce the heat and simmer for 1 minute. Drain the beans and barley and add them to the meat in the casserole. Pour the stock into the casserole and add a bouquet garni, consisting of 1 bay leaf and sprigs of parsley and thyme tied together. Bring to the boil and cover the casserole. Reduce the heat and simmer for 1 hour. Alternatively, bake in the oven at 350°F (180°C) for 1 hour.

Remove the bouquet garni from the casserole. Add 8 small white onions, 4 sliced medium-sized carrots and 2 small turnips, cut into quarters. Cover the casserole again and continue to bake for 30 to 45 minutes, or until the vegetables are tender.

Sprinkle with 2 tablespoons of chopped parsley and serve immediately.

INGREDIENTS TO SERVE FOUR:
¼ **cup (50 g) flageolets or navy beans**
¼ **cup (50 g) pearl barley**
2 lb (1 kg) boneless shoulder of lamb
1 tablespoon (15 ml) corn oil
1 large onion
1 tablespoon (15 ml) flour
2½ cups (600 ml) lamb or beef stock
1 tablespoon (15 ml) tomato paste
salt
pepper
1 bouquet garni, consisting of 1 bay leaf and sprigs of parsley and thyme
8 small white onions
4 medium-sized carrots
2 small turnips
2 tablespoons (30 ml) chopped parsley

Noisettes of Lamb Provençal

Noisettes are slices cut from boned lamb rib chops. The meat is tightly rolled up and tied at 1½-inch intervals with string. The rolled meat is then sliced between the strings to make lean and succulent portions.

Cut 1 garlic clove in half. Rub the garlic over both sides of 4 noisettes of lamb. Sprinkle the noisettes with salt and pepper and put them into a bowl. Pour in ⅔ cup of dry vermouth or dry white wine and add 4 sprigs of rosemary. Marinate the noisettes for at least 1 hour, turning them occasionally.

Remove the noisettes from the marinade and put under a hot broiler. Broil for about 5 minutes, turning them once, until both sides have browned.

Cut the bones from the meat.

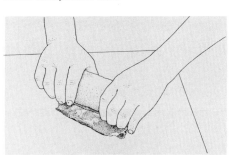

Roll the meat up tightly and tie at intervals with string.

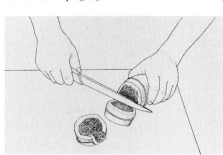

Slice the meat between the string.

Meanwhile, prepare the sauce. Pour the marinade into a saucepan. Blanch and peel 1½ pounds of tomatoes. Cut the tomatoes into halves and remove the seeds. Remove the seeds from 1 green pepper and cut it into thin strips. Add the tomatoes and pepper to the pan. Bring to the boil. Cover the pan, reduce the heat and simmer gently for 5 minutes, or until the tomatoes have reduced to a pulp.

When the noisettes have browned, drain off any excess fat and add them to the sauce in the pan. Spoon the sauce over the noisettes, cover the pan and continue to simmer gently for 10 minutes.

Transfer the noisettes to a warmed serving dish. If the sauce is too liquid, boil uncovered for 2 minutes, then pour it over the meat. Serve immediately, garnished with sprigs of watercress.

INGREDIENTS TO SERVE FOUR:
1 garlic clove
4 noisettes of lamb
salt
pepper
⅔ **cup (150 ml) dry vermouth or dry white wine**
4 rosemary sprigs
1½ **lb (700 g) tomatoes**
1 green pepper
watercress sprigs

Lamb Chops Tartare

Preheat the oven to 375°F (190°C).

Pour 1¼ cups of yogurt into a bowl and add 1 tablespoon of chopped gherkins, 1 tablespoon of capers, 2 tablespoons of chopped parsley and 4 chopped stuffed olives. Mix well. Season to taste with salt and pepper.

Put 4 lamb chops into a shallow baking dish. Pour the yogurt mixture over the chops.

Bake for 1 hour, or until the lamb is tender and the yogurt has set.

Garnish with slices of stuffed olives and parsley sprigs and serve immediately.

INGREDIENTS TO SERVE FOUR:
1¼ **cups (300 ml) yogurt**
1 tablespoon (15 ml) chopped gherkins
1 tablespoon (15 ml) capers
parsley sprigs
stuffed olives
salt
pepper
4 lamb chops

Bobatie

Preheat the oven to 350°F (180°C).

Heat 1 tablespoon of corn oil in a large saucepan. Add 2 cups of sliced onions to the pan and fry for 3 minutes, or until the onions are just beginning to brown. Add 1½ pounds of ground beef with 1 chopped small tart apple and fry, stirring constantly, for 3 minutes.

Add 1 tablespoon of curry powder, ⅓ cup of seedless raisins, ½ cup of peanuts, the juice of 1 small lemon, salt and pepper. Mix well. Cook over very low heat for 5 minutes.

Transfer the beef mixture to an ovenproof dish or casserole. Press 2 bay leaves into the top, cover and bake for 45 minutes.

Beat 1 egg with ⅔ cup of milk. Remove the cover from the dish, discard the bay leaves and pour the liquid over the meat. Return the dish to the oven and bake for 15 to 20 minutes more, or until the topping is set.

INGREDIENTS TO SERVE FOUR :
1 tablespoon (15 ml) corn oil
2 cups (250 g) sliced onions
1½ lb (700 g) ground beef
1 small tart apple
1 tablespoon (15 ml) curry powder
⅓ cup (50 g) seedless raisins
½ cup (50 g) peanuts
1 small lemon
salt
pepper
2 bay leaves
1 egg
⅔ cup (150 ml) milk

Pot au Feu

This classic French dish is actually two dishes—a delicious beef broth and a main course of tender boiled beef and vegetables. Several different kinds of meat—beef, pork, veal and chicken—are often used as well as bones or an oxtail for extra flavor.

Roll a 4-pound piece of brisket of beef and tie it securely with string. Put ¼ pound of beef liver into a large pan and put the brisket on top of it. Sprinkle the meat with salt, then pour in cold water to cover. Add to the pan 3 stalks of celery, cut into 4 pieces, 1 large onion, studded with 2 cloves, a bouquet garni, consisting of 2 bay leaves and sprigs of parsley and thyme, 3 peppercorns and 2 garlic cloves. Bring to the boil slowly, over moderate heat, skimming off the scum. Reduce the heat to very low and simmer gently for two hours.

Peel and quarter 4 carrots, 4 turnips, 4 parsnips and 4 onions and add them to the pan. Cover the pan and simmer over very low heat for 1 hour.

Cut 1 medium-sized cabbage into wedges. Cut 2 leeks into 4 pieces. Add the cabbage and the leeks to the beef with 3 tablespoons of

drained capers. Cook the stew for 30 minutes more, or until the beef is tender.

Drain the beef and cut and discard the string. Put the beef on a large, hot serving dish. Drain the vegetables and arrange them around the meat. Strain the cooking stock, skim off any fat and serve some of it with the beef.

The remaining stock may be served as a clear soup.

INGREDIENTS TO SERVE EIGHT TO TEN :
4 lb (2 kg) beef brisket
¼ lb (125 g) beef liver
salt
3 celery stalks
1 large onion studded with 2 cloves
1 bouquet garni, consisting of 2 bay leaves, parsley sprigs and thyme sprigs
3 peppercorns
2 garlic cloves
4 carrots
4 turnips
4 parsnips
4 onions
1 medium-sized cabbage
2 leeks
3 tablespoons (45 ml) drained capers

ROLLING BRISKET OF BEEF

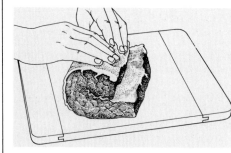

Roll a piece of brisket of beef up tightly.

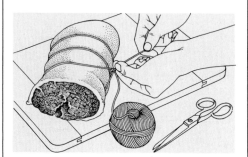

Tie the rolled meat securely at intervals with string.

Steak with Mushrooms and Red Wine

Rub 4 lean sirloin steaks (1½ pounds in total) with 1 cut clove of garlic.

Pour ⅔ cup of dry red wine into a bowl. Mix in 1 bay leaf, 4 sprigs of thyme, a little salt and freshly ground black pepper. Put the steaks into the marinade. Baste them well then marinate them for at least 30 minutes.

Take the steaks from the marinade and put them under a hot broiler. (The cooking time will depend on the thickness of the steaks and how rare or well done you like them.)

Meanwhile, prepare the sauce. Wash 2 cups of mushrooms. Slice them and put them into a large saucepan. Add the wine marinade and ⅔ cup of beef stock. Cover the pan and bring to the boil. Then reduce the heat and simmer for 2 minutes.

Add the broiled steaks to the pan, baste them with the sauce, cover the pan and simmer gently for 1 minute.

Put the steaks on a hot serving dish. Boil the sauce for 1 minute, then pour it over the steaks.

Serve immediately, sprinkled with 2 tablespoons of chopped parsley.

INGREDIENTS TO SERVE FOUR :
1½ lb (700 g) sirloin steak
1 garlic clove
⅔ cup (150 ml) dry red wine
1 bay leaf
4 thyme sprigs
salt
pepper
2 cups (150 g) mushrooms
⅔ cup (150 ml) beef stock
2 tablespoons (30 ml) chopped parsley

Stuffed Beef Rolls

Preheat the oven to 350°F (180°C).

Cut 1½ pounds of rump roast into 4 thin slices. Lay the slices on a piece of waxed paper. Cover them with another piece of waxed paper. Flatten them, using a rolling pin or a meat mallet.

For the stuffing, heat 2 tablespoons of margarine in a saucepan. Add 1 chopped onion and fry for 3 minutes, stirring frequently. Add 1 cup of coarsely chopped mushrooms to the pan. Fry them for 2 minutes. Remove the pan from the heat and stir in 1 cup of fresh bread crumbs, 1 tablespoon of chopped parsley, 1 teaspoon of chopped thyme, the grated rind of 1 lemon, salt and pepper.

Spread the stuffing on the slices of steak. Roll the slices up neatly and secure them with string or toothpicks. Arrange the beef rolls in a shallow ovenproof dish or casserole.

Blanch and peel 2 medium-sized tomatoes. Cut the tomatoes into quarters and remove the seeds. Put the tomatoes around the beef rolls with 2 bay leaves. Pour in 1¼ cups of beef stock or dry red wine.

Cover the dish and bake for 1 hour, or until the beef rolls are tender.

INGREDIENTS TO SERVE FOUR:
1½ lb (700 g) rump roast
2 tablespoons (25 g) margarine
1 onion
1 cup (100 g) chopped mushrooms
1 cup (50 g) fresh bread crumbs
1 tablespoon (15 ml) chopped parsley
1 teaspoon (5 ml) chopped thyme
1 lemon
salt
pepper
2 medium-sized tomatoes
2 bay leaves
1¼ cups (300 ml) beef stock or dry red wine

PREPARING BEEF ROLLS

Flatten slices of steak with a rolling pin.

Spread with stuffing and roll the slices up.

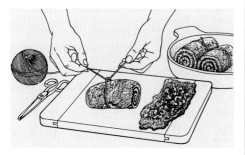

Tie the rolls and put into an ovenproof dish.

Beef in Yogurt Sauce

This is a delicious, less rich, version of the classic Beef Stroganoff.

Cut 1 pound of lean steak (sirloin, for example) into strips about ½ by 2 inches (1 by 5 cm).

Peel and slice 1 large onion. Prepare 1½ cups of washed and sliced mushrooms. Blanch and peel 2 ripe medium-sized tomatoes. Cut them into halves and remove the seeds. Chop the tomatoes coarsely.

Heat 2 tablespoons of corn oil in a large, heavy frying pan. Add the onions and fry them for 2 minutes, stirring frequently. Add the mushrooms and fry for 2 minutes more. Using a slotted spoon, transfer the onions and mushrooms to a bowl and keep warm.

Add the beef strips to the pan and, stirring constantly, fry quickly until they are no longer red.

Return the onions and mushrooms to the pan with the chopped tomatoes. Season well with salt and pepper. Cook over low heat, stirring constantly, for two minutes.

Stir in ⅔ cup of yogurt and heat gently. Do not allow the sauce to boil as the yogurt may curdle.

Serve immediately, sprinkled with 1 tablespoon of chopped parsley.

INGREDIENTS TO SERVE FOUR:
1 lb (500 g) lean steak
1 large onion
1½ cups (150 g) sliced mushrooms
2 ripe medium-sized tomatoes
2 tablespoons (30 ml) corn oil
salt
pepper
⅔ cup (150 ml) yogurt
1 tablespoon (15 ml) chopped parsley

Cassoulet

Wash 1 cup of navy beans. Put the beans into a bowl, cover with cold water and soak them for at least 12 hours.

Preheat the oven to 325°F (170°C).

Chop 8 slices of bacon and put them into an ovenproof casserole. Add 1 pound of salt pork, cut into 1-inch (2-cm) cubes, 4 small chicken or rabbit quarters and ½ pound of garlic sausage cut into ½-inch (1-cm) pieces.

Drain the beans and add them to the casserole with 4 scant cups of chicken stock and ¾ cup of blanched, peeled and coarsely chopped tomatoes. Add a bouquet garni, consisting of 1 bay leaf and sprigs of parsley and thyme tied together. Season with salt and pepper. Mix well. Cover the casserole and bake for 1½ hours.

Discard the bouquet garni. If the mixture looks dry add a little more stock. Sprinkle 2 cups of fresh bread crumbs over the top and continue to bake the casserole, uncovered, for 1 hour more.

INGREDIENTS TO SERVE FOUR TO SIX:
1 cup (250 g) navy beans
8 slices (100 g) bacon
1 lb (500 g) salt pork
4 small chicken or rabbit quarters
½ lb (250 g) garlic sausage
4 scant cups (850 ml) chicken stock
¾ cup (250 g) chopped tomatoes
1 bouquet garni, consisting of 1 bay leaf and parsley and thyme sprigs
salt
pepper
2 cups (100 g) fresh bread crumbs

Pork and Cabbage Soup

For this Chinese soup all the ingredients are cut into small pieces so that they cook very quickly.

Cut ½ pound of pork tenderloin or boned pork chops into thin strips. Put them into a large saucepan.

Prepare ½ cup of thinly sliced small mushrooms. Finely shred ½ pound of cabbage. Finely chop 1 scallion. Add the mushrooms, cabbage and scallion to the pan.

Cut a ¼-inch (6-mm) slice of ginger root. Peel off and discard the skin. Chop the ginger finely. Add it to the pan. Pour in 4 scant cups of well-seasoned chicken stock.

Bring to the boil. Reduce the heat and simmer for 10 minutes, or until the pork is cooked. Season with salt and pepper. Serve immediately.

INGREDIENTS TO SERVE FOUR:
½ lb (250 g) pork tenderloin or boned pork chops
½ cup (50 g) sliced small mushrooms
½ lb (250 g) cabbage
1 scallion
ginger root
4 scant cups (850 ml) well-seasoned chicken stock
salt
pepper

Pork Goulash

Slice 4 medium-sized onions. Cut 1 pound of lean boned shoulder or pork tenderloin into 2-inch (5-cm) cubes. Blanch, peel and quarter 2 tomatoes.

Heat 1 tablespoon of corn oil in a large saucepan. Add the onions to the pan and fry them for 3 minutes, stirring frequently. Add the pork to the pan and fry until the cubes are well browned. Stir in 1 tablespoon of paprika and 1 tablespoon of flour and cook for 1 minute, stirring constantly.

Add 2½ cups of well-seasoned chicken stock, the quartered tomatoes, 2 tablespoons of tomato paste, the grated rind of 1 lemon, salt and pepper. Bring to the boil, stirring constantly. Cover the pan, reduce the heat and simmer gently for 1 to 1½ hours, or until the meat is tender.

Add 1 cup of small mushrooms to the goulash and continue to cook for 10 minutes.

Just before serving put ⅔ cup of yogurt into a small saucepan. Warm the yogurt over very low heat, but do not allow it to boil. Mix the warmed yogurt into the goulash. Sprinkle with a little paprika and serve.

INGREDIENTS TO SERVE FOUR:
4 medium-sized onions
1 lb (500 g) boned pork shoulder or
**   tenderloin**
2 tomatoes
1 tablespoon (15 ml) corn oil
paprika
1 tablespoon (15 ml) flour
2½ cups (600 ml) chicken stock
2 tablespoons (30 ml) tomato paste
1 lemon
salt
pepper
1 cup (100 g) small mushrooms
⅔ cup (150 ml) yogurt

Pâté de Campagne

Line the bottom and sides of a large loaf pan or terrine with 8 slices of bacon, laying the slices crosswise in the pan. If any bacon is left chop it finely.

Put 1 pound of ground pork and 1 pound of ground veal into a mixing bowl with the chopped bacon. Finely chop or grind ½ pound of pig's liver and add it to the bowl. Crush 2 garlic cloves and add them with 2 teaspoons of salt and freshly ground black pepper to taste.

Grate in the rind of 1 orange, then add the squeezed juice with 2 tablespoons of brandy. Add 1 tablespoon of chopped sage and 1 tablespoon of chopped thyme. Mix well. Refrigerate for 2 hours.

Preheat the oven to 325°F (170°C).

Press the meat mixture into the bacon-lined pan. Level the top and press in 2 bay leaves and 4 sage leaves. Cover the pan

and put it into a roasting pan. Half fill the roasting pan with water. Bake for 1½ hours.

Let the pâté cool slightly, then put a weight on top of it until it has cooled completely. Cover and refrigerate for at least 4 hours before serving.

Serve the pâté from the terrine or turn it out of the pan onto a plate and cut it into slices.

INGREDIENTS TO SERVE SIX TO EIGHT:
8 slices (250 g) bacon
1 lb (500 g) ground pork
1 lb (500 g) ground veal
½ lb (250 g) pig's liver
2 garlic cloves
2 teaspoons (10 ml) salt
freshly ground black pepper
1 orange
2 tablespoons (30 ml) brandy
sage leaves
1 tablespoon (15 ml) chopped thyme
2 bay leaves

MAKING PÂTÉ

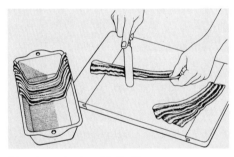

Line a pan or terrine with sliced bacon.

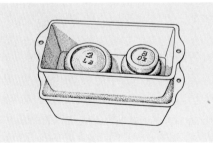

Weight the pâté while it is cooling.

Somerset Stuffed Pork

Preheat the oven to 350°F (180°C).

Put ½ cup of finely chopped or ground roasted hazelnuts into a mixing bowl with salt and pepper. Peel and core 1 small cooking apple and grate half of it into the bowl. Add just enough beaten egg to bind the ingredients. Mix well.

Trim any fat off 1 large or 2 small pork tenderloins or steaks (1 to 1½ pounds). Cut halfway through the steaks lengthwise. Open out the steaks. Put each of them between 2 pieces of waxed paper and flatten them with a rolling pin or a mallet. Spread the stuffing mixture down the centers of the steaks and roll them up tightly lengthwise. Tie the rolls with string.

Put 2 cups of sliced onions into a roasting pan or ovenproof dish. Slice the remaining ½ apple and arrange the slices on top of the onions. Put the stuffed meat on top of the apple and onions. Sprinkle 3 tablespoons of whole hazelnuts around the meat. Pour in 1¼ cups of hard cider. Season the meat with salt and pepper.

Cover and bake for 45 minutes, then uncover and cook, basting occasionally, for 20 to 30 minutes more, or until the pork is brown.

INGREDIENTS TO SERVE FOUR:
⅔ cup (100 g) chopped roasted hazelnuts
salt
pepper
1 small cooking apple
1 egg
1 to 1½ lb (500 to 700 g) pork tenderloin
**   or steak**
2 cups (250 g) sliced onions
1¼ cups (300 ml) hard cider

Stuffed Veal

Have a 3½-pound (1.65-kg) shoulder or breast of veal boned and flattened.

Preheat the oven to 375°F (190°C).

Put the veal, boned side up, on a board. Sprinkle it with salt and pepper.

Arrange 4 thin slices of prosciutto or any cured ham on top of the veal. Put 4 thin slices of Gruyère cheese on top of the ham with 8 sage leaves. Roll the veal up neatly and tie it with string. Put the veal roll into a roasting pan. Pour in ⅔ cup of chicken stock and ⅔ cup of dry white wine.

Cover the pan with aluminum foil and bake for 1 hour. Remove the foil and baste the meat. Continue to cook for 30 minutes more, or until the veal is brown. Lift it out onto a warmed serving dish and keep hot.

Mix 2 teaspoons of cornstarch with 2 tablespoons of cold water. Put the roasting pan over low heat. Stir the cornstarch mixture into the cooking liquid. Stirring constantly, bring to the boil. Continue to boil and stir the sauce until it has thickened. Season to taste with salt and pepper.

Garnish the veal roll with sage leaves. Pour the sauce into a gravy boat and serve.

INGREDIENTS TO SERVE SIX:
3½-lb (1.65-kg) shoulder or breast of veal, boned and flattened
salt
pepper
4 thin slices of prosciutto or any cured ham
4 thin slices of Gruyère cheese
sage leaves
⅔ cup (150 ml) chicken stock
⅔ cup (150 ml) dry white wine
2 teaspoons (10 ml) cornstarch

Veal Scallops with Orange

Cut 1 pound of veal into 4 scallops. Put each of the scallops between two pieces of waxed paper. Flatten them with a rolling pin until they are ¼ inch (6 mm) thick. Heat 2 tablespoons of safflower oil in a frying pan. Add the scallops to the pan and fry over high heat until they are browned on both sides. Lift the scallops out of the pan and keep them warm.

Finely chop 1 medium-sized onion and add it to the pan. Stirring frequently, fry the onion for 5 minutes, or until it is soft and translucent. Stir in 1 tablespoon of flour. Stirring constantly, gradually add 1¼ cups of chicken stock.

Add the grated rind and juice of 1 orange. Peel and remove the pith from another orange. Cut the membrane from the fruit segments. Add the segments to the pan with 3 tablespoons of sweet Madeira and salt and pepper. Bring to the boil. Reduce the heat and simmer for 1 minute.

Return the scallops to the pan. Cover and simmer gently for 10 minutes.

Transfer the scallops to a warmed serving dish, pour the sauce over them, garnish with sprigs of watercress and serve immediately.

INGREDIENTS TO SERVE FOUR:
1 lb (500 g) veal
2 tablespoons (30 ml) safflower oil
1 medium-sized onion
1 tablespoon (15 ml) flour
1¼ cups (300 ml) chicken stock
2 oranges
3 tablespoons (45 ml) sweet Madeira
salt
pepper
watercress sprigs

Kidneys and Mushrooms in Wine

Slice 1 onion. Remove the skins from 1 pound of lamb kidneys. Cut the kidneys into halves and remove the cores.

Heat 1 tablespoon of corn oil in a large, heavy frying pan. Add the onion and fry for 3 minutes. Add the kidneys to the pan with 1 cup of small mushrooms. Continue to fry, stirring occasionally, until the mushrooms are tender.

Stir in 1 tablespoon of flour. Stirring constantly, gradually add ⅔ cup of red wine and bring to the boil. Add a bouquet garni, consisting of 1 bay leaf and sprigs of parsley and thyme. Cover the pan, reduce the heat and simmer gently for 10 minutes, or until the kidneys are cooked. (Overcooking will toughen them.)

Remove the bouquet garni. Season to taste with salt and pepper. Sprinkle with 1 tablespoon of chopped parsley and serve immediately.

INGREDIENTS TO SERVE FOUR:
1 onion
1 lb (500 g) lamb kidneys
1 tablespoon (15 ml) corn oil
1 cup (100 g) small mushrooms
1 tablespoon (15 ml) flour
⅔ cup (150 ml) red wine
1 bouquet garni, consisting of 1 bay leaf and parsley and thyme sprigs
salt
pepper
1 tablespoon (15 ml) chopped parsley

PREPARING KIDNEYS

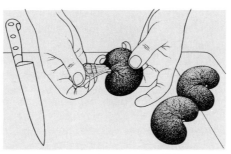

Pierce and remove the fine outer skin of kidneys.

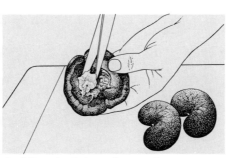

Cut kidneys into halves and remove the cores.

Chicken Liver Pâté

Put ½ pound of chicken livers into a saucepan with 4 chopped slices of bacon. Add 1 chopped small onion, 1 crushed garlic clove, 1 bay leaf, 1 sprig of thyme, salt, pepper and ¼ cup of chicken stock.

Cover the pan and cook over low heat, stirring occasionally, for 15 minutes. Remove the bay leaf. Pour the mixture into a blender. Add 1 tablespoon of brandy. Blend to a smooth paste.

Transfer the pâté to a serving dish. Chill for at least 2 hours before serving.

INGREDIENTS TO SERVE FOUR:
½ lb (250 g) chicken livers
4 slices (50 g) bacon
1 small onion
1 garlic clove
1 bay leaf
1 thyme sprig
salt
pepper
¼ cup (60 ml) chicken stock
1 tablespoon (15 ml) brandy

Braised Liver and Vegetables

Preheat the oven to 350°F (180°C).

Thinly slice 1 medium-sized onion, separate the slices into rings and put them into an ovenproof casserole or dish.

Thinly slice 1 pound of zucchini and put the slices on top of the onions. Sprinkle with 1 tablespoon of chopped thyme, salt and pepper.

Arrange 1 pound of sliced lamb's liver on top of the zucchini. Sprinkle with salt and pepper. Pour in ⅔ cup of tomato juice.

Cover the casserole and bake for 40 to 45 minutes, or until the liver and vegetables are cooked.

INGREDIENTS TO SERVE FOUR:
1 medium-sized onion
1 lb (500 g) zucchini
1 tablespoon (15 ml) chopped thyme
salt
pepper
1 lb (500 g) sliced lamb's liver
⅔ cup (150 ml) tomato juice

No prizes for guessing whether brown or white eggs are best—they are equally nutritious, rich in proteins that have all the essential amino acids. It is the breed of hen that determines shell color. And the grim battery system can produce as fine an egg as the free-range run. But no egg is perfect, for a high cholesterol content mars the magnificence of the golden yolk.

FEW PEOPLE NOW BELIEVE that the universe was created out of one great Mother Egg, or that witches use the shells as boats—although they may think it safer to smash the empty shells in the egg cups. But most English people—and most Bostonians—persist in believing that brown eggs are better than white, while New Yorkers believe the opposite. It is far more difficult to sort egg facts from egg fallacies than to separate yolks from whites.

One estimate is that more than two hundred thousand million eggs are eaten throughout the world every year, and most of them are hen's eggs. Among the wild birds' eggs, those of the quail are most popular, the once much-prized plovers' eggs now being rightly protected. The original jungle fowl from which the modern hen is descended might lay about twenty eggs a year; her intensively raised descendant must lay at the rate of at least two hundred and fifty eggs a year if she is to go on living.

The laying hen is the prime victim of factory farming, whether kept on deep litter or in batteries. Under the battery system the hens, which by nature are scratching, scavenging birds, are hatched in electric incubators, raised indoors by hundreds for five months and then caged in twos or threes in batteries of wire cages. There they spend nearly a year laying an egg almost every day. Feeding, with processed feeds, watering, collecting of eggs and removal of droppings is likely to be entirely automated, making it possible for one person to be in charge of about ten thousand birds.

In the West the vast majority of eggs are produced in this way. In Britain fewer than 8 percent of hens are now kept outdoors, their number being quite incapable of laying all the eggs offered for sale as "free range." It is not easy to distinguish battery eggs from other eggs, although if they have faint black lines almost circling the shell, they are most certainly from batteries, for

these lines are caused by the eggs rolling along the wire base of the cage.

You may well object to hens being incarcerated, but if they have been properly fed their eggs will have the same nutritional value as free-range eggs, and, again, with the right diet, there need be no difference in flavor. The color of the shell, which depends on the breed of the hen, bears no relationship to the nutritional value of the egg. The color of the yolk, from pale yellow to vivid orange, can be manipulated through the hen's diet. Free range or battery, the egg is 12 percent protein, 12 percent fat (almost all of it in the yolk) and 74 percent water, giving a Calorie value of about 90 for a two-ounce egg. It is also a good source of iron and vitamins A and D.

To describe an egg as free range is either true or false, but to describe it as fresh is meaningless. It is impossible to buy a really fresh egg in a store; to get that you will have to keep your own hens.

An egg will stay fresh for twelve days at ordinary room temperature, three weeks in a domestic refrigerator and up to nine months in commercial cold storage. The freshness affects nutritional value little, but flavor and, above all, texture will deteriorate as the egg gets older. The white of an egg boiled on the day it is laid will stay milky; it cannot be beaten successfully until it is about three days old; and it will not set firmly when it is hard-boiled until the end of a week or more.

The rate at which an egg declines into staleness depends on how well it is stored. It should be kept cool and in the dark, to cut down loss of moisture through the shell, and pointed end downward so that the air space within the broad end of the egg remains at the top.

Even within its shell an egg cannot hide its age if you put it in water. A fresh egg sinks, an aging egg floats. When you break open an egg the yolk of a fresh one sits firmly in the center of the white; that of an aging egg breaks as it emerges from the shell.

Eggs remain an eminently wholesome food, even when they are produced under intensive conditions. They can be vexatious at times, cracking while they boil, turning into scrambled rubber when your back is turned and, as Mr. Mantalini said in Dickens's *Nicholas Nickleby* when he was complaining about them being messy to eat, "yolk runs down the waistcoat, and yolk of egg does not match any waistcoat but a yellow waistcoat, dammit."

Science accuses the egg of a more serious fault. The yolk is rich in cholesterol, which is suspected of promoting arteriosclerosis. Some experiments suggest that the danger is lessened if the fowls are fed unsaturated fatty acids in, for example, sunflower seed oil.

Eggs are exceptionally versatile as well as

The Nutrients in Eggs
Eggs are particularly high in protein, fat, iron and vitamins A and D and a two-ounce egg provides about 90 Calories.

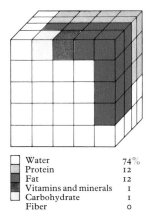

☐ Water	74%
☐ Protein	12
■ Fat	12
■ Vitamins and minerals	1
☐ Carbohydrate	1
☐ Fiber	0

IF CHICKENS EVER STOPPED LAYING...

All birds' eggs are edible, although many people might balk at a three-and-a-half-pound ostrich egg that takes forty minutes to boil. Of the domesticated birds, the egg of a duck is richer in fat than a hen's egg, and is also more likely to carry organisms that cause food poisoning. Turkey and guinea fowl eggs are delicately flavored, but a goose egg, which weighs about half a pound, is stronger tasting. Egg sizes are compared in the illustration below.

guinea fowl egg

duck egg

chicken egg

turkey egg

goose egg

nutritious. At the end of the eighteenth century the Irish poet Thomas Moore conceded that whatever the faults of the French, one could not "help loving the land who has taught us six hundred and eighty ways to dress eggs." And besides the immense number of dishes in which an egg remains recognizably an egg, there are many more in which the egg submerges its identity for the betterment of another food.

Until recently it might have been said with confidence that the whole art of cake making could not exist without eggs. But no longer, thanks to man's diabolical ingenuity. Fish and skimmed milk are now treated to provide substitutes for eggs in commercial baking, and animal blood plasma is used in place of egg whites. Fortunately, no one has yet produced a totally artificial egg, complete with white and yolk in a shell, although doubtless someone, somewhere, is trying hard to make hens redundant. So far even other birds have also failed to do that.

Egg-white Omelet with Herbs

This fluffy omelet is suitable for those on a low-cholesterol diet and is a good way to use extra egg whites.

Beat 2 egg whites until they are stiff. Fold in 1 tablespoon of yogurt, a pinch of chopped mixed herbs and salt and pepper to taste.

Lightly grease a small, nonstick frying pan and put it over moderate heat. Pour in the egg mixture and spread it to cover the bottom of the pan. Cook gently until it is brown underneath.

Sprinkle with 1 teaspoon of grated Parmesan cheese. Put the pan under a moderate broiler until the top is set and golden brown.

Fold the omelet in half, garnish with parsley and serve immediately.

INGREDIENTS TO SERVE ONE:
2 egg whites
1 tablespoon (15 ml) yogurt
mixed herbs
salt
pepper
1 teaspoon (5 ml) grated Parmesan cheese
parsley sprigs

SEPARATING EGGS

Working over a bowl crack the egg in half.

Drain the white keeping the yolk in the shell.

Spanish Pepper Omelet

Serve this large flat omelet cut into wedges and straight from the pan in which it is cooked.

Heat 2 tablespoons of olive oil in a large frying pan. Add 1 thinly sliced onion and 1 thinly sliced green pepper and fry gently for 3 minutes, or until the onion is soft and translucent.

Add 2 blanched, peeled, seeded and chopped tomatoes and ½ crushed clove of garlic. Season to taste with salt and pepper. Cook for 2 minutes more.

Lightly beat 6 eggs, season with salt and pepper and pour over the vegetables. Cook, stirring occasionally from the outside to the center. When the omelet is almost set, lower the heat and stop stirring.

When the omelet is just set and lightly browned underneath remove the pan from the heat. Sprinkle the omelet with 1 tablespoon of chopped parsley or chopped mixed herbs and serve immediately.

INGREDIENTS TO SERVE FOUR:
2 tablespoons (30 ml) olive oil
1 onion
1 green pepper
2 tomatoes
½ garlic clove
salt
pepper
6 eggs
parsley or mixed herbs

Mushrooms and Eggs en Cocotte

Preheat the oven to 375°F (190°C).

Heat 1 tablespoon of corn oil in a saucepan. Add 1 chopped small onion and fry for 3 minutes, stirring occasionally. Add 1 cup of chopped mushrooms and fry for 2 minutes more. Season to taste with salt and pepper.

Spoon the mixture into 4 cocottes or individual ovenproof dishes. Break 1 egg into each dish and sprinkle with salt and pepper.

Bake the cocottes for 5 to 10 minutes, or until the whites of the eggs are set but the yolks are still soft. Serve immediately.

INGREDIENTS TO SERVE FOUR:
1 tablespoon (15 ml) corn oil
1 small onion
1 cup (100 g) chopped mushrooms
salt
pepper
4 eggs

Leek Eggah

Cut into slices or squares, this Arabic dish can be eaten hot or cold, as a first course or as a light lunch or supper dish.

Preheat the oven to 350°F (180°C). Lightly grease a rectangular ovenproof dish.

Put 3 cups of thinly sliced young leeks into a saucepan with ½ cup of boiling salted water to which the juice of ½ lemon has been added. Reduce the heat and simmer for 5 to 10 minutes, or until the leeks are just tender. Drain the leeks and put them into the prepared dish.

Beat 6 eggs with 4 tablespoons of milk. Season to taste with salt and pepper. Pour the egg mixture over the leeks.

Bake for 30 to 35 minutes, or until the mixture is firm and golden brown.

INGREDIENTS TO SERVE FOUR:
3 cups (500 g) thinly sliced young leeks
½ lemon
6 eggs
4 tablespoons (60 ml) milk
salt
pepper

Onion Quiche

Preheat the oven to 400°F (200°C).

Make 1½ cups of cheese pastry with whole-wheat flour (see quiche lorraine). Roll it out and line an 8-inch (20-cm) flan ring or pie pan. Bake blind for 15 minutes. Remove the paper and beans and bake for 5 minutes more.

Prepare 4 cups of peeled and thinly sliced onions. Heat 2 tablespoons of corn oil in a frying pan. Add the onions to the pan, cover, and cook over moderate heat for 10 minutes, or until the onions are soft and translucent. Uncover and continue to fry until the onions are lightly browned. Season with salt, pepper and a pinch of grated nutmeg. Arrange the cooked onions in the pastry shell.

Beat 2 eggs with ⅔ cup of milk or light cream. Pour the mixture over the onions.

Bake for 30 to 35 minutes, or until the filling is set. Serve hot or cold.

INGREDIENTS TO SERVE FOUR TO SIX:
1½ cups (150 g) cheese pastry made with whole-wheat flour (see quiche lorraine)
4 cups (500 g) thinly sliced onions
2 tablespoons (30 ml) corn oil
salt
pepper
grated nutmeg
2 eggs
⅔ cup (150 ml) milk or light cream

Quiche Lorraine

Cheese pastry is not traditionally used for this popular French dish, but it makes a pleasant change from plain pie crust.

Preheat the oven to 400°F (200°C). Put an 8-inch (20-cm) flan ring on a greased baking sheet.

Combine 1½ cups of flour, ¼ teaspoon of salt and a pinch of pepper in a mixing bowl. Add 6 tablespoons of margarine or butter and cut it into small pieces with a table knife. Rub the fat into the flour with your fingertips until the mixture resembles fine bread crumbs. Stir in ¾ cup of finely grated sharp Cheddar cheese.

In a small bowl beat 1 egg yolk with 1 tablespoon of cold water. Make a well in the flour mixture and pour in the egg and water. Mix quickly with a knife and then with your fingertips to form a firm dough.

Turn the dough out onto a lightly floured surface and knead it gently until it is smooth.

Roll the pastry out and line the flan ring (see page 34) or an 8-inch (20-cm) pie pan. Line the pastry with waxed paper, weight it down with dried beans and bake for 15 minutes. Remove the paper and beans and bake for 5 to 10 minutes more, or until the pastry is just beginning to brown. Take it out of the oven.

Lower the oven temperature to 350°F (180°C).

Chop 8 slices of bacon and fry for 2 minutes. Add 4 tablespoons of chopped onion and 1 cup of sliced small mushrooms and fry for 2 minutes more, or until the onion is soft. Pour off the fat and spoon the bacon, onions and mushrooms into the pastry shell.

Beat together 2 eggs and ⅔ cup of light cream. Season to taste with salt and pepper. Pour the egg mixture into the pastry shell and sprinkle 4 tablespoons of grated Cheddar cheese over the top.

Bake the quiche for 25 to 30 minutes, or until the filling is set and lightly browned.

INGREDIENTS TO SERVE FOUR TO SIX:
1½ cups (150 g) flour
salt
pepper
6 tablespoons (75 g) margarine or butter
1 cup (100 g) finely grated sharp Cheddar cheese
2 eggs plus 1 egg yolk
8 slices bacon
4 tablespoons (60 ml) chopped onion
1 cup (100 g) sliced small mushrooms
⅔ cup (150 ml) light cream or milk

Egg and Pickle Mousse

Put 1¼ cups of milk into a saucepan with 1 small onion, cut into quarters, 2 sprigs of parsley and 1 bay leaf and bring to the boil. Remove the pan from the heat. Season to taste with salt and pepper and leave the milk to infuse for 10 minutes, then strain it.

Melt 2 tablespoons of margarine in a saucepan. Stir in 4 tablespoons of flour. Stirring constantly, gradually add the milk and bring to the boil. Reduce the heat and simmer for 1 minute. Adjust the seasoning. Cover the pan and set aside.

When the milk mixture is cool, stir into it

Dissolve gelatin in a cup set in hot water.

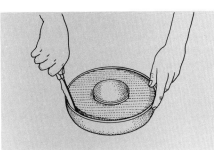

Run a knife between the mold and the mousse.

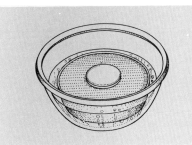

Dip the mold up to the rim in hot water.

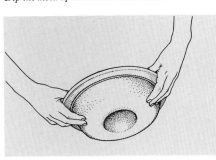

Cover with a plate, invert and remove the mold.

¼ pound of cottage cheese, ⅔ cup of yogurt, 4 finely chopped hard-boiled eggs, 2 tablespoons of finely chopped pickles and 1 tablespoon of Worcestershire sauce.

Dissolve 1½ tablespoons of gelatin in 2 tablespoons of water in a cup set in a pan of hot water. Mix the gelatin into the other ingredients.

Pour the mousse into a dampened 4-cup ring mold. Cover and put into the refrigerator to set, about 6 hours.

To turn out, loosen the edges of the mousse with a knife and dip the mold into a bowl of hot water. Cover the mold with a plate and invert. Fill the center of the mousse with sprigs of watercress and serve.

INGREDIENTS TO SERVE FOUR:
1¼ cups (300 ml) milk
1 small onion
2 parsley sprigs
1 bay leaf
salt
pepper
2 tablespoons (25 g) margarine
4 tablespoons (25 g) flour
¼ lb (100 g) cottage cheese
⅔ cup (150 ml) yogurt
4 hard-boiled eggs
2 tablespoons (30 ml) finely chopped pickles
1 tablespoon (15 ml) Worcestershire sauce
1½ tablespoons (15 g) powdered gelatin
watercress sprigs

Cottage Scramble

Chop 8 slices of bacon coarsely and fry it in a small frying pan for 3 minutes, or until it is cooked.

Lightly beat 6 eggs. Season with salt and pepper and pour over the bacon. Cook gently, stirring occasionally, until the egg is scrambled. Stir in ½ pound of cottage cheese and continue to cook over low heat until the cheese is heated through.

Meanwhile, toast 4 slices of whole-wheat bread. Pile the scrambled eggs on the toast. Garnish with sprigs of watercress and serve immediately.

INGREDIENTS TO SERVE FOUR:
8 slices bacon
6 eggs
salt
pepper
½ lb (250 g) cottage cheese
4 slices whole-wheat bread
watercress sprigs

Eggs Florentine

A perfect combination, poached eggs on a
bed of spinach and topped with cheese sauce
make a delicious lunch or supper dish.

Thoroughly wash 1 pound of spinach in
cold water, drain it well and put it into a
large saucepan. Add 1 teaspoon of salt, cover
the pan and cook for 10 minutes, or until the
spinach is tender. Drain the spinach well and
chop it coarsely. Put the spinach into a
flameproof dish and keep it hot.

In a small saucepan combine 1¼ cups of
yogurt with 1 egg yolk, 1 tablespoon of flour,
1 teaspoon of Dijon mustard and
2 tablespoons of grated Parmesan cheese.
Season to taste with grated nutmeg, salt and
pepper. Heat gently, stirring constantly,
until the sauce boils and thickens. Remove
the pan from the heat immediately.

Poach 4 eggs and put them on top of the
spinach. Pour the cheese sauce over the eggs
and sprinkle with 1 tablespoon of grated
Parmesan cheese.

Put the dish under a hot broiler until the
sauce is lightly browned and bubbling. Serve
immediately.

INGREDIENTS TO SERVE FOUR:
1 lb (500 g) spinach
salt
1¼ cups (300 ml) yogurt
1 egg yolk
1 tablespoon (15 ml) flour
1 teaspoon (5 ml) Dijon mustard
3 tablespoons (45 ml) grated Parmesan
** cheese**
nutmeg
pepper
4 eggs

POACHING EGGS

*Poach eggs in gently simmering water to which a little
vinegar has been added.*

Beef and Egg Loaf

This beef loaf can be served hot as a main
dish or cold.

Preheat the oven to 350°F (180°C). Grease
a large loaf pan.

Put ¾ pound of ground beef into a large
mixing bowl with ¼ pound of sausage meat
and 2 cups of fresh bread crumbs. Finely chop
2 stalks of celery and add them to the bowl
with 1 grated onion, 1 grated carrot,
1 tablespoon of chopped parsley and
½ teaspoon of dried mixed herbs. Season
well with salt and pepper. Mix until the
ingredients are blended.

In a small bowl lightly beat 1 egg with
2 tablespoons of tomato paste. Stir it into the
meat mixture. Put half of the meat mixture
into the prepared loaf pan and press it well
down with the back of a spoon. Put
2 hard-boiled eggs in the center and cover
them with the remaining meat mixture. Put
1 bay leaf on top and cover the pan with foil.

Bake for 1 to 1¼ hours, or until the meat is
tender and has shrunk slightly away from the
sides of the pan.

Turn the loaf out of the pan and serve
immediately or allow it to cool in the pan.

INGREDIENTS TO SERVE FOUR TO SIX:
¾ lb (350 g) ground beef
¼ lb (100 g) sausage meat
2 cups (100 g) fresh bread crumbs
2 celery stalks
1 onion
1 carrot
1 tablespoon (15 ml) chopped parsley
½ teaspoon (2.5 ml) dried mixed herbs
salt
pepper
1 egg
2 tablespoons (30 ml) tomato paste
2 hard-boiled eggs
1 bay leaf

Eggs and Chicken in Aspic

Pour 2 scant cups of well-seasoned chicken
stock into a saucepan and bring to the boil.
Skim any fat and scum from the surface of the
stock. Let the stock cool slightly, then strain
it through cheesecloth.

Return the stock to the saucepan. Stir in
⅔ cup of dry white wine, 2 tablespoons of
lemon juice and 1½ tablespoons of powdered
gelatin. Heat gently, stirring occasionally,
until the gelatin has dissolved. Bring to the
boil and remove the pan from the heat. Strain
the aspic into a pitcher. Stand the pitcher in a
bowl of hot water to keep the aspic from
setting.

Dampen a 1-quart (850-ml) mold with
cold water and pour in a layer of the aspic.
Chill the mold for 10 to 15 minutes, or until
the aspic is firm.

Meanwhile, prepare 2 cups of chopped

cooked chicken and slice 4 hard-boiled eggs.
Put a layer of chicken meat and egg slices over
the aspic in the mold. Cover with more of the
soft aspic and chill again.

Repeat the layers, finishing with a layer of
aspic, until all the chicken, eggs and aspic
have been used up. Chill each layer of aspic.

Chill until the aspic has set completely.
Dip the mold in hot water for a few seconds.
Cover with a plate and invert. Surround the
mold with sprigs of watercress and serve.

INGREDIENTS TO SERVE FOUR:
2 scant cups (450 ml) well-seasoned
** chicken stock**
⅔ cup (150 ml) dry white wine
2 tablespoons (30 ml) lemon juice
1½ tablespoons (15 g) powdered gelatin
2 cups (250 g) chopped cooked chicken
4 hard-boiled eggs
watercress sprigs

Curried Eggs

Coarsely chop 1 large onion. Peel, core and
chop ½ cooking apple. Heat 2 tablespoons
of corn oil in a saucepan. Add the onion and
fry for 3 minutes. Add the apple to the onion.

Stir in 2 teaspoons of curry powder with
1 tablespoon of flour. Cook for 1 minute,
stirring constantly.

Add 1¼ cups of chicken or vegetable stock
and bring to the boil, stirring constantly,
until the sauce is thick and smooth. Add 1 bay
leaf, 1 sprig of thyme and salt and pepper to
taste. Cover the pan, reduce the heat and
simmer gently for 30 minutes.

Hard boil 6 eggs, remove the shells and
cut the eggs into halves lengthwise. Arrange
the eggs in a serving bowl and pour the curry
sauce over them.

Serve at once or reheat in the oven at 400°F
(200°C) for 20 minutes.

INGREDIENTS TO SERVE FOUR:
1 large onion
½ cooking apple
2 tablespoons (30 ml) corn oil
2 teaspoons (10 ml) curry powder
1 tablespoon (15 ml) flour
1¼ cups (300 ml) chicken or vegetable
** stock**
1 bay leaf
1 thyme sprig
salt
pepper
6 eggs

Eggs Mornay

Immerse 6 eggs in simmering water for 10 minutes. Transfer the eggs to a bowl of cold water.

For the sauce, heat 2 tablespoons of margarine in a saucepan. Stir in 2 tablespoons of flour. Beat in 1¼ cups of milk. Bring to the boil, stirring constantly, until the sauce is thick and smooth. Remove from the heat and stir in ½ cup of grated sharp Cheddar cheese, a pinch of mustard, salt and pepper.

Remove the shells from the cooled hard-boiled eggs. Slice the eggs and arrange them in an ovenproof dish. Pour the hot sauce over the eggs.

Sprinkle ¼ cup of grated Cheddar cheese over the top. Put the dish under a hot broiler for 3 to 4 minutes, or until the sauce is bubbling and lightly browned on top.

Garnish with sprigs of parsley and serve immediately.

INGREDIENTS TO SERVE FOUR:
6 eggs
2 tablespoons (25 g) margarine
2 tablespoons (30 ml) flour
1¼ cups (300 ml) milk
¾ cup (75 g) grated sharp Cheddar cheese
mustard
salt
pepper
parsley sprigs

Egg Flower Soup

This is a Chinese soup into which beaten eggs are stirred, forming strands resembling a flower.

Bring 5 cups of well-seasoned chicken stock to the boil. Add 1 tablespoon of soy sauce, 1 teaspoon of lemon juice and ¼-inch (6-mm) slice of ginger root, peeled and finely chopped or grated.

Just before serving, beat 4 eggs with a little salt and pepper. Pour the eggs slowly into the boiling soup. The eggs should form threads and float. Remove the soup from the heat.

Sprinkle 2 finely sliced scallions and 1 tablespoon of chopped parsley over the soup and serve immediately.

INGREDIENTS TO SERVE FOUR TO SIX:
5 cups (1 liter) well-seasoned chicken stock
1 tablespoon (15 ml) soy sauce
1 teaspoon (5 ml) lemon juice
ginger root
4 eggs
salt
pepper
2 scallions
1 tablespoon (15 ml) chopped parsley

Pickle Stuffed Eggs

Dill pickles give the filling for these eggs an unusual flavor and a delicate color.

Immerse 6 eggs in simmering water for 10 minutes. Transfer the eggs to a bowl of cold water.

For the stuffing, cream ¼ pound of pot cheese with 4 tablespoons of yogurt. Add 4 tablespoons of chopped dill pickles, ½ teaspoon of lemon juice and salt and pepper to taste.

When the eggs are cold, remove their shells and cut the eggs into halves lengthwise. Carefully scoop out the yolks and rub them through a strainer into the stuffing. Beat the stuffing until it is smooth and well blended.

Pipe or spoon the stuffing into the center of the egg whites. Chill in the refrigerator until needed.

INGREDIENTS TO SERVE FOUR TO SIX:
6 eggs
¼ lb (125 g) pot cheese
4 tablespoons (60 ml) yogurt
4 tablespoons (60 ml) chopped dill pickles
½ teaspoon (2.5 ml) lemon juice
salt
pepper

Spinach and Egg Roulade

Preheat the oven to 400°F (200°C). Line a shallow 9- by 12-inch (23- by 32-cm) baking pan with waxed paper. Brush the paper lightly with oil.

Thoroughly wash ¾ pound of spinach in cold water. Put it into a large saucepan. Add 1 teaspoon of salt, cover the pan and cook for 10 minutes, or until the spinach is tender. Drain the spinach well and chop it coarsely.

Put the spinach into a large mixing bowl. Beat in 4 egg yolks and ⅔ cup of sour cream. Season to taste with salt and pepper. Beat 4 egg whites until stiff and fold them into the mixture.

Pour the roulade mixture into the prepared pan and level the surface. Bake for 10 to 15 minutes, or until the roulade is well risen, firm and just beginning to brown.

Meanwhile, prepare the filling. In a small saucepan combine 1¼ cups of milk, 1 small onion, quartered, 1 bay leaf and 2 parsley sprigs. Bring to the boil. Remove the pan from the heat. Season the milk to taste with salt and pepper and leave it to infuse for 10 minutes. Strain it. Hard boil 4 eggs.

Melt 2 tablespoons of margarine in a saucepan. Stir in 2 tablespoons of flour. Stirring constantly, gradually add the strained milk. Bring to the boil, reduce the heat and simmer for 1 minute. Adjust the seasoning and leave to cool. Coarsely chop the hard-boiled eggs and stir into the filling.

Sprinkle 1 tablespoon of grated Parmesan cheese over a large piece of waxed paper. Turn the roulade out onto the paper. Peel off the waxed paper on which it was baked. Spread the egg sauce over the roulade, leaving a 1-inch (2-cm) margin all around. Roll the roulade like a jelly roll by gently lifting the waxed paper so that the roulade folds over. Carefully lift it onto a serving dish and serve immediately.

INGREDIENTS TO SERVE FOUR:
¾ lb (350 g) spinach
salt
8 eggs
⅔ cup (150 ml) sour cream
pepper
1¼ cups (300 ml) milk
1 small onion
1 bay leaf
2 parsley sprigs
2 tablespoons (25 g) margarine
2 tablespoons (30 g) flour
1 tablespoon (15 ml) grated Parmesan cheese

MAKING A ROULADE

Turn the roulade out and remove the baking paper.

Spread the roulade with filling.

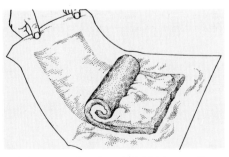

Lift the paper so that the roulade folds into a roll.

91

Baked Eggs

Preheat the oven to 400°F (200°C). Grease a 1-quart (850-ml) ovenproof dish.

Scrub and thickly slice 1½ pounds of potatoes. Put the potatoes into a saucepan, cover with salted water and bring to the boil. Cover the pan, reduce the heat and simmer for 15 minutes, or until the potatoes are tender.

Finely chop 1 large onion. Heat 1 tablespoon of corn oil in a frying pan. Add the onion and fry until it is soft and translucent. Spread the onion in the prepared dish.

Drain the potatoes and mash them with salt, pepper and ground nutmeg to taste. Add 2 tablespoons of milk to the potato and beat it in well with a fork.

Spoon the mashed potato over the onions and level the surface. Make 4 hollows in the potato with the back of a spoon and crack 1 egg into each hollow.

Prepare 1 cup of grated sharp Cheddar cheese and sprinkle over the eggs and potato and bake for 20 minutes, or until the eggs have set and the cheese is golden brown on top.

INGREDIENTS TO SERVE FOUR:
1½ lb (700 g) potatoes
salt
1 large onion
1 tablespoon (15 ml) corn oil
pepper
ground nutmeg
2 tablespoons (30 ml) milk
4 eggs
1 cup (100 g) grated sharp Cheddar cheese

Macaroni Carbonara

Cook ½ pound (2 cups) of macaroni in a large pan of salted boiling water until tender. Drain well.

In a large pan heat 2 tablespoons of margarine. Add 8 slices of chopped bacon or 1 cup of chopped cooked ham and fry. Add the drained pasta to the pan and toss lightly.

Beat 4 eggs with salt and pepper in a bowl and pour over the pasta. Stir gently over low heat until the eggs begin to thicken.

Stir in ½ cup of grated Parmesan cheese and season to taste with salt and pepper.

Serve immediately.

INGREDIENTS TO SERVE FOUR:
½ lb, 2 cups, (250 g) macaroni
2 tablespoons (25 g) margarine
8 slices bacon or 1 cup (200 g) chopped cooked ham
4 eggs
salt
pepper
½ cup (50 g) grated Parmesan cheese

Oeufs Provençal

Preheat the oven to 375°F (190°C).

Heat 1 tablespoon of corn oil in a saucepan. Add 1 chopped large onion and 1 crushed garlic clove and fry for 3 minutes.

Blanch and peel 4 medium-sized tomatoes. Coarsely chop the tomatoes and add them to the pan. Add 1 bay leaf, 1 teaspoon of chopped oregano or marjoram, 1 teaspoon of chopped basil and salt and pepper to taste. Cover the pan and cook over low heat for 15 to 20 minutes, or until the tomatoes are reduced to a purée.

Divide the purée between 4 ramekins and make a hollow in the center of each. Break 1 egg into each ramekin and sprinkle with salt and pepper.

Bake for 10 minutes, or until the eggs are set.

Serve immediately.

INGREDIENTS TO SERVE FOUR:
1 tablespoon (15 ml) corn oil
1 large onion
1 garlic clove
4 medium-sized tomatoes
1 bay leaf
1 teaspoon (5 ml) chopped oregano or marjoram
1 teaspoon (5 ml) chopped basil
salt
pepper
4 eggs

Eggs and Zucchini

Preheat the oven to 350°F (180°C). Grease a 1-quart (850-ml) ovenproof dish.

Heat 2 tablespoons of corn oil in a large deep frying pan. Add 1 crushed garlic clove and fry over low heat for 1 minute. Add 1½ pounds of sliced zucchini and continue to fry, stirring occasionally, until they are well browned.

Thinly slice 1 large onion and add it to the pan with 1 teaspoon of chopped tarragon and salt and pepper to taste. Continue to cook until the onions are soft.

Meanwhile, beat 4 eggs with 4 tablespoons of yogurt. Transfer the zucchini mixture to the prepared dish and pour in the eggs and yogurt.

Bake for 20 minutes, or until the eggs and yogurt have set and are golden brown on top.

INGREDIENTS TO SERVE FOUR:
2 tablespoons (30 ml) corn oil
1 garlic clove
1½ lb (700 g) zucchini
1 large onion
1 teaspoon (5 ml) chopped tarragon
salt
pepper
4 eggs
4 tablespoons (60 ml) yogurt

Hazelnut and Coffee Soufflé

This is a deliciously light dessert with a rich flavor and unusual texture.

Tie a double strip of waxed paper around a 1-quart (850-ml) soufflé dish. The paper should form a collar which stands 3 inches (8 cm) above the rim of the dish.

In the top of a double-boiler, over simmering water, beat 3 egg yolks with ¼ cup of sugar until the mixture is thick and creamy. Remove from the heat and continue beating until the mixture is cool. Stir in ⅔ cup of yogurt.

In a cup set in a pan of simmering water dissolve 2 teaspoons of powdered gelatin in ⅔ cup of strong black coffee.

Reserve 3 tablespoons from 1 cup of chopped toasted hazelnuts and stir the remainder into the soufflé mixture with the coffee and gelatin.

Beat 3 egg whites until they are stiff and fold them into the soufflé. Pour the soufflé into the prepared dish. Chill for about 6 hours, or until set.

Carefully remove the paper from the dish. Coat the sides of the soufflé with the reserved chopped nuts. Decorate the top with a few whole hazelnuts.

INGREDIENTS TO SERVE FOUR TO SIX:
3 eggs
¼ cup (50 g) sugar
⅔ cup (150 ml) yogurt
2 teaspoons (10 ml) powdered gelatin
⅔ cup (150 ml) strong black coffee
1 cup (100 g) chopped toasted hazelnuts
whole toasted hazelnuts

PREPARING A SOUFFLÉ DISH

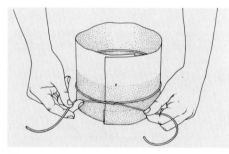

Tie a strip of waxed paper around the dish.

Plum and Orange Custard

This delightful pudding is a fruity version of a simple custard.

Preheat the oven to 350°F (180°C).

Halve and pit ½ pound of plums. Divide the plums among 4 individual soufflé or ovenproof dishes. Peel and remove the pith from 1 orange. Cut the membrane from the segments of fruit. Divide the segments among the dishes.

To make the custard, beat together 1¼ cups of yogurt, 2 eggs and 1 tablespoon of sugar. Add the grated rind of ½ orange. Pour the custard into the dishes.

Put the dishes into a roasting pan. Pour in enough hot water to reach halfway up the sides of the dishes.

Bake for 20 minutes, or until the custard is set and firm to the touch. Serve immediately.

INGREDIENTS TO SERVE FOUR:
½ lb (250 g) plums
1½ oranges
1¼ cups (300 ml) yogurt
2 eggs
1 tablespoon (15 ml) sugar

BAKING IN A BAIN-MARIE

Put dishes in a pan half-filled with hot water.

Candied Bread and Butter Pudding

Remove the crusts from 6 thin slices of whole-wheat bread. Spread thinly with ¼ cup of margarine or butter. Line the bottom of a 1- to 1½-quart (850-ml to 1-liter) greased baking dish with 3 slices of the bread.

Mix ¼ pound of candied peel with 2 tablespoons of sugar. Sprinkle half of the peel and sugar mixture over the bread. Arrange the remaining bread slices on top and sprinkle with the rest of the peel and sugar.

Beat 3 eggs with 2½ cups of milk. Strain over the bread. Let stand for 30 minutes to allow the custard to soak into the bread.

Meanwhile, preheat the oven to 350°F (180°C).

Bake the pudding for 30 to 40 minutes, or until the custard is set and the top is crisp and golden brown.

Serve hot.

INGREDIENTS TO SERVE FOUR:
6 thin slices whole-wheat bread
¼ cup (50 g) margarine or butter
¼ lb (100 g) candied peel
2 tablespoons (30 ml) sugar
3 eggs
2½ cups (600 ml) milk

Confectioner's Custard

This custard has a smooth texture and may be used instead of cream.

Pour ⅔ cup of milk into a small saucepan and heat to just below boiling point.

Beat 1 egg in a bowl with 1 tablespoon of cornstarch, 1 tablespoon of sugar and ¼ teaspoon of vanilla extract.

Pour the hot milk into the bowl and mix well. Pour the mixture into the pan and slowly bring to the boil, stirring constantly, until the custard thickens.

Let cool, stirring occasionally to prevent a skin forming.

Beat in 5 tablespoons (75 ml) of yogurt.

INGREDIENTS TO MAKE TWO-THIRDS OF A CUP (150 ML):
⅔ cup (150 ml) milk
1 egg
1 tablespoon (15 ml) cornstarch
1 tablespoon (15 ml) sugar
¼ teaspoon (1 ml) vanilla extract
5 tablespoons (75 ml) yogurt

White Mayonnaise

This light and foamy mayonnaise is made from only the white of an egg. It will remain frothy for up to 1 week if stored in the refrigerator.

In a mixing bowl, beat 1 egg white until it is thick but not too stiff. Beat in ⅔ cup of corn oil, olive oil or safflower oil a little at a time, beating well after each addition.

Beat in 1 tablespoon of lemon juice, ½ teaspoon of mustard, ¼ teaspoon of salt and freshly ground black pepper. Chill until required.

INGREDIENTS TO DRESS A SALAD TO SERVE FOUR:
1 egg white
⅔ cup (150 ml) corn, olive or safflower oil
1 tablespoon (15 ml) lemon juice
½ teaspoon (2.5 ml) mustard
¼ teaspoon (1 ml) salt
freshly ground black pepper

Mayonnaise

This mayonnaise requires only half the amount of oil used in a traditional mayonnaise.

Put 1 egg yolk, ½ teaspoon of Dijon mustard, ¼ teaspoon of salt and freshly ground black pepper into a mixing bowl. Beat the ingredients to mix them. Add ¼ cup of corn oil, olive oil or safflower oil, a few drops at a time, beating constantly until the mayonnaise has thickened.

Stir in 2 tablespoons of yogurt and 2 teaspoons of lemon juice and beat again. Beat 1 egg white until it is stiff and fold it into the mayonnaise. Use immediately.

INGREDIENTS TO DRESS A SALAD TO SERVE FOUR:
1 egg
½ teaspoon (2.5 ml) Dijon mustard
¼ teaspoon (1 ml) salt
freshly ground black pepper
¼ cup (60 ml) corn, olive or safflower oil
2 tablespoons (30 ml) yogurt
2 teaspoons (10 ml) lemon juice

Yogurt Hollandaise Sauce

This is a lighter version of a true hollandaise. Serve it with fish and vegetable dishes.

In a small saucepan combine 3 tablespoons of wine vinegar, 5 peppercorns, 1 bay leaf and 1 mace blade and bring to the boil. Continue boiling until the liquid has reduced to 2 teaspoons.

Beat 3 egg yolks in the top of a double-boiler. Strain the vinegar into them. Heat over simmering water, stirring constantly, until the yolks are thick.

Add ⅔ cup of yogurt and continue stirring until the sauce is thick enough to coat the back of a spoon. Be careful not to overheat or the sauce will curdle.

Serve lukewarm.

INGREDIENTS TO MAKE ⅔ CUP (150 ml) OF SAUCE:
3 tablespoons (45 ml) wine vinegar
5 peppercorns
1 bay leaf
1 mace blade
3 egg yolks
⅔ cup (150 ml) yogurt

A BREAST-FED INFANT and a suckled calf are both getting their perfect food—mother's milk. If the child is switched to cow's milk, however, it will be given something which is less than perfect. Although the milk of all mammals has the same constituents, the proportions of the constituents differ. Human milk contains far less protein and more carbohydrate than cow's milk.

But even though it cannot be described as "perfect," milk is still the most valuable of all foods in the human diet. Its quality will vary according to the breed of the cow, the quality of its fodder and the season. In the summer, for example, milk is the best quality and three glasses a day will provide an adult with 25 to 30 percent of the protein needed (including most of the essential amino acids), at least 10 percent of the calories, more than the daily requirement of calcium, 50 percent of the riboflavin, 30 percent of the vitamin A and 17 percent of the thiamine he or she requires.

It is thanks to Pasteur, the great nineteenth-century French chemist, that milk is now a safe as well as a nutritious food. The process of pasteurization named after him involves heating the milk to destroy disease-carrying organisms and bacteria that make it sour quickly. Pasteurization destroys some of the thiamine and vitamin C, but far less than is destroyed if you boil milk at home. The flavor of milk is also changed by pasteurization, but it is a deprivation in the cause of health that we learn to live with. (In most countries in the West people have no option, since by law almost all milk sold has to be pasteurized.)

It is the nature of fresh milk to go sour because the bacteria in the milk convert the milk sugar, called lactose, into lactic acid. This accounts for the sharpness of sour-milk products, but the particular flavor of the product depends on which bacteria have been at work. Souring is commonly produced by *Lactobacillus acidophilus*, but it is *Lactobacillus bulgaricus* that is responsible for the special flavor of yogurt.

When the souring milk reaches a certain level of acidity the protein, which was in solution in the milk, changes into a curd. The curd floats in the clear liquid whey that remains. The curds can be eaten as they are or made into cheesecake, but their main role is in the making of cheese, a "natural" convenience food with a recorded history of six thousand years. Armies have marched on it. David was on his way to Saul's headquarters with ten cheeses for the troops when he encountered Goliath. The wrestlers of ancient Greece trained on it and the armies of Caesar and Genghis Khan conquered on it. But even so cheese has none of the aggressive associations of meat and is the staple food of many vegetarians. Most cheese is richer in protein than meat,

IN PRAISE OF YOGURT

There is no proven recipe for longevity, but yogurt is one food that has long been associated with the attainment of great age. Like most Bulgarians, the centenarian above eats yogurt every day. The Bulgarians, however, are extremely health conscious and their diet is very well balanced. Certainly, yogurt contains more protein and riboflavin than milk itself and is also more easily digested, but it can't by itself work miracles of rejuvenation.

fish or poultry. It is a good source of the vitamins A, D, E and riboflavin and it is rich in phosphorus and calcium.

Whole curd is the basis of all cheese, but several thousand different types are made from it. The texture and flavor of the cheese will vary according to the type of milk used, the bacteria involved and the manufacturing process. Cow's milk is now most widely used in cheesemaking, but goat's milk is popular in many parts of Europe. Ewe's milk, the richest milk of the three, is less popular for cheesemaking, although it does produce the famous Roquefort.

Whatever the milk the starting point of cheese is the curd. The simplest process is the one used to make what the French call *fromage blanc*. The curd of soured skimmed milk is hung in a muslin bag through which the whey drips. Refinements of this process produce the low-fat cottage cheese (skimmed milk, heated and soured) and the high-fat cream cheeses (cow's milk with added cream) such as French Petit Suisse, Gervais and demi-sel. These fresh soft cheeses do not keep.

The manufacture of the world-famous cheeses is far more complicated. It may involve not only the use of rennin, an enzyme usually obtained from a calf's stomach, which (as in the making of junket) coagulates milk without souring it, but also the heating of the curd and, to produce the blue-veined cheeses, inoculating it with molds.

Roquefort is a prime example of what can be involved in the making of a cheese. It is made

Cheese is an excellent source of protein and also of calcium, riboflavin and vitamin A. But, with the exception of such low-fat cheeses as cottage cheese, it is also high in saturated fat and cholesterol. Above, left to right, front row: Brie, cottage cheese and Ricotta; center: a natural Tomme, Roquefort and Parmesan; back row: Edam and American Cheddar.

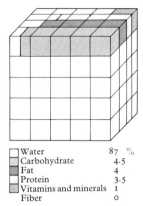

The Nutrients in Milk
Milk is a well-balanced food containing first-class protein, and three and a half ounces (100 g) provide about 65 Calories.

Water	87 %
Carbohydrate	4.5
Fat	4
Protein	3.5
Vitamins and minerals	1
Fiber	0

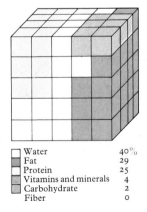

The Nutrients in Cheese
Cheese is rich in protein, fat and calcium. Three and a half ounces (100 g) of Cheddar, for example, provide about 400 Calories.

Water	40 %
Fat	29
Protein	25
Vitamins and minerals	4
Carbohydrate	2
Fiber	0

during the lambing season from the unskimmed milk of ewes, and is a mixture of morning and evening milkings; the morning milk is richer in fat. Rennin from a lamb's stomach is added and the whey is drained from the resulting curd. The curd is then placed between layers of bread crumbs on which the mold *Penicillium glaucum roqueforti* has been grown. The pressed cheese is then stored in the damp and cool limestone caves of Roquefort in the French Massif Central. It ripens slowly, turning into a cheese fit, as the

cliché goes, for kings and popes. Fermented curds can also be made into such soft cheeses as Brie and Camembert, or into such hard cheeses as Cheshire, Wensleydale, Edam, Stilton and Gorgonzola.

There is also processed cheese. This is the twentieth-century invention of two Swiss scientists and consists of several types of cheese which have been heated and emulsified and packaged. Its claim to virtue is that it keeps well—and it is indeed best kept and not eaten.

Homemade Cottage Cheese

Any type of milk may be used to make cottage cheese, but skim milk contains less fat. Use commercial skim milk or 7 rounded tablespoons of skim milk powder to 2½ cups of water. For extra flavor, yogurt, herbs or spices may be added.

In a saucepan heat 2½ cups of milk until it is just tepid. Add 1½ teaspoons of rennet and mix well. Pour the milk into a bowl. Leave it in a warm place for 15 minutes, or until the milk has set and curds have formed.

Pour the milk mixture into the top of a double-boiler and gently heat over hot water to a temperature of 110°F (43°C). (Cool enough to hold your finger in without discomfort.) Stir constantly until the curds and the whey separate. Put a strainer over a bowl and line it with several layers of cheesecloth. Pour in the curds and whey. Tie the corners of the cheesecloth together to form a bag and suspend the bag over the bowl for 12 to 24 hours to drain. If, however, the bag is squeezed gently from time to time, the cheese should be drained in 2 to 3 hours.

Put the drained curd in a bowl, mash it with a fork and season it to taste with salt and pepper. Cover and store in the refrigerator. It will keep for up to 1 week.

INGREDIENTS TO MAKE A QUARTER-POUND
(100 g) OF CHEESE:
2½ cups (600 ml) milk
1½ teaspoons (7.5 ml) rennet
salt
pepper

MAKING COTTAGE CHEESE

Tie the curds and whey in cheesecloth and drain.

Cheese and Onion Pie

Preheat the oven to 400°F (200°C).

Peel and thinly slice 8 medium-sized onions. Put into a saucepan with 1¼ cups of water. Cover the pan, bring to the boil and simmer for 10 minutes, or until the onions are soft. Drain the onions and let them cool.

Cut ½ pound of sharp Cheddar cheese into ½-inch (1-cm) cubes.

Put half of the onions into a 1 quart (850 ml) baking dish. Scatter the cubes of cheese and 3 tablespoons of seedless raisins over the onions. Sprinkle with salt, pepper and a generous pinch of grated nutmeg.

Arrange the remaining onions on top and sprinkle with more seasoning.

Make 1½ cups of shortcrust pastry with whole-wheat flour (see page 34) and roll it out a little bigger than the dish. Cut a ½-inch (1-cm) strip from around the edge of the pastry and press it onto the dampened rim of the dish. Brush the strip of pastry lightly with water, then cover the pie with the remaining pastry. Press the edges of the pastry together to seal them. Trim off any excess pastry. Flute the edges of the pastry and decorate the pie with leaves cut from the pastry trimmings.

Brush the pie with beaten egg or milk. Bake for 45 minutes, or until the pastry is crisp and browned.

Serve immediately.

INGREDIENTS TO SERVE FOUR:
8 medium-sized onions
½ lb (250 g) sharp Cheddar cheese
3 tablespoons (25 g) seedless raisins
salt
pepper
grated nutmeg
1½ cups (150 g) shortcrust pastry made
**   with whole-wheat flour (see page 34)**
1 egg or milk

Tartare Party Dip

Serve this dip with pieces of celery, carrot, green pepper, cauliflower and whole mushrooms.

Put ½ pound of cottage cheese and ⅔ cup of yogurt into a mixing bowl. Add 1 grated small onion, 1 tablespoon of chopped pickle, 1 tablespoon of finely chopped celery, 1 tablespoon of finely chopped green pepper, 1 tablespoon of chopped parsley and the grated rind of ½ lemon. Mix well. Season to taste with salt and pepper.

Chill. Serve sprinkled with ground paprika.

INGREDIENTS TO SERVE FOUR TO SIX:
½ lb (250 g) cottage cheese
⅔ cup (150 ml) yogurt
1 small onion
1 tablespoon (15 ml) chopped pickle
1 tablespoon (15 ml) chopped celery
1 tablespoon (15 ml) chopped green
**   pepper**
1 tablespoon (15 ml) chopped parsley
½ lemon
salt
pepper
paprika

Cottage Cheese and Tuna Cocottes

Preheat the oven to 400°F (200°C).

Lightly brush with oil 4 individual ramekins. Put them on a baking sheet.

Put ½ pound of cottage cheese into a mixing bowl and beat in 2 eggs. Drain a 7-ounce can of tuna fish and flake it. Add it to the cheese mixture with the grated rind and the juice of ½ lemon and 1 tablespoon of chopped parsley. Mix well. Season to taste with salt and pepper. Spoon the mixture into the prepared dishes.

Bake for 10 to 15 minutes, or until the mixture is lightly set and golden brown on top. Garnish with sprigs of parsley and serve immediately.

INGREDIENTS TO SERVE FOUR:
½ lb (250 g) cottage cheese
2 eggs
7 oz (198 g) canned tuna fish
½ lemon
1 tablespoon (15 ml) chopped parsley
salt
pepper
parsley sprigs

Coeur à la Crème

Serve this version of a traditional French dessert with berries or a fruit purée.

Sieve ½ pound of cottage cheese into a mixing bowl. Stir in ⅔ cup of heavy cream and ⅔ cup of sour cream. Add 2 tablespoons of sugar and mix well. Beat 2 egg whites until they are stiff, then fold them into the cheese mixture.

Press the mixture into 6 individual heart-shaped molds that have holes in the bottom for the mixture to drain. Put the molds onto a deep plate. Alternatively, line a strainer with several layers of cheesecloth and put it over a bowl. Pour the mixture into the strainer. Leave the molds or the strainer in the refrigerator overnight to drain and chill. Turn out onto a plate.

INGREDIENTS TO SERVE SIX:
½ lb (250 g) cottage cheese
⅔ cup (150 ml) heavy cream
⅔ cup (150 ml) sour cream
2 tablespoons (30 ml) sugar
2 egg whites

Pashka

This traditional Russian Easter dish can be eaten as a dessert or spread on cakes and breads. It is especially good with gingerbread.

Sieve $\frac{1}{2}$ pound of cottage cheese into a mixing bowl. Beat in $\frac{2}{3}$ cup of sour cream. Add 2 tablespoons of chopped blanched almonds, 2 tablespoons of chopped mixed candied peel, $\frac{1}{3}$ cup of seedless raisins and the grated rind of $\frac{1}{2}$ lemon. Mix well.

Line a strainer with several layers of cheesecloth and put the strainer over a bowl. Spoon the mixture into the strainer. Leave it in the refrigerator for 12 to 24 hours to drain. When the pashka is solid, turn it out onto a serving dish.

INGREDIENTS TO SERVE FOUR:
$\frac{1}{2}$ **lb (250 g) cottage cheese**
$\frac{2}{3}$ **cup (150 ml) sour cream**
2 tablespoons (25 g) chopped blanched
   almonds
2 tablespoons (25 g) mixed candied peel
$\frac{1}{3}$ **cup (50 g) seedless raisins**
$\frac{1}{2}$ **lemon**

Orange Cheese Puffs

Preheat the oven to 400°F (200°C). Grease a large baking sheet.

Make $\frac{3}{4}$ cup of choux paste (see page 35). Use either a pastry tube or a spoon to shape small rounds of dough onto the baking sheet. Bake for 20 minutes. Slit each puff, lower the oven temperature to 350°F (180°C) and bake the puffs for 10 minutes more. Cool the puffs on a wire rack.

To make the filling, sieve $\frac{3}{4}$ pound of cottage cheese into a mixing bowl. Add the grated rind and juice of 1 orange and 2 to 3 tablespoons of milk. Stir the ingredients well; the mixture should have a creamy consistency. Stir in 1 tablespoon of sugar.

To make the sauce, in a small saucepan blend 2 teaspoons of cornstarch with $\frac{2}{3}$ cup of water. Stir in 4 tablespoons of orange marmalade and the juice of $\frac{1}{2}$ lemon. Stirring constantly, bring the mixture to the boil. Lower the heat and simmer for 5 minutes, stirring frequently.

Fill the puffs with the cheese filling. Pile them into a serving bowl and pour the hot sauce over them. Serve immediately.

INGREDIENTS TO SERVE FOUR TO SIX:
$\frac{3}{4}$ **cup (75 g) choux paste (see page 35)**
$\frac{3}{4}$ **lb (350 g) cottage cheese**
1 orange
2 to 3 tablespoons (30 to 45 ml) milk
1 tablespoon (15 ml) sugar
2 teaspoons (10 ml) cornstarch
4 tablespoons (60 ml) orange
   marmalade
$\frac{1}{2}$ **lemon**

Orange and Lemon Cheesecake

If you do not have a spring form cake pan, first put the cheesecake mixture into a regular cake pan and chill it until it is set. Then press the crumb crust lightly on top of the cheesecake and chill again. Cover the pan with a plate, invert, remove the pan and serve.

Grease a 7- to 8-inch (18- to 20-cm) spring form cake pan. Put about 15 graham crackers into a plastic bag and crush them with a rolling pin. (Or the crackers may be crushed in a blender.) They should make $1\frac{1}{2}$ cups of crumbs.

Melt 6 tablespoons of margarine or butter in a saucepan. Add the crumbs and stir until

Put cookies into a bag and crush with a rolling pin.

Press the crumb and butter mixture into a pan.

they are well mixed.

Pour the crumbs into the prepared cake pan and press them down with the back of a spoon. Put the pan into the refrigerator for 30 minutes.

Meanwhile, in the top of a double-boiler, beat 2 egg yolks with $\frac{1}{4}$ cup of sugar until the mixture is thick and creamy. Stir in the grated rind and juice of 1 orange and 1 lemon. Cook over simmering water, stirring constantly, until the mixture is thick enough to coat the back of a spoon. Pour it into a large mixing bowl.

In a cup set in a pan of hot water, dissolve $1\frac{1}{2}$ tablespoons of powdered gelatin in 2 tablespoons of water. Stir into the egg mixture. Allow to cool slightly. Sieve $\frac{3}{4}$ pound of cottage cheese into the bowl. Add $\frac{2}{3}$ cup of sour cream and mix well.

Beat 2 egg whites until they are stiff and fold them in. Pour the cheesecake mixture into the cake pan. Chill in the refrigerator until the mixture has set.

Run a knife around the edge of the cheesecake and remove it from the pan. Decorate the top with orange and lemon slices.

INGREDIENTS TO SERVE SIX TO EIGHT:
15 graham crackers
6 tablespoons (75 g) margarine or butter
2 eggs
$\frac{1}{4}$ **cup (50 g) sugar**
2 oranges
2 lemons
$1\frac{1}{2}$ **tablespoons (15 g) powdered gelatin**
$\frac{3}{4}$ **lb (350 g) cottage cheese**
$\frac{2}{3}$ **cup (150 ml) sour cream**

Baked Cheesecake

This rich-tasting cheesecake can be made with a plain or rich shortcrust, with spiced or almond pastry, or without the pastry if you are counting calories.

Preheat the oven to 400°F (200°C).

Make 1 cup of shortcrust pastry (see page 34). Roll out the pastry and line the bottom of a 7- to 8-inch (18- to 20-cm) spring form cake pan with it. Line the pastry with foil or waxed paper, weight it down with dried beans and bake it for 15 minutes. Remove the paper and beans and bake for 5 minutes more, or until the pastry is just beginning to brown. Let the pastry cool.

Reduce the oven temperature to 350°F (180°C).

Meanwhile, make the filling. Put $\frac{1}{2}$ pound of pot cheese into a large mixing bowl. Stir in $\frac{2}{3}$ cup of yogurt, $\frac{1}{4}$ cup of sugar, $\frac{1}{4}$ cup of cornstarch, $\frac{1}{2}$ cup of seedless raisins and the grated rind and juice of 1 lemon. Stir until well mixed. Stir in 2 egg yolks.

Beat 2 egg whites until they are stiff. Fold them into the cheese mixture.

Pour the cheesecake mixture into the pan. Bake for 30 to 35 minutes, or until it has set and the top is golden brown. Cool before serving.

INGREDIENTS TO SERVE SIX TO EIGHT:
1 cup (100 g) shortcrust pastry (see
   page 34)
$\frac{1}{2}$ **lb (250 g) pot cheese**
$\frac{2}{3}$ **cup (150 ml) yogurt**
$\frac{1}{4}$ **cup (50 g) sugar**
$\frac{1}{4}$ **cup (25 g) cornstarch**
$\frac{1}{2}$ **cup (75 g) seedless raisins**
1 lemon
2 eggs

Blue Cheese Dip

In a mixing bowl, mash $\frac{1}{2}$ pound of a blue cheese, such as Roquefort or Blue Cheese.

Sieve $\frac{1}{4}$ pound of cottage cheese into the bowl. Add $\frac{2}{3}$ cup of yogurt. Mix until well blended.

Store in the refrigerator for up to 2 days. Serve the dip at room temperature.

INGREDIENTS TO SERVE FOUR TO SIX :
$\frac{1}{2}$ **lb (250 g) Roquefort or Blue Cheese**
$\frac{1}{4}$ **lb (100 g) cottage cheese**
$\frac{2}{3}$ **cup (150 ml) yogurt**

Chilled Watercress Soup

Melt 2 tablespoons of margarine in a large saucepan. Add 1 chopped onion and fry over low heat for 5 minutes, or until the onion is soft but not browned.

Add $2\frac{1}{2}$ cups of chicken stock, the grated rind and juice of $\frac{1}{2}$ lemon, salt and pepper. Add 2 cups of diced peeled potatoes to the pan. Bring to the boil. Cover the pan, reduce the heat and simmer gently for 15 to 20 minutes, or until the potatoes are cooked.

Thoroughly wash 2 bunches of watercress. Reserve a few sprigs for garnish. Remove the coarse stalks. Coarsely chop the watercress

and add it to the pan. Simmer the soup for 2 minutes more. Pour the soup into a blender and purée it.

Pour the soup into a tureen. Allow it to cool slightly and then beat in $1\frac{1}{4}$ cups of yogurt. Chill it thoroughly. Garnish with the reserved sprigs of watercress and serve.

INGREDIENTS TO SERVE FOUR TO SIX :
2 tablespoons (35 g) margarine
1 onion
$2\frac{1}{2}$ cups (600 ml) chicken stock
$\frac{1}{2}$ lemon
salt
pepper
2 cups (250 g) diced peeled potatoes
2 bunches watercress
$1\frac{1}{4}$ cups (300 ml) yogurt

Cheese and Bacon Pudding

Preheat the oven to 400°F (200°C).

Put 3 cups of small bread cubes, about $\frac{1}{2}$ inch (1 cm) square, into a lightly greased large baking dish.

In a mixing bowl beat together 3 eggs and 2 scant cups of milk. Add 1 cup of grated sharp Cheddar cheese. Season to taste with salt and pepper. Mix well. Pour the cheese

mixture over the bread cubes. Let the mixture stand for 15 minutes. Put 4 slices of bacon on top.

Bake for 30 to 40 minutes, or until the bacon is cooked and the custard is well risen, golden brown and set. Pour off the excess fat from the bacon and serve at once.

INGREDIENTS TO SERVE FOUR :
3 cups (150 g) small bread cubes
3 eggs
2 scant cups (450 ml) milk
1 cup (100 g) grated sharp Cheddar cheese
salt
pepper
4 slices bacon

Cottage Cheese and Salami Quiche

This tasty quiche with its unusual combination of flavors will not brown when it is cooked. If it is overcooked, however, the filling will split, so remove it from the oven as soon as it has set.

Preheat the oven to 400°F (200°C).

Roll out $1\frac{1}{2}$ cups of shortcrust pastry (see page 34) and use it to line an 8-inch (20-cm) flan ring or pie pan. Line the pastry with

waxed paper weighted down with dried beans and bake it for 15 minutes. Remove the paper and beans and bake the pastry for 5 to 10 minutes more, or until it is just beginning to brown.

Reduce the oven temperature to 350°F (180°C).

Reserving 3 slices for garnish, arrange ¼ pound of thinly sliced salami on the bottom of the pastry shell.

In a mixing bowl lightly beat 2 eggs. Stir in ½ pound of cottage cheese, 1 grated small onion, ½ teaspoon of dried mixed herbs and a pinch of salt and of pepper. Mix well. Spoon the mixture into the pastry shell. Bake the quiche for 25 to 30 minutes, or until the filling is set.

Let the quiche cool slightly. Garnish it with the reserved salami and serve.

INGREDIENTS TO SERVE FOUR TO SIX:
1½ cups (150 g) shortcrust pastry (see page 34)
¼ lb (100 g) thinly sliced salami
2 eggs
½ lb (250 g) cottage cheese
1 small onion
dried mixed herbs
salt
pepper

Raspberry Cheese Mousse

Sieve ½ pound of raspberries into a mixing bowl, or purée them in a blender and then sieve them. Stir in ½ pound of sieved cottage cheese. Add ⅔ cup of yogurt and the grated rind and juice of ½ lemon. Mix well.

Dissolve 1½ tablespoons of powdered gelatin in 3 tablespoons of water in a cup set in a pan of hot water. Stir the dissolved gelatin into the raspberry mixture.

Beat 2 egg whites until they are stiff and fold them into the mixture. Fold in 1 tablespoon of sugar.

Pour the mixture into a 2-pint (1.20-liter) ring mold or an 8-inch (20-cm) cake pan. Chill in the refrigerator until the mousse has set.

To turn out, dip the mold in hot water for 10 seconds. Cover the mold with a plate and invert.

To decorate, blanch, peel and slice 3 peaches. Dip the slices into 1 tablespoon of lemon juice to keep them from browning. Pile the peaches in the center of the ring or arrange them on top of the mousse.

INGREDIENTS TO SERVE SIX TO EIGHT:
½ lb (250 g) raspberries
½ lb (250 g) cottage cheese
⅔ cup (150 ml) yogurt
½ lemon, plus 1 tablespoon (15 ml) lemon juice
1½ tablespoons (15 g) powdered gelatin
2 egg whites
1 tablespoon (15 ml) sugar
3 peaches

Cheese and Tomato Soufflé

A mixture of eggs, milk, cheese and air—the perfect soufflé should be firm on the outside but creamy in the middle.

Preheat the oven to 375°F (190°C).

Melt 2 tablespoons of margarine in a large saucepan and stir in 4 tablespoons of flour. Stirring constantly, gradually add ⅔ cup of milk. Bring to the boil, reduce the heat and cook gently for 1 minute. Remove the pan from the heat.

Add 1 cup of grated sharp Cheddar cheese and stir until it has melted. Stir in 1 tablespoon of tomato paste and ½ teaspoon of dried basil. Season to taste with salt and pepper.

Add 2 blanched, peeled and coarsely chopped medium-sized tomatoes and 4 egg yolks. Beat well.

Beat 4 egg whites until they are stiff. Add 2 tablespoons of the egg whites to the cheese mixture and stir well. Carefully fold in the

Milk, yogurt and cheese make refreshing and exciting fare for summer buffets: from left to right, Chilled Watercress Soup, Cottage Cheese and Salami Quiche and Blue Cheese Dip.

remainder of the egg whites.

Pour the mixture into an 8-inch (20-cm) soufflé dish and bake for 35 to 40 minutes, or until the soufflé is well risen and the top is golden brown. Serve immediately.

INGREDIENTS TO SERVE FOUR:
2 tablespoons (25 g) margarine
4 tablespoons (25 g) flour
⅔ cup (150 ml) milk
1 cup (100 g) grated sharp Cheddar cheese
1 tablespoon (15 ml) tomato paste
dried basil
salt
pepper
2 medium-sized tomatoes
4 eggs

Cheese and Apple Rarebit

Grate ½ pound of Cheddar cheese into a mixing bowl. Peel and core 2 apples and grate them into the bowl. Add 1 teaspoon of Dijon mustard and 2 tablespoons of milk. Mix well. Season to taste with salt and pepper.

Core 1 apple and cut it into 4 rings. Sprinkle the rings with 1 tablespoon of lemon juice.

Toast 4 slices of whole-wheat bread. Pile the cheese and apple mixture onto each slice. Cook under a moderate broiler for 3 minutes, or until the top is golden brown and bubbling.

Garnish each rarebit with an apple ring and a sprig of watercress. Serve immediately.

INGREDIENTS TO SERVE FOUR:
½ lb (250 g) Cheddar cheese
3 apples
1 teaspoon (5 ml) Dijon mustard
2 tablespoons (30 ml) milk
salt
pepper
1 tablespoon (15 ml) lemon juice
4 slices whole-wheat bread
4 watercress sprigs

Homemade Yogurt

The taste of homemade yogurt is very different and far superior to commercial varieties. Easy to make, it can be prepared from whole milk or skim milk. Special equipment that keeps the yogurt at a constant warm temperature is available, but is not necessary for producing good results. For yogurt to set properly and quickly it requires a temperature of about 85° to 90°F (29° to 32°C). A thermos bottle or the oven of an electric stove at its lowest setting are equally suitable.

Pour 2½ cups of milk into a saucepan and bring to the boil. Cover the pan, remove it from the heat and let the milk cool to a temperature of 110°F (43°C)—cool enough to hold your finger in without discomfort.

Add 3 tablespoons of yogurt to the cooled milk and mix well. Pour the milk and yogurt mixture into a warmed, wide-necked thermos bottle. Close the thermos and leave it undisturbed for 10 hours or overnight for the yogurt to set.

Alternatively, pour the milk and yogurt mixture into a bowl and leave it in an 85° to 90°F (29° to 32°C) oven overnight.

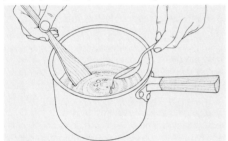

Bring the milk to the boil, cool and stir in yogurt.

Seal in a warmed thermos bottle overnight.

Chill the set yogurt in a covered container.

The longer the yogurt is left to incubate, the thicker and more acidic in taste it will become.

When the yogurt is set, put it in a covered container and chill in the refrigerator. It will keep for up to 1 week.

INGREDIENTS TO MAKE 2½ CUPS (600 ml):
2½ cups (600 ml) milk or skim milk
3 tablespoons (45 ml) yogurt

Blueberry Yogurt Sherbet

This sparkling, richly flavored sherbet is most refreshing at the end of a hearty meal.

Put ½ pound of blueberries and 2 to 3 tablespoons of water into a saucepan. Cook gently for 5 minutes, or until the fruit is tender. Reserve 2 tablespoons of the blueberries and sieve the remainder. Stir the reserved blueberries, 1¼ cups of yogurt and the juice of ½ lemon into the purée. Add sugar to taste.

In a small bowl set in a pan of hot water dissolve 2 tablespoons of powdered gelatin in 2 tablespoons of water. Add to the purée and mix well. Chill until the mixture just begins to set.

Beat 2 egg whites until they are stiff and fold them into the purée. Spoon into an ice-cube tray or other container and freeze until firm.

INGREDIENTS TO SERVE FOUR:
½ lb (250 g) blueberries
1¼ cups (300 ml) yogurt
½ lemon
sugar
2 teaspoons (10 ml) powdered gelatin
2 egg whites

Cucumber Raita Salad

This cool salad from India makes a marvelous accompaniment to hot, spicy dishes.

Peel and thinly slice 2 large cucumbers. Put the cucumber slices into a colander, sprinkle them with ½ teaspoon of salt and let drain for 30 minutes.

Put 1¼ cups of yogurt into a serving bowl with 1 tablespoon of chopped mint. Add the cucumber, season with freshly ground black pepper and stir well. Chill well.

Before serving garnish with 1 tablespoon of chopped mint.

INGREDIENTS TO SERVE FOUR:
2 large cucumbers
½ teaspoon (2.5 ml) salt
1¼ cups (300 ml) yogurt
2 tablespoons (30 ml) chopped mint
freshly ground black pepper

Yogurt Cheese

Vary the fresh sharp flavor of yogurt cheese by beating in chopped chives, crushed garlic or herbs.

In a bowl mix 1¼ cups of yogurt with ¼ teaspoon of salt. Put a strainer over another bowl and line it with cheesecloth. Pour in the yogurt mixture and leave it to drain for 3 hours. Much of the liquid will drain out, leaving a smooth "creamy" cheese.

INGREDIENTS TO MAKE ONE-QUARTER POUND (100 g) OF CHEESE:
1¼ cups (300 ml) yogurt
¼ teaspoon (1 ml) salt

Mint Yogurt Dressing

Wash 1 sprig of mint and remove the leaves from the stalk. Chop the leaves finely and put into a mixing bowl. Add salt and pepper and ⅔ cup of yogurt. Mix well.

Alternatively, mix all the ingredients together in a blender.

INGREDIENTS TO DRESS A SALAD TO SERVE FOUR:
1 mint sprig
salt
pepper
⅔ cup (150 ml) yogurt

Ginger Junket

Rennet is used to coagulate the milk in this light, finely flavored dessert.

Gently heat 2½ cups of milk in a saucepan until it reaches body temperature (just warm to the touch). Add 1 tablespoon of sugar and stir until it has dissolved.

Finely chop 2 pieces of preserved ginger. Stir it into the warm milk with 1 teaspoon of rennet.

Pour the mixture into 4 individual serving dishes or glasses immediately. Let set at room temperature.

Sprinkle with ground ginger and serve.

INGREDIENTS TO SERVE FOUR:
2½ cups (600 ml) milk
1 tablespoon (15 ml) sugar
2 pieces preserved ginger
1 teaspoon (5 ml) rennet
ground ginger

Brown Bread Ice Cream

This ice cream is not too rich and has an unusual and pleasant flavor. Toast the bread crumbs to give a crunchy texture.

Beat $\frac{2}{3}$ cup of heavy cream until it is thick. Fold in $\frac{2}{3}$ cup of yogurt and 2 lightly beaten egg yolks. Stir 1 cup of fresh whole-wheat bread crumbs and 1 tablespoon of sherry or rum into the cream mixture.

Beat 2 egg whites until they are stiff. Beat in 2 tablespoons of confectioner's sugar.

Fold the beaten egg whites into the cream mixture and pour into an ice-cube tray or plastic container and freeze.

For a smoother ice cream, when the mixture is half frozen, turn it out into a bowl and beat it for 2 minutes. Return it to the freezing tray and freeze until firm.

INGREDIENTS TO SERVE FOUR:
$\frac{2}{3}$ cup (150 ml) heavy cream
$\frac{2}{3}$ cup (150 ml) yogurt
2 eggs
1 cup (50 g) fresh whole-wheat
   bread crumbs
1 tablespoon (15 ml) sherry or rum
2 tablespoons (25 g) confectioner's sugar

Yogurt Cream

Serve this mixed with fresh summer fruit.

Beat $\frac{2}{3}$ cup of heavy cream in a bowl until it is thick. Fold in $\frac{2}{3}$ cup of yogurt.

Spoon the cream and yogurt mixture into a serving dish and sprinkle with 1 tablespoon of brown sugar. Chill overnight.

INGREDIENTS TO SERVE FOUR:
$\frac{2}{3}$ cup (120 ml) heavy cream
$\frac{2}{3}$ cup (120 ml) yogurt
1 tablespoon (15 ml) brown sugar

Syllabub

This smooth, creamy dessert, with just a hint of tartness, makes a perfect complement to a rich meal.

Grate the rind and squeeze the juice of 1 large lemon into a large mixing bowl. Add 5 tablespoons of dry white wine, 1 tablespoon of brandy, 4 tablespoons of sugar and $1\frac{1}{4}$ cups of heavy cream. Beat until the mixture stands in soft peaks. Add $\frac{2}{3}$ cup of yogurt and beat until the mixture is thick.

Spoon the syllabub into individual serving dishes or glasses. Put a twist of lemon on each. Serve at once or chill in the refrigerator for several hours.

INGREDIENTS TO SERVE FOUR TO SIX:
1 large lemon
5 tablespoons (75 ml) dry white wine
1 tablespoon (15 ml) brandy
4 tablespoons (50 g) sugar
$1\frac{1}{4}$ cups (300 ml) heavy cream
$\frac{2}{3}$ cup (150 ml) yogurt
4 to 6 lemon slices

Apricot Yogurt Whip

To make this light, frothy dessert in advance, set it lightly with 2 teaspoons of powdered gelatin dissolved in 2 tablespoons of water.

Put $\frac{1}{4}$ pound of dried apricots into a bowl and cover with $1\frac{1}{4}$ cups of water. Soak overnight.

Put the apricots and water into a small saucepan and simmer for 20 to 25 minutes, or until the apricots are tender. Blend the apricots or sieve them to a purée. Stir in 2 cups of yogurt and 1 tablespoon of sugar. In another bowl beat 2 egg whites until they are stiff. Fold them into the purée.

Spoon into individual serving bowls or glasses, decorate with $\frac{1}{4}$ cup of chopped toasted hazelnuts and serve immediately.

INGREDIENTS TO SERVE FOUR:
$\frac{1}{4}$ lb (100 g) dried apricots
2 cups (450 g) yogurt
1 tablespoon (15 ml) sugar
2 egg whites
$\frac{1}{4}$ cup (25 g) chopped toasted hazelnuts
2 teaspoons (10 ml) powdered gelatin
   (optional)

Chilled Yogurt and Tomato Soup

In a large mixing bowl beat together $2\frac{1}{2}$ cups of yogurt and $2\frac{1}{2}$ cups of tomato juice. Add the grated rind and juice of 1 lemon. Mix well.

Peel 1 medium-sized cucumber. Reserving a 1-inch (2-cm) piece for garnish, cut the cucumber into $\frac{1}{4}$-inch (6-mm) cubes. Stir the cubes into the yogurt mixture. Season to taste with salt and pepper. Chill until needed.

Before serving slice the reserved piece of cucumber and $\frac{1}{2}$ lemon. Garnish the soup with slices of cucumber and lemon and 1 tablespoon of chopped chives.

INGREDIENTS TO SERVE FOUR TO SIX:
$2\frac{1}{2}$ cups (600 ml) yogurt
$2\frac{1}{2}$ cups (600 ml) tomato juice
$1\frac{1}{2}$ lemons
1 medium-sized cucumber
salt
pepper
1 tablespoon (15 ml) chopped chives

Ranch-style Salad Dressing

To vary the flavor of this piquant salad dressing add finely chopped herbs or green pepper. It will keep for up to 1 week in the refrigerator.

In a small bowl, beat together $\frac{2}{3}$ cup of buttermilk with $\frac{2}{3}$ cup of yogurt.

Stir in 1 teaspoon of grated onion and $\frac{1}{4}$ teaspoon of crushed garlic. Season to taste with salt and pepper.

Cover the bowl and refrigerate.

INGREDIENTS TO DRESS A SALAD TO SERVE FOUR:
$\frac{2}{3}$ cup (150 ml) buttermilk
$\frac{2}{3}$ cup (150 ml) yogurt
1 teaspoon (5 ml) grated onion
$\frac{1}{4}$ teaspoon (1 ml) crushed garlic
salt
pepper

Orange Egg Flip

This nourishing breakfast drink is ideal for people in a hurry.

Beat together 1 egg, $\frac{2}{3}$ cup of yogurt and the juice of 1 orange. Drink immediately.

INGREDIENTS TO SERVE ONE:
1 egg
$\frac{2}{3}$ cup (150 ml) yogurt
1 orange

FOR A VEGETABLE WHICH WAS, according to a Turkish myth, the devil's creation, the onion has been credited with some remarkable virtues, both magical and medical. It has been said that if a man sleeps with an onion under his pillow he will dream of his future wife, or if he rubs onion juice on his bald head his hair will rapidly grow again. It has been asserted that onions cure boils, restore bad eyesight, reduce blood pressure, increase lust, clean out the bowels and induce sleep. There is no end to the claims made for them and none of them has been substantiated. It is much the same for other members of the onion family. Garlic has been reputed to make peasants work harder and Roman soldiers fight more stubbornly and roses smell more sweetly if it is planted among them. Leeks, according to the Roman emperor Nero, ensure that you are in good voice.

But does all this add up to the greatest vegetable confidence trick of all time? What are the qualities that make onions the most universally used and apparently the most indispensable vegetable? They are insignificant as a source of energy—one pound of boiled onions provides only 60 Calories. Pyramid building was hard work and the slaves who built them required a large number of calories each day. They must have eaten a lot of bread and drunk copious amounts of beer with their supposedly staple diet of onions. Onions provide no carotene or vitamin D and their vitamin C content is far behind that of the brassicas, the cabbage family. Their contribution to our mineral needs is not outstanding. Even in sulfur, which is their strong point, they are no better than cabbage, and Brussels sprouts leave them far behind.

Whatever their virtue, however, there is no denying their attraction. The English, for example, eat about a quarter of a million tons of onions a year. Most of them are imported, and when imports were stopped during the Second World War the deprivation felt was greater than could be accounted for simply by the loss of flavor. Whatever the nutritional analysis shows, perhaps there is something magical in an onion. On the other hand, there may be a danger in eating them to excess because they contain an alkaloid that has been shown to cause anemia in dogs and may do the same in humans.

Onions can be eaten raw or cooked in a host of ways—boiled, fried, baked, made into soups and sauces, used in stews and other spicy dishes and pickled.

They vary in the intensity of their flavor—some are more pungent, others sweeter. While all need the sun to ripen them, the greater the heat the milder the onion will taste. The mild varieties are usually sold as Bermuda onions. Red-colored varieties have a stronger flavor. Those grown in cooler climates are smaller, stronger and keep better. But wet weather produces large, soft-fleshed bulbs which soon rot.

Onions are available in the stores all year round, because crops ripen at different times in various parts of the world. But to provide a year-round supply from your own garden is difficult, because stored onions will sprout or rot before the new crop is ready.

Leeks, which can be harvested during the fall, winter and spring, are a better alternative as a garden crop. Because they are hardy they can stay in the ground during the winter and can be dug up as you need them and eaten fresh, when they taste their best. Leeks have a far more subtle taste than onions, and they are more nutritious both in vitamins (notably carotene and vitamin C in the leaves) and minerals (including twice as much sulfur, potassium and calcium). They are popular throughout Europe, but less so in the United States.

The Nutrients in Onions
Onions are high in sulfur, and unless fried they are low in calories. Three and a half ounces (100 g) provide about 30 Calories.

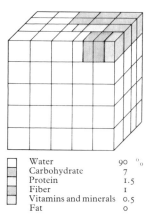

Water	90	%
Carbohydrate	7	
Protein	1.5	
Fiber	1	
Vitamins and minerals	0.5	
Fat	0	

Members of the onion family have little nutritional value, but their wide range of flavors are indispensable. The most delicately flavored white onion is the shallot. The large Bermuda onions are so sweet that they are delicious eaten raw. The "ordinary onion" is more pungent and ideal for flavoring cooked dishes. Garlic is also strong, but develops a sweetness when cooked. Of the green onions, chives and scallions are best eaten in salads. Leeks have the sweetest flavor of all. Below, clockwise: shallots (in the box), pots of chives, leeks, garlic and bundles of scallions, surrounding Bermuda and "ordinary onions."
Onions are best stored on strings (right).

THE MEDICINAL ONION

Although the onion has little nutritional value, for centuries it has been widely revered as a food. Possibly this is because it is known to stimulate the natural contractions of the intestine and to improve the circulation of the blood. It has now been discovered that onions reduce serum cholesterol, thus helping to lessen the likelihood of coronary heart disease. It is doubtful, however, that onions, when fried, can do more than ameliorate the effect of the fat in which they are cooked. But pickled onions would stand a good chance of becoming the health food of the future were it not for their unfortunate effect on the breath.

Onions and leeks are the two members of the onion family used as vegetables—the others are used for flavoring. Shallots are a smaller, somewhat less pungent version of the onion with the merest hint of garlic. Introduced into Europe in the Middle Ages, supposedly one of the spoils of war of the returning Crusaders, shallots achieved particular esteem in French cooking. Unfortunately, they are not widely cultivated elsewhere.

Chives, the smallest and most subtle of the onions, were being used by the Chinese five thousand years ago. By having a pot of them indoors for use in the winter and the spring and by planting them in window boxes or in a corner of the garden, you can be assured of a supply of chives all year. The bulbs are left in the soil to produce more leaves.

Home-grown Welsh onions are useful as a winter substitute for scallions which, although available all year, are expensive.

Garlic has an onion flavor with a difference. It is best treated with a certain discretion, although there are some dishes—aioli, the Provençal mayonnaise, and gazpacho, Spanish cold vegetable soup—in which garlic is used with abandon for a throat-tingling effect. Dishes containing garlic are not suitable for freezing for they often develop an unpleasant flavor.

In the Middle Ages it was thought that garlic warded off werewolves and vampires. Today health-food literature still frequently gives the impression that garlic will cure all ills. But even ignoring such extravagant claims garlic is worth growing, especially since cloves for planting are cheap and easily cultivated.

Leek and Bacon Quiche

Preheat the oven to 400°F (200°C).

Make 1½ cups of shortcrust pastry with whole-wheat flour (see page 34). Roll it out and line an 8-inch (20-cm) flan ring or pie pan. Bake blind for 15 minutes. Remove the paper and the beans and bake for 5 minutes more.

Reduce the oven temperature to 375°F (190°C).

Make the filling. Wash 3 cups of sliced leeks thoroughly and drain well.

Chop 8 slices of bacon. Fry it gently in a large saucepan until the fat runs. Add the leeks, cover the pan and cook over very low heat, stirring occasionally, for 10 minutes, or until the leeks are tender.

Using a slotted spoon, transfer the leeks and bacon to the pastry shell.

Beat 2 eggs with ⅔ cup of milk. Season to taste with salt and pepper. Pour over the leeks. Sprinkle with 1 tablespoon of grated Parmesan cheese.

Bake for 30 minutes, or until the filling is set and lightly browned on top.

Serve hot or cold.

INGREDIENTS TO SERVE FOUR TO SIX:
**1½ cups (100 g) shortcrust pastry made with whole-wheat flour (see page 34)
3 cups (500 g) sliced leeks
8 slices bacon
2 eggs
⅔ cup (150 ml) milk
salt
pepper
1 tablespoon (15 ml) grated Parmesan cheese**

Leek and Tomato Casserole

Preheat the oven to 350°F (180°C).

Prepare 3 cups of sliced leeks. Wash them thoroughly. Put half of the leeks into a casserole or ovenproof dish.

Slice 2 medium-sized tomatoes and put them in a layer over the leeks, sprinkling them with salt, pepper, the juice of ½ lemon and 1 crushed garlic clove.

Put the remaining leeks on top of the tomatoes. Sprinkle them with the juice of ½ lemon and salt and pepper.

Cover and bake for 30 to 40 minutes, or until the leeks are just tender. Serve hot or cold.

INGREDIENTS TO SERVE FOUR:
**3 cups (500 g) sliced leeks
2 medium-sized tomatoes
1 lemon
salt
pepper
1 garlic clove**

Leeks Vinaigrette

Trim 12 young leeks and cut them lengthwise almost to the root end. Wash them thoroughly. Tie them together neatly.

In a large saucepan bring 1¼ cups of salted water to the boil. Add the leeks, cover the pan, reduce the heat and simmer gently for 15 minutes, or until the leeks are tender. Drain the leeks. Put them into a shallow bowl to cool. Untie them.

In a small bowl mix together 1 teaspoon of Dijon mustard, salt, pepper, 1 teaspoon of lemon juice and 2 tablespoons of corn oil.

Pour the dressing over the leeks. Marinate them for at least 2 hours. Serve them chilled.

INGREDIENTS TO SERVE FOUR:
**12 young leeks
salt
1 teaspoon (5 ml) Dijon mustard
pepper
1 teaspoon (5 ml) lemon juice
2 tablespoons (30 ml) corn oil**

PREPARING LEEKS

Trim the roots and leaves.

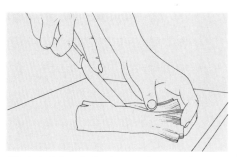

Slit the leeks lengthwise almost to the root end.

Rinse thoroughly under cold running water.

Garlic Sauce

Serve this sauce with lamb or a strong-flavored fat fish such as mackerel.

Peel 1 large bulb of garlic, about 16 cloves. Put them into a saucepan. Add 1 sprig of rosemary, ½ cup of fresh bread crumbs, salt and pepper. Pour in 1¼ cups of beef stock and ⅔ cup of milk. Bring to the boil, cover the pan, reduce the heat and simmer for 30 minutes, stirring occasionally.

Sieve the sauce or blend it to a purée. Pour it back into the pan, correct the seasoning and reheat.

INGREDIENTS TO SERVE FOUR:
**1 large garlic bulb (about 16 cloves)
1 rosemary sprig
½ cup (25 g) fresh bread crumbs
salt
pepper
1¼ cups (300 ml) beef stock
⅔ cup (150 ml) milk**

Garlic Soup

Peel 8 large garlic cloves and put them into a saucepan. Peel 2 medium-sized potatoes, dice them into ½-inch (1-cm) pieces and add them to the pan.

Pour in 4 scant cups of water. Add 1 bay leaf, 1 thyme sprig, 1 sage leaf, 1 basil leaf, salt and pepper.

Bring to the boil, cover the pan, reduce the heat and simmer for 30 minutes.

Pour the soup into a blender and purée it. Return the soup to the pan, reheat and adjust the seasoning. Serve hot.

INGREDIENTS TO SERVE FOUR:
**8 large garlic cloves
2 medium-sized potatoes
1 bay leaf
1 thyme sprig
1 sage leaf
1 basil leaf
salt
pepper**

French Onion Soup

Peel and thinly slice 6 medium-sized onions. Melt 2 tablespoons of butter in a large saucepan with 1 tablespoon of corn oil. Add the onions to the pan. Cover the pan and cook the onions over moderate heat, stirring occasionally, for about 15 minutes, or until they are tender and translucent.

Raise the heat to moderately high and stir in 1 teaspoon of salt and ½ teaspoon of sugar. Cook the onions, stirring frequently, for about 30 minutes, or until they are a deep golden brown.

Stir in 4 cups of beef stock, 1¼ cups of red wine, 1 bay leaf and ½ teaspoon of dried sage. Cover the pan, reduce the heat and simmer gently for 30 to 40 minutes. Season to taste with salt and pepper.

Serve the soup hot with slices of toasted French bread sprinkled with grated Parmesan cheese.

INGREDIENTS TO SERVE FOUR:
6 medium-sized onions
2 tablespoons (25 g) butter
1 tablespoon (15 ml) corn oil
salt
½ teaspoon (2.5 ml) sugar
4 cups beef stock
1¼ cups (300 ml) red wine
1 bay leaf
½ teaspoon dried sage
French bread
grated Parmesan cheese

Braised Onions

Peel 5 medium-sized onions. Cut them into quarters and put them into a saucepan. Add ⅔ cup of water, 2 tablespoons of wine vinegar, ⅔ cup of seedless raisins, ⅓ cup of coarsely chopped walnuts, 1 crushed garlic clove, 2 thyme sprigs, 1 bay leaf, salt and pepper.

Bring to the boil, cover the pan, reduce the heat and simmer, stirring occasionally, for 15 to 20 minutes, or until the onions are just tender and the water has evaporated. If the water has not completely evaporated during cooking, continue to cook uncovered for a few minutes.

Serve hot.

INGREDIENTS TO SERVE FOUR:
5 medium-sized onions
2 tablespoons (30 ml) wine vinegar
⅔ cup (100 g) seedless raisins
⅓ cup (50 g) coarsely chopped walnuts
1 garlic clove
2 thyme sprigs
1 bay leaf
salt
pepper

CRUSHING GARLIC

Crush finely chopped garlic with a knife blade.

Onion and Sage Stuffing

Onion and sage stuffing is traditionally served with pork. Use this to stuff a boneless, rolled pork roast or a 2- to 3-pound chicken.

Peel and chop 2 large onions. Put them into a saucepan and cover with cold water. Bring to the boil, reduce the heat and simmer for 5 minutes, or until the onions are tender.

Chop 4 slices of bacon. Put the bacon into a frying pan and fry it in its own fat. Remove the pan from the heat and stir in 2 cups of fresh bread crumbs.

Peel, core and finely chop 1 small tart apple. Add the apple to the bread crumbs with 2 tablespoons of chopped sage (or 2 teaspoons of dried sage), salt and pepper.

Drain the onion, add it to the stuffing and mix well.

INGREDIENTS TO SERVE FOUR:
2 large onions
4 slices (50 g) bacon
2 cups (100 g) fresh bread crumbs
1 small tart apple
2 tablespoons (30 ml) chopped sage
or 2 teaspoons (10 ml) dried sage
salt
pepper

Onion and Caper Sauce

This creamy onion sauce, flavored with mustard and capers, is particularly good with lamb or beef.

Peel and finely chop 2 onions. In a saucepan heat 2 tablespoons of margarine with 1 tablespoon of corn oil. Add the onions and fry over low heat for 5 minutes, until they are soft but not colored.

Stir in 2 tablespoons of flour. Still stirring, gradually add 2 scant cups of milk and bring to the boil. Continue to boil, stirring constantly, until the sauce thickens.

Reduce the heat and stir in 1 teaspoon of Dijon mustard, 1 tablespoon of capers and salt and pepper to taste. Simmer for 5 minutes, stirring occasionally.

Serve hot.

INGREDIENTS TO SERVE FOUR:
2 onions
2 tablespoons (25 g) margarine
1 tablespoon (15 ml) corn oil
2 tablespoons (30 ml) flour
2 scant cups (450 ml) milk
1 teaspoon (5 ml) Dijon mustard
1 tablespoon (15 ml) capers
salt
pepper

Raw Onion Salad

Peel and thinly slice 3 medium-sized onions. Put them into a serving bowl. Thinly slice 3 large tomatoes and 1 cucumber and add to the onions.

Cut 2 green chilies into halves and discard the seeds. Chop the chilies and sprinkle them over the salad with 1 tablespoon of chopped coriander leaves. (If you don't like the hotness of chilies use ½ green pepper instead.)

In a small bowl combine 1 tablespoon of wine vinegar, ¼ cup of corn oil and salt and pepper to taste.

Pour the dressing over the salad and toss lightly. Marinate for at least 30 minutes before serving.

INGREDIENTS TO SERVE FOUR TO SIX:
3 medium-sized onions
3 large tomatoes
1 cucumber
2 green chilies or ½ green pepper
1 tablespoon (15 ml) chopped coriander leaves
1 tablespoon (15 ml) wine vinegar
¼ cup (60 ml) corn oil
salt
pepper

SLICING AND CHOPPING ONIONS

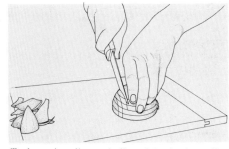

To chop onion, slice vertically and then horizontally.

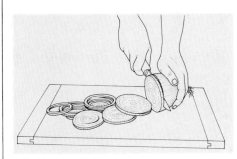

To cut onion rings, slice the onion horizontally.

VEGETABLE FRUIT/The Exotics of the Vegetable World

YOU ARE UNLIKELY to grow fat on vegetable fruit. All except one are more than 90 percent water and contain only the merest trace of fat and very little carbohydrate. The exception is the avocado, which stands out among vegetables (or fruit) because it contains about 17 percent fat. But obesity brought about by a surfeit of avocados must be rare.

Some vegetable fruit have nutritionally little merit except the negative virtue of being non-fattening, but our diet would be the poorer without them. Cucumbers may be 97 percent water, but what deliciously flavored water. And the equally moist zucchini certainly serves as a tasty and convenient container for stuffing.

The vegetable fruit that excels all others in flavor is the tomato. Eaten raw it is also a good source of carotene and vitamin C, and is low in calories; half a pound of raw tomatoes provides only 35 Calories. As vegetables go the tomato is a comparative newcomer. Its original home was Mexico and Peru and it was introduced into Europe only in the mid-sixteenth century, first into Italy and then spreading northward through France. When it reached England the tomato was admired for its decorativeness but mistrusted as food, possibly because of its association with other members of its family—not only the then still suspect potato and the tobacco plant, but the poisonous mandrake and deadly nightshade. And it was not until the middle of the nineteenth century that the tomato became generally accepted in the United States.

Depending on the variety and where they are grown there are great differences in the flavor and the degree of sweetness or acidity of tomatoes. Under a hot sun they grow large and sweet. The sweet Italian tomatoes are outstanding; they are, indeed, the only canned vegetable worth eating.

Unhappily, as tomatoes have become more popular over the past thirty years they have deteriorated in flavor because, for commercial reasons, the sole aim of growers is to obtain heavy yields of tomatoes with tough skins so that they travel well. It is not even easy to find the older varieties to grow yourself, but it is worth trying. Eating a tomato when it is freshly picked from the garden, the greenhouse or even from a window box is an experience that can never be obtained from one bought in a store. With such a poor choice of good tomatoes it is unfortunate that there is a prejudice against yellow tomatoes, the skins of which are softer and the flesh sweeter.

The more you enjoy a food the more perfection you demand. In honesty it has to be admitted that there are tomatoes, eaten raw, that are dis-appointing. Happily the tomato is versatile when it is cooked—in soups, sauces, stews, soufflés or stuffed in endless ways. It must be remembered, however, that if they are fried, the cooking oil may increase the calorific value of the tomatoes by as much as five times.

For many thousands of years the world has been divided into cucumber-eaters and cucumber-haters. The case against cucumbers was summed up by the erudite third-century writer on food Athenaeus: "The cucumber is hard to digest and to purge from the system, moreover it causes chilliness, provokes bile and inhibits coition." With care these dangers—at least about indi-gestibility—can be avoided. If you grow your own cucumbers you can choose the new variety of the easily cultivated ridge cucumber which has the self-explanatory name of Burpless, or the white cucumber, which is popular in Europe. All

Vegetable fruit are full of flavor, and, with the exception of avocados, they are low in calories. Clockwise below: a golden pumpkin to cook in a pie or casserole; tomatoes, a good source of vitamins A and C; hot chilis for flavoring; avocados, a useful source of B vitamins; green peppers, packed with vitamin C; zucchini, the most flavorful of squashes; refreshing cucumbers; and eggplant, only low in calories if they are not cooked in oil.

cucumbers can be made less indigestible by thinly slicing the unpeeled cucumber, sprinkling it with salt and then after about an hour pouring off the resulting liquid. Only then do you add dressing, preferably a sharp one to contrast with the clean sweetness of the cucumber.

The old herbalists set great store by the health-giving properties of cucumber, but we scarcely eat enough for them to be regarded as nutritionally important. Even their vitamin C is often wasted through peeling. But the cucumber, raw or cooked, has a unique flavor.

Sweet peppers are the only other popular vegetable fruit that can be enjoyed both raw and cooked; squashes, pumpkins and eggplant are totally unpalatable when they are raw. The peppers used as a vegetable are the milder varieties of *Capsicum annuum*. They are eaten immature and green or when they have ripened to a striking redness and taste sweeter and less pungent.

Varieties of *Capsicum annuum*, some mild, some hot, are dried and ground to make paprika, especially in Hungary and Spain. The small, hot, red peppers, or chilis, which are the fruits of *Capsicum frutescens*, are used not as a vegetable but for flavoring or making into red, or cayenne, pepper. None of the capsicums have any connection with the plant *Piper nigrum* that provides us with black and white pepper.

Mature squashes are best thought of as nutritionally harmless containers in which to stuff and cook more interesting food, for they have but little nourishment or flavor of their own. But picked in their infancy as zucchini and gently fried they are a most subtle-tasting vegetable. Pumpkins are more nourishing than squashes, but in pumpkin pie their simple health-giving qualities get rather lost among the pastry, eggs, sugar and spices. It is not every day, however, that you have Thanksgiving.

Eggplant is more potentially treacherous, because of the insatiable way in which it soaks up the olive oil or butter in which it is cooked. The dish known as Iman Bayildi requires vast amounts of oil and serves as a warning. The story goes that when the *iman*, or priest, married a girl who was unrivaled in cooking eggplant he asked for her dowry to be given in twelve large jars of olive oil to cook them in. In the first eleven nights of their marriage the eggplant had used up all the dowry. On being told the news the *iman* fainted. He could have suffered a worse fate—saturation with saturated fat.

The Nutrients in Vegetable Fruit
Vegetable fruit are largely water. Three and a half ounces (100 g) of tomatoes, for example, provide 15 Calories.

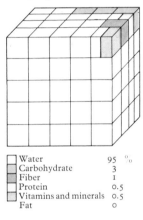

Water	95 %
Carbohydrate	3
Fiber	1
Protein	0.5
Vitamins and minerals	0.5
Fat	0

Sweet peppers (left) are red when ripe, green when less mature. An exceptionally good source of vitamin C, they contain about six times as much as tomatoes. Peppers add a pleasant smoky pungency to stews and casseroles and can be stuffed, but they are better nutritionally eaten raw in salads, so that none of the water-soluble vitamin C is lost in cooking.

Tomato and Rosemary Soup

This delicious hot soup may be made from tomatoes that are too ripe and soft to use for a salad.

Put 4 medium-sized very ripe tomatoes into a saucepan. Add 1 chopped large onion and 3 cups of peeled and diced potatoes. Grate in the rind of ½ lemon and then squeeze in the juice. Pour in 2½ cups of well-seasoned chicken or vegetable stock with 4 rosemary sprigs and salt and pepper to taste. Cover the pan and simmer the soup gently for 30 minutes, or until the tomatoes are very soft.

Sieve the soup or blend it and then strain it to remove the tomato seeds.

Return the puréed soup to the pan, reheat it and adjust the seasoning to taste.

INGREDIENTS TO SERVE FOUR:
4 medium-sized ripe tomatoes
1 large onion
3 cups (350 g) peeled diced potatoes
½ lemon
2½ cups (600 ml) well-seasoned chicken or vegetable stock
4 rosemary sprigs
salt
pepper

Tomato Sauce

Heat 1 tablespoon of corn oil in a saucepan. Add 1 chopped slice of bacon, 1 chopped small onion, 1 chopped small carrot and ½ stalk of celery, chopped. Fry over low heat for 5 minutes, stirring frequently, until the vegetables have softened but are not colored.

Cut 4 medium-sized ripe tomatoes into halves. Add the tomatoes to the pan with 1¼ cups of well-seasoned beef or vegetable stock, the grated rind of ½ lemon, 1 bay leaf and salt and pepper to taste. Cover the pan and simmer over very low heat for 30 minutes.

Sieve the sauce or blend and then strain it.

Return the puréed sauce to the pan and reheat it, adjusting the seasoning to taste.

INGREDIENTS TO MAKE TWO CUPS (600 ML) OF SAUCE:
1 tablespoon (15 ml) corn oil
1 slice bacon
1 small onion
1 small carrot
½ celery stalk
4 medium-sized ripe tomatoes
1¼ cups (300 ml) beef or vegetable stock
½ lemon
1 bay leaf
salt
pepper

Tomato and Mint Water Ice

Frozen into a water ice, tomatoes flavored with lemon and mint make a refreshing start to a meal.

Cut 6 medium-sized ripe tomatoes into quarters. Put them into a saucepan with 1 chopped small onion and the grated rind and juice of ½ lemon. Add 4 large sprigs of mint, 2 teaspoons of Worcestershire sauce and salt and pepper. Cover the pan and cook over very low heat for 10 minutes, or until the tomatoes are soft.

Blend the mixture until it is smooth, then sieve it to remove the tomato skins and seeds. Adjust the seasoning. Set aside to cool.

Pour the tomato mixture into a rigid container, cover it tightly and freeze it until it is solid.

Remove the water ice from the freezer and leave it at room temperature for 15 minutes to soften slightly so that the ice can be spooned out or crushed.

Pile the water ice into individual bowls, garnish with sprigs of mint and serve immediately.

INGREDIENTS TO SERVE FOUR:
6 medium-sized ripe tomatoes
1 small onion
½ lemon
8 mint sprigs
2 teaspoons (10 ml) Worcestershire sauce
salt
pepper

PREPARING TOMATOES

Blanch tomatoes in boiling water and peel.

Cut the tomato in half and scoop out the seeds.

Baked Stuffed Eggplant

First make the stuffing. Heat 1 tablespoon of olive oil in a large saucepan. Chop 2 large onions and fry them, stirring frequently, for 5 minutes, or until they are soft and translucent.

Blanch and peel 2 medium-sized tomatoes. Cut the tomatoes in half and remove the seeds. Coarsely chop the tomatoes and add them to the pan.

Preheat the oven to 350°F (180°C).

Cut 2 large eggplant into halves lengthwise. Scoop out the flesh, chop it and add it to the pan. Reserve the shells. Simmer over low heat for 10 minutes, then stir in 1 tablespoon of chopped parsley and salt and pepper to taste.

Divide the filling between the 4 shells. Put the eggplants in a lightly greased, ovenproof dish. Cover with foil and bake for 40 minutes. Serve immediately.

INGREDIENTS TO SERVE FOUR:
1 tablespoon (15 ml) olive oil
2 large onions
2 medium-sized tomatoes
2 large eggplant
1 tablespoon (15 ml) chopped parsley
salt
pepper

Zucchini with Lemon and Herbs

Preheat the oven to 350°F (180°C).

Wash and thickly slice 8 medium-sized zucchini. In a small bowl mix together the grated rind of ½ lemon, 1 tablespoon of chopped parsley, 1 tablespoon of chopped thyme leaves, salt and pepper.

Arrange the zucchini slices in an ovenproof dish, sprinkling each layer with the herb mixture.

Squeeze the juice of the ½ lemon into a small bowl and add 5 tablespoons of chicken stock. Pour the liquid over the zucchini.

Cover and bake for 30 minutes, or until the zucchini are just tender but not soft.

INGREDIENTS TO SERVE FOUR:
8 medium-sized zucchini
½ lemon
1 tablespoon (15 ml) chopped parsley
1 tablespoon (15 ml) chopped thyme
salt
pepper
5 tablespoons (75 ml) chicken stock

Ratatouille

This delicious vegetable casserole is usually cooked in lots of oil. In this recipe, however, the vegetables cook in their own juices for a more concentrated flavor.

Chop 1 large onion and put it into a large saucepan with 1 crushed garlic clove, 3 cups of sliced zucchini and 3 cups of coarsely diced eggplant.

Cut 1 green pepper into quarters lengthwise. Remove the white pith and the seeds. Cut the pepper into eighths and add it to the pan.

Blanch and peel 4 medium-sized tomatoes. Cut them into quarters and remove the seeds.

Add the tomatoes to the pan with 1 tablespoon of dried oregano. Season to taste with salt and pepper.

Cover the pan and cook over very low heat, stirring occasionally, for 30 minutes, or until the vegetables are tender. Serve hot or cold.

INGREDIENTS TO SERVE FOUR:
1 large onion
1 garlic clove
3 cups (500 g) sliced zucchini
3 cups (500 g) coarsely diced eggplant
1 green pepper
4 medium-sized tomatoes
1 tablespoon (15 ml) dried oregano
salt
pepper

PREPARING PEPPERS FOR STUFFING

Carefully cut a lid from the top of the pepper.

Scoop out the pith and the seeds.

Iced Cucumber and Mint Soup

Dice 2 peeled cucumbers into $\frac{1}{2}$-inch (1-cm) cubes, reserving a 2-inch (5-cm) piece for garnish. Put the cucumbers into a saucepan. Peel and chop 1 small onion and 1 small potato and add to the cucumbers in the pan.

Add $2\frac{1}{2}$ cups of chicken stock, the grated rind and juice of 1 large lemon, 2 tablespoons of chopped mint and salt and pepper. Cover the pan and simmer over low heat for 15 to 20 minutes, or until the cucumbers and potato are tender.

Sieve or blend the soup to a smooth purée. Let it cool. Stir in $\frac{2}{3}$ cup of yogurt and adjust the seasoning.

Serve the soup well chilled, garnished with thin slices of the reserved cucumber and sprigs of mint.

INGREDIENTS TO SERVE FOUR:
2 cucumbers
1 small onion
1 small potato
$2\frac{1}{2}$ cups (600 ml) chicken stock
1 large lemon
1 small bunch mint
salt
pepper
$\frac{2}{3}$ cup (150 ml) yogurt

Hot Cucumber Sauce

Serve this sauce with fish.

Melt 2 tablespoons of margarine in a saucepan. Finely chop 1 small onion. Fry it over low heat for 3 minutes, stirring frequently, until it is soft and translucent.

Peel 1 cucumber. Cut the cucumber into $\frac{1}{4}$-inch (6-mm) slices and then dice them. Add the diced cucumber to the onion in the pan. Cover and cook over very low heat for 5 minutes.

Stir in 4 tablespoons of flour. Still stirring, gradually add $1\frac{1}{4}$ cups of milk. Then add 1 tablespoon of chopped mint and salt and pepper. Bring the sauce to the boil, stirring. Reduce the heat and simmer for 1 minute.

Serve hot.

INGREDIENTS TO SERVE FOUR:
2 tablespoons (30 ml) margarine
1 small onion
1 cucumber
4 tablespoons (60 ml) flour
$1\frac{1}{4}$ cups (150 ml) milk
1 tablespoon (15 ml) chopped mint
salt
pepper

Chilled Avocado Soup

Cut 2 large ripe avocados into halves and remove the seeds. Scoop out the flesh and put it into a blender with the juice of $\frac{1}{2}$ lemon, $2\frac{1}{2}$ cups of well-seasoned chicken stock and $\frac{2}{3}$ cup of yogurt. Season to taste with salt and pepper. Blend until the ingredients are smooth.

Pour the soup into a bowl or a tureen. Cover and chill it well before serving. (To keep the soup from discoloring, add the avocado seeds to the soup and remove them just before serving.)

Serve the soup cold, garnished with 2 tablespoons of chopped chives.

INGREDIENTS TO SERVE FOUR:
2 large ripe avocados
$\frac{1}{2}$ lemon
$2\frac{1}{2}$ cups (600 ml) well-seasoned chicken stock
$\frac{2}{3}$ cup (150 ml) yogurt
salt
pepper
2 tablespoons (30 ml) chopped chives

Avocado Mousse

This smooth, pale-green mousse makes an appetizing start to a meal.

Pour $1\frac{1}{4}$ cups of strong, well-seasoned chicken stock into a blender. Add $\frac{2}{3}$ cup of yogurt, $\frac{1}{4}$ lb of pot cheese, the grated rind and juice of $\frac{1}{2}$ lemon and $\frac{1}{2}$ small onion.

Cut 2 large ripe avocados into halves and remove the seeds. Scoop out all the flesh and add it to the other ingredients.

Blend until the mixture is smooth. In a cup set in a pan of hot water dissolve $\frac{1}{2}$ ounce of powdered gelatin in 2 tablespoons of cold water. Pour the dissolved gelatin into the mousse. Blend for 10 seconds more.

Pour the mousse into a 4-cup soufflé dish or mold. Chill in the refrigerator until set. Serve in the dish or unmold just before serving.

INGREDIENTS TO SERVE FOUR:
$1\frac{1}{4}$ cups (300 ml) strong well-seasoned chicken stock
$\frac{2}{3}$ cup (150 ml) yogurt
$\frac{1}{4}$ lb (100 g) pot cheese
$\frac{1}{2}$ lemon
$\frac{1}{2}$ small onion
2 large ripe avocados
$\frac{1}{2}$ oz (15 g) powdered gelatin

Summer Squash and Tomato Casserole

Preheat the oven to 350°F (180°C).

Peel a large summer squash, about 2 pounds. Cut it in half and scoop out the seeds from the center. Cut the squash into cubes, about 1 inch (2 cm) square. Blanch and peel 3 medium-sized tomatoes and cut them into quarters. Chop 1 medium-sized onion.

Arrange layers of squash, tomato and onion in a casserole, sprinkling each layer with salt and pepper. Top with ½ cup of grated Gruyère cheese.

Cover the casserole and bake for 20 minutes. Uncover the casserole and bake for 15 minutes more.

INGREDIENTS TO SERVE FOUR:
1 summer squash, about 2 pounds (1 kg)
3 medium-sized tomatoes
1 medium-sized onion
salt
pepper
½ cup (50 g) grated Gruyère cheese

Pumpkin Ring

Make this unusual vegetable dish in a ring mold and fill the center with cooked peas, tiny whole onions or mushrooms.

Preheat the oven to 350°F (180°C).

Cut a 3-pound pumpkin in half. Remove the seeds, the stringy portion and the outside shell. Cut the pumpkin flesh into small pieces and put them into a saucepan. Add boiling water to cover and cook, covered, for 20 minutes, or until the pumpkin is tender. Drain the pumpkin and mash it well.

Served with diced cucumber, tomato and green pepper for garnish, Gazpacho is a delicious cold soup to serve on a hot day.

Beat in 4 tablespoons of melted butter or margarine, ¼ cup of milk and ¼ cup of fresh bread crumbs. Beat 3 eggs and add them to the pumpkin. Grate 1 small onion and add it with salt and pepper to taste. Mix well.

Put the mixture into a buttered 1-quart (850-ml) ring mold. Put the mold into a roasting pan half-filled with hot water. Bake for 45 minutes, or until the pumpkin is firm.

Turn out onto a serving dish.

INGREDIENTS TO SERVE SIX TO EIGHT:
3-lb pumpkin
4 tablespoons (60 ml) butter or margarine
¼ cup (50 ml) milk
¼ cup (25 g) fresh bread crumbs
3 eggs
1 small onion
salt
pepper

Peperonata

Heat 1 tablespoon of olive oil in a large, heavy frying pan. Slice 1 large onion. Add it to the pan and cook over low heat for 3 minutes.

Cut 4 medium-sized green peppers into halves lengthwise. Remove the seeds and pith. Cut the peppers into long narrow strips and add them to the onion in the pan. Cover and cook over low heat for 10 minutes, stirring occasionally.

Blanch and peel 3 medium-sized tomatoes. Cut the tomatoes into quarters and add them to the pan. Cover and simmer gently for 20 minutes, or until the tomatoes have reduced to a sauce around the peppers. Add pepper and salt to taste. Serve hot or cold.

INGREDIENTS TO SERVE FOUR:
1 tablespoon (15 ml) olive oil
1 large onion
4 medium-sized green peppers
3 medium-sized tomatoes
pepper
salt

Gazpacho

This famous cold "salad" soup from Spain is very easy to make. In warm weather, put a few ice cubes into the soup before serving it, to keep it cool.

Blanch and peel 4 ripe medium-sized tomatoes. Cut the tomatoes into halves and remove the seeds. Reserve 1 tomato half and put the remainder into a blender. Chop 1 small onion and add it to the tomatoes with 1 garlic clove. Cut 1 large green pepper in half, remove the pith and the seeds. Reserve a quarter of the pepper and coarsely chop the rest of it. Add it to the blender. Slice 1½ cucumbers and add them to the other

ingredients with 1 tablespoon of wine vinegar and the grated rind and juice of 1 small lemon.

Blend all the ingredients until the mixture is smooth. Pour the soup into a tureen or a bowl and stir in enough cold water to give a "creamy" consistency. Chill well.

Finely dice ½ cucumber and the reserved tomato and green pepper and serve with the soup.

INGREDIENTS TO SERVE FOUR:
4 ripe medium-sized tomatoes
1 small onion
1 garlic clove
1 large green pepper
2 cucumbers
1 tablespoon (15 ml) wine vinegar
1 small lemon

Stuffed Peppers

Preheat the oven to 375 F (190 C).

First prepare the filling. Cook ¾ cup of brown rice in 1¼ cups of water for 30 minutes, or until the rice is tender and the water has been absorbed.

Blanch and peel 2 tomatoes. Cut them into halves and remove the seeds. Chop the tomatoes and put them into a mixing bowl with the cooked rice.

Add ½ cup of cooked and shelled shrimp, 1 large onion, finely chopped or grated, 1 small can of anchovies, drained, and 1 crushed garlic clove. Add 1 tablespoon of chopped parsley, 1 tablespoon of chopped thyme leaves, 8 sliced stuffed olives and salt and pepper. Mix well.

Cut a slice off the tops of 4 green peppers. Remove the white pith and the seeds. Put the peppers upright, cutting a small slice off the bottom if necessary, in an ovenproof dish or small roasting pan. Divide the filling among the peppers.

Pour 5 tablespoons of vegetable or chicken stock around the peppers. Cover the dish with foil. Bake for 30 to 40 minutes, or until the peppers are done.

Serve hot or cold.

INGREDIENTS TO SERVE FOUR:
¾ cup (125 g) brown rice
2 tomatoes
½ cup (100 g) cooked, shelled shrimp
1 large onion
1 small can anchovies
1 garlic clove
1 tablespoon (15 ml) chopped parsley
1 tablespoon (15 ml) chopped thyme
8 stuffed olives
4 green peppers
5 tablespoons (75 ml) vegetable or chicken stock

A rich filling, varied in flavor and texture, transforms Stuffed Peppers into a tasty dish for lunch or supper.

THERE MAY BE more nutritious vegetables than the stalks and shoots we eat, but few are as delicious. They come from many plant families. Asparagus, for example, is a lily, artichokes and cardoons are thistles and various chards are from the beet family. Their flavors are just as diverse as their classification.

Celery, now one of the most flavorsome of these vegetables, was used in the Middle Ages mainly as medicine, since at that time it was appropriately bitter and evil-smelling. Then Italian gardeners took it in hand and developed it into an acceptable vegetable, which became popular throughout Europe in the seventeenth and eighteenth centuries. It was the Italians who began the technique of blanching, which involves banking up the soil to cover the celery stalks as they grow so that they become sweet and crisp. Celeriac is the version of celery grown as a root, but the stalks can be cooked and eaten like those of sea kale. Although neither celery nor celeriac rates high in the nutritional charts, they taste good

—and that is really quite enough in this case.

Asparagus, however, contains a considerable amount of protein, a fair amount of ascorbic acid and is exceptionally rich in folic acid (although much of the vitamin content is lost in cooking). There are cheaper ways of satisfying these nutritional requirements, but there is no other way of enjoying the flavor of asparagus. What we eat are the immature shoots, which appear in the spring and grow into ferns if they are not picked.

Self-sufficiency enthusiasts could use the young shoots of elder, or even of hops, in the same way. A far more rewarding substitute for asparagus was grown in English cottage gardens for centuries, but is not now widely cultivated. The early colonists took it to America, but it is now neglected here, too. Among the many names of this plant are Poor Man's Asparagus and Good King Henry. (Henry VIII was supposed to have eaten it to bring relief to his painful legs.) The young blanched shoots are used as asparagus, the leaves as spinach and the flower buds as them-

SUCCULENT BAMBOO SHOOTS

The edible shoots of bamboo are cut soon after they emerge through the soil, but usually when they are longer than asparagus spears and three inches (8 cm) or more in diameter. Their flavor makes up for their nutritional value, for they have little except small amounts of vitamin C. The tender winter shoots, which taste somewhat like artichokes, are considered to have the best flavor. Unfortunately, since bamboo shoots are grown mainly in Southeast Asia, people in the West are unlikely to taste them fresh and must be content to eat those which have been canned.

The young shoots, or spears, of asparagus are richer in protein and flavor than are most stalks and shoots. In Britain and America, where green-tipped asparagus are preferred, the spears are allowed to grow several inches above ground (right) before being cut. The French and Germans, however, like white asparagus, so they cut the spears below the soil just as the tips emerge through the soil.

selves. Their nutritional distinction is that, for vegetables, they are rich in iron.

Artichokes were introduced into England in the seventeenth century but never became popular. They are expensive to buy and harder to grow in the English climate than in southern Europe and in California, where they flourish with the abandon of weeds. As an inconvenience food the artichoke is outstanding. Each scale of the many-layered "globe" has to be broken off, dipped in a sauce to enhance the flavor and sucked to extract what little flesh there is inside it. That done, you are confronted with the center, or choke, of tightly packed stamens, which have to be removed cleanly with a knife or fork. Beneath the choke is the really delectable heart, or fond.

Artichokes, like many other plants, can be used to produce chards, a name confusingly applied not only to forced, blanched shoots, but also to the midribs of leaves of sea kale beet, which is also known as Swiss chard. Raw or boiled, it is a delicious winter vegetable.

The nutty-tasting cardoon, a close relative of the artichoke, also provides forced stalks in winter, but they are more likely to be found on the Continent than in Britain or in the United States. Their flavor vaguely suggests both artichoke and celery. To enjoy the chards of young stems of salsify and scorzonera you may have to grow these root vegetables yourself; it is quite easy to do so.

The bulbous stem base of Florence fennel has a sweet aniseed flavor and is milder, but even sweeter, when cooked as a vegetable than when used as flavoring or eaten raw in salads. The Greeks believed it made them slim, courageous and long-lived and improved their eyesight. Pliny saw another virtue in it; since the stems are light, they made excellent walking sticks for the aged.

The fruits of many plants are used as vegetables, but rhubarb is a vegetable which is usually used as a fruit. The Poles, however, mix rhubarb and potatoes as a vegetable dish.

The Nutrients in Stalks and Shoots
These are low in calories. Three and a half ounces (100 g) of celery, for example, provide 15 Calories.

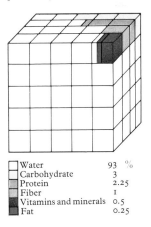

☐ Water	93 %
☐ Carbohydrate	3
☐ Protein	2.25
☐ Fiber	1
☐ Vitamins and minerals	0.5
■ Fat	0.25

Delicious low-calorie vegetables, stalks and shoots such as celery (far left) and Florence fennel (left) also add crunch and flavor to salads. Asparagus (far left) and artichokes (left) must be cooked.

Rhubarb, although a vegetable, is eaten as a fruit. It is a pity that the oxalic acid in the stalks makes rhubarb so sour, because if it could be eaten without sugar it would contain only 1 Calorie per ounce.

Fennel Braised with Tomato

Wash 2 fennel bulbs, then cut them into quarters lengthwise. Put the fennel into a saucepan with 4 blanched, peeled and chopped large tomatoes and $\frac{1}{4}$ cup of water. Grate in the rind of 1 lemon, then add the squeezed juice, 1 teaspoon of dried oregano and salt and pepper to taste.

Bring to the boil, cover the pan, reduce the heat and simmer gently, stirring occasionally, for about 30 minutes, or until the fennel is tender.

Stir in 1 tablespoon of chopped mint. Serve hot.

INGREDIENTS TO SERVE FOUR:
2 fennel bulbs
4 large tomatoes
1 lemon
1 teaspoon (5 ml) dried oregano
salt
pepper
1 tablespoon (15 ml) chopped mint

Fennel Braised with Apple

Preheat the oven to 350°F (180°C).

Wash 2 large fennel bulbs and cut them into quarters lengthwise. Put the fennel into a casserole or ovenproof dish.

Peel and core 1 large tart apple. Cut the apple into slices and put the slices into the casserole with $\frac{2}{3}$ cup of chicken stock, 1 tablespoon of lemon juice and salt and pepper to taste.

Cover and bake for 30 minutes, or until the fennel is tender but not soft.

Fennel Braised with Apple makes an ideal accompaniment to pork or fish.

Drain the stock off into a saucepan and boil it for about 3 minutes, or until it is reduced to 3 tablespoons. Pour the sauce over the fennel, sprinkle with 1 tablespoon of chopped parsley and serve.

INGREDIENTS TO SERVE FOUR:
2 large fennel bulbs
1 large tart apple
$\frac{2}{3}$ cup (150 ml) chicken stock
1 tablespoon (15 ml) lemon juice
salt
pepper
1 tablespoon (15 ml) chopped parsley

Fennel Salad

First make the dressing. Pour $\frac{2}{3}$ cup of yogurt into a large salad bowl. Stir in 1 tablespoon of lemon juice and salt and pepper to taste.

Wash 2 medium-sized fennel bulbs and cut them into thin slices. Put the fennel slices into the salad bowl with the dressing. Slice 4 medium-sized tomatoes and add them to the fennel. Cut $\frac{1}{2}$ cucumber into slices and then into quarters and add to the salad.

Toss well, until all the ingredients are coated with the yogurt dressing.

INGREDIENTS TO SERVE FOUR:
$\frac{2}{3}$ cup (150 ml) yogurt
1 tablespoon (15 ml) lemon juice
salt
pepper
2 medium-sized fennel bulbs
4 medium-sized tomatoes
$\frac{1}{2}$ cucumber

Asparagus

To appreciate the real flavor of asparagus it is best to cook it very gently and then serve it simply with melted margarine or butter or a yogurt hollandaise sauce.

Wash 2 pounds—about 24 spears—of asparagus carefully. Using a knife or vegetable peeler, scrape the lower part of the stems. Trim the spears so that they are all the same length, cutting off any tough woody parts at the bottom.

Tie the asparagus together—at the base and just below the tips—in bundles of about 12 spears.

The best way to cook asparagus is in a special asparagus steamer—a tall, narrow saucepan which contains a basket in which the stalks cook in boiling water while the tips cook in the steam. You can, however, easily improvise by putting the bundles of asparagus upright into a jar covered with perforated foil. Immerse the jar in a pan of simmering water and cook for 20 to 30 minutes, just until the stalks and tips are tender, but not limp.

When the asparagus is cooked, remove the bundles from the pan, drain them, put them on serving dishes and remove the strings.

Serve the asparagus hot with individual bowls of melted margarine or butter flavored with lemon juice, chopped parsley and salt and pepper or with a yogurt hollandaise sauce (see page 93). Asparagus may also be served cold with a vinaigrette dressing (see page 153).

INGREDIENTS TO SERVE FOUR:
2 lb (1 kg) asparagus
$\frac{3}{4}$ cup (150 g) margarine or butter, lemon juice, parsley, salt and pepper or
$\frac{2}{3}$ cup (150 ml) yogurt hollandaise sauce (see page 93) or
$\frac{2}{3}$ cup (150 ml) basic vinaigrette dressing (see page 153)

Cream of Asparagus Soup

Wash and scrape the woody stalks of 1 pound of asparagus. Cut off some of the tips and reserve for the garnish. Chop the remaining asparagus.

Melt 2 tablespoons of margarine in a large saucepan. Add 1 chopped medium-sized onion to the pan and fry for 3 minutes, or until it is soft and translucent. Then stir in 4 tablespoons of flour. Stirring constantly, gradually add 4 cups of chicken stock and bring to the boil. Add the chopped asparagus. Cover the pan, reduce the heat and simmer for 20 minutes, or until the asparagus is tender.

Meanwhile, cook the reserved asparagus tips separately in a little simmering water for 5 to 10 minutes, or until they are just tender. Drain the tips.

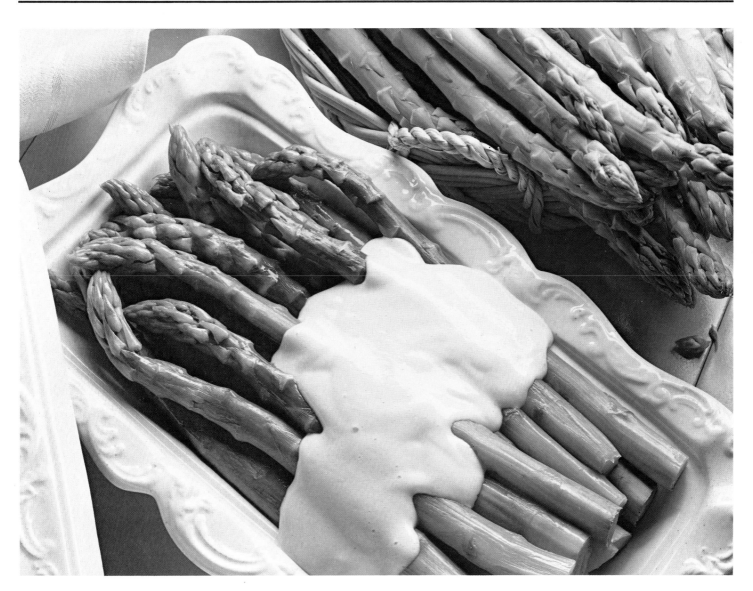

A truly gourmet dish, asparagus served with Yogurt Hollandaise Sauce.

When the asparagus is cooked, blend the soup or sieve it and then return it to the pan. Stir in $\frac{2}{3}$ cup of milk, 1 teaspoon of lemon juice and salt and pepper to taste. Reheat but do not boil.

Serve hot or cold, garnished with the asparagus tips.

INGREDIENTS TO SERVE FOUR TO SIX:
1 lb (500 g) asparagus spears
2 tablespoons (25 g) margarine
1 medium-sized onion
4 tablespoons (25 g) flour
4 cups (850 ml) chicken stock
$\frac{2}{3}$ cup (150 ml) milk
1 teaspoon (5 ml) lemon juice
salt
pepper

Asparagus Quiche

This quiche may be served hot or cold, but it is probably at its best about 1 hour after it is baked, when it is still warm.

Preheat the oven to 400°F (200°C).

Make 1$\frac{1}{2}$ cups of shortcrust pastry with whole-wheat flour (see page 34). Line an 8-inch (20-cm) flan ring or pie pan with the pastry. Bake the pastry blind for 15 minutes. Remove the waxed paper and the beans and bake for 5 minutes more.

Reduce the oven temperature to 350°F (180°C).

Meanwhile, cook 8 large or 12 small spears of asparagus until they are just tender. Drain them well. Arrange the asparagus in the pie shell with the spears radiating out from the center like spokes of a wheel. Trim the asparagus stalks if necessary and reserve to add to the filling.

For the filling, beat together 2 eggs, $\frac{2}{3}$ cup of light cream or milk, the grated rind of $\frac{1}{2}$ lemon and salt and pepper to taste. Finely

chop the reserved asparagus stalks and add them. Pour the filling over the asparagus, then sprinkle it with 1 tablespoon of grated Parmesan cheese.

Bake for 25 to 30 minutes, or until the filling is set.

Garnish the center of the quiche where the spears meet with 2 twists of lemon.

INGREDIENTS TO SERVE FOUR TO SIX:
1$\frac{1}{2}$ cups (150 g) shortcrust pastry made with whole-wheat flour (see page 34)
8 large or 12 small asparagus spears
2 eggs
$\frac{2}{3}$ cup (150 ml) light cream or milk
1 lemon
salt
pepper
1 tablespoon (15 ml) grated Parmesan cheese

Asparagus au Gratin

Cook 1 pound of asparagus until just tender. Drain the asparagus, reserving the liquid for the sauce. Put the asparagus into a flameproof dish with ⅔ cup of sliced and diced cooked ham and 1 cup of sliced mushrooms which have been lightly poached and drained.

For the sauce, melt 2 tablespoons of margarine in a small saucepan. Stir in 4 tablespoons of flour. Stirring constantly, gradually add 1¼ cups of milk and 4 tablespoons of the reserved cooking liquid. Bring to the boil, stirring constantly, until the sauce is smooth and has thickened. Add 1 teaspoon of lemon juice and salt and pepper to taste. Simmer the sauce for 1 minute, then pour it over the asparagus. Sprinkle with 2 tablespoons of grated Parmesan cheese. Put the dish under a hot broiler for 5 minutes, or until the sauce is brown and bubbling.

INGREDIENTS TO SERVE FOUR:
1 lb (500 g) asparagus
⅔ cup (100 g) sliced cooked ham
1 cup (100 g) sliced mushrooms
2 tablespoons (25 g) margarine
4 tablespoons (25 g) flour
1¼ cups (300 ml) milk
1 teaspoon (5 ml) lemon juice
salt
pepper
2 tablespoons (30 ml) grated Parmesan cheese

COOKING ASPARAGUS

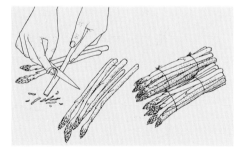

Scrape, trim and tie asparagus stalks in bundles.

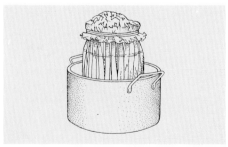

You can improvise if you do not have an asparagus pan.

Celery Soup

Separate the stalks of 1 head of celery. Wash them well. Reserve some of the inner leaves for garnish and coarsely chop the rest with the stalks.

Put the chopped celery into a saucepan with 1 chopped large onion and ½ pound of potatoes that have been peeled and coarsely chopped. Add 2½ cups of well-seasoned chicken or vegetable stock, the grated rind of ½ lemon and salt and pepper to taste.

Bring to the boil, cover, reduce the heat and simmer for 30 minutes, or until the celery and potatoes are tender. Blend or sieve the vegetables to a purée.

Return the soup to the pan. Stir in 1¼ cups of milk. Reheat, but do not boil. Adjust the seasoning. Serve sprinkled with 4 tablespoons of grated Cheddar cheese and the reserved celery leaves.

INGREDIENTS TO SERVE FOUR:
1 head celery
1 large onion
½ lb (250 g) potatoes
2½ cups (600 ml) chicken or vegetable stock
½ lemon
salt
pepper
1¼ cups (300 ml) milk
4 tablespoons (25 g) grated Cheddar cheese

Celery Provençal

Wash a large head of celery. Drain it well and cut it into 2-inch (5-cm) lengths. Blanch, peel and coarsely chop 6 ripe medium-sized tomatoes. Finely chop 8 anchovies.

Put the celery, tomatoes and anchovies into a saucepan with 8 pitted black olives and ⅔ cup of boiling water.

Cover the pan and simmer over low heat for 20 minutes, or until the celery is cooked but still crisp. Uncover the pan and simmer for 5 minutes to reduce the sauce.

Serve hot.

INGREDIENTS TO SERVE FOUR:
1 large head celery
6 ripe medium-sized tomatoes
8 anchovies
8 pitted black olives

Celery Salad

This crunchy salad in an orange dressing is ideal to serve in the winter months, when there are fewer salad ingredients available.

Separate the stalks from ½ large celery head or from 1 small celery head. Wash and drain them. Squeeze 1 tablespoon of lemon juice into a bowl.

Slice the celery stalks and put them into a salad bowl with ⅓ cup of seedless raisins and 3 tablespoons of chopped walnuts.

Cut 1 large apple into quarters and remove the core. Chop the apple coarsely. Toss the chopped apple in the lemon juice to keep it from browning, then add the apple to the salad.

For the dressing, beat together the remaining lemon juice with the grated rind and juice of 1 orange, 3 tablespoons of corn oil and salt and pepper.

Pour the dressing over the salad and toss well. Garnish with a few celery leaves.

INGREDIENTS TO SERVE FOUR:
½ large or 1 small head celery
1 tablespoon (15 ml) lemon juice
⅓ cup (50 g) seedless raisins
3 tablespoons (25 g) chopped walnuts
1 large apple
1 orange
3 tablespoons (45 ml) corn oil
salt
pepper

Rhubarb Crumble

The crumble topping for this dish is made with rolled oats instead of flour.

Preheat the oven to 375°F (190°C).

Wash 1 pound of rhubarb and cut the stalks into 1-inch (2-cm) lengths.

Put the rhubarb into a deep pie pan or baking dish. Add 2 tablespoons of sugar and the juice of ½ orange and mix well.

For the topping, put 1¼ cups of rolled oats into a mixing bowl. Add ¼ cup of margarine or butter, ⅓ cup of brown sugar and 1 teaspoon of ground cinnamon. Rub the ingredients together with your fingers until well mixed. Spoon the topping on top of the rhubarb.

Bake for 30 to 40 minutes, or until the topping is golden brown.

INGREDIENTS TO SERVE FOUR:
1 lb (500 g) rhubarb
2 tablespoons (30 ml) sugar
½ orange
1¼ cups (100 g) rolled oats
¼ cup (50 g) margarine or butter
⅓ cup (50 g) brown sugar
1 teaspoon (5 ml) ground cinnamon

Artichokes

Simply cooked and served hot with a little melted butter or yogurt hollandaise sauce, or cold with mayonnaise or vinaigrette dressing, artichokes are a marvelous dish to choose if you are dieting—it takes a long time to eat very little, but what there is is delicious.

Wash 4 artichokes in salted water. Cut off the stalks at the base of the leaves and pull off any of the outer leaves that are dried or discolored. Use scissors to trim off the points of the outer leaves. Rub the cut surfaces with lemon juice.

The chokes may be removed before or

Trim artichoke stalks and remove the outer leaves.

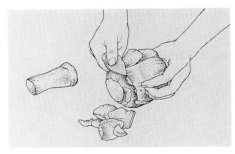

Trim the tops and the leaves of the artichoke.

To remove the choke, pull out the inner leaves.

Scoop out the choke and rub cut areas with lemon.

after cooking. If they are removed before cooking, the artichokes will take less time to cook. To remove the choke, spread the top leaves apart, pull out the small inside leaves to reveal the hairy choke. Scrape away the choke with a teaspoon leaving the heart exposed.

Cook the artichokes, uncovered, in a large pan of boiling salted water until the leaves pull off easily. This will take 20 to 40 minutes, depending on the size and age of the artichokes. Remove the artichokes from the pan and put them upside down on a plate to drain thoroughly.

INGREDIENTS TO SERVE FOUR:
4 artichokes
lemon juice
¾ cup (150 g) margarine or butter or
⅔ cup (150 ml) yogurt hollandaise (see page 93) or
⅔ cup (150 ml) mayonnaise (see page 93) or
⅔ cup (150 ml) basic vinaigrette dressing (see page 53)

Artichoke Heart Salad

Prepare and cook 4 large artichokes. Pull off and discard all the artichoke leaves. Scrape off the choke until you are left with just the artichoke heart.

(The hearts may be removed from the rest of the artichoke before cooking, rubbed with lemon juice to prevent browning and then simmered in water to which a few drops of lemon juice have been added for 15 to 20 minutes, or until tender.)

After the artichoke hearts have cooled, arrange them on lettuce leaves on a serving dish or on individual dishes.

In a mixing bowl, combine ¼ cup of yogurt, 1 teaspoon of lemon juice, 1 tablespoon of chopped chives, salt and pepper. Add 1 cup of shelled cooked shrimp and mix well. Spoon the dressing onto the artichoke hearts and serve.

INGREDIENTS TO SERVE FOUR:
4 large artichokes
lettuce leaves
¼ cup (60 ml) yogurt
1 teaspoon (5 ml) lemon juice
1 tablespoon (15 ml) chopped chives
salt
pepper
1 cup (100 g) shelled cooked shrimp

Stuffed Artichokes

Cook 4 large artichokes in boiling salted water for 20 to 40 minutes, or until the leaves pull off easily. Drain the artichokes and remove the choke and some of the inner leaves so that there is room for the stuffing.

Preheat the oven to 375°F (190°C).

For the stuffing, finely chop 6 slices of bacon and cook in a saucepan until the fat runs. Chop 1 large onion and add it to the bacon. Fry for 5 minutes, stirring frequently, until the onion is soft and translucent. Take the pan from the heat and stir in 1½ cups of fresh bread crumbs, the grated rind and juice of 1 lemon, 1 tablespoon of chopped parsley and salt and pepper to taste. Mix well. Divide the stuffing between the artichokes.

Put the artichokes into an ovenproof dish or roasting pan. Pour 1¼ cups of chicken stock around them. Cover the dish with foil and bake for 20 minutes.

Serve hot.

INGREDIENTS TO SERVE FOUR:
4 large artichokes
salt
6 slices bacon
1 large onion
1½ cups (75 g) fresh bread crumbs
1 lemon
1 tablespoon (15 ml) chopped parsley
pepper
1¼ cups (300 ml) chicken stock

Braised Artichokes with Mushrooms

Cut the stems off 2 artichokes and trim off the tops of the leaves so that the artichokes are about 2 inches (5 cm) high. Cut the artichokes into quarters and remove the choke from each quarter.

Preheat the oven to 350°F (180°C).

Fill a saucepan with salted water. Bring the water to the boil and drop in the artichoke quarters. Simmer for 10 minutes. Drain the artichokes well.

Put the drained artichokes into a casserole with 1¼ cups of chicken stock and 2 tablespoons of lemon juice. Cover and bake for 20 minutes.

Wash ¼ pound of small mushrooms and cut them into quarters. Add the mushrooms to the casserole, stirring them into the liquid. Bake for 10 minutes longer, or until the mushrooms are cooked.

If there is too much liquid, drain it off into a saucepan and boil it for a few minutes until it is reduced. Then pour it over the artichokes.

Serve hot or cold sprinkled with 2 tablespoons of chopped parsley.

INGREDIENTS TO SERVE FOUR:
2 artichokes
salt
1¼ cups (300 ml) chicken stock
2 tablespoons (30 ml) lemon juice
¼ lb (100 g) small mushrooms
2 tablespoons (30 ml) chopped parsley

The Nutrients in Brassicas
These vegetables are high in vitamins and three and a half ounces (100 g) of broccoli, for example, provide only 35 Calories.

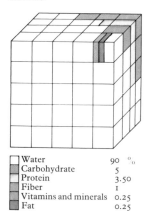

☐ Water	90	%
▨ Carbohydrate	5	
☐ Protein	3.50	
▨ Fiber	1	
▨ Vitamins and minerals	0.25	
▨ Fat	0.25	

IF WE ATE TO PEOPLE'S HEALTH instead of drinking to it the toasts might appropriately be consumed in turnip tops—a daunting thought. It is one of the sadnesses of life that what is particularly good for you is not necessarily desirable, for turnip tops are among the most nutritious, but are the least palatable, of all the eminently worthy green vegetables. Fortunately, there are far more acceptable leaf vegetables and brassicas that contain a wealth of vitamins and minerals.

Some of the carotene in vegetables can be converted into vitamin A in the human body. In the analysis of vegetables, therefore, it is the carotene content that is given rather than the vitamin A value. The amount of carotene in the leaves of vegetables is more or less related to how much of the green pigment chlorophyll they contain. The dark green and tougher outer leaves of cabbage, for example, may have fifty times as much carotene as the white, and more tender, heart.

On most nutritional counts boiled spinach would be the most desirable green vegetable to eat. It has about five grams of protein per hundred grams, about five hundred and ninety-five milligrams of calcium, four milligrams of iron, six milligrams of carotene and twenty-five milligrams of vitamin C, or ascorbic acid. But, unfortunately, spinach also contains a considerable amount of oxalic acid and that locks up the calcium and iron, making them unavailable to the body. It is, of course, still a valuable food as a source of carotene and vitamin C.

One hundred grams of boiled broccoli tops contain one hundred and sixty milligrams of calcium, one and a half milligrams of iron and forty milligrams of vitamin C. Above all, they taste good, especially the variety known as calabrese. Calabrese is available much of the year fresh, and all year round frozen. The coarser white and purple sprouting broccoli are excellent standbys for winter and early spring. Smaller sprigs with thin stalks are more tender, and for best eating the flower buds should be tightly closed.

Kale should probably come next on the list—it is strong in carotene and ascorbic acid and has the ability to survive through bitter winters—but few people enjoy it. It is cultivated mainly as animal feed.

There are other brassicas that may be eaten—and enjoyed—just as well raw as cooked, and as a result their vitamin C content will be much higher. Cauliflower can be chewed after it has been broken into small florets, but cabbage and Brussels sprouts need shredding, and that means losing about one-fifth of the vitamin C through exposure to the air. This, however, is not as bad as the loss brought about by boiling, for vitamin C dissolves in water. Raw cauliflower has seventy milligrams of ascorbic acid in one hundred grams,

ANATOMY OF A BRUSSELS SPROUT

Brussels sprouts, like all the brassicas, are high in sulfur—hence their characteristic smell. They are also high in vitamin C—eaten raw there are about eighty milligrams in one hundred grams. Although the heart (see section below) makes enjoyable eating, it is the darker green outer leaves that contain the most carotene. So discard these sparingly.

and only half of that when it is boiled. Cabbage suffers an even worse loss when it is cooked. Raw it has about fifty milligrams of ascorbic acid and three-quarters of this is lost when it is cooked. Winter cabbage and savoys are higher in calcium than cauliflowers or sprouts and all four are rich in potassium.

The most subtle-tasting and least sulfurous brassica is the Chinese cabbage, although it, too, becomes strong in sulfur when it is old and huge. The Chinese have used this vegetable for fifteen centuries, but it is only now beginning to be appreciated in the West. It is equally good raw or briefly cooked, as in stir-frying, to retain its crispness.

All of the brassicas can suffer at the hands of an unfeeling cook, ending up as a soggy mess of leaves or a mush of curds. Not only are their flavor and texture annihilated, but their nutritional worth is sacrificed. What is needed is a code of conduct for the cooking of cabbage, cauliflower and all the other brassicas.

The wealth of vitamins and minerals in these vegetables is all too easily lost in preparing them for cooking. Leave their preparation until the last possible moment because vitamin C is lost through oxidation and cutting up the vegetables exposes a greater surface to the air and greatly increases vitamin C losses. Above all, never leave cut vegetables standing in water. All you need do is briskly wash off any possible traces of insecticides. The reason is simple: vitamin C is readily soluble in water and will be leached out and minerals may also be lost.

Never put bicarbonate of soda in the water in which vegetables are to be cooked. Although the bicarbonate may make them stay green, all their vitamin C will be lost in the alkaline water.

Cook vegetables in a minimum of boiling, not cold, water. If cold water is used the enzymes which cause oxidization and vitamin loss become very destructive as the temperature rises. Boiling water immediately inactivates these enzymes.

Cover the pan when cooking vegetables in order to cut down on cooking time. Drain them while they still have some bite and as much of their flavor and food value as is possible. There is no danger that they will be indigestible, since most of them are perfectly digestible raw.

Even when you have done everything you can to minimize the loss of vitamins, by the time you serve the vegetables you will probably still have lost up to a half of their vitamin C content and up to 40 percent of their thiamine, riboflavin and niacin content. You will lose still more vitamin C if you do not eat them immediately, but leave them to keep warm on the stove.

For the sake of your taste buds and the good of your health it is worth the time to take a little extra care.

Spinach (above) and such brassicas as cauliflower, cabbage, Chinese cabbage and broccoli (below) are all nutritious vegetables. They contain a wealth of vitamins and minerals and also contribute some protein to the diet. With the exception of spinach, they are important sources of calcium and iron and they all provide valuable amounts of vitamins C, K and carotene and the B vitamins folic acid and riboflavin.

Brussels Sprouts with Chestnuts

Make a small cut through the shells of
½ pound of chestnuts (about 20). Put them
into a large saucepan with enough water to
cover. Bring to the boil and cook until the
shells split. Or the chestnuts may be put on a
baking sheet on the top shelf of a hot oven and
roasted for 5 to 10 minutes, or until the shells
crack.

Drain the chestnuts and peel off the shells
and the inner skins while they are still warm.

Chop 8 slices of bacon and put into a
large saucepan. Fry until the fat runs. Add
the peeled chestnuts and fry, stirring
constantly, for 3 minutes, or until they are
lightly browned.

PREPARING BRUSSELS SPROUTS

Trim the stems and outer leaves of Brussels sprouts.

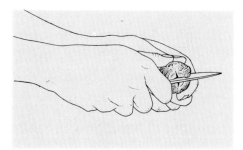

Cut a cross in each stem to ensure even cooking.

Pour in ⅔ cup of chicken or turkey stock.
Reduce the heat, cover the pan and simmer
gently for 20 minutes, or until the chestnuts
are almost tender.

Trim and wash 1 pound of Brussels sprouts
and add them to the pan. Cover the pan and
continue to simmer over low heat for 5 to
10 minutes, or until the chestnuts and sprouts
are just tender. (Add more stock if necessary.)
Serve immediately.

INGREDIENTS TO SERVE FOUR TO SIX:
½ lb (250 g) chestnuts
8 slices bacon
⅔ cup (150 ml) chicken or turkey stock
1 lb (500 g) Brussels sprouts

Brussels Sprouts and Green Grapes

Trim the outer leaves from 1 pound of
Brussels sprouts and wash them thoroughly.
Steam them in about 1 inch (2 cm) of boiling
water for 10 to 12 minutes, or until they are
just done. Season them with salt and pepper.

When the sprouts are tender, add ½ pound
of seedless green grapes. Cook just until the
grapes look plump and are hot.

Drain the sprouts and grapes well and put
them into a serving bowl. Add 2 tablespoons
of butter or margarine. Toss lightly until the
butter or margarine is melted. Serve
immediately.

INGREDIENTS TO SERVE FOUR:
1 lb (500 g) Brussels sprouts
salt
pepper
½ pound (250 g) seedless green grapes
2 tablespoons (30 ml) butter or
      margarine

Brussels Salad

Trim and wash 1 pound of Brussels sprouts.
Put them into a large saucepan with a little
boiling salted water and cook for 5 minutes,
or until they are tender but still crisp. Drain
and cool.

Core and slice 2 apples. Toss the slices
immediately in 1 tablespoon of lemon juice to
keep them from turning brown. Add them
to the sprouts with ⅓ cup of chopped walnuts.

In a small bowl combine 1 tablespoon of
wine vinegar with ¼ cup of corn oil, salt and
freshly ground black pepper. Pour the
dressing over the salad and toss well.

INGREDIENTS TO SERVE FOUR:
1 lb (500 g) Brussels sprouts
salt
2 apples
1 tablespoon (15 ml) lemon juice
⅓ cup (50 g) chopped walnuts
1 tablespoon (15 ml) wine vinegar
¼ cup (60 ml) corn oil
freshly ground black pepper

Spinach Quiche

Preheat the oven to 400°F (200°C).

Make 1½ cups of shortcrust pastry with
whole-wheat flour (see page 34). Roll it out
and line an 8-inch (20-cm) flan ring or pie pan.
Bake the pastry blind for 15 minutes. Remove
the waxed paper and the beans and bake for
5 to 10 minutes more, or until the pastry is
slightly colored.

Reduce the oven temperature to 350°F
(180°C).

Meanwhile, prepare the filling. Remove
and discard the coarse stalks from 1 pound of

spinach. Wash the spinach thoroughly and
put it into a large saucepan with only the
water that clings to the leaves after washing.
Cover the pan and cook over low heat for
10 minutes, or until the spinach is tender.
Drain the spinach, pressing it down well with
the back of a wooden spoon to squeeze out all
the liquid. Finely chop the spinach.

Put the chopped spinach into a mixing
bowl with the juice of ½ lemon, ¼ teaspoon of
grated nutmeg, salt and pepper.

In a small bowl beat 2 eggs with ¼ cup of
yogurt. Stir the egg mixture into the
spinach. Add ½ pound of sieved cottage
cheese and 2 tablespoons of grated Parmesan
cheese. Mix well.

Spoon the filling into the pastry shell and
level the surface. Bake for 30 minutes, or
until the filling is set and the top is lightly
browned.

INGREDIENTS TO SERVE FOUR TO SIX:
1½ cups (150 g) shortcrust pastry made
      with whole-wheat flour (see page 34)
1 lb (500 g) spinach
½ lemon
¼ teaspoon (1 ml) grated nutmeg
salt
pepper
2 eggs
¼ cup (60 ml) yogurt
½ lb (250 g) cottage cheese
2 tablespoons (30 ml) grated Parmesan
      cheese

Baked Spinach Parmesan

Preheat the oven to 375°F (190°C).

Remove the coarse stalks from 1 pound of
spinach. Coarsely chop the larger leaves.
Wash the spinach well and put it into a large
saucepan. (Do not drain the spinach. Drops
of water should still be clinging to the leaves.)
Cover the pan and, stirring occasionally,
cook for 3 minutes, until the spinach is just
tender. Drain the spinach well.

In a mixing bowl beat 3 eggs, then stir in
½ cup of grated Parmesan cheese, salt and
pepper. Stir in the drained spinach. Spoon
the spinach mixture into a shallow ovenproof
dish. Sprinkle with ¼ cup of grated Parmesan
cheese. Bake for 10 to 15 minutes, or until the
eggs are set.

Serve at once.

INGREDIENTS TO SERVE FOUR:
1 lb (500 g) spinach
3 eggs
¾ cup (75 g) grated Parmesan cheese
salt
pepper

Spinach with Bacon and Coconut

Chop 8 slices of bacon. Chop 1 small onion. Remove and discard the coarse stalks from 1 pound of spinach. Coarsely chop the large leaves. Wash the spinach thoroughly. Do not drain it.

Heat 1 tablespoon of corn oil in a large saucepan. Add the bacon and the onion to the pan and fry over very low heat, stirring frequently, for 5 minutes. Add ½ cup of unsweetened shredded coconut. Fry for 1 minute, until the coconut is beginning to brown. Add the spinach to the pan with 1 tablespoon of lemon juice. Fry over very low heat, stirring frequently, for 3 to 5 minutes, until the spinach is just tender and is still a bright green. Season to taste with salt and pepper.

Serve immediately.

INGREDIENTS TO SERVE FOUR:

8 slices bacon
1 small onion
1 lb (500 g) spinach
1 tablespoon (15 ml) corn oil
½ cup (50 g) unsweetened shredded coconut
1 tablespoon (15 ml) lemon juice
salt
pepper

Spinach Soup

Wash and drain 1 pound of spinach. Remove any coarse stalks. Coarsely chop the spinach. Put it into a large saucepan with 1 chopped small onion, salt, pepper and ½ teaspoon of grated nutmeg. Grate in the rind of ½ lemon then squeeze in the juice. Pour in 2½ cups of well-seasoned chicken stock. Cover the pan and simmer over low heat for 10 minutes.

Pour the contents of the pan into a blender. Blend until smooth. Return the soup to the pan. Stir in ⅔ cup of yogurt. Adjust the seasoning. Reheat, but do not allow the soup to boil or the yogurt might curdle.

Serve the soup hot or chilled, garnished with thin slices of lemon.

INGREDIENTS TO SERVE FOUR:

1 lb (500 g) spinach
1 small onion
salt
pepper
½ teaspoon (2.5 ml) grated nutmeg
1 lemon
2½ cups (600 ml) well-seasoned chicken stock
⅔ cup (150 ml) yogurt

Raw Spinach Salad

Wash ½ pound of small young spinach leaves thoroughly and drain them well. Put them into a salad bowl.

Cut ½ cucumber into thin slices and add them to the spinach.

To make the dressing, heat 2 tablespoons of corn oil in a frying pan. Add 8 chopped slices of bacon. Fry until the bacon is well done and very crisp. Add the juice of 1 lemon, salt and pepper to the pan. Let the dressing cool slightly, then pour it over the spinach.

Toss the salad well. It may be kept in the refrigerator, covered, for several hours before serving.

INGREDIENTS TO SERVE FOUR:

½ lb (250 g) small young spinach leaves
½ cucumber
2 tablespoons (30 ml) corn oil
8 slices bacon
1 lemon
salt
pepper

Baked Cabbage

Preheat the oven to 400°F (200°C).

Prepare 4 cups of shredded green cabbage. Put half of it into an ovenproof casserole or baking dish. Spread ⅓ cup of yogurt over the cabbage. Sprinkle with ⅓ cup of seedless raisins, ½ cup of peanuts, salt and pepper.

Put the remaining cabbage into the casserole, then spread it with ⅓ cup of yogurt.

Sprinkle ½ cup of grated Cheddar cheese and a little grated nutmeg over the top.

Bake for 15 to 20 minutes, or until the top is lightly browned. Serve immediately.

INGREDIENTS TO SERVE FOUR:

4 cups (350 g) shredded green cabbage
⅔ cup (150 ml) yogurt
⅓ cup (50 g) seedless raisins
½ cup (50 g) peanuts
salt
pepper
½ cup (50 g) grated Cheddar cheese
grated nutmeg

Stuffed Cabbage Leaves

Preheat the oven to 375°F (190°C).

Blanch 8 large cabbage leaves in boiling salted water for 2 minutes. This should soften the leaves sufficiently so that they can easily be rolled up around the stuffing.

For the stuffing, heat 1 tablespoon of corn oil in a saucepan. Add 1 chopped onion and fry gently for 5 minutes. Add ¾ pound of ground beef and fry, stirring frequently, until it is brown.

Blanch and peel 4 tomatoes. Cut them into halves and remove the seeds. Coarsely chop the tomatoes and add them to the meat with 1 tablespoon of chopped parsley, a pinch of dried mixed herbs, salt and pepper.

Cover the pan, reduce the heat and simmer gently for 15 minutes, stirring occasionally. If the mixture is still a little liquid, boil, uncovered, for 2 minutes, stirring constantly.

Divide the stuffing between the blanched cabbage leaves. Roll up the leaves around the stuffing, folding in the edges so that the meat is completely enclosed.

Put the stuffed cabbage leaves into a shallow ovenproof dish. Cover the dish and bake for 20 minutes. Serve immediately with hot tomato sauce (see page 108).

INGREDIENTS TO SERVE FOUR:

8 large cabbage leaves
salt
1 tablespoon (15 ml) corn oil
1 onion
¾ lb (350 g) ground beef
4 tomatoes
1 tablespoon (15 ml) chopped parsley
dried mixed herbs
pepper
tomato sauce (see page 108)

STUFFING CABBAGE LEAVES

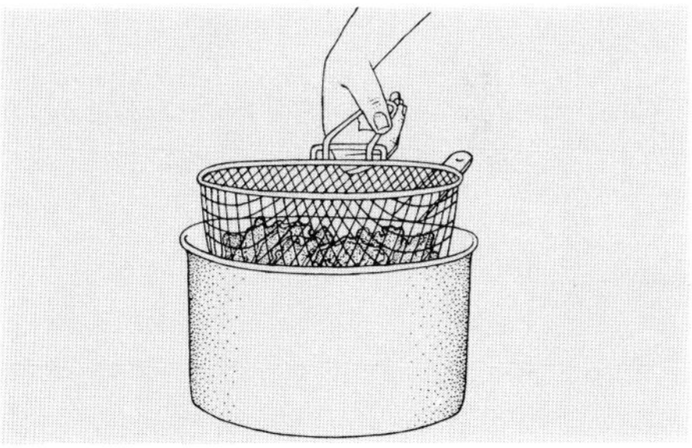

Blanch the leaves in boiling water to soften them.

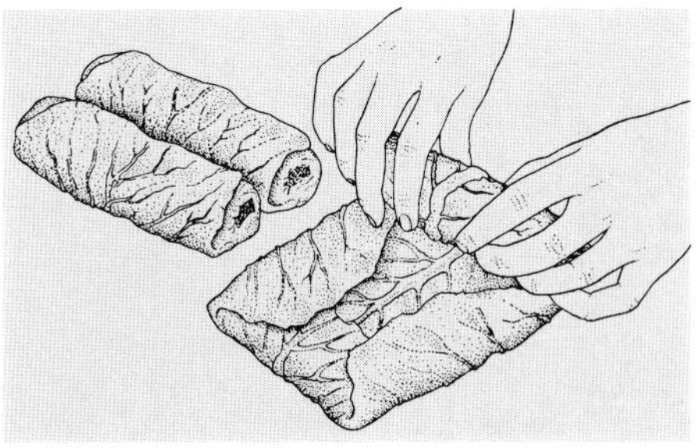

Roll the cabbage leaves around the filling.

Coleslaw

Put $\frac{2}{3}$ cup of yogurt into a large mixing bowl. Season to taste with salt and pepper.

Add 3 cups of finely shredded white cabbage to the bowl with 2 grated large carrots.

Cut 2 firm green apples into quarters, core them and cut them into thin slices. Put them into a small bowl with the juice of $\frac{1}{2}$ lemon. Lightly toss the apple in the lemon juice and add to the cabbage with $\frac{1}{4}$ pound of seedless green grapes, $\frac{1}{4}$ cup of coarsely chopped pecans and 2 tablespoons of chopped chives.

Toss well so that all the ingredients are coated with the yogurt dressing.

INGREDIENTS TO SERVE SIX:
$\frac{2}{3}$ **cup (150 ml) yogurt**
salt
pepper
3 cups (250 g) shredded white cabbage
2 large carrots
2 green apples
$\frac{1}{2}$ **lemon**
$\frac{1}{4}$ **lb (100 g) seedless green grapes**
$\frac{1}{4}$ **cup (50 g) chopped pecans**
2 tablespoons (30 ml) chopped chives

Chinese Cabbage with Bean Sprouts

Chop 1 large onion. Shred 1 pound (about 6 cups) of Chinese cabbage. Blanch and peel 2 tomatoes and cut them into quarters.

Heat 1 tablespoon of peanut oil in a *wok* or a large, heavy frying pan. Add the chopped onion and fry over high heat, stirring constantly, for 2 minutes.

Add the Chinese cabbage to the pan and stir-fry for 2 minutes. Add the tomatoes, $\frac{1}{4}$ pound of bean sprouts, 1 tablespoon of soy sauce and pepper to taste. Stir-fry for 2 minutes more, or until the cabbage is just tender but is still crisp.

Serve immediately.

INGREDIENTS TO SERVE FOUR:
1 large onion
1 lb (500 g) Chinese cabbage
2 tomatoes
1 tablespoon (15 ml) peanut oil
$\frac{1}{4}$ **lb (100 g) bean sprouts**
1 tablespoon (15 ml) soy sauce
pepper

Cabbage Casserole

Preheat the oven to 375°F (190°C).

Cut $\frac{1}{2}$ medium-sized white cabbage, about 1 pound, into 4 to 6 wedges. Put them into a casserole or ovenproof dish.

Thinly slice 1 large carrot and add it to the cabbage with 1 finely chopped onion. Peel, core and slice 1 cooking apple and add it to the casserole. Season with salt and pepper, then pour in $\frac{2}{3}$ cup of vegetable or chicken stock and 1 tablespoon of wine vinegar.

Cover the casserole and bake for 30 to 40 minutes, or until the cabbage is just tender.

INGREDIENTS TO SERVE FOUR:
$\frac{1}{2}$ **medium-sized white cabbage**
1 large carrot
1 onion
1 cooking apple
salt
pepper
$\frac{2}{3}$ **cup (150 ml) vegetable or chicken stock**
1 tablespoon (15 ml) wine vinegar

Cabbage and Apple Soup

Put 3 cups of shredded cabbage into a large saucepan.

Chop 1 large onion and add it to the pan with 1 crushed garlic clove. Peel, core and coarsely chop 1 large tart apple. Add the apple to the pan.

Cut a $\frac{1}{4}$-inch (6-mm) slice from a piece of ginger root. Peel and finely chop the ginger and add it to the pan. (If ginger root is not available, $\frac{1}{4}$ teaspoon of ground ginger may be substituted.)

Pour in 4 cups of well-seasoned chicken stock.

Bring to the boil, cover the pan, reduce the heat and simmer for 10 minutes, or until the cabbage and apple are tender. Pour the

contents of the pan into a blender and blend to a purée.

Return the soup to the pan, adjust the seasoning, reheat and serve.

INGREDIENTS TO SERVE FOUR:
3 cups (250 g) shredded cabbage
1 large onion
1 garlic clove
1 large tart apple
ginger root or $\frac{1}{4}$ teaspoon (2.5 ml) ground ginger
4 cups (850 ml) chicken stock
salt
pepper

Braised Broccoli

Divide $1\frac{1}{2}$ pounds of broccoli into spears. Wash them well and put into a large saucepan.

Drain 1 small can of anchovies. Separate the fillets and add them to the broccoli with $\frac{1}{2}$ cup of sliced Brazil nuts and 8 stuffed olives. Pour in $\frac{2}{3}$ cup of chicken or vegetable stock.

Bring to the boil. Cover the pan, reduce the heat and simmer gently for 5 to 10 minutes, or until the broccoli is just tender.

Lift out the broccoli and arrange it on a warm serving dish. Boil the stock rapidly for a few minutes to reduce it and then pour it over the broccoli.

Serve immediately.

INGREDIENTS TO SERVE FOUR:
$1\frac{1}{2}$ **lb (700 g) broccoli**
1 small can anchovies
$\frac{1}{2}$ **cup (50 g) sliced Brazil nuts**
8 stuffed olives
$\frac{2}{3}$ **cup (150 ml) chicken or vegetable stock**

Baked Broccoli

Preheat the oven to 375°F (190°C).

Divide 1½ pounds of broccoli into spears or florets, wash well and put into a large saucepan. Pour in ⅔ cup of water and sprinkle with salt and pepper. Bring to the boil. Cover the pan, reduce the heat and simmer gently for 5 to 10 minutes, or until the broccoli is tender but still crisp.

Drain the broccoli and arrange it in an ovenproof dish.

Mix ⅔ cup of yogurt with 1 beaten egg, 1 tablespoon of grated Parmesan cheese, salt and pepper. Pour the yogurt sauce over the broccoli and sprinkle with 1 tablespoon more of grated Parmesan cheese.

Bake for 15 to 20 minutes, or until the sauce is bubbling and lightly browned on top.

INGREDIENTS TO SERVE FOUR:
1½ lb (700 g) broccoli
salt
pepper
⅔ cup (150 ml) yogurt
1 egg
2 tablespoons (30 ml) grated Parmesan cheese

Roman Broccoli

Cauliflower may also be cooked in this way.

Chop 1 large onion. Heat 1 tablespoon of olive oil in a large saucepan. Add the onion with 1 crushed garlic clove to the pan and fry for 3 minutes.

Blanch and peel 2 medium-sized tomatoes. Slice the tomatoes and add to the onions. Pour ⅔ cup of well-seasoned chicken or vegetable stock into the pan. Add 1 tablespoon of chopped oregano, marjoram or basil. Bring to the boil and simmer for 2 minutes. Stir in 8 stuffed olives.

Divide 1 medium-sized broccoli head into large florets, wash well and add to the pan. Cover the pan and simmer for 5 to 10 minutes, or until the broccoli is tender.

Sprinkle with 1 tablespoon of chopped parsley and serve immediately.

INGREDIENTS TO SERVE FOUR:
1 large onion
1 tablespoon (15 ml) olive oil
1 garlic clove
2 medium-sized tomatoes
⅔ cup (150 ml) well-seasoned chicken or vegetable stock
1 tablespoon (15 ml) chopped oregano, marjoram or basil
8 stuffed olives
1 medium-sized broccoli head
1 tablespoon (15 ml) chopped parsley

Cauliflower au Gratin

Divide 1 medium-sized cauliflower into large florets, wash well and put them into a saucepan. Pour in 1¼ cups of water and season with salt and pepper. Bring to the boil. Cover the pan, reduce the heat and simmer for 5 to 10 minutes, or until the cauliflower is tender but still crisp.

Drain the cauliflower, reserving the cooking liquid. Arrange the cauliflower in a hot flameproof dish and keep warm. Add enough milk to the cooking liquid to bring it up to 1¼ cups.

For the sauce, chop 4 slices of bacon. Heat 2 tablespoons of margarine in a saucepan. Add the bacon and 1 chopped small onion to the pan and fry for 3 minutes. Add 4 tablespoons of split blanched almonds and continue to fry until the almonds are lightly browned. Stir in 1 tablespoon of flour. Still stirring, gradually add the reserved liquid and milk. Bring to the boil, stirring constantly; and continue to cook until the sauce is thick and smooth. Add ½ cup of grated sharp Cheddar cheese. Remove the pan from the heat and stir until the cheese has melted. Season the sauce with salt and

Stir flour rapidly into the melted fat.

Stirring briskly, gradually add the liquid.

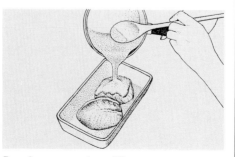
Pour the sauce over the cauliflower.

pepper. Pour it over the cauliflower. Sprinkle with ¼ cup more of grated Cheddar cheese.

Put the dish under a hot broiler for 2 to 3 minutes, or until the sauce is bubbling and golden brown on top.

INGREDIENTS TO SERVE FOUR:
1 medium-sized cauliflower
salt
pepper
milk
4 slices bacon
2 tablespoons (25 g) margarine
1 small onion
4 tablespoons (25 g) split blanched almonds
1 tablespoon (15 ml) flour
¾ cup (75 g) grated sharp Cheddar cheese

Cream of Cauliflower Soup

Discard the outside leaves and the bottom of the stalk of 1 small cauliflower. Cut and coarsely chop the remaining stalk and leaves from the cauliflower head. Divide the cauliflower into small florets and put them into a saucepan with the chopped leaves and stalk. Pour in 2½ cups of well-seasoned chicken stock or vegetable stock and 1¼ cups of milk. Grate in the rind of ½ lemon and squeeze in the juice. Add a pinch of grated nutmeg and salt and pepper to taste.

Bring to the boil. Cover the pan, reduce the heat and simmer for 10 to 15 minutes, or until the cauliflower is tender. Reserving a few cauliflower florets for garnish, pour the rest into a blender and blend to a smooth purée. Return the soup to the pan and reheat.

Serve hot, garnished with 1 tablespoon of chopped parsley and the reserved cauliflower florets.

INGREDIENTS TO SERVE FOUR:
1 small cauliflower
2½ cups (600 ml) well-seasoned chicken or vegetable stock
1¼ cups (300 ml) milk
½ lemon
grated nutmeg
salt
pepper
1 tablespoon (15 ml) chopped parsley

Cauliflower, Mushroom and Ham Salad

This crisp salad with a mustard dressing may be served as a light main dish or as a first course.

Divide 1 small cauliflower into small florets. Wash well and drain.

Put them into a bowl with ½ cup of sliced small mushrooms and 1 cup of chopped cooked ham.

For the dressing, beat 2 tablespoons of wine vinegar with 5 tablespoons of corn oil and 2 teaspoons of Dijon mustard. Stir in 1 tablespoon of finely chopped chives. Season to taste with salt and freshly ground black pepper. Pour the dressing over the salad.

Toss the salad and let it marinate for at least 30 minutes before serving.

INGREDIENTS TO SERVE FOUR:
1 small cauliflower
½ cup (50 g) sliced small mushrooms
1 cup (100 g) chopped cooked ham
2 tablespoons (30 ml) wine vinegar
5 tablespoons (75 ml) corn oil
2 teaspoons (10 ml) Dijon mustard
1 tablespoon (15 ml) chopped chives
salt
freshly ground black pepper

Gado Gado

This mixed vegetable salad is an Indonesian specialty. The lightly cooked vegetables are served cold with a peanut sauce.

Cook the following vegetables separately in a little water until they are tender, but still very crisp: 3 cups of chopped white cabbage, ½ pound of spinach, 2 cups of cauliflower florets, 2 cups of sliced carrots. Drain the vegetables and let them cool.

Hard boil 2 eggs. Let them cool, then peel them and slice them.

Put a layer of each vegetable into a salad bowl. Top with 2 ounces of bean sprouts and then put the hard-boiled egg slices on top. Pour in 1¼ cups of peanut sauce (see pork saté, page 200). Sprinkle with ¼ cup of unsweetened shredded coconut.

INGREDIENTS TO SERVE FOUR TO SIX:
3 cups (250 g) chopped white cabbage
½ lb (250 g) spinach
2 cups (250 g) cauliflower florets
2 cups (250 g) sliced carrots
2 eggs
2 oz (50 g) bean sprouts
1¼ cups (300 ml) peanut sauce (see pork saté, page 200)
¼ cup (25 g) unsweetened shredded coconut

Pickled Cauliflower and Cabbage

A good accompaniment to cold meats, this cauliflower and cabbage pickle will keep for up to 1 month.

Cut 1 medium-sized cauliflower into small florets and wash well. Prepare 3 cups of coarsely shredded red cabbage.

Fill two 2-pound Mason jars with layers of cauliflower florets, red cabbage and the leaves of 8 stalks of celery. Sprinkle 2 teaspoons of salt into each jar. Pour ⅔ cup of wine vinegar into each jar. Fill up the jars with water.

Seal the jars and leave at room temperature for 1 week to mature.

INGREDIENTS TO MAKE FOUR POUNDS (2 kg) OF PICKLE:
1 medium-sized cauliflower
3 cups (250 g) shredded red cabbage
celery leaves
4 teaspoons (20 ml) salt
1⅓ cups (300 ml) wine vinegar

PREPARING CAULIFLOWER AND CABBAGE

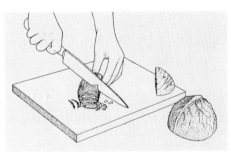

Coarsely shred cabbage using a sharp knife.

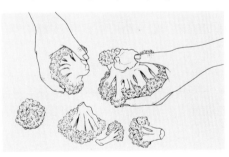

Divide cauliflower into florets.

Lemon and Herb Cauliflower

Remove and coarsely chop the leaves from 1 medium-sized cauliflower. Divide the cauliflower into large florets.

Put the florets and the chopped leaves into a large saucepan. Pour in ⅔ cup of boiling water and 1 tablespoon of lemon juice. Sprinkle with salt and pepper.

Cover the pan and simmer over low heat for 5 to 8 minutes, or until the cauliflower is tender but still crisp.

Transfer the cauliflower to a warm serving dish and keep warm. Boil the cooking liquid rapidly for 2 minutes, or until it is reduced to 4 tablespoons. Stir in 1 tablespoon of chopped parsley and 1 tablespoon of chopped chives. Pour over the cauliflower.

Serve immediately.

INGREDIENTS TO SERVE FOUR:
1 medium-sized cauliflower
1 tablespoon (15 ml) lemon juice
salt
pepper
1 tablespoon (15 ml) chopped parsley
1 tablespoon (15 ml) chopped chives

Cauliflower in Cider

Divide 1 medium-sized cauliflower into large florets. Wash the florets and put them into a saucepan. Pour 1¼ cups of hard cider over the florets and sprinkle them with salt and pepper. Bring to the boil, cover the pan and simmer for 5 to 10 minutes, or until the cauliflower is tender.

Drain the florets, reserving the cooking liquid and arrange them in a warm ovenproof dish.

For the sauce, chop 4 slices of bacon. Put 2 tablespoons of margarine into a saucepan with the bacon and fry until the bacon is crisp. Stir in 2 tablespoons of flour. Bring the cooking liquid up to 1¼ cups with more cider and add it to the saucepan.

Bring to the boil, stirring constantly. Continue to cook, stirring, until the sauce is thick and smooth. Season to taste with salt, pepper and grated nutmeg.

Pour the sauce over the cauliflower and serve immediately.

INGREDIENTS TO SERVE FOUR:
1 medium-sized cauliflower
hard cider
salt
pepper
4 slices bacon
2 tablespoons (25 g) margarine
2 tablespoons (30 ml) flour
grated nutmeg

PUT AWAY THE PEELER

Up to a quarter of a potato's protein is lost by peeling because the protein is most highly concentrated just below the skin. And if a peeled potato is boiled, up to half of its vitamin C content is dissolved in the cooking water. So to retain as much goodness as possible, bake or boil unpeeled potatoes. Green skin, however, should be removed — it contains a detrimental alkaloid.

Although the underground stems, or tubers, of potatoes, yams and artichokes are more than three-quarters water, if they are eaten in quantity they provide a substantial amount of energy-giving starch. Sweet potatoes and Jerusalem artichokes have a sweeter taste than that of other tubers because they also contain some sugars. Clockwise: a sackful of old potatoes; a tub of new potatoes; on the ground a basket of Jerusalem artichokes and a box of yams and sweet potatoes (of the red variety).

THE POTATO, having gone through a period of nutritional disgrace, has been rehabilitated. It is now bread, which has three times as many calories, that is taking the blame for putting extra inches on our waistlines.

Although the potato has been a familiar food since the first century A.D., wherever it has been introduced it has taken a long time to become accepted. It was brought to Europe from its original home in South America by Spanish conquerors in the second half of the sixteenth century. But more than a century passed before it became widely eaten in the British Isles; the Scots and Irish at first rejected it because it was not mentioned in the Bible. By the end of the eighteenth century, however, it had become one of the major crops not only of Ireland but of continental Europe.

Poverty and the potato have often gone together, and as standards of living have risen people have turned to other foods. But in wartime, when food is scarce, potatoes have always come into their own. Today, even in the midst of peaceful affluence, the potato, a valuable source of vitamin C, is an important part of the diet.

Like many other foods the potato has been assailed by technology. It has been washed and prepacked mechanically, canned, turned into chips, frozen French fries and instant mashed potato (for which credit, if that is the word, is claimed by the Eastern Research Center of the United States Agriculture Department in Wyndmoor, Pennsylvania).

Potatoes have suffered even more at the hands of farmers. Of the many varieties that are theoretically available, only a handful provide almost all of the United States commercial crop, and excellence of flavor is generally the least of the farmer's reasons for growing them.

One of the most widely grown varieties is Majestic, which has been around for sixty-six years. It crops well and keeps satisfactorily, and little else can be said for it. The tubers are given to cracking, their texture is soapy, their flavor insipid and they tend to go black when boiled. Newer varieties have recently been challenging Majestic, but they do not taste much better, while many established varieties with superior texture and flavor have gone out of commercial cultivation altogether because they crop less profitably.

To the drawback of poor flavor of the potatoes you buy must be added the damage done by mechanical harvesting. One potato in every five is damaged, according to a recent survey. The potatoes get a further battering when they are washed and prepacked. Buying the "convenience" of prepacked potatoes is folly. Their bruises turn black and have to be cut away and in the humid atmosphere inside the plastic bag the potatoes quickly go bad and the skins become green and

toxic as the result of prolonged exposure to light.

The English and Americans prefer starchy, floury potatoes, while the French like them waxy. The preferences are related—not to nationality, but to different methods of cooking; whether it is done in fat or oil or in water. Americans traditionally bake potatoes in their skins, or mash or boil them (the French call boiled potatoes Pommes à l'anglaise) and for this they need floury potatoes. Potato hawkers went through the streets of London a hundred years ago shouting "Taters 'ot! All 'ot and floury!" and tastes have not greatly changed since then. But the French are fonder of potatoes cooked in oil or butter, and for this waxy potatoes are best. That is the simple choice, but shoppers are often denied it. Vegetable gardeners do, however, have a choice, and as they cook so should they grow. A few varieties —floury, waxy or early—would be adequate for the five hundred or so ways potatoes can be cooked.

The sweet potato, which is the tuberous root of a tropical vine, is unrelated to the common potato and is altogether different. Its flesh is yellow, sweet and faintly scented. Nutritionally it is useful for its carotene and vitamin C content, but amounts of these vary considerably. The sweet potato arrived in Europe in the sixteenth century and the buccaneering Sir Francis Drake, who brought it to Britain, thought it more delicious than the sweetest apple. In spite of such sponsorship it never became popular in Britain. In France, where sweet potatoes had Louis XV and the Empress Josephine as royal patrons, they have fared a little better, although not as well as in Spain. They are popular in the United States, especially in the South.

Some tubers which are sold as yams in the United States are in fact a variety of sweet potatoes. The true yams, which are an important food in parts of West Africa, Vietnam and Cambodia, are the tubers of a family of climbing plants which are grouped together on the basis that some species twine counterclockwise when climbing and some twine clockwise. One way or the other their nutritional value is similar to other tubers; they are starchy vegetables that contain little protein but useful amounts of carotene and vitamin C.

There are two other tubers that are somewhat alike in flavor and texture although they come from opposite ends of the world. One is the Jerusalem artichoke, which is not an artichoke and which comes from North America, and the other is the Chinese (or Japanese) artichoke, which although also not an artichoke does come from China. Jerusalem artichokes look like tormented potatoes and Chinese artichokes have been described as looking like petrified worms. But they have a pleasantly sweet flavor.

The Nutrients in Potatoes
Potatoes provide useful amounts of starch, vitamin C, thiamine and niacin and three and a half ounces (100 g) provide about 80 Calories.

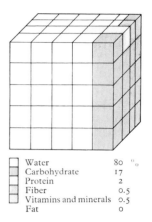

Water	80 %
Carbohydrate	17
Protein	2
Fiber	0.5
Vitamins and minerals	0.5
Fat	0

Herb Baked New Potatoes

Preheat the oven to 400°F (200°C).

Scrub 1½ pounds of new potatoes, but do not peel them.

Grease a sheet of foil that is large enough to enclose the potatoes. Put the potatoes in the center and sprinkle them with salt and freshly ground black pepper. Put 4 mint sprigs and 4 parsley sprigs among the potatoes. Fold the foil around the potatoes and seal the edges.

Bake for 30 to 45 minutes, depending on the size of the potatoes, or until they are tender.

Remove the potatoes from the foil and put them into a serving bowl. Sprinkle with 1 tablespoon of chopped mint and 1 tablespoon of parsley.

INGREDIENTS TO SERVE FOUR:
1½ lb (700 g) new potatoes
salt
freshly ground black pepper
1 small bunch mint
1 small bunch parsley

Piquant New Potato Salad

Scrub but do not peel 1½ pounds of small new potatoes. Cook them in boiling salted water until they are just tender.

Meanwhile make the dressing. In a small mixing bowl combine ¼ cup of corn oil with 1 tablespoon of wine vinegar. Add 1 tablespoon of capers, 1 tablespoon of chopped gherkins, 1 tablespoon of chopped parsley and salt and pepper to taste. Mix well.

Drain the potatoes and put them into a salad bowl. (Cut the larger potatoes into halves or quarters.) Pour the dressing over the potatoes while they are still hot. Toss lightly but well.

Broil 4 slices of bacon until they are very crisp. Let the bacon cool, then crumble it over the potatoes.

Serve the salad warm or cold.

INGREDIENTS TO SERVE FOUR:
1½ lb (700 g) small new potatoes
¼ cup (60 ml) corn oil
1 tablespoon (15 ml) wine vinegar
1 tablespoon (15 ml) capers
1 tablespoon (15 ml) chopped gherkins
1 tablespoon (15 ml) chopped parsley
salt
pepper
4 slices bacon

Potato and Tuna Salad

This tasty dish can be served as a first course or as a main dish.

Scrub 4 medium-sized potatoes. Put them into a pan with 2½ cups of boiling salted water and cook them until they are just tender. Drain well. Let the potatoes cool, then slice them thickly into a salad bowl.

Drain and coarsely flake 7 ounces of canned tuna fish and add it to the potatoes. Add ½ cup of thinly sliced small mushrooms to the salad with 8 sliced stuffed olives.

For the dressing, mix ⅔ cup of yogurt with the grated rind and juice of 1 lemon, 1 tablespoon of chopped parsley, salt and pepper. Pour over the salad and toss lightly.

INGREDIENTS TO SERVE FOUR TO SIX:
4 medium-sized potatoes
salt
7 oz (198 g) canned tuna fish
½ cup (50 g) sliced small mushrooms
8 stuffed olives
⅔ cup (150 ml) yogurt
1 lemon
1 tablespoon (15 ml) chopped parsley
pepper

Scalloped Potatoes with Yogurt

Preheat the oven to 400°F (200°C).

Peel and thinly slice 6 medium-sized potatoes.

Finely chop or grate 1 small onion. In a small bowl mix the onion with salt, pepper and 1¼ cups of yogurt.

Layer the potato slices in a casserole, spreading each layer with the yogurt mixture. Arrange the top layer of potatoes attractively in overlapping circles, then spread with the remaining yogurt.

Cover and bake for 30 minutes. Uncover and bake for 30 minutes more, or until the potatoes are cooked and the top is crisp and brown.

Serve hot.

INGREDIENTS TO SERVE FOUR:
6 medium-sized potatoes
1 small onion
salt
pepper
1¼ cups (300 ml) yogurt

Potatoes Baked with Salami

Preheat the oven to 375°F (190°C).

Peel 6 medium-sized potatoes and cut them into thin slices. Slice 2 medium-sized tomatoes. Thinly slice ¼ pound of salami.

In a casserole or ovenproof dish arrange the potatoes in layers with the tomatoes and salami. Season each layer with salt and pepper.

Cover and bake for 1 hour, or until the potatoes are tender.

Serve hot.

INGREDIENTS TO SERVE FOUR:
6 medium-sized potatoes
2 medium-sized tomatoes
¼ lb (100 g) salami
salt
pepper

Potato and Carrot Boulangère

Preheat the oven to 400°F (200°C).

Peel and thinly slice 4 medium-sized potatoes. Wash and thinly slice 3 medium-sized carrots. Thinly slice 1 small onion and separate the slices into rings. Finely chop 4 slices of bacon.

In a casserole arrange the potatoes in layers with the carrots, onion, bacon and ¾ cup of grated Gruyère cheese, salt and pepper. Finish with a layer of potato arranged attractively on the top.

Pour in 1¼ cups of chicken or vegetable stock. Cover and bake for 30 minutes. Uncover, brush the top with corn oil and bake for 30 minutes more, or until the potatoes are cooked and browned on top.

Serve hot.

INGREDIENTS TO SERVE FOUR:
4 medium-sized potatoes
3 medium-sized carrots
1 small onion
4 slices bacon
¾ cup (75 g) grated Gruyère cheese
salt
pepper
1¼ cups (300 ml) chicken or vegetable stock
corn oil

Potatoes à l'Orange

Preheat the oven to 375°F (190°C).

Peel 6 medium-sized potatoes and cut them into thin slices. Arrange half of the potatoes in a casserole or ovenproof dish.

Grate the rind of 1 orange over the potatoes, then squeeze in the juice. Peel and remove the pith from another orange and, working over the casserole to catch the juice, cut the membrane away from the segments of fruit. Arrange the orange segments on top of the potatoes. Sprinkle with 3 tablespoons of blanched almonds, 1 chopped scallion, salt and pepper.

Arrange the remaining potato slices on top. Sprinkle with 3 tablespoons of blanched almonds, 1 chopped scallion, salt and pepper. Squeeze in the juice of 1 more orange.

Cover and bake for 1 hour, or until the potatoes are tender.

INGREDIENTS TO SERVE FOUR:
6 medium-sized potatoes
3 oranges
6 tablespoons (50 g) blanched almonds
2 scallions
salt
pepper

Duchesse Potatoes with Parsnips

These whirls of creamed potato and parsnip may be made in advance and heated before serving. The parsnips give a sweetness to the potatoes, but the dish may be made only with potatoes.

Peel and thickly slice 3 medium-sized potatoes. Peel and thickly slice 3 medium-sized parsnips. Put the potatoes and the parsnips into a saucepan with 1¼ cups of salted water. Cover the pan and bring to the boil. Reduce the heat and simmer for about 20 minutes, or until the potatoes and parsnips are tender.

Preheat the oven to 400°F (200°C).

Drain the vegetables well, then mash them to a smooth purée. Beat 1 egg with salt and pepper. Beat into the potato and parsnip purée.

Let the purée cool slightly, then spoon it into a pastry tube fitted with a large star nozzle. Pipe whirls of potato onto a lightly greased baking sheet. Top each whirl with a blanched almond.

The potatoes may be made in advance up to this stage and then heated before serving.

Bake for 10 to 15 minutes until heated through and golden brown.

INGREDIENTS TO SERVE FOUR:
3 medium-sized potatoes
3 medium-sized parsnips
1 egg
salt
pepper
blanched almonds

Baked Cheese Soufflé Potatoes

Preheat the oven to 400°F (200°C).

Scrub 2 very large potatoes or 4 smaller potatoes. Bake for 1 to 1½ hours, depending on the size, until the potatoes are cooked and soft when pressed.

Cut large potatoes in half or cut a slice off the top of smaller potatoes. Scoop the potato out of the centers, leaving shells about ¼ inch (6 mm) thick. Mash the potato.

Separate 2 eggs into 2 mixing bowls. Beat the egg yolks slightly then stir in the mashed potato, ½ cup of grated sharp Cheddar cheese, 2 chopped scallions, a pinch of grated nutmeg, salt and pepper.

Beat the egg whites until they are stiff and fold them into the cheese and potato mixture. Spoon into the potato skins. Put the stuffed potatoes on a lightly greased baking sheet. Bake for 15 to 20 minutes, until risen and golden brown on top. Serve at once.

INGREDIENTS TO SERVE FOUR:
2 very large or 4 smaller potatoes
2 eggs
½ cup (50 g) grated sharp Cheddar cheese
2 scallions
grated nutmeg
salt
pepper

STUFFING POTATOES

Scoop the cooked potato out of its skin.

Mash the potato well.

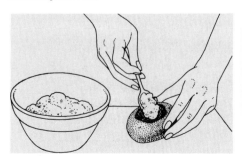

Spoon the filling back into the potato skin.

Potatoes Braised in Red Wine

Preheat the oven to 375°F (190°C).

Peel 6 medium-sized potatoes and cut them into ¼-inch (6-mm) slices. Put the potatoes into a casserole or ovenproof dish and pour in 1¼ cups of dry red wine.

Sprinkle with 2 tablespoons of chopped thyme, 2 tablespoons of chopped parsley, salt and pepper. Mix lightly so that the potatoes are coated with wine and herbs.

Cover and bake for 1 hour, or until the potatoes are tender and almost all the wine has been absorbed. The potatoes will be a delicate pink color on the outside but still white inside.

Serve hot.

INGREDIENTS TO SERVE FOUR:
6 medium-sized potatoes
1¼ cups (300 ml) dry red wine
2 tablespoons (30 ml) chopped thyme
2 tablespoons (30 ml) chopped parsley
salt
pepper

Potato and Eggplant Casserole

Cut 2 medium-sized eggplant into thin slices. Spread the slices on a plate and sprinkle them liberally with salt. Leave for at least 30 minutes. Wash the slices and drain them well.

Preheat the oven to 375°F (190°C).

Put 4 cups of thinly sliced, peeled potatoes into a bowl. Grate 1 small onion and mix it with 1 cup of grated Gruyère cheese.

In an ovenproof casserole arrange layers of potato and eggplant slices, sprinkling each layer with a little of the grated onion and cheese and salt and pepper. Arrange the top layer so that there are alternating slices of potato and eggplant overlapping in a circle.

Pour in ⅔ cup of chicken or vegetable stock.

Brush the top layer with 1 tablespoon of corn oil.

Bake the casserole for 1 hour, or until the vegetables are tender and the top is browned.

INGREDIENTS TO SERVE FOUR:
2 medium-sized eggplant
4 cups (500 g) thinly sliced potatoes
1 small onion
1 cup (100 g) grated Gruyère cheese
salt
pepper
⅔ cup (150 ml) chicken or vegetable stock
1 tablespoon (15 ml) corn oil

Irish Potato Cakes

These little potato cakes, or scones, may be made with leftover mashed potatoes.

Preheat the oven to 425°F (220°C). Lightly grease a baking sheet.

Peel and slice 4 medium-sized potatoes. Put them into a saucepan with boiling salted water to cover. Simmer for 15 minutes, or until the potatoes are tender. Drain the potatoes and mash them well.

Add to the mashed potatoes 2 teaspoons of chopped sage, 2 chopped scallions, 1 teaspoon of salt and freshly ground black pepper. Stir in 1 cup of self-rising flour. Mix well. Add a little more flour if necessary to make a soft dough that will roll out.

On a lightly floured surface roll out the potato dough to a 7-inch (18-cm) circle. Cut it into 8 wedges and put them on the baking sheet.

Bake for 20 minutes, or until the cakes have risen and are crisp and golden brown. Alternatively, the cakes may be fried in a lightly greased pan until they are brown on both sides.

Serve hot.

INGREDIENTS TO SERVE FOUR :
4 medium-sized potatoes
2 teaspoons (10 ml) chopped sage
2 scallions
salt
freshly ground black pepper
1 cup (100 g) self-rising flour

Shepherd's Pie

This recipe specifies ground beef, but lean chopped or sliced leftover beef or lamb may be used. The pie can be prepared in advance and baked just before serving.

Put 2 chopped slices of bacon into a saucepan and fry over low heat until the fat runs. Add 1 chopped onion and 2 cups of thinly sliced carrots to the pan. Continue to fry gently, stirring occasionally, for 3 minutes. Add 1 cup of sliced mushrooms and cook for 2 minutes more. Add 1 pound of ground beef and fry, stirring constantly, until the meat has browned.

Stir in 1 tablespoon of flour. Stirring constantly, add 1 tablespoon of tomato paste, gradually pour in ⅔ cup of beef stock and bring to the boil.

Reduce the heat and simmer gently for 20 to 30 minutes, or until the meat is tender. Season to taste with salt and pepper. Transfer the mixture to an ovenproof dish.

Preheat the oven to 375°F (190°C).

Meanwhile, prepare 6 cups of peeled and coarsely chopped potatoes. Put the potatoes into a saucepan with enough boiling salted water to cover. Bring to the boil and cook for 15 to 20 minutes, or until the potatoes are tender. Drain the potatoes. Add a little milk,

margarine, salt and pepper and mash them well.

Spread the mashed potatoes over the meat mixture and level the surface with a fork. Bake for 25 to 30 minutes, or until the potato is crisp and brown on top.

INGREDIENTS TO SERVE FOUR :
2 bacon slices
1 onion
2 cups (250 g) thinly sliced carrots
1 cup (100 g) sliced mushrooms
1 lb (500 g) ground beef
1 tablespoon (15 ml) flour
1 tablespoon (15 ml) tomato paste
⅔ cup (150 ml) beef stock
salt
pepper
6 cups (700 g) chopped potatoes
milk
margarine

Potato Soup

Peel 4 medium-sized potatoes, slice them and put them into a large saucepan. Chop 1 large onion and add it to the pan with 2 sprigs of thyme, ¼ teaspoon of grated nutmeg and salt and pepper.

Pour in 3¾ cups of well-seasoned beef stock. Cover the pan and bring to the boil. Reduce the heat and simmer for 30 minutes, or until the potatoes are tender. Blend or sieve the soup to a purée. Return the soup to the pan, reheat and adjust the seasoning.

Serve hot, sprinkled with 2 tablespoons of

PURÉEING VEGETABLES

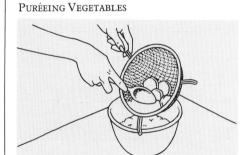

Press cooked vegetables through a strainer to purée.

grated Parmesan cheese and 1 tablespoon of chopped chives.

INGREDIENTS TO SERVE FOUR :
4 medium-sized potatoes
1 large onion
2 thyme sprigs
¼ teaspoon (1 ml) grated nutmeg
salt
pepper
3¾ cups (850 ml) beef stock
2 tablespoons (30 ml) grated Parmesan cheese
1 tablespoon (15 ml) chopped chives

Vichysoisse

Peel and chop 3 medium-sized onions and put them into a large saucepan. Wash 3 cups of trimmed and thinly sliced leeks thoroughly, then add them to the pan with 4 cups of peeled and sliced potatoes.

Pour in 5 cups of well-seasoned chicken stock, the grated rind and juice of ½ lemon and salt and pepper to taste. Bring to the boil, cover the pan, reduce the heat and simmer for 30 minutes, or until the vegetables are tender.

Blend the soup or sieve it to a purée. Stir in ⅔ cup of milk or light cream. Adjust the seasoning.

Chill well before serving.

INGREDIENTS TO SERVE SIX :
3 medium-sized onions
3 cups (500 g) thinly sliced leeks
4 cups (500 g) peeled and sliced potatoes
5 cups (1 liter) chicken stock
½ lemon
salt
pepper
⅔ cup (150 ml) milk or light cream

Stuffed Baked Potatoes

Preheat the oven to 400°F (200°C).

Scrub 4 large potatoes. With a sharp knife score them around the middle lengthwise. Bake the potatoes for 50 to 60 minutes, or until they are cooked.

Cut the potatoes into halves lengthwise and carefully scoop the potato out of the skins into a mixing bowl. Reserve the skins. Mash the potato well and season to taste with salt and pepper.

Broil or fry 4 slices of bacon until crisp. Drain well and then crumble the bacon into the mashed potato.

Stir ½ pound of cottage cheese, 2 tablespoons of chopped chives or scallions and 1 tablespoon of chopped parsley into the potatoes. Add enough milk to bind the ingredients together and mix well.

Spoon the stuffing back into the reserved potato skins and sprinkle ½ cup of grated Cheddar cheese over them.

Return the stuffed potatoes to the oven for 10 to 15 minutes, or until the filling is slightly brown on top.

INGREDIENTS TO SERVE FOUR :
4 large potatoes
salt
pepper
4 slices bacon
½ lb (250 g) cottage cheese
2 tablespoons (30 ml) chopped chives or scallions
1 tablespoon (15 ml) chopped parsley
milk
½ cup (50 g) grated Cheddar cheese

Normandy Sweet Potatoes

This sweet potato dish is particularly good served with pork.

Preheat the oven to 350°F (180°C).

Peel and thinly slice 1 pound of sweet potatoes. Peel, core and thickly slice 1 large cooking apple.

In a small bowl mix 3 tablespoons of seedless raisins with the juice and grated rind of 1 lemon and salt and pepper to taste.

In a casserole or ovenproof dish make layers of the sweet potato and apple slices. Sprinkle each layer with the raisin mixture. Pour in ⅔ cup of chicken stock.

Cover and bake for 45 minutes, or until the potatoes are tender.

Serve hot.

INGREDIENTS TO SERVE FOUR:
1 lb (500 g) sweet potatoes
1 large cooking apple
3 tablespoons (25 g) seedless raisins
1 lemon
salt
pepper
⅔ cup (150 ml) chicken stock

Sweet Potato and Avocado Casserole

Preheat the oven to 375°F (190°C).

Scrub 8 small sweet potatoes. Put them into a large saucepan with enough boiling water to cover. Cover the pan, bring to the boil and cook for 25 minutes, or until the potatoes are tender. When the potatoes are cool enough to handle, peel them and mash them or purée them in a blender.

Peel 1 medium-sized avocado and remove the seed. Mash it well, then beat it into the puréed sweet potatoes. Grate in the rind of 1 orange, then squeeze in the juice. Season with salt, pepper and a large pinch of grated nutmeg.

Spoon into a lightly greased ovenproof dish. Bake for 20 to 30 minutes, or until brown on top.

Serve hot.

INGREDIENTS TO SERVE FOUR:
8 small sweet potatoes
1 medium-sized avocado
1 orange
salt
pepper
grated nutmeg

Creamed Mixed Potatoes

Peel and slice ¾ pound of sweet potatoes and ¾ pound of white potatoes. Put them into a saucepan with boiling salted water to cover. Simmer for about 20 minutes, or until the potatoes are tender. Drain well.

Mash the potatoes until they are smooth. Beat in ¼ cup of milk. Add more milk if necessary for a creamy consistency. Season to taste with salt and pepper.

Serve hot, sprinkled with a large pinch of grated nutmeg.

INGREDIENTS TO SERVE FOUR TO SIX:
¾ lb (350 g) sweet potatoes
¾ lb (350 g) white potatoes
¼ cup (60 ml) milk
salt
pepper
grated nutmeg

Braised Jerusalem Artichokes

Wash 1½ pounds of small Jerusalem artichokes. Cut them into ¼-inch (6-mm) slices. Put them into a saucepan with the grated rind and juice of 1 lemon, 2 tablespoons of chopped thyme and salt and pepper to taste. Pour in ⅔ cup of water.

Cover the pan and bring to the boil. Reduce the heat and simmer for about 10 minutes, or until the artichokes are tender and almost all the water has evaporated.

Serve hot or cold, sprinkled with 1 tablespoon of chopped parsley.

INGREDIENTS TO SERVE FOUR:
1½ lb (700 g) Jerusalem artichokes
1 lemon
2 tablespoons (30 ml) chopped thyme
salt
pepper
1 tablespoon (15 ml) chopped parsley

Jerusalem Artichoke Soup

Peel and coarsely chop 1 pound of Jerusalem artichokes. Peel and chop 1 medium-sized onion. Put the artichokes and the onion into a large saucepan with 2½ cups of well-seasoned chicken stock, 1¼ cups of milk, salt and pepper. Cover the pan and bring to the boil. Reduce the heat and simmer for 20 minutes, or until the artichokes are tender.

Sieve the soup or blend it to a smooth purée. Return the soup to the pan, reheat and adjust the seasoning.

Serve hot, garnished with 2 tablespoons of chopped parsley.

INGREDIENTS TO SERVE FOUR TO SIX:
1 lb (500 g) Jerusalem artichokes
1 medium-sized onion
2½ cups (600 ml) well-seasoned chicken stock
1¼ cups (300 ml) milk
salt
pepper
2 tablespoons (30 ml) chopped parsley

Jerusalem Artichoke and Ham Soufflé

Preheat the oven to 375°F (190°C).

Peel 1 pound of Jerusalem artichokes. (If the artichokes are very nubbly and difficult to peel, cook them first, then the skins can be peeled off easily.) Simmer the artichokes in a saucepan in a little salted water for about 20 minutes, or until they are tender.

In a large mixing bowl, mash the artichokes well. Stir in ⅔ cup of yogurt and salt and pepper to taste. Alternatively, put the artichokes into a blender with the yogurt, salt and pepper and blend to a smooth purée. Mix ½ cup of chopped cooked ham into the purée.

PREPARING JERUSALEM ARTICHOKES

Cook nubbly artichokes before peeling.

Separate 3 large eggs. Stir the yolks into the artichoke mixture. Beat the whites until they are stiff. Fold them in.

Pour the mixture into a 2-quart (1½-liter) soufflé dish. Bake for 40 to 45 minutes, or until the soufflé is well risen, firm to the touch and golden brown.

Serve at once.

INGREDIENTS TO SERVE FOUR:
1 lb (500 g) Jerusalem artichokes
⅔ cup (150 ml) yogurt
salt
pepper
½ cup (100 g) chopped cooked ham
3 large eggs

EVEN IN PREHISTORIC TIMES when man was still a hunter his diet was not all meat. What evidence there is at least establishes this fact. Many writers have shown great imagination in conjuring up the details of the likely scene—the women scouring the countryside for anything edible while their men were away on the chase. In the spring and the summer they would pick young shoots and leaves and in the autumn they would gather berries and nuts. Then in the bleak midwinter the women would be reduced to scrabbling in the earth for the wild roots that would help avert starvation until spring came again.

This scenario, however accurate, is hard to associate with, for example, the celebrated French dish Carottes Vichy, in which tender young carrots are cooked in butter, sugar and Vichy water, then glazed and sprinkled with parsley. Nonetheless, although people and their roots have changed considerably since prehistoric times, it is difficult to dispel the air of impoverishment that hangs over the roots we usually eat. The fault is ours, for we, like our prehistoric ancestors, tend to eat roots in the winter because there is little else to choose. We are therefore eating them when they are at their worst. Not only are they old, woody or stringy, but they become less and less nutritious every week they are stored. There obviously is a place for roots in a winter diet, but the time to enjoy them is in late spring or summer when they are young and small, tender and sweet. Among roots, with one exception, small really is beautiful. Celeriac alone is better larger and is worth saving as a winter choice.

Carrots are undoubtedly the most useful of all roots. Teeth permitting, they are good to chew raw and in a dish of crudités they are usually the first to disappear. When young, carrots are delicious grated in salads or gently cooked in butter. In winter they are invaluable in stews, for they do not lose their color or their shape in long cooking. Carotene, which is converted into vitamin A in the body, is the major nutritional reason for eating carrots. To ensure that this vitamin is not squandered, the carrots should not be scraped or peeled, for the greatest concentration is in the skin or just beneath it.

Other roots, such as beets, turnips, rutabaga and parsnips, contain either no carotene or the merest trace. Some have a moderate amount of vitamin C. Kohlrabi, for example, contains as much vitamin C as oranges.

The main positive virtue of most roots lies in their mineral content, but they also have the negative virtue of being reasonably low in calories, so that they fill without fattening. There is also the likelihood that you will at least enjoy some of them, if not all, for their flavor.

The most subtle of the root vegetable flavors is that of the raw, very young, white turnip, but

The Nutrients in Roots
A high water content makes starchy roots low in calories and three and a half ounces (100 g) of carrots, for example, provide about 20 Calories.

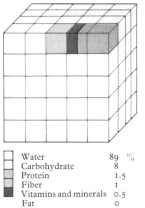

Water	89 %
Carbohydrate	8
Protein	1.5
Fiber	1
Vitamins and minerals	0.5
Fat	0

Many roots are valued for their low-calorie bulk. Radishes and beets, however, are flavorful additions to green salads and contribute not more than 30 Calories per hundred grams. Carrots have the additional merit of being very rich in carotene, which the body converts into vitamin A. In the basket (right) next to the carrots is scorzonera, or black salsify, and grouped on the ground are turnips, rutabagas, parsnips, beets and radishes.

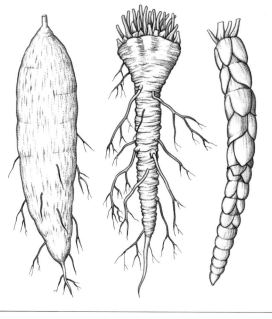

UNUSUAL ROOTS

Staple foods in some tropical countries, cassava (right) and arrowroot (far right) are roots with an unusually high starch content. Tapioca flour, made from cassava, and powdered arrowroot, which is used to thicken sauces, may be 85 percent starch and provide as many as 350 Calories in one hundred grams. Horseradish (center) is only slightly higher in starch than most roots, but it is outstandingly high in vitamin C, providing one hundred and twenty milligrams of this vitamin in one hundred grams. But no one could eat so much, and should not, since horseradish is poisonous except in small quantities.

even then its skin is likely to be tough and must be peeled. As an older vegetable the turnip is useful in stews for it has the valuable property of absorbing the rich flavors of whatever is cooked with it. The yellow-fleshed rutabaga is more domineering, and is best used alone. It can be boiled, mashed and then chastened with a little butter, cream and pepper. Above all, rutabaga must be eaten young and small.

Kohlrabi is woody and flavorless when it is old and large, but when the vegetable is young it has a somewhat nutty turnip flavor.

The sweetest tasting roots are the creamy fleshed parsnips, which because of their extreme hardiness are a reliable winter vegetable, and the red-fleshed beets. Beets are available much of the year, but are at their best in the early summer—again when they are young and small.

Celeriac is the most distinctively flavored root, and the ugliest, but it must not be missed if you like the taste of celery. It is best to choose roots about six inches in diameter and it is essential to peel them. They can be grated raw for salads or cooked. There is a hint of celeriac in the flavor of the root of Hamburg parsley, but in shape it resembles a parsnip.

A curiously large number of roots have lost their one-time popularity. The delicately flavored salsify, or so-called oyster plant, was popular until Victorian times, but has now almost been forgotten. So, too, has its black-skinned version, scorzonera. The sweet-potato flavor of skirret, a great favorite in sixteenth-century England, is now no longer appreciated and neither are the turnip-flavored rampion nor the turnip-rooted chervil, which tastes of aniseed.

Salsify au Gratin

The delicate flavor of salsify, or oyster plant, is complemented by a lemon and herb sauce and grated cheese.

Pour 1¼ cups of water into a saucepan. Add the grated rind and juice of 1 lemon.

Peel 1½ pounds of salsify, about 8 large roots. Cut into 2-inch (5-cm) pieces and drop immediately into the saucepan. This will keep the salsify from turning brown. Add 1 large sprig of thyme, the stalks from 1 small bunch of parsley and salt and pepper to taste.

Cover the pan and bring to the boil. Reduce the heat and simmer gently for 10 minutes, or until the salsify is just tender. Transfer the salsify to a flameproof serving dish and keep warm. Reserve the cooking liquid.

Melt 2 tablespoons of margarine or butter in a saucepan, then stir in 1 tablespoon of flour to make a roux. Add milk to the cooking liquid to bring it to 1¼ cups. Stirring constantly, gradually add it to the roux. Bring to the boil, stirring, and cook until the sauce has thickened. Reduce the heat, stir in 2 tablespoons of chopped parsley, salt and pepper and simmer gently for 2 minutes.

Pour the sauce over the salsify, then sprinkle with grated Parmesan cheese. Put under a hot broiler for 2 to 3 minutes, until the top is brown and bubbling.

INGREDIENTS TO SERVE FOUR:
1 lemon
1½ lb (700 g) salsify
1 large thyme sprig
1 small bunch parsley
salt
pepper
2 tablespoons (25 g) margarine or butter
1 tablespoon (15 ml) flour
milk
grated Parmesan cheese

Carrots Braised with Apples

Preheat the oven to 350°F (180°C).

Scrub and slice 1 pound of carrots. Put them into a casserole or an ovenproof dish.

Peel, core and thickly slice 1 tart apple. Put the apple slices on top of the carrots. Grate in the rind of ½ lemon then squeeze in the juice. Pour in ⅔ cup of water. Season with salt and pepper. Sprinkle with ⅓ cup of seedless raisins.

Cover and bake for 1 hour, or until the carrots are just tender.

INGREDIENTS TO SERVE FOUR:
1 lb (500 g) carrots
1 tart apple
½ lemon
salt
pepper
⅓ cup (50 g) seedless raisins

Sweet and Sour Carrots

Chop 4 slices of bacon. Cut a ¼-inch (6-mm) slice of ginger root. Peel and finely chop it. Scrub 1½ pounds of carrots and thinly slice them. Chop 4 scallions.

In a large, heavy frying pan fry the bacon until the fat runs. Add the chopped ginger and 1 crushed garlic clove and fry for 1 minute.

Add the carrots and the scallions to the pan and fry over moderate heat, stirring constantly, for 3 minutes.

Add 6 tablespoons of water mixed with 2 tablespoons of wine vinegar, 1 tablespoon of soy sauce, 1 tablespoon of brown sugar and salt and pepper to taste. Cover the pan, reduce the heat and simmer for 10 minutes. Uncover and simmer for 3 to 5 minutes more, or until the liquid is reduced and the carrots are tender but still a little crunchy.

PREPARING GINGER ROOT

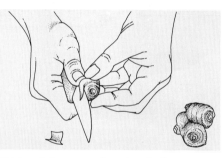

Thinly peel ginger root using a sharp knife.

Chop the ginger very finely before cooking.

Serve at once, sprinkled with 1 tablespoon of chopped coriander or parsley.

INGREDIENTS TO SERVE FOUR:
4 slices bacon
ginger root
1½ lb (700 g) carrots
4 scallions
1 garlic clove
2 tablespoons (30 ml) wine vinegar
1 tablespoon (15 ml) soy sauce
1 tablespoon (15 ml) brown sugar
salt
pepper
1 tablespoon (15 ml) chopped coriander
**   or parsley**

Sherried Carrots

Preheat the oven to 350°F (180°C).

Scrub 1½ pounds of carrots. Quarter them and cut them into sticks about 3 inches (8 cm) long. Put the carrots into a casserole with ⅓ cup of blanched almonds, ⅔ cup of medium or sweet sherry and ⅔ cup of water. Season with salt and pepper.

Cover and bake for 1 hour, or until the carrots are just tender and most of the liquid has been absorbed.

Serve hot, garnished with 1 tablespoon of chopped parsley.

INGREDIENTS TO SERVE FOUR:
1½ lb (700 g) carrots
⅓ cup (50 g) blanched almonds
⅔ cup (150 ml) medium or sweet sherry
salt
pepper
1 tablespoon (15 ml) chopped parsley

Spiced Carrot Cake

Grated carrots give a delicious moistness to this cake, which is flavored with orange and spices.

Preheat the oven to 350°F (180°C). Grease an 8-inch (20-cm) round cake pan and line it with waxed paper. Grease the paper.

In a large mixing bowl cream ½ cup of soft margarine and ⅔ cup of brown sugar until the mixture is light and fluffy.

Beat in 2 eggs, one at a time, alternating with 1 tablespoon from 1 cup of self-rising flour.

Scrub 2 medium-sized carrots and coarsely grate them into the batter. Grate in the rind of ½ orange then squeeze in the juice. Add ½ cup of ground almonds. Beat until well mixed.

Mix ½ teaspoon of ground ginger and ½ teaspoon of ground cinnamon with the remaining flour. Fold it into the cake mixture.

Spoon the batter into the prepared cake pan. Bake for 45 to 55 minutes, or until the cake is well risen, golden brown and firm to the touch.

INGREDIENTS TO MAKE AN EIGHT-INCH (20-CM) CAKE:
½ cup (100 g) soft margarine
⅔ cup (100 g) brown sugar
2 eggs
1 cup (100 g) self-rising flour
2 medium-sized carrots
½ orange
½ cup (50 g) ground almonds
½ teaspoon (2.5 ml) ground ginger
½ teaspoon (2.5 ml) ground cinnamon

Glazed Carrots

Scrub 1½ pounds of young carrots. Leave the small carrots whole, cut larger ones into halves lengthwise. Put them into a saucepan with the grated rind and juice of ½ lemon, 1¼ cups of chicken stock and salt and pepper to taste.

Bring to the boil, cover the pan, reduce the heat and simmer for 10 to 15 minutes, or until the carrots are just tender. Transfer the carrots to a serving bowl and keep warm.

Boil the cooking liquid rapidly until it is reduced to about 6 tablespoons. Remove the pan from the heat and stir in 2 tablespoons of chopped chives or parsley. Pour the sauce over the carrots and serve.

INGREDIENTS TO SERVE FOUR:
1½ lb (700 g) young carrots
½ lemon
1¼ cups (300 ml) chicken stock
salt
pepper
2 tablespoons (30 ml) chopped chives or parsley

Carrot and Orange Salad

First make the dressing. In a salad bowl beat ¼ cup of corn oil with the grated rind and juice of 1 orange, the juice of 1 lemon, salt and pepper. Add ⅓ cup of seedless raisins and let soak for at least 1 hour so that the raisins will swell up and absorb the orange flavor.

Scrub 1 pound of carrots. Coarsely grate them into the salad bowl. Add 2 ounces of bean sprouts. Toss well to coat the carrots and bean sprouts with the dressing.

INGREDIENTS TO SERVE FOUR:
¼ cup (60 ml) corn oil
1 orange
1 lemon
salt
pepper
⅓ cup (50 g) seedless raisins
1 lb (500 g) carrots
2 oz (50 g) bean sprouts

Chilled Carrot and Orange Soup

Scrub and coarsely chop 1 pound of carrots. Put them into a large saucepan with 1 chopped medium-sized onion and 2 scant cups of well-seasoned chicken stock. Add the grated rind and juice of 2 oranges. Season with salt and pepper.

Cover the pan and bring to the boil. Reduce the heat and simmer for 30 minutes, or until the carrots are tender.

Blend or sieve the soup to a purée. Let it cool. Adjust the seasoning.

Chill the soup. Serve garnished with 1 tablespoon of chopped chives.

INGREDIENTS TO SERVE FOUR:
1 lb (500 g) carrots
1 medium-sized onion
2 scant cups (850 ml) well-seasoned chicken stock
2 oranges
salt
pepper
1 tablespoon (15 ml) chopped chives

Cream of Winter Soup

Peel and coarsely chop ½ pound of potatoes. Scrub ½ pound of carrots and cut into thick slices. Peel and coarsely chop ½ pound of parsnips, rutabagas or turnips. Slice 2 stalks of celery.

Put all the vegetables into a large saucepan with 5 cups of well-seasoned chicken stock, 4 sage leaves, 1 bay leaf, 1 parsley sprig, salt and pepper.

Cover the pan and bring to the boil. Reduce the heat and simmer for 40 minutes, or until the vegetables are tender.

Sieve or blend the soup to a purée. Return the soup to the pan and reheat. Adjust the seasoning. Serve hot.

INGREDIENTS TO SERVE SIX:
½ lb (250 g) potatoes
½ lb (250 g) carrots
½ lb (250 g) parsnips, rutabagas or turnips
2 celery stalks
5 cups (1 liter) well-seasoned chicken stock
4 sage leaves
1 bay leaf
1 parsley sprig
salt
pepper

Rutabagas with Lemon and Carrots

Peel 1 pound of young rutabagas and cut them into ½-inch (1-cm) cubes. Scrub ½ pound of carrots and cut them into ½-inch (1-cm) cubes.

Put the rutabagas and carrots into a saucepan with the grated rind and juice of ½ lemon, ⅔ cup of chicken stock and salt and pepper.

Cover the pan and bring to the boil. Reduce the heat and simmer for 10 minutes, or until the vegetables are just tender and most of the stock has been absorbed.

Transfer to a serving dish, garnish with 1 tablespoon of chopped chives.

Serve immediately.

INGREDIENTS TO SERVE FOUR:
1 lb (500 g) young rutabagas
½ lb (250 g) carrots
½ lemon
⅔ cup (150 ml) chicken stock
salt
pepper
1 tablespoon (15 ml) chopped chives

DICING RUTABAGA

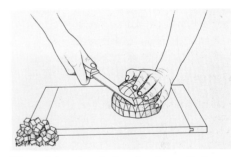

Slice peeled rutabaga in three directions to dice it.

Orange Glazed Turnips

Put 5 cups of peeled and thinly sliced turnips into a saucepan with the grated rind of 1 orange and the juice of 2 large oranges. Season with salt and pepper.

Cover the pan and bring to the boil. Reduce the heat and simmer gently for 10 to 15 minutes, or until the turnips are just tender.

Transfer the turnips to a warm serving dish, sprinkle with 2 tablespoons of chopped parsley and serve.

INGREDIENTS TO SERVE FOUR:
5 cups (700 g) sliced turnips
2 large oranges
salt
pepper
2 tablespoons (30 ml) chopped parsley

Turnips Braised with Bacon

Chop 8 slices of bacon. Chop 1 small onion. Peel 1½ pounds of turnips and cut them into quarters, or sixths if they are large.

Put the bacon into a large saucepan and fry over low heat until the fat runs. Add the onion and fry for 3 minutes.

Add the turnips to the pan with 1¼ cups of beef stock, 1 tablespoon of chopped sage, salt and pepper.

Cover the pan and bring to the boil. Reduce the heat and simmer for 15 minutes, or until the turnips are just tender.

Transfer the turnips to a serving dish and keep warm.

Reduce the cooking liquid to about 5 tablespoons by boiling rapidly. Pour over the turnips.

Serve immediately.

INGREDIENTS TO SERVE FOUR:
8 slices bacon
1 small onion
1½ lb (700 g) turnips
1¼ cups (300 ml) beef stock
1 tablespoon (15 ml) chopped sage
salt
pepper

Roast Parsnips and Bacon

This is one of the most delicious ways to cook parsnips. Don't peel them, because the skin will get crisp while the inside stays sweet and tender and absorbs the flavor of the bacon. Serve with roast meat.

Preheat the oven to 400°F (200°C).

Scrub 1 pound of parsnips. Trim off the root ends. Cut into quarters lengthwise, or sixths if the parsnips are very large. Put the parsnips into a small roasting pan or ovenproof dish. Cover with 8 slices of bacon.

Bake, uncovered, for 30 minutes, or until the bacon is crisp and the parsnips are tender.

Serve immediately.

INGREDIENTS TO SERVE FOUR:
1 lb (500 g) parsnips
8 bacon slices

Parsnip, Tomato and Cheese Casserole

This delicious vegetable casserole makes a light lunch or supper dish. Serve it with boiled rice.

Preheat the oven to 375°F (190°C).

Scrub 1½ pounds of parsnips and cut them into thin slices. Slice 2 medium-sized tomatoes. Prepare 1 cup of grated Gruyère cheese.

Put a layer of the sliced parsnips into a casserole or ovenproof dish. Cover with a layer of tomato slices. Sprinkle with some of the grated cheese and salt and pepper.

Repeat the layers, finishing with a layer of parsnips. Spread ⅔ cup of yogurt over the top and sprinkle with the remaining cheese.

Cover the dish and bake for 40 to 45 minutes, or until the parsnips are almost tender. Uncover the dish and continue to bake for 10 to 15 minutes more, or until the top is crisp and browned.

Serve hot.

INGREDIENTS TO SERVE FOUR AS A MAIN DISH:
1½ lb (700 g) parsnips
2 medium-sized tomatoes
1 cup (100 g) grated Gruyère cheese
salt
pepper
⅔ cup (150 ml) yogurt

PREPARING PARSNIPS

Cut the tops off the parsnips.

Scrub the parsnips with a stiff brush.

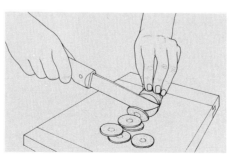

Cut them into thin slices.

Citrus Braised Parsnips

Scrub 1½ pounds of young parsnips. Quarter them and cut them into sticks about 3 inches (7 cm) long.

Put the parsnips into a saucepan with the grated rind and juice of 1 orange and 1 lemon. Add a pinch of grated nutmeg and salt and pepper to taste.

Pour in ⅔ cup of chicken stock. Cover the pan and bring to the boil. Reduce the heat and simmer for 10 minutes, or until the parsnips are just tender.

Transfer the parsnips to a serving dish and keep warm. Reduce the cooking liquid to about 6 tablespoons by boiling rapidly for a few minutes. Pour over the parsnips and serve.

INGREDIENTS TO SERVE FOUR TO SIX:
1½ lb (700 g) parsnips
1 orange
1 lemon
grated nutmeg
salt
pepper
⅔ cup (150 ml) chicken stock

Bortsch

Thinly peel 1 pound of beets and shred them into a large saucepan. Chop 1 large onion and prepare 1½ cups of shredded cabbage. Add the onion and the cabbage to the saucepan with the grated rind and juice of 1 small lemon, 2 tablespoons of tomato paste and 2 bay leaves. Pour in 5 cups of beef stock. Season with salt and pepper.

Cover the pan and bring to the boil. Reduce the heat and simmer for 45 minutes, or until the vegetables are tender.

Before serving add sour cream to taste.

INGREDIENTS TO SERVE FOUR TO SIX:
1 lb (500 g) beets
1 large onion
1½ cups (100 g) shredded cabbage
1 small lemon
2 tablespoons (30 ml) tomato paste
2 bay leaves
5 cups (1 liter) beef stock
salt
pepper
sour cream

Beet and Yogurt Salad

Serve this tangy salad with cold meat.

Put 2 cups of sliced cooked beets into a mixing bowl.

Thinly slice 1 large stalk of celery. Core and chop 1 apple. Add the celery and apple to the beets.

For the dressing, stir the grated rind and juice of ½ lemon into ⅔ cup of yogurt. Season with salt and pepper. Pour the dressing over the beet mixture and toss lightly until well mixed.

Transfer to a serving bowl. Chill before serving.

INGREDIENTS TO SERVE FOUR:
2 cups (500 g) sliced cooked beets
1 celery stalk
1 apple
½ lemon
⅔ cup (150 ml) yogurt
salt
pepper

Beet Ragoût

This sweet and sour beet stew makes a good accompaniment to roast or broiled meat, particularly pork.

Peel 2 medium-sized potatoes and cut them into ½-inch (1-cm) cubes. Put the potatoes into a saucepan with 1¼ cups of beef stock, salt and pepper. Cover the pan and bring to the boil. Reduce the heat and simmer for 5 minutes.

Cook 1 pound of beets in boiling salted water until they are tender. Thinly peel the beets and cut them into thick slices. Cut the slices into halves or quarters, depending on how large the beets are. Peel, core and thinly slice 1 tart apple.

Add the beets and apple slices to the saucepan with ⅓ cup of seedless raisins, 2 tablespoons of wine vinegar, 1 bay leaf and salt and pepper to taste.

Cover the pan and simmer gently for 10 minutes, or until the potatoes are cooked. Serve hot.

INGREDIENTS TO SERVE FOUR:
2 medium-sized potatoes
1¼ cups (300 ml) beef stock
salt
pepper
1 lb (500 g) beets
1 tart apple
⅓ cup (50 g) seedless raisins
2 tablespoons (30 ml) wine vinegar
1 bay leaf

Beets with Orange

Steam 1½ pounds of beets or boil them in a small amount of water.

Peel the beets, then slice them. Put them into a saucepan with the grated rind and juice of 3 oranges. Season with salt and pepper to taste.

Cover the pan and cook over low heat for 5 minutes, or until the beets are hot and most of the orange juice has been absorbed.

Serve hot or cold.

INGREDIENTS TO SERVE FOUR:
1½ lb (700 g) beets
3 oranges
salt
pepper

Celeriac and Salami Salad

This crunchy salad with a yogurt and mustard dressing makes a delicious first course.

Peel ¾ pound of celeriac (celery root) and cut into julienne sticks. Blanch the celeriac for 1 minute in boiling salted water to which

Peel the rough skin off the celeriac.

Slice the celeriac into very thin sticks.

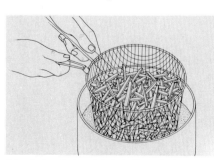

Blanch the celeriac sticks in boiling salted water.

the juice of ½ lemon has been added. Drain and cool.

For the dressing, put ⅔ cup of yogurt into a mixing bowl. Stir in 1 to 2 teaspoons of Dijon mustard, salt and pepper.

Reserve 4 slices from ¼ pound of sliced salami and cut the rest into quarters.

Add the celeriac and salami to the dressing and mix well.

Arrange a bed of lettuce on a serving dish or individual plates. Spoon the salad on top and garnish with the reserved slices of salami.

INGREDIENTS TO SERVE FOUR:
¾ lb (350 g) celeriac
½ lemon
⅔ cup (150 ml) yogurt
1 to 2 teaspoons (5 to 10 ml) Dijon mustard
salt
pepper
¼ lb (100 g) salami
1 small lettuce

Radish Salad

Trim about 30 large radishes. Wash the radishes well and cut them into thin slices and put the slices into a salad bowl.

For the dressing, pour ⅔ cup of yogurt into a mixing bowl. Add 1 tablespoon of chopped parsley, 1 tablespoon of chopped chives, 1 tablespoon of chopped tarragon or chervil, 1 tablespoon of lemon juice and salt and pepper to taste. Stir until well mixed and pour over the radishes.

Chill thoroughly before serving.

INGREDIENTS TO SERVE FOUR:
30 large radishes
⅔ cup (150 ml) yogurt
1 tablespoon (15 ml) chopped parsley
1 tablespoon (15 ml) chopped chives
1 tablespoon (15 ml) chopped tarragon or chervil
1 tablespoon (15 ml) lemon juice
salt
pepper

Horseradish Sauce

Serve this sauce with roast beef.

Put 3 tablespoons of grated horseradish into a mixing bowl. Stir in ⅔ cup of yogurt, salt and pepper.

Set aside for at least 1 hour before serving to allow the flavor to develop.

INGREDIENTS TO SERVE FOUR:
3 tablespoons (45 ml) grated horseradish
⅔ cup (150 ml) yogurt
salt
pepper

HIGH IN FOOD VALUE and fine in flavor, peas and beans come as near to being perfect vegetables as is possible. Whether fresh or dried, they provide more energy and protein than either root or green vegetables. They are a good source of B vitamins and fresh and frozen peas and broad beans contain a reasonable amount of vitamin C. They are valuable in any diet and invaluable to vegetarians.

Nevertheless, during their long history—possibly as long as nine thousand years—the popularity of these vegetables has waxed and waned. The ancient Egyptians connected beans with death and in medieval Europe dried peas and beans were associated with famine, when there was little else to eat, and with Lent, when so many other foods were forbidden. But any danger that these vegetables might fall so much out of favor as to slide into oblivion, in the way vegetables do, was eliminated when they began to be eaten fresh rather than dried.

From its ancient home in Central and South America the green bean (alias French bean, haricot vert, snap bean and string bean) was brought to Europe early in the sixteenth century. A hundred years later the runner bean followed, but it was first grown for its flowers rather than for its pods. Today the runner bean is most popular in Britain and the countries of the eastern Mediterranean. In the United States the runner bean is almost unknown. Nutritionally there is little to choose between French beans and runner beans when they are boiled, but if they are eaten raw runner beans have twice as much vitamin C.

The eating of fresh peas spread northward from Italy in the sixteenth century. In Britain they were made fashionable by Charles II and in France by Louis XIV, who almost stuffed himself to death with them. The popularity of peas was given further boosts when they became the first vegetable to be canned and then the first to be frozen. But in the process of canning, fresh peas lose most of their vitamin C value and so much of their color that green dye has to be added to them. Peas do not lose their vitamin C when they are frozen.

As rich in protein as meat, and strong in B vitamins and iron, legumes would seem to be worthy of a prominent place in the diet. Unfortunately, before they can be eaten, dried peas and beans must be soaked and cooked. When this is done their water content increases from about 12 percent to 70 percent and in lentils, for example, the protein content falls to a quarter, and the energy value falls from almost 300 Calories to about 95 in one hundred grams. In the basket (left) clockwise: orange lentils, chick-peas, kidney beans, soybeans, green split peas, yellow split peas. In the small basket are green lentils and mung beans. On the ground are flageolet beans and black-eyed peas are in the bowl.

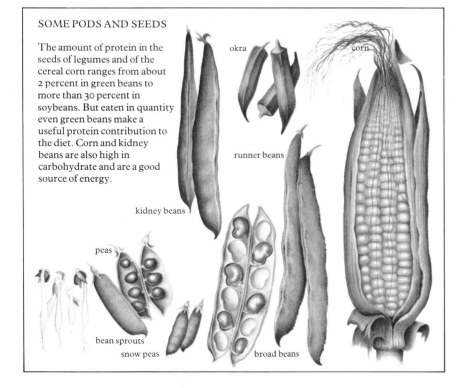

SOME PODS AND SEEDS

The amount of protein in the seeds of legumes and of the cereal corn ranges from about 2 percent in green beans to more than 30 percent in soybeans. But eaten in quantity even green beans make a useful protein contribution to the diet. Corn and kidney beans are also high in carbohydrate and are a good source of energy.

okra

corn

runner beans

kidney beans

peas

bean sprouts

snow peas

broad beans

Once—and not so many years ago—"fresh" peas and beans belonged to summer, but today, frozen, they are vegetables for all seasons. Peas are the most successful of all frozen vegetables, monotonously so, for if food is predictably and uniformly acceptable you escape disappointment by sacrificing any peak of excellence. Moreover, those people who eat frozen peas all year miss that impatient expectancy the rest of us enjoy while waiting for the first crops of early summer and the heightened enjoyment when they arrive. Even this enjoyment is threatened, however, unless we grow our own, for the canners and freezers, in league with agribusiness, grab the best peas.

For centuries, dried peas and beans and other legumes were the staple winter diet and their canned and frozen rivals have only partly ousted them. In the Middle Ages the dried beans were broad beans, but haricot beans, or flageolets, have since taken their place. They have many uses— simply as a vegetable, as baked beans, in stews and as the basis of countless dishes.

There are many other beans to choose from as well. Pale green lima beans have a delicate flavor. Dark red kidney beans are extremely good when they are baked. There are also black-eyed beans, rose cocoa beans and dappled pink pintos, or frijoles. The small, round and red adzuki beans from Japan and China are particularly sweet. On the other hand, the most nutritious bean, the soybean, has a bitter aftertaste unless it is heavily disguised by other flavors.

Dried beans and peas are bursting with protein —about 20 percent. It puts them on a par with meat. The same is true of chick peas and other legumes such as lentils, whether the small orange Egyptian variety or the more flavorsome French green or brown lentils.

Dried legumes lack vitamin C, but by sprouting them they can be made rich in both C and B vitamins. The small green mung beans are the most widely used for sprouting, but soybeans, lentils and chick peas will also do as long as they have not been split.

The Nutrients in Peas
Peas are a useful source of B vitamins, vitamin C and carotene and three and a half ounces (100 g) provide about 70 Calories.

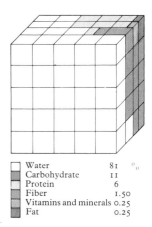

Water	81	%
Carbohydrate	11	
Protein	6	
Fiber	1.50	
Vitamins and minerals	0.25	
Fat	0.25	

The Nutrients in Kidney Beans
These beans are as high in protein as meat and three and a half ounces (100 g) provide about 330 Calories.

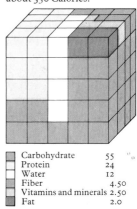

Carbohydrate	55	%
Protein	24	
Water	12	
Fiber	4.50	
Vitamins and minerals	2.50	
Fat	2.0	

Only peas that are eaten straight from the pod (left) taste as they really should. Canned peas have lost most of their original flavor. To retain the nutrients in peas they must be cooked with care. Boiling, for example, can result in a loss of a quarter of their riboflavin and almost half of their niacin.

Green Beans with Garlic and Sage

Snip the ends off 1 pound of green beans and string them if necessary. Cut the beans into diagonal slices about 1 inch (2 cm) long.

Heat 1 tablespoon of corn oil in a saucepan. Add 2 crushed garlic cloves and fry gently for 1 minute until lightly browned.

Stir in 1 tablespoon of chopped sage leaves. Add the beans, $\frac{2}{3}$ cup of water and salt and pepper.

Cover the pan and bring to the boil. Reduce the heat and simmer for about 5 minutes, or until the beans are tender but still slightly crisp.

Serve hot or cold, sprinkled with 1 tablespoon of chopped parsley.

INGREDIENTS TO SERVE FOUR :
1 lb (500 g) green beans
1 tablespoon (15 ml) corn oil
2 garlic cloves
1 tablespoon (15 ml) chopped sage
salt
pepper
1 tablespoon (15 ml) chopped parsley

Green Beans Provençal

This dish may be served hot as a vegetable accompaniment or cold as a first course.

Slice 3 medium-sized onions. Blanch and peel 2 medium-sized tomatoes. Cut them into halves and remove the seeds. Cut 1 small green pepper in half. Remove the seeds and cut away the white pith. Chop the pepper. Snip the ends off 1 pound of green beans.

Heat 2 tablespoons of corn oil in a saucepan. Add the onions and 1 crushed garlic clove and fry for 3 minutes, stirring frequently.

Add the tomatoes and pepper to the pan with 1 tablespoon of chopped oregano and salt and pepper to taste. Cover the pan and simmer gently for 5 minutes, or until the tomatoes are reduced to a pulp.

Add the beans to the pan and simmer, stirring occasionally, for 5 to 10 minutes, or until the beans are tender but still crisp.

Serve hot or cold.

INGREDIENTS TO SERVE FOUR :
3 medium-sized onions
2 medium-sized tomatoes
1 small green pepper
1 lb (500 g) green beans
2 tablespoons (30 ml) corn oil
1 garlic clove
1 tablespoon (15 ml) chopped oregano
salt
pepper

Green Beans with Mushrooms and Yogurt

Snip the ends off 1 pound of green beans and string them if necessary. Slice the beans thinly. Put them into a saucepan.

Add 1 cup of thinly sliced small mushrooms to the pan with the grated rind and juice of $\frac{1}{2}$ lemon, $\frac{1}{4}$ cup of water, salt and pepper. Cover the pan and bring to the boil. Reduce the heat and simmer gently for 5 to 8 minutes, or until the beans and mushrooms are just tender.

Stir in $\frac{2}{3}$ cup of yogurt. Cook gently to heat the yogurt through, but do not boil or it may curdle.

Serve immediately.

INGREDIENTS TO SERVE FOUR :
1 lb (500 g) green beans
1 cup (100 g) sliced small mushrooms
$\frac{1}{2}$ lemon
salt
pepper
$\frac{2}{3}$ cup (150 ml) yogurt

PREPARING GREEN BEANS

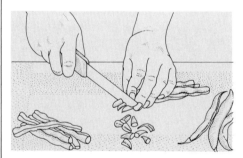

Cut the ends off green beans.

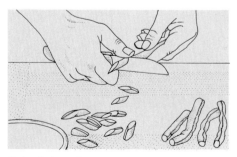

String the beans if necessary and slice them.

Green Beans with Grapes

Snip the ends off 1 pound of green beans and put them into a saucepan.

Add 1 cup of seedless green grapes to the pan with the grated rind and juice of $\frac{1}{2}$ lemon, $\frac{2}{3}$ cup of water, salt and 2 tablespoons of chopped, blanched almonds.

Cover the pan and bring to the boil. Reduce the heat and simmer for 10 minutes, or until the beans are tender but still crisp and most of the water has evaporated. Boil uncovered for 2 to 3 minutes more, or until the cooking liquid is reduced to about 4 tablespoons.

Serve immediately.

INGREDIENTS TO SERVE FOUR :
1 lb (500 g) green beans
1 cup (100 g) seedless green grapes
$\frac{1}{2}$ lemon
salt
2 tablespoons (25 g) chopped, blanched almonds

Salad Niçoise

Snip the ends off $\frac{1}{2}$ pound of green beans. Cook them, covered, in a small amount of boiling salted water until they are barely tender. Drain the beans, rinse them in cold water and put them into a salad bowl.

Cut 1 small green pepper into narrow strips, discarding the pith and seeds. Cut 3 medium-sized tomatoes into small wedges and add to the beans with the green pepper strips.

Drain and flake 7 ounces of canned tuna fish and arrange in the bowl with 2 hard-boiled eggs cut into quarters.

Garnish with 8 anchovies, cut into halves, and 10 pitted black olives.

Just before serving add $\frac{2}{3}$ cup of basic vinaigrette dressing (see page 153) flavored with garlic.

INGREDIENTS TO SERVE FOUR :
$\frac{1}{2}$ lb (250 g) green beans
1 small green pepper
3 medium-sized tomatoes
7 oz (198 g) canned tuna fish
2 hard-boiled eggs
8 anchovies
10 pitted black olives
$\frac{2}{3}$ cup (150 ml) basic vinaigrette dressing flavored with garlic (see page 153)

Green Bean, Lemon and Almond Salad

Snip the ends off 1 pound of green beans. Cook them, covered, in a small amount of boiling salted water for 3 to 5 minutes, or until barely tender.

Drain the beans and rinse them in cold water to cool them. Put them into a salad bowl.

For the dressing, heat 2 tablespoons of corn oil in a saucepan. Add ¼ cup of split blanched almonds and fry gently for about 3 minutes, or until the almonds are lightly browned. Remove the pan from the heat and stir in 1 tablespoon of lemon juice, 1 tablespoon of chopped parsley, salt and pepper. Pour immediately over the beans and toss well to coat all the beans in the lemon dressing.

Chill before serving.

INGREDIENTS TO SERVE FOUR TO SIX:
1 lb (500 g) green beans
2 tablespoons (30 ml) corn oil
¼ cup (50 g) split blanched almonds
1 tablespoon (15 ml) lemon juice
1 tablespoon (15 ml) chopped parsley
salt
pepper

Snow Peas with Bacon and Lemon

In this dish the snow peas are stir-fried in the Chinese style, so that they cook quickly and retain their crispness.

Wash 1 pound of snow peas. Snip the ends off and string them if necessary.

Chop 4 slices of bacon. Put the bacon into a *wok* or a large frying pan with 1 tablespoon of corn oil. Fry for 2 minutes, stirring constantly.

Add the snow peas and fry, stirring constantly, for 1 minute.

Add 5 tablespoons of chicken stock, the juice of 1 small lemon and salt and pepper. Cook over moderate heat, stirring constantly, for about 5 minutes, or until the peas are tender but still crisp and most of the stock has evaporated.

Serve immediately.

INGREDIENTS TO SERVE FOUR:
1 lb (500 g) snow peas
4 slices bacon
1 tablespoon (15 ml) corn oil
5 tablespoons (75 ml) chicken stock
1 small lemon
salt
pepper

Green Pea Soup

Hull 1 pound of peas and put them into a large saucepan. Shred ½ head of lettuce and add to the peas.

Chop 1 small onion and add it to the pan with 1 sprig of rosemary, salt and pepper.

Pour in 3¾ cups of chicken stock. Add the grated rind and juice of ½ lemon.

Cover the pan and bring to the boil. Reduce the heat and simmer for 30 minutes. Blend or sieve the soup to a purée.

Adjust the seasoning and reheat.

INGREDIENTS TO SERVE FOUR:
1 lb (500 g) unhulled peas
½ head of lettuce
1 small onion
1 rosemary sprig
salt
pepper
3¾ cups (850 ml) chicken stock
½ lemon

Pea Purée

Hull 2 pounds of peas. Put them into a saucepan with ¼ cup of chicken stock, salt and pepper. Chop 1 small onion and add it to the peas.

Cover the pan and bring to the boil slowly. Reduce the heat and simmer gently, stirring occasionally, for 15 minutes, or until the peas are tender and all the stock has been absorbed. Add more stock if necessary.

Put the peas into a blender with ¼ cup of yogurt. Blend to a smooth purée.

Return the purée to the pan and reheat, beating, but do not boil. Adjust the seasoning. Serve hot or cold garnished with 1 tablespoon of chopped parsley.

INGREDIENTS TO SERVE FOUR TO SIX:
2 lb (1 kg) unhulled peas
¼ cup (60 ml) chicken stock
salt
pepper
1 small onion
¼ cup (60 ml) yogurt
1 tablespoon (15 ml) chopped parsley

HULLING PEAS

Open the pod and push the peas out.

Peas with Grapefruit and Mint

Hull 2 pounds of peas and put them into a saucepan with the grated rind and juice of 1 grapefruit.

Cut the peel and pith from another grapefruit, then, working over the pan, cut the membrane away from the segments of fruit. Add the grapefruit segments to the peas with 1 tablespoon of chopped mint, salt and pepper.

Cover the pan and bring to the boil slowly. Reduce the heat and simmer gently for 15 minutes, or until the peas are just tender and almost all the grapefruit juice has been absorbed.

Serve hot garnished with sprigs of mint.

INGREDIENTS TO SERVE FOUR:
2 lb (1 kg) unhulled peas
2 grapefruit
1 small bunch mint
salt
pepper

Peas with Rice and Tomatoes

This vegetable risotto makes a substantial lunch or supper dish.

Chop 4 slices of bacon. Chop 1 large onion. Blanch and peel 4 medium-sized tomatoes, cut them into quarters and remove the seeds.

Heat 1 tablespoon of corn oil in a saucepan. Add the bacon and the onion and fry for 3 minutes, stirring frequently. Add the tomatoes to the pan, cover and cook for 2 minutes.

Add 1¼ cups of brown rice to the pan with 2½ cups of chicken stock and salt and pepper to taste. Cover the pan and simmer for 20 minutes.

Hull 1 pound of peas. Add the peas to the pan and continue to cook, covered, for 20 minutes more, or until the rice is tender, but still a little chewy, the peas are cooked and all the stock is absorbed.

Serve hot, sprinkled with 2 tablespoons of grated Parmesan cheese and 1 tablespoon of chopped parsley.

INGREDIENTS TO SERVE FOUR:
4 slices bacon
1 large onion
4 medium-sized tomatoes
1 tablespoon (15 ml) corn oil
1¼ cups (250 g) brown rice
2½ cups (600 ml) chicken stock
1 lb (500 g) unhulled peas
salt
pepper
2 tablespoons (30 ml) grated Parmesan cheese
1 tablespoon (15 ml) chopped parsley

Pois à la Française

This French method of cooking peas with lettuce and scallions makes a delicious dish.

Wash but do not drain the leaves of 1 Boston lettuce. Put the large outside leaves into a saucepan.

Hull 2 pounds of peas and put them on top of the lettuce.

Chop 4 scallions and add them to the pan with 1 tablespoon of chopped mint, salt and pepper. Shred the remaining lettuce and put it on top of the peas. Add 4 tablespoons of water.

Cover the pan, bring slowly to the boil, then reduce the heat and simmer gently for 15 minutes, or until the peas are tender.

Transfer to a serving bowl with the cooking liquid, garnish with sprigs of mint and serve.

INGREDIENTS TO SERVE FOUR TO SIX:
1 head Boston lettuce
2 lb (1 kg) unhulled peas
4 scallions
1 small bunch mint
salt
pepper

Baby Lima Beans in the Pod

When Lima beans are very young they are delicious eaten in the pod like snow peas.

Snip the ends off 1 pound of baby Lima beans. Cut them diagonally into pieces about 2 inches (5 cm) long and put them into a saucepan.

Add ⅔ cup of chicken stock or water, the juice of 1 small lemon, salt and pepper.

Cover the pan and bring to the boil. Reduce the heat and simmer, stirring occasionally, for 5 to 10 minutes, or until the beans are just tender but still a little crisp. All the liquid should have evaporated by the time the beans are cooked.

Serve at once, sprinkled with 1 tablespoon of chopped parsley.

INGREDIENTS TO SERVE FOUR:
1 lb (500 g) baby Lima beans
⅔ cup (150 ml) chicken stock or water
1 small lemon
salt
pepper
1 tablespoon (15 ml) chopped parsley

Lima Beans in Yogurt Sauce

Hull 2 pounds of Lima beans. Put them into a saucepan with ⅔ cup of water, salt and pepper.

Cover the pan and bring to the boil. Reduce the heat and simmer for 5 to 10 minutes, depending on the size and age of the beans, until just tender.

Drain the beans and return them to the pan.

For the sauce, pour ⅔ cup of yogurt into a mixing bowl. Stir in 2 tablespoons of chopped parsley and 2 tablespoons of chopped chives or scallions, salt and pepper.

Pour the yogurt sauce over the beans and reheat, but do not boil or the yogurt may curdle.

Serve hot or cold.

INGREDIENTS TO SERVE FOUR:
2 lb (1 kg) unhulled Lima beans
salt
pepper
⅔ cup (150 ml) yogurt
2 tablespoons (30 ml) chopped parsley
2 tablespoons (30 ml) chopped chives or scallions

HULLING BEANS

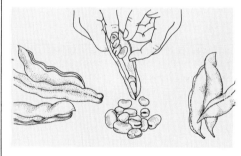

Open the pod and push the beans out with your thumb.

Lima Beans Creole

Hull 2 pounds of young Lima beans. Put the beans into a saucepan with a small amount of boiling salted water, cover the pan and boil rapidly for 20 to 30 minutes, or until the beans are tender. Drain the beans.

Chop 1 medium-sized onion. Cut 1 small green pepper in half and remove the seeds and the white pith. Chop the pepper. Blanch and peel 6 ripe medium-sized tomatoes. Cut them into halves and remove the seeds.

Fry two slices of bacon in a saucepan until crisp. Remove the bacon from the pan with a slotted spoon. Add the chopped onion and pepper to the pan and fry, stirring frequently, for 5 minutes, or until tender but not brown. Add the tomatoes, cover the pan and cook, stirring occasionally, for 15 minutes. Add the beans and season to taste with salt and pepper. Cook for 3 minutes more.

Transfer to a serving dish. Crumble the bacon over the vegetables and serve.

INGREDIENTS TO SERVE FOUR:
2 lb (500 g) unhulled young Lima beans
1 medium-sized onion
1 small green pepper
6 ripe medium-sized tomatoes
2 slices bacon
salt
pepper

Okra Stew

Wash 1 pound of young, tender okra pods. Cut off the stems without cutting into the pods. Chop 1 medium-sized onion. Blanch, peel and quarter 2 medium-sized tomatoes.

Heat 1 tablespoon of corn oil in a saucepan. Add the chopped onion to the pan with 1 crushed garlic clove. Fry, stirring frequently, for 3 minutes.

Add the tomatoes to the pan with ½ teaspoon of ground coriander, the grated rind and juice of ½ lemon, salt and pepper. Cover the pan and cook over low heat for 5 minutes, or until the tomatoes are reduced to a pulp.

Add the okra to the pan, cover and continue to cook for 8 to 10 minutes, or until the okra is tender. Serve hot or cold.

INGREDIENTS TO SERVE FOUR:
1 lb (500 g) young okra
1 medium-sized onion
2 medium-sized tomatoes
1 tablespoon (15 ml) corn oil
1 garlic clove
½ teaspoon (2.5 ml) ground coriander
½ lemon
salt
pepper

PREPARING OKRA

Trim the stems of okra, leaving the pods intact.

Chinese Bean Sprouts

Chop 4 slices of bacon and 4 scallions. Peel and finely chop ¼-inch (6-mm) slice of ginger root. Thinly slice 4 stalks of celery. Prepare 1 cup of sliced mushrooms.

Heat 1 tablespoon of peanut oil in a large frying pan or a *wok*. Add the bacon, scallions, celery and ginger to the pan and fry over high heat, stirring constantly, for 3 minutes. Add the mushrooms and stir-fry for 1 minute.

Add 1 pound of bean sprouts, 5 tablespoons of chicken stock and 1 tablespoon of soy sauce. Continue to stir-fry for 2 to 3 minutes, or until the bean sprouts are hot and well coated in the sauce, but are still crisp.

INGREDIENTS TO SERVE FOUR TO SIX:
4 slices bacon
4 scallions
ginger root
4 celery stalks
1 cup (100 g) sliced mushrooms
1 tablespoon (15 ml) peanut oil
1 lb (500 g) bean sprouts
5 tablespoons (75 ml) chicken stock
1 tablespoon (15 ml) soy sauce

Corn on the Cob

For corn kernels, cook the whole ears of corn first. Then cut the kernels off the cob with a sharp knife. A medium-sized ear gives about ½ cup of kernels.

Remove the husks and silk from 4 medium-sized ears of corn. Line a large saucepan with the husks. Add 1 inch (2 cm) of boiling water. Drop the ears in one by one so that the temperature of the water does not drop. Cover the pan and boil for 4 to 10 minutes, depending on how old the corn is.

Drain and serve with margarine or butter, salt and freshly ground black pepper.

INGREDIENTS TO SERVE FOUR:
4 medium-sized ears corn
margarine or butter
salt
freshly ground black pepper

Corn Chowder

Chop 1 large onion and 8 slices of bacon. Heat 1 tablespoon of corn oil in a large saucepan. Add the onion and bacon to the pan and fry, stirring frequently, for 3 minutes.

Peel 4 medium-sized potatoes and cut them into ½-inch (1-cm) cubes. Add the potatoes to the pan with 2 scant cups of water and salt and pepper to taste. Bring to the boil, cover the pan, reduce the heat and simmer for 15 minutes, or until the potatoes are tender.

Add 1 cup of cooked corn kernels. Stir in 1¼ cups of milk and continue to simmer for 5 minutes. Adjust the seasoning. Serve hot, sprinkled with ½ cup of grated Cheddar cheese and 1 tablespoon of chopped parsley.

INGREDIENTS TO SERVE FOUR TO SIX:
1 large onion
8 slices bacon
1 tablespoon (15 ml) corn oil
4 medium-sized potatoes
salt
pepper
1 cup (250 g) cooked corn kernels
1¼ cups (300 ml) milk
½ cup (50 g) grated Cheddar cheese
1 tablespoon (15 ml) chopped parsley

Corn Quiche

Preheat the oven to 400 F (200 C).

Make 1½ cups of shortcrust pastry (see page 34) and line an 8-inch (20-cm) flan ring or pie pan. Bake blind for 15 minutes. Remove the baking paper and beans and bake for 5 to 10 minutes more, or until the pastry is just beginning to color.

Reduce the oven temperature to 350 F (180 C)

Spread 1 cup of corn kernels and ½ cup of chopped cooked ham in the pastry shell.

Beat 2 eggs with ⅔ cup of milk. Grate in 1 small onion. Season with salt and pepper

Pour the mixture into the pastry shell and bake for 25 minutes, or until set.

INGREDIENTS TO SERVE FOUR TO SIX:
1½ cups (150 g) shortcrust pastry (see page 34)
1 cup (250 g) corn kernels
½ cup (100 g) chopped cooked ham
2 eggs
⅔ cup (150 ml) milk
1 small onion
salt
pepper

Mealie Bread

Preheat the oven to 375 F (190 C). Grease a loaf pan.

Put 2 eggs and 1½ cups of corn kernels into a blender and blend for 1 minute. Add 1 tablespoon of softened margarine or butter, 1 tablespoon of sugar, 1 teaspoon of baking powder and 1 teaspoon of salt and blend to a smooth purée. Alternatively, the corn may be mashed in a bowl and the remaining ingredients beaten in.

Transfer the purée to the prepared loaf pan and cover with foil. Bake for 1 hour.

Turn the loaf out onto a wire rack to cool.

INGREDIENTS TO MAKE 1 SMALL LOAF:
2 eggs
1½ cups (350 g) corn kernels
1 tablespoon (15 ml) margarine or butter
1 tablespoon (15 ml) sugar
1 teaspoon (5 ml) baking powder
1 teaspoon (5 ml) salt

Chili con Carne

This is a moderately hot version of the famous Mexican dish. More chilli powder or finely chopped fresh chilies can be added, with caution.

Soak ¾ cup of kidney beans in cold water overnight. Blanch, peel and coarsely chop 1 pound of ripe tomatoes.

Heat 2 tablespoons of corn oil in a large saucepan. Add 2 sliced onions with 1 crushed garlic clove. Fry for 3 minutes, stirring frequently. Cut any excess fat from 1 pound of chuck roast. Cut the beef into small cubes. Add the meat to the pan and fry, stirring constantly, until it is brown.

Stir in 1 tablespoon of flour and 2 teaspoons of chilli powder. Drain the kidney beans well and add them to the pan with the tomatoes, 1¼ cups of water, salt and pepper. Cover the pan, reduce the heat and simmer for 1 hour, or until the beans are cooked. Stir occasionally during cooking and add a little more water if the mixture becomes too dry.

Adjust the seasoning and serve immediately.

INGREDIENTS TO SERVE FOUR:
¾ cup (250 g) kidney beans
1 lb (500 g) ripe tomatoes
2 tablespoons (30 ml) corn oil
2 onions
1 garlic clove
1 lb (500 g) chuck roast
1 tablespoon (15 ml) flour
2 teaspoons (10 ml) chilli powder
salt
pepper

BEFORE DRIED LEGUMES CAN BE COOKED they must be soaked. This can be done in one of three ways, depending on the time available. Dried legumes should be soaked in the proportion of 1 cup of dried legumes to $2\frac{1}{2}$ cups of water. The legumes absorb a lot of water and after soaking they should have doubled in size and weight.

SOAKING OVERNIGHT
Put 1 cup of dried legumes into a bowl. Pour in $2\frac{1}{2}$ cups of cold water. Soak the legumes for 8 to 12 hours.

SOAKING FOR TWO HOURS
Put 1 cup of dried legumes into a bowl. Pour in $2\frac{1}{2}$ cups of boiling water. Soak the legumes for 2 hours.

SOAKING FOR ONE HOUR
Put 1 cup of dried legumes into a saucepan with $2\frac{1}{2}$ cups of cold water. Bring to the boil and cook the legumes for 2 minutes. Remove the pan from the heat and let the legumes soak for 1 hour.

Lima Bean Soup

Soak 1 cup of dried Lima beans in $2\frac{1}{2}$ cups of water.

Drain the Lima beans and reserve the water. Put the beans into a large saucepan with 1 chopped onion, 2 chopped celery stalks, 1 sliced large carrot, the grated rind and juice of $\frac{1}{2}$ lemon and 1 bay leaf. Add 3 to 4 cups of beef stock to the soaking liquid to make it up to 5 cups. Pour it over the beans and vegetables. Season with salt and pepper. Cover the pan and bring to the boil. Reduce the heat and simmer gently for 2 hours, or until the beans are tender.

Blend or sieve the soup. Return the soup to the pan and reheat. Adjust the seasoning and add more stock if necessary.

INGREDIENTS TO SERVE FOUR:
1 cup (250 g) dried Lima beans
1 onion
2 celery stalks
1 large carrot
$\frac{1}{2}$ lemon
3 to 4 cups (700 to 900 ml) beef stock
1 bay leaf
salt
pepper

Lima Beans Hors d'oeuvre

Dried Lima beans cooked with garlic and herbs make a delicious and unusual first course.

Soak 1 cup of dried Lima beans in $2\frac{1}{2}$ cups of water.

Drain the beans and reserve the water. Put the beans into a saucepan with 1 chopped large onion, 1 or 2 large garlic cloves, crushed, 2 tablespoons of chopped parsley, 1 tablespoon of chopped thyme and 1 tablespoon of chopped marjoram or oregano. Add the grated rind and juice of 1 small lemon, 1 bay leaf and salt and pepper. Add water to make the soaking water up to $2\frac{1}{2}$ cups and pour it into the saucepan.

Cover the pan and bring to the boil. Reduce the heat and simmer for about 2 hours, or until the beans are tender.

Drain the beans. Reserve the cooking liquid. Put the beans into a bowl. Return the cooking liquid to the pan and boil rapidly until it has reduced to about $\frac{2}{3}$ cup, then pour it over the beans.

Serve cold, sprinkled with 1 tablespoon of chopped parsley.

INGREDIENTS TO SERVE FOUR AS A STARTER:
1 cup (250 g) dried Lima beans
1 large onion
1 or 2 large garlic cloves
3 tablespoons (30 ml) chopped parsley
1 tablespoon (15 ml) chopped thyme
**1 tablespoon (15 ml) chopped marjoram
  or oregano**
1 small lemon
1 bay leaf
salt
pepper

Lima Beans Provençal

Soak 1 cup of dried Lima beans in $2\frac{1}{2}$ cups of water.

Drain the beans, reserving the soaking water, and put them into a saucepan. Add more water to make the soaking water up to $2\frac{1}{2}$ cups. Pour it over the beans. Cover the pan and bring to the boil. Reduce the heat and simmer for 45 to 60 minutes, or until the beans are almost tender. Drain the beans and reserve the cooking liquid.

For the sauce, chop 4 slices of bacon. Chop 3 medium-sized onions and 1 garlic clove. Blanch and peel 3 medium-sized tomatoes, then cut them into quarters. Cut 1 small green pepper into strips, discarding the seeds and the pith.

Heat 1 tablespoon of corn oil in a saucepan. Add the chopped bacon, onions and garlic. Fry for 3 minutes, stirring frequently, until the onions are lightly browned.

Add the tomatoes and green pepper and $\frac{2}{3}$ cup of the strained cooking liquid. Season with salt and pepper. Bring to the boil. Add

the Lima beans and 12 stuffed olives, halved.

Cover the pan, reduce the heat and simmer, stirring occasionally, for 45 to 60 minutes, or until the beans are tender.

Serve hot or cold.

INGREDIENTS TO SERVE FOUR:
1 cup (250 g) dried Lima beans
4 slices bacon
3 medium-sized onions
1 garlic clove
3 medium-sized tomatoes
1 small green pepper
1 tablespoon (15 ml) corn oil
salt
pepper
12 stuffed olives

Lima Bean Goulash

Soak 1 cup of dried Lima beans in $2\frac{1}{2}$ cups of water. Drain the beans and reserve the soaking water.

Chop 8 slices of bacon. Slice 3 medium-sized onions and 2 celery stalks. Blanch and peel 2 medium-sized tomatoes and cut them into quarters.

Over low heat, fry the bacon in a saucepan until the fat runs. Add the chopped onions and celery and fry, stirring frequently, for 3 minutes, or until lightly browned. Stir in 1 tablespoon of paprika and cook for 1 minute. Add the tomatoes to the pan.

Add water to make the soaking water up to $2\frac{1}{2}$ cups. Stir it into the pan. Add the grated rind and juice of $\frac{1}{2}$ lemon, salt and pepper. Bring to the boil. Add the Lima beans. Cover the pan and simmer for 2 hours, or until the beans are tender.

Add 1 cup of sliced mushrooms. Cover the pan and cook for 10 to 15 minutes more, or until the mushrooms are cooked.

Serve hot.

INGREDIENTS TO SERVE FOUR:
1 cup (250 g) dried Lima beans
8 slices bacon
3 medium-sized onions
2 celery stalks
2 medium-sized tomatoes
1 tablespoon (15 ml) paprika
$\frac{1}{2}$ lemon
salt
pepper
1 cup (100 g) sliced mushrooms

Curried Soybeans

Soak 1 cup of dried soybeans in 2½ cups of water.

Drain the soybeans, reserving the water, and put them into a saucepan. Add water to make up the soaking water to 5 cups and pour it over the beans. Cover the pan and bring to the boil. Reduce the heat and simmer for 2 to 3 hours, or until the beans are tender.

Drain the beans, reserving the cooking liquid.

Grind spices in a mortar to mix a curry powder.

Meanwhile, heat 2 tablespoons of corn oil in a saucepan. Add 1 chopped large onion and 1 crushed large garlic clove and fry for 3 minutes, stirring frequently. Peel and finely chop 1-inch (2-cm) slice of ginger root and add it to the pan with 1 finely chopped seeded green chili and continue frying.

In a mortar grind together 1 teaspoon of turmeric, 2 teaspoons of ground coriander, 1 teaspoon of ground cumin, ½ teaspoon of cayenne pepper and 1 teaspoon of ground paprika. Add enough cold water to make a paste.

Add the paste to the onion mixture and fry, stirring constantly, for 5 minutes. Stir in 1 to 2 tablespoons of the bean stock if the mixture gets too dry.

Pour in 1 pint of bean stock and mix well. Bring to the boil, stirring occasionally, then add the soybeans. Cover the pan and simmer for 1 hour, or until the beans are tender and have absorbed the flavor of the curry. Season to taste with salt. Alternatively, cook in the oven, covered, at 350°F (180°C), for 1 hour.

INGREDIENTS TO SERVE FOUR:
**1 cup (250 g) dried soybeans
2 tablespoons (30 ml) corn oil
1 large onion
1 large garlic clove
ginger root
1 green chili
1 teaspoon (5 ml) turmeric
2 teaspoons (10 ml) ground coriander
1 teaspoon (5 ml) ground cumin
½ teaspoon (2.5 ml) cayenne pepper
1 teaspoon (5 ml) ground paprika
salt**

Soybean Casserole

Soybeans baked with onions, tomatoes and cheese makes a substantial main-course dish.

Soak 1 cup of dried soybeans in 2½ cups of water.

Drain the beans, reserving the soaking water, and put them into a saucepan. Add water to make the soaking water up to 5 cups and pour it over the beans. Cover the pan and bring to the boil. Reduce the heat and simmer for 2 to 3 hours, or until the beans are tender. Drain the beans and reserve the cooking liquid.

Preheat the oven to 350°F (180°C).

Thinly slice 1 large onion and 3 medium-sized tomatoes.

In a small bowl combine 1 tablespoon of grated Parmesan cheese, 1 tablespoon of chopped parsley, 1 tablespoon of chopped mixed herbs and salt and pepper.

Put half of the drained beans into a casserole or ovenproof dish. Arrange half of the onions and tomatoes on the beans and sprinkle with the cheese mixture. Make another layer of beans and another layer of onions and tomatoes. Pour in 1¼ cups of the cooking liquid or beef stock. Sprinkle with 1 tablespoon of grated Parmesan cheese.

Cover the dish and bake for 1 hour, uncovering the dish for the last 20 minutes to brown the top.

INGREDIENTS TO SERVE FOUR:
**1 cup (250 g) dried soybeans
1 large onion
3 medium-sized tomatoes
2 tablespoons (30 ml) grated Parmesan cheese
1 tablespoon (15 ml) chopped parsley
1 tablespoon (15 ml) chopped mixed herbs
salt
pepper
1¼ cups (300 ml) beef stock (optional)**

Baked Soybean Cakes

These onion- and cheese-flavored soybean cakes may be served hot, with tomato sauce, or cold.

Soak 1 cup of dried soybeans in 2½ cups of water. Drain the beans, reserving the soaking water, and put the beans into a saucepan. Add water to make the soaking water up to 5 cups and pour it over the beans. Cover the pan and bring to the boil. Reduce the heat and simmer for about 3 hours, or until the beans are soft enough to mash. Drain the beans.

Preheat the oven to 425°F (220°C).

Mash the soybeans well. Add 1 grated small onion, ½ cup of grated sharp Cheddar cheese, 2 tablespoons of chopped parsley, salt and pepper. Mix well. Beat 1 egg and stir it into the mixture.

Divide the mixture into 8 and shape into round cakes. Put the cakes on a greased baking sheet and bake for 20 to 30 minutes, or until they are brown and crisp.

INGREDIENTS TO SERVE FOUR:
**1 cup (250 g) dried soybeans
1 small onion
½ cup (50 g) grated sharp Cheddar cheese
2 tablespoons (30 ml) chopped parsley
salt
pepper
1 egg**

Bean Cassoulet

Soak 1 cup of dried white beans or navy beans in 2½ cups of water.

Drain the beans, reserving the water, and put them into a saucepan. Add water to make the soaking water up to 2½ cups and pour it into the saucepan. Cover the pan and bring to the boil. Reduce the heat and simmer for 1 hour, or until the beans are just tender. Drain the beans.

Preheat the oven to 350°F (180°C).

Slice 3 medium-sized onions. Scrub 3 medium-sized carrots and slice them thinly. Slice 2 celery stalks. Cut ¼ pound of sliced salami into half slices. Slice ¼ pound of garlic sausage, then cut the slices into halves. Blanch, peel and coarsely chop 4 large ripe tomatoes.

Layer the beans in a casserole or ovenproof dish with the onions, carrots, celery, salami and garlic sausage. Put the chopped tomatoes on top, pour in ⅔ cup of water and sprinkle with salt and pepper. Put 1 bay leaf on top.

Bake, covered, for 1½ hours, stirring occasionally.

INGREDIENTS TO SERVE FOUR:
**1 cup (250 g) dried white beans or navy beans
3 medium-sized onions
3 medium-sized carrots
2 celery stalks
¼ lb (100 g) sliced salami
¼ lb (100 g) garlic sausage
4 large ripe tomatoes
salt
pepper
1 bay leaf**

Baked Beans

Soak 1 cup of dried white beans or navy beans in 2½ cups of water.

Drain the beans, reserving the soaking water, and put them into a saucepan. Add water to make the soaking water up to 2½ cups and pour it over the beans. Cover the pan and bring to the boil. Reduce the heat and simmer for 1 hour, or until the beans are tender, adding more water if necessary. Drain the beans and reserve the cooking liquid.

Preheat the oven to 350°F (180°C).

In a bowl combine 1¼ cups of the cooking liquid, 1 chopped onion, 1 tablespoon of dark molasses, 2 tablespoons of tomato paste, 2 teaspoons of dried mustard, 2 teaspoons of Worcestershire sauce and 1 teaspoon of salt.

Put the beans into a casserole or baking dish. Pour in the spicy liquid and mix well. Arrange 6 thick slices of bacon or ½ lb of sliced salt pork on top.

Cover the casserole and bake for 1½ hours, then uncover and bake for 30 minutes more. Alternatively, the beans may be cooked in a very slow oven for about 5 hours, uncovering the casserole for the last hour. Add a little more cooking liquid if the beans become dry during cooking.

INGREDIENTS TO SERVE FOUR:
1 cup (250 g) dried white beans or navy
   beans
1 onion
1 tablespoon (15 ml) dark molasses
2 tablespoons (30 ml) tomato paste
2 teaspoons (10 ml) dried mustard
2 teaspoons (10 ml) Worcestershire
   sauce
salt
6 thick slices bacon or
   ½ lb (250 g) salt pork

Beans Bourguignonne

Soak 1 cup of dried white beans or navy beans in 2½ cups of water. Add water to make the soaking water up to 2½ cups. Put the beans and the water into a saucepan and bring to the boil. Cover the pan, reduce the heat and simmer for 1 hour, or until the beans are almost tender. Drain the beans and reserve the cooking liquid.

For the sauce, chop 8 slices of bacon. Chop 1 large onion. Prepare 1 cup of sliced mushrooms.

Fry the bacon gently in a saucepan until the fat runs. Add the chopped onion and fry for 3 minutes, stirring frequently. Add the mushrooms to the pan and fry for 2 minutes.

Pour ⅔ cup of the cooking liquid and 1¼ cups of red wine into the pan. Season with salt and pepper and bring to the boil. Add the drained beans, cover the pan, reduce the heat and simmer gently for 45 to 60 minutes, or

until the beans are cooked and the wine sauce has reduced and thickened slightly.

Serve hot, sprinkled with 1 tablespoon of chopped parsley.

INGREDIENTS TO SERVE FOUR:
1 cup (250 g) dried white beans or navy
   beans
8 slices bacon
1 large onion
1 cup (100 g) sliced mushrooms
1¼ cups (300 ml) red wine
salt
pepper
1 tablespoon (15 ml) chopped parsley

Bean and Tuna Salad

This piquant Italian dish from Tuscany makes a substantial first course.

Soak 1 cup of dried white beans or navy beans in 2½ cups of water.

Drain the soaked beans, reserving the water, and put them into a saucepan. Add water to make the soaking water up to 2½ cups and pour it into the pan. Add ½ teaspoon of salt. Cover the pan and bring to the boil. Reduce the heat and simmer for 45 to 60 minutes, or until the beans are tender. Drain the beans and set aside to cool.

Put the cooled beans into a bowl. Drain and flake 7 ounces of canned tuna fish and add it to the beans with 1 finely chopped small onion, 4 tablespoons of chopped parsley and the grated rind of 1 lemon.

Pour in 1¼ cups of vinaigrette dressing (see page 153). Toss well. Marinate in the refrigerator for at least 2 hours. Before serving toss again, then sprinkle with 1 tablespoon of chopped parsley.

INGREDIENTS TO SERVE SIX AS A FIRST COURSE:
1 cup (250 g) dried white beans or navy
   beans
7 oz (198 g) canned tuna fish
1 small onion
1 small bunch parsley
1 lemon
1¼ cups (300 ml) vinaigrette dressing
   (see page 153)

Sweet and Sour Beans

Soak 1 cup of dried white beans or navy beans in 2½ cups of water.

Put the beans into a saucepan. Add water to make the soaking water up to 2½ cups. Pour it into the saucepan. Cook the beans, covered, for 1 hour, or until tender. Drain the beans and reserve the cooking liquid.

Chop 8 slices of bacon. Chop 1 small onion. Scrub 3 medium-sized carrots and dice them. Peel and core 1 large tart apple and slice it thickly. Shred ½ pound of white cabbage.

Put the bacon into a large saucepan and fry over low heat until the fat runs. Add the onion and fry, stirring frequently, for 3 minutes.

Add the diced carrots, the sliced apple, ⅓ cup of seedless raisins and the drained beans to the pan. Add water to make the cooking liquid up to 2½ cups. Add it to the pan with 1 tablespoon of wine vinegar and salt and pepper. Simmer, covered, for 20 minutes.

Add the cabbage and continue to cook, covered, for 5 to 10 minutes, or until all the vegetables are cooked.

Serve hot.

INGREDIENTS TO SERVE FOUR TO SIX:
1 cup (250 g) dried white beans or navy
   beans
8 slices bacon
1 small onion
3 medium-sized carrots
1 large tart apple
½ lb (250 g) white cabbage
⅓ cup (50 g) seedless raisins
1 tablespoon (15 ml) wine vinegar
salt
pepper

Hopping John

This southern recipe is a mixture of black-eyed peas, rice and tomatoes.

Soak 1 cup of dried black-eyed peas in 2½ cups of water.

Drain the peas, reserving the soaking water, and put them into a saucepan. Add water to make up the soaking water to 2½ cups and pour it over the peas. Cover the pan and bring to the boil. Reduce the heat and simmer for 1 hour, or until the beans are tender.

Blanch and peel 2 medium-sized ripe tomatoes. Cut them into halves and remove the seeds. Coarsely chop the tomatoes and add to the peas with ⅔ cup of brown rice.

Cover the pan and continue to simmer, stirring occasionally and adding a little more water if necessary, for about 40 minutes, or until the peas and rice are cooked and all the water has been absorbed. Season to taste with salt and pepper.

Serve hot, sprinkled with 2 tablespoons of chopped parsley.

INGREDIENTS TO SERVE FOUR:
1 cup (250 g) dried black-eyed peas
2 medium-sized ripe tomatoes
⅔ cup (100 g) brown rice
salt
pepper
2 tablespoons (30 ml) chopped parsley

Mexican Kidney Beans

Soak ¾ cup of dried kidney beans in 4 scant cups of water. Drain the beans.

Slice 3 medium-sized onions. Cut 1 large green pepper into strips, discarding the seeds and pith. Blanch, peel and coarsely chop 4 ripe large tomatoes.

Heat 2 tablespoons of corn oil in a saucepan. Add the sliced onions and 1 large clove of garlic, crushed, and fry for 3 minutes, stirring frequently. Stir in ½ teaspoon of chilli powder with the green pepper and fry for 1 minute.

Add the tomatoes, 3 cups of water and salt and pepper. Bring to the boil, stirring occasionally, then add the drained kidney beans.

Cover the pan, reduce the heat and simmer for 1½ hours, or until the beans are tender. Stir in ½ cup of peanuts and cook for 10 minutes more.

Serve hot.

INGREDIENTS TO SERVE FOUR:
¾ cup (250 g) dried kidney beans
3 medium-sized onions
1 large green pepper
4 ripe large tomatoes
1 large garlic clove
2 tablespoons (30 ml) corn oil
½ teaspoon (2.5 ml) chilli powder
salt
pepper
½ cup (50 g) peanuts

Pease Pudding

This old English pudding of dried peas is traditionally served with pork.

Soak 1 cup of dried peas in 2½ cups of water.

Put the peas and the soaking water into a saucepan with 1 sprig of mint, 1 sprig of parsley and 1 sprig of thyme. Cover the pan and bring to the boil. Reduce the heat and simmer for 1 hour, or until the peas are tender. Stir occasionally and add a little more water if necessary.

Preheat the oven to 350°F (180°C).

Drain the peas then blend or sieve them. Beat 1 egg, then stir it into the pea purée. Season with salt and pepper.

Lightly grease a baking dish. Spoon the pea mixture into it and level the surface. Bake for 30 minutes.

Serve hot.

INGREDIENTS TO SERVE FOUR:
1 cup (250 g) dried peas
1 mint sprig
1 parsley sprig
1 thyme sprig
1 egg
salt
pepper

Lentil and Nut Rissoles

Put ¾ cup of split red lentils into a saucepan. Chop 1 small onion and add it to the pan. Pour in 2 cups of water. Cover the pan and bring to the boil. Reduce the heat and simmer gently, stirring occasionally, for 40 to 45 minutes, or until the lentils are soft and all the water has been absorbed.

Preheat the oven to 400°F (200°C). Spread ½ cup of chopped almonds on a board.

Let the lentil purée cool, then beat in ¼ pound of pot cheese, 1 cup of fresh bread crumbs, 2 tablespoons of chopped parsley and salt and pepper.

Divide the mixture into 8 and shape into rolls. Coat them with the chopped almonds.

Put the rolls on a greased baking sheet and bake for 20 to 30 minutes, or until they are golden brown.

Serve hot or cold.

INGREDIENTS TO SERVE FOUR:
¾ cup (150 g) split red lentils
1 small onion
½ cup (100 g) chopped almonds
¼ lb (100 g) pot cheese
1 cup (50 g) fresh bread crumbs
2 tablespoons (30 ml) chopped parsley
salt
pepper

PREPARING LENTIL RISSOLES

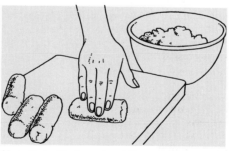

Shape the lentil mixture into rolls.

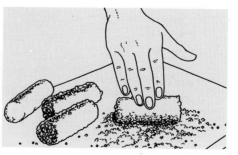

Roll the lentil rissoles in chopped nuts.

Lentil and Ham Soup

Put ½ cup of split red lentils into a large saucepan.

Chop 1 large onion. Slice 1 large carrot. Finely slice 2 stalks of celery. Add the onion, carrot and celery to the pan with ½ cup of chopped cooked ham. Pour in 5 cups of well-seasoned beef stock.

Cover the pan and bring to the boil. Reduce the heat and simmer, stirring occasionally, for 45 to 60 minutes, or until the lentils have cooked and have thickened the soup.

Adjust the seasoning and serve hot.

INGREDIENTS TO SERVE FOUR TO SIX:
½ cup (100 g) split red lentils
1 large onion
1 large carrot
2 celery stalks
½ cup (100 g) chopped cooked ham
5 cups (1 liter) well-seasoned beef stock
salt
pepper

Hummus

This Middle Eastern purée of chick peas may be used as a spread or a dip.

Soak 1 cup of chick peas in 2½ cups of water.

Put the chick peas and soaking water into a saucepan with 1 crushed garlic clove. Cover the pan and bring to the boil. Reduce the heat and simmer for 30 to 40 minutes, or until the chick peas are tender, adding more water if necessary.

Drain the chick peas if necessary. Mash them to a purée, then stir in ⅔ cup of yogurt, the juice of ½ lemon, salt and pepper. Beat until smooth. Alternatively, put all the ingredients into a blender and blend until smooth.

Sprinkle with paprika and serve hot or cold.

INGREDIENTS TO SERVE FOUR:
1 cup (250 g) chick peas
1 garlic clove
⅔ cup (150 ml) yogurt
½ lemon
salt
pepper
paprika

THE SIMPLEST SALAD is made with raw green leaves. It may be of one type of leaf, usually lettuce, or a mixture of several types. Either way it is called a green salad. The English and French eat it with meat, fish and poultry, while in the United States a green salad is usually served as a separate course, often at the start of a meal. The American way is nutritionally more sensible. You are likely to eat more health-promoting salad when you are hungry than when you are satiated with other food, particularly with meat.

The image of the "simple salad" is of cool, crisp, tender greenness. The reality on the plate is too often a pile of badly savaged lettuce doused in oil and vinegar. If you are able to grow your own salad vegetables, and grow them well, nothing should go wrong. The most important quality of salad ingredients is freshness, for without that there can be no crispness.

The lettuce is the most popular salad plant. Grown either outdoors or under glass it is available year-round, and yet one seldom tires of it. The soft Boston or butterhead type has the tenderest leaves, but they soon wilt. The large Iceberg lettuce has a dense heart, which will keep crisp in the salad compartment of a refrigerator. The inner leaves of the elongated Romaine lettuce are tender and sweet, but the dark green outside leaves can be tough.

We are always being encouraged to eat the outer leaves of lettuce because they are richer in vitamin C. But some common-sense compromise is needed here. The outer leaves of lettuces bought in a store are those most likely to have been exposed to pesticides when they were growing, and to have wilted in marketing. The outer leaves of lettuces grown in our own gardens have probably suffered the attentions of slugs and the

The Nutrients in Salad Leaves
Salad leaves have few calories. Three and a half ounces (100 g) of lettuce, for example, provide less than 20 Calories.

All the crisp green salad vegetables, right, are very low in calories and they are also filling. In the bowl, clockwise from the front are: mustard greens, Belgian endive, Romaine lettuce and Iceberg lettuce surrounding a Boston lettuce. These salad plants are all a reasonably good source of vitamin C.

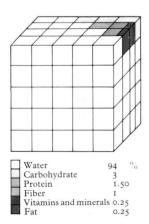

☐ Water	94	%
☐ Carbohydrate	3	
☐ Protein	1.50	
☐ Fiber	1	
☐ Vitamins and minerals	0.25	
■ Fat	0.25	

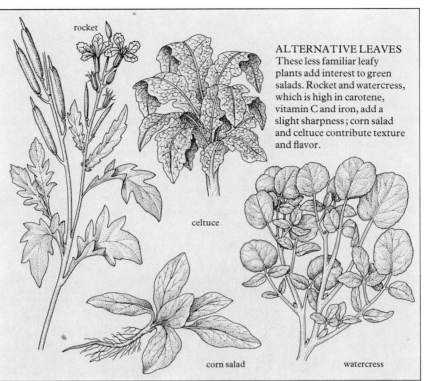

rocket

ALTERNATIVE LEAVES
These less familiar leafy
plants add interest to green
salads. Rocket and watercress,
which is high in carotene,
vitamin C and iron, add a
slight sharpness; corn salad
and celtuce contribute texture
and flavor.

celtuce

corn salad

watercress

Nutritionally exceptional,
salad alfalfa (above) has the
added virtue of needing only a
jam jar and water to sprout.
Full of protein and vitamins,
particularly vitamin C, and
such minerals as calcium, iron
and phosphorus, salad alfalfa
is ready to eat in three to four
days. It has a crunchy texture
and a taste reminiscent of
fresh, sweet garden peas. But
unlike peas it can be grown
with almost no effort all year
round.

neighbor's pets. The solution is to discard the outer leaves and eat more of the heart, which is, anyway, so much more enjoyable. There is no danger of obesity from eating a lot of lettuce because it is so low in calories. On the contrary, the bulkiness of salad, and the time taken to eat it, may lessen your intake of more fattening food.

In a simple salad many other greens may be substituted for lettuce. The most likely alternatives are curly chicory and the broad-leaved escarole. Belgian or French endive is another variant. What we eat are the forced blanched chicons; if these tightly packed bundles of leaves are exposed to the light they soon become flabby and bitter. Celtuce, a lettuce on a stem, is rarely available in stores, but it is quite easy to grow. Although not primarily a salad plant, shredded Chinese cabbage makes beautifully crisp eating. It is less chewy than finely shredded white cabbage, which is also used in salads.

The cresses—watercress, the comparable American cress and garden cress, usually found in partnership with mustard—introduce a variety of warm to hot tastes to salads. Dandelion leaves and corn salad provide other sharp tastes. Both grow wild, but there are more succulent cultivated varieties.

Such are the possible ingredients of a simple green salad. In what are called mixed salads, tomatoes, cucumber, beets and scallions may be added. Sliced raw vegetables, tomato or cucumber, for example, or such fruits as orange and pineapple served on a bed of lettuce with a vinaigrette dressing, make very attractive salads.

Any salad, particularly a green salad, may be improved or ruined by a dressing. A little salt seems natural, since the word for salad in many languages is derived from *sal*, the Latin word for salt. But oil, vinegar or lemon juice will change the texture and flavor. If that is what you want there is no harm in it. Lemon juice will give added vitamin C and you can substitute such polyunsaturated oils as corn oil or safflower oil for olive oil, whatever food snobs say.

You may also enjoy tossing salads as a gastronomic performance. The washed leaves must be dried in a towel, cotton bag or wire basket. The softer the leaves the greater the care that must be taken to keep them from becoming sodden with dressing. How much oil to use is largely a matter of taste, but even a large salad will not need much. Then toss the salad to spread the oil over the leaves. The method is to lift them about six inches in the air with a large wooden salad fork and spoon, and then give them a whirl as you let them fall back into the bowl. When the leaves are reasonably well coated, add the lemon juice and vinegar (preferably wine or cider vinegar) and the salt and pepper, and toss them again.

Salads can also be eaten with only salt and a bit of freshly ground black pepper. Dressers and tossers may find them surprisingly good and different. Thousand Island, Russian and similar dressings which are souped up with tabasco or catsup, should certainly be avoided with green salads.

Chicory Salad with Mushrooms and Ham

Cut the stalk from 1 head of chicory, separate the leaves and wash and drain them well.

Put $\frac{1}{2}$ cup of thinly sliced small mushrooms into a salad bowl. Add 6 tablespoons of basic vinaigrette dressing or tomato juice dressing (see page 153) and toss until all the mushrooms are coated. Marinate the mushrooms for 30 minutes.

Cut 4 thin slices of cooked ham into strips about $\frac{1}{4}$ by 1 inch (6 mm by 2 cm) and add them to the mushrooms.

Wash and thinly slice 1 small bulb of fennel and add it to the salad with 2 tomatoes cut into wedges. Add the chicory. Toss well before serving.

INGREDIENTS TO SERVE FOUR:
1 head chicory
$\frac{1}{2}$ cup (50 g) sliced small mushrooms
6 tablespoons (100 ml) basic vinaigrette
or tomato juice dressing (see page 153)
4 thin slices cooked ham
1 small fennel bulb
2 tomatoes

Endive, Watercress and Orange Salad

Separate the leaves from 2 large heads of Belgian endive. Wash and dry them. Put the larger leaves around the edge of a salad bowl with the leaves pointing upward. Slice the remaining endive and put it in the center.

Wash and drain 1 large bunch of watercress. Remove the coarse stalks. Add half of the watercress to the endive in the center and reserve the rest.

Peel and remove the pith from 3 oranges. Cut the fruit into thin slices and arrange them in the center of the bowl. Put the remaining watercress in a ring between the oranges and endive.

Pour in 6 tablespoons of basic vinaigrette dressing made with lemon juice (see page 153).

Sprinkle $\frac{1}{4}$ cup of chopped walnuts over the top.

Serve immediately.

INGREDIENTS TO SERVE FOUR:
2 large heads Belgian endive
1 large bunch watercress
3 oranges
6 tablespoons (100 ml) basic vinaigrette
dressing made with lemon juice (see
page 153)
$\frac{1}{4}$ cup (25 g) chopped walnuts

This tempting display of crisp salads includes, clockwise, Endive, Watercress and Orange Salad, Tossed Salad, Caesar Salad, Cress and Egg Salad and Chicory Salad with Mushrooms and Ham.

Cress and Egg Salad

Hard boil and cool 4 eggs. Wash and dry
1 small lettuce and arrange the leaves in
1 large or 4 individual salad bowls.

Peel the eggs, cut them into halves
lengthwise and arrange them on the lettuce.
Pour ⅔ cup of watercress yogurt dressing (see
page 153) over the eggs.

Slice 8 red or white radishes into thin
rounds and arrange them around the eggs.

Garnish the salad generously with
watercress.

INGREDIENTS TO SERVE FOUR:
4 large eggs
1 small head lettuce
⅔ cup (150 ml) watercress yogurt
 dressing (see page 153)
8 red or white radishes
watercress

Tossed Salad

About 1 hour before you are going to make
the salad, wash and drain 1 medium-sized
head of Romaine lettuce and a variety of
other greens, including chicory, endive,
escarole, watercress and young spinach leaves.

Rub the inside of a large salad bowl with
½ garlic clove. Discard the garlic. Tear the
greens into fairly large pieces and put them
into the bowl. Cut 2 ripe medium-sized
tomatoes into wedges and add them to the
salad. Peel and slice ½ cucumber and add it
with 2 coarsely chopped scallions. Separate
and wash a small bunch of seedless green
grapes and add them. Slice 4 crisp red
radishes into the bowl. Sprinkle with
2 tablespoons of crumbled Roquefort or blue
cheese. Pour in the contents of 1 small can of
anchovies rolled with capers.

Toss the salad lightly. Add ¼ cup of olive
oil or corn oil, 1½ tablespoons of wine vinegar
and salt and pepper to taste. Toss well and
serve.

INGREDIENTS TO SERVE FOUR TO SIX:
1 medium-sized head Romaine lettuce
Other greens as available: chicory,
 endive, escarole, watercress and
 young spinach leaves
½ garlic clove
2 ripe medium-sized tomatoes
½ cucumber
2 scallions
small bunch seedless green grapes
4 radishes
2 tablespoons (30 ml) crumbled
 Roquefort or blue cheese
1 small can anchovies, preferably
 rolled with capers
¼ cup (60 ml) olive oil or corn oil
1½ tablespoons (22 ml) wine vinegar
salt
pepper

Caesar Salad

Preheat the oven to 325°F (170°C).

Cut 2 slices of bread into cubes. Put them on a baking sheet and bake them, turning them occasionally, for 15 to 20 minutes, or until they are crisp and lightly browned. Cook 1 egg in simmering water for 1 minute. Coarsely chop 8 anchovies.

Put 1 teaspoon of salt in the bottom of a large salad bowl. Crush 1 garlic clove into the salt. Add freshly ground black pepper.

Wash 1 large head of Romaine lettuce and drain the leaves well. Tear the lettuce leaves into bite-sized pieces and add them to the

Drain washed salad leaves in a salad basket.

salad bowl with the croûtons and anchovies. Add ½ cup of olive oil or corn oil and 2 tablespoons of lemon juice and toss well. Sprinkle with 2 tablespoons of grated Parmesan cheese. Break the coddled egg into the bowl and toss thoroughly. Sprinkle with 1 tablespoon of Parmesan cheese.

Serve immediately.

INGREDIENTS TO SERVE FOUR:
2 slices of bread
1 egg
8 anchovies
1 teaspoon (5 ml) salt
1 garlic clove
freshly ground black pepper
1 large head Romaine lettuce
½ cup (120 ml) olive oil or corn oil
2 tablespoons (30 ml) lemon juice
3 tablespoons (45 ml) grated Parmesan cheese

Lettuce Soup

Lettuce makes a soup with a surprisingly strong flavor. It is an ideal way to use lettuce that is not quite crisp enough to use in a salad.

Wash 1 large head of lettuce. Shred it and put it into a saucepan. Grate 1 medium-sized onion and add it to the lettuce. Grate in the rind of ½ lemon, then squeeze in the juice. Add ¼ teaspoon of grated nutmeg, 2½ cups of well-seasoned chicken stock and salt and pepper to taste.

Bring to the boil, cover the pan, reduce the heat and simmer for 15 minutes. Sieve or blend the soup. Return it to the pan and pour in 2 scant cups of milk.

Reheat and serve hot.

INGREDIENTS TO SERVE FOUR:
1 large head lettuce
1 medium-sized onion
½ lemon
¼ teaspoon (1 ml) grated nutmeg
2½ cups (600 ml) chicken stock
salt
pepper
2 scant cups (450 ml) milk

Baked Stuffed Lettuce

Preheat the oven to 350°F (180°C).

Keeping them whole, wash and dry 2 heads of lettuce.

For the stuffing, drain and flake 7 ounces of canned tuna fish into a mixing bowl. Add 1 cup of fresh bread crumbs, 1 tablespoon of chopped parsley and 8 black olives that have been pitted and chopped. Stir in 1 tablespoon of lemon juice, 1 crushed garlic clove and salt and pepper. Mix well.

Spread open the centers of the lettuces and spoon in the stuffing.

Pour 5 tablespoons of water into a casserole, then put in the 2 stuffed lettuces.

Cover the casserole and bake for 15 minutes.

Serve at once.

INGREDIENTS TO SERVE FOUR:
2 heads lettuce
7 oz (198 g) canned tuna fish
1 cup (50 g) fresh bread crumbs
1 tablespoon (15 ml) chopped parsley
8 black olives
1 tablespoon (15 ml) lemon juice
1 garlic clove
salt
pepper

STUFFING LETTUCE

Open the leaves and stuff the lettuce.

Seafood, Avocado and Grape Salad

Wash 1 head of Romaine lettuce and drain the leaves well. Tear the leaves into bite-sized pieces and put them into a large salad bowl. Add 1 cup of cooked crab meat, 1 cup of shelled cooked shrimp and ¼ pound of seedless green grapes.

Peel and remove the large seed from 1 medium-sized avocado. Dice the avocado into a small bowl. Lightly toss the avocado with 1 tablespoon of lemon juice then add it to the salad bowl.

Pour in special salad dressing. Toss well and serve.

INGREDIENTS TO SERVE FOUR:
1 head Romaine lettuce
1 cup (250 g) cooked crab meat
1 cup (250 g) shelled cooked shrimp
¼ lb (100 g) seedless green grapes
1 medium-sized avocado
1 tablespoon (15 ml) lemon juice
special salad dressing

Watercress and Grapefruit Salad

Wash and drain 2 large bunches of watercress. Remove the coarse stalks and put the watercress into a salad bowl.

Thinly slice ½ small cucumber. Cut the slices into quarters and add them to the watercress.

Brown ¼ cup of shelled hazelnuts under a hot broiler for 1 to 2 minutes or on a baking sheet on the top shelf of a hot oven for 5 to 10 minutes. (Watch them carefully because they burn easily.) Remove the thin brown skins by rubbing the nuts together in a clean dish towel. Discard the skins and put the hazelnuts in the salad bowl.

Peel and remove the pith from 1 grapefruit. Holding the grapefruit over the salad bowl to catch the juice, cut the fruit into segments between the membrane. Squeeze the juice from another half grapefruit over the salad. Season with salt and pepper to taste and toss

INGREDIENTS TO SERVE FOUR:
2 large bunches watercress
½ small cucumber
¼ cup (50 g) shelled hazelnuts
1½ grapefruit
salt
pepper

Watercress and Endive Salad

Wash and drain 1 bunch of watercress. Remove and discard the coarse stalks. Put the watercress into a salad bowl.

Cut 4 heads of Belgian endive into halves lengthwise. Wash and drain well, then break them into bite-sized pieces and put into the salad bowl.

In a small bowl combine $\frac{1}{2}$ cup of corn oil, 3 tablespoons of wine vinegar and 1 tablespoon of chopped chives. Add a pinch of paprika, season to taste with salt and pepper and mix well.

Just before serving pour the dressing over the watercress and endive and toss lightly.

INGREDIENTS TO SERVE FOUR:
1 bunch watercress
4 heads Belgian endive
$\frac{1}{2}$ cup (120 ml) corn oil
3 tablespoons (45 ml) wine vinegar
1 tablespoon (30 ml) chopped chives
paprika
salt
pepper

Braised Endive

Preheat the oven to 350°F (180°C).

Cut 4 heads of Belgian endive into halves lengthwise. Wash and drain them. Put them into a casserole or an ovenproof dish.

Pour in $\frac{2}{3}$ cup of chicken stock mixed with the juice of 1 orange, salt, pepper and a pinch of grated nutmeg.

Cover and bake for 15 to 20 minutes, or until the endive is tender but still crisp.

Drain the endive, pouring the stock into a saucepan. Keep the endive warm in the casserole.

Boil the stock for a few minutes until it is reduced to about 4 tablespoons, then pour it over the endive. Serve at once.

INGREDIENTS TO SERVE FOUR:
4 large heads Belgian endive
$\frac{2}{3}$ cup (150 ml) chicken stock
1 orange
salt
pepper
grated nutmeg

PREPARING ENDIVE

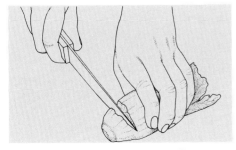

With a sharp knife trim the base of the endive.

Watercress Yogurt Dressing

Wash 1 small bunch of watercress and remove the coarse stalks. Chop the watercress finely and put it into a mixing bowl with 1 teaspoon of lemon juice, $\frac{2}{3}$ cup of yogurt, salt and pepper. Mix well. Alternatively, put all the ingredients into a blender and blend well.

INGREDIENTS TO DRESS A SALAD TO SERVE FOUR:
1 small bunch watercress
1 teaspoon (5 ml) lemon juice
$\frac{2}{3}$ cup (150 ml) yogurt
salt
pepper

Piquant Yogurt Dressing

Mix $\frac{2}{3}$ cup of yogurt with the grated rind of $\frac{1}{2}$ lemon, 1 tablespoon of chopped parsley, 1 tablespoon of chopped chives or scallions and 1 teaspoon of chopped gherkins. Season to taste with salt and freshly ground black pepper and mix well.

INGREDIENTS TO DRESS A SALAD TO SERVE FOUR:
$\frac{2}{3}$ cup (150 ml) yogurt
$\frac{1}{2}$ lemon
1 tablespoon (15 ml) chopped parsley
1 tablespoon (15 ml) chopped chives or scallions
1 teaspoon (5 ml) chopped gherkins
salt
freshly ground black pepper

Tomato Juice Dressing

Beat together $\frac{1}{4}$ cup of tomato juice with 2 tablespoons of lemon juice. Stir in 1 tablespoon of chopped parsley, chives or mint. Season to taste with salt and freshly ground black pepper.

INGREDIENTS TO DRESS A SALAD TO SERVE FOUR
$\frac{1}{4}$ cup (60 ml) tomato juice
2 tablespoons (30 ml) lemon juice
1 tablespoon (15 ml) chopped parsley, chives or mint
salt
freshly ground black pepper

Special Salad Dressing

In a small bowl mix together 1 crushed garlic clove, $\frac{1}{4}$ cup of corn oil or olive oil, 1 tablespoon of wine vinegar, 1 teaspoon of Dijon mustard and 1 tablespoon of yogurt or light cream. Stir until well blended.

INGREDIENTS TO DRESS A SALAD TO SERVE FOUR:
1 garlic clove
$\frac{1}{4}$ cup (60 ml) corn oil or olive oil
1 tablespoon (15 ml) wine vinegar
1 teaspoon (5 ml) Dijon mustard
1 tablespoon (15 ml) yogurt or light cream

Basic Vinaigrette Dressing

One tablespoon of chopped herbs, such as parsley, chives, mint, tarragon, oregano or basil, may be added to this basic vinaigrette dressing.

Put 2 tablespoons of wine vinegar or lemon juice into a small bowl with 5 to 6 tablespoons of corn oil, olive oil or safflower oil. Add a pinch of dried mustard and salt and freshly ground black pepper to taste. Beat until well blended.

INGREDIENTS TO DRESS A SALAD TO SERVE FOUR:
2 tablespoons (30 ml) wine vinegar or lemon juice
5 to 6 tablespoons (75 to 90 ml) corn oil, olive oil or safflower oil
dried mustard
salt
freshly ground black pepper

CHOPPING HERBS

Chop herbs with a sharp knife on a board,

or with a curved blade in a wooden bowl.

The word mushroom has various meanings. It is sometimes used to denote all club-shaped fungi in the class Basidiomycetes or, more specifically, any edible species belonging to the Agaricaceae family. It can also mean any umbrella-shaped edible fungus. More often, however, the word is used to mean all edible fungi, including truffles and morels.

The parasol mushroom (*Lepiota procera*, right) is delicately flavored with a large cap up to about six inches (15 cm) across covered with brown scales, and a long mottled brown stem. It is found during the summer and fall, often growing near, but not under, trees.

MOST PEOPLE IN THE UNITED STATES are afraid to eat any mushrooms except supermarket mushrooms—guaranteed safe if not satisfying. In fact, few mushrooms are dangerous to eat, but many are not worth the effort and some are indeed deadly.

The mystery of mushrooms has fascinated people since the beginning of history—their lifestyle is so different from other plants. Like the other members of the fungi group they do not contain chlorophyll, and instead of converting inorganic substances into organic, as green plants do, they have, like animals, to feed on organic material. Furthermore, unlike most plants, mushrooms do not flower but reproduce themselves by spores, not by seeds. This makes them fascinating, but why it should make us so suspicious of them is inexplicable.

In most parts of Europe numerous varieties of wild mushrooms are eaten, and it would be considered almost criminal not to do so. People grow up with a taste for them, and acquire a knowledge of which are safe to pick and which are dangerous. Anyone without such experience who is planning to eat wild mushrooms should buy and study well a first-rate field guide that includes the poisonous species. After that, if in doubt throw out.

"Mushroom" has increasingly come to mean only the common field mushroom and the mass-produced cultivated mushroom, which has been

The chanterelle (*Cantharellus cibarius*, left) has an unmistakable shape, color and odor. The cap looks like a fluted funnel with the gills clearly visible. Both the cap and the short stem are yellow, and the aroma is faintly reminiscent of apricots. The delicately flavored flesh is firmer than that of other mushrooms and needs to be cooked slightly longer. It is common in deciduous woods in the summer and fall.

The cep (*Boletus edulis*, left) has a light, shiny, bronze-colored cap that looks like the top half of a bun. The underside is spongy and lacks pronounced gills. The thick, pale brown stalk has fine white veins toward the top. The flesh is white and may be tinged with pink. Ceps can be found in the summer and fall in deciduous woods throughout Europe, but they are especially abundant in France, where they are the most highly prized of the mushrooms.

The field mushroom (*Agaricus campestris*, above) looks like the familiar cultivated mushroom. The cap is white and the gills turn pink and then dark brown. It is most likely to be found in the early fall in fields that are permanently used as pasture. The deadly Destroying Angel (*Amanita virosa*) has a similar shape to the field mushroom but grows in woods. Fortunately it is uncommon, and differs from a field mushroom in being totally white. The highly poisonous Death Cap (*Amanita phalloides*) is sometimes confused with the field mushroom, but its cap has an olive tinge and the white gills and stem may also be slightly tinged with green. It appears in deciduous woods or adjoining fields in summer and early fall.

derived from it. The cultivated mushroom is invaluable if only because it is available all year. But to neglect the wild species involves the loss of some incomparable flavors. It is for flavor rather than nutritional value that mushrooms are eaten, but even for that they are not to be scorned. Many wild mushrooms have appreciable amounts of vitamin D, which is not found in green vegetables. And both wild and cultivated mushrooms are good sources of niacin as well as potassium and phosphorus.

Seaweeds, which are a kind of algae, are almost as mysterious as mushrooms, but they are far more nutritious. They are rich in minerals—the gamut runs from aluminum to zinc, with a particular abundance of calcium, potassium and sodium. Iodine is also present and is a strong selling point. Some health-food enthusiasts make the most extravagant claims for the virtues of seaweed. It certainly is nutritionally valuable, but in anything like their natural state most species taste like salt with the consistency of rubber.

The Celts, Japanese and Chinese share a taste for seaweeds, but in general in the West they are not popular. Most of us eat more seaweed than we realize, however, in the form of vegetable gelatins, in ice cream, salad dressing, soups and sauces and as sausage skins. But the time may come when we shall appreciate this nutritious and neglected harvest of the sea as a food itself.

EDIBLE SEAWEED

An excellent source of vitamins and minerals, red seaweed can be eaten as a vegetable. Laver (*Porphyra umbilicalis*, top right), once a traditional breakfast accompaniment to bacon and eggs in South Wales, can be bought boiled and chopped, smelling like cabbage and looking like brown spinach. It is then rolled in oatmeal and fried. Laver can also be broiled and eaten on toast. Although many of the larger brown seaweeds are inedible, the common bladder wrack (*Fucus vesiculosus*, below right), which makes a popping sound when it is walked on, contains useful nutrients. It is usually eaten in pills which are available from health-food stores.

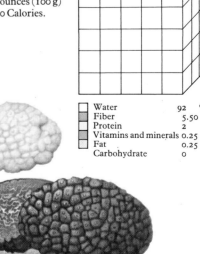

In Japan, brown seaweed, or kelp, gathered from the sea shore, is laid out to dry (left) before being fried or made into soup. The Japanese, who consume large quantities of seaweed, also use kelp as a seasoning or as a garnish for rice.

The morel (*Morchella esculenta*, left) is a richly flavored mushroom, both fresh and dried. The cap has a distinctive criss-cross of ridges, but varies in shape from conical to round and also in color from ochre to deep brown. When young the stem is whitish, but it turns yellow or reddish as it ages. Morels appear in the spring in deciduous woods, most commonly wherever the ground has been disturbed or swept by fire. In France the battlefields of the First World War produced a great morel harvest when peace came.

The bluet, or blewit, (*Tricholoma personatum*, right) is an edible mushroom popular in parts of England. The cap is gray or pale brown tinged with lilac and the stem is streaked with blue. It is found in pastureland in the fall.

Truffles are the aristocrats among fungi. Because these woodland plants grow underground all year long most people are unlikely to encounter any except in cans and jars. They have more aroma than flavor and a little goes a long way in cooking. The most sought after is the Périgord truffle (*Tuber melanosporum*, below right). The white flesh of the young truffle gradually turns gray and then almost violet-black. The so-called white truffle of Italy (top right) has a somewhat peppery flavor.

The Nutrients in Mushrooms
Mushrooms are a useful source of B vitamins and three and a half ounces (100 g) provide about 10 Calories.

Water	92 %
Fiber	5.50
Protein	2
Vitamins and minerals	0.25
Fat	0.25
Carbohydrate	0

Mushroom Armenienne

This mushroom dish makes an interesting start to a meal.

Slice 1 large onion, 1 large carrot and 1 stalk of celery. Blanch and peel 2 medium-sized tomatoes. Cut the tomatoes into quarters and remove the seeds.

Heat 2 tablespoons of olive oil in a large saucepan. Add the sliced onion, carrot and celery and fry for 3 minutes, stirring frequently. Crush 1 large garlic clove, add it to the pan and fry for 1 minute more.

Add ⅔ cup of red wine, a bouquet garni consisting of sprigs of thyme and parsley and 1 bay leaf, and salt and pepper to taste. Stir in the tomatoes and 1 pound of washed, whole small mushrooms.

Bring to the boil, then reduce the heat and simmer gently for 15 minutes.

Let cool and then remove the bouquet garni. Put into the refrigerator to chill for at least 1 hour before serving.

Serve sprinkled with 2 tablespoons of chopped parsley.

INGREDIENTS TO SERVE FOUR:
1 large onion
1 large carrot
1 celery stalk
2 medium-sized tomatoes
2 tablespoons (30 ml) olive oil
1 garlic clove
⅔ cup (150 ml) red wine
1 bouquet garni, consisting of sprigs of thyme and parsley and 1 bay leaf
salt
pepper
1 lb (500 g) small mushrooms
2 tablespoons (30 ml) chopped parsley

Stuffed Mushrooms

Preheat the oven to 375°F (190°C).

Wash 8 large flat mushrooms but do not peel them. Cut off and finely chop the stalks. Put the mushroom caps into a lightly greased ovenproof dish.

Finely chop 8 slices of bacon. Finely chop 1 medium-sized onion. Put the bacon into a saucepan and fry over low heat until the fat runs. Add the onion and 1 crushed garlic clove and fry with the bacon, stirring frequently, for about 3 minutes. Add the chopped mushroom stalks to the pan and fry for 2 minutes more.

Remove the pan from the heat and stir in the grated rind of 1 lemon, 2 tablespoons of chopped parsley, salt, pepper and a pinch of grated nutmeg.

Add 1½ cups of fresh bread crumbs and 2 tablespoons of dry sherry and mix well.

Divide the filling between the mushroom caps. Sprinkle them with grated Parmesan cheese.

Bake for 20 minutes, or until the

mushrooms are tender and the stuffing is lightly browned on top. Serve immediately.

INGREDIENTS TO SERVE FOUR:
8 large flat mushrooms
8 slices bacon
1 medium-sized onion
1 garlic clove
1 lemon
2 tablespoons (30 ml) chopped parsley
salt
pepper
grated nutmeg
1½ cups (75 g) fresh bread crumbs
2 tablespoons (30 ml) dry sherry
grated Parmesan cheese

STUFFING MUSHROOMS

Wash and trim the stalks of large flat mushrooms.

Spoon the filling onto the mushrooms.

Mushroom Pie

Preheat the oven to 400°F (200°C).

Make 1½ cups of shortcrust pastry with whole-wheat flour (see page 34) and line an 8-inch (20-cm) flan ring or pie pan. Bake for 15 minutes. Remove the baking paper and beans and bake for 5 minutes more.

Reduce the oven temperature to 350°F (180°C).

Wash and slice ½ pound of small mushrooms. Put them into a saucepan with the grated rind and juice of ½ lemon, 2 sprigs of thyme, salt and pepper. Cover the pan and heat gently for 5 minutes, or until the mushrooms are tender.

Strain the mushrooms and reserve the juice. Put the mushrooms into the pastry shell.

Beat 2 eggs with ⅔ cup of milk and the

reserved mushroom juice. Season with salt and pepper. Pour over the mushrooms.

Bake for 30 minutes, or until the filling is set.

Serve warm or cold.

INGREDIENTS TO SERVE FOUR TO SIX:
1½ cups (150 g) shortcrust pastry made with whole-wheat flour (see page 34)
½ lb (250 g) small mushrooms
½ lemon
2 thyme sprigs
salt
pepper
2 eggs
⅔ cup (150 ml) milk

Mushroom Duxelles

This thick, concentrated mushroom sauce is very versatile. It can be used as a sauce or as flavoring for many dishes.

Finely chop 1 medium-sized onion. Finely chop ½ pound of flat mushrooms, including the stalks.

Heat 2 tablespoons of corn oil in a saucepan. Add the onion and fry, stirring frequently, for 3 minutes.

Add the mushrooms and fry for 3 minutes. Stir in ¼ teaspoon of dried mixed herbs and ¼ teaspoon of paprika and cook for 1 minute.

Add ⅔ cup of dry white wine, ⅔ cup of beef stock and 1 teaspoon of lemon juice. Simmer, uncovered, until the liquid has reduced and the sauce is thick. Season to taste with salt and pepper.

If not to be used at once the duxelles can be stored in the refrigerator, in a tightly covered jar, for 1 week.

INGREDIENTS TO MAKE ONE PINT (600 ML) OF SAUCE:
1 medium-sized onion
½ lb (250 g) flat mushrooms
2 tablespoons (30 ml) corn oil
¼ teaspoon (1 ml) dried mixed herbs
¼ teaspoon (1 ml) paprika
⅔ cup (150 ml) dry white wine
⅔ cup (150 ml) beef stock
1 teaspoon (5 ml) lemon juice
salt
pepper

Mushrooms Poached with Lemon and Herbs

Trim the stalks and wash 1 pound of mushrooms. Cut large mushrooms into halves or quarters and leave the small ones whole.

Put the mushrooms into a saucepan with the grated rind and juice of 1 lemon, salt, pepper, 4 sprigs of thyme and 1 large sprig of parsley.

Cover the pan and cook over very low heat, for about 2 minutes, to draw out the juices. Then raise the heat and simmer gently for 5 minutes, or until the mushrooms are tender. (Overcooking will toughen the mushrooms.)

Serve hot or cold.

INGREDIENTS TO SERVE FOUR:
1 lb (500 g) mushrooms
1 lemon
salt
pepper
4 thyme sprigs
1 large parsley sprig

Mushroom Soup

Wash and slice $\frac{1}{2}$ pound of mushrooms and put them into a saucepan with 1 chopped medium-sized onion and the grated rind and juice of $\frac{1}{2}$ lemon.

Pour in $2\frac{1}{2}$ cups of chicken stock and $1\frac{1}{4}$ cups of milk. Add 1 sprig of thyme and salt and pepper to taste.

Cover the pan and bring to the boil. Reduce the heat and simmer for 5 minutes. Remove a few sliced mushrooms for garnish and continue to simmer the soup for 10 minutes.

Blend the soup and pour it back into the pan. Reheat and adjust the seasoning.

Serve hot.

INGREDIENTS TO SERVE FOUR TO SIX:
$\frac{1}{2}$ lb (250 g) mushrooms
1 medium-sized onion
$\frac{1}{2}$ lemon
$2\frac{1}{2}$ cups (600 ml) chicken stock
$1\frac{1}{4}$ cups (300 ml) milk
1 thyme sprig
salt
pepper

Makizushi

For this Japanese hors d'oeuvre, vinegared rice, or sushi, and tuna fish are wrapped in thin sheets of nori, dried laver seaweed. Short-grained rice should be used for this dish because it sticks together.

Put $1\frac{1}{4}$ cups of short-grained rice into a saucepan. Add $2\frac{1}{2}$ cups of water and a little salt. Cover the pan and bring to the boil. Reduce the heat and simmer the rice for about 15 minutes, or until the rice is tender and all the water is absorbed. Remove the pan from the heat and leave covered for 5 minutes so that the rice becomes sticky.

Transfer the cooked rice to a mixing bowl. Add 4 tablespoons of white wine vinegar and mix well. Let the rice cool slightly.

Pass 6 sheets of dried nori quickly over a gas flame. This turns the nori from black to green and improves the flavor.

Lay the sheets of nori on a flat surface. Divide the warm vinegar rice between the nori sheets. Spread the rice over the seaweed except for a margin of 2 inches (5 cm) along one of the shortest sides. Drain and flake 7 ounces of canned tuna fish. Put the fish along the center of the nori sheets.

Tightly roll up the nori toward the uncovered end like a jelly roll, sealing the join. Let stand for 5 minutes then cut the rolls into 1-inch (2-cm) slices, trimming off the ends if necessary.

Serve cold with drinks or as a first course.

INGREDIENTS TO SERVE SIX TO EIGHT:
$1\frac{1}{4}$ cups (250 g) short-grained rice
4 tablespoons (60 ml) white wine vinegar
6 sheets dried nori seaweed
$\frac{3}{4}$ cup (150 g) tuna fish

MAKING MAKIZUSHI

Pass sheets of dried seaweed rapidly over a flame.

Cover with filling and roll the dried seaweed up.

Slice the makizushi.

Seaweed Baked Fish

Cod, haddock or halibut fillets or a whole round fish, such as mackerel, can be substituted for the fillets and baked on seaweed.

Preheat the oven to 350°F (180°C).

Put 2 ounces of dried wakame seaweed into an ovenproof dish. Pour in $1\frac{1}{4}$ cups of water and toss the seaweed in it.

Cover the dish and bake for 30 minutes, or until the seaweed softens, absorbs the water and becomes plump. Stir the seaweed once or twice during cooking to prevent the top from becoming dry. (Alternatively, this preliminary cooking of the seaweed may be done in a saucepan for about 20 minutes.)

When the seaweed is tender put 4 rolled fillets of white fish or the whole round fish on top of it. Add a little more water if the seaweed looks dry.

Cover the dish and bake for 20 to 30 minutes, depending on the size of the fish.

Serve hot, garnished with lemon wedges.

INGREDIENTS TO SERVE FOUR:
2 oz (50 g) dried wakame seaweed
4 fish fillets
1 lemon

Irish Moss Ginger Mold

Irish moss or carrageen seaweed can be used for setting foods instead of gelatin. Agar agar, which is a powdered form of dried seaweed, can be substituted.

Measure $\frac{1}{2}$ ounce of carrageen. Rinse off the salt that is used to preserve it, by stirring it briskly in hot water and removing it immediately.

Put the carrageen into a saucepan with 1 quart of milk and the grated rind of 1 lemon and 1 orange. Add 2 tablespoons of chopped ginger root to the milk.

Bring to the boil, reduce the heat and simmer gently, stirring occasionally, for 15 minutes, or until the mixture thickens and coats the back of the spoon.

Wet a 1-quart (850-ml) ring mold and pour the mixture into it. Refrigerate for at least 3 hours before serving.

To serve turn out on to a plate and fill the center with sliced oranges or bananas.

INGREDIENTS TO SERVE FOUR TO SIX:
$\frac{1}{2}$ oz (15 g) carrageen seaweed
1 quart (850 ml) milk
1 lemon
1 orange
2 tablespoons (25 g) chopped ginger root
sliced bananas or oranges

IN RECENT YEARS it has become fashionable to rhapsodize about the bounty of Nature and to moan about our neglect of it. Books written in the rosy glow of enthusiasm make us feel that the Garden of Eden is still there for the picking, or at least in a medieval version, for the Middle Ages have a particular fascination for the wild-fooders.

But there are several things to bear in mind before you set off in the car in search of, for example, Billy Buttons, Rags and Tatters, Chucky Cheeses, Goodnight-at-Moon, Flibberty Gibbets, or any other of the folksy names given to the mallow (*Malva sylvestris*), in order, with the help of an electric blender, to make a passable imitation of melokhia, the supposedly aphrodisiac Arab peasant soup. In the first place, although the ancient Romans liked mallows, medieval peasants had already come to regard them as famine fare. More important, in the Middle Ages there was far more countryside and there were far fewer people, and no automobiles. If the two-car families of the West seriously took to hunting for wild food what countryside remains would quickly be ravaged.

Furthermore where would you search—road-sides polluted by the exhaust of cars or sprayed with labor-saving herbicides, or on farmland, trampling on cultivated crops on which your existence depends? Or would you crowd into forests, wiping out the already diminishing number of species?

There is another consideration. Some of these supposedly desirable roadside plants have gone out of favor simply because the cultivated varieties are so much better. This applies particularly to roots, of which the wild specimens are miserably small and bitter. Many leaves are also not only bitter but tough, because we pick them when we happen to be in the country and not at the exact moment when they are young and succulent.

You are more likely to catch them at that stage if you have a weed-choked garden of your own. Then, for most of the year, the leaves of wild dandelions will provide you with a sharp addition to salads or they can be cooked like spinach. If you fertilized them and drew soil around the leaves you would have a substitute for endive. Their roots, roasted and ground, are a substitute for coffee, and wine can be made from the flowers. Chickweed is a very persistent garden weed, and

hazelnuts

rose hips

sloes

wild strawberries

sorrel

cranberries

it is worthwhile stewing it in butter as a change from putting it on the compost heap. Since ground elder (or bishop's weed, according to one's ecclesiastical prejudices) is virtually impossible to get rid of, it is worth eating as a substitute for spinach. Yet another spinach substitute is the nettle. It should be picked only in the early spring-time of its youth, for in summer it becomes horribly bitter and undesirably laxative.

The real countryside, when you find it, undoubtedly does offer some beautiful flavors. While roots have been improved by cultivation, many fruits have suffered. Tiny wild strawberries, wild raspberries and blackberries have flavors that cannot be matched by garden varieties. It is, however, politic to curb your greed and leave some of these berries for the birds so that they may scatter the remaining good seed on the land and thereby provide more fruit in future years.

There are other plentiful berries that make excellent jellies. Rose hips, mixed with a few crab apples to make them set, make an excellent jelly to go with game. A good jelly can be made with the haws of hawthorn if they, too, are mixed with crab apples. Elderberries are better used with blackberries than on their own. If you can get them before the birds do, the beautiful scarlet berries of the rowan, or mountain ash, make a delicious preserve. Dark blue sloes are the tartest of all berries, totally inedible until they have matured for a few months in gin, although it is actually for the refreshingly flavored gin that you go to this trouble. Sloes also make a very brightly colored, bright-tasting jelly. The best jelly of all is made from another sour fruit—the wild crab apple.

After berries, nuts are the most desirable way-side food, but even if you are lucky enough to live near a nut-bearing roadside, your choice will be quite restricted, and will depend on the climate.

If you do go foraging, pick with restraint. Do not strip plants of their leaves or berries or nuts; take a little here and there. Do not snap off branches to reach berries or nuts that are out of arm's reach. Do not wrench mushrooms or other fungi out of the ground, merely twist the stalks. Do not pull up roots. There is then a better chance that something will be left for the following year, both for you and for the wildlife that depends far more than humans do on this food.

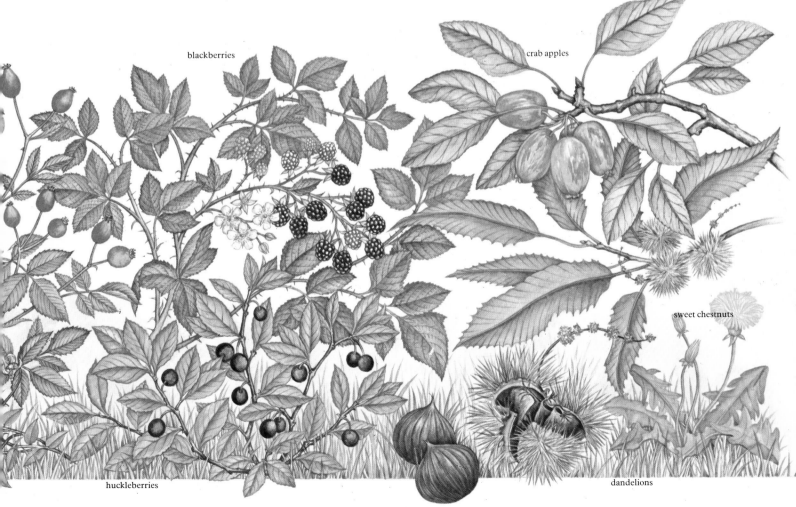

blackberries

crab apples

sweet chestnuts

huckleberries

dandelions

Nettle Soup

Nettles make a delicious soup in spring and early summer when the nettles are young and tender. Cut off the shoots from the tops of 30 nettles, taking off about the top 2 inches (5 cm), including the stalk and the leaves. Cut them with a pair of scissors or wear gloves to prevent the nettles from stinging you.

Chop 1 large onion and put it into a large saucepan. Peel and chop 2 medium-sized potatoes. Put the potatoes into the pan. Add 2 sprigs of mint, 3¾ cups of chicken stock, salt, pepper and the juice of ½ lemon.

Cover the pan and bring to the boil. Reduce the heat and simmer for 20 minutes.

Wash the nettle tops and add to the soup. Simmer gently for 1 minute. Blend and then strain the soup.

Return the soup to the pan and reheat. Adjust the seasoning, adding a little more stock or milk if a thinner consistency is desired. Serve hot or chilled.

INGREDIENTS TO SERVE FOUR TO SIX:
30 nettle tops
1 large onion
2 medium-sized potatoes
2 mint sprigs
3¾ cups (850 ml) chicken stock
salt
pepper
½ lemon

Dandelion Greens with Bacon

Chop 8 slices of bacon. Put the bacon into a saucepan and fry over low heat until the fat runs.

Wash ½ pound of dandelion leaves and add to the bacon. Fry, stirring constantly, for 1 minute.

Add 5 tablespoons of water, salt and pepper. Cover the pan and cook over low heat for about 2 minutes, or until the leaves are tender but still a bright green color.

Serve hot.

INGREDIENTS TO SERVE FOUR:
8 slices bacon
½ lb (250 g) dandelion leaves
salt
pepper

Sorrel Purée

Sorrel cooks to a purée in the same way as spinach does, but sorrel has a stronger lemon flavor, which makes it a delicious accompaniment to egg dishes as well as to fish, poultry and veal. The purée may be blended to make a smooth sauce.

Remove the stalks and wash 1 pound of sorrel leaves. Put the leaves into a saucepan without draining them.

Cover the pan and cook over low heat, stirring occasionally, for 2 to 3 minutes, until the sorrel wilts. Stir in salt and pepper and a pinch of grated nutmeg.

Serve hot.

INGREDIENTS TO SERVE FOUR:
1 lb (500 g) sorrel
salt
pepper
grated nutmeg

Hazelnut Torte

Preheat the oven to 350°F (180°C). Lightly grease two 8-inch (20-cm) cake pans and line them with waxed paper.

Separate 4 eggs. Put the whites and the yolks into large mixing bowls. Beat the egg whites until stiff. Do not wash the beater.

Add ⅔ cup of brown sugar to the egg yolks and beat with the same beater until the mixture is thick and creamy.

Grind ⅔ cup of hazelnuts. (Leave the thin brown skins on the hazelnuts because this improves the flavor.)

Fold the egg whites, the ground hazelnuts and the grated rind of 1 lemon into the beaten egg yolks until well blended.

Pour the mixture into the prepared pans.

Bake for 25 to 30 minutes, or until the layers have risen, are lightly browned and springy to the touch.

Let the cakes cool in the pans until they shrink from the sides and then turn out.

When the layers are completely cool, sandwich them together using ½ pound of crushed strawberries, raspberries or apricot purée for the filling.

INGREDIENTS TO SERVE SIX:
4 eggs
⅔ cup (100 g) brown sugar
⅔ cup (100 g) shelled hazelnuts
1 lemon
½ lb (250 g) strawberries, raspberries or apricot purée

Crab Apple Compote

These small tart apples, which are usually made into jelly or jam, are also delicious cooked in a spicy syrup.

For the syrup, pour 2½ cups of water into a saucepan. Add ½ cup of sugar, a strip of thinly pared lemon rind, the juice of ½ lemon, 1 cinnamon stick and 2 cloves.

Cook over low heat until the sugar is dissolved, then bring to the boil. Reduce the heat and simmer for 5 minutes.

Wash and core 1½ pounds of crab apples. Add the apples to the syrup. Simmer gently for 15 to 20 minutes, or until the apples are tender. Do not overcook or they will burst.

Using a slotted spoon transfer the apples to a serving bowl. Boil the syrup for about 5 minutes, or until it has reduced and thickened slightly. Strain the syrup over the apples.

Serve hot or cold.

INGREDIENTS TO SERVE FOUR TO SIX:
½ cup (100 g) sugar
½ lemon
1 cinnamon stick
2 cloves
1½ lb (700 g) crab apples

Rose Hip Soup

This Scandinavian fruit soup is really a purée of rose hips that can be served as a dessert.

Trim the ends from 1 pound of rose hips. Wash the rose hips well and put them into a saucepan with 2½ cups of water. Cover the pan and bring to the boil. Reduce the heat and simmer for 20 to 30 minutes, or until the rose hips are tender.

Blend the rose hips with the water and then strain the purée into a saucepan.

Blend 2 tablespoons of arrowroot with a little of the purée, then stir into the fruit purée in the pan.

Bring to the boil, stirring constantly, and boil until the soup thickens. Sweeten to taste with a little sugar or honey and simmer for 2 minutes more.

Pour into individual serving bowls or 1 large bowl and leave to cool.

Serve chilled, sprinkled with 3 tablespoons of sliced almonds.

INGREDIENTS TO SERVE FOUR:
1 lb (500 g) rose hips
2 tablespoons (30 ml) arrowroot
sugar or honey
3 tablespoons (25 g) sliced almonds

Roast Chestnuts

This is one of the most enjoyable ways to eat chestnuts and the simplest method of preparing them for a number of other dishes.

Preheat the oven to 400°F (200°C).

Cut 2 slits in the skins of 2 pounds of chestnuts using a sharp knife. Put the chestnuts on a baking sheet in the top of the oven and roast them for 10 to 15 minutes, or until the skins split.

Pile the chestnuts onto a plate and serve immediately. Peel off both layers of skin while the chestnuts are still warm.

INGREDIENTS TO SERVE FOUR TO SIX:
2 lb (1 kg) chestnuts

Chestnut Stuffing

Prepare and peel 1 pound of chestnuts. Chop 4 slices of bacon. Chop 1 large onion.

Over low heat fry the bacon in a saucepan until the fat runs.

Add the onion to the pan and fry for 3 minutes. Remove the pan from the heat and stir in 2 cups of fresh whole-wheat bread crumbs, the grated rind of 1 lemon and 1 tablespoon of chopped parsley.

Put the peeled chestnuts into a saucepan, cover with water and bring to the boil. Simmer for 30 minutes, or until the chestnuts are tender. Drain the chestnuts and either chop them for a coarse stuffing, or blend them for a smoother stuffing.

Add the chestnuts to the bread-crumb mixture. Mix well and season with salt, pepper and grated nutmeg. Add 1 tablespoon of brandy if desired. Beat 1 egg and stir it into the stuffing.

INGREDIENTS TO STUFF ONE TWELVE-POUND (6-KG) TURKEY:
1 lb (500 g) chestnuts
4 slices bacon
1 large onion
2 cups (100 g) fresh whole-wheat
**   bread crumbs**
1 lemon
1 tablespoon (15 ml) chopped parsley
salt
pepper
grated nutmeg
1 tablespoon (15 ml) brandy (optional)
1 egg

Mont Blanc

This famous puréed chestnut dessert is made much lighter by using yogurt instead of cream and by the addition of a stiffly beaten egg white.

Prepare and peel 1 pound of chestnuts.

Put the chestnuts into a saucepan with 1 vanilla bean. Add water to cover. Bring to the boil, then reduce the heat and simmer for 20 to 30 minutes, or until the chestnuts are tender.

Remove and discard the vanilla bean and drain the chestnuts. Blend them to a purée.

Put the purée into a mixing bowl and stir in ⅔ cup of yogurt and 1 tablespoon of brandy or lemon juice. Add 1 to 2 tablespoons of brown sugar.

Beat 1 egg white until just stiff, then fold into the chestnut purée.

Carefully spoon the chestnut mixture into a mountain on a serving dish. Spoon 2 tablespoons of yogurt on the top to cap the mountain with snow.

Serve chilled.

INGREDIENTS TO SERVE FOUR:
1 lb (500 g) chestnuts
1 vanilla bean
⅔ cup plus 2 tablespoons (180 ml) yogurt
1 tablespoon (15 ml) brandy or lemon
**   juice**
1 to 2 tablespoons (15 to 30 ml) brown
**   sugar**
1 egg white

Elderflower Water

Elderflowers make a refreshing summer drink which may be stored in a cool place for several weeks.

Cut a large bunch of elderflowers, about 2½ cups of the tightly packed flower heads. Put them into a large bowl with the grated rind and juice of 2 lemons and 1 cup of sugar.

Pour in 2 quarts of boiling water and stir until the sugar is dissolved.

Cover the bowl and leave to stand overnight, then strain the liquid and pour it into bottles. Serve chilled.

INGREDIENTS TO MAKE 2 QUARTS (1.60 LITERS) OF WATER:
large bunch elderflowers
2 lemons
1 cup (250 g) sugar

Sloe Gin

Made in the fall when sloes are ripe, this unusual liqueur matures in time for Christmas, but properly sealed it will keep indefinitely. Serve the sloes with the gin or separately as a dessert.

Remove the stalks from 1 pound of sloes. Wash the sloes and prick them well with a large needle.

Put the sloes into a large preserving jar. Add ½ cup of sugar. Pour 1 quart of gin into the jar.

Seal the jar and store in a cool dark place for 2 to 3 months, shaking the bottle occasionally.

Serve with 1 or 2 sloes in the glass. The sloes will have lost their bitterness.

INGREDIENTS TO MAKE 1 QUART (850 ML) OF LIQUEUR:
1 lb (500 g) sloe berries
½ cup (100 g) sugar
1 quart (850 ml) gin

MAKING SLOE GIN

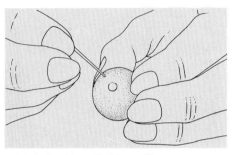

Prick the sloe skins well with a needle.

Put into a jar, add sugar and gin to cover.

Seal the jar and store, shaking occasionally.

IT HAS NEVER BEEN VERY CLEAR what it is in the daily apple that is supposed to keep the doctor away. There are many other popular fruits and vegetables that are far better sources of vitamins and minerals. But the popular trust in apples may be more justified than most nutritional charts suggest.

Consider, for example, our estimated requirements of vitamin C and the quantity an apple provides—and an apple is not a fruit that is associated with vitamin C. It is generally accepted that ten milligrams of ascorbic acid a day will prevent scurvy. But recommended intakes are always far more generous to allow for individual variation and increased utilization of vitamin C in times of stress. In the United States the recommended intake of vitamin C for an adult male is sixty milligrams a day.

An average-sized, three-and-a-half-ounce raw apple is estimated to contain five milligrams of vitamin C. And if its health-giving virtue lies in its vitamin C content it would take a dozen apples a day to keep an American doctor away.

The vitamin and mineral content of an apple varies, however, according to its variety, the kind of soil in which it was grown, how ripe it is and how long it has been stored. The amount of vitamin C in an apple increases as it ripens and falls as it is stored. But the most striking differences in the amounts of vitamin C depend, it appears, on the variety. The range is from less than three milligrams to more than thirty milligrams in a medium-sized apple.

It is a comforting thought that some of the most nutritious apples are also the best flavored. Of the American apples, the richest in vitamin C is Northern Spy with almost eighteen milligrams. The ubiquitous Golden Delicious, however, has only eight milligrams and the rather tasteless

The Nutrients in Apples, Pears and Quinces
These are quite high in fiber and three and a half ounces (100 g) of pears, for example, provide about 60 Calories.

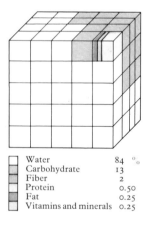

Water	84	%
Carbohydrate	13	
Fiber	2	
Protein	0.50	
Fat	0.25	
Vitamins and minerals	0.25	

EXTRACTING APPLE JUICE

Sweet-tasting apple juice is not the easiest of juices to squeeze out, so most people buy it bottled. The cider press (left) is no longer used, but more modern presses play a part in making both unfermented apple juice and fermented cider. The fruit is first ground into a pulp or pomace, then fed into the press which converts it into "cheeses." Wrapped in open-meshed cloths, layers of these cheeses lie on slatted wooden racks while the juice drips through. To make cider, the juice is then fermented, usually with the natural yeasts on apples and without the need for additional sugar, but to stop apple juice fermenting it is pasteurized. To prevent the juice oxidizing, extra vitamin C is often added.

Rome Beauty cannot even manage four milligrams. All apples contain fructose and glucose to give you energy—a medium-sized apple provides about 60 Calories—and they are a valuable source of roughage.

Apples have been cultivated for more than three thousand years, since they were developed from the wild crab apple, *Malus pumila*. Of the seven thousand named varieties in the United States the big eight are Red and Golden Delicious, McIntosh, Rome Beauty, Jonathan, Winesap, York and Stayman.

The image of an apple is crunchiness, but cooking it provides other beautiful flavors and textures—tart in sauce, sweet in pies and uniquely frothy when baked. Crab apples provide a jelly that is beautiful in color and flavor, and from other astringent but cultivated varieties unfermented apple juice (sweet cider) and fermented cider (hard cider) are obtained.

Apples are the fruit that many people count on for instant goodness. They provide energy because they are relatively high in sugar and three and a half ounces (100 g) provide about 60 Calories. They add roughage to the diet and are a good source of minerals and vitamin C, although the amount of vitamin C depends on how ripe the apple is and how long it has been stored. Pears (in the smaller basket, center) are similar to apples in their nutritional potential, as are the less familiar quinces (inset).

Apples are the major fruit crop of temperate climates, and indeed in the world as a whole they are beaten only by grapes, oranges and bananas. We eat far fewer pears—only a third of the apple consumption. This is understandable, for while the apple is a very dependable fruit, the pear is infuriatingly unreliable. One day it is hard and then, almost while your back is turned, it has become mealy. It is deceitful, fooling you by turning rotten from the inside instead of from the outside. But caught at just the right moment of ripeness, all its failings are forgiven. Even if its mouth-watering succulence can be embarrassing, it is perfection. And pears, like apples, provide energy, vitamins, minerals and roughage.

As with apples, there are thousands of varieties of pears, and a few of the best have been cultivated for centuries. The Jargonelle, for example, goes back to 1600. The three outstanding pears are Conference, an English pear of the late nineteenth century, Comice and Bartlett. This is the pear that cans extremely well.

These and other dessert pears are far better for cooking than the so-called cooking pears, which need long slow cooking to make them soft. Just as apples are used to make cider, there are bitter pears that are rich in tannin which have been used for more than twenty-five hundred years to make pear cider, or perry.

Quinces have an equally long history and the trees themselves can live a century or more. They are now not widely grown—which is a pity, for a quince tree when it is covered in white or pink blossoms is a beautiful sight. The fruit, however, even when it is left on the tree until November, is hard and acid, and impossible to eat raw. But quinces do have a honeylike aroma, and they make excellent pies, jams and jellies. They are made into a kind of sweet pâté in Spain, Germany and France.

French Apple Pie

Preheat the oven to 400°F (200°C).

Make 1½ cups of almond pastry (see page 35). Roll it out on a floured surface and line an 8-inch (20-cm) fluted flan ring or a pie pan.

Bake blind for 15 minutes. Remove the beans and paper and bake for 5 minutes more.

Lower the oven temperature to 375°F (190°C).

Peel and core 2 pounds of tart apples. Slice the apples thinly into a bowl. Add the juice of 1 lemon and 1 tablespoon of sugar and toss lightly.

Arrange the apple slices neatly in overlapping circles in the pastry shell.

For the glaze, put 2 tablespoons of apricot jam into a saucepan with 2 tablespoons of water and the lemon juice remaining from the apples. Cook over very low heat until the jam has dissolved, then, stirring constantly, bring to the boil.

Brush half of the glaze over the apples. Bake for 30 minutes, or until the apples are tender and lightly browned.

Remove the pie from the oven. Reheat the remaining glaze and brush it over the apples.

Serve hot or cold.

INGREDIENTS TO SERVE FOUR TO SIX:
1½ cups (150 g) almond pastry (see page 35)
2 lb (1 kg) tart apples
1 lemon
1 tablespoon (15 ml) sugar
2 tablespoons (30 ml) apricot jam

PREPARING FRENCH APPLE PIE

Overlap apple slices in circles in the pastry shell.

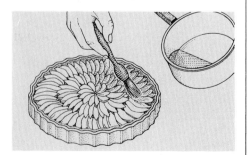

Brush the apple slices with apricot jam glaze.

Apple and Mint Sauce

Serve this sauce with lamb, pork or poultry.

Peel and core 1 pound of tart apples. Slice the apples and put them into a saucepan with 2 tablespoons of lemon juice, 4 tablespoons of water and 2 tablespoons of chopped mint.

Cover the pan and cook over low heat for 10 to 15 minutes, or until the apples are reduced to a pulp.

Blend the apples to a smooth purée. Return the purée to the pan and reheat, adding 1 tablespoon of sugar if desired.

INGREDIENTS TO SERVE FOUR TO SIX:
1 lb (500 g) tart apples
2 tablespoons (30 ml) lemon juice
2 tablespoons (30 ml) chopped mint
1 tablespoon (15 ml) sugar (optional)

Baked Apple Custard

Preheat the oven to 350°F (180°C).

Peel and core 1½ pounds of tart apples. Slice the apples and put them into a saucepan with 2 tablespoons of rum or lemon juice, 1 to 2 tablespoons of sugar and ¼ teaspoon of ground cinnamon. Cover the pan and cook over low heat, stirring occasionally, for 10 to 15 minutes, or until the apples are reduced to a pulp. Sieve or blend the apples to a smooth purée.

Beat 4 eggs with ⅔ cup of milk. Beat the mixture into the apple purée.

Pour the apple mixture into a 4- to 5-cup (850-ml) ring mold or tube pan. Put the mold into a roasting pan half-filled with water.

Bake for 1 hour, or until the custard is set and firm to the touch.

To serve the custard hot, leave it in the mold for 5 minutes before turning it out. To serve cold leave it in the mold until it is cold, then turn it out.

Core and slice 1 red apple and arrange the slices in the center of the mold.

INGREDIENTS TO SERVE FOUR:
1½ lb (700 g) tart apples
2 tablespoons (30 ml) rum or lemon juice
¼ teaspoon (1 ml) ground cinnamon
4 eggs
⅔ cup (150 ml) milk
1 red apple

Apple and Red Currant Snow

Peel and core 1½ pounds of tart apples. Slice the apples and put them into a saucepan with 3 tablespoons of red currant jelly and the juice of ½ lemon. Cover the pan and cook over low heat, stirring occasionally, for 15 minutes, or until the apples are reduced to a pulp.

Sieve or blend the apples to a smooth purée. Let the apple purée cool, then stir in ⅔ cup of yogurt.

Beat 2 egg whites until stiff, then fold into the apple and yogurt mixture.

Spoon into a serving bowl or individual dishes or glasses.

Over low heat, cook 1 tablespoon of red currant jelly in a saucepan with 1 tablespoon of water until the jelly is dissolved. Add ¼ cup of sliced almonds to the pan. Stir lightly until the almonds are glazed. Turn out onto a plate or a piece of foil and let cool. Arrange the glazed almonds on top of the apple snow.

INGREDIENTS TO SERVE FOUR:
1½ lb (700 g) tart apples
4 tablespoons (60 ml) red currant jelly
½ lemon
⅔ cup (150 ml) yogurt
2 egg whites
¼ cup (50 g) sliced almonds

Orange Candied Apples

Peel and core 2 pounds of tart apples. Slice the apples. Put them into a saucepan with the grated rind and juice of 2 oranges, ⅓ cup of candied orange peel, ⅓ cup of currants and 1 tablespoon of honey, if desired.

Cover the pan and cook over low heat for 10 to 15 minutes, or until the apples are tender but still in whole slices.

Serve hot or cold.

INGREDIENTS TO SERVE FOUR TO SIX:
2 lb (1 kg) tart apples
2 oranges
⅓ cup (50 g) candied orange peel
⅓ cup (50 g) currants
1 tablespoon (15 ml) honey (optional)

Apple Roulade

Peel and core 1 pound of tart apples. Slice them and put them into a saucepan with the grated rind and juice of 1 lemon and 2 tablespoons of sugar.

Cover the pan and cook over low heat, stirring occasionally, for 15 minutes, or until the apples are reduced to a pulp. Sieve or blend the apples to a smooth purée. Put the purée into a bowl and stir in ½ cup of ground almonds. Cool slightly.

Preheat the oven to 400°F (200°C). Separate 4 eggs, beating the yolks into the cool apple purée. Beat the egg whites until stiff then fold lightly into the apple purée.

Line a 9- by 13-inch (23- by 32-cm) jelly-roll pan or a baking sheet with a raised rim with waxed paper and brush lightly with oil. Spread the apple mixture in the pan.

Bake for 10 to 15 minutes, or until firm and beginning to brown lightly.

Dust a large sheet of waxed paper with 1 tablespoon of sugar. Turn the roulade out onto the prepared paper and peel off the baking paper.

Spread ½ pound of raspberries over the top to within 1 inch (2 cm) of the edges. Roll up, like a jelly roll, by lifting up the waxed paper so that the roulade turns over on itself.

Carefully lift onto a serving dish. Serve hot or cold.

INGREDIENTS TO SERVE FOUR TO SIX :
1 lb (500 g) tart apples
1 lemon
3 tablespoons (45 ml) sugar
½ cup (50 g) ground almonds
4 eggs
½ pound (250 g) raspberries

Apples Baked in Cider

Preheat the oven to 350°F (180°C).

Peel and core 2 pounds of apples. Slice the apples and put them into a baking dish with ⅔ cup of seedless raisins and 1¼ cups of hard cider.

Cover the dish and bake for 20 minutes. Uncover the dish, baste the apples with the cider and bake for 10 minutes more.

Serve hot or cold.

INGREDIENTS TO SERVE SIX :
2 lb (1 kg) apples
⅔ cup (100 g) seedless raisins
1¼ cups (300 ml) hard cider

Baked Apples

Put ½ cup of coarsely chopped dried apricots into a bowl with 2 tablespoons of brandy. Soak the apricots for several hours or, preferably, overnight.

Preheat the oven to 350°F (180°C).

Core 4 large tart apples. Make a shallow cut through the skin around the center of each apple.

Put the apples into a baking dish. Spoon 1 teaspoon of brown sugar into the center of each apple. Press the apricots into the centers.

Spoon 4 tablespoons of water around the apples and bake for 45 minutes, or until the apples are tender.

Serve hot with the juice from the dish. Top each apple with 1 tablespoon of yogurt.

PREPARING BAKED APPLES

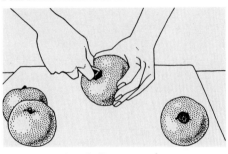

Use a corer or sharp knife to core apples.

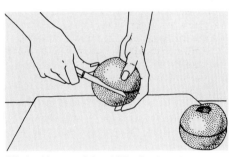

Slit the skin around the middle of each apple.

Fill the hollow centers of the apples.

INGREDIENTS TO SERVE FOUR :
½ cup (100 g) chopped dried apricots
2 tablespoons (30 ml) brandy
4 large tart apples
4 teaspoons (20 ml) brown sugar
4 tablespoons (60 ml) yogurt

Apple Layer Pudding

Preheat the oven to 350°F (180°C). Grease an 8-inch (20-cm) spring form cake pan.

Peel and core 2 pounds of tart apples and put them into a saucepan. Add 1 tablespoon of water, 6 cloves and 3 tablespoons of light brown sugar. Heat gently, stirring continuously, until the apples are tender.

Sieve the apples into a bowl. Stir in 2 tablespoons of melted butter and the grated rind of 1 lemon. Set aside to cool slightly.

Meanwhile, mix 2 cups of dry whole-wheat bread crumbs with ⅓ cup of light brown sugar and 1 teaspoon of ground cinnamon.

Beat 2 eggs into the apple mixture and spoon one-third of it into the prepared pan. Level the surface. Cover with a layer of the bread-crumb mixture. Repeat the layers twice more, ending with a layer of bread crumbs.

Bake the pudding for 20 minutes, or until the top is golden brown.

Beat ⅔ cup of yogurt and spread it over the top of the pudding. Remove the ring from the pan and serve immediately or allow the pudding to cool in the pan before removing the ring.

INGREDIENTS TO SERVE SIX TO EIGHT :
2 lb (1 kg) tart apples
6 cloves
½ cup (75 g) light brown sugar
2 tablespoons (25 g) melted butter
1 lemon
2 cups (150 g) dry whole-wheat bread crumbs
1 teaspoon (5 ml) ground cinnamon
2 eggs
⅔ cup (150 ml) yogurt

Apple Crème

Preheat the oven to 350°F (180°C).

Peel and core 1½ pounds of tart apples. Slice the apples thickly. Heat 2 tablespoons of butter in a saucepan. Add the apples, ¼ teaspoon of ground cinnamon and 6 cloves to the pan and cook them gently for 10 minutes, stirring constantly. Transfer the apples to a greased baking dish.

Make 1¼ cups of custard. Beat 2 eggs with 1¼ cups of warm milk and 1 tablespoon of sugar. Pour over the apples.

Bake for 40 to 45 minutes. Serve immediately or let the custard cool, then chill thoroughly before serving.

INGREDIENTS TO SERVE FOUR :
1½ lb (700 g) tart apples
2 tablespoons (25 g) butter
¼ teaspoon (1 ml) ground cinnamon
6 cloves
2 eggs
1¼ cups (300 ml) warm milk
1 tablespoon (15 ml) sugar

Spiced Apple and Hazelnut Pie

Preheat the oven to 400°F (200°C).

Put the grated rind and juice of 1 lemon into a large mixing bowl. Add ¼ teaspoon of ground ginger, ¼ teaspoon of ground cinnamon, ¼ teaspoon of grated nutmeg and 1 to 2 tablespoons of brown sugar. Add ⅓ cup of seedless raisins. Mix well.

Peel and core 1½ pounds of tart apples. Slice them into the bowl. Toss lightly to coat the apple slices in the spice mixture.

Arrange the apples in a 1-quart (850-ml) pie pan.

Make 1½ cups of shortcrust pastry with whole-wheat flour (see page 34), adding ½ cup of chopped roasted hazelnuts. On a floured surface roll the pastry out to a circle a little larger than the top of the pie pan. Cut a ½-inch (1-cm) strip of pastry from around the edge and press it onto the dampened rim of the pie pan. Dampen the strip of pastry and put the pastry circle on top. Seal the edges together and flute them. Cut the pastry trimmings into leaves and decorate the top of the pie with them. Brush the pastry with beaten egg or milk.

Bake for 30 to 35 minutes, or until the pastry is crisp and brown. After 15 minutes, if the pastry is getting too brown, lower the oven temperature to 350°F (180°C).

INGREDIENTS TO SERVE SIX:
1 lemon
¼ teaspoon (1 ml) ground ginger
¼ teaspoon (1 ml) ground cinnamon
¼ teaspoon (1 ml) grated nutmeg
1 to 2 tablespoons (15 to 30 ml) brown sugar
⅓ cup (50 g) seedless raisins
1½ lb (700 g) tart apples
1½ cups (150 g) shortcrust pastry made with whole-wheat flour (see page 34)
½ cup (50 g) chopped roasted hazelnuts
1 egg or milk

Apple and Ginger Mousse

Put the grated rind and juice of 1 lemon into a saucepan. Peel, core and slice 2 pounds of tart apples and put them into the saucepan. Toss lightly to coat all the apples with the lemon juice. Add 1 tablespoon of honey. Cover the pan and cook over low heat, stirring occasionally, for about 15 minutes, or until the apples are reduced to a pulp.

Blend or sieve the apples to a smooth purée. Put the purée into a large bowl.

Separate 2 eggs, adding the yolks to the apple purée. Beat the yolks into the apple

Familiar fruit, apples and pears make wonderful desserts. From left to right: Apple and Ginger Mousse, Spiced Apple and Hazelnut Pie and Pears in Red Wine.

purée with 1¼ cups of yogurt. Finely chop 1 piece of preserved ginger and stir it into the purée with 1 tablespoon of the ginger syrup.

In a cup set in a pan of hot water dissolve 1½ tablespoons of powdered gelatin in 2 tablespoons of water. Stir the gelatin into the apple mixture.

When the apple mixture is just beginning to thicken, beat the 2 egg whites until they are stiff and fold them in.

Around the top of a 1-quart (850-ml) soufflé dish tie a strip of waxed paper to come 2 inches (5 cm) above the rim. Pour the mousse into the dish.

Refrigerate for 2 to 3 hours before serving.

Carefully remove the paper collar and decorate the top of the mousse with yogurt

cheese (see page 100) and preserved ginger.

INGREDIENTS TO SERVE FOUR TO SIX:
1 lemon
2 lb (1 kg) tart apples
1 tablespoon (15 ml) honey
2 eggs
1¼ cups (150 ml) yogurt
preserved ginger in syrup
1½ tablespoons (15 g) powdered gelatin
yogurt cheese (see page 100)

Pear and Yogurt Custard Pie

Preheat the oven to 400°F (200°C).

Make 1½ cups of shortcrust pastry using

whole-wheat flour and ground cinnamon (see page 34). Roll out the pastry on a floured surface and line an 8-inch (20-cm) flan ring or pie pan. Bake blind for 15 minutes. Remove the paper and beans and bake for 10 minutes more. Reduce the oven temperature to 350°F (180°C).

Cut 3 pears into halves, remove the cores and peel thinly. Put the pear halves into a saucepan with 1 tablespoon of water and the juice of ½ lemon. Cover the pan and poach the pears gently for 5 minutes, or until they are just tender. Remove the pears from the pan with a slotted spoon and drain well.

For the custard, beat 2 eggs in a mixing bowl, then beat in 1¼ cups of yogurt with 1 tablespoon of sugar. Spoon half of the custard into the pastry shell and bake for 20 minutes.

Arrange the pear halves on top of the custard, cut side downward. Spoon the remaining custard around the pears and return to the oven for 10 to 15 minutes more, or until the custard is just set.

INGREDIENTS TO SERVE SIX:
1½ cups (150 g) shortcrust pastry made with whole-wheat flour and cinnamon (see page 34)
3 pears
½ lemon
2 eggs
1¼ cups (300 ml) yogurt
1 tablespoon (15 ml) sugar

Pears in Red Wine

Put 1¼ cups of red wine and 1¼ cups of water into a large saucepan with 3 strips of lemon rind, ¼ cup of sugar, 2 tablespoons of red currant jelly and 1 stick of cinnamon. Cook over very low heat until the sugar and jelly are dissolved.

Use 4 to 6 ripe pears, preferably with stems. Leaving the pears whole, peel off the skin. Put the pears into the pan, submerging them as much as possible in the wine mixture.

Cover the pan and cook over low heat for about 20 minutes, or until the pears are tender.

Carefully lift out the pears and put them into a serving bowl.

Strain the wine sauce and return it to the pan.

Blend 1 tablespoon of arrowroot with a little cold water, then pour it into the pan. Bring to the boil, stirring constantly, until the sauce is lightly thickened, then reduce the heat and simmer for 2 minutes.

Pour the wine sauce over the pears.
Serve cold.

INGREDIENTS TO SERVE FOUR TO SIX:
1¼ cups (300 ml) red wine
1 lemon
¼ cup (50 g) sugar
2 tablespoons (30 ml) red currant jelly
1 cinnamon stick
4 to 6 ripe pears
1 tablespoon (15 ml) arrowroot

Broiled Pears and Blue Cheese

This is a delicious dish with which to either start or end a meal.

Cut 4 pears into quarters and remove the cores. Slice each pear into an individual flameproof dish.

Cut ½ pound of Blue cheese into thin slices and arrange them on top of the pear slices.

Put under a hot broiler for 3 to 5 minutes, until the cheese is bubbling and browned.

Serve at once.

INGREDIENTS TO SERVE FOUR:
4 pears
½ lb (250 g) Blue cheese

Pear and Honey Sherbet

Cut 2 pounds of pears into quarters. Remove the cores and peel. Slice the pears into a saucepan. Add the grated rind and juice of 1 lemon and 2 to 3 tablespoons of honey.

Cover the pan and cook over low heat for 15 minutes, or until the pears are tender.

Blend or sieve the pears to a smooth purée.

Pour the pear purée into a plastic bowl and put it into the freezer for 1 hour, or until the purée is half-frozen. Beat well.

Beat 1 egg white until stiff and fold it into the pear purée.

Return to the freezer until solid, then cover tightly. The sherbet may be stored in the freezer for up to 3 months.

To serve, let the sherbet soften slightly in the refrigerator or at room temperature, then spoon into individual serving dishes or glasses.

INGREDIENTS TO SERVE FOUR TO SIX:
2 lb (1 kg) pears
1 lemon
2 to 3 tablespoons (30 to 45 ml) honey
1 egg white

Pear, Cucumber and Mint Cocktail

Cut 4 pears into quarters. Remove the cores. Slice the pears and put them into a bowl.

Cut 1 cucumber into slices, then cut the slices into quarters and add to the pears.

For the dressing, beat together 2 tablespoons of lemon juice with 2 tablespoons of corn oil and 1 tablespoon of chopped mint. Pour the dressing over the pears and cucumber and toss lightly but well.

Marinate in the refrigerator for at least 2 hours before serving.

Serve in individual dishes garnished with sprigs of mint.

INGREDIENTS TO SERVE FOUR TO SIX:
4 pears
1 cucumber
2 tablespoons (30 ml) lemon juice
2 tablespoons (30 ml) corn oil
1 small bunch mint

Pear and Ginger Fool

Cut 4 large pears into quarters. Peel them, remove the cores and slice them into a saucepan.

Add the grated rind and juice of $\frac{1}{2}$ lemon, $\frac{1}{4}$ teaspoon of ground ginger and 1 tablespoon of ginger syrup from a jar of preserved ginger.

Cover the pan and cook over low heat, stirring occasionally, for 10 to 15 minutes, or until the pears are tender.

Sieve the pears to a smooth purée. Stir in $\frac{2}{3}$ cup of yogurt. Alternatively, put the cooked

pears into a blender with the yogurt and blend to a smooth purée. Pour into 4 individual serving dishes.

Serve chilled and decorated with slices of preserved ginger.

INGREDIENTS TO SERVE FOUR:
4 large pears
$\frac{1}{2}$ lemon
1 tablespoon (15 ml) ginger syrup
$\frac{2}{3}$ cup (150 ml) yogurt
preserved ginger

PREPARING PEARS

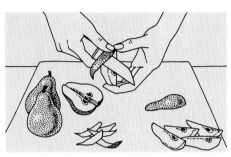

Cut pears into quarters and peel them.

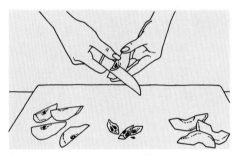

Cut out the cores with a sharp knife.

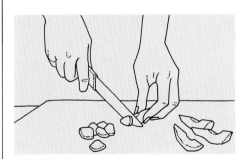

Thinly slice the quartered pears.

Stuffed Pears

Preheat the oven to 350°F (160°C).

Cut a thin slice from the base of 4 large ripe pears so that they stand upright. Peel the pears and slice a 1-inch (2-cm) piece off the top of each to make a lid. Scoop the cores out with a teaspoon.

Mix $\frac{1}{3}$ cup of chopped pitted dates with $\frac{1}{3}$ cup of sliced blanched almonds and 2 tablespoons of honey. Spoon the mixture into the hollow pears. Cover with the lids.

Stand the pears in a greased baking dish and pour $\frac{2}{3}$ cup of dry white wine over them. Bake for 30 minutes, or until the pears are tender.

Serve immediately.

INGREDIENTS TO SERVE FOUR:
4 large ripe pears
$\frac{1}{3}$ cup (50 g) chopped pitted dates
$\frac{1}{3}$ cup (50 g) sliced blanched almonds
2 tablespoons (30 ml) honey
$\frac{2}{3}$ cup (150 ml) dry white wine

Pears with Beans

Peel and core 1 pound of firm pears. Chop the pears into large chunks and put them into a saucepan. Add 2 scant cups of dry white wine and the peeled rind of 1 lemon. Simmer gently over low heat for 10 minutes.

Snip the ends off 1 pound of green beans. Wash the beans, slice them and add them to the pears. Continue to simmer until the beans are tender.

Meanwhile, make $\frac{2}{3}$ cup of yogurt hollandaise sauce (see page 93). Drain the pears and beans and put them into a serving dish.

Spoon the sauce over the pears and beans or serve it separately in a gravy boat. Serve immediately.

INGREDIENTS TO SERVE FOUR:
1 lb (500 g) firm pears
2 scant cups (450 ml) dry white wine
1 lemon
1 lb (500 g) green beans
$\frac{2}{3}$ cup (150 ml) yogurt hollandaise sauce (see page 93)

Autumn Pudding

Preheat the oven to 350°F (180°C). Lightly grease a deep 1-quart (850-ml) ovenproof dish.

Cut the crust from 1 small loaf of whole-wheat bread. Thinly slice the bread.

Dip the bread slices into ⅓ cup of melted margarine or butter. Line the dish with the bread slices, overlapping them slightly so that they completely cover the inside of the dish.

Peel, core and thinly slice 1 pound of tart apples. Wash and hull ¾ pound of blackberries. Put the apples and blackberries into a saucepan with ¼ cup of sugar, the grated rind and juice of ½ lemon and 2 tablespoons of water. Cover the pan and slowly bring to the boil. Reduce the heat and simmer for 1 minute.

Spoon the fruit mixture into the bread-lined dish. Cover the fruit with overlapping slices of bread. Put an ovenproof plate and weight on top of the pudding.

Bake for 40 to 45 minutes. Turn the pudding out onto a plate and serve immediately or chill and serve cold.

INGREDIENTS TO SERVE FOUR TO SIX:
1 small whole-wheat loaf
⅓ cup (75 g) margarine or butter
1 lb (500 g) tart apples
¾ lb (375 g) blackberries
¼ cup (50 g) sugar
½ lemon

Apple, Date and Celery Salad

Separate the stalks of 1 medium-sized head of celery. Wash well and chop into ½-inch (1-cm) pieces. Thinly slice ⅔ cup of pitted dates. Wash and core ½ pound of tart apples. Cut the apples into ½-inch (1-cm) cubes. Put the celery, dates and apples into a salad bowl.

In a small mixing bowl combine 2 tablespoons of honey, 1¼ cups of yogurt and 1 tablespoon of finely chopped mint.

Pour the yogurt mixture over the celery and fruit and toss gently. Serve chilled, sprinkled with 3 tablespoons of chopped pistachio nuts.

INGREDIENTS TO SERVE FOUR:
1 medium-sized head celery
⅔ cup (100 g) pitted dates
½ lb (250 g) tart apples
2 tablespoons (30 ml) honey
1¼ cups (300 ml) yogurt
1 tablespoon (15 ml) chopped mint
3 tablespoons (25 g) chopped pistachio nuts

Apple Chutney

Serve this delicious fruit chutney with cold pork or ham. Stored in sealed jars, it will keep for 2 to 3 weeks.

Wash 1 pound of cooking apples and grate them coarsely into a large mixing bowl. Discard the cores. Peel and coarsely grate 3 medium-sized onions and add them to the apples.

Cut 1 large green pepper in half and remove the seeds and pith. Finely chop the pepper and ⅓ cup of pitted dates. Add the pepper and dates to the bowl with ⅔ cup of seedless raisins and 2 tablespoons of finely chopped crystallized ginger.

In a small bowl mix 2 tablespoons white wine vinegar with 1 teaspoon of salt and 1 teaspoon of sugar. Pour over the chopped fruit and onions and mix well.

Spoon the chutney into sterilized jars, seal and store.

INGREDIENTS TO MAKE TWO AND A QUARTER POUNDS (1 KG) OF CHUTNEY:
1 lb (500 g) cooking apples
3 medium-sized onions
1 large green pepper
⅓ cup (50 g) pitted dates
⅔ cup (100 g) seedless raisins
2 tablespoons (25 g) chopped crystallized ginger
2 tablespoons (30 ml) white wine vinegar
1 teaspoon (5 ml) salt
1 teaspoon (5 ml) sugar

Spiced Apple Drink

Wash 2 pounds of apples and grate them coarsely into a clean 5-quart (4-liter) wide-necked container, such as a plastic bucket or bowl. Add the cores and cover the apples with 5 quarts of cold water. Put in a cool place for 1 week and stir once a day.

Add 4 cups of sugar, 2 tablespoons of ground ginger, 2 tablespoons of ground cinnamon, 1 tablespoon of cloves and 1 tablespoon of allspice. Stir the liquid until the sugar has dissolved. Let stand for 1 day more, then strain the liquid through several layers of cheesecloth. Siphon or pour the liquid into clean bottles.

Lightly cork the bottles and leave them in a cool place for 1 week before drinking.

INGREDIENTS TO MAKE 5 QUARTS (4 LITERS):
2 lb (1 kg) apples
4 cups (500 g) sugar
2 tablespoons (30 ml) ground ginger
2 tablespoons (30 ml) ground cinnamon
1 tablespoon (15 ml) cloves
1 tablespoon (15 ml) allspice

Quince Preserve

The strong flavor of quince makes it ideal for preserving. Serve with cold or hot meat, poultry or game.

Wash 3 pounds of quinces. Chop them coarsely, including the cores, and put them into a large saucepan.

Coarsely chop 1 unpeeled orange and add it to the pan. Pour in enough water to just cover the quinces. Simmer gently for 30 to 40 minutes, or until the fruit is very soft.

Strain the quince pulp and measure the purée.

Return the purée to the pan and stir in 1½ cups of sugar for every 2 cups of purée.

Cook over low heat, stirring constantly, until the sugar is dissolved, the preserve is thick and a firm line can be drawn through it with a wooden spoon.

Lightly grease the inside of clean, dry, warm Mason jars so that the preserve can be turned out easily, as it sets quite solid. Pour the preserve into the jars.

Cover the preserve with waxed disks, waxed side down. Wipe cellophane disks with a clean damp cloth and put them on top of the jars. Secure with rubber bands. Label the jars and store in a cool dark place. It is best to let the preserve mature for 3 months.

To serve, turn the preserve out of the jars and cut into slices.

INGREDIENTS TO MAKE ABOUT FOUR POUNDS (2 KG) OF PRESERVE:
3 lb (1.40 kg) quinces
1 orange
sugar

TESTING QUINCE PRESERVE FOR SETTING

When the preserve is ready it will retain a clear line.

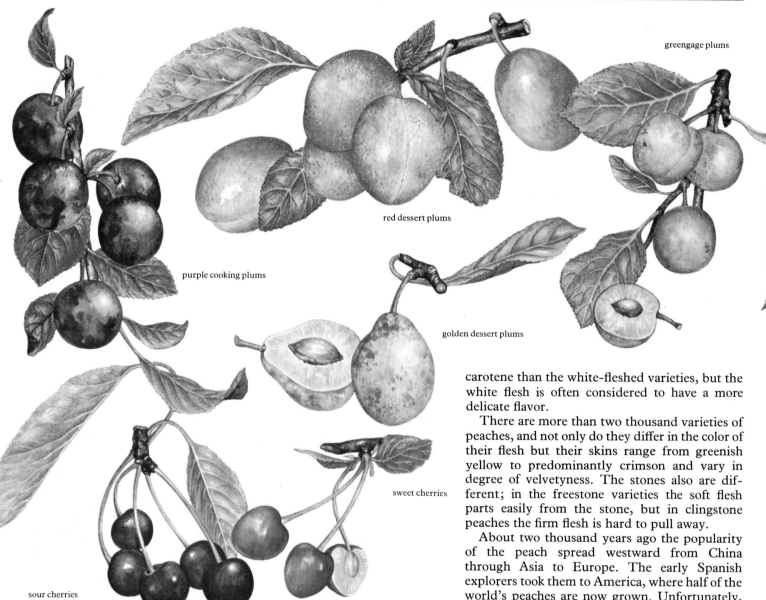

greengage plums

red dessert plums

purple cooking plums

golden dessert plums

sweet cherries

sour cherries

All the luscious fruit illustrated above are species of the genus *Prunus*. They are valued more for their flavor and succulence than their nutritional value. But they do contain small amounts of vitamin C, and their yellow flesh is a clue to their carotene content, which is particularly high in nectarines, apricots and peaches. They all contain useful minerals.

THAT "ABSENCE MAKES THE HEART GROW FONDER," is just as true of the stomach as of the heart. Some of the enjoyment of apples is lost because they are there for the biting all year round; there is nothing to look forward to. Not so with the more fleeting cherries, plums, apricots, peaches and nectarines. There are months of pleasurable anticipation, and then the brief spell of luscious, gluttonous plenty.

By a wise dispensation the most succulent of these orchard fruits—the nectarine, a smooth-skinned form of peach—is the most nutritious, brimming with vitamin C, carotene and thiamine, as well as juice. Apricots have somewhat less vitamin C, but provide more carotene and a good contribution of riboflavin. Peaches are more variable nutritionally, depending on the variety. The yellow-fleshed types contain far more carotene than the white-fleshed varieties, but the white flesh is often considered to have a more delicate flavor.

There are more than two thousand varieties of peaches, and not only do they differ in the color of their flesh but their skins range from greenish yellow to predominantly crimson and vary in degree of velvetyness. The stones also are different; in the freestone varieties the soft flesh parts easily from the stone, but in clingstone peaches the firm flesh is hard to pull away.

About two thousand years ago the popularity of the peach spread westward from China through Asia to Europe. The early Spanish explorers took them to America, where half of the world's peaches are now grown. Unfortunately, many of them are put into cans, from which they emerge with their taste and texture remarkably altered. They bear even less similarity to the original when they are dried.

Nectarines and peaches are even more difficult to catch at their prime than are pears, because they will not ripen satisfactorily off the tree. The lucky connoisseur who grows his own nectarines and peaches can seek out a likely victim early in the morning and if he has chosen correctly it will fall into his palm at the lightest touch. By lunchtime it will have been eaten.

Apricots, like peaches, come from China, but have a much longer history. They have also traveled farther, for American astronauts took them to the moon as a pleasantly rich source of minerals, especially potassium and magnesium.

Nutritionally, cherries lag somewhat behind peaches and apricots, but they are by no means inferior in flavor. There are two species of cherries:

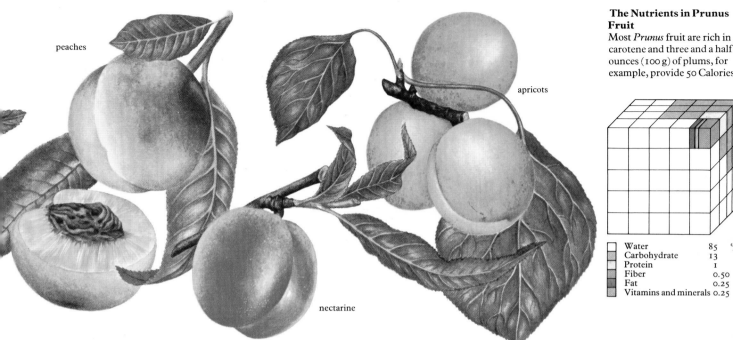

peaches

apricots

nectarine

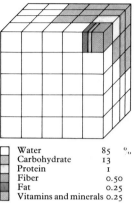

The Nutrients in Prunus Fruit
Most *Prunus* fruit are rich in carotene and three and a half ounces (100 g) of plums, for example, provide 50 Calories.

Water	85 %
Carbohydrate	13
Protein	1
Fiber	0.50
Fat	0.25
Vitamins and minerals	0.25

the sour one is used in cooking, and the sweet one is eaten as dessert. Cherries grow wild in many parts of Europe, perhaps as a result of the Roman soldier's habit of eating them while on the march and spitting out the pits.

The main sour varieties are the black Morellos and red Amarelles. The important sweet groups are the firm-fleshed and sweet bigarreau varieties, such as Black hearts and White hearts, and the softer-fleshed juicy guignes, such as Tartarian. Hybrids of the sour and sweet species are known as Dukes or Royals. Each variety has its proper role, eaten raw, stewed, in pies, jams or made into brandy or as a flavoring for gin.

Plums do not have the aura of luxury that still surrounds peaches, even though now more peaches than plums are being grown. But the right variety, grown in favorable conditions and picked when sweet, juicy and fully ripe, is out of this world.

Wild species of plums still survive in the Northern Hemisphere along with their cultivated descendants. The wild plum of western Europe is the blackthorn, or sloe, and the wild plum of western Asia is the cherry plum. These are the progenitors of European plums. Many of the dessert plums grown in the United States and Australia are, however, descended from the so-called Japanese plum, which hails from China. The flavor is generally inferior to that of the best European plums.

For aroma and sweetness there is nothing to beat a ripe gage—christened for Sir Thomas Gage, who brought it to England from the Continent in the eighteenth century. The gage is a round plum, with pale green or yellow flesh and

a ripe sensuous smell. It also makes excellent jam and preserves. The most succulent varieties are Early Transparent, and two of American upbringing—Jefferson and Denniston's Superb.

The Victoria, which is ripe in late summer, is the most popular dessert plum; it also jams and bottles successfully. Of the later varieties the best are Kirke's Blue, a beautiful, rich-tasting purple plum, and Coe's Golden Drop. Cooking plums are less juicy and not so rich in flavor.

Damsons are the least popular of plums, because they are small and usually sour, but nevertheless they make excellent preserves. And if the wind has not blown them off the trees by late fall they become surprisingly sweet.

As if the fruit of apricot, peach, cherry and plum was not prize enough their delicate blossoms are one of the great joys of spring.

Fruit can be stored and preserved in many different ways and *Prunus* fruit are particularly versatile. Plums, for example, can be canned, bottled and used to make jam or preserves. They can be frozen whole or as a purée. For centuries they have been dried to make prunes. The Chinese preserve them in salt. Below, left to right, back row: canned plums, plum jam, plum purée, plum preserve. Front row: salted plums, bottled plums, fresh plums and prunes.

Apricot Ring

Cut 1½ pounds of apricots into halves and remove the pits. Put the apricots into a saucepan with 1¼ cups of water. Bring to the boil then reduce the heat and simmer gently for 10 to 15 minutes, or until the apricots are tender.

Drain the apricots and reserve about one-third of them.

Put the remaining apricots into a blender with 1¼ cups of yogurt. Blend until smooth. Add sugar to taste.

In a cup set in a pan of hot water, dissolve 2 teaspoons of powdered gelatin in the juice of 1 lemon. Stir the dissolved gelatin into the apricot purée.

Pour into a 1-quart (850-ml) ring mold or tube pan. Refrigerate for at least 3 hours before serving.

To serve, turn the ring out by running a knife around the edge and dipping the mold into hot water for a few seconds. Then invert onto a serving plate. Fill the center of the ring with the reserved apricots.

INGREDIENTS TO SERVE FOUR TO SIX:

1½ lb (700 g) apricots
1¼ cups (300 ml) yogurt
2 teaspoons (10 ml) powdered gelatin
1 lemon

PREPARING APRICOTS

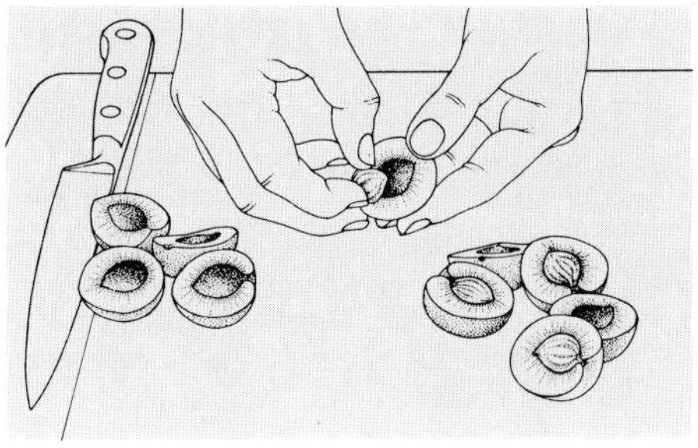

Cut apricots into halves and remove the pits.

Apricot and Almond Pie

Preheat the oven to 400°F (200°C).

Make 1½ cups of almond pastry (see page 35) and line an 8-inch (20-cm) flan ring or pie pan. Bake blind for 15 minutes. Remove the baking paper and beans and bake for 5 more minutes.

Reduce the oven temperature to 350°F (180°C).

Cut 1 pound of apricots into halves and remove the pits. Arrange the apricots in the pastry shell. Sprinkle with 1 tablespoon of brown sugar. Scatter ¼ cup of split blanched almonds over the apricots.

Bake for 20 to 30 minutes, or until the apricots are tender.

To make the glaze put 4 tablespoons of apricot jam into a small saucepan. Add the juice of ½ lemon and cook over very low heat until the jam has melted.

Spoon the hot apricot glaze over the baked pie.

Serve hot or cold.

INGREDIENTS TO SERVE FOUR TO SIX:

1½ cups (150 g) almond pastry (see page 35)
1 lb (500 g) apricots
1 tablespoon (15 ml) brown sugar
¼ cup (25 g) split blanched almonds
4 tablespoons (60 ml) apricot jam
½ lemon

Apricot and Hazelnut Trifle

Cut 1 pound of apricots into halves and remove the pits. Put the apricots into a saucepan with ⅔ cup of water and 2 tablespoons of brown sugar. Bring to the boil slowly, then reduce the heat and simmer gently for 5 minutes. Stir in 2 tablespoons of brandy. Let the apricots cool in the syrup.

Put ½ pound of small macaroons into the bottom of a serving bowl, preferably a glass bowl so that the layers can be seen. Pour the apricots and the syrup over the macaroons.

Make 1¼ cups of confectioner's custard (see page 93) using 2 egg yolks. Beat ⅔ cup of yogurt into the custard and pour it on top of the apricots.

Beat 2 egg whites until stiff, then fold in 1¼ cups of yogurt. Heap on top of the custard and sprinkle with ¼ cup of toasted hazelnuts.

INGREDIENTS TO SERVE SIX:

1 lb (500 g) apricots
2 tablespoons (30 ml) brown sugar
2 tablespoons (30 ml) brandy
½ lb (250 g) small macaroons
1¼ cups (300 ml) confectioner's custard (see page 93)
2 scant cups (450 ml) yogurt
2 eggs
¼ cup (25 g) toasted hazelnuts

Apricot Crème

Preheat the oven to 250°F (108°C).

Pour 2½ cups of milk into a saucepan and cook over low heat until it is hot, but not boiling.

Break 4 eggs into a mixing bowl. Add 1 tablespoon of sugar and ½ teaspoon of vanilla extract and beat well.

Pour into the hot milk and stir well. Strain the custard into a 1-quart (850-ml) soufflé dish or cake pan.

Put the soufflé dish into a roasting pan half-filled with hot water. Bake for 45 to 50 minutes, or until the custard is set.

Let the custard cool in the soufflé dish and then refrigerate, preferably overnight.

To turn the custard out, run a knife around the edge and invert onto a serving dish.

For the sauce, remove the pits from ½ pound of apricots. Put the apricots into a saucepan with the juice of 1 large orange. Cover the pan and simmer over low heat for 5 minutes, or until the apricots are very tender. Blend or sieve the apricots with the orange juice. Add sugar to taste if desired. Let the sauce cool, then pour it over the custard cream.

INGREDIENTS TO SERVE FOUR TO SIX:

2½ cups (600 ml) milk
4 eggs
1 tablespoon (15 ml) sugar
½ teaspoon (2.5 ml) vanilla extract
½ lb (250 g) apricots
1 large orange
sugar (optional)

Cheese and Apricot Salad

Remove the pits from ½ pound of apricots. Cut the apricots into ¼-inch (6-mm) cubes.

Blend ½ pound of ricotta cheese with ⅔ cup of yogurt. Fold in the apricots and 2 ounces of shelled pistachio nuts. Chill for at least 1 hour.

Remove the coarse stalks from 1 large bunch of watercress. Wash and drain the watercress thoroughly. Line 4 individual serving dishes with the watercress.

Spoon the cheese and fruit mixture on top of the watercress and serve immediately.

INGREDIENTS TO SERVE FOUR:

½ lb (250 g) apricots
½ lb (250 g) ricotta cheese
⅔ cup (150 ml) yogurt
2 oz (50 g) shelled pistachio nuts
1 large watercress bunch

Cherry Clafouti

Preheat the oven to 425°F (220°C).

Put 2 tablespoons of margarine or butter into a baking dish. Heat the dish in the oven until the fat has melted and is bubbling.

Put 1 cup of all-purpose flour and ¼ teaspoon of salt into a mixing bowl. Beat 1 egg with ⅔ cup of milk. Make a well in the flour and pour in the egg and milk. Mix to a smooth batter. Beat in another ⅔ cup of milk.

Put ¾ pound of pitted cherries into the dish. Pour the batter over the cherries.

Bake for 35 to 40 minutes, or until the clafouti is well risen and brown.

Serve hot or warm.

INGREDIENTS TO SERVE FOUR:
2 tablespoons (25 g) margarine or butter
1 cup (100 g) all-purpose flour
¼ teaspoon (1 ml) salt
1 egg
1⅓ cups (300 ml) milk
¾ lb (350 g) pitted cherries

Spiced Cherries in Wine

Remove the pits from 1½ pounds of cherries.

Pour 1¼ cups of red wine into a saucepan. Add 2 tablespoons of red currant jelly, 2 tablespoons of sugar and 1 cinnamon stick. Cook over very low heat until the sugar and jelly have dissolved, then bring to the boil.

Add the cherries to the pan, reduce the heat and simmer gently for 5 minutes, or until the cherries are tender but not wrinkled.

Using a slotted spoon, remove the cherries and put them into a serving bowl. Boil the wine syrup for a couple of minutes to reduce and slightly thicken it. Remove the cinnamon stick then pour the syrup over the cherries.

Chill before serving.

INGREDIENTS TO SERVE FOUR TO SIX:
1½ lb (700 g) cherries
1¼ cups (300 ml) red wine
2 tablespoons (30 ml) red currant jelly
2 tablespoons (30 ml) sugar
1 cinnamon stick

Cherry and Almond Snow

Remove the stalks and pits from 1 pound of cherries.

Blend the cherries or chop them finely. Put the cherries into a mixing bowl with ⅓ cup of ground almonds, 1 tablespoon of brown sugar, the grated rind of 1 lemon, ¼ teaspoon of ground cinnamon and ⅔ cup of yogurt. Mix well.

Beat 2 egg whites until stiff, then fold into the cherry mixture.

Spoon into 4 individual glasses or dishes and chill.

INGREDIENTS TO SERVE FOUR:
1 lb (500 g) cherries
⅓ cup (50 g) ground almonds
1 tablespoon (15 ml) brown sugar
1 lemon
¼ teaspoon (1 ml) ground cinnamon
⅔ cup (150 ml) yogurt
2 egg whites

PITTING CHERRIES

A special cherry pitter is easy to use.

Summer Salad

Remove the pits from 2 large peaches. Thinly slice the peaches. Core 2 large firm apples and cut the apples into thin slices. Thinly slice 2 bananas. Remove the pits from ¼ pound of black cherries. Remove the seeds from ¼ pound of green grapes. Hull ¼ pound of strawberries and cut the strawberries into halves.

Squeeze the juice from 1 lemon into a large serving bowl. Add the fruit and toss well in the lemon juice.

Squeeze the juice from 2 large oranges into a bowl. Stir in 2 tablespoons of Cointreau and pour over the fruit. Chill well.

INGREDIENTS TO SERVE SIX:
2 large peaches
2 large firm apples
2 bananas
¼ lb (100 g) black cherries
¼ lb (100 g) green grapes
¼ lb (100 g) strawberries
1 lemon
2 large oranges
2 tablespoons (30 ml) Cointreau

Spiced Plum Charlotte

Preheat the oven to 375°F (190°C).

Remove the pits from 1½ pounds of cooking plums. Put half of them into a baking dish.

Put 3 cups of fresh whole-wheat bread crumbs into a mixing bowl with the grated rind of 1 lemon, ⅓ cup of brown sugar and 1 teaspoon of ground cinnamon or ginger. Mix well. Arrange half of the crumb mixture on top of the plums.

Repeat the layers once more.

Bake for 30 to 40 minutes, or until the topping is crisp and browned.

Serve hot.

INGREDIENTS TO SERVE FOUR TO SIX:
1½ lb (700 g) cooking plums
3 cups (150 g) fresh whole-wheat bread crumbs
1 lemon
⅓ cup (50 g) brown sugar
1 teaspoon (5 ml) ground cinnamon or ginger

Plum and Apple Mold

Wash and remove the pits and any stalks from ½ pound of plums. Peel, core and thinly slice ½ pound of tart apples.

Melt ¼ cup of butter in a large saucepan. Stir in 2 tablespoons of cold water. Add the prepared fruit and simmer gently, stirring occasionally, until tender.

Pour the contents of the pan into a blender and purée. Return the purée to the pan and add sugar to taste. Continue to cook over low heat, stirring constantly, until the purée has thickened.

Remove the pan from the heat and beat in 2 eggs. Put the pan over a low heat again and stir constantly until the mixture thickens. Let cool.

Beat ⅔ cup of yogurt and stir it into the mixture. Spoon into a serving bowl or mold and chill for at least 1 hour. Dip the mold or bowl into hot water for 10 seconds and then invert onto a serving plate.

INGREDIENTS TO SERVE FOUR:
½ lb (250 g) plums
½ lb (250 g) tart apples
¼ cup (50 g) butter
sugar
2 eggs
⅔ cup (150 ml) yogurt

Plums Poached with Oranges

Preheat the oven to 350°F (180°C).

Wash 1 pound of plums and put them into a baking dish.

Grate the rind of ½ orange over the plums then pour in the juice of 2 oranges. Cut the peel and pith from 1 orange. Working over the dish, cut the membrane away from the segments of fruit. Add the orange segments to the plums. Spoon 2 tablespoons of honey over the fruit.

Cover the dish and bake for 20 to 30 minutes, or until the plums are tender.

Serve hot or cold.

INGREDIENTS TO SERVE FOUR:
1 lb (500 g) plums
3 oranges
2 tablespoons (30 ml) honey

Plum and Red Currant Pie

Preheat the oven to 400°F (200°C).

Make 1½ cups of sweet pie pastry with whole-wheat flour and add cinnamon (see page 35) to the dough. Line an 8-inch (20-cm) flan ring or pie pan. Bake blind for 15 minutes. Remove the baking paper and beans and bake for 5 to 10 minutes more to cook the bottom of the pastry.

For the custard filling, make 1¼ cups of confectioner's custard (see page 93). Then beat in ⅔ cup of yogurt and 1 tablespoon of sherry. Let the custard cool, then spoon it into the cooled pastry shell and level the surface.

Cut 1 pound of cooking plums into halves and remove the pits.

Put 4 tablespoons of red currant jelly into a large saucepan and cook over very low heat until the jelly has melted. Put the plums into the pan, cut sides down. Cover the pan and

bring to the boil. Reduce the heat and simmer gently for 5 to 10 minutes, or until the plums are tender.

Arrange the plums on top of the custard, with the cut sides upward. Pour the syrup from the pan over the plums.

Serve cold.

INGREDIENTS TO SERVE FOUR TO SIX:
1½ cups (150 g) sweet pie pastry made with whole-wheat flour and cinnamon (see page 35)
1¼ cups (300 ml) confectioner's custard (see page 93)
⅔ cup (150 ml) yogurt
1 tablespoon (15 ml) sherry
1 lb (500 g) cooking plums
4 tablespoons (60 ml) red currant jelly

Cheese and Yogurt Peach Pie

A refreshing summer dessert, this pie may be made with other fruit such as raspberries, strawberries, apricots or oranges, or a mixture of fruit.

Make 1½ cups of cookie crust (see orange and lemon cheesecake, page 97) and line a 7- to 8-inch (18- to 20-cm) spring form cake pan with it. Chill the crust for 30 minutes.

Meanwhile, in a large mixing bowl beat ½ pound of pot cheese or sieved cottage cheese with 1¼ cups of yogurt. Stir ⅓ cup of brown sugar into the cheese and yogurt mixture. Add ⅓ cup of coarsely chopped walnuts and ⅓ cup of coarsely chopped pitted dates. Mix well.

Thinly slice 4 ripe large peaches. Reserving a few for decoration, arrange the peach slices on the cookie crust. Spoon the cheese and yogurt mixture on top of the peaches.

Arrange the reserved peach slices and a few

walnut halves on top of the mixture. Chill, preferably overnight.

INGREDIENTS TO SERVE SIX:
1½ cups (150 g) cookie crust (see orange and lemon cheesecake, page 97)
½ lb (250 g) pot cheese or cottage cheese
1¼ cups (300 ml) yogurt
⅓ cup (50 g) coarsely chopped walnuts
⅓ cup (50 g) coarsely chopped pitted dates
⅓ cup (50 g) brown sugar
4 ripe large peaches
walnut halves

Frozen Peach Yogurt

Peaches that are overripe may be used for this lovely dessert.

Blanch, peel and pit 4 ripe large peaches. Put the peaches into a mixing bowl with the grated rind of 1 lemon and the juice of 1 lemon and 1 orange. Mash well then beat in ⅔ cup of yogurt. (Alternatively, all the ingredients may be mixed in a blender.) Add sugar to taste, if desired.

Pour the peach mixture into a rigid container. Freeze until almost solid, then remove from the freezer and beat well. Return to the freezer until firm.

Cover, seal and store in the freezer until needed.

INGREDIENTS TO SERVE FOUR:
4 ripe large peaches
1 lemon
1 orange
⅔ cup (150 ml) yogurt
sugar (optional)

Baked Stuffed Peaches

Preheat the oven to 350°F (180°C).

Cut 4 large peaches into halves. Remove the pits. Scoop out and reserve some of the peach flesh to make more room for the filling.

Beat 1 egg in a large mixing bowl. Stir in 3 tablespoons of ground almonds, 3 tablespoons of sliced almonds and the reserved peach pulp. Add ⅓ cup of raspberries and toss lightly but well.

Spoon the filling into the peach halves. Put the peaches into a baking dish.

In a small saucepan, over very low heat, dissolve ¼ cup of sugar in ⅔ cup of white wine or water. Pour the syrup over the peaches.

Plum and Red Currant Pie is a mouth-watering dessert of ripe plums on custard, glazed with red currant jelly.

Bake for 20 to 30 minutes, or until the peaches are heated through and are tender. Serve hot.

INGREDIENTS TO SERVE FOUR:
4 large peaches
1 egg
3 tablespoons (25 g) ground almonds
3 tablespoons (25 g) sliced almonds
⅓ cup (50 g) raspberries
¼ cup (50 g) sugar
⅔ cup (150 ml) white wine or water

A sophisticated dessert such as Baked Stuffed Peaches can be simply achieved by combining subtle flavors and textures.

Spiced Brandied Peaches

Preheat the oven to 350°F (180°C).

Cut 4 large peaches into halves and remove and reserve the pits. Put the peaches into a baking dish.

Put the juice of 2 oranges into a small saucepan with 2 tablespoons of red currant jelly, 1 cinnamon stick and 2 cloves. Cook over very low heat until the jelly melts, then bring to the boil. Pour the syrup over the peaches.

Cover the dish and bake, basting occasionally, for 15 minutes, or until the peaches are heated through and just tender.

(Alternatively, the peaches may be poached in the syrup in a saucepan for 5 to 10 minutes.)

Remove the cinnamon and cloves and scatter 2 tablespoons of chopped almonds over the peaches when they come out of the oven.

To serve the peaches hot, warm 4 tablespoons of brandy, pour over the peaches and ignite. Serve flaming.

INGREDIENTS TO SERVE FOUR:
4 large peaches
2 oranges
2 tablespoons (30 ml) red currant jelly
1 cinnamon stick
2 cloves
4 tablespoons (60 ml) brandy
2 tablespoons (30 ml) chopped almonds

UNLESS THE "GOLDEN APPLE" of Greek mythology was an orange, as some insist, this most popular of citrus fruits is a comparative newcomer in the West. Most of the citrus family come from China, where references to them date from as early as 2000 B.C. But it was only when vitamin C became one of the gods of the twentieth century that almost magical qualities were attributed to them.

Citrus fruit certainly is rich in vitamin C, but there are richer sources. And while some fruits contain more vitamin C when they are ripe, the riper an orange is the less vitamin C it has. Assuming that an orange weighing three and a half ounces contains about fifty milligrams of ascorbic acid, the same weight of black currants with a content of two hundred milligrams is way ahead. You would even do better eating raw cabbage or cauliflower, although perhaps they would be less appetizing. Nor are oranges generally the most important source of vitamin C. In some parts of the Western World that honor belongs to potatoes. Nevertheless, the orange deserves a high rank among the good ingredients for it is refreshing and although it is sweet it is low in calories—a medium-sized orange contains about 40 Calories.

The charm of citrus fruit is that they provide a readily available source of vitamin C. Although they are not in fact as rich in vitamin C as, for example, black currants or green peppers, they do make a valuable contribution to health, either eaten whole or squeezed for their juice. On the hamper right are blood oranges, whose nutritional value is the same as ordinary oranges—their color is due to a red pigment. Below them are clockwise: Jaffa oranges, grapefruit, uglis (a cross between the tangerine and grapefruit), lemons and limes.

The taste of a citrus fruit is unmistakable, but within the group there is a delectable range of flavors. These depend on the proportions of sugars and acids in the juice. In most species, most notably oranges, there is a preponderance of sugar, while in lemons and limes there is more acid. There are, however, bitter oranges—the bigarades, or Seville oranges (*Citrus aurantium*), which the Arabs took from Asia to Spain. These have thick aromatic peel, little and sour juice and innumerable seeds.

There are dozens of varieties of sweet oranges (*Citrus sinensis*) and some of them are worldwide

Grapefruit (above) are overrated as an aid to dieting. Although low in sugar their fruit acid content is calorific. Three and a half ounces (100 g) provide about 22 Calories.

household names. Jaffa oranges from Israel are large, oval, juicy and sweet. Valencias are round, thin skinned, almost seedless and full of sweet juice. Washington navel oranges are large, seedless, easy to recognize from their navellike protrusion and satisfyingly easy to peel. They originated in Brazil, and their introduction into the United States by Mrs. Eliza Tibbets in 1873 is commemorated by a monument in her memorial park in Riverside, California. The rough-skinned Malta oranges get their name of blood oranges from the color of their sweet, juicy flesh.

A whole group of deliciously sweet oranges is related to the Chinese Mandarin orange (*Citrus reticulata*). They are smaller than the sweet orange, all have loose, easy-to-peel skins, but many suffer from an inordinate number of seeds. The tangerine, a darker skinned variety than those usually sold as mandarins, is full of seeds. The clementine, ortanique and the Temple orange, or tangor, are crosses between the orange and the tangerine. Both tangelos and uglis are hybrids of the tangerine and grapefruit.

A Captain Shaddock gave his name to a coarse

citrus fruit which he took to Barbados in the West Indies at the end of the seventeenth century. The more familiar grapefruit (*Citrus paradisi*) was developed from it, but did not become popular until the twentieth century. As well as popularity it has gathered some of the more weird of the modern dietary myths—the most absurd being that it actually burns up fat in the body. Admittedly, grapefruit is low in calories—unless you smother it with sugar—but every single calorie beyond your needs will be turned into fat, whatever its source. There is, however, no argument that grapefruit is a pleasant source of vitamin C, and the pink-fleshed varieties also contain some carotene.

Lemons (*Citrus limon*) and limes (*Citrus aurantifolia*) are too acid to eat, but their very acidity makes them invaluable in cooking. The two species are closely related and during a long history of some four thousand years they have often been confused. The lime, however, is a tropical fruit, while the lemon grows in areas with a subtropical or Mediterranean-type climate. Both were used for centuries to prevent sailors from dying of scurvy on lengthy sea voyages, long before the cause of the disease—lack of vitamin C —was understood.

Like limes and lemons, the citron (*Citrus medica*) is too sour to eat, but its thick rough skin can be wonderfully transformed into candied peel. The kumquat (*Fortinella species*) is not a true citrus, although it looks like a small orange.

The Nutrients in Citrus Fruit

Citrus fruit is rich in vitamin C and a three-and-a-half ounce (100 g) orange provides 40 Calories.

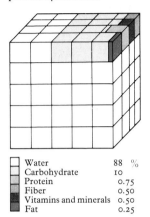

☐	Water	88 %
	Carbohydrate	10
	Protein	0.75
	Fiber	0.50
	Vitamins and minerals	0.50
■	Fat	0.25

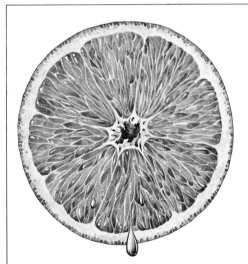

FRUIT IN YOUR JUICE

No commercial drink matches freshly squeezed juice for flavor or for naturally occurring vitamin C. Some fruit-flavored drinks are not made from fruit at all, but contain artificial ingredients. The description "whole fruit" drink is also deceptive, implying goodness but in fact meaning a drink whose fruit content has been strained from the fruit pulp instead of containing a definite proportion of real fruit juice. The fruit content of various drinks varies and is compared below. Most of them also contain artificial sweeteners.

PURE JUICE

Fresh fruit juice is full of vitamin C. A small wine glass of fresh orange juice can supply the total day's requirement. Canned or bottled juices can provide about the same amount of vitamin C.

FRUIT DRINKS

Noncarbonated fruit drinks usually contain less than 50 percent pure fruit juice before dilution, but the vitamin C level is boosted to the level of that in pure fruit juice.

CARBONATED DRINKS

Fizzy fruit drinks need not by law contain any fruit at all. 'Ades are usually about one-third fruit juice and fruit flavored drinks often have only artificial flavoring and no fruit content.

MARMALADE IS A JAM MADE WITH CITRUS FRUIT. It should have a good bright color, a fresh fruity flavor and should set well and keep well. Basically all jams are made by boiling fruit with sugar until the mixture sets lightly when it is cold.

SUGAR

To help the sugar dissolve more rapidly, warm it in a slow oven before adding it to the fruit.

TO TEST FOR SETTING

Chill some small plates in the refrigerator beforehand. Remove the pan from the heat and put a little marmalade on a cold plate and let it cool. If it wrinkles when pushed with your finger it is ready.

A faster and more reliable method is to use a candy thermometer. Keep the thermometer in hot water in between testing. Stir the marmalade and insert the thermometer into the center without touching the bottom of the pan. The temperature needed for a set is 220°F (104°C), but sometimes 222°F (105°C) may give better results.

STORING

When the marmalade is ready skim off the scum. Let the marmalade cool until a skin forms, about 15 minutes. This gives the marmalade time to thicken and to suspend the fruit evenly. Stir it, then pour the marmalade into clean, dry, warm Mason jars.

Wipe the necks of the jars. Cover first with waxed disks, wax side down and then with transparent cellophane or plastic covers. Secure with rubber bands. Or use the screw-on Mason tops. Label, date and store in a cool, dark, ventilated cupboard.

There are few more satisfying sights than shelves well stocked with such preserves as dark and light Orange Marmalade, Lemon, Honey and Ginger Marmalade and Grapefruit Marmalade.

TO PRESERVE SLICED CITRUS FRUIT

Sliced oranges, lemons, grapefruits and limes may be preserved in syrup or alcohol; use honey or sugar, brandy or wine.

Try pickling citrus fruit in a spiced wine vinegar syrup. The addition of such spices as cloves, cinnamon and mace produces unusual preserves which can be served with cold duck or turkey.

Lime Marmalade

This recipe makes a clear marmalade in which there are shreds of peel. To make a somewhat cloudier marmalade with slices of the fruit use the same quantities, but boil the whole limes in the water for 1½ to 2 hours, or until they are very tender. Remove the limes from the pan and slice them very thinly, discarding the seeds. Return the sliced fruit and the juice to the pan. Then add the sugar.

Wash 1½ pounds of limes. Thinly peel them. Cut the peel into thin shreds and put into a large enamel or stainless-steel pan.

Cut the limes into halves and squeeze the juice. Strain the juice into the pan. Tie the seeds and the lime pulp in a piece of cheesecloth and add it to the pan with 2 quarts of water. Bring to the boil. Reduce the heat and simmer gently for 1½ hours, or until the peel is very soft and the contents of the pan have reduced by about half.

Remove the cheesecloth bag, squeezing all the juice into the pan.

Add 6 cups of warm sugar and stir until it is dissolved.

Boil rapidly until the setting point is reached, 220°F (104°C) on a candy thermometer.

When the marmalade is set let it cool for 15 to 20 minutes, then pour it into jars. Seal and store.

INGREDIENTS TO MAKE ABOUT 4 PINTS (2 LITERS) OF MARMALADE:
1½ lb (700 g) limes
6 cups (1.40 kg) sugar

Orange Marmalade

For a darker marmalade simmer the peel longer, so that the water reduces and becomes darker. Then add only 9 cups of warm sugar and simmer until the setting point is reached and the marmalade has darkened. This will make about 16 cups of marmalade. For an even darker marmalade 2 tablespoons of molasses may be added with the sugar.

Wash 3 pounds of Valencia oranges and 2 large lemons. Cut the oranges and lemons into halves. Squeeze the juice and strain it into a large, heavy enamel or stainless-steel pan. Tie the seeds in a piece of cheesecloth and add them to the pan.

Shred the orange rinds finely or coarsely, depending on preference.

Add the shredded peel to the pan with 4 quarts of water. Bring to the boil, then reduce the heat and simmer for 1½ hours, or until the peel is very soft when squeezed between the fingers. Remove the cheesecloth bag, squeezing all the juice into the pan.

Add 12 cups of warm sugar. Cook over low heat, stirring constantly, until the sugar is dissolved. Then boil until the setting point is reached, 220°F (104°C) on a candy thermometer.

When the marmalade is set let it cool for 15 minutes before pouring it into jars.

INGREDIENTS TO MAKE ABOUT 10 PINTS (5 LITERS) OF MARMALADE:
3 lb (1.40 kg) Valencia oranges
2 large lemons
12 cups (2.80 kg) sugar

Well worth the time involved in making them are, clockwise, Lemon Curd, Limes Preserved in Honey Syrup, Lime Marmalade, Spiced Pickled Oranges and Oranges Preserved in Brandy.

Lemon, Honey and Ginger Marmalade

This tart marmalade is set with honey instead of sugar.

Wash 8 large lemons. Cut them into halves and squeeze the juice. Strain the juice into a large enamel or stainless-steel pan. Tie the seeds in a piece of cheesecloth with 2 tablespoons of peeled and coarsely chopped ginger root. Add the muslin bag to the pan.

Cut the lemon rinds in half again, then cut the rinds into thin strips and add to the pan with 5 cups of water.

Bring to the boil, then reduce the heat and simmer gently for $1\frac{1}{2}$ hours, or until the peel is very soft when squeezed between the fingers.

Remove the cheesecloth bag, squeezing out all the juice into the pan.

Coarsely chop $\frac{1}{2}$ cup of preserved ginger and add it to the pan with the ginger syrup and 6 cups of clear honey.

Cook over low heat until the honey is dissolved. Then boil rapidly until setting point is reached, 220°F (104°C) on a candy thermometer.

When the marmalade is set let it cool for 15 minutes before pouring it into jars.

INGREDIENTS TO MAKE ABOUT THREE AND A HALF PINTS ($1\frac{3}{4}$ LITERS) OF MARMALADE:
8 large lemons
2 tablespoons (25 g) coarsely chopped ginger root
$\frac{1}{2}$ cup (250 g) preserved ginger in syrup
6 cups (1.40 kg) clear honey

Lemon Curd

Lemon curd makes an excellent pie or cake filling or it can be spread on bread like jam. Oranges may be substituted for the lemons to make a flavorsome orange curd.

Put the grated rind and juice of 4 large lemons into the top of a double-boiler. Add $\frac{1}{2}$ cup of margarine or butter and 1 cup of sugar.

Beat 4 eggs, then strain them into the lemon mixture.

Stir over simmering water until the sugar has dissolved and the margarine or butter has melted.

Continue to cook, stirring constantly, until the curd thickens and coats the back of a spoon. It will thicken more when it cools.

Pour the curd into clean, dry, warm Mason jars and cover as for marmalade. It will keep in a cool place for up to 1 month.

INGREDIENTS TO MAKE ABOUT ONE AND A HALF CUPS (500 G TO 700 G) OF CURD:
4 large lemons
$\frac{1}{2}$ cup (100 g) margarine or butter
1 cup (250 g) sugar
4 eggs

Grapefruit Marmalade

The proportion of sugar to fruit is comparatively low in this recipe, so the grapefruit flavor is concentrated and the marmalade is not too sweet.

Wash 2 large grapefruit and 4 large lemons. Using a potato peeler thinly cut off the peel. Cut the peel into narrow strips and put it into a large enamel or stainless-steel pan.

Cut off the pith with a sharp knife. Coarsely chop the fruit and add it to the pan with any juice. Tie the seeds and the pith in a large piece of cheesecloth and put it into the pan. Add 2 quarts of water.

Bring to the boil, then reduce the heat and simmer gently for 1 to $1\frac{1}{2}$ hours, or until the contents of the pan are reduced by about half.

Remove the cheesecloth bag, squeezing all the juice into the pan.

Add 6 cups of warm sugar and cook over low heat, stirring, until it is dissolved. Boil rapidly until the setting point is reached, 220°F (104°C) on a candy thermometer.

Let the marmalade cool for 15 minutes before putting it into jars.

INGREDIENTS TO MAKE ABOUT THREE PINTS ($1\frac{1}{2}$ LITERS) OF MARMALADE:
2 large grapefruit
4 large lemons
6 cups (1.40 kg) sugar

Pork Chops Braised with Cabbage and Grapefruit

Preheat the oven to 375°F (190°C).

Put 4 cups of shredded red cabbage into an ovenproof dish or casserole.

Peel and remove the pith from 2 small grapefruit. Working over the dish, cut the membrane away from the segments of fruit. Add the grapefruit segments, $\frac{1}{3}$ cup of seedless raisins, salt and pepper to the cabbage and mix well.

Trim the fat from 4 pork loin chops. Arrange the chops on top of the cabbage and grapefruit mixture.

Cover the dish and bake for 45 to 60 minutes, or until the pork is tender and the cabbage is cooked but still crisp.

INGREDIENTS TO SERVE FOUR:
4 cups (350 g) shredded red cabbage
2 small grapefruit
$\frac{1}{3}$ cup (50 g) seedless raisins
salt
pepper
4 pork loin chops

Baked Spiced Grapefruit

These spiced hot grapefruit halves make a refreshing start or finish to a meal.

Preheat the oven to 400°F (200°C).

Cut 2 grapefruit into halves. Using a grapefruit knife, cut between the segments and between the flesh and skin to loosen them. Remove and discard the seeds.

Put the grapefruit onto a baking sheet. Sprinkle with 2 tablespoons of medium sherry.

Mix 3 tablespoons of brown sugar with $\frac{1}{2}$ teaspoon of ground mixed spice and sprinkle over the grapefruit halves.

Bake for 10 minutes, or until heated through.

Serve hot.

INGREDIENTS TO SERVE FOUR:
2 grapefruit
2 tablespoons (30 ml) medium sherry
3 tablespoons (25 g) brown sugar
$\frac{1}{2}$ teaspoon ground mixed spice

PREPARING GRAPEFRUIT

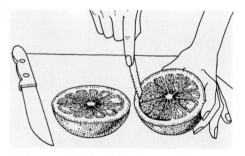

Cut between the flesh and skin of a grapefruit.

Cut between each segment. Use a serrated knife.

Grapefruit Mousse

Separate 4 eggs and put the yolks into the top of a double-boiler with $\frac{1}{2}$ cup of sugar, the grated rind of 1 large grapefruit and the juice of $\frac{1}{2}$ the grapefruit.

Beat over simmering water until the mixture is pale and thick. Remove from the heat.

Squeeze $\frac{1}{2}$ grapefruit and pour the juice into a small bowl. Sprinkle $1\frac{1}{2}$ tablespoons of powdered gelatin into the grapefruit juice. Put the bowl into a pan of hot water and stir until the gelatin is dissolved.

Stir $\frac{2}{3}$ cup of yogurt and the dissolved gelatin into the egg mixture.

Cut the peel and pith from 1 grapefruit and cut the membrane away from the segments of fruit. Coarsely chop the segments and stir into the mousse.

Let the mousse cool until it is beginning to set. Beat the 4 egg whites until just stiff, then fold them into the mousse.

Transfer the mousse to a serving bowl. Refrigerate for at least 2 hours before serving.

INGREDIENTS TO SERVE SIX:
4 large eggs
$\frac{1}{2}$ cup (100 g) sugar
2 large grapefruit
1$\frac{1}{2}$ tablespoons (15 g) powdered gelatin
$\frac{2}{3}$ cup (150 ml) yogurt

Orange Soufflé

Preheat the oven to 350°F (180°C).

Melt 2 tablespoons of margarine or butter in a large saucepan. Add 4 tablespoons of flour and cook over low heat, stirring constantly, for 1 minute. Stir in the grated rind and juice of 3 oranges and 1 lemon. Bring to the boil and cook, stirring constantly, until the mixture is thick and smooth. Stir in 2 tablespoons of brandy or orange liqueur and 4 tablespoons of sugar. Let the mixture cool slightly.

Separate 4 eggs. Beat the yolks into the orange mixture.

Cut the peel and pith from 1 orange. Cut the membrane away from the segments of fruit. Stir the orange segments into the orange mixture. (The soufflé may be made in advance up to this point.)

Beat 5 egg whites until stiff, then fold them into the orange mixture.

Pour into a 5-cup (1-liter) soufflé dish.

Bake for 45 minutes, or until the soufflé is well risen, set and the top is golden brown.

INGREDIENTS TO SERVE FOUR:
2 tablespoons (25 g) margarine or butter
4 tablespoons (25 g) flour
4 oranges
1 lemon
2 tablespoons (30 ml) brandy or orange liqueur
4 tablespoons (50 g) sugar
4 eggs plus 1 egg white

Orange and Green Pepper Salad

Wash two medium-sized green peppers and cut them into thin rings. Cut away the white pith and the seeds.

Using a grapefruit knife and with a sawing motion, cut away the peel, pith and outer membrane from two large seedless oranges. Slice the oranges.

Arrange the pepper and orange slices on 4 individual salad plates or 1 serving platter.

For the dressing, combine $\frac{1}{4}$ cup of corn oil with the juice of 1 orange, 1 crushed garlic clove and salt to taste. Mix well.

Pour the dressing over the salad just before serving.

INGREDIENTS TO SERVE FOUR:
2 medium-sized green peppers
3 large seedless oranges
$\frac{1}{4}$ cup (60 ml) corn oil
1 garlic clove
salt

SEPARATING ORANGE SEGMENTS

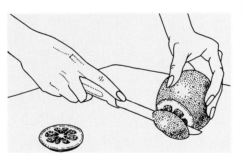

Slice the top and bottom off an orange.

Cut away the peel and pith in strips.

Cut away the membrane from the segments of fruit.

Oranges in Wine

Using a potato peeler, thinly peel 3 large seedless oranges. Cut the peel into thin strips and put them into a small saucepan. Cover with cold water, bring to the boil and then drain. (This initial blanching will remove the bitterness from the peel.) Cover the orange shreds with clean cold water and bring to the boil. Reduce the heat and simmer for 20 minutes. Drain well.

Cut the pith and outer membrane from the 3 peeled oranges and the peel, pith and membrane from 3 more oranges. (Use a grapefruit knife and cut around with a sawing motion.) Slice the oranges and put them into a serving bowl.

Pour $\frac{2}{3}$ cup of red or white wine into a saucepan. Add the juice of 1 orange, 1 tablespoon of red currant jelly, 1 stick of cinnamon and the shredded peel. Cook over low heat until the jelly is dissolved, then bring to the boil. Remove the cinnamon stick then pour the sauce over the oranges.

Serve chilled.

INGREDIENTS TO SERVE FOUR TO SIX:
7 large seedless oranges
$\frac{2}{3}$ cup (150 ml) red or white wine
1 tablespoon (15 ml) red currant jelly
1 cinnamon stick

Avgolemeno

Put 5 cups of well-seasoned chicken stock into a saucepan. Add $\frac{1}{3}$ cup of brown rice, the grated rind of 1 large lemon, 1 sprig of thyme and 1 sprig of parsley.

Cover the pan and bring to the boil. Reduce the heat and simmer for 30 minutes, or until the rice is tender. Remove the herbs.

Beat 2 eggs until they are light and frothy, then beat in the juice of the lemon. Stir in a little hot soup, then pour the mixture back into the soup in the pan. Season to taste with salt and pepper.

Reheat, stirring constantly. The soup must not boil or the egg will curdle.

Serve hot.

INGREDIENTS TO SERVE FOUR:
5 cups (1 liter) well-seasoned chicken stock
$\frac{1}{3}$ cup (50 g) brown rice
1 large lemon
1 thyme sprig
1 parsley sprig
2 eggs
salt
pepper

MORE GRAPES ARE GROWN than any other fruit. Most of them we consume as wine, and even those that are eaten as fruit are about 80 percent water. The melon, another fruit that grows on a vine, can beat that, with more than 90 percent water. What makes both fruits so desirable is the flavor of that water; their juices are among the most agreeable means imaginable of getting our quota of minerals, particularly potassium. Unfortunately, melons will not grow without warmth and grapes will not ripen without sun—therefore they are considered a luxury in the colder parts of the world.

Most of the grapes we eat or drink belong to the species *Vitis vinifera*, known as the European grape vine, although it probably originally came from western Asia. It is one of the most venerable of food plants, for it has been in cultivation for at least six thousand years.

There are American species, among them *Vitis labrusca* (Fox grapes) and *Vitis rotundifolia* (muscadine grapes), but they do not have the standing of *Vitis vinifera*. Vinifera grapes may be white, which is anything from green to yellow, or black, which may be various shades of red or purple. Some varieties are better for dessert, others for wine-making, but the flavor is affected to an extraordinary degree by the soil in which the vines are grown and by the climate.

The British have to rely on Spain and South Africa for most of their grapes, but in their own hothouses they produce the most succulent, and possibly the most expensive grapes in the world. There is no need for Americans to import grapes, but although grapes grow in many parts of the United States about 90 percent of dessert grapes come from California.

An American dessert favorite is the yellowish-green Thompson Seedless, also used for drying as raisins. Others include the red Flame Tokay, the purple Ribier and the red Malagas. These are varieties of the European grape vine, but some descendants of American species are popular in New York State—the dark purple Concord, the

THIRST-QUENCHING MELONS

Melons are more than 90 percent water and it is this that makes them refreshing and low in calories. Melons are also a reasonable source of vitamin C and in addition yellow melons provide carotene. On the left is a watermelon with its distinctive red flesh and an ogen melon from Israel. On the right is the thicker skinned winter melon.

redder Catawba and the pinkish Delaware, for example.

The flesh of ripe melon tastes sweeter than that of grapes even though it contains far less sugar: 5 percent as against about 17 percent. A melon contributes a whole range of minerals and vitamin C and yellow melons are a useful source of carotene.

India, tropical Africa and Iran have all been credited with being the original home of melons. Today they are grown in many of the warm temperate, subtropical and tropical parts of the world. They are annual and, like their relatives the cucumbers, have tendrils, which they attach to anything that will support them.

Melons are to be found in all shapes and sizes and have different star ratings for lusciousness. The most popular types are cantaloupe and musk melons, but, confusingly, musk melons are often called cantaloupes in the United States. The cantaloupe, which was developed in Cantalupo in Italy in the seventeenth century, has a warty and often grooved skin and sweet juicy flesh which is usually orange colored. Charentais melons are a small aromatic type of cantaloupe which are becoming increasingly popular in Europe. A recent addition has been the ogen melon, an Israeli variety named after the kibbutz where it was developed. This has an orange skin and sweet green flesh.

Musk melons may be spherical or oval (hence their other name in England—nutmeg melons), the skin yellow or green and the flesh anything between pale green and red. What they have in common is that the skin is covered with a raised lacy network.

Other familiar names are honeydew and winter melons, both used somewhat indiscriminately. They are thick skinned and the flesh is not strongly aromatic. The real honeydew has a creamy or yellowish skin and pale green flesh. One winter melon that is often miscalled honeydew has dark green corrugated skin and creamy insipid flesh. Because these melons travel well they persistently make the journey from Spain to Britain, deceiving the natives by their false name.

All these melons are varieties of *Cucumis melo*, but the watermelon is *Citrullus vulgaris*. It is common in the warmer parts of Europe and Asia and Africa; in Britain it needs to be grown in glasshouses, and is not considered worth the effort. The early colonists took watermelons to the Americas and they are now grown in about half of the states, but mainly in California, Florida, Texas, Georgia and South Carolina. They are juicily refreshing when ripe and as they are often sold cut into slices it is possible to judge their ripeness. The flesh should be red and firm and the seeds brown or black and not white and immature.

Grapes are more than 80 percent water, which makes them equally as refreshing as melons. They are, however, more calorific because they contain more sugars. Their sweet flavor is due to the fact that they contain not only glucose but fructose. This is more than twice as sweet as most sugars. They also provide useful amounts of vitamin C and small amounts of such minerals as potassium. The most widely cultivated grapes are those of the species *Vitis vinifera* (shown in the vineyard above and the inset

bottom right). Most American dessert grapes of the species *Vitis labrusca* and *Vitis rotundifolia* are grown in California, but the dark purple Concord grapes (inset top right) are popular in New York State. All the varieties of dessert grapes make succulent additions to both vegetable and fruit salads, and are also delicious with cheese.

The Nutrients in Grapes
Grapes are mostly water and contain the sugars glucose and fructose. Three and a half ounces (100 g) provide about 75 Calories.

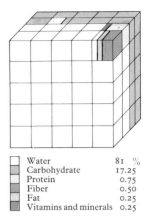

Water	81 %
Carbohydrate	17.25
Protein	0.75
Fiber	0.50
Fat	0.25
Vitamins and minerals	0.25

The Nutrients in Melons
Melons contain a high percentage of water and are low in calories. Three and a half ounces (100 g) provide about 25 Calories.

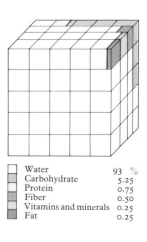

Water	93 %
Carbohydrate	5.25
Protein	0.75
Fiber	0.50
Vitamins and minerals	0.25
Fat	0.25

Grapes Baked with Oranges

Preheat the oven to 350°F (180°C).

Remove the seeds from 1 pound of white grapes, keeping them whole if possible. (This is easy to do with a tapestry or carpet needle.) Put the grapes into a baking dish.

Pour in the juice of 2 oranges.

Cut the peel and pith from 2 more oranges. Working over the dish, cut the membrane away from the segments of fruit. Put the orange segments into the dish.

Cover the dish and bake for 15 to 20 minutes, or until the grapes are hot but not cooked enough to wrinkle.

Serve hot.

INGREDIENTS TO SERVE FOUR:
1 lb (500 g) white grapes
4 oranges

SEEDING GRAPES

Cut grapes into halves and remove the seeds.

Remove grape seeds with the eye of a large needle.

Grape and Grapefruit Pie

Make 1½ cups of cookie crust (see orange and lemon cheesecake, page 97). Use it to line an 8-inch (20-cm) pie pan. Refrigerate while making the filling.

Squeeze the juice of 1 large grapefruit and add water to make ⅔ cup of liquid. Pour into a saucepan and bring to just below boiling point.

In a mixing bowl beat 1 egg, then stir in 1 tablespoon of cornstarch and 2 tablespoons of sugar. Stirring constantly, gradually add the hot grapefruit juice. Pour the mixture into the pan. Bring to the boil, stirring constantly, until the custard thickens and boils. Remove from the heat and beat in

5 tablespoons of yogurt. Cover the pan and let the custard cool, stirring occasionally to prevent a skin from forming.

Spoon the cooled custard into the pie shell.

Cut ¾ pound of grapes into halves and remove the seeds. Put the halved grapes on top of the custard.

For the grapefruit glaze, heat the juice of 1 grapefruit in a small saucepan to just below boiling point. In a small bowl blend 1 teaspoon of arrowroot with 1 to 2 tablespoons of sugar and a little of the fruit juice, then stir in all of the hot grapefruit juice. Return the mixture to the pan and bring to the boil, stirring constantly, until the glaze thickens and clears. Pour the glaze over the grapes. Refrigerate for at least 2 hours before serving.

INGREDIENTS TO SERVE SIX:
1½ cups (150 g) cookie crust (see orange and lemon cheesecake, page 97)
2 grapefruit
1 egg
1 tablespoon (15 ml) cornstarch
3 to 4 tablespoons (45 to 60 ml) sugar
5 tablespoons (75 ml) yogurt
¾ lb (350 g) grapes
1 teaspoon (5 ml) arrowroot

Grape Snow

Reserving a few whole grapes for decoration cut 1 pound of grapes into halves and remove the seeds. Finely chop half of the grapes.

Just before serving, beat 3 egg whites until stiff. Fold in 1¼ cups of yogurt with the grated rind of 1 orange and the chopped grapes. Add 1 tablespoon of sugar if desired.

In individual glasses arrange the halved grapes in layers with the grape snow.

Decorate with the whole grapes and serve immediately.

INGREDIENTS TO SERVE FOUR:
1 lb (500 g) grapes
3 egg whites
1¼ cups (300 ml) yogurt
1 orange
1 tablespoon (15 ml) sugar (optional)

Grape Wine Gelatin

Pour 2½ cups of sweet white wine into a saucepan. Add 1½ tablespoons of powdered gelatin, 2 tablespoons of sugar and the grated rind and juice of 1 lemon. Cook over low heat, stirring constantly, until the sugar and gelatin are dissolved, then bring to the boil and remove the pan from the heat.

Strain into a pitcher. Stand the pitcher in a pan or bowl of hot water to keep the gelatin from setting.

Rinse out a dessert mold with cold water,

then pour in a layer of gelatin about ½ inch (1 cm) deep.

Halve ½ pound of grapes and remove the seeds.

Arrange a layer of grapes over the gelatin and put the mold into the refrigerator for 10 to 15 minutes, or until the gelatin begins to set.

Continue making layers of gelatin and grapes, refrigerating between each layer, so that the grapes will be distributed evenly.

Finish with a layer of gelatin and refrigerate until completely set.

To serve, dip the mold in hot water for a few seconds, place a serving plate on top and invert.

INGREDIENTS TO SERVE SIX:
2½ cups (600 ml) sweet white wine
1½ tablespoons (25 g) powdered gelatin
2 tablespoons (25 g) sugar
1 lemon
½ lb (250 g) grapes

Grape Mincemeat

Used for mincemeat pies, this traditional Christmas preserve of dried fruits is deliciously moist because of the addition of grapes. It may be stored, however, for only 2 weeks.

Put 1⅓ cups of seedless raisins and ⅔ cup of currants into a mixing bowl.

Add ⅓ cup of chopped candied mixed peel, ⅓ cup of sliced almonds, ⅔ cup of brown sugar and the grated rind and juice of ½ lemon.

Peel and core ½ pound of cooking apples. Coarsely grate the apples into the bowl. Cut ½ pound of grapes into halves and remove the seeds. Cut the grapes into halves again and add them to the mincemeat with ½ teaspoon of ground allspice, ¼ teaspoon of grated nutmeg and 2 tablespoons of brandy. Stir the mincemeat well.

Cover the bowl and leave overnight. Pack the mincemeat into clean dry jars and cover as for marmalade (see page 178).

INGREDIENTS TO MAKE TWO AND A HALF POUNDS (1.20 KG) OF MINCEMEAT:
1⅓ cups (100 g) seedless raisins
⅔ cup (100 g) currants
⅓ cup (50 g) candied mixed peel
⅓ cup (50 g) sliced almonds
⅔ cup (100 g) brown sugar
½ lemon
½ lb (250 g) cooking apples
½ lb (250 g) grapes
½ teaspoon (2.5 ml) ground allspice
¼ teaspoon (1 ml) grated nutmeg
2 tablespoons (30 ml) brandy

Grape and Lemon Layer Pudding

Preheat the oven to 350°F (180°C).

Cut ½ pound of white grapes into halves and remove the seeds. Arrange the halved grapes in the bottom of a baking dish.

Cream ¼ cup of margarine, 4 tablespoons of sugar and the grated rind of 1 large lemon. Beat until light and fluffy.

Separate 2 eggs. Add the yolks to the creamed mixture and beat well. Stir in 1¼ cups of milk, the juice of the lemon and ½ cup of self-rising flour. The consistency will be curdlike.

Beat the 2 egg whites until just stiff, then fold into the mixture. Spoon it on top of the grapes.

Put the dish into a roasting pan half-filled with hot water and bake for 40 to 45 minutes, or until the top is set, firm to the touch and golden brown.

INGREDIENTS TO SERVE FOUR:
½ lb (250 g) white grapes
¼ cup (50 g) margarine
4 tablespoons (60 ml) sugar
1 large lemon
2 eggs
1¼ cups (300 ml) milk
½ cup (50 g) self-rising flour

Grape Stuffed Onions

Preheat the oven to 375°F (190°C).

Peel 4 large onions and put them into a saucepan. Pour in 2½ cups of boiling water. Cover the pan, reduce the heat and simmer the onions for 25 minutes. Drain the onions and set them aside until they are cool enough to handle.

Cut ¼ pound of green grapes into halves and remove the seeds. Put the grapes into a mixing bowl with 3 tablespoons of blanched almonds, 2 tablespoons of yogurt and salt and pepper to taste. Mix well.

Cut a slice off the top of each of the onions. Carefully remove the centers, leaving ½-inch (1-cm) thick shells. (Reserve the centers of the onions for another dish.)

Divide the filling among the onions. Put them into an ovenproof dish and bake for 20 to 30 minutes, or until the onions are tender. Serve hot.

INGREDIENTS TO SERVE FOUR:
4 large onions
¼ lb (100 g) green grapes
3 tablespoons (25 g) blanched almonds
2 tablespoons (30 ml) yogurt
salt
pepper

Melon and Grape Salad

Cut a slice for the lid from the top of a ripe, medium-sized honeydew melon. Cut a small slice off the bottom so that the melon will stand.

Scoop out and discard the seeds. Cut out the flesh and then dice it or scoop it out in balls. Put the melon into a mixing bowl.

Cut ½ pound of white grapes into halves and remove and discard the seeds. Add the grapes to the melon with the grated rind and juice of 1 large orange and 1 tablespoon of chopped mint. Toss lightly but well.

Transfer the melon and grape mixture to the melon shell. Sprinkle with 1 tablespoon of blanched and split pistachio nuts and a few mint leaves.

Replace the melon lid and chill well before serving.

INGREDIENTS TO SERVE FOUR:
1 medium-sized honeydew melon
½ lb (250 g) white grapes
1 large orange
mint sprigs
1 tablespoon (15 g) split pistachio nuts

MAKING MELON BALLS

Cut the top off a melon and scoop out the seeds.

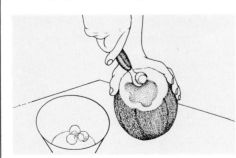

Use a small scoop to remove the fruit in balls.

Melon and Shrimp Cocktail

Melon and shrimp, with a dressing of grapefruit juice, make this a refreshing first course.

Cut 1 small honeydew melon into quarters. Discard the seeds and dice the melon into ½-inch (1-cm) pieces. Put the melon into a mixing bowl.

Peel and devein ¾ pound of cooked shrimp and add them to the melon pieces.

Pour the juice of 1 grapefruit over the melon and shrimp and toss lightly.

Shred ½ small head of lettuce. Divide the lettuce between 6 individual serving glasses. Spoon the melon and shrimp on top, pouring in any grapefruit juice from the bowl.

Serve chilled.

INGREDIENTS TO SERVE SIX:
1 small honeydew melon
¾ lb (350 g) unpeeled cooked shrimp
1 grapefruit
½ small head lettuce

Melon and Ginger Sherbet

Cut 1 small honeydew melon into quarters. Remove the seeds and the skin. Coarsely chop the melon and put it into a saucepan with 1 teaspoon of ground ginger, 2 tablespoons of brown sugar and the grated rind and juice of 1 small lemon.

Cover the pan and cook over low heat for 10 to 15 minutes, or until the melon is tender. Pour the contents of the pan into a blender and blend until smooth. Pour the puréed melon into a bowl. Put it into the freezer until the purée is half-frozen.

Beat 2 egg whites until stiff, then beat the melon purée. Fold the whites into the purée and transfer to a rigid container. Return to the freezer until solid. Cover, seal and label the sherbet and store in the freezer until needed.

INGREDIENTS TO SERVE FOUR TO SIX:
1 small honeydew melon
1 teaspoon (5 ml) ground ginger
2 tablespoons (30 ml) brown sugar
1 small lemon
2 egg whites

EXOTIC FRUIT/Nature's Sweet Luxuries

The Nutrients in Exotic Fruit

These are high in sugar. Three and a half ounces (100 g) of banana, for example, provide about 80 Calories.

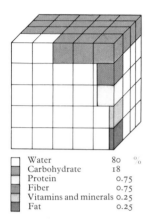

Water	80	%
Carbohydrate	18	
Protein	0.75	
Fiber	0.75	
Vitamins and minerals	0.25	
Fat	0.25	

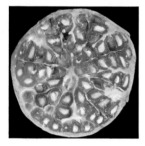

The refreshing juice of the pomegranate makes it worth the tedium of sucking the flesh from hundreds of tiny seeds (above).

NO PRECISE DEFINITION OF EXOTIC is possible. What is exotica in one corner of the earth may be commonplace elsewhere. To people who live in temperate zones the fruit that will grow only in the tropics seem particularly desirable (or outlandish). Some of the exotic image persists even when a tropical fruit becomes a regular part of Western diet. If you live in a high-rise you might imagine a garden of your own filled with strawberries, raspberries and apples, but not with bananas, although they are the third most popular fruit in the world.

From being rare and expensive at the beginning of the twentieth century, bananas have now become a cheap product of agribusiness. America is supplied by Central America (the "banana republics") and the West Indies. Europeans get theirs from the Caribbean and West Africa. Almost all the imports are of dessert bananas, which have a high sugar content of between 17 and 20 percent. Cooking bananas, often called plantains, which are a staple food in some African countries, have more starch and less sugar. There are numerous varieties of bananas, but only the very few which travel well and ripen in storage appear in the stores. A banana is at its best when it is entirely yellow with a few brown specks. Bananas with tips that are still green will ripen in a day or two at room temperature. Canary bananas, which grow in such subtropical climates as the Canary Islands and Israel, are small, thin-skinned, curved and very sweet with a real banana fragrance. The only drawback to them is that they tend to make you dissatisfied with other bananas. Nutritionally there is little to choose between the different varieties. They are all reasonable sources of the vitamins C, carotene and riboflavin. A good source of energy, a medium-sized banana has about 80 Calories.

The succulence of a ripe pineapple is hard to beat, but also hard to experience. Unlike the banana the pineapple will not ripen satisfactorily except on the plant, where it may even double its sugar content in the final stage of ripening. Then it has to face a long journey to the markets from its tropical homelands.

The pineapple is a native of South America, but more than half of the pineapples we eat come from Hawaii, where until less than a century ago the plant was regarded as a pernicious weed. Although fresh pineapples travel badly, they are still agreeable when canned, as most of them are. In canning, however, the texture and flavor is greatly changed, and two-thirds of their rich supply of vitamin C is lost.

Other exotic fruit are more likely to add variety than nourishment to our diet, since they are generally too expensive to be eaten in quantity. Such is the mango, the fruit most commonly eaten in the tropics, but a luxury in the West. It has a marvelously delicate flavor—hard to pin down—with perhaps a hint of pear or melon, or perhaps pineapple or apricot. In other words, it tastes like a mango. Eaten in the kind of quantities that would be nice, mangoes would be a good source of carotene.

Lichees, natives of China and now grown in many tropical countries, are becoming more available and fashionable. They look like plums that are covered in warts, but they have sweet juicy flesh. Lichees travel well, and even benefit from travel because their flavor becomes more aromatic.

It is a game of chance, with the odds heavily against you, to buy a fresh fig at that critical stage when its ripeness is just bursting through the skin. The chances are more in your favor if you travel to your figs instead of having them brought to you. (Try Provence, Sicily or Smyrna, for example.) Alternatively, you can eat them dried, canned or preserved.

The curse of figs is seeds and these, un-

fortunately, afflict some other pleasant exotic fruits. The purple, plum-sized passion fruit has sweet (even too sweet) juicy pulp riddled with small blackish seeds. The fruit was given its name by Jesuits who arrived in South America in the sixteenth century and saw in the flower symbols of the passion of Christ, the five stamens representing his five wounds, the stigma the three nails and the ten sepals and petals the faithful disciples. The guava has no legend to distinguish it, but it does have a notably high content of vitamin C— even higher than that of citrus fruits. Whether this makes up for the mass of seeds embedded in the slightly sharp pulp is another matter. As for the pomegranate, the two Latin words that make up its name give it away—"the many-seeded apple." There are so many seeds that the fruit inevitably became a symbol of fertility.

The Japanese persimmon presents a different problem, for when it is unripe it is extremely sour and when ripe it can be cloyingly sweet. For centuries the Japanese persimmon has been cultivated in Japan, China and in Mediterranean countries and now it is grown in the United States.

There are hundreds more exotic tropical fruit that are popular where they grow, but impossible to market abroad in perfect condition. There is no better example than the durian, a large and prickly Malaysian fruit with creamy flesh, which when ripe is said to taste of rich cheese, peanuts, garlic, pineapple, apricots and sherry, but when overripe suggests nothing but sewage. It would be exciting, however, to have the fruit of *Monstera deliciosa* (the ubiquitous potted plant which will not fruit in captivity), for its flavor is said to be a combination of all the most beautiful fruit.

Guavas (below) are extremely rich in vitamin C. Like black currants they have four times as much vitamin C as oranges. The juicy fruit, which turns from green to light yellow as it ripens, has a slightly sharp flavor and is, therefore, often stewed or made into jam or jelly.

Exotic fruit have intriguing flavors, are high in carbohydrate and are a source of vitamins and minerals. Chinese gooseberries, for example, are high in vitamin C and persimmons and mangoes are rich in carotene. Dates have an exceptionally high sugar content of more than 60 percent and contain carotene, B vitamins and minerals. Left, clockwise: a pineapple, a mango, Chinese gooseberries, a papaya, passion fruit, rambutans and bananas. In the foreground are a date, a persimmon and a cut passion fruit and rambutan.

187

Baked Spiced Pineapple

Preheat the oven to 350°F (180°C).

Cut the skin from 1 small pineapple. Slice the pineapple and remove the core. Arrange the rings in a baking dish.

Mix the juice of 1 large orange with 2 tablespoons of brandy and 1 to 2 tablespoons of brown sugar. Pour over the pineapple rings. Add 1 stick of cinnamon and 2 cloves to the dish.

Bake for 20 minutes.

Serve hot or cold.

INGREDIENTS TO SERVE FOUR:
1 small pineapple
1 large orange
2 tablespoons (30 ml) brandy
1 to 2 tablespoons (15 to 30 ml) brown sugar
1 cinnamon stick
2 cloves

PREPARING PINEAPPLE

Slice the top, bottom and skin from pineapple.

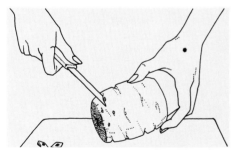

Cut any remaining eyes out with spiraling cuts.

Slice the pineapple and remove the core.

Pineapple Mousse

Separate 4 eggs. Put the yolks into the top of a double-boiler with ½ cup of sugar. Beat over simmering water until the mixture is pale and thick. Remove from the heat.

Cut the skin from 1 medium-sized pineapple. Slice the pineapple and remove the core. Reserving 1 slice for decoration, coarsely chop the pineapple then blend to a frothy purée.

Beat the pineapple purée into the egg yolks and sugar.

In a cup set in a pan of hot water dissolve 1½ tablespoons of powdered gelatin in the juice of 1 large lemon.

Pour the dissolved gelatin into the pineapple mixture and mix well.

When the pineapple mousse is just beginning to set, beat the 4 egg whites until just stiff, then fold them in.

Pour into a serving dish and chill until set. Decorate with the reserved pineapple.

INGREDIENTS TO SERVE SIX:
4 eggs
½ cup (100 g) sugar
1 medium-sized pineapple
1½ tablespoons (15 g) powdered gelatin
1 large lemon

Pineapple Ice

Cut the skin from 1 small pineapple. Slice the pineapple and remove the core. Coarsely chop the pineapple and then blend to a purée.

Pour the pineapple purée into a bowl. Stir in the juice of 1 large lemon and 1 large orange. Add sugar to taste, if desired.

Freeze until half-frozen then remove from the freezer.

Beat 2 egg whites until stiff. Beat the half-frozen pineapple purée, then fold in the egg whites. Pour into a rigid container and freeze until solid. Cover, seal and label and store in the freezer until needed.

INGREDIENTS TO SERVE FOUR TO SIX:
1 small pineapple
1 large lemon
1 large orange
sugar (optional)
2 egg whites

Pineapple in Red Kirsch

This classic French way of serving a pineapple could not be simpler—soaked in kirsch and mixed with oranges and cherries.

Cut the skin from 1 small pineapple, then cut it into slices. Remove the central core and put the pineapple rings into a serving bowl. Pour in 3 tablespoons of kirsch. Let the pineapple soak for at least 1 hour.

Cut the peel and pith from 2 large oranges. Slice the oranges and arrange on top of the pineapple rings.

Pit ¼ pound of cherries and arrange the cherries on top.

Serve chilled.

INGREDIENTS TO SERVE SIX:
1 small pineapple
3 tablespoons (45 ml) kirsch
2 large oranges
¼ lb (100 g) cherries

Frozen Banana and Hazelnut Yogurt

Peel 4 medium-sized bananas. Put them into a bowl and mash them well. Then beat in the grated rind and juice of 1 lemon and 1 to 2 tablespoons of rum.

Add 1¼ cups of yogurt and 2 tablespoons of brown sugar. Mix well.

Beat 2 egg whites until stiff, then fold into the banana mixture.

Put the bowl into the freezer until the mixture is half-frozen.

Remove from the freezer and beat well. Stir in ⅓ cup of chopped toasted hazelnuts. Spoon into a rigid container and return to the freezer until frozen solid.

Cover, seal and label and store in the freezer until needed.

INGREDIENTS TO SERVE FOUR:
4 medium-sized bananas
1 lemon
1 to 2 tablespoons (15 to 30 ml) rum
1¼ cups (300 ml) yogurt
2 tablespoons (30 ml) brown sugar
2 egg whites
⅓ cup (50 g) chopped toasted hazelnuts

Baked Stuffed Bananas

Preheat the oven to 375°F (190°C).

Slit the skins of 4 bananas along the length of the inside curve. Carefully remove the bananas, keeping the skins whole.

Put the bananas into a mixing bowl and mash them well. Stir in the grated rind and juice of ½ lemon, ¼ teaspoon of ground mixed spice and 3 tablespoons of seedless raisins.

Beat 1 egg white until stiff, then fold into the banana mixture.

Open out the banana skins and spoon in

the filling. Put the bananas into a baking dish, slit side upward. Put them close together so they won't fall over.

Bake for 15 minutes, or until the filling is puffed up and lightly browned.

Serve at once.

INGREDIENTS TO SERVE FOUR:

4 bananas
½ lemon
¼ teaspoon (1 ml) ground mixed spice
3 tablespoons (25 g) seedless raisins
1 egg white

Caribbean Baked Bananas

Preheat the oven to 375°F (190°C).

Peel 4 large bananas. Cut them into halves lengthwise and put them into a baking dish.

Mix the juice of 2 oranges with ¼ teaspoon of ground cinnamon and 1 tablespoon of rum and pour over the bananas.

Sprinkle with ¼ cup of shredded coconut.

Bake for 15 minutes, or until the bananas are soft and heated through.

Serve at once.

INGREDIENTS TO SERVE FOUR:

4 large bananas
2 oranges
¼ teaspoon (1 ml) ground cinnamon
1 tablespoon (15 ml) rum
¼ cup (25 g) shredded coconut

Banana Cheese Whip

Peel 4 bananas and mash them well with the juice of 1 orange.

Beat ⅔ cup of yogurt into ½ pound of pot cheese until smooth. Beat the cheese mixture into the mashed bananas. Add 1 to 2 tablespoons of honey to taste.

Spoon into individual dishes or glasses. Serve chilled.

INGREDIENTS TO SERVE FOUR:

4 bananas
1 orange
⅔ cup (150 ml) yogurt
½ lb (250 g) pot cheese
1 to 2 tablespoons (15 to 30 ml) honey

Papaya and Lime Mousse

Cut 1 medium-sized papaya in half and remove the black seeds. Scoop out the fruit, scraping it away from the skin.

Mash the papaya with the juice of 1 large lime. Beat in ⅔ cup of yogurt. (Alternatively, put the papaya fruit into a blender with the lime juice and yogurt and blend until smooth.) Add sugar, if desired.

In a cup set in a pan of hot water dissolve 2 teaspoons of powdered gelatin in 2 tablespoons of water. Stir into the mousse.

When the mousse is just beginning to set, beat 2 egg whites until just stiff then fold them in.

Spoon into 4 individual dishes and chill for at least 3 hours before serving.

INGREDIENTS TO SERVE FOUR:

1 medium-sized papaya
1 large lime
⅔ cup (150 ml) yogurt
sugar (optional)
2 teaspoons powdered gelatin
2 egg whites

PREPARING PAPAYA

Cut the papaya in half and scoop out the seeds.

Scoop the flesh out, down to the skin.

Balinese Fruit Salad

Cut ½ pineapple into ½-inch (1-cm) slices, cut off the skin and remove the core. Cut the pineapple into chunks.

Slice 1 small mango, peel off the skin and remove the seed. Cut the fruit into cubes.

Cut the peel and pith from 1 pomelo, or 1 large grapefruit. Divide into segments.

Remove the seeds and peel from ½ small papaya and dice the fruit.

Remove the brown fuzzy skin from 4 kiwi fruit. Slice the fruit.

Cut 1 passion fruit in half and scoop out the flesh with the seeds.

Peel and slice 2 bananas.

Put all the fruit into a large bowl. Add the juice of 2 large limes and toss lightly to coat the fruit. Sweeten to taste with a little sugar if desired.

INGREDIENTS TO SERVE SIX:

½ pineapple
1 small mango
1 pomelo or large grapefruit
½ small papaya
4 kiwi fruit
1 passion fruit
2 bananas
2 large limes
sugar (optional)

Mango Fool

Peel 2 medium-sized mangoes.

Cut the fruit away from the large seed and put the fruit into a mixing bowl. Mash the mango until smooth, then beat in the juice of 1 large lime or 1 small lemon and ⅔ cup of yogurt. (Alternatively, blend the mango with the lime juice and yogurt.)

Spoon into individual dishes and chill for at least 2 hours before serving.

INGREDIENTS TO SERVE FOUR:

2 medium-sized mangoes
1 large lime or 1 small lemon
⅔ cup (150 ml) yogurt

Figs with Yogurt and Honey

Cut the stems from 1 pound of ripe figs. Cut the figs into quarters, or sixths if they are large, and put them into a glass serving bowl.

Put 1¼ cups of yogurt into a mixing bowl and stir in the grated rind of 1 lemon and 2 tablespoons of honey. Pour the yogurt mixture over the figs and sprinkle with 1 tablespoon of brown sugar. Chill before serving.

INGREDIENTS TO SERVE FOUR:

1 lb (500 g) ripe figs
1¼ cups (300 ml) yogurt
1 lemon
2 tablespoons (30 ml) honey
1 tablespoon (15 ml) brown sugar

Botanically a berry is a fruit with seeds enclosed in pulp, and by that definition the banana is included. But most people associate the word berry with the lush fruits of summer and fall—strawberries, raspberries, black and red currants and blackberries, although many of them are not true berries. They are the exotic fruits of temperate climates.

Much of a berry is water—between 80 and 90 percent—and which berry you prefer depends how much you like your water flavored. Besides water, most of the berries are quite prodigal with vitamin C, carotene, thiamine and riboflavin. Strawberries and raspberries have niacin as well. Berries also provide reasonable amounts of such minerals as potassium.

Cultivated strawberries have two American species as parents, but it was not until they were introduced into Europe that they were interbred. The first species to arrive, in the seventeenth century, was *Fragaria virginiana* from the woodlands of the eastern states. A century later *Fragaria chiloensis* followed from the west coast. In the United States they had been separated by mountains, but in Europe innumerable hybrids were bred from them during the nineteenth century. Scientific breeding in the twentieth century put more emphasis on productivity, ability to travel and resistance to disease than on flavor and texture. Nevertheless a freshly picked ripe strawberry is still something to savor.

Growing your own strawberries can give a wider range of flavors than buying them at the store. When they are unripe all strawberries tend to be acid, but when ripe there are considerable differences from variety to variety in the degree and character of their sweetness. In some varieties, along with the strawberry flavor, is a background of pineapple, a trait for which the west coast ancestor is responsible. Although strawberries are conventionally served with sugar and cream, the flavor of ripe sweet berries is remarkably enhanced by a few drops of wine vinegar.

Wild strawberries have a more pronounced flavor and something of the same richness and sweetness is found in the small Alpine strawberries. Both are extravagantly improved if champagne is poured over them.

Out-of-season strawberries are a disappointing luxury. It is axiomatic that the sooner ripe strawberries are eaten after being picked the better they will be, so they inevitably suffer on a flight of several thousand miles. These imported strawberries also diminish the longing for the first strawberries of the season without satisfying the craving for them. But Remontant varieties do fruit into very late fall and they help to fill the time gap naturally.

Raspberries have a less aggressive, more velvety flavor than strawberries, and raspberry enthusiasts

raspberries

blueberries

blackberries

strawberries

Berries are a flavorful gift of summer. Although almost 90 percent water, they are relatively rich in such minerals as calcium, and in the vitamins thiamine, riboflavin and carotene. They are a good source of vitamin C—black currants have four times as much as citrus fruit. Strawberries have less vitamin C, but like raspberries they contain niacin. Blackberries have the least vitamin C, but they are a source of calcium.

gooseberries

huckleberries

red currants

black currants

never understand why strawberries are more popular. One reason is simple and unavoidable; raspberries should be eaten as soon as they are picked because their delicate flavor begins to evaporate after even a few hours. Wild raspberries are richer but less fleshy, and many of the modern varieties have lost in flavor what they have gained in size. There are many summer- and fewer fall-fruiting raspberries. While most are red there are particularly sweet yellow varieties, as well as the popular black raspberries.

Like strawberries and raspberries, the wild blueberry tastes better than the cultivated one, but cannot compete for size. Only since it was bred for plumpness in the last fifty years has it achieved its current popularity. Those who prefer the wild blueberry can still find it growing in many of the barren places of the world, from the Arctic to South America.

Both the English and the American species of blackberry are indubitably better wild, for even when they are ripe the cultivated varieties retain a certain acidity. The loganberry, which is almost certainly a cross between a blackberry and a raspberry, is even more acid. Other hybrids have proliferated, differing more in their names than in their characteristics. Of these the boysenberry is probably the best known.

The other berries—black and red currants and gooseberries—are used more for cooking than as

dessert, although all of them become sweet enough to eat raw if they are left on the bushes longer than usual. Gooseberries have been popular in Britain since the Middle Ages, and in the north of England in Victorian times there was a craze for gooseberry clubs, which competed to grow the most gigantic berries. A few of these clubs still exist. As well as being rich in vitamins C and thiamine (even when cooked) and a moderate source of carotene, gooseberries have the virtue of being the earliest berries of the year.

The most health-giving berries are black currants because of their wealth of vitamin C and minerals. In Britain they are the most popular of the currants, whereas the less nutritious red and white currants are more popular in the United States.

One ancient berry enjoyed by the Romans is seldom grown today. This is the black mulberry. King James 1 planted several hundred acres of mulberries in the heart of London at the beginning of the seventeenth century, and one tree survives in the gardens of Buckingham Palace. His idea was to establish a silkworm industry in Britain. But it is the leaves of the white mulberry on which the silkworm feeds, and King James had mistakenly planted the black. Mulberries are used in similar ways to blackberries, but they must be eaten at just the right moment—when they are falling off the trees with ripeness.

The Nutrients in Berries

Berries are a source of vitamins and minerals and three and a half ounces (100 g) of strawberries, for example, provide 40 Calories.

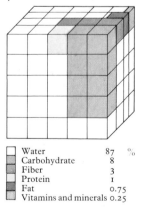

Water	87	%
Carbohydrate	8	
Fiber	3	
Protein	1	
Fat	0.75	
Vitamins and minerals	0.25	

Blueberry Pie

Preheat the oven to 400°F (200°C).

Wash 1 pound of blueberries and remove the stems. Put the blueberries into a deep 9-inch (23-cm) pie pan. Sprinkle with 2 to 4 tablespoons of sugar depending on how sour the berries are.

Make 1½ cups of sweet pie pastry with whole-wheat flour (see page 35). On a lightly floured surface roll out the pastry to ½ inch (2 cm) larger in diameter than the top of the pie pan. Cut a ½-inch (2-cm) strip from the edge of the pastry. Dampen the rim of the pie pan and press the strip of pastry onto it.

Cut a strip from the edge of the pastry.

Press the strip onto the rim of the pan.

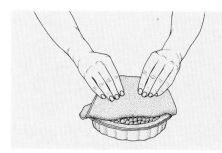

Cover with the remaining pastry.

Flute the edges of the pastry to seal.

Dampen the strip of pastry and cover the pie pan with the remaining pastry. Trim and press the edges of the pastry together. Flute to seal.

Cut any pastry trimmings into leaves and use to decorate the top of the pie. Brush the pastry with beaten egg to glaze.

Bake for 30 to 35 minutes, or until the pastry is crisp and brown on top.

Serve warm or cold.

INGREDIENTS TO SERVE SIX:
1 lb (500 g) blueberries
2 to 4 tablespoons (30 to 60 ml) sugar
1½ cups (150 ml) sweet pie pastry made with whole-wheat flour (see page 35)
1 egg

Spiced Cranberry Sauce

Grate the rind of 1 orange into a saucepan. Add the juice of 2 oranges, ⅔ cup of brown sugar, 1 stick of cinnamon, 1 clove and a pinch of grated nutmeg. Cook over very low heat until the sugar dissolves, then bring to the boil.

Add ½ pound of cranberries and continue to boil, uncovered, for 5 to 10 minutes, or until the cranberries have popped and the liquid has thickened slightly.

Remove the cinnamon and clove and let cool.

Serve chilled.

INGREDIENTS TO SERVE FOUR TO SIX:
2 oranges
⅔ cup (100 g) brown sugar
1 cinnamon stick
1 clove
grated nutmeg
½ lb (250 g) cranberries

Gooseberry Fool

Remove the stems and blossom ends from 1 pound of gooseberries. Put the berries into a saucepan with 4 tablespoons of sugar and 4 tablespoons of water. Cover the pan and cook over low heat for 15 minutes, or until the gooseberries are tender.

Make ⅔ cup of confectioner's custard (see page 93). Let the custard cool slightly, then beat in ⅔ cup of yogurt.

Sieve the gooseberries into a mixing bowl. Add the custard to the gooseberry purée and mix well. Turn into a large serving bowl or individual glasses or dishes. Serve chilled.

INGREDIENTS TO SERVE FOUR:
1 lb (500 g) gooseberries
4 tablespoons (60 ml) sugar
⅔ cup confectioner's custard (see page 93)
⅔ cup (150 ml) yogurt

Gooseberry and Almond Sauce

Serve this tart sauce with fat fish, such as mackerel and trout, or with duck or goose.

Wash ½ pound of gooseberries. Remove the stems and blossom ends. Put the berries into a saucepan with 1¼ cups of water. Cover the pan and bring to the boil. Reduce the heat and simmer for 5 minutes, or until the gooseberries are tender.

Blend the gooseberries with the cooking liquid, then strain them.

PREPARING GOOSEBERRIES

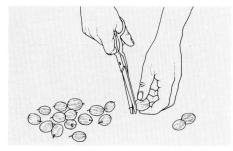

Trim gooseberries with scissors.

Melt 2 tablespoons of margarine or butter in a saucepan. Add ¼ cup of coarsely chopped blanched almonds and fry gently until they are golden brown. Stir in 1 tablespoon of flour and then the gooseberry purée. Heat gently, stirring constantly, until the sauce thickens and boils. Simmer for 1 minute. Add salt and pepper to taste and a pinch of grated nutmeg.

Serve hot or cold.

INGREDIENTS TO SERVE FOUR:
½ lb (250 g) gooseberries
2 tablespoons (25 g) margarine or butter
¼ cup (50 g) coarsely chopped blanched almonds
1 tablespoon (15 ml) flour
salt
pepper
grated nutmeg

Gooseberry and Orange Compote

Wash 1 pound of gooseberries. Remove the stems and blossom ends. Put the berries into a saucepan with the grated rind of 1 orange, the juice of 2 oranges and 4 tablespoons of sugar. Cover the pan and cook over low heat until the juice simmers. Continue to simmer very gently for about 3 minutes, or until the gooseberries are just tender.

Remove the peel and pith of 2 more oranges. Working over the pan, cut the membrane away from the segments of fruit. Carefully stir the orange segments into the gooseberries and let cool.

Transfer to a serving dish and chill. Serve cold.

INGREDIENTS TO SERVE SIX:
1 lb (500 g) gooseberries
4 oranges
4 tablespoons (50 g) sugar

Gooseberry Squares

Preheat the oven to 400°F (200°C).

Clean ½ pound of gooseberries. Wash and drain them and put them into a large saucepan with ¼ cup of sugar and 3 tablespoons of dry white wine. Heat the gooseberries gently, stirring occasionally, until they have reduced to a purée.

Add the grated rind of 1 lemon and ⅓ cup of split blanched almonds to the gooseberries and mix well.

Make and roll out thinly 3 cups of cheese pastry (see quiche lorraine, page 89). Cut out eight 4-inch (10-cm) squares. Transfer 4 of the squares to a greased baking sheet.

Spoon the gooseberry mixture onto the squares on the baking sheet. Dampen the edges of the pastry. Use the remaining squares to cover the gooseberry mixture. Press the edges of the pastry squares together to seal them. Cut a slit in the top of each square and brush the tops with beaten egg.

Bake for 15 to 20 minutes, or until the pastry is crisp and golden. Serve immediately.

INGREDIENTS TO SERVE FOUR:
½ lb (250 g) gooseberries
¼ cup (50 g) sugar
3 tablespoons (45 ml) dry white wine
1 lemon
⅓ cup (50 g) split blanched almonds
3 cups (375 g) cheese pastry (see quiche lorraine, page 89)
1 egg

Strawberry Yogurt Whip

This light fluffy dessert may be made just before serving or in advance and set with gelatin.

Hull ½ pound of strawberries and sieve or blend them to purée.

Stir in 1¼ cups of yogurt and the grated rind and juice of ½ orange or lemon. Add 1 tablespoon of sugar, if desired.

If the whip is being made in advance dissolve 2 teaspoons of powdered gelatin in the juice of ½ orange or lemon and stir it into the strawberry purée with the yogurt.

Beat 2 egg whites until stiff, then fold into the strawberry mixture.

Serve at once decorated with whole strawberries. If set with gelatin, chill until set.

INGREDIENTS TO SERVE FOUR:
½ lb (250 g) strawberries
1¼ cups (300 ml) yogurt
½ orange or lemon
1 tablespoon (15 ml) sugar (optional)
2 teaspoons (10 ml) powdered gelatin (optional)
2 egg whites

HULLING STRAWBERRIES

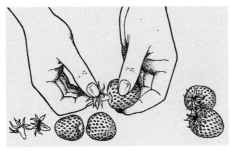

Pull leaves, stalk and soft center from strawberries.

Strawberry Crème Brûlée

A traditional crème brûlée is a rich custard made with cream and egg yolks and topped with burned sugar. This custard is made with yogurt and eggs and is poured on top of strawberries. It has a tangy flavor and a rich texture.

Hull and slice ½ pound of strawberries. Divide them between 4 ovenproof dishes.

To make the custard, put 2½ cups of yogurt into the top of a double-boiler. Add ½ vanilla bean or 1 teaspoon of vanilla extract and a pinch of grated nutmeg.

Cook over simmering water until the yogurt is lukewarm.

Beat 4 egg yolks with 2 tablespoons of sugar and stir into the warm yogurt. Continue to heat, stirring constantly, until the custard thickens and coats the back of a spoon.

Strain the custard over the strawberries. Chill for at least 2 hours. The custard will set and thicken when it cools.

Sprinkle the top with 2 tablespoons of light brown sugar to cover the custard. Stand the dishes in a baking pan filled with ice cubes then put under a hot broiler for 1 to 2 minutes, or until the sugar browns and caramelizes. Return the crème brûlées to the refrigerator and chill before serving.

INGREDIENTS TO SERVE FOUR:
½ pound (250 g) strawberries
2½ cups (600 ml) yogurt
½ vanilla bean or 1 teaspoon (5 ml) vanilla extract
grated nutmeg
4 egg yolks
2 tablespoons (30 ml) sugar
2 tablespoons (30 ml) light brown sugar

Strawberry Cloud

Hull and slice 1 pound of strawberries. Put the strawberries into a serving bowl. Sprinkle with 2 tablespoons of Grand Marnier, if desired.

Just before serving, beat 2 egg whites until stiff. Carefully fold in 1¼ cups of yogurt, the grated rind of ½ lemon and 1 tablespoon of sugar, if desired. Fold the strawberries into the foam.

Sprinkle with ¼ cup of toasted sliced almonds and serve.

INGREDIENTS TO SERVE FOUR:
1 lb (500 g) strawberries
2 tablespoons (30 ml) Grand Marnier (optional)
2 egg whites
1¼ cups (300 ml) yogurt
½ lemon
1 tablespoon (15 ml) sugar (optional)
¼ cup (25 g) toasted sliced almonds

Strawberries à l'Orange

Hull 1 pound of strawberries. Cut them into halves and put them into a serving bowl.

Cut 1 small bunch of green grapes into halves and remove the seeds. Add the grapes to the strawberries.

Cut the peel and pith from 2 oranges. Working over the bowl, cut the membrane away from the segments of fruit. Add the orange segments to the strawberries.

Mix the juice of 1 large orange with 3 tablespoons of Grand Marnier or brandy. Stir in 1 tablespoon of sugar, if desired, then pour over the strawberries.

Refrigerate for at least 1 hour before serving.

INGREDIENTS TO SERVE FOUR:
1 lb (500 g) strawberries
1 small bunch (100 g) green grapes
3 oranges
3 tablespoons (45 ml) Grand Marnier or brandy
1 tablespoon (15 ml) sugar (optional)

Strawberry and Cheese Tartlets

This recipe may be used to make one 8-inch (20-cm) pie instead of tartlets.

Preheat the oven to 400°F (200°C).

Make 1½ cups of almond pastry with whole-wheat flour (see page 35). Roll out the pastry on a lightly floured surface. Using a 2½-inch (6-cm) round fluted cutter cut out 18 circles and use them to line tartlet pans. Prick the pastry well with a fork and bake blind for 10 minutes. Let cool.

For the filling, put ½ pound (250 g) of pot

cheese into a mixing bowl. Beat in ¼ cup of yogurt, 1 tablespoon of honey and the grated rind of 1 lemon.

Divide the filling between the baked pastry shells.

Hull ½ pound of strawberries, cut them into halves if they are large and arrange on top of the tartlets.

For the glaze, put 2 tablespoons of red currant jelly into a small saucepan with the juice of 1 lemon. Cook over low heat until the jelly is dissolved, then spoon the glaze over the strawberries.

INGREDIENTS TO MAKE EIGHTEEN TARTLETS:
1½ cups (150 g) almond pastry made with whole-wheat flour (see page 35)
½ lb (250 g) pot cheese
¼ cup (60 ml) yogurt
1 tablespoon (15 ml) honey
1 lemon
½ lb (250 g) strawberries
2 tablespoons (30 ml) red currant jelly

Strawberry Wine Punch

Squeeze the juice of 4 lemons into a large punch bowl. Hull 1 pound of strawberries and cut them into halves. Peel and remove the seeds from 1 medium-sized melon. Cut the melon into 1-inch (2-cm) cubes. Add the strawberries and melon to the bowl and toss in the lemon juice.

Sprinkle ¼ cup of sugar over the fruit and squeeze in the juice of 4 oranges. Pour 1 bottle of dry red wine and 2½ cups of soda water into the bowl. Mix well and chill thoroughly.

Thinly slice 1 orange and 1 lemon and add them to the bowl. Serve immediately.

INGREDIENTS TO MAKE 5 PINTS OF PUNCH:
5 lemons
1 lb (500 g) strawberries
1 medium-sized melon
¼ cup (50 g) sugar
5 oranges
1 bottle dry red wine
2½ cups (600 ml) soda water

Raspberry Sherbet

Sieve ½ pound of raspberries into a bowl. Or blend them and then strain to remove the seeds.

Stir in 1¼ cups of yogurt, the juice of ½ lemon and 2 tablespoons of sugar.

Put the bowl into the freezer until the purée is half-frozen.

Beat 2 egg whites until stiff.

Beat the purée, then fold in the egg whites.

Pour into a rigid container and freeze until the sherbet is firm. Cover, seal and label and store in the freezer until needed.

INGREDIENTS TO SERVE FOUR TO SIX:
½ lb (250 g) raspberries
1¼ cups (300 ml) yogurt
½ lemon
2 tablespoons (30 ml) sugar
2 egg whites

The season of berries is short and they are at their best for only a brief time, but during that time we can enjoy such memorable dishes as Strawberry à l'Orange, left, Raspberry Sherbet, right, and Summer Pudding, far right.

Raspberry Cheese Fool

Put 1 pound of raspberries into a mixing bowl, reserving a few for decoration. Mash the raspberries.

Beat ½ pound of cottage cheese with 1¼ cups of yogurt in a mixing bowl. Add the mashed raspberries with 1 to 2 tablespoons of sugar to taste and mix well.

Just before serving, beat 2 egg whites until stiff, then fold into the raspberry mixture. Spoon into individual serving dishes or a serving bowl and decorate with the reserved raspberries.

INGREDIENTS TO SERVE FOUR TO SIX:
1 lb (500 g) raspberries
½ lb (250 g) cottage cheese
1¼ cups (300 ml) yogurt
1 to 2 tablespoons (15 to 30 ml) sugar
2 egg whites

Summer Pudding

This is a glorious pudding, incorporating as many different soft summer fruits as you care to include.

Lightly grease a 1-quart (850-ml) bowl.

Cut the crusts from a small loaf of thinly sliced white bread. Cut 1 slice of bread into a circle to fit the bottom of the bowl. Line the sides of the bowl with more bread, cutting to shape so that the slices fit closely together.

Wash and hull 1½ pounds of soft summer fruit, using a mixture of raspberries, strawberries, cherries and currants. Cut large strawberries into halves and pit the cherries.

Put the fruit into a saucepan with ¼ cup of sugar, the grated rind and juice of ½ lemon and 2 tablespoons of water. Cover the pan and bring to the boil slowly. Reduce the heat and simmer for 1 minute.

Reserving 3 tablespoons of the juice, spoon the contents of the pan into the bread-lined bowl.

Cover the fruit with the remaining slices of bread, trimming the edges to fit the top of the bowl.

Put a small plate on top and then weight it down with a heavy can. Refrigerate, preferably overnight.

Turn the pudding out onto a serving plate. Pour the reserved juice over any parts of the bread that have not been soaked through and colored pink by the fruit juices.

INGREDIENTS TO SERVE FOUR TO SIX:
1 small thinly sliced white bread loaf
1½ lb (700 g) mixed soft summer fruits (raspberries, strawberries, cherries and currants)
¼ cup (50 g) sugar
½ lemon

Frozen Raspberry Yogurt

Frozen flavored yogurt is a marvelous substitute for ice cream. Other fruits can be substituted, but the sugar must then be adjusted to taste.

Sieve ½ pound of raspberries or blend and then strain to remove the seeds.

Stir 2½ cups of yogurt and 2 tablespoons of sugar into the purée. Mix well.

Pour into a plastic container, seal, label and freeze until firm.

Store in the freezer until needed.

INGREDIENTS TO SERVE FOUR TO SIX:
½ lb (250 g) raspberries
2½ cups (600 ml) yogurt
2 tablespoons (30 ml) sugar

Raspberry Melba Sauce

This sharp colorful sauce is particularly good with peaches and strawberries.

Put ½ pound of raspberries into a saucepan with the grated rind and juice of ½ lemon and 4 tablespoons of red currant jelly.

Cover the pan and cook over low heat until the jelly melts and the juices run from the raspberries. Uncover and continue to cook, stirring constantly, until the raspberries are mushy.

Sieve the raspberries and return to the pan.

The sauce may be thickened a little more by blending 1 teaspoon of arrowroot with 1 tablespoon of water and adding it to the sauce. Reheat, stirring constantly, until the sauce thickens and becomes clear.

Serve hot or cold.

INGREDIENTS TO SERVE FOUR:
½ lb (250 g) raspberries
½ lemon
4 tablespoons (60 ml) red currant jelly
1 teaspoon (5 ml) arrowroot (optional)

Raspberry Zabaglione

Sieve ½ pound of raspberries into the top of a double-boiler. Add 4 egg yolks, 6 tablespoons of sugar and ⅔ cup of dry white wine.

Beat over simmering water until the custard is very foamy and thick.

Pour into individual dishes or glasses and serve immediately.

INGREDIENTS TO SERVE FOUR:
½ lb (250 g) raspberries
4 egg yolks
6 tablespoons (75 g) sugar
⅔ cup (150 ml) dry white wine

Chilled Raspberry Soufflé

Reserving a few berries for decoration, sieve 1 pound of raspberries, or blend and then strain them to remove the seeds.

Separate 4 eggs, putting the yolks into the top of a double-boiler. To the yolks add 6 tablespoons of sugar and the grated rind of 1 lemon. Beat over simmering water until the mixture is thick. Remove from the heat and beat until cool.

Stir in the raspberry purée and ⅔ cup of yogurt. Mix well.

Squeeze the juice from the lemon into a small bowl set in a pan of hot water. Dissolve 1½ tablespoons of powdered gelatin in the lemon juice. Stir the dissolved gelatin into the raspberry mixture.

When the mixture is beginning to set beat the egg whites until just stiff, then fold in.

Turn into a 1-quart (850-ml) soufflé dish prepared with a band of waxed paper tied around it so that it stands 2 inches (5 cm) above the rim. Alternatively, pour the soufflé into a serving bowl. Refrigerate for at least two hours before serving.

To serve, carefully remove the waxed paper and decorate with the reserved raspberries.

INGREDIENTS TO SERVE FOUR TO SIX:
1 lb (500 g) raspberries
4 eggs
6 tablespoons (75 g) sugar
1 lemon
⅔ cup (150 ml) yogurt
1½ tablespoons (15 g) powdered gelatin

Raspberries and Peaches in Wine

Put 1 pound of raspberries into a serving bowl.

Blanch and peel 2 peaches. Cut the peaches into halves and remove the pits. Slice the peaches into the bowl of raspberries.

Pour in ⅔ cup of white wine and toss lightly to mix. Sweeten if desired with a little sugar.

Chill for at least 1 hour before serving.

INGREDIENTS TO SERVE FOUR:
1 lb (500 g) raspberries
2 peaches
⅔ cup (150 ml) white wine
sugar (optional)

Hot Raspberry Snow

Preheat the oven to 400°F (200°C).

Put 1 pound of raspberries into a baking dish. Sprinkle with 1 tablespoon of sugar, if desired.

Put ⅔ cup of yogurt into a mixing bowl. Separate 2 eggs. Beat the egg yolks into the yogurt with 2 tablespoons of flour and 4 tablespoons of ground almonds.

Beat the egg whites until they are stiff. Fold them into the yogurt mixture.

Spoon the topping over the raspberries and sprinkle with 2 tablespoons of brown sugar.

Bake for 15 to 20 minutes, or until the topping has risen and browned.

INGREDIENTS TO SERVE FOUR TO SIX:
1 lb (500 g) raspberries
1 tablespoon (15 ml) sugar (optional)
⅔ cup (150 ml) yogurt
2 eggs
2 tablespoons (30 ml) flour
4 tablespoons (25 g) ground almonds
2 tablespoons (30 ml) brown sugar

Red Fruit Compote

Wash ½ pound of red currants and strip them from the stems. Put the currants into a saucepan.

Pit ½ pound of cherries and add them to the pan with the juice of 1 orange and 2 tablespoons of red currant jelly. Add 1 to 2 tablespoons of sugar, if desired.

Cover the pan and cook over low heat until the juice comes to the boil. Remove the pan from the heat and set aside for 10 minutes to soften the fruit.

Carefully stir in 1 pound of raspberries, then spoon into a serving bowl.

Serve chilled.

INGREDIENTS TO SERVE FOUR TO SIX:
½ lb (250 g) red currants
½ lb (250 g) cherries
1 orange
2 tablespoons (50 ml) red currant jelly
1 to 2 tablespoons (15 to 30 ml) sugar (optional)
1 lb (500 g) raspberries

Red Currant Jelly

Red currant jelly is very good to have on hand. It can be used to sweeten, flavor and glaze numerous dishes.

Wash 3 pounds of red currants. It is not necessary to remove the stems.

Put the red currants into a saucepan with $2\frac{1}{2}$ cups of water. Bring to the boil, reduce the heat and simmer gently until the currants are reduced to a pulp. They must be thoroughly cooked in order to extract as much juice as possible.

Strain the currants through a jelly bag, preferably overnight, until all the juice has dripped through. Do not squeeze the bag of fruit because this will make the jelly cloudy. (A clean dish towel or a piece of cheesecloth may be used instead of a jelly bag.)

Measure the juice and pour it into a saucepan. To each cup of juice add $\frac{3}{4}$ to 1 cup of sugar. Cook over low heat, stirring constantly, until the sugar is dissolved. Boil rapidly until the setting point is reached. (See directions for making marmalade, page 178.)

Skim the jelly then pour at once into clean, dry warm jars. Wipe the jars and cover as for marmalade.

INGREDIENTS (yield varies according to ripeness of the fruit and straining time):
3 lb (1.40 kg) red currants
sugar

STRAINING RED CURRANT JELLY

Strain the juice of red currants through a jelly bag.

Cumberland Sauce

This red currant sauce is traditionally served with ham, but it is also good with lamb and game.

Thinly cut the peel from 2 large oranges and 1 large lemon, then cut the peel into thin strips. Put them into a small saucepan, cover with water and bring to the boil. Reduce the heat and simmer for 15 minutes. Drain well.

Squeeze the juice from the oranges and lemon into a saucepan. Add $\frac{3}{4}$ cup of red currant jelly. Cook over low heat until the jelly melts, then bring to the boil.

Blend 2 teaspoons of arrowroot with 4 tablespoons of port, then stir the mixture into the sauce. Stirring constantly, bring to the boil and cook until the sauce thickens and clears.

Add the orange and lemon peel, reduce the heat and simmer for 5 minutes.

Serve warm or cold.

INGREDIENTS TO SERVE FOUR:
2 large oranges
1 large lemon
$\frac{3}{4}$ cup (250 g) red currant jelly
2 teaspoons (10 ml) arrowroot
4 tablespoons (60 ml) port

Rødgrød

This delicious Danish red fruit pudding is a purée of mixed fruits.

Put 2 pounds of mixed red berries (red or black currants, raspberries and strawberries) into a saucepan. Add the grated rind and juice of 1 lemon. Cover the pan and slowly bring to the boil. Simmer gently for 5 minutes until the fruit is just soft.

Sieve the fruit with the juices or purée it in a blender and then strain it. Return the fruit purée to the saucepan.

Blend 2 tablespoons of arrowroot with a little of the purée, then stir it into the pan. Bring to the boil, stirring constantly, until the mixture thickens. Add sugar to taste, reduce the heat and simmer for 2 minutes.

Let the rødgrød cool, then spoon it into individual serving dishes or glasses and decorate with $\frac{1}{4}$ cup of sliced almonds.

INGREDIENTS TO SERVE SIX:
2 lb (1 kg) mixed red berries (red or black currants, raspberries and strawberries)
1 lemon
2 tablespoons (30 ml) arrowroot
sugar
$\frac{1}{4}$ cup (25 g) sliced almonds

Currant Cottage Cheese Delight

Wash 1 pound of red or white currants, or a mixture of both, and remove the stems.

Put $\frac{3}{4}$ pound of cottage cheese, $\frac{2}{3}$ cup of yogurt and 2 tablespoons of honey into a blender and blend until smooth. Alternatively, sieve the cottage cheese then stir in the yogurt and honey.

Fold in the currants and the grated rind of 1 lemon.

Pile into a serving bowl and refrigerate until well chilled.

INGREDIENTS TO SERVE FOUR:
1 lb (500 g) red or white currants (or a mixture of both)
$\frac{3}{4}$ lb (350 g) cottage cheese
$\frac{2}{3}$ cup (150 ml) yogurt
2 tablespoons (30 ml) honey
1 lemon

Black Currant Mousse

Remove the stems from 1 pound of black currants. Put the fruit into a saucepan with the grated rind and juice of 1 large orange and 2 sprigs of mint. Cover the pan and cook over low heat until the juices come to the boil. Reduce the heat and simmer gently for 5 minutes, or until the currants are soft.

Separate 3 eggs. Add 6 tablespoons of sugar to the yolks and beat until thick and pale. Add the cooked black currants while they are still warm and beat well. (The black currants may be blended or sieved for a smoother texture.)

In a cup set in a pan of hot water dissolve 2 teaspoons of powdered gelatin in 1 tablespoon of water. Stir the dissolved gelatin into the black currant mixture. Add $\frac{2}{3}$ cup of yogurt and mix well.

When the mousse begins to set, beat the egg whites until just stiff, then fold in.

Pour into a serving dish and chill for at least 2 hours before serving.

INGREDIENTS TO SERVE FOUR TO SIX:
1 lb (500 g) black currants
1 large orange
2 mint sprigs
3 eggs
6 tablespoons (75 g) sugar
2 teaspoons (10 ml) powdered gelatin
$\frac{2}{3}$ cup (150 ml) yogurt

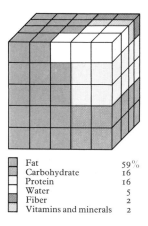

Fat	59%
Carbohydrate	16
Protein	16
Water	5
Fiber	2
Vitamins and minerals	2

PEOPLE HAVE BEEN EATING NUTS from time immemorial. Archeological sites in the Near East indicate that pistachio nuts and acorns were being eaten in about 10,000 B.C., possibly because other food was scarce. Today people in the West would eat acorns only out of dire necessity, while pistachios suggest cocktail-hour affluence.

There is a bewildering variety of nuts, but not all are used as food. Some are used as beads, some are made into varnish, hair oil or soap, and the *Ophiocaryon paradoxum* from Guyana has a reputation as a charm against snake bites. The most important edible nuts are filberts and hazels, pecans, walnuts, almonds, peanuts, cashews, Brazils, chestnuts, pistachios and macadamias.

Vegetarians apart, people in the West eat few nuts. Most people think of nuts as something to nibble, rather than as a serious food. But nuts are staggeringly nutritious and even a nibble provides a considerable amount of protein and fat and a wide range of minerals. Vegetarians would have a lean time without them, and there is no

reason why they should cover up nuts' delicious natural flavors by turning them into imitation meat dishes.

The nutritional value of different nuts varies considerably. Most are outstandingly rich in protein: almonds have 20 percent, cashews 17 percent, Brazils 13 percent and walnuts 12 percent. Even richer are pine nuts and peanuts, although neither of them is, botanically, a nut.

Pine nuts, or kernels, the seeds of the Stone Pine, may reach a surprising 31 percent protein and only a few meats achieve or excel that. They have something of an almond flavor, but are softer than true dessert nuts.

Peanuts are the pods of a leguminous plant of South America, and may be 28 percent protein. Also known as groundnuts and earthnuts, peanuts are eaten raw or roasted. They are ground to make peanut butter and the oil that is extracted from them is used for cooking and for making margarine.

Strictly speaking, neither almonds nor Brazils are nuts either. The Brazil is a seed and the almond is a drupe, that is, a fleshy fruit enclosing a stone in which is a kernel. There are sweet and bitter almonds, but the bitter almonds are so bitter as to be inedible—fortunately so, since they contain a poison called prussic acid. After refining, however, the flavoring oil made from the kernels is perfectly safe and is widely used in cooking. Sweet almonds are equally delicious eaten raw, roasted, toasted or fried and used in either sweet or savory dishes, especially fish and chicken dishes.

A very tall South American forest tree produces the very odd fruit that provides the highly desirable Brazil nut. The fruit itself is a large woody sphere, weighing several pounds, which crashes to the ground when it is ripe and is hazardous to harvesters. Inside are about twenty of the familiar nuts, tightly packed like the segments of an orange. These are the shells with which we struggle to reach the large creamy colored kernel within.

Walnuts are true nuts and among the most distinguished. The best flavored is the English (alias Persian) walnut from the beautiful *Juglans regia* tree, which grows throughout Europe and Asia. The black walnut (*Juglans nigra*) is a native of North America and the kernel, when you get to it through the immensely hard shell, has a stronger flavor than the English walnut. Another North American walnut is *Juglans cinerea*, known as the butternut or white walnut, which has a rich flavor but does not keep long. When they are ripe walnuts are usually used in sweet, rather than spicy, cooking. Pickled walnuts, made from the whole walnuts before the shell has hardened (around midsummer), have no rival as companions to cold meats and cheese. In ancient Roman times the nuts were thrown at brides, as rice or confetti

NUTS FROM THE GROUND

Not true nuts, peanuts are actually the pods of a leguminous plant of South American origin. Because of the curious way in which they grow they have earned their other names—groundnuts and earthnuts. After the plant's flowers have been pollinated the stalks bearing them bend to the ground and grow longer, forcing the young pods into the soil. There, as illustrated left, they mature to produce two, three or four nuts within each shell. These nuts are a precious food because they are very rich in protein, fat, thiamine and niacin.

The coconut is the most versatile of nuts. It supplies milk as well as "meat." Coconut milk is easily digested and is low in calories, but the meat is full of energy-giving oil and contains such minerals as iron. Shredded coconut is used in cooking to add flavor and texture. Oil, for cooking and to make margarine, is extracted from the meat.

are today, but of course they are too precious for that now.

Two nuts in growing demand in the West are the pistachio and the macadamia. The pistachio is a pretty green, mild in flavor, unusually rich in iron and expensive. The macadamia, a native of Australia, which looks like a large hazelnut, has become popular in the United States. Although not rich in protein as nuts go, the macadamia is notable for its fat content of more than 70 percent.

Another cocktail-time nut is the cashew, less plebeian than the peanut, but the way in which it grows is equally singular. The tropical tree produces a crop of fleshy fruits and from the base of each hangs a single olive-colored nut. This contains a particularly irritant oil, which has to be driven off by roasting before the nut is shelled to release the sweet kernel.

The most famous nuts of temperate climates are filberts, the related hazels and the sweet chestnuts. The wild hazel is one of the most ancient of nuts, but its cultivation is comparatively recent. The names hazel and filbert are often used indiscriminately. It is possible to distinguish between them. The hazelnut is more likely to be round and the filbert oval, but the husk is the more reliable indicator; that on the filbert is longer than on the hazel and it folds over and hugs the top of the nut closely.

The sweet, or Spanish, chestnut is a nut with a high moisture content—about 50 percent. It contains little more than 2 percent protein and about the same amount of fat, so it is far less fattening than most nuts. Chestnuts have innumerable uses in cooking. They associate well with poultry, game and many other meats, as well as with the cabbage tribe. The French cook them in sugar to make marrons glacés, or purée them with ice cream to make the exotic Nesselrode pudding. The Italians cook them in wine. The British and New Yorkers like them roasted, and as winter approaches hot-chestnut vendors do a brisk trade roasting and selling them in the streets.

Nuts are a highly concentrated source of energy. They can be as much as 70 percent fat and some nuts are as high as meat in carbohydrate and protein. They also contain B vitamins and such minerals as iron. Clockwise below from top left: pecans, very high in fat; Brazil nuts, a good source of niacin; pistachios, rich in iron; almonds, a source of calcium; and walnuts, which, unlike most nuts, have more polyunsaturated than saturated fat.

Nut Pâté

Preheat the oven to 375°F (190°C).

Chop 4 slices of bacon. Peel and chop 3 medium-sized onions.

Heat 1 tablespoon of corn oil in a saucepan and fry the bacon, the onions and 1 crushed garlic clove for 5 minutes, or until the onions are lightly browned.

Remove the pan from the heat and stir in 2 cups of chopped mixed nuts (cashews, almonds, Brazil nuts and walnuts).

Add 2 cups of fresh whole-wheat bread crumbs, 1 tablespoon of chopped parsley, 1 tablespoon of chopped sage, salt and pepper. Stir well. Beat 1 egg then stir it into the mixture.

Turn into a lightly greased loaf pan. Alternatively, shape into a loaf on a greased baking sheet.

Bake for 40 to 45 minutes, or until browned.

Turn out onto a serving dish and serve hot or cold. (If the pâté is to be served cold it is better to let it cool in the pan before turning it out.)

INGREDIENTS TO SERVE FOUR TO SIX:
**4 slices bacon
3 medium-sized onions
1 tablespoon (15 ml) corn oil
1 garlic clove
2 cups (250 g) chopped mixed nuts
2 cups (100 g) fresh whole-wheat
 bread crumbs
1 tablespoon (15 ml) chopped parsley
1 tablespoon (15 ml) chopped sage
salt
pepper
1 egg**

Pork Saté

This specialty of Southeast Asia makes an unusual cocktail snack or first course. The strips of pork, marinated, cooked and served on bamboo sticks or small skewers, are dipped into a spicy sauce.

Cut 1 pound of pork tenderloin or boned pork chops into slices ¼ inch (6 mm) thick. Cut the slices into strips about 1 inch (2 cm) long and ½ inch (1 cm) wide. Skewer 3 to 4 pieces of meat close together on the end of a bamboo stick. (You will need about 30 sticks.) Put the sticks into a shallow bowl.

To make the marinade, in a small bowl combine 1 tablespoon of clear honey, 1 tablespoon of soy sauce, 1 teaspoon of peanut oil, 1 teaspoon of water, 1 teaspoon of grated onion, 1 crushed garlic clove, salt and pepper. Mix well. Pour the marinade over the meat on the sticks. Marinate the meat for at least 1 hour at room temperature or overnight in the refrigerator. Turn the sticks occasionally.

For the sauce, heat 3 teaspoons of peanut oil in a small saucepan. Add 1 crushed garlic clove and fry, stirring constantly, until it is lightly browned. Stir in ½ teaspoon of chilli powder and fry for 1 minute. Add 1 cup of chopped or ground roasted salted peanuts to the pan. Stir in ⅔ cup of water and 1 tablespoon of lemon juice. Bring to the boil, stirring constantly. Reduce the heat and simmer gently for 5 minutes, or until the sauce has thickened enough to coat the back of a spoon. Season to taste with salt and pepper.

Remove the meat from the marinade and cook over a charcoal fire or under a moderate broiler, turning the sticks frequently, for 4 to 5 minutes, or until the meat has browned.

Pour the hot sauce into a bowl. Pile the saté on a serving dish. Garnish with sticks of cucumber and serve immediately.

INGREDIENTS TO SERVE SIX:
**1 lb (500 g) pork tenderloin or boned
 pork chops
1 tablespoon (15 ml) clear honey
1 tablespoon (15 ml) soy sauce
4 teaspoons (20 ml) peanut oil
1 teaspoon (5 ml) grated onion
2 garlic cloves
salt
pepper
½ teaspoon (2.5 ml) chilli powder
1 cup (100 g) chopped or ground roasted
 salted peanuts
1 tablespoon (15 ml) lemon juice
cucumber sticks**

MAKING SATÉ

Cut lean pork into thin strips.

Thread the pork onto bamboo sticks.

Brazil Patties

Ground Brazil nuts flavored with thyme make a tasty and satisfying meat substitute. The patties may be fried or baked. Serve them with a mushroom sauce or a tomato sauce.

Coarsely grind ½ pound of shelled Brazil nuts in a blender (or chop them very finely) and put them into a mixing bowl.

Add 1 cup of fresh whole-wheat bread crumbs, 1 tablespoon of chopped thyme, salt and pepper and mix well. Beat 1 egg and stir it in.

Divide the mixture into 4 and shape into cakes about ½ inch (1 cm) thick and 3 inches (8 cm) in diameter.

Fry the patties in a little corn oil for 5 minutes, turning once so that both sides brown. Alternatively, put them on a lightly greased baking sheet and bake at 400°F (200°C) for 20 minutes.

Serve hot or cold.

INGREDIENTS TO SERVE FOUR:
**½ lb (250 g) shelled Brazil nuts
1 cup (50 g) fresh whole-wheat
 bread crumbs
1 tablespoon (15 ml) chopped thyme
salt
pepper
1 egg
corn oil**

Walnut, Cheese and Tomato Loaf

Serve this dish as a first course or as a light main dish.

Preheat the oven to 400°F (200°C).

Grind 2 cups of shelled walnuts in a blender. Put the nuts into a large mixing bowl.

Blanch and peel 2 medium-sized tomatoes. Slice them thinly and add to the ground walnuts with 1 cup of grated Cheddar cheese, 1 grated onion, 1 tablespoon of chopped marjoram or oregano, salt and pepper. Mix well. Beat 1 egg and stir it in.

Spoon the mixture into a lightly greased loaf pan and press it down well. Bake for 30 to 40 minutes, or until browned.

Cool the loaf in the pan and then turn it out onto a serving dish.

INGREDIENTS TO SERVE FOUR TO SIX:
**2 cups (250 g) shelled walnuts
2 medium-sized tomatoes
1 cup (100 g) grated Cheddar cheese
1 onion
1 tablespoon (15 ml) chopped marjoram
 or oregano
salt
pepper
1 egg**

Mushroom and Nut Loaf

Preheat the oven to 350°F (180°C).

Chop 3 medium-sized onions. Chop ½ pound of mushrooms. Coarsely grind ½ pound of shelled Brazil nuts.

Heat 2 tablespoons of corn oil in a large saucepan. Add the onions and fry, stirring frequently, for 3 minutes. Add the mushrooms and fry for 2 minutes.

Remove the pan from the heat and stir in the Brazil nuts and 2 cups of fresh whole-wheat bread crumbs.

Beat 1 egg with 2 teaspoons of Worcestershire sauce, salt and pepper and add to the mushroom and nut mixture. Mix well. Press the mixture into a lightly greased large loaf pan.

Bake for 1 hour, or until the loaf is lightly browned.

Turn out of the pan and serve hot. To serve cold, cool in the pan and then turn out.

INGREDIENTS TO SERVE SIX:
3 medium-sized onions
½ lb (250 g) mushrooms
½ lb (250 g) shelled Brazil nuts
2 tablespoons (30 ml) corn oil
2 cups (100 g) fresh whole-wheat bread crumbs
1 egg
2 teaspoons (10 ml) Worcestershire sauce
salt
pepper

Cream of Peanut Soup

Chop 1 onion and put it into a saucepan with 2½ cups of chicken stock. Cover the pan and bring to the boil. Reduce the heat and simmer for 10 minutes, or until the onion is soft.

Add 1 cup of ground or finely chopped salted peanuts to the pan with 1¼ cups of milk. Bring to the boil, stirring constantly.

Blend the soup and then return it to the pan.

Blend 2 teaspoons of cornstarch with 3 tablespoons of dry sherry and add it to the soup. Bring to the boil, stirring constantly, until the soup has thickened. Season to taste with salt and pepper and simmer for 1 minute.

Serve hot, sprinkled with ¼ cup of chopped salted peanuts.

INGREDIENTS TO SERVE FOUR TO SIX:
1 onion
2½ cups (600 ml) chicken stock
1¼ cups (150 g) finely chopped salted peanuts
1¼ cups (300 ml) milk
2 teaspoons (10 ml) cornstarch
3 tablespoons (45 ml) dry sherry
salt
pepper

Hazelnut and Apricot Stuffing

This dried apricot and hazelnut stuffing can be used for chicken, turkey or a rolled pork roast.

Put ⅔ cup of chopped dried apricots into a mixing bowl with ⅔ cup of chopped hazelnuts, 1 cup of fresh whole-wheat bread crumbs, the grated rind of ½ lemon, ¼ teaspoon of ground allspice, salt and pepper. Mix well, then stir in 1 beaten egg to bind the stuffing.

INGREDIENTS TO MAKE TWO AND A HALF CUPS (250 G) OF STUFFING:
⅔ cup (100 g) chopped dried apricots
⅔ cup (100 g) chopped hazelnuts
1 cup (50 g) fresh whole-wheat bread crumbs
½ lemon
¼ teaspoon (1 ml) ground allspice
salt
pepper
1 egg

Walnut and Dried Fruit Stuffing

Use this unusual crunchy stuffing for chicken, duck or a rolled pork or lamb roast.

Put ⅔ cup of finely chopped walnuts into a mixing bowl.

Add ⅔ cup of seedless raisins and 1 cup of fresh whole-wheat bread crumbs.

Peel, core and finely chop 1 small apple and add it to the stuffing with 2 chopped scallions. Season to taste with salt and pepper. Mix well.

Bind the stuffing with 1 to 2 tablespoons of chicken stock.

INGREDIENTS TO MAKE TWO AND A HALF CUPS (300 G) OF STUFFING:
⅔ cup (100 g) finely chopped walnuts
⅔ cup (100 g) seedless raisins
1 cup (50 g) fresh whole-wheat bread crumbs
1 small apple
2 scallions
salt
pepper
1 to 2 tablespoons (15 to 30 ml) chicken stock

Bakewell Pie

Preheat the oven to 400°F (200°C).

Make 1½ cups of shortcrust pastry with whole-wheat flour (see page 34) and line a 7- to 8-inch (18- to 20-cm) flan ring or pie pan. Bake blind for 15 minutes. Remove the baking paper and the beans and bake for 5 minutes more.

Spread the bottom of the pastry shell with 2 tablespoons of lemon curd (see page 180).

For the filling, cream 4 tablespoons of

margarine with ⅓ cup of light brown sugar until pale and fluffy. Beat in 1 egg, 4 tablespoons of flour and ½ teaspoon of baking powder. Stir in ⅔ cup of ground almonds and the grated rind and juice of 1 lemon.

Beat 1 egg white until stiff, then carefully fold it into the filling.

Spoon the filling into the pastry shell and bake for 10 minutes.

Reduce the oven temperature to 350°F (180°C) and continue to bake for 15 to 20 minutes more, or until the filling has risen and is golden brown.

Serve hot or cold.

INGREDIENTS TO SERVE SIX:
1½ cups (150 g) shortcrust pastry made with whole-wheat flour (see page 34)
2 tablespoons (30 ml) lemon curd (see page 180)
4 tablespoons (50 g) margarine
⅓ cup (50 g) light brown sugar
1 egg
4 tablespoons (25 g) flour
½ teaspoon (2.5 ml) baking powder
⅔ cup (100 g) ground almonds
1 lemon
1 egg white

BLANCHING ALMONDS

Pour boiling water over the almonds.

Slide the skins off.

DRIED FRUIT/Concentrated Energy

FOR MANY THOUSANDS OF YEARS the only way to hoard food for the winter was to dry it. The principle behind drying is simple—bacteria need moisture to grow and as moisture content is reduced bacterial growth is inhibited. It was discovered that meat and fish were best dehydrated in a cold wind, and fruit was best dried by the heat of the sun. One early simple method was to bury dates and figs in the hot desert sand.

Most fruit is still dried by warmth, much of it in the natural heat of the sun, but more, with all the benefits of modern technology, by artificial heat. It is now possible, however, to dry fruit by freezing it at very low temperatures. It is then transferred to a vacuum chamber, where the ice crystals turn into vapor without first becoming liquid. The finished product is not frozen but dried, and has a moisture content that may be as low as 2 percent.

The most ancient and still most popular dried fruit are dates, figs and dried grapes (raisins and currants).

The origin of the date palm is lost in time, but it has been in cultivation for more than five thousand years. It is the universal provider of the Arab world. The fruit is delicious eaten ripe straight from the palm and many varieties of date keep well when dried. Sugar and wine are made from the tree's sap, oil from the seeds and rope from the fibers. The palm fruits prodigiously, more than a hundred pounds (45 kg) of dates a year, and a tree may live for a century.

The world's most popular date is the variety Deglet Noor. This is the one that was introduced to California in the early years of the twentieth century and is now the variety most grown in the United States. When fresh and ripe it is amber in color, but it is a darker brown when dried. Deglet Noor dates are exported in large quantities from North Africa and are often sold in the familiar round-ended box with the soft and juicy fruit still attached to a stalk. Two-thirds or more of a date is sugar, so it is a fruit to be enjoyed in moderation, in spite of the natural temptation to sneak just one more. Like most other dried fruits dates are rich in niacin, and also have some carotene, thiamine and riboflavin.

The fig tree is less versatile than the date palm and, except for Adam and Eve and sculptors, interest in it is confined to the fruit. Fresh figs are thin skinned and suffer if they have to travel, but there are no problems when they have been dried. This is usually done in the sun, and a deposit of sugar (which makes up half of a dried fig) appears on the skin. As well as being rich in sugar figs are notably rich in a whole range of minerals (the iron content, for example, is four milligrams in one hundred grams), and raw or stewed figs are often included in the diet as a pleasant and gentle laxative.

The Nutrients in Dried Fruit

Dried fruit is a good source of energy. Three and a half ounces (100 g) of raisins provide about 300 Calories.

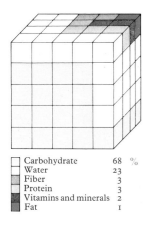

☐ Carbohydrate	68 %
☐ Water	23
▨ Fiber	3
▨ Protein	3
▨ Vitamins and minerals	2
▧ Fat	1

A selection of the more familiar dried fruit is shown in the jar (left).

Dried figs are high in fiber and protein as well as in B vitamins. Their gentle laxative action adds to their health-giving properties.

Dates are the sweetest of all dried fruit but are no more calorific.

Apples are one of the few fruits that retain all their vitamin C when dried.

Prunes, or dried plums, contain less sugar than most other dried fruit and half the number of calories.

Golden raisins are dried seedless white grapes.

Dried pears provide about six times as many calories as their fresh counterparts.

Dark raisins, like dried currants, are only shriveled grapes. Nutritionally raisins and currants are the same.

Dried apricots are a good source of vitamin C with twelve milligrams in three and a half ounces (100 g).

Currants, not to be confused with fresh red currants, white currants and black currants, have a reasonably high content of iron, but unfortunately this is poorly absorbed by the body.

Grapes when they are dried may be dark or golden raisins or currants, depending on which varieties of vines are used. Many are sun dried. The best dark raisins, large and sweet, are the so-called Malaga raisins, which are dried muscat grapes. Many are dried in the sun, the branches either left on the vine with the stalks partially severed or, more generally, spread out in the sun. Wine grapes are most commonly used for drying because they contain more sugar. Golden raisins are dried white seedless grapes. The best golden raisins come from Turkey, but they are cultivated in many parts of the Near East and in Australia and South Africa. In the United States the variety most widely grown for drying is Thompson Seedless. Although they are sweet and juicy, golden raisins are used most in cooking. Currants are dried small black grapes, which have been grown in Greece since classical times. They were long known as raisins of Corinth and in French still are, but in English Corinth has been corrupted to currant. Although currants taste tarter than dark or golden raisins they all contain similar amounts of sugar—about 70 percent. They all are fairly rich in minerals, although they have only half as much iron as figs.

Prunes are made from plums with a high sugar content and can be dried without removing the pits. Many plums ferment if they are dried unpitted. The United States is a major producer of prunes, either by sun-drying, as in California, or by artificial heat. Most American varieties are of European origin, the plums brought over by the early settlers. Prunes have only about half as much sugar as dates, figs and raisins and only half as many calories. Like figs they have a following among those haunted by constipation.

Other dried fruits are of lesser importance. Dried apricots have a most delicious flavor and contain more protein than any other dried fruit. Peaches are less attractive when dried, but for

Dates are still prepared by the traditional method of drying in the sun. Using this method most of the vitamin C in the dates is destroyed by oxidation. Modern factory drying in ovens or in streams of air, quickly and at controlled temperatures, results in fresher flavor and less vitamin C loss.

dried fruit they contain an astonishing amount of iron (nearly seven milligrams in a hundred grams compared with the one and a half milligrams in raisins). Dried bananas ("banana figs") are often to be found in health-food stores. Apples (peeled, cored and cut into rings) and dessert pears (halved) are easily dried at home. Put them on racks in a very slow oven (not more than 150°F, 65°C) for several hours with the oven door slightly ajar.

GRAPES VERSUS CURRANTS

When dried, a pound of grapes reduces to about three and a half ounces (100 g) of currants. The three and a half ounces of currants shown on the right-hand side of the scales provide more than 240 Calories, while the same weight of grapes shown on the left-hand side of the scales provides a mere 60 Calories. This is because grapes contain more than 80 percent water, which provides no calories at all. Currants, however, contain only 20 percent water and the rest is mostly sugar.

Stuffed Dates

Fresh or dried dates can be stuffed with this cheese and herb mixture, but the fresh dates are plumper and easier to handle.

Slit 1 side of ½ pound of dates and carefully remove the pits.

For the stuffing, put ¼ pound of pot cheese into a bowl. Beat in 2 to 3 tablespoons of yogurt. The consistency should be thick and creamy.

Finely chop 2 scallions or 1 small bunch of chives and beat into the cheese with 1 tablespoon of chopped parsley, 1 tablespoon of chopped sage and the grated rind of 1 orange. Mix well. Stuff the mixture into the pitted dates.

INGREDIENTS TO MAKE ABOUT 30 STUFFED DATES:
½ lb (250 g) dates
¼ lb (100 g) pot cheese
2 to 3 tablespoons (30 to 45 ml) yogurt
2 scallions or small bunch chives
1 tablespoon (15 ml) chopped parsley
1 tablespoon (15 ml) chopped sage
1 orange

Spiced Raisin and Wine Sauce

Raisins cooked in spiced red wine make a delicious sauce to serve with pork and ham.

Put ⅔ cup of seedless raisins into a saucepan with 2 cloves, 1 stick of cinnamon, 1¼ cups of red wine and ⅔ cup of water.

Cover the pan and bring to the boil. Reduce the heat and simmer gently for 10 minutes. Remove the cloves and the cinnamon.

In a small bowl blend 2 teaspoons of cornstarch with 2 tablespoons of brown sugar and 2 tablespoons of lemon juice. Stir the mixture into the sauce. Bring to the boil, stirring constantly. Boil until the sauce thickens then reduce the heat and simmer for 2 minutes.

Serve hot or cold.

INGREDIENTS TO MAKE TWO CUPS (450 ML) OF SAUCE:
⅔ cup (100 g) seedless raisins
2 cloves
1 cinnamon stick
1¼ cups (300 ml) red wine
2 teaspoons (10 ml) cornstarch
2 tablespoons (30 ml) brown sugar
2 tablespoons (30 ml) lemon juice

Devils on Horseback

Prunes stuffed with almonds, wrapped in bacon and broiled can be served as a snack.

Remove the pits from 8 large prunes. Stuff the prunes with 8 blanched almonds.

Stretch 4 slices of bacon with the blade of a knife, then cut them into halves.

Wrap 1 half piece of bacon around each prune and secure with a toothpick.

Broil, turning frequently, for about 5 minutes, or until the bacon is crisp and browned.

Serve hot.

INGREDIENTS TO SERVE FOUR:
8 large prunes
8 blanched almonds
4 slices bacon

MAKING DEVILS ON HORSEBACK

Carefully remove the pits from large prunes.

Fill each prune with a blanched almond.

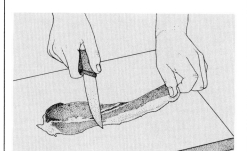
Stretch bacon slices with the back of a knife.

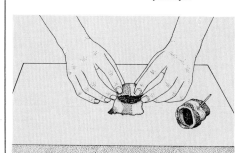
Wrap each prune in a half slice of bacon.

Spinach and Prune Beef Stew

Heat 1 tablespoon of corn oil in a large saucepan. Add 1 chopped large onion and fry for 3 minutes.

Cut any excess fat from 1 pound of chuck roast. Cut the meat into 2-inch (5-cm) cubes. Add the cubes to the pan and fry for 3 minutes, stirring constantly, until they are brown on all sides.

Add 1¼ cups of beef stock, the grated rind and juice of 1 lemon, ¼ teaspoon of grated nutmeg, salt and pepper. Bring to the boil, stirring constantly, then add ¼ pound of pitted prunes. Cover the pan, reduce the heat and simmer gently for 1½ to 2 hours, or until the meat is tender.

Meanwhile, thoroughly wash ½ pound of spinach and drain it well. Coarsely chop the large spinach leaves leaving the small leaves whole. Press the spinach into the pan on top of the beef stew. Cover the pan and cook for 10 minutes more so that the spinach cooks in the steam from the stew.

Stir the spinach into the stew and serve immediately.

INGREDIENTS TO SERVE FOUR:
1 tablespoon (15 ml) corn oil
1 large onion
1 lb (500 g) chuck roast
1¼ cups (300 ml) beef stock
1 lemon
¼ teaspoon (1 ml) grated nutmeg
salt
pepper
¼ lb (100 g) pitted prunes
½ lb (250 g) spinach

Dried Fruit Compote

Put 1 pound of mixed dried fruit into a bowl. (Use dried apricots, prunes, peaches, pears, apples, figs and raisins.)

Pour in 2½ cups of water and add 1 large strip of lemon peel, 1 clove and 1 stick of cinnamon. Soak the fruit overnight.

Transfer the fruit, liquid and spices to a saucepan. Cover and bring to the boil. Reduce the heat and simmer gently for 20 minutes, or until the fruit is tender, adding water if the syrup is absorbed.

Remove the peel, clove and cinnamon. Serve the compote warm or cold.

INGREDIENTS TO SERVE FOUR TO SIX:
1 lb (500 g) mixed dried fruit (dried apricots, peaches, prunes, apples, pears, figs and raisins)
1 large strip lemon peel
1 clove
1 cinnamon stick

Christmas Pudding

Put 2 cups of fresh whole-wheat bread crumbs into a large mixing bowl with 1 cup of whole-wheat flour, 1 teaspoon of baking powder, ⅓ cup of brown sugar, ½ teaspoon of ground allspice, ½ teaspoon of ground ginger, ½ teaspoon of ground cinnamon and ¼ teaspoon of grated nutmeg. Mix well.

Stir in 2 cups of seedless raisins, ⅓ cup of currants, ⅓ cup of chopped mixed candied peel and ½ cup of ground almonds.

Peel and core ½ pound of cooking apples. Coarsely grate the apples into the bowl. Add the grated rind of 1 orange and 1 lemon.

Squeeze the juice from the orange and the lemon into a bowl. Beat in 1 large egg, 2 tablespoons of milk and 2 tablespoons of brandy. Pour into the dry ingredients and mix well.

Spoon the mixture into a 5-cup (850-ml) pyrex bowl or pudding basin which has been lightly greased. The mixture should fill about three-quarters of the bowl.

Cover the bowl with waxed paper or foil, allowing room for the pudding to rise, but sealed at the edges.

Put the bowl into a saucepan half-full of simmering water. Cover the pan and steam the pudding for 4 to 5 hours, adding more water when necessary.

Allow the pudding to cool in the bowl. Cover with new foil or cloth and store in a cool place until needed.

Steam the pudding for 2 hours before serving, then turn out onto a serving plate and serve hot.

INGREDIENTS TO SERVE SIX :
2 cups (100 g) fresh whole-wheat bread crumbs
1 cup (100 g) whole-wheat flour
1 teaspoon (5 ml) baking powder
⅓ cup (50 g) brown sugar
½ teaspoon (2.5 ml) ground allspice
½ teaspoon (2.5 ml) ground ginger
½ teaspoon (2.5 ml) ground cinnamon
¼ teaspoon (1 ml) grated nutmeg
2 cups (250 g) seedless raisins
⅓ cup (50 g) currants
⅓ cup (50 g) chopped mixed candied peel
½ cup (50 g) ground almonds
½ lb (250 g) cooking apples
1 orange
1 lemon
1 large egg
2 tablespoons (30 ml) milk
2 tablespoons (30 ml) brandy

Whole-wheat Apricot Éclairs

Put ¼ pound of dried apricots into a small bowl with 2½ cups of water. Soak the apricots overnight.

Preheat the oven to 425°F (220°C). Grease a large baking sheet.

Make ½ cup plus 2 tablespoons of choux pastry with whole-wheat flour (see page 35). Pipe strips of pastry, about 3 inches (4 cm) long, onto the prepared baking sheet. Bake for 20 minutes. Slit the éclairs, lower the oven temperature to 375°F (190°C) and continue baking for 10 minutes more. Cool the éclairs on a wire rack.

Fill the éclairs with ½ pound of yogurt cheese (see page 100).

Put the apricots and water into a saucepan and bring to the boil. Cover the pan, reduce the heat and simmer for 1 hour, or until the apricots are tender and almost all the water has evaporated. Blend the apricots to a smooth purée. Spread the purée along the tops of the éclairs and let set.

INGREDIENTS TO MAKE TWELVE ECLAIRS :
¼ lb (100 g) dried apricots
½ cup plus 2 tablespoons (75 g) choux pastry (see page 35)
½ lb (250 g) yogurt cheese (see page 100)

FILLING A PIPING BAG

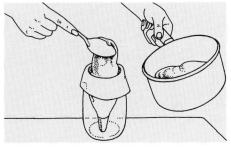

Support the bag in a jar and spoon in the dough.

Winter Salad

Put ⅔ cup of seedless raisins into a salad bowl. Add the juice of 1 large orange. Season with salt and pepper and mix well. Let the raisins soak for at least 30 minutes.

Slice 2 stalks of celery and add to the raisins. Peel, core and chop, or coarsely grate, 1 large sweet apple and add to the salad.

Toss lightly but well to coat all the ingredients in the orange juice. Top with ¼ cup of chopped walnuts and serve.

INGREDIENTS TO SERVE FOUR :
⅔ cup (100 g) raisins
1 large orange
salt
pepper
2 celery stalks
1 large sweet apple
¼ cup (25 g) chopped walnuts

Apricot Soufflé

Put 1 cup of dried apricots into a bowl. Add the grated rind and juice of 1 lemon and 1¼ cups of water. Soak the apricots overnight.

Preheat the oven to 400°F (200°C).

Put the apricots and the soaking liquid into a saucepan, cover and bring to the boil. Reduce the heat and simmer gently for 20 minutes, or until the apricots are tender.

Drain the apricots and reserve the liquid. If necessary add water to make the liquid up to ⅔ cup. Put the apricots and liquid into a blender and blend to a purée.

Sweeten to taste with a little sugar.

Beat 4 egg whites until just stiff and then fold them into the apricot purée.

Pour into a soufflé dish and bake for 20 minutes, or until the soufflé has risen and the top is lightly browned. Serve at once.

INGREDIENTS TO SERVE FOUR TO SIX :
1 cup (150 g) dried apricots
1 lemon
sugar
4 egg whites

Khoshaf

This Middle Eastern fruit salad is made of dried apricots, prunes, raisins and figs which are soaked in scented water for 2 days.

Put ¼ pound of dried apricots, ¼ pound of prunes, ⅔ cup of seedless raisins and ¼ pound of dried figs into a large bowl.

Pour in 1 pint of water and 1 tablespoon of rose water or orange blossom water.

Soak the fruit for at least 2 days, when the syrup will be rich and golden.

Sprinkle with ½ cup of sliced blanched split almonds and ¼ cup of split pistachio nuts before serving.

INGREDIENTS TO SERVE FOUR TO SIX :
¼ lb (100 g) dried apricots
¼ lb (100 g) prunes
⅔ cup (100 g) seedless raisins
¼ lb (100 g) dried figs
1 tablespoon (15 ml) rose water or orange blossom water
½ cup (50 g) sliced blanched split almonds
¼ cup (25 g) split pistachio nuts

HERBS ARE BACK IN FASHION, although sometimes it seems that people are more eager to read about them than actually use them. This is not surprising, in view of all the dire warnings about using herbs with discretion. The proper way to use herbs is with common sense. Start with a little, nothing more than the proverbial pinch, adding more the second time you make the same dish until you find the level that you and your family enjoy. Common sense will tell you when you are spoiling the flavor of the food, and you will then know when to cut down.

Furthermore, as you gain confidence, do not be rigidly bound by someone else's rules about which herbs go with which foods—experiment. You may make a minor mistake, or discover a new and exciting combination of flavors. Parsley sauce, for example, goes with fish and, therefore, it keeps on and on going with fish. But there are fennel, chervil, dill leaves, chives, basil or sage which, used creatively, will go just as well.

The safer herbs, those which give a wide margin of error in the quantities used—are parsley, chives and lemon thyme. Common thyme, sage,

The Nutrients in Herbs
Herbs are not eaten in enough quantity to be a great source of nutrients, but they do contain some valuable vitamins and minerals.

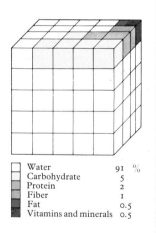

Water	91	%
Carbohydrate	5	
Protein	2	
Fiber	1	
Fat	0.5	
Vitamins and minerals	0.5	

THE USE OF HERBS IN MEDICINE

Herbs have long been used for treating various ailments. The seventeenth-century German illustration below shows a scholarly discussion of their merits. The twelfth-century herbal above recommends, for example, catmint for upset stomachs and *Cynoglossa*, or hound's tooth, for bruises or coughs.

Parsley contains almost as much protein as peas, but is low in carbohydrate. It has a wealth of carotene, vitamin C, iron, potassium and phosphorus. But it also contains apiol, a narcotic substance, which rules it out as a major vegetable. But in small amounts it is a garnish worth eating. Flat-leaved parsley has a stronger flavor than curly-leaved varieties.

Sweet basil is an annual with shiny green, slightly hairy leaves. These have a strong, sweet aroma and a powerful, spicy flavor. Delicious with tomato salads, basil is used in Italy for making the distinctive green sauce called *pesto* that is served with pasta. It can also be used with meat and fish.

Dill is a hardy annual. The leaves taste somewhat like parsley with a hint of orange peel, and the more pungent seeds are like those of caraway. Dill goes well with fish, and dill sauce is eaten with roast meat. The seeds are used in pickling, especially for pickled cucumbers.

Sweet marjoram has the more distinctive flavor, but pot marjoram is a hardier plant. The grayish-green, slightly hairy leaves of sweet marjoram are sweet and spicy, with a hint of nutmeg. Used sparingly, marjoram goes well with pork, poultry and game and enhances sausages and rissoles. In stuffings for veal and poultry it keeps its savor and penetrates the meat, but in soups and stews the flavor tends to get lost.

Common thyme, an evergreen with narrow leaves, has a strong, sweet, clovelike flavor. It can easily dominate other herbs, but it complements thick stews, baked fish and roasts, and is useful in stuffings for poultry and veal. Lemon thyme (bottom left) has wider, lemon-scented leaves and adds flavor to custards.

Sage, a perennial with greyish-green, often furry leaves, has a strong, slightly bitter flavor. In forcemeat it traditionally accompanies pork and duck and it is also used with liver and veal, stews and bean dishes. But try fresh sage with eel, or between the pieces of meat in kebabs, or chopped and sprinkled over a salad.

The mint family contains several subtly different flavors, but the most common is spearmint. Mint sauce, or jelly, is the traditional accompaniment to lamb, and sprigs of mint enhance the flavor not only of peas and new potatoes but also of baby carrots and French beans.

Rosemary, an evergreen with pale flowers, has a fragrant aroma and needlelike green-gray leaves. These contain a volatile oil, comparable to eucalyptus oil, with a powerful flavor. The Italians like rosemary with young lamb and sucking pig. Elsewhere it is widely used in stuffings or in marinades for meat and strong-flavored fish. It can be sprinkled lightly over poultry or other meats before roasting, or over cooked cauliflower and baked potatoes. And it can even be used in a claret cup.

marjoram, garlic, rosemary, bay, tarragon and chervil are strongly flavored. Dried herbs have a more definite flavor than fresh herbs, but the flavor of dried herbs is never the same as that of fresh herbs. If you have a garden it is foolish not to grow some herbs. A window box or indoor pots may also be used. However, you cannot hope to have fresh herbs all year long, and you will have to fall back on dried herbs or, in some instances, frozen herbs, which have even less flavor.

In classic cuisine, bouquet garni, which is used in soups, stews and meat dishes, means three sprigs of parsley, one sprig of thyme and a bay leaf tied together so that they can be removed when the dish is ready to serve. But there is nothing to stop you from adding others—basil, chervil, marjoram, rosemary or tarragon, for example. *Fines herbes* usually means a mixture of parsley, chervil, tarragon and chives and is used for flavoring omelets, chicken, broiled fish and steak. Dried mixed herbs are most likely to be a combination of parsley, thyme, marjoram and savory.

A GUIDE TO HERBS

Your choice of herbs is a matter of personal taste, but as a guide here are some frequently used combinations of foods and herbs.

Lamb: *rosemary, garlic, dill, bay*

Beef: *horseradish, marjoram, thyme, basil*

Veal: *lemon thyme, rosemary, sage*

Pork: *sage, chives, parsley, basil, bay*

Casseroles: *parsley, thyme, chives, garlic, sage, rosemary, bay, dill, marjoram, tarragon*

Poultry: *parsley, thyme, fennel, rosemary, sage, tarragon*

White fish: *parsley, chervil, dill, savory*

Fat fish: *basil, bay, fennel, marjoram, rosemary, tarragon, sage, balm, thyme*

Pasta: *parsley, thyme, mint, garlic, basil*

Salads: *parsley, chives, fennel, garlic, dill, mint*

French or yogurt dressings: *chives, tarragon, chervil, garlic*

Vinegars: *tarragon, garlic, sage, rosemary*

Jellies: *mint, parsley, lemon verbena*

Sour fruits: *sweet cicely, angelica, lemon balm*

INDIAN CURRY SPICES

Indian curries are made with a blend of up to thirty spices including turmeric, cinnamon, cumin, cloves, mace, coriander, chilies, cardamom, ginger, saffron and peppercorns. These spices not only tempt appetites jaded by the heat but also act as a food preservative. Right: spices on sale in Panjim, on the west coast of India.

Some of the wonderful range of spices that add subtle or rich flavors to spicy and sweet dishes. Top row, left to right: cinnamon sticks, aniseed, peppercorns, cloves. Middle row: caraway seeds, coriander seeds and sea salt, not really a spice. Front row: mustard seeds, mace, chili powder. In the foreground, clockwise: sesame seeds (in the scoop), allspice, nutmeg and turmeric powder.

AROMATIC PLANTS ARE THE SOURCE of the spices and herbs that are so important in cooking for their flavor and aroma. The distinction usually made between them is that spices come from the tropics and culinary herbs come from temperate regions. The original home of almost all spices was the Orient. The Western Hemisphere has contributed only three of importance—allspice, chilies and vanilla.

The history of spices in the Far East goes back at least four thousand years. In pre-Christian times the Arabs grew rich by their monopoly of the trade in spices from the East. The Romans broke this monopoly in the first century A.D. when they realized that, with the help of the monsoon winds, they could sail from Egypt to India and back in less than a year, while the Arabs' overland camel route took at least two years.

With the fall of the Roman Empire the spice trade also collapsed. It was revived in the Middle Ages by the Crusaders, who were more effective in introducing their fellow Christians to spices than the infidels to Christianity.

The spices for which the world was explored, wars fought and people enslaved have been used for preserving food, for embalming, as perfumes and as medicines attributed with almost magical qualities, but, above all, they have been used to add flavor to our food. Throughout history and throughout the world pepper has always been, and still is, the most important spice. In the West pepper is closely followed by mustard. Cloves, cinnamon, ginger and nutmeg complete the list of the top six spices.

If possible it is wiser not to buy spices as powder. When ground they lose aroma and flavor more rapidly. Moreover, it is impossible to judge their quality, and spices have a bad record of adulteration. Always try to buy whole peppercorns, nutmegs, allspice and sticks of cinnamon, for example, and grind them yourself.

The nutritional value spices have is almost irrelevant because of the small amounts we eat. Mustard is almost one-third protein and one-third fat, but that still adds up to almost nothing in the smear we put on our food. The preservative qualities of spices are also meaningless in the quantities we usually use in the West, and their medicinal virtues are debatable. But certainly the aroma and flavor of spices do increase the flow of saliva and gastric juices. And by the use of spices, uninteresting but otherwise wholesome food may be made more appetizing.

Salt is not a spice, however indissolubly wedded pepper and salt are in our minds. It is a mineral called sodium chloride, which is obtained by evaporating sea water (sea salt), or by mining the crystalline deposits in the earth (rock salt). Salt may be mixed with ground dehydrated herbs (celery salt, garlic or onion salt, for example) or with spices. Although salt does not, strictly speaking, enhance the flavor of food, many people find that without salt some food tastes flat. Salt, which is an essential part of the diet, exists, however, in many foods without our adding it to them. Spices (excluding allspice and mace) may be used instead of salt to add interest to a salt-restricted diet.

Monosodium glutamate (MSG), a salt of glutamic acid, although almost flavorless itself, does enhance the flavor of food, especially meats, by making our taste buds more sensitive. It has little effect on sweet flavors. It is widely used in Chinese and Japanese cooking, but some people are allergic to it.

The old spice wars between nations are things of the past; the battle is now between the genuine spices and the synthetic flavorings that are taking their place. There are thousands of them, made out of wood pulp, coal tar and a whole gamut of chemicals. They cannot totally achieve the flavor of the natural spice, but they often get near enough to fool us. These are the substances that put the taste of butter into margarine and the vanilla into ice cream. St. Anthony was once the patron saint of the ancient guilds of spicers, pepperers and grocers. Today we have the International Organization of the Flavor Industry.

Yeast, mainly used in baking and brewing, also adds flavor to many spicy dishes. Extremely rich in protein, minerals and such B vitamins as thiamine, niacin and riboflavin, it can be eaten in powdered form—added to drinks or sprinkled on cereals—or as liquid yeast extract. Both fresh and dried baker's yeast is nutritionally inferior but has a valuable role in bread making. Without yeast, bread would be unattractively flat and hard, or "unleavened."

dried baker's yeast

yeast extract

fresh baker's yeast

powdered yeast

SUGARS/The Dangerous Seducers

WHOEVER COINED THE PHRASE "I have a sweet tooth" has a lot to answer for. Those who repeat it seem to regard it as total justification for shoveling sugar into coffee and tea, using it lavishly in cooking and cramming themselves with ice cream, cakes, cookies, candy and chocolates. If there were such a thing as a sweet tooth, and it could be located, the right course would be to have it extracted.

Sweetness is the great seducer and in this context a little seduction should go a long way. But in practice it does not. On average sugar consumption in Britain works out at about two pounds a week for every man, woman and child. In the United States it is minimally less, because Americans are not as addicted to sweets as the British, the world's greatest sweet-eaters.

Those two pounds of sugar provide about 4,000 Calories, or almost 600 Calories a day, and this is between one-quarter and one-sixth of the daily energy requirement of most people. It would not matter if sugar were a balanced food. However, it is the most unbalanced food there is because it provides nothing but energy. For proteins, fats, minerals and vitamins it is necessary to turn to other food and since these also provide energy, if people are also eating sweets they are consuming more calories than they need.

There are, unfortunately, other ways in which sugar plays the villain. It increases the amount of triglycerides in the blood and, therefore, may be associated with coronary heart diseases. It may raise the amount of uric acid in the blood and increase the risk of gout. It encourages dental decay, the metaphorical sweet tooth thus destroying the real ones.

There is certainly a strong case for reducing the amount of sugar in the diet. With comparatively little will power sugar intake can be cut by a third or a half. Like giving up smoking it is difficult and unpleasant to begin with, but before long the palate adjusts and very sweet dishes can even become nauseating. When you reduce the amount of sugar you use, you discover the real flavors of foods, for they are no longer lost under a predominant sugariness. You realize that fruit, for example, suffers if too much sugar is added.

Homemade puddings and other desserts often have more sugar in them than is good for either their flavor or your health. Their sugar content, is, however, under our control, but if we buy processed food we have no say. Food manufacturers are mistakenly liberal in their use of sugar, which is cheap, and they are as likely to add it to soup as to a pudding. The alternative is, of course, wholesome home cooking in which sugar is used sparingly.

Constant consumption of cookies, sugary cakes and candy often has nothing to do with hunger and a lot to do with habit. It is, of course, im-

Dioscoreophyllum berries

Thaumatococcus seeds

MIRACLE FRUITS

Chemists have now discovered some surprising natural alternatives to sugar. Among the most promising are thaumatin and monellin, which are proteins isolated from the African *Thaumatococcus* and *Dioscoreophyllum* berries. Thaumatin is more than four thousand times as sweet as sugar. If these natural, low-calorie sweeteners can be isolated they could provide a satisfactory alternative to sugar.

possible to totally remove sugar from our diet, because it occurs naturally in foods. It is also sensible to use it to make acceptable those foods that would be too sour without it. And it makes wonderful preserves. It is not deprivation that is needed but discrimination.

More nonsense is written about honey than about any other food. In a strict sense it is hardly the "natural" food that health-food devotees revere; it has been elaborately processed by bees. The nectar of flowers, which is mainly sucrose (sugar), is converted by enzymes in the body of the bee into fructose and glucose. Because it does not need further digestion, this "invert" sugar provides instant energy for humans. Honey is 70 to 80 percent invert sugar.

But honey is also the most beautiful of all sweeteners. The flavors, some subtle, some rich, of the seasons may be captured in it: heather, wild rose, clover, lavender, lime, orange blossom, hawthorn. It is worth cutting down on other sugars to be able to spread this delicious food on your bread.

Inevitably, to avoid the excessive use of sugar, synthetic sweeteners have been invented. These have proved as controversial as sugar itself. Saccharin (ortho-sulfobenzimide), an American discovery of the late nineteenth century, is five hundred to six hundred times sweeter than sugar. Its disadvantage is that it leaves a slightly bitter aftertaste. Cyclamate, another American discovery, is only about thirty times as sweet as sugar, but it has no bitter aftertaste. Cyclamates were first used in the United States in 1950 and in Britain in 1964, but after American research showed that in high doses they could produce bladder cancer in rats they were banned in 1969 in the United States and Britain, as well as in several other countries. After similar research with saccharin, the United States has imposed limits on its use, and even proposed a ban. Many people, however, feel that saccharin is less harmful than excessive use of sugar.

Whether white or brown, sugar is just sucrose. Brown sugar boasts slightly more minerals than white, but both contain virtually nothing except calories (about 400 Calories in one hundred grams). Syrup—a thick solution of partially refined sugar—has fewer calories (300 Calories in one hundred grams) simply because it contains more water; molasses, with 230 Calories in one hundred grams, is even more dilute. However, you will not save calories by using syrup instead of sugar because syrup tastes less sweet and you will probably use more. The exception is honey which, calorie for calorie, is sweeter than sucrose and contains detectable amounts of essential fatty acids, minerals and vitamin C. Left, clockwise: a honeycomb, coarse-grained brown sugar, granulated sugar, unrefined brown sugar and fine-grained brown sugar. In the center: molasses (unrefined sugar syrup).

FATS/Only in Moderation

THE REASONS why we should limit the amount of sugar we eat are simple, but the reasons why we should cut down on fat are more complicated.

The difference between fats may be described in several ways. They may be animal or vegetable. They may be visible, like butter or the fat on a chop, or invisible, as is the considerable amount in nuts or the trace in most vegetables. They may be described as fats or oils according to whether they are solid or liquid at room temperature.

The distinction increasingly made in recent years, however, is between polyunsaturated fats, which have gained the reputation of "goodies," and saturated fats, which are the "baddies." As it happens most animal fats are high in saturated fatty acids and most vegetable fats are higher in polyunsaturated acids. Consequently, animal fats have been dubbed bad and most vegetable fats have been extolled.

The current preoccupation with fats in the diet is the result of the fearful increase in deaths, in the past twenty-five years in many parts of the West, from what is loosely called heart disease. Many causes have been suggested, among them smoking, obesity, high blood pressure, lack of exercise, heredity, stress and diet. In the diet the main villains are considered to be an excess of sugar or of fats, especially of saturated fats, or a combination of both.

The so-called experts often disagree about the most important causal factor, but there is evidence that heart attacks are associated with a high level of blood fats—triglycerides and cholesterol—and the accumulation of fat on the inner walls of the arteries. Saturated fats—the solid fats—increase the level of cholesterol and triglycerides in the blood and lead to deposits in the arteries. Polyunsaturated fats—the soft fats or oils of fish and vegetables—cause blood cholesterol to fall. Hence the advice to eat fewer saturated fats and increase the proportion of polyunsaturated fats.

It is impossible to eat only fat that is completely unsaturated—because all fat includes both saturated and unsaturated fatty acids, and it is the proportions of each that vary. Although the more unsaturated the fat the lower its calorific value, both types of fat are high in calories, so you can

Corn oil has about 40 percent of linoleic acid which makes it 60 percent saturated. In the polyunsaturate league it trails well behind the more polyunsaturated sunflower oil and safflower oil, both of which have more than 60 percent linoleic acid.

Peanut oil, with only 30 percent linoleic acid, is well down in the vegetable oil league for polyunsaturation. Unlike such oils as safflower oil it has its own definite taste which it imparts to the food cooked in it. It is used in Chinese cooking.

Soybean oil is not only a good polyunsaturated oil with about 60 percent linoleic acid, but it is relatively cheap because of the high productivity and fat content of the soybean. It is the third most favorable oil in terms of polyunsaturation.

Coconut oil is the villain of vegetable oils, with only 2 percent linoleic acid. Although it is a saturated fat it is liquid because the saturated fatty acids are in shorter chains than in other oils. It is especially likely to cause heart disease.

Olive oil, with about 10 percent linoleic acid, is mostly rich in monounsaturated fatty acids which do not contribute to heart disease. Its popularity as an ingredient in salad dressing is rivaled by the equally palatable safflower seed oil.

put on weight if you eat too much of either. The widely quoted recommendations of the American Heart Association to people with a high level of blood fats are that the total amount of fat in the diet should not account for more than 35 percent of an individual's energy intake, and that the saturated fats should be less than 10 percent.

The most delicious of all fats is an animal fat—butter. It accounts for about a quarter of the world's fat consumption. Americans, however, have made a remarkable switch in the last twenty-five years. From eating almost twice as much butter as margarine they are now eating more than twice as much margarine as butter. Such is the effect of all the publicity about heart disease.

For people in good health the flavor of butter is something not to be willingly sacrificed. Once again a compromise is necessary; polyunsaturated types of margarine can be used for cooking, and the butter used at the table can be offset by cutting down on more expendable saturated fats.

Butter is an ancient food, but margarine is little more than a century old. It was invented by a French chemist's assistant, Hippolyte Mège Mouriès, and consisted largely of beef suet, under the mistaken belief that this was the basis of cow's milk. Only after the process of hydrogenation had been discovered early in the twentieth century was it possible to harden almost any oil to produce a substance with the consistency of butter. But hydrogenation produces a saturated margarine, and it was not until the 1960s that soft margarine, which has a fair proportion of poly-unsaturated fat, was invented. There is no point in changing from butter to hard margarine. And even in the soft margarines the proportion of saturated fats ranges from slightly less than 60 percent to 80 percent.

Fat accounts for much of the flavor in meat, but most people now prefer their meat lean, and animals are bred that way. Even the amount of marbling in the meat of intensively reared animals has decreased since the 1960s. The leanest meat, with the highest proportion of polyunsaturated fat, is, however, from "free-range" animals.

Vegetable oils can certainly be used for cooking, but some oils are considered more virtuous than others. They can be rated according to their richness in linoleic acid, a polyunsaturated fatty acid that cannot be synthesized in the body, and must therefore be absorbed from the food we eat.

Safflower oil, bland and almost without odor, has, for example, between 70 and 80 percent of linoleic acid. But although production is increasing it is not yet one of the major oils. Olive oil has only about 15 percent of the polyunsaturated linoleic acid. Coconut oil is a vegetable oil to avoid; although vegetable and liquid it is heavily saturated, with only a miserable 2 percent of linoleic acid.

SOFT MARGARINES—WATCH THE LABEL!

Margarine was originally made of hardened vegetable oils, but with the evidence linking polyunsaturation to heart disease manufacturers started making some margarines only from unhardened, unsaturated oils. These are the more healthy polyunsaturated margarines that remain soft at refrigerator temperature. There are, however, ways of making soft, but more saturated, margarines, such as mixing hard margarine and water ("low calorie spreads") or by chemically adjusting hard margarines. Polyunsaturated margarine is always labeled as such.

Animal fats vary in their degree of saturation. Fish oils are as healthy as vegetable oils, but butter (above left) is about 95 percent saturated and beef dripping, or unprocessed lard (above right) averages about 90 percent. Unfortunately, manufacturers harden lard to make totally saturated, rock-hard suets (bottom).

HAMLET was thoroughly wide of the mark when he complained of his "too, too solid flesh." He was, like the rest of us are, at least two-thirds, and maybe three-quarters, water. It is much the same with our food. With few exceptions much of it, or most of it, is drink.

Deprived of water for only a few days, a human being dies. Without food most people could survive for several weeks. The functioning of the body depends on water, both within the cells and outside them. The fluid within the cells accounts for most of the water in the body, up to fifty-two pints (30 liters). Another seventeen pints (10 liters) surround the cells. In the blood plasma there are three and a half pints (2 liters). The total amount of body water is, therefore, more than seventy-two pints (42 liters).

The level of water within the body remains remarkably constant. It is lost through the breath and in urine and sweat. It is replaced by the liquids that we drink when we are thirsty, by the water in our food and the water formed during digestion. This may total more than five pints (3 liters) a day. For no apparent reason some people drink more than others. Some drink more because they sweat more and everyone drinks more in hot weather.

Natural thirst is a fairly reliable indicator of the amount of water we need, but it tends to be over-ruled when it comes to sweet or alcoholic drinks. The kidneys very efficiently rid the body of any excess fluid, along with sodium and other minerals, but they cannot prevent the obesity created by too many carbohydrate-rich drinks.

Except in certain rare diseases water is not responsible for overweight; fat is the cause. Restricting intake of water will not make people thin. On the other hand, cutting down on liquor, beer, wine and sweet soft drinks will certainly help.

According to its source water acquires different characteristics and flavors. Rain is contaminated as it falls through an atmosphere polluted by industry. If the gathering grounds for reservoirs are peaty the water will be soft and acid (and soft water is now being suggested as yet another predisposing factor in heart disease). If the water has run through limestone country it will be hard and alkaline, providing a source of calcium for the body. Other minerals become dissolved in it as it passes through the soil. The most common are sodium chloride and carbonates of sodium, calcium and magnesium. A little of such minerals add to the palatability of water, but some waters taste more like medicine, and they are either drunk as such or bathed in.

The sparkle in mineral waters is caused by the presence of carbon dioxide. It can also be created artificially by impregnating ordinary water with carbon dioxide. The natural mineral waters are superior because although they are less fizzy to

begin with, they will retain their fizziness longer.

The addition of one mineral—fluoride—to ordinary drinking water is the cause of endless controversy. Fluoride is being added to water supplies in many parts of the world in order to arrest tooth decay. Those opposed to fluoridation argue that it is not as effective as claimed, may be harmful and in any event enforced medication is an infringement of personal liberty.

Fluoride is found naturally in our bones and teeth. Adding more to a diet low in fluoride reduces tooth decay in the very young, far less in those children who are ten years old and over and very little in adults. Beyond a certain concentration in the body fluoride can produce unsightly mottling of the teeth.

Water is one of our most essential foods. Impure water can start deadly epidemics, but the only water that is totally pure—distilled water—is undrinkably boring. The piped water of the Western World is quite safe to drink, however, after it has been carefully filtered and chlorinated. Chlorine is added to water to kill germs, and then as much as possible is extracted to remove the unpleasant taste.

Spas became fashionable in the eighteenth and nineteenth centuries. The waters at the English spa town of Bath, illustrated in this eighteenth-century cartoon "Comforts of Bath" (inset left) by the satirist John Rowlandson, had a clear, bitter taste and was recommended for the cure of gout. While there is scant scientific evidence to support the medicinal value of spa waters, drinking calorie-free water is surely a beneficial alternative to drinking wine with its attendant dangers of obesity.

MINERAL WATERS

All water except distilled water contains some minerals and without them it is unpalatable. Some mineral water, such as that near Biarritz (left), is protected for local consumption. Bottled mineral waters are drunk by people who distrust the local water supply, or who drink them to help their digestion. These mineral waters vary considerably in taste. The popular French Vichy water, for example, contains about forty minerals, especially sodium bicarbonate, and has a markedly salty taste. In contrast, English Malvern water is very pure and absolutely tasteless. Evian, from France, is also neutral and a good companion to wine.

Most foods contain only minute amounts of fluoride; water in some areas has scarcely any, but at the other extreme there may be fourteen parts of fluoride in a million parts of water. Adding fluoride to drinking water to ensure that there is one part per million of fluoride in the water would roughly double the average intake of fluoride without in general making it excessive.

Tea contains an unusually large amount of fluoride and several cups of strong tea a day would probably provide adequate amounts in the diet. But such avid tea drinkers are unlikely to be of the age when it will benefit their teeth. The alternative to fluoridation, of course, is to avoid the sugar that is responsible for tooth decay in the first place.

STIMULATION WITHOUT INEBRIATION is the quality that coffee and tea have in common. The mild stimulants that are responsible, and that also stir up a certain amount of controversy, are theophylline and caffeine. Most people enjoy their effect, others complain of all kinds of side effects, particularly insomnia. These drinks are, therefore, best avoided on medical grounds by certain people (those with peptic ulcers, for example), but in general they are pleasantly harmless.

Coffee contains the greatest amount of caffeine, which stimulates the brain. Tea may have only half as much caffeine, but it is richer in theophylline, which increases the heart rate and acts as a diuretic. However, we absorb so little of the stimulants in coffee or tea that we would have to drink a great deal, or be unusually sensitive, to be upset by them. Coffee can be bought, at an even higher price, decaffeinated, but that seems rather like dealcoholizing beer.

Cocoa has gained the reputation of being a more innocuous drink than coffee or tea. It does, however, contain mild stimulants, but unlike tea and coffee it does not keep you awake because the body does not absorb them. There is, however, no substance in cocoa (except, perhaps, the added milk) to send you to sleep.

Coffee is like the famous little girl who had a little curl: "When she was good she was very, very good, but when she was bad she was horrid." There is no point wasting time making horrid coffee when with a little more care it can be made to perfection. The steps to success are to buy good fresh coffee beans, roasted to the degree you

want, to grind them as you need them and to brew the coffee with care.

There are more than a hundred types of coffee beans, but they are usually sold blended. There is also a bewildering range of roasts, from those that are light and thin-tasting, to the darkest Italian or espresso. Experiment until you get the combination you most enjoy.

Roasted beans will remain reasonably fresh if they are kept in a tightly sealed jar in the refrigerator. They will keep fresh for two or three months in sealed jars in a freezer, but to avoid waste use several small jars and not one large one because once removed from the freezer the beans are likely to go moldy if they are put back again. They can, however, be stored in the refrigerator. Once a can of vacuum-packed ground coffee has been opened even if it is stored in the refrigerator the flavor is lost in little more than a week.

HERBAL TEAS, OR TISANES

Infusions made from fresh or dried herbs have long been attributed with health-giving properties and are particularly good for the digestion. Providing a vast range of interesting flavors, herbal teas, for example mint, lavender and camomile, should be left to infuse for about six minutes and then served without milk, although they may be flavored with a thin slice of lemon or orange.

Camomile tea, recommended for soothing the nerves, has a slightly bitter tang.

Peppermint leaves make a very refreshing tea that is said to relieve indigestion.

Lemon verbena tea is tasty and fragrant. It is excellent after a heavy, rich meal.

Rose petals are used to make a pleasantly sweet tisane that is said to relieve headaches.

Lavender makes a highly aromatic infusion that is recommended as a tonic.

powder was made may have contained 30 percent more soluble solids than the optimum. In some processing all the aroma vanishes but is put back artificially so that for a short time after the jar is opened there is at least a smell of coffee.

It is easier to make a good cup of tea than good coffee, as long as you buy good tea in the first place. While many British people reject instant tea, more than a third of the tea drunk in the United States is instant. Excellent tea can be made with tea bags if the tea in them is excellent. But most mass-marketed tea bags are filled with blends that vary between nondescript and vicious. It is safer to use loose tea.

There are three main kinds of loose tea: black tea has been fermented, green tea has not and oolong tea is halfway between the two. Such names as Pekoe, Orange Pekoe, Broken Orange Pekoe and Souchong given to black teas indicate only leaf sizes and not flavor. The pungent un-blended Indian teas are likely to be from Assam and Darjeeling. Ceylon teas are gentler; they sometimes form the base of the famous Earl Grey tea, which is scented with bergamot.

To make good tea, first warm the teapot by rinsing it with boiling water and then put in one teaspoon (or tea bag) for every cup of tea you need. Pour boiling water on the tea and let it stand for three to five minutes: the smaller the leaf the shorter the infusion time. As the tea stands, caffeine and flavor are dissolved; left longer the tannin will build up and make the tea bitter. If you want a second cup that is as good as the first, brew another pot of tea.

Coffee and tea make refreshing and stimulating drinks and are a rich source of niacin. They also contain some riboflavin and thiamine. Without milk or sugar they have no Calories. From left to right: a box of Ceylon tea, a bag of coffee beans, a caddy of Jasmine tea and, in the grinder, roasted coffee beans.

The fineness of the grind depends on how the coffee is to be brewed. There are many types of coffee pots, but basically there are only two methods of brewing; decoction, in which the coffee is boiled in the water, and infusion, in which the boiling water is poured onto the coffee, which is allowed to steep.

The purpose of brewing is to dissolve the soluble solids in the beans. Those which give coffee its pleasant flavor and aroma are the first to be dissolved. The coffee that is most generally acceptable contains not more than 20 percent of these dissolvable solids, and extraction beyond that makes the coffee bitter.

In the presence of lovingly prepared coffee it is almost blasphemous to mention instant coffee. It has nothing to recommend it except convenience. In the first place instant coffee is not made from the best beans and the brew from which the

To make cocoa powder, cocoa beans (left) are fermented under palm leaves (above) before being dried, roasted and ground. Although some of the calorific cocoa butter fat is removed during this process, the amount of powder used to make one cup of cocoa contains up to 50 Calories. As many as 200 extra Calories may be provided by the sugar and milk that are added to the powder.

Spiced Tea

Tea flavored with spices, orange and lemon makes a refreshing hot or cold drink.

Put 2 tablespoons of tea leaves into a tea pot.

Pour 5 cups of water into a saucepan. Add the juice of 1 large orange and 1 large lemon, 1 cinnamon stick and 2 cloves. Bring to the boil and then pour onto the tea leaves.

Let stand for 3 to 5 minutes, then serve hot with slices of orange and lemon.

To serve cold, strain the tea into a pitcher when it has cooled. Chill before serving. Pour into glasses filled with ice cubes and decorate with orange and lemon slices.

INGREDIENTS TO SERVE SIX:
2 tablespoons (30 ml) tea leaves
2 large oranges
2 large lemons
1 cinnamon stick
2 cloves

Mint Tisane

Coarsely chop 8 large sprigs of mint, including the stalks. Put the mint into a pitcher or a bowl.

Pour in 2½ cups of boiling water. Cover and let stand for 3 minutes.

Strain out the mint leaves and serve hot.

INGREDIENTS TO MAKE 1 PINT (600 ML):
8 large mint sprigs
2½ cups (600 ml) boiling water

MAKING HERBAL TISANES

Pour boiling water over the chopped herbs.

Let stand, then strain before serving.

Irish Fruit Cake

Dried fruit that has been soaked in cold tea gives this traditional Irish fruit cake its moist texture.

Put 2 cups of mixed dried fruit into a large bowl and pour 1¼ cups of cold strong tea over it. Soak the fruit for at least 12 hours.

Preheat the oven to 350°F (180°C). Grease a 7-inch (18-cm) square cake pan and line it with waxed paper.

In a large mixing bowl beat ⅓ cup of brown sugar and 1 egg together. Stir 2 cups of self-rising flour into the egg and sugar mixture. Add the drained fruit and mix well.

Spoon the mixture into the prepared cake pan. Bake the cake for 1¼ to 1½ hours, or until it is brown and firm to the touch. Remove the cake from the oven and turn it out of the pan onto a wire rack to cool.

INGREDIENTS TO MAKE ONE SEVEN-INCH (18-CM) CAKE:
2 cups (500 g) mixed dried fruit
1¼ cups (300 ml) cold strong tea
⅓ cup (50 g) brown sugar
1 egg
2 cups (250 g) self-rising flour

Chocolate and Ginger Custard

Preheat the oven to 350°F (180°C).

Put ¼ pound of semisweet chocolate into the top of a double-boiler over boiling water. Stir occasionally until the chocolate has melted, then remove from the heat.

In a small saucepan heat 1¼ cups of milk to lukewarm.

Beat 2 eggs. Stir the eggs into the melted chocolate with 1 tablespoon of brown sugar and the warm milk. Mix well.

Finely chop 2 pieces of preserved ginger and stir it into the chocolate custard.

Spoon into 4 small ovenproof dishes. Put the dishes into a baking pan and pour in hot water to come halfway up the sides of the dishes.

Bake for 35 to 40 minutes, or until the custards are set.

Serve chilled.

INGREDIENTS TO SERVE FOUR:
¼ lb (100 g) semisweet chocolate
2 eggs
1 tablespoon (15 ml) brown sugar
1¼ cups (300 ml) milk
2 pieces preserved ginger

Chocolate and Orange Mousse

If you cannot resist chocolate mousse, then try this one which is made without cream, butter or egg yolks. It should be prepared several hours in advance, but if it is made the day before it is served, a little of the egg white may separate out.

Put 6 ounces of semisweet chocolate and the grated rind and juice of 1 orange into the top of a double-boiler over boiling water. Stir until the chocolate has melted.

Remove from the heat and stir in 1 tablespoon of brandy. Let the mixture cool and thicken slightly.

Beat 4 egg whites until stiff, then carefully fold them into the chocolate mixture.

Spoon the mousse into 4 small serving dishes. Refrigerate for at least 2 hours before serving.

INGREDIENTS TO SERVE FOUR:
6 oz (150 g) semisweet chocolate
1 orange
1 tablespoon (15 ml) brandy
4 egg whites

Chocolate Cake

This rich moist cake may be served plain or cut in half and filled with mashed strawberries, bananas or pears. Decorate the top with sliced fruit.

Preheat the oven to 350°F (180°C).

In a large mixing bowl cream ½ cup of margarine with ⅔ cup of dark brown sugar.

Separate 2 eggs and add the yolks to the creamed mixture. Stir in ⅓ cup of ground almonds and beat well.

Dissolve 2 tablespoons of unsweetened cocoa in 4 tablespoons of boiling water and mix until smooth. Add to the creamed mixture and beat well.

Fold in 1 teaspoon of baking powder mixed with 1 cup of whole-wheat flour.

Beat the 2 egg whites until stiff and then fold into the cake mixture.

Transfer to a 7- or 8-inch (18- or 20-cm) round cake pan.

Bake for 30 minutes, or until the cake has risen and is just firm to touch.

INGREDIENTS TO MAKE ONE SEVEN-INCH (18-CM) CAKE:
½ cup (100 g) margarine
⅔ cup (100 g) dark brown sugar
2 eggs
⅓ cup (50 g) ground almonds
2 tablespoons (30 ml) unsweetened cocoa
1 teaspoon (5 ml) baking powder
1 cup (100 g) whole-wheat flour

Mocha Raspberry Roulade

Preheat the oven to 375°F (190°C). Line a 9- by 13-inch (22- by 32-cm) baking sheet with a raised rim with waxed paper and brush lightly with oil.

Put ¼ pound of semisweet chocolate and 2 tablespoons of strong black coffee into the top of a double-boiler over boiling water. Stir occasionally until the chocolate has melted.

Separate 4 eggs. Add ⅔ cup of brown sugar to the egg yolks and beat well. Beat in the melted chocolate. Stir in ⅓ cup of ground almonds.

Beat the egg whites until stiff. Beat 2 tablespoons into the chocolate mixture, then fold in the rest.

Spoon the chocolate mixture into the prepared pan. Level the surface.

Bake for 15 minutes, or until the roulade has risen and is just firm to the touch.

Cover the roulade with a clean dampened dish towel to prevent a crust from forming. Set aside until cold.

Lightly sprinkle a large sheet of waxed paper with powdered sugar. Turn the roulade out onto the paper. Peel off the baking paper.

Scatter ½ pound of raspberries over the roulade. Roll it up like a jelly roll by lifting up the waxed paper from one end so that the roulade falls into a roll. Chill for at least 1 hour before serving.

INGREDIENTS TO SERVE SIX:
¼ lb (100 g) semisweet chocolate
2 tablespoons (30 ml) strong black coffee
4 eggs
⅔ cup (100 g) brown sugar
⅓ cup (50 g) ground almonds
powdered sugar
½ lb (250 g) raspberries

Frozen Coffee and Almond Yogurt

Pour 1¼ cups of yogurt into a mixing bowl. Stir in 2 tablespoons of very strong black coffee and 2 tablespoons of dark brown sugar.

Beat 2 egg whites until stiff, then fold into the coffee yogurt with ⅓ cup of toasted sliced almonds.

Pour into 4 individual dishes and freeze until firm.

Put the dishes into the refrigerator for 30 minutes before serving.

INGREDIENTS TO SERVE FOUR:
1¼ cups (300 ml) yogurt
2 tablespoons (30 ml) very strong black coffee
2 tablespoons (30 ml) dark brown sugar
2 egg whites
⅓ cup (50 g) toasted sliced almonds

Coffee Bavarois Ring

Pour 2 scant cups of milk into a saucepan. Add 2 tablespoons of medium ground coffee and bring to the boil. Remove the pan from the heat and stir well. Set aside for 15 minutes.

Separate 2 eggs. Add 2 tablespoons of brown sugar to the egg yolks and beat well. Strain in the milk and stir until well blended.

Pour the custard mixture into a saucepan and cook over low heat, stirring constantly, until it thickens slightly. Do not let it boil or the eggs may curdle.

In a cup set in a pan of hot water dissolve 1½ tablespoons of powdered gelatin in 2 tablespoons of water. Stir the gelatin into the custard.

Let cool, stirring occasionally, until the custard thickens and begins to set.

Beat the 2 egg whites until stiff and then fold into the coffee custard.

Pour into a 1-quart (850 ml) ring mold or tube pan and refrigerate for at least 2 hours before serving.

To serve, loosen the edges of the mold with a knife, then dip the mold into hot water for a few seconds and immediately invert onto a plate and remove the mold.

INGREDIENTS TO SERVE FOUR TO SIX:
2 scant cups (450 ml) milk
2 tablespoons (30 ml) medium ground coffee
2 eggs
2 tablespoons (30 ml) brown sugar
1½ tablespoons (15 g) powdered gelatin

Irish Coffee Ice

This is an unusual dessert. Brandy may be substituted for Irish whiskey.

Put ½ cup of medium ground coffee into a saucepan. Pour in 2½ cups of water and bring to the boil. Remove the pan from the heat and let stand for 15 minutes.

Strain the coffee into a bowl. Stir in ⅔ cup of brown sugar and 2 tablespoons of Irish whiskey. Put the bowl into the freezer until the ice is almost frozen.

Whip 2 egg whites until stiff. Beat the coffee mixture and then fold in the egg whites.

Pour the ice into a rigid container and return to the freezer until it is solid. Cover, seal, label and store in the freezer until needed.

INGREDIENTS TO SERVE FOUR:
½ cup (50 g) medium ground coffee
⅔ cup (100 g) brown sugar
2 tablespoons (30 ml) Irish whiskey
2 egg whites

Coffee Swiss Roll

Preheat the oven to 425°F (210°C).

Line a 9- by 12-inch (22- by 30-cm) jelly-roll pan with waxed paper and brush lightly with oil.

Break 3 eggs into the top of a double-boiler. Stir in ½ cup of brown sugar. Beat over simmering water until the mixture is thick and pale colored. (Alternatively, beat with an electric mixer.) Add 1 tablespoon of freeze-dried coffee dissolved in 1 tablespoon of hot water and beat until well blended. Carefully fold in ¾ cup of whole-wheat flour.

Spoon the cake mixture into the prepared pan and level the surface.

Bake for 10 minutes, or until the cake is well risen, golden brown and springy to the touch.

Lightly sprinkle a large sheet of waxed paper with powdered sugar. Turn the cake out onto the paper. Peel off the baking paper. Trim off the crusty edges of the cake on the long sides so that it will roll up easily.

Put a sheet of waxed paper on top and, with the paper inside, roll the cake up loosely, lifting up the bottom piece of paper so that it falls into a roll.

For the filling make ⅔ cup of confectioner's custard (see page 93) and beat in 1 teaspoon of freeze-dried coffee dissolved in 1 teaspoon of hot water.

When the cake is cold unroll it and remove the paper. Spread with the filling and roll up again.

INGREDIENTS TO SERVE SIX TO EIGHT:
3 eggs
½ cup (75 g) brown sugar
1 tablespoon plus 1 teaspoon (20 ml) freeze-dried coffee
¾ cup (75 g) whole-wheat flour
powdered sugar
⅔ cup (150 ml) confectioner's custard (see page 93)

PREPARING SWISS ROLL

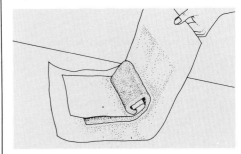

Roll up Swiss roll with paper inside, let it cool.

IT WAS INEVITABLE that alcohol should be discovered, since fermentation, in which alcohol is produced through the reaction of sugar and yeasts in the presence of moisture, is a fundamental natural process.

The grape is a do-it-yourself wine maker, for it has both the necessary sugar and the natural yeasts. To make wines from other fruits and to make beer from grains, either sugar or yeast, or both, have to be added. Natural fermentation continues until the level of alcohol reaches 14 to 15 percent, then the yeast stops working. To reach a higher level of alcohol, distillation is needed and the more potent product is drunk as liquor, or added to some wines to make them stronger. These so-called fortified wines, which include port, sherry and vermouths such as Martini, Cinzano and Noilly Prat, Dubonnet and Campari, have an alcohol content of 15 percent. Ordinary table wines usually have no more than 10 or 11 percent alcohol. Beers range from 2.5 to 6 percent and liquor is 30 to 40 percent alcohol.

Alcoholic drinks are high in calories. Pure alcohol provides about 160 Calories per fluid ounce. One fluid ounce (30 ml) of wine provides about 20 Calories; one fluid ounce of fortified wine between 35 and 45 Calories and one fluid ounce of 70 degree proof liquor about 70 Calories. This is one reason why you should keep a sharp watch on how much you drink: from the point of view of obesity alcohol is even more dangerous than sugar. But beer and wines, unlike sugar, do contain some minerals and vitamins. Liquor has no vitamins and very few minerals. Depending to any degree on alcoholic drinks for energy throws a diet entirely out of balance. This is quite apart from the more obvious disadvantage of hangovers, and the possible psychological and physical disasters of alcoholism. As with eating, so with drinking—the fault is in the excess.

On the other hand, drinking in moderation, especially at meals, is enjoyable. And because it depresses the centers of anxiety in the brain it can be an aid to relaxation.

There is, too, everything to be said for using beer and wine in cooking, for while all the alcohol will evaporate delicious flavors will be left behind. Beer and cider add a rich flavor to stews and make good marinades. Wine does not add its own flavor to food, but rather makes the dish richer. Liquor is less often used in cooking. Brandy, however, provides flavor and, in flambéing, an opportunity for the exhibitionist to perform.

Pinot Noir grapes (right) are carried in willow baskets to the presses to make champagne. The juice of these dusky skinned grapes, which are grown near Rheims, is white.

WINE

Wine can be made from the fermented juice of any fruit. The grape, however, is unique in producing within it the sugar and, on its skin, the natural yeasts needed for fermentation. Crushing grapes begins the process. White wine can be made from white grapes, black grapes or a mixture of both, since only the almost colorless juice is fermented. To make red wine, both the skins and juice are present during fermentation. Rosé wine is made either by leaving some skins with the juice or by adding a red wine to a white one. To produce a sparkling wine, such as champagne, the wine is bottled before fermentation is finished and natural carbon dioxide is still being produced. Fortified wines have brandy or pure alcohol added. To make port, brandy is added to stop the fermenting process; to make sherry, pure alcohol is added afterwards.

One fluid ounce of wine provides about 20 Calories, one fluid ounce of sherry about 35 Calories and one fluid ounce of port provides about 45 Calories.

LIQUOR

Most liquor is distilled from the alcohol made from grains, grapes and sugar cane and its products. The fermented brew is heated in a still to separate the alcohol from the water. Above 173°F (78.3°C) but below 212°F (100°C) the alcohol becomes a vapor, but the water does not boil. The alcohol vapor is collected and cooled back into a liquid.

The malt whiskeys of Scotland are made entirely from malted barley and are matured in wooden casks, sometimes for more than fifteen years. Blended Scotch whiskey, which includes other unmalted grains, must by law be matured for three years, but in practice five years is often the minimum. Irish whiskey is made from a mixture of barley, wheat, rye and oats, and is matured for at least seven years. Bourbon (above) must include at least 51 percent corn in its mash; other components are barley and rye, and it is aged for at least four years. Rye whiskey must be made from at least a 51 percent rye base. Gin is a highly refined liquor, slightly flavored with such spices as juniper, coriander or cassia. It needs no maturing.

Vodka can be made from potatoes, but wheat or rye are usually used.

Rum is distilled from fermented molasses. Most comes from the Caribbean: light rums from Cuba, dark, heavy-bodied rums from Jamaica and aromatic rums from Barbados, Puerto Rico and Martinique.

One fluid ounce of 70 proof liquor provides about 70 Calories; 90 proof more than 100 Calories.

LIQUEURS AND APERITIFS

By distilling wine, brandy is obtained. Although French brandies such as Cognac and Armagnac are the most famous, there are many others. More brandy is, in fact, distilled in California than in France. Brandies are made from fruits other than grapes. Normandy's Calvados and American applejack are made from apples, Yugoslav slivovitz from plums and German kirsch from cherries.

Most liqueurs are made from sweetened and flavored brandy. Bénédictine and Chartreuse, both devised by monks, are cognacs flavored with secret mixtures of innumerable herbs. Green Chartreuse is stronger; yellow is sweeter. Crème de menthe is flavored with peppermint, Kummel with caraway seeds, and Curaçao, Cointreau (above) and Grand Marnier with orange peel. Other fruit-flavored liqueurs are apricot brandy and cherry brandy. Drambuie, however, is based not on brandy but on Scotch whiskey flavored with honey and herbs.

One fluid ounce of liqueur provides approximately 70 Calories.

Of the popular apéritifs, vermouths, such as Martini, Cinzano and Noilly Prat, are made from a mixture of wine, grape spirit and herbs; Dubonnet is a sweetened fortified wine flavored with quinine and bittersweet Campari is more heavily fortified and flavored with herbs.

One fluid ounce of dry vermouth provides about 33 Calories.

BEER

Most beer is made from barley, hops, sugar, yeast and water. The barley is first soaked in water, allowed to germinate and then dried. The result is malt. This is then milled, made into a mash with water and cooked until the malt is further broken down into its component sugars. The liquid, called wort, is run off and boiled with hops. When it cools, yeast is added to cause fermentation, which converts the sugars into alcohol and carbon dioxide. Most beers are then pasteurized.

Two types of fermentation are used in beer making. British beers, or ales, are made by top fermentation —the spent yeast rises to the top of the brew—and the beer is drunk fresh. American beer, or lager, is made by bottom fermentation—the spent yeast sinks to the bottom— and the beer is refrigerated for several weeks or even months to mellow it. Differences of flavor in beer are determined by the proportions of malt and hops—the more hops the more bitter the brew. And beer varies in color according to the temperatures used in malting the barley. The amount of froth depends on how much carbon dioxide has been put into it.

Twelve fluid ounces of beer provide between 100 and 250 Calories depending on its strength.

Coq au Vin

Preheat the oven to 350°F (180°C).

Cut a 2½-pound chicken into 8 pieces. Chop 8 slices of bacon. Peel ½ pound of small white onions.

Heat 1 tablespoon of corn oil in a large saucepan and fry the bacon over low heat until the fat runs. Add the chicken pieces and fry quickly to brown lightly on all sides. Using a slotted spoon remove the chicken from the pan and put it into a casserole.

Add the onions to the pan and fry until lightly browned. Add 1 crushed garlic clove and cook for 1 minute more.

Stir in 1 tablespoon of flour. Stirring constantly, gradually add 1¼ cups of dry red wine and ⅔ cup of chicken stock. Bring to the boil. Season with salt, pepper and a little grated nutmeg.

Pour the wine sauce over the chicken. Add a bouquet garni, consisting of 1 bay leaf and sprigs of parsley and thyme.

Cover the casserole and bake for 45 minutes, or until the chicken is tender.

Stir in 1 cup of small mushrooms and bake for 10 to 15 minutes more, or until the mushrooms are cooked.

Remove the bouquet garni and serve sprinkled with 2 tablespoons of chopped parsley.

INGREDIENTS TO SERVE FOUR:
2½-lb (1.20-kg) chicken
8 slices (100 g) bacon
½ lb (100 g) small white onions
1 tablespoon (15 ml) corn oil
1 garlic clove
1 tablespoon (15 ml) flour
1¼ cups (300 ml) dry red wine
⅔ cup (150 ml) chicken stock
salt
pepper
grated nutmeg
1 bouquet garni, consisting of 1 bay leaf
  and parsley and thyme sprigs
1 cup (100 g) small mushrooms
2 tablespoons (30 ml) chopped parsley

Carbonnade of Beef

Preheat the oven to 325°F (170°C).

Prepare 4 cups of peeled and sliced onions. Trim any fat from 1½ pounds of lean boneless chuck. Cut into 2-inch (5-cm) cubes.

Heat 2 tablespoons of corn oil in a large saucepan. Add the onions to the pan and fry until lightly browned. With a slotted spoon remove the onions from the pan and put them into a casserole.

Add the meat to the pan and fry over high heat until it is lightly browned.

Remove the meat from the pan and put it into the casserole.

Stir 1 tablespoon of flour into the remaining oil in the pan. Cook over low heat,

stirring, for 1 minute. Stirring constantly, gradually add 2½ cups of beer. Bring to the boil. Season with salt and pepper and pour over the beef and onions in the casserole.

Cover and bake for 2 to 2½ hours, or until the meat is tender.

INGREDIENTS TO SERVE FOUR:
4 cups (500 g) peeled sliced onions
1½ lb (700 g) boneless chuck
2 tablespoons (30 ml) corn oil
1 tablespoon (15 ml) flour
2½ cups (600 ml) beer
salt
pepper

Guinness Cake

Preheat the oven to 325°F (170°C).

In a large mixing bowl combine 2 cups of whole-wheat flour with 2 teaspoons of baking powder and 1 teaspoon of ground mixed spice.

Rub in ½ cup of margarine and then stir in ⅔ cup of brown sugar.

Add 1⅓ cups of seedless raisins, ⅔ cup of chopped walnuts and ⅓ cup of chopped candied mixed peel. Mix well.

Beat 2 eggs with ⅔ cup of Guinness. Pour it into the flour mixture and blend thoroughly.

Spoon into a greased and lined 8-inch (20-cm) cake pan and level the surface.

Bake for 1½ to 2 hours, or until the top of the cake is brown and firm to the touch.

Let the cake cool and then remove it from the pan. Turn the cake upside down. Prick the bottom of the cake with a fork, then pour 4 tablespoons of Guinness over it.

INGREDIENTS TO MAKE ONE CAKE:
2 cups (250 g) whole-wheat flour
2 teaspoons (10 ml) baking powder
1 teaspoon (5 ml) mixed ground spice
½ cup (100 g) margarine
⅔ cup (100 g) brown sugar
1⅓ cups (100 g) seedless raisins
⅔ cup (100 g) chopped walnuts
⅓ cup (50 g) chopped candied mixed peel
2 eggs
⅔ cup plus 4 tablespoons (210 ml)
  Guinness

Grand Marnier Soufflé

Preheat the oven to 350°F (180°C).

Melt 2 tablespoons of margarine in a saucepan. Stir in 4 tablespoons of flour, then pour in ⅔ cup of milk. Bring to the boil, stirring, until the sauce thickens. Reduce the heat, stir in the finely grated rind and juice of 1 orange and simmer for 1 minute. Cool slightly.

Separate 5 eggs, adding 4 of the yolks to the saucepan. Beat in the egg yolks well and then beat in 3 tablespoons of Grand Marnier.

Beat the egg whites until stiff. Stir 2 tablespoons into the pan, then fold in the remaining whites until well blended.

Pour the soufflé mixture into a 1-quart (1-liter) soufflé dish.

Bake for 45 minutes, or until the soufflé is well risen, set and golden brown.

Serve immediately.

INGREDIENTS TO SERVE FOUR:
2 tablespoons (25 g) margarine
4 tablespoons (25 g) flour
⅔ cup (150 ml) milk
1 orange
5 eggs
3 tablespoons (45 ml) Grand Marnier

Crème de Menthe Mousse

Put ¼ cup of sugar into the top of a double-boiler.

Separate 4 eggs. Add the yolks to the sugar

Beat the sugar mixture over simmering water until thick. Remove from the heat and beat until cool.

Add 2 tablespoons of crème de menthe liqueur and ⅔ cup of yogurt and beat until well mixed.

In a cup set in a pan of hot water dissolve 1½ tablespoons of powdered gelatin in 3 tablespoons of water. Stir into the mousse.

When the mousse is beginning to set, beat the 4 egg whites until stiff and then fold them into the mousse.

Pour the mousse into a glass serving dish or individual glasses and chill until set.

INGREDIENTS TO SERVE FOUR:
¼ cup (50 g) sugar
4 eggs
2 tablespoons (30 ml) crème de menthe
  liqueur
⅔ cup (150 ml) yogurt
1½ tablespoons (25 g) powdered gelatin

Rum Sauce

This "hard" sauce may be served at Christmas with mincemeat pies or Christmas pudding. It may be made with brandy instead of rum.

Put ½ cup of margarine into a mixing bowl with ⅔ cup of brown sugar and the grated rind of 1 lemon. Beat until the mixture is pale and creamy.

Gradually beat in 2 tablespoons of rum. Transfer to a serving bowl. Chill well before serving.

INGREDIENTS TO SERVE FOUR TO SIX:
½ cup (100 g) margarine
⅔ cup (100 g) brown sugar
1 lemon
2 tablespoons (30 ml) rum

Orange and Madeira Sauce

Serve this richly flavored sauce with duck, veal, ham or pork.

Put 4 tablespoons of soft brown sugar into a saucepan with 5 tablespoons of wine vinegar. Cook over low heat until the sugar has dissolved. Boil for 2 to 3 minutes, until the syrup is brown and thick.

Remove the pan from the heat and stir in ¼ pint of chicken stock, ¼ pint of madeira and the grated rind and juice of 2 large oranges.

Bring to the boil then reduce the heat and simmer gently for 15 minutes.

Blend 2 teaspoons of cornstarch with 1 tablespoon of water and add it to the sauce. Bring to the boil, stirring constantly.

Peel and remove the pith from 1 orange. Cut the membrane away from the segments of fruit. Add the orange segments to the sauce and simmer for 5 minutes.

Serve hot.

INGREDIENTS TO MAKE A HALF PINT (300 ML) OF SAUCE:
4 tablespoons (60 ml) soft brown sugar
5 tablespoons (75 ml) wine vinegar
¼ pint (150 ml) chicken stock
¼ pint (150 ml) madeira
3 large seedless oranges
2 teaspoons (10 ml) cornstarch

Wine Sherbet

This sherbet is particularly good if it is served layered with strawberries.

Grate the rind of 2 oranges and 2 lemons into a saucepan and then add the juice of each and ½ cup of sugar. Cook over low heat until the sugar is dissolved, then simmer gently for 3 minutes. Remove the pan from the heat and leave to cool.

Pour 2½ cups of medium to sweet white wine into a bowl. Strain in the fruit juice mixture.

Put the bowl into the freezer until the sherbet is half-frozen.

Beat 2 egg whites until stiff, then beat the sherbet to break down the ice crystals. Fold in the egg whites until well blended.

Pour the sherbet into a rigid container for freezing and return to the freezer until solid. Cover, seal and label and store in the freezer.

INGREDIENTS TO SERVE FOUR TO SIX:
2 oranges
2 lemons
½ cup (100 g) sugar
2½ cups (600 ml) medium or sweet white wine
2 egg whites

MAKING SHERBET

Beat the sherbet to break down the ice crystals.

Fold in stiffly beaten egg whites.

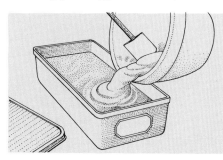

Pour into a rigid container and freeze.

Mulled Wine

Pour 1¼ cups of water into a large saucepan. Add ⅔ cup of brown sugar, 2 cinnamon sticks, 4 cloves, 1 thinly sliced lemon and 1 thinly sliced orange.

Cook over low heat until the sugar is dissolved and then bring to the boil. Let stand for at least 10 minutes so that the flavors will develop.

Pour in 1 bottle of dry red wine and heat to just below boiling point. Remove the pan from the heat and stir in 2 tablespoons of brandy. Serve hot.

INGREDIENTS FOR EIGHT LARGE GLASSES:
⅔ cup (100 g) brown sugar
2 cinnamon sticks
4 cloves
1 lemon
1 orange
1 bottle dry red wine
2 tablespoons (30 ml) brandy

Wassail Cup

Serve this hot spiced drink at winter parties.

Pour 5 cups of beer into a large saucepan.

Thinly peel 1 lemon and add the peel to the pan with the juice of the lemon, ⅓ cup of brown sugar, ¼ teaspoon of grated nutmeg, ¼ teaspoon of ground ginger and 1 cinnamon stick.

Cut 1 apple into quarters and remove the core. Thinly slice the apple into the pan.

Stir in ⅔ cup of brandy or rum.

Cook over low heat until the sugar is dissolved, then bring to just below boiling point.

Serve hot.

INGREDIENTS FOR TEN TO TWELVE GLASSES:
5 cups (1 liter) beer
1 lemon
⅓ cup (50 g) brown sugar
¼ teaspoon (1 ml) grated nutmeg
¼ teaspoon (1 ml) ground ginger
1 cinnamon stick
1 apple
⅔ cup (150 ml) brandy or rum

No recommendations exist for the growth rate of children, but the average growth rate found in a survey of American female children is illustrated right. The graph shows average weights and heights at each age and the columns indicate daily calorie requirements. While different children may grow faster or slower at different ages, their weight and height should remain the same proportionately. Weights given include light clothing.

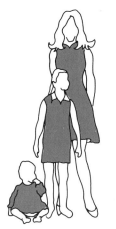

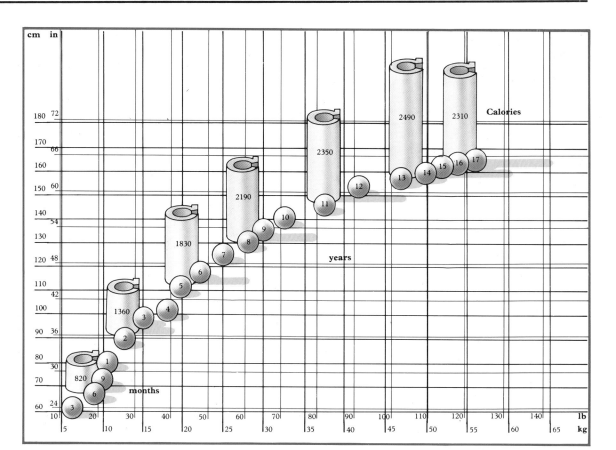

The graph right shows the average growth rates found in a survey of American male children. The graph shows average weight and height at each age and the columns indicate daily calorie requirements. Weights given include light clothing.

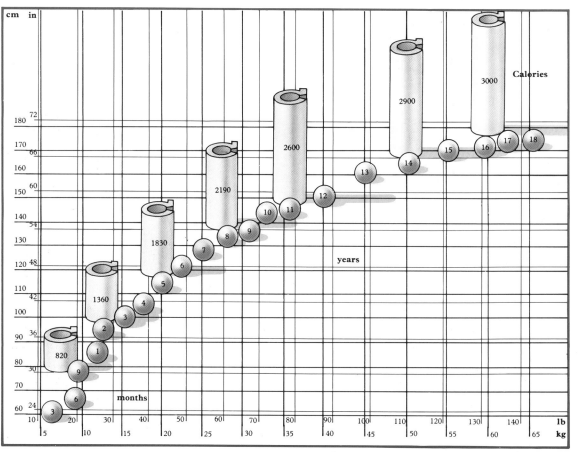

This graph shows ideal weights for adult females at each height and for each build. The weights include light clothing, and heights assume two-inch (5-cm) heels.

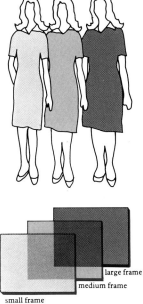

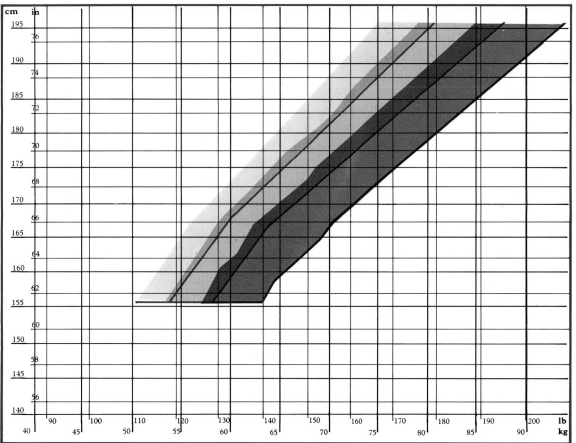

small frame
medium frame
large frame

This graph shows ideal weight for adult males at each height and for each build. The weights include light clothing and heights assume one-inch (2-cm) heels.

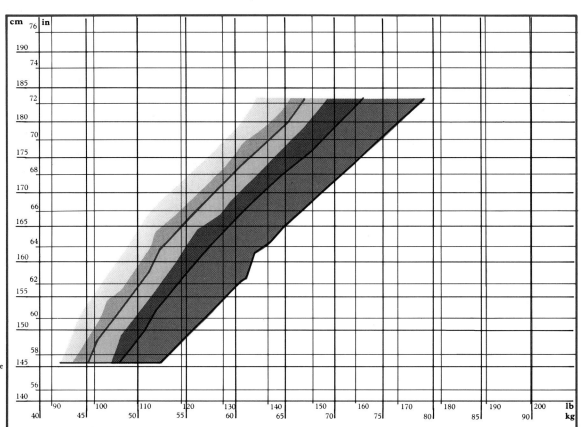

small frame
medium frame
large frame

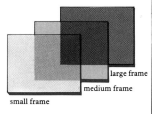

Calories are easy to come by and hard to spend. Every little snack provides us with some, and, as the chart illustrates, exercise costs us far fewer than is usually realized. The nine dishes shown are recipes given in this book. The calories provided by a single portion of each dish increase from Mushrooms and Eggs en Cocotte (113 Calories) to Dutch Apple Cake (550 Calories). Also shown are eight levels of activity which cost progressively more energy. And the clocks indicate the hours and minutes of each activity that are needed to dispose of the calories in each portion of food.

	Mushrooms and Eggs en Cocotte		Raw Spinach Salad		Apple and Ginger Mousse		Orange Capered Halibut	
	113		141		178		211	
	Calories per portion		Calories per portion		Calories per portion		Calories per portion	
	men	women	men	women	men	women	men	women
Sleeping	1 hr 45 min	2 hr 6 min	2 hr 11 min	2 hr 17 min	2 hr 45 min	3 hr 18 min	3 hr 15 min	3 hr 54 min
Sitting quietly	1 hr 21 min	1 hr 38 min	1 hr 41 min	2 hr 8 min	2 hr 8 min	2 hr 35 min	2 hr 32 min	3 hr 3 min
Driving	1 hr 11 min	1 hr 26 min	1 hr 28 min	1 hr 47 min	1 hr 51 min	2 hr 15 min	2 hr 12 min	2 hr 40 min
Cooking	55 min	1 hr 6 min	1 hr 8 min	1 hr 23 min	1 hr 26 min	1 hr 45 min	1 hr 42 min	2 hr 4 min
Walking	31 min	38 min	38 min	47 min	48 min	59 min	57 min	1 hr 10 min
Doing housework	26 min	32 min	33 min	40 min	41 min	51 min	49 min	1 hr
Playing tennis	18 min	23 min	23 min	28 min	28 min	36 min	34 min	42 min
Chopping wood	13 min	16 min	16 min	20 min	21 min	26 min	25 min	31 min

Chinese Fried Rice		Baked Cheese Soufflé Potatoes		Steak with Mushrooms		Blueberry Pie		Dutch Apple Cake	
225		**248**		**352**		**414**		**550**	
Calories per portion		Calories per portion		Calories per portion		Calories per portion		Calories per portion	
men	women	men	women	men	women	men	women	men	women
3 hr 28 min	4 hr 10 min	3 hr 50 min	4 hr 36 min	5 hr 26 min	6 hr 31 min	6 hr 23 min	7 hr 40 min	8 hr 29 min	10 hr 11 min
2 hr 42 min	3 hr 16 min	2 hr 58 min	3 hr 36 min	4 hr 13 min	5 hr 6 min	4 hr 58 min	6 hr	6 hr 36 min	7 hr 58 min
2 hr 21 min	2 hr 50 min	2 hr 35 min	3 hr 8 min	3 hr 40 min	4 hr 27 min	4 hr 19 min	5 hr 14 min	5 hr 44 min	6 hr 57 min
1 hr 49 min	2 hr 12 min	2 hr	2 hr 26 min	2 hr 50 min	3 hr 27 min	3 hr 20 min	4 hr 4 min	4 hr 26 min	5 hr 23 min
1 hr 1 min	1 hr 15 min	1 hr 7 min	1 hr 23 min	1 hr 35 min	1 hr 57 min	1 hr 52 min	2 hr 18 min	2 hr 29 min	3 hr 3 min
52 min	1 hr 4 min	58 min	1 hr 11 min	1 hr 22 min	1 hr 41 min	1 hr 36 min	1 hr 58 min	2 hr 8 min	2 hr 37 min
36 min	45 min	40 min	50 min	56 min	1 hr 10 min	1 hr 6 min	1 hr 23 min	1 hr 28 min	1 hr 50 min
26 min	33 min	29 min	36 min	41 min	51 min	48 min	1 hr	1 hr 4 min	1 hr 20 min

227

Vitamins are sensitive chemicals and the destructive barrage of conditions to which we subject them in food preparation is designed for our palate and not their survival. Cooking, processing and letting food stand can all contribute to a loss of vitamins. This can be illustrated if we take as a standard an extremely simple meal of, for example, fresh fruit juice, steak tartare, spinach salad, tomato salad, bread and fresh pineapple—the most vitamin-rich preparation of each food that is palatable—and then consider the alternative preparations for each food. With each variation some vitamins will be lost. The loss is represented as a percentage of the amount of the vitamin in the standard meal.

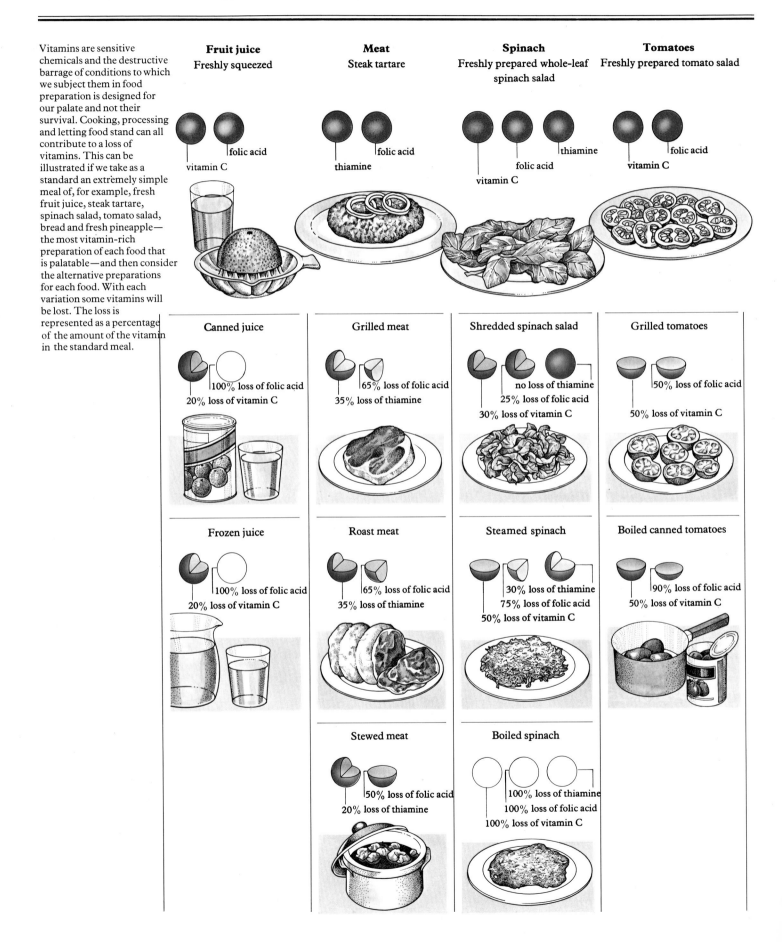

Fruit juice
Freshly squeezed

vitamin C   folic acid

Meat
Steak tartare

thiamine   folic acid

Spinach
Freshly prepared whole-leaf spinach salad

vitamin C   folic acid   thiamine

Tomatoes
Freshly prepared tomato salad

vitamin C   folic acid

Canned juice

100% loss of folic acid
20% loss of vitamin C

Grilled meat

65% loss of folic acid
35% loss of thiamine

Shredded spinach salad

no loss of thiamine
25% loss of folic acid
30% loss of vitamin C

Grilled tomatoes

50% loss of folic acid
50% loss of vitamin C

Frozen juice

100% loss of folic acid
20% loss of vitamin C

Roast meat

65% loss of folic acid
35% loss of thiamine

Steamed spinach

30% loss of thiamine
75% loss of folic acid
50% loss of vitamin C

Boiled canned tomatoes

90% loss of folic acid
50% loss of vitamin C

Stewed meat

50% loss of folic acid
20% loss of thiamine

Boiled spinach

100% loss of thiamine
100% loss of folic acid
100% loss of vitamin C

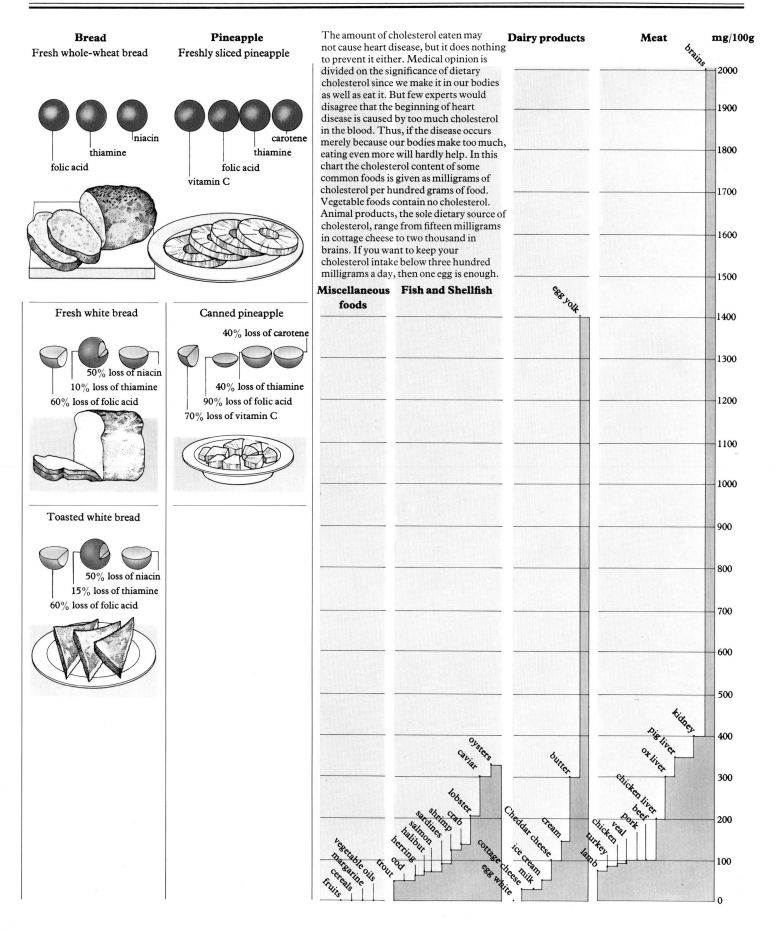

Bread
Fresh whole-wheat bread

niacin
thiamine
folic acid

Pineapple
Freshly sliced pineapple

carotene
thiamine
folic acid
vitamin C

Fresh white bread

50% loss of niacin
10% loss of thiamine
60% loss of folic acid

Toasted white bread

50% loss of niacin
15% loss of thiamine
60% loss of folic acid

Canned pineapple

40% loss of carotene
40% loss of thiamine
90% loss of folic acid
70% loss of vitamin C

The amount of cholesterol eaten may not cause heart disease, but it does nothing to prevent it either. Medical opinion is divided on the significance of dietary cholesterol since we make it in our bodies as well as eat it. But few experts would disagree that the beginning of heart disease is caused by too much cholesterol in the blood. Thus, if the disease occurs merely because our bodies make too much, eating even more will hardly help. In this chart the cholesterol content of some common foods is given as milligrams of cholesterol per hundred grams of food. Vegetable foods contain no cholesterol. Animal products, the sole dietary source of cholesterol, range from fifteen milligrams in cottage cheese to two thousand in brains. If you want to keep your cholesterol intake below three hundred milligrams a day, then one egg is enough.

Dairy products

Meat

mg/100g

brains 2000

1900

1800

1700

1600

1500

egg yolk 1400

1300

1200

1100

1000

900

800

700

600

500

kidney
pig liver 400
ox liver
butter
caviar
oysters
chicken liver 300

lobster
crab
shrimp
sardines
salmon
halibut
Cheddar cheese
cream
ice cream
milk
beef
pork
veal
chicken
turkey
lamb 200

herring
cod
trout
vegetable oils
margarine
cottage cheese
egg white 100

cereals
fruits 0

Miscellaneous foods

Fish and Shellfish

Storing food is not encouraged, but there are occasions when it may be necessary. The chart, right, is therefore a guide to how long various wholesome foods can be stored in a cool room, a refrigerator or a freezer. Times are approximate and assume that the food is in good condition to begin with. Fruit storage times are for whole fruit. Always clean shellfish, fish and poultry. Do not store French bread—it always deteriorates. Wash leaf vegetables and herbs before storage, but not root vegetables or soft fruit. Store root vegetables in the dark. Only freeze fruit and vegetables if they are cooked or blanched. Store eggs pointed end down. Only freeze yogurt if sugar has been added. Fats vary in the length of time they can be stored according to the degree of saturation—the more saturated they are the longer they keep.

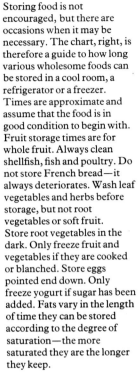

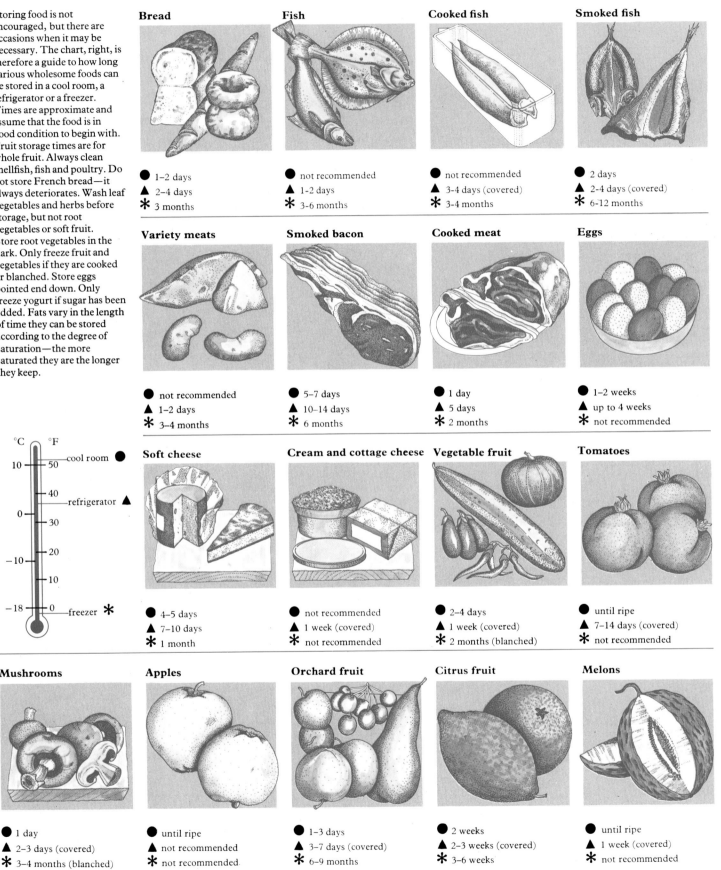

Bread
- ● 1–2 days
- ▲ 2–4 days
- ✳ 3 months

Fish
- ● not recommended
- ▲ 1–2 days
- ✳ 3–6 months

Cooked fish
- ● not recommended
- ▲ 3–4 days (covered)
- ✳ 3–4 months

Smoked fish
- ● 2 days
- ▲ 2–4 days (covered)
- ✳ 6–12 months

Variety meats
- ● not recommended
- ▲ 1–2 days
- ✳ 3–4 months

Smoked bacon
- ● 5–7 days
- ▲ 10–14 days
- ✳ 6 months

Cooked meat
- ● 1 day
- ▲ 5 days
- ✳ 2 months

Eggs
- ● 1–2 weeks
- ▲ up to 4 weeks
- ✳ not recommended

Soft cheese
- ● 4–5 days
- ▲ 7–10 days
- ✳ 1 month

Cream and cottage cheese
- ● not recommended
- ▲ 1 week (covered)
- ✳ not recommended

Vegetable fruit
- ● 2–4 days
- ▲ 1 week (covered)
- ✳ 2 months (blanched)

Tomatoes
- ● until ripe
- ▲ 7–14 days (covered)
- ✳ not recommended

Mushrooms
- ● 1 day
- ▲ 2–3 days (covered)
- ✳ 3–4 months (blanched)

Apples
- ● until ripe
- ▲ not recommended
- ✳ not recommended

Orchard fruit
- ● 1–3 days
- ▲ 3–7 days (covered)
- ✳ 6–9 months

Citrus fruit
- ● 2 weeks
- ▲ 2–3 weeks (covered)
- ✳ 3–6 weeks

Melons
- ● until ripe
- ▲ 1 week (covered)
- ✳ not recommended

°C °F
- cool room ●
- refrigerator ▲
- freezer ✳

Shellfish
- ● not recommended
- ▲ 1 day
- ✳ 1 month

Chicken
- ● 2 days
- ▲ 3–4 days
- ✳ 10–12 months

Large pieces of meat
- ● 1 day (covered)
- ▲ 4 days
- ✳ 6–8 months

Small cuts of meat
- ● 1 day (covered)
- ▲ 2–3 days
- ✳ 4 months

Ground meat
- ● not recommended
- ▲ 2–4 days
- ✳ 3 months

Hard-boiled eggs in shell
- ● 1 day
- ▲ 5–7 days
- ✳ not recommended

Milk
- ● 1 day (in dark)
- ▲ 3–4 days
- ✳ 2 months (homogenized)

Yogurt
- ● not recommended
- ▲ 7 days
- ✳ 2 months (sugar added)

Hard cheese
- ● 5–10 days (covered)
- ▲ 1–4 weeks (covered)
- ✳ 3 months

Grated cheese
- ● 2–3 days (covered)
- ▲ 1–2 weeks (covered)
- ✳ 4–6 months

Stalks and shoots
- ● 2–4 days
- ▲ 5–7 days (covered)
- ✳ 2 months (blanched)

Brassicas and leaf vegetables
- ● 1 day (in dark)
- ▲ 5 days (covered)
- ✳ 6–9 months

Potatoes and root vegetables
- ● 1 week (in dark)
- ▲ not recommended
- ✳ 6–9 months (carrots only)

Pods and seeds
- ● 1 day (unshelled)
- ▲ 1–2 days (shelled)
- ✳ 6–9 months (blanched)

Salad leaves
- ● 1 day (covered)
- ▲ 3–7 days (covered)
- ✳ not recommended

Pineapples
- ● until ripe
- ▲ 10 days (covered)
- ✳ not recommended

Soft fruit
- ● 1 day
- ▲ 2–3 days (not bananas)
- ✳ 7–9 months (not bananas)

Fresh herbs
- ● 1–2 days (in water)
- ▲ 1 week (covered)
- ✳ 6–9 months

Butter and margarine
- ● 3–7 days
- ▲ 7–14 days
- ✳ 1 month

Oils
- ● up to 6 months
- ▲ not recommended
- ✳ not recommended

This index covers only those pages that contain general information. (Preparation of food and recipes are covered in the index that begins on page 236.) Italics indicate entries that are illustrated.

RECIPE INDEX

The recipes are listed under their main ingredients, with the exception of bread, cakes, pastry and salad dressings.

RECIPE INDEX

ACKNOWLEDGEMENTS

The publishers wish to acknowledge the following people: A.E. Bicknell, Lis Blackburn, Andrew Duncan, Joan Faller, Mike Janson, Ethne Rose

Indexer: Donald Cameron

Artists: Javed Badar, David Baxter (The Garden Studio), Ray Burrows, Patricia Capon (Joan Farmer), Lyn Cawley, Richard Corfield (John Martin and Artists Ltd), Patrick Cox, Brian Delf, Chris Forsey, Gary Hincks, Ingrid Jacob, Richard Jacobs, Coral Milla, Marion Mills (Joan Farmer), Peter Morter, Keith Palmer (Arka Graphics), Andrew Popkiewicz, Christine Robins (The Garden Studio), Philip Rymer (The Garden Studio), Posy Simmonds, Glen Stewards (John Martin and Artists Ltd), David Watson (The Garden Studio), Sidney Woods

Fact Finder charts designed by Mike Blore

Photographic stylists: Maggi Heinz, Roisin Nield

Studio services: Face Photosetting, J.D. Colour Studios, Mitchell Beazley Studio, Negs Photography, PLS Typesetters, Sally Slight, Summit Art Studios

Original photography: Frank Apthorp 86, 102-3, 106-7, 119 bottom left, 118-19, 126-7, 133, 138, 176, 182 bottom left, 2nd bottom right; Bryce Attwell 17 top left, 19 top right, 20 far left, 38 far left, 66-7, 70, 74-5, 95, 98-9, 110 bottom left, 110-11, 114 bottom left, 114-15, 122-3, 149, 150-1, 166-7, 171 bottom right, 174 bottom left, 175, 178-9, 186-7, 194-5, 199, 202, 203 bottom, 208 top, 209, 211, 212, 213, 216 bottom left, 216-17; Steve Bicknell cover, 12 top right, 46-7, 52; Michael Freeman 13 top right, 21 far left, 70-1, 78-9 top right, 162-3; Michael Kaye 27 bottom left, bottom right and center right

Additional photographs: A-Z Botanical Collection 187 top right; Ardea, London (Photo: John Mason) 186 top left; Barnaby's Picture Library 155, 203 top right; Battle Creek Sanitarium Hospital 22; The Bettmann Archive 206 bottom left; Bodleian Library, Oxford, from color film strip 186 H, Ms. Ashmole 1462, folio 37v and 38, 206 top left; Cadbury Limited 217 bottom left and far right; Camera Press 23; Kay Casebourne 15 top right; Bruce Coleman 10 center (Photo: C.B. Frith), 20 top left (Photo: Hans Reinhard), 71 left inset (Photo: Hans Reinhard), 182-3 center (Photo: Sandro Prato), 183 bottom inset (Photo: Sandro Prato); Colorific 10 left (Photo: Penny Tweedie); Douglas Dickins 58, 198 bottom; Robert Estall 71 bottom right inset; Mary Evans Picture Library 18 top center, 59; Explorer 8 far left, 8-9; Werner Forman Archive 47 top right; Archiv Gerstenberg 207; Robert Harding Associates 79 left inset, 220-1; Alan Hutchison 208 bottom; Imperial Chemical Industries Limited 20 inset; King Features (Walter Tuckwell and Associates) 15 top far left; The Mansell Collection 18 top right, 215 inset; Mitchell Beazley Archive 27 top right inset; Natural History Photographic Agency (Photo: Joe Blossom) 71 top right inset; New Zealand Dairy Board 20 center top; Picturepoint 13 bottom right, 26-7, 163 inset, 177, 183 top right inset, 186 bottom left, 215 bottom left; Jean Ribière 18 top left; Harry Smith Horticultural Collection 138-9; Sofia Press, Bulgaria 94; Spectrum 112 bottom left, 214-15; *The Sunday Times Magazine* 9 far right; Tate & Lyle 210; Michael Warren 107; ZEFA 10 right, 47 top left, 71 center inset, 113 bottom right, 162

The publishers also wish to acknowledge the kind cooperation of the following organizations for the loan of various items for use in photography and for reference for artwork: The Conran Shop, London SW3; The Craftsmen Potters Shop, London W1; Cucina, London NW3; Elizabeth David, London W1; Dodo Old Advertising, London W11; Habitat, London SW3; David Mellor, London SW1; Richard Morris, London SW6; The New Neal Street Shop, London WC2; Old Pine, London SW6; The Pine Mine, London SW6; The Potshop, London NW3; Thompson & Morgan, Ipswich; The Warehouse, London WC2; World's End Tiles and Flooring Ltd, London SW10